# marketing
## REAL PEOPLE, REAL DECISIONS

second canadian edition

# marketing
## REAL PEOPLE, REAL DECISIONS

**Michael R. Solomon**
Auburn University

**Elnora W. Stuart**
The American University in Cairo

**J. Brock Smith**
University of Victoria

**Ajay K. Sirsi**
Schulich School of Business,
York University

PEARSON

Prentice
Hall

Toronto

**Library and Archives Canada Cataloguing in Publication**

Marketing: real people, real decisions/Michael R. Solomon ... [et al.].—2nd Canadian ed.

Includes index.
ISBN 0-13-127273-X

1. Marketing—textbooks.  I. Solomon, Michael R.

HF5415.M3696 2005          658.8          C2004-904205-X

0-13-127273-X

Vice President, Editorial Director: Michael J. Young
Acquisitions Editor: Laura Forbes
Director of Marketing, Business and Economics: Bill Todd
Senior Developmental Editor: Paul Donnelly
Production Editor: Marisa D'Andrea
Copy Editor: Jennifer Therriault
Proofreader: Catharine Haggert
Production Coordinator: Andrea Falkenberg
Page Layout: Nelson Gonzalez
Photo and Literary Permissions Researcher: Lisa Brant
Art Director: Julia Hall
Interior and Cover Design: Miguel Acevedo
Front and Back Cover Images: Masterfile/Zefa, L. Moses

2 3 4 5     09 08 07 06 05

Printed and bound in the United States.

*To Gail, Amanda, Zachary, and Alexandra—my favourite market segment*
—M.S.

*To Sonny, Patrick, and Marge*
—E.S.

*To Claudia, Ford, and Reed—thanks for your patience*
—J.B.S.

*To Tammara and Belvedere, constant companions*
—A.K.S.

# BRIEF CONTENTS

# CONTENTS

## Chapter 5    Consumer Buying Behaviour    **147**

## Chapter 6    Organizational Buying Behaviour    **181**

---

**PART III**   Developing Marketing Strategies   **211**

### Chapter 7   Product Strategy   **213**

### Chapter 8   Product Management   **241**

## Chapter 9    Pricing Strategy                                           265

# PREFACE

The complexity of the decisions faced by Canadian marketers in today's technology-intensive, hyper-competitive, global business environment is both exciting and challenging. The main goal of this textbook is to help students develop the skills necessary to meet these challenges by immersing them in authentic decision-making experiences.

Unlike other introductory marketing textbooks, *Marketing: Real People, Real Decisions*, Second Canadian Edition, focuses on the decision *maker*, not just on decision making. Students are encouraged to assume the role of a marketing manager and practise making *real* marketing decisions supported by key theories, concepts, and principles. Students also learn from decisions made by others—experienced and successful international marketers in a variety of industries, companies, and contexts. We believe that this combination of learning by doing and learning from others will engage students in active learning and excite them about careers in marketing, both in Canada and internationally.

Marketing in the Canadian context is not simply a scaled-down version of U.S. practices—in this book, we capture the uniqueness of the Canadian decision environment in which students will be working. The discussion of multicultural marketing in Chapter 5, for instance, presents a uniquely Canadian perspective. In addition, most of the examples, exhibits, vignettes, and cases in the book provide a broad array of Canadian examples, but these are balanced with the need for Canadians to have an international perspective and understand international decision environments. The examples, exhibits, vignettes, and cases were also chosen to represent a variety of industries to give students a broad perspective on marketing contexts: for-profit and not-for-profit; large established firms and entrepreneurial start-ups; and services, durable-goods, packaged-goods, retail, and e-tail businesses.

Similarly, the text has been updated to reflect the rapidly changing technological context of marketing decisions, particularly as it relates to the way Canadian companies use the Internet. Additionally, the role of marketing in small- and medium-sized businesses is well integrated throughout the book in recognition of the importance of these businesses to the Canadian economy. Much has happened since the initial printing of the first Canadian edition. Domestic and global events have had a profound effect on how we think about marketing and our marketing decisions. To ensure the book's currency and, where possible, to deepen its international perspective, we have made some significant changes to the text. Here are the highlights:

- The text is more strategic in focus, introducing strategic marketing concepts such as the development of market-driven strategies, positioning strategies, and sources of sustainable competitive advantage. This allows students to fully appreciate the strategic nature and implications of their decisions.

- At the same time, the text focuses on decision making by taking marketing managers' perspectives and showing students how core marketing concepts, theories, and principles are used to make key marketing decisions.

- We changed the order in which material relating to understanding and identifying markets is presented, moving the discussion of segmentation and positioning before the discussion of market research, consumer behaviour, and organizational buying behaviour. This change recognizes that many students prefer to understand the "big picture" of segmentation before getting into the details about approaches, theories, concepts, and principles that are useful for developing rich segment profiles.

- In this second Canadian edition, we have taken a more concise, streamlined approach to the material:

  - We integrated the material on international marketing and ethics throughout each chapter to stress to students that international and ethical dimensions of decision making should form a part of their everyday thinking. Chapter 2 also contains a separate section on ethics and international marketing.

  - We seamlessly integrated material from goods and services into one chapter (Chapter 7) to highlight the importance of thinking about products as a continuum from pure goods to pure services.

— We united material on pricing strategies and methods into one chapter (Chapter 9) to clearly demonstrate the application of theories and concepts.

— We combined and condensed material on marketing communications decisions (from three chapters in the previous edition) to create two chapters on communication strategy and communication tactics (Chapters 12 and 13).

- We have enhanced the text with new content:

  — We added two new chapters to this edition: Chapter 14, "Developing and Implementing a Marketing Plan," and Chapter 15, "Customer Satisfaction and Retention."

  — We included new material on supply chain strategies (Chapter 10) to keep students up to date on the latest developments in channel strategies.

  — We added two new appendices to Chapter 4. Appendix 4.A focuses on statistical tools commonly used by marketers to analyze data to make key marketing decisions. Appendix 4.B focuses on sales forecasting methods. Not all instructors will want to cover this material in an introductory course, but those with a more analytical focus can expose their students to the analytic side of marketing decision making.

  — We added new concepts and theories to each chapter, concentrating on the marketing implications of the Internet and current e-commerce trends.

  — We enhanced the text with new contexts to provide students with an even greater diversity of industries and organizations in which to pursue their careers.

  — We updated the profiles of decision makers in our series of *Real People, Real Decisions*: Henrik Kaas at Sony Nordic (Chapter 2), Marion Lay, CEO of 2010 Legacies Now (Chapter 6), Dee Dee Gordon at Lambesis (Chapter 7), Julie Desrosier at one of Canada's largest mutual fund companies (her company in Chapter 8 is kept a secret until students read to the end of the chapter), Leanne Cadden at the Brentwood Bay Lodge & Spa (Chapter 9), Mike Nomura at Weldwood of Canada (Chapter 10), Dawn Robertson at Federated Direct (Chapter 11), Mario Demers at Saputo Dairy Products (Chapter 13), Leonard Hendricks at TELUS Communications (Chapter 14), and Jamie Chiarotto at TD Canada Trust (Chapter 15). We updated our *Real People, Real Decisions* profiles of key decision makers at Army & Navy (Chapter 1) and MegaBloks (Chapter 5).

  — All the video cases are new. Each chapter contains one video case that illustrates content discussed in the chapter.

  — New to *Spotlight on Real People* are features on Gateway to Excellence (Chapter 4), Monsterpin (Chapter 5), Adform Marketing (Chapter 6), Industrial Research Assistance Program (Chapter 7), Bluenile.com (Chapter 11), Rethink Ad Agency (Chapter 12), Cara Operations (Chapter 13), Sangam Dairy (Chapter 14), and Subaru (Chapter 15). We also updated our *Spotlight on Real People* features on JobDirect, Aliah Inc., The Body Blocker Company, and McAfee Associates.

  — New *Marketing in Action* cases discuss such subjects as learning about marketing from a German maker of domestic appliances (Miele Domestic Appliances in Chapter 1), marketing strategy in an international context (Wal-Mart in Japan, Chapter 2), ethical issues in segmentation and positioning (Chapter 3), Kraft Foods' obesity initiative (Chapter 5), product strategies (Boeing in Chapter 7), brand management strategies (Unilever in Chapter 8), pharmaceutical pricing strategies (Chapter 9), channels strategy (Moosehead Brewery in Chapter 10), electronic retailing strategies (e-tailing and luxury brands in Chapter 11), integrated marketing communications (L'Oréal Canada, Chapter 12), repositioning campaigns (Dairy Farmers of Ontario and the BC Dairy Foundation in Chapter 13), marketing plans and strategies (Google in Chapter 14), and customer satisfaction and retention (McDonald's in Chapter 15).

# APPROACH AND ORGANIZATION

The text is organized into 15 chapters grouped into four parts.

- Part I (Understanding Marketing) provides an overview of the world of marketing (Chapter 1) and strategic marketing decisions (Chapter 2).

- Part II (Preparing for Marketing Strategies) teaches students the foundations of developing marketing strategies: market segmentation (Chapter 3), marketing research (Chapter 4), consumer buying behaviour (Chapter 5), and organizational buying behaviour (Chapter 6). These chapters help students identify creative segmentation schemes, develop rich segment profiles, and evaluate the appropriateness of alternative targeting strategies.

- Part III (Developing Marketing Strategies) arms the student with the marketing mix to develop superior marketing strategies: product strategies (Chapter 7), product management (Chapter 8), pricing strategy (Chapter 9), channels supply chain strategy (Chapter 10), retailing and e-tailing (Chapter 11), integrated marketing communications (Chapter 12), and communications mix and tactics (Chapter 13).

- Part IV (Managing the Marketing Effort) introduces students to how marketing plans are developed and implemented (Chapter 14), and customer satisfaction and customer retention strategies (Chapter 15).

Each chapter starts with a profile of a marketing decision maker who occupies a position students might expect to have within a few years after graduation. A decision that the marketer has recently faced is described and alternative courses of action are proposed. At this point, students are asked to step into the shoes of the profiled marketer, evaluate the alternatives, and recommend and defend a course of action. At the end of the chapter, we discuss what decision the marketer made and why, and provide a summary of the known consequences of that decision.

We try to make it clear that the decision made by the marketer is not necessarily the most appropriate one. Our aim is to show the rationale underpinning the decision and to help students understand how that rationale is informed by the decision maker's perspective. This format allows students to take an active role in applying the marketing concepts they are learning, such as deciding what markets to target (Jacqui Cohen of Army & Navy), what products to introduce (Dee Dee Gordon of Lambesis), or how to satisfy customers (Jamie Chiarotto of TD Canada Trust).

We include decision makers from a variety of organizations, ranging from large, well-known companies like TELUS and TD Canada Trust, to small not-for-profit organizations and family businesses like Army & Navy Department Stores, to Internet-based businesses like SurveySite. This allows students to see how marketing issues and decisions change across organizations, and also how they are similar.

One of our objectives for this book is to be as current as possible so that the content is relevant for the marketplace that students will face when they graduate. To that end, we integrated Internet marketing throughout the book and devoted a major part of Chapter 11 ("Retailing and E-tailing") to business and consumer electronic commerce.

# KEY FEATURES

This book contains many special features that facilitate learning and enhance understanding of core concepts and their applications.

- **Chapter Objectives** at the beginning of each chapter clearly summarize the core concepts explored in that chapter.

- **Key Terms** are boldfaced where they are defined in the text, and are listed at the end of each chapter for easy reference.

- **Figures, Tables,** and **Exhibits** throughout the book each carry explanatory captions.

- **Real People, Real Decisions** vignettes frame each chapter by introducing a decision maker and dilemma faced at the beginning and discussing the decision reached at the end.

- **Spotlight on Real People** boxes profile entrepreneurs in small- and medium-sized businesses. Wherever possible, we have highlighted the activities of young Canadian entrepreneurs to whom students can relate as peers.

- Recognizing that ethics play a crucial role in marketing and business, we have included **Good or Bad Decision?** boxes in each chapter that prompt students to consider ethical dilemmas faced by decision makers.

- **Marketing in Action** cases at the end of each chapter provide an opportunity for students to make marketing decisions related to key chapter concepts in up-to-date, relevant decision situations.

- **Video Cases** (at the end of each chapter) are based on segments from the CBC shows *Venture* and *Marketplace* that deal topically with the practice of marketing, often in a small business context.

- **Weblinks** in the margins direct users to useful and relevant Internet sites.

- Extensive **Chapter Summary** material helps students understand chapter concepts and issues. **Testing Your Knowledge** and **Discussing Choices and Issues** stimulate recall and critical thinking. **Applying What You've Learned** exercises ask students to assume the role of marketing professional and apply concepts and theory to marketing decisions. **Learning by Doing** invites students to learn outside the classroom by talking with marketing professionals, observing phenomena in the marketplace, or conducting primary and secondary research.

- **Real People, Real Surfers** exercises help students learn about resources available on the Internet and encourage them to explore first-hand the many permutations of Web-based marketing.

- The **Appendix** offers a sample marketing plan integrated with the marketing plan template in Chapter 14.

## SUPPLEMENTS

Instructors will enjoy access to the following supplements, which are offered together on a single CD-ROM:

- The *Instructor's Manual* provides an overview of each chapter's suggested activities, projects, and topics for class discussions. Moreover, it offers direction on overcoming barriers to effective learning, assigning in-class projects, and developing class plans. It also includes teaching notes for the end-of-chapter and CBC video cases.

- *Electronic Transparencies in PowerPoint* incorporate exhibits and Weblinks from the text. The presentations are available in both Extended and Express versions.

- The *Pearson Education Canada TestGen,* containing over 2700 questions, has been thoroughly revised to provide the optimum number of questions of each format (true/false, multiple choice, and short answer), degree of difficulty (easy, moderate, difficult), and type of cognitive skill tested (recall/application). The TestGen program enables instructors to edit existing questions, add new questions, and generate tests.

- *CBC/Pearson Education Canada Video Library* is a compilation of video segments drawn from the CBC's *Venture* and *Marketplace* programs upon which the video cases in the book are based.
- *Digital Image Gallery* consists of figures and exhibits featured in the book.

For students, we have prepared the following supplements:

- *Study Guide*, organized by chapter, provides students with outlines, overviews, review questions, and application exercises to aid in the understanding of the textbook and to encourage class discussion.
- *Companion Website* contains numerous resources for students, including review exercises and quizzes, online access to the PowerPoint slides, hyperlinks to the text's Weblinks, and search tools that facilitate further research into key organizations and topics discussed in the text. For instructors, it additionally provides access to the Instructor's Manual and TestGen, and contains a syllabus builder as well as other materials.
- A *Course Management System (CMS)* is available in WebCT, BlackBoard, and CourseCompass. Instructors can use the CMS to enhance traditional course content with an online component, or to deliver the entire course online. The CMS created for this text features a number of study resources for students (review questions, exercises, Weblinks), and valuable teaching and course administration tools for instructors (all instructor's supplements that accompany this text), including the Test Item File for online testing, and Communication Tools including threaded discussion areas and e-mail accounts for each student instructor.

## ACKNOWLEDGMENTS

We would first of all like to express our thanks to the U.S. authors of this text, Michael R. Solomon and Elnora W. Stuart, for their vision of a marketing text that reflects the activities and priorities of real marketers. Their student-centred approach to the text is refreshing and inspiring, and we hope we have maintained their vision in the second Canadian edition.

We also would like to thank the many other people who have made significant contributions to this book. We greatly appreciate the time that each of the "Real People" generously spent to help us write the *Real People, Real Decisions* profiles. Without their willingness to be involved, we could not have provided students with the decision maker focus that is so central to this book.

We would also like to thank the people at Pearson Education Canada who worked so hard on the preparation of the book, especially Paul Donnelly, Laura Forbes, Marisa D'Andrea, and Andrea Falkenberg.

We are grateful to the following reviewers, instructors, and real marketers who provided valuable feedback during the development of this edition:

Cathy Ace, University of British Columbia
Patricia Browne, Kwantlen University College
Peter Burgess, George Brown College
Brahm Canzer, John Abbott College
Gary Dover, Georgian College
Craig Dyer, Red River College
Dwight Dyson, Centennial College
Mary Louise Huebner, Seneca College
Philip Jones, Algonquin College
Steve Lee, Algonquin College
Marcel Massie, independent consultant
Peter Mitchell, British Columbia Institute of Technology
Lesley J. Moffitt, Assiniboine Community College
Miguel Morales, St. Mary's University
Keith Murray, Langara College
Ron Rubin, independent consultant
Reginald Sheppard, University of New Brunswick
Harvey Skolnick, Sheridan College

Our families also deserve a great deal of thanks for enduring with us through the writing process and for being understanding in spite of too many evenings and weekends spent working. To Claudia, Ford, and Reed Smith, and Tammara Sirsi, we thank you for your patience and support.

Finally, we have had the privilege, through 30 years of combined teaching, to interact with outstanding students of marketing. It is those students who have provided much of the inspiration for this book. We wish to thank all of our previous and current students for providing us with the motivation to do this book, and for helping us better understand what students need and want in a marketing textbook.

**J. Brock Smith**  *University of Victoria*
**Ajay K. Sirsi**  *Schulich School of Business, York University*

## *A Great Way to Learn and Instruct Online*

The Pearson Education Canada Companion Website is easy to navigate and is organized to correspond to the chapters in this textbook. Whether you are a student in the classroom or a distance learner you will discover helpful resources for in-depth study and research that empower you in your quest for greater knowledge and maximize your potential for success in the course.

Companion
Website

**[www.pearsoned.ca/solomon]**

Prentice Hall

Jump to...    http://www.pearsoned.ca/solomon    ⬍    Home  Search  Help  Profile    Companion Website

Home >

### PH Companion Website

*Marketing: Real People, Real Decisions,* Second Canadian Edition, by Solomon, Stuart, Smith, and Sirsi

#### Student Resources

This online study guide provides students with tools for learning course material. Each chapter includes:

- Chapter Objectives
- Chapter Overview
- Quizzes
- Internet Exercises
- Weblinks

In the quiz modules students can send answers to the grader and receive instant feedback on their progress through the Results Reporter. Coaching comments and references to the textbook may be available to ensure that students take advantage of all available resources to enhance their learning experience.

#### Instructor Resources

Links will direct instructors to a secure, password-procted site that provides access to a variety of teaching aids, including PowerPoint Presentations, downloadable Instructor's Manual, and TestGen test bank. To get a password, simply contact your Pearson Education Canada Representative or call Faculty Sales and Services at 1-800-850-5813.

# PART I

Societal Success • Business Success • Customer Success • Societal Success

Part I • Part II • Part III • Part IV

# Understanding Marketing

**Marketing.** The term conjures up two common misconceptions. Some people will tell you that marketing is all about advertising. Others tend to equate marketing with selling something to someone. As you will learn in this Part, marketing is first and foremost a disciplined approach used to solve business problems such as lacklustre sales and low brand awareness. At the end of Part I you will also recognize that leading businesses achieve their success by focusing on the welfare of customers and society.

SINCE 1919
ARMY & NAVY

ISSUE 1  11/01

# A STORE IS BORN

**LANGLEY, B.C. OPENS
SATURDAY, NOVEMBER 3**

## GOOD JEANS
**WE HAVE THE BLUES
FROM $12**

## CAREER GEAR
**CORPORATE CLASSICS
FROM KAREN ELISE**

BARGAINS WITH BITE
**FABULOUS FOOD SAVINGS**

**SALE STARTS:
SATURDAY
NOVEMBER 3RD**

Low rise jeans $29

**You won't believe what's in store.**

# CHAPTER 1
## What Is Marketing?

## CHAPTER OBJECTIVES

WHEN YOU HAVE COMPLETED YOUR STUDY OF THIS CHAPTER, YOU SHOULD BE ABLE TO

1. Define the marketing concept.
2. Describe what tools marketers use to create value for customers: the marketing mix.
3. Outline the basics of marketing planning.
4. Describe the evolution of the marketing concept.
5. Explain marketing's role within an organization.

# Real People, Real Decisions

## Meet **Jacqui Cohen,** a Decision Maker at Army & Navy

Jacqui Cohen has good instincts. A self-described "trust fund brat," who spent years living the high life with the international and Hollywood jet set, Cohen is now president of Army & Navy Department Stores, a chain her grandfather Sam Cohen built into a Western Canadian retail empire. The only surviving grandchild, Jacqui Cohen felt a strong pull to continue the family legacy and, in 1998, assumed the presidency of the $50 million operation after it had been managed by non-family members for three decades. She is the charismatic visionary who sets the direction for the organization and generally makes things happen. She makes all the major corporate decisions after seeking input from her management team. This flat structure allows Cohen to stay close to suppliers, store managers, and customers and to keep her finger on the pulse of the 800-employee operation.

She grew up in the business, attended board meetings, and worked as a buyer for a year. With no formal business education, Cohen has relied on her instincts, knowledge of trends and fashion picked up during her years of travel, and marketing street smarts picked up growing up in the retail business and from her celebrity friends and their advisors. She is actively involved in the marketing strategy of the chain and works closely with her marketing team to make key marketing mix decisions. She is well respected for listening to ideas and suggestions from others, but is the intellectual spark behind Army & Navy's marketing strategy.

Army & Navy was once a $100-million business that provided value to customers by buying merchandise from bankrupt or overstocked merchants and passing on the savings. Sales are now about half that. Large retailers such as Wal-Mart and Zellers are rapidly increasing their market share with the cost-conscious customer, and discount clubs such as Costco have adopted a similar strategy to that which made Army & Navy successful.

The location of the flagship Army & Navy store on Hastings Street in downtown Vancouver has also changed, not physically, but demographically. Once the upscale business centre of Vancouver, Hastings Street, next to trendy Gastown, is now run down and dirty, the centre of Vancouver's drug trade, and is perceived by many to be seedy and unsafe. Woolworth's, Woodwards, and Sears, once retail neighbours of Army & Navy, have moved or have gone out of business, replaced by pawn shops, tattoo parlours, and offices for social programs. Loyal Army & Navy customers, once young parents, are now seniors, and new generations of customers are unaware of what Army & Navy is all about. Declining sales were not just observed in the downtown Vancouver store; sales had been declining throughout the Army & Navy chain. They had lost touch with their traditional customer base and had lost their unique positioning in the marketplace.

Army & Navy was in trouble, and Jacqui Cohen and her team realized that something had to be done—walk away or try to fix it. Although a new marketing strategy was clearly needed, it was uncertain if the store should risk a large investment when cash flow was short. They also had to decide whom to target—current older shoppers or, going back to their roots, young adults and parents with young families. The first thing Cohen decided to do was gather information from potential customer groups to find out what they thought about the stores. Mostly, the researchers were given the task of finding out why particular shoppers did not think to visit Army & Navy. They asked four focus groups of six people each to spend $20 at the Army & Navy store in Vancouver or New Westminster. Two groups were shoppers aged 25 to 35, and two were shoppers aged 35 to 49. All of the guest shoppers made regular purchases at Zellers or Wal-Mart and none of them had ever been to an Army & Navy store. The study concluded that the problem for Army & Navy was in brand perception—no one knew what to expect going into Army & Navy; the name had no meaning to them. Also, the stores were perceived to be untidy and disorganized. Armed with this information, Cohen needed to decide what to do with the chain.

### Option 1.

The first option Cohen considered was selling the stores. She could live very comfortably on the proceeds of selling the business and could spend more time with her daughter and in running her "Face the World" charity. "Sell" was the advice from her peers, some of whom were heirs of other prominent department store families. This, however, would end 80 years of Cohen ownership and the family legacy.

### Option 2.

Re-establish the traditional positioning of Army & Navy as a place for young adults and young families to buy unique merchandise, find "deals," and have an original retro-style destination shopping experience. This would require a million-dollar advertising campaign aimed at enticing younger, "hipper" clientele to come into the store for the first time. It would also require a revitalized merchandizing strategy, presenting the current mix of unique and interesting retro merchandise in a way that made for a fun shopping adventure, with neat stuff around every corner. With cash flow being tight, this option was financially risky. Attracting younger consumers could also alienate their current older shoppers if they perceived that the store was no longer for them. Certainly there were no guarantees that younger shoppers would come back to Army & Navy.

### Option 3.

A third option was to try to re-establish the traditional positioning of Army & Navy, with a scaled down advertising campaign focusing on just the Vancouver market. Cohen was not sure whether customers in Calgary, Edmonton, Regina, and Saskatoon had the same shopping preferences and values as those in Vancouver and was concerned that young adults in those cities may not be attracted to an "original-retro" concept store. The strategy for the other cities would be to focus on current and previous customers, reminding them of the value of shopping at Army & Navy.

Now, join the Army & Navy decision team: Which option would you choose, and why?

## THE WHO OF MARKETING: MARKETERS AND CUSTOMERS

This book is about marketing. After you have read it, you will learn that success in the competitive world of business is not accidental; organizations that succeed (such as Army & Navy) do so because they develop and implement superior marketing strategies that create value for their customers.

After reading this book you will have taken the first steps on the road to developing and executing superior marketing strategies that will enable you, your organization, and society to succeed. But, first, you need to know more about marketing as a business function.

Your road to thinking like a marketing strategist begins with this book. At the beginning of each chapter, we will introduce you to professionals like Jacqui Cohen in a box called "Real People, Real Decisions." We'll tell you about a specific decision the marketer had to make and give you the possible options that person considered. That way, you'll be able to form your own opinion about which choice is the best. To conclude each chapter, we'll tell you what the decision maker decided and what happened. It is important to recognize that the decision maker may not have made the most appropriate decision. In fact, there are no "right answers" in business and, ultimately, consumers are the only judges of whether we, as marketers, have made good decisions. What you want to practise is making and defending your decisions based on appropriate analysis, application of marketing theory, concepts, and principles, and your judgment. Do not worry if you think that you might not have good judgment yet. That comes with experience and practice in making decisions.

## WHAT IS MARKETING?

Marketing. Lots of people talk about it, but what is it? When you ask people to define marketing, you get many answers and there are many misconceptions about what marketing is. Some say, "That's what happens when a pushy salesperson tries to sell me something I don't want." Others say, "Oh, that's simple—advertising." Others might say "merchandizing," "pricing," "packaging," or "telephone soliciting."

As you can see, the term *marketing* means different things to different people (in England, it is even used as a synonym for shopping). However, marketing is none of the above terms. As you will see in this book, these terms are tools used by a marketing strategist to accomplish certain goals. The term marketing refers to three things—a business function, a business philosophy, and a decision-making process.

## Marketing As a Business Function and a Business Philosophy

As a business function, marketing's primary role is to provide the business with a long-term competitive advantage in the **marketplace** by understanding the needs of, and creating value for, the lifeblood of any business—the customers. This is done by focusing on a

**marketplace** Any location or medium used to conduct an exchange.

**marketing concept** A business orientation that focuses on achieving organizational objectives by understanding customer needs, the associated costs of satisfying them, and thinking about the best way to satisfy those needs.

business philosophy, the **marketing concept**, which is concerned with the mindset, or orientation, business people have with respect to operating their business. The marketing concept suggests that organizational objectives such as long-term profitability are best met by understanding what customers need and the associated costs of satisfying them—thus making informed decisions of how best to provide products that satisfy those needs.

Successful firms realize that the basic marketing concept applies to all aspects of the firm's activities. As a result, there has been a trend toward integrating marketing with other business functions instead of setting it apart as a separate function. In such organizations, marketing managers work with financial and accounting officers to figure out whether products are profitable, to set marketing budgets, and to determine prices. They work with people in manufacturing to be sure that products are produced on time, in the right quantities, and to quality specifications.

Marketers also must work with research and development (R&D) specialists to create products that meet customers' needs. The experience of Stratos Product Development, a Seattle industrial design firm, illustrates how teamwork creates products that offer more value. When it set about developing a passenger video player for British Airways, Stratos brought together mechanical specialists, customers, and British Airways personnel in brainstorming sessions, where everyone could propose new ideas. The system came together in four months, one-third of the time estimated for the project.[1]

**Stratos Product Development**
www.stratos.com

## Marketing as a Process

As the marketing concept suggests, marketing is primarily a decision-making *process* that allows organizations to achieve objectives by satisfying customer needs and wants. The American Marketing Association, the world's largest professional marketing association, uses this definition of marketing: "**Marketing** is the *process* [emphasis added] of planning and executing the conception, pricing, promotion, and distribution of ideas, goods, and services to create exchanges that satisfy individual and organizational objectives."[2] To better understand the process of marketing, it is helpful to examine this definition in some detail. Use Figure 1.1 to do this. Let's start at the end of the definition and work backwards.

**marketing** The process of planning and executing the conception, pricing, promotion, and distribution of ideas, goods, and services to create exchanges that satisfy individual and organizational objectives.

## Marketing Satisfies Needs

The most important part of the marketing definition is "...satisfy individual and organizational objectives." It tells us about the central aspect of marketing: satisfying the needs of both buyers and sellers. A **consumer** is the ultimate user of a good or service. Consumers can be individuals or organizations (although we usually use the term "customer" when referring to an organization), whether a company, government, or charity, all with different needs. But the seller, or marketer, also has needs—to make a profit, achieve organizational goals (such as eliminating homelessness, in the case of a not-for-profit organization), and to remain in business. So products are *sold* to satisfy marketers' and consumers' objectives. Thus, marketing is all about satisfying needs. A **need** is the difference between a consumer's actual state and some ideal or desired state. When the difference is big enough, the consumer is motivated to take action to satisfy the need. When you're hungry, you buy a snack. A business that has low brand awareness may decide to advertise to bolster brand awareness levels.

**consumer** The ultimate user of a good or service. Can be an individual or an organization.

**need** Recognition of any difference between a consumer's actual state and some ideal or desired state.

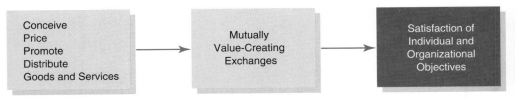

**Figure 1.1** Marketing as a Process

Needs can be related to physical functions, such as eating, or to psychological ones, such as wanting to look good. Research has shown, for example, that people wear such clothes as Roots hats to say important things about themselves and their desired image; the clothes satisfy the wearer's need for self-expression. Consumers can become very attached to their clothes; Levi Strauss, for example, occasionally receives in the mail a pair of beat-up pants with a letter from the owner requesting that they be given a proper burial.[3]

A **want** is a desire for a particular product to satisfy a need in specific ways; it is influenced culturally and socially. For example, two classmates' stomachs rumble during a lunchtime lecture and both need food. However, how each person satisfies this need might be quite different. The first student may be concerned about his health and so he thinks about munching on a big handful of trail mix, whereas the second person may be equally enticed by a greasy cheeseburger and fries. So, the first student's want is trail mix, while the second student's want is fast food.

A product delivers a **benefit** when it satisfies a need or want. For marketers to be successful, they must develop products that provide one or more benefits. The challenge is to identify what benefits people look for, develop a product that delivers those benefits, and then convince buyers that it does so better than a competitor's. As the management expert Peter Drucker wrote, "The aim of marketing is to make selling superfluous."[4] What Drucker means is if we succeed in creating a product that meets the needs of the customer, he or she will happily buy it without any "persuasion" from a salesperson.

The marketing definition talks about satisfying both individual and organizational objectives. A recent movement in marketing is the **social marketing concept**, which emphasizes that customer needs must be satisfied in ways that also benefit society. Large and small firms alike practise this philosophy (see Exhibit 1.1). These efforts include satisfying society's environmental and social needs for a cleaner, safer environment by developing recyclable packaging; adding extra safety features like side-impact car air bags; voluntarily modifying a manufacturing process to reduce pollution; and sponsoring campaigns to address social problems. For example, McCain Foods Ltd., one of the world's largest makers of frozen french fries, refuses to process genetically altered potatoes.[5]

## Marketing Is an Exchange of Value

Central to the philosophy reflected in the marketing concept is an understanding that organizations exist to create value for consumers where it is neither efficient nor effective for consumers to attempt to satisfy their needs themselves.[6] The phrase "to create exchanges…" in our definition of marketing, as shown in Figure 1.2, identifies the heart of every marketing act. An **exchange** occurs when something of value is obtained by one party for something of value offered in return to another. Typically, a buyer receives a good, service, or idea that satisfies a need, and a seller receives money in exchange.

For an exchange to occur, at least two people or organizations must be willing to make a trade, and each must have something the other wants. Both parties must perceive the exchange as being a good deal—that is, each must believe that what they are receiving in an exchange is worth the same or more than what they are offering in return. Both parties can feel this way because value is perceived—different parties have different ideas about how to best satisfy their needs. Therefore, the challenge to the marketer is to create, price, distribute, and communicate an attractive value proposition to the customer.

## Anything Can Be Marketed

The "…ideas, goods, and services…" part of the marketing definition shows that just about anything can be marketed. Indeed, some of the best marketers come from the ranks of service companies such as American Express or not-for-profit organizations such as Greenpeace. Even politicians, athletes, and performers use marketing to their advantage. Ideas, such as democracy, religion, and art, also compete for acceptance in a "marketplace."

**want** The desire to satisfy needs in specific ways that are culturally and socially influenced.

**benefit** The outcome sought by a customer that motivates buying behaviour.

**social marketing concept** An orientation that focuses on satisfying consumer needs while also addressing the needs of the larger society.

**exchange** The process by which some transfer of value occurs between a buyer and a seller.

**Exhibit 1.1**

Social marketing, such as Durex Condoms' sponsorship of Saskatoon band Wide Mouth Mason, applies marketing principles to the promotion of social ideas and issues.

| Conceive Price Promote Distribute Goods and Services | → | Mutually Value-Creating Exchanges | → | Satisfaction of Individual and Organizational Objectives |

**Figure 1.2** Marketing Is an Exchange of Value

**product** A tangible good, a service, an idea, or some combination of these that, through the exchange process, satisfies consumer or business customer needs; a bundle of attributes including features, functions, benefits, and uses.

In this book, we'll refer to any good (physical product), service (intangible product), or idea that can be marketed as a **product**, even though what is being sold may not take a physical form. These products may be directed at consumers for personal or family use, or at other organizations for use in their operations (such as office equipment) or for incorporation in their consumer products (such as component parts). Although consumer goods are more visible, in reality more goods are sold to businesses and other organizations than to consumers.

**NOT-FOR-PROFIT MARKETING** You don't have to be a business person to use marketing principles. Many not-for-profit organizations, including museums, churches, and animal rights organizations (see Exhibit 1.2), practise the marketing concept. Even local govern-

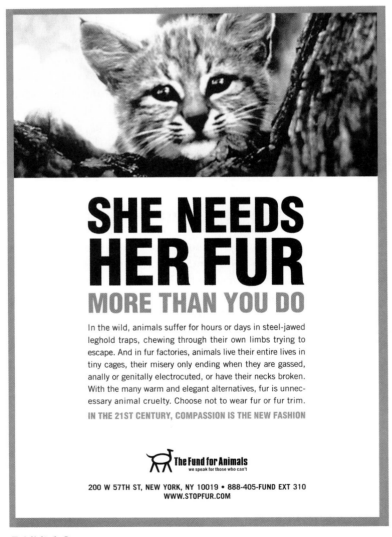

**Exhibit 1.2**

Not-for-profit organizations also practise the marketing concept.

ments are getting into the act, as they adopt marketing techniques to create more effective taxpayer services and to attract new businesses and industries to their regions and cities. The intense competition for support of civic and charitable activities means that only those not-for-profits that meet the needs of their constituents and donors will survive.

**IDEA, PLACE, AND PEOPLE MARKETING** Marketing principles are also used to get people to endorse ideas or to change their behaviours in positive ways. Many organizations work hard to convince consumers to use seat belts, engage in safe sex, not litter, not smoke, and not drink and drive.

In addition to ideas, places and people are also marketed. We are all familiar with tourism marketing, whether for resorts like Club Med or for provinces such as "explore, relax, indulge, enjoy" Prince Edward Island and "Super-Natural" British Columbia.

Tourist events, sports, and other entertainment activities do not just happen; people must plan them. Whether for a sports team or a ballet company, the application of sound marketing principles helps ensure that fans will continue to support the activity and buy tickets. Today, sports and the arts are hotbeds of activity for marketing. A big part of these efforts involves promoting the athletes and artists who create these experiences. You may have heard the expression, "Stars are made, not born." It means that many of the famous people you pay to see got famous with the help of some shrewd marketing: They (and their handlers) developed a "product" that they hoped would appeal to some segment of the population. For example, basketball player Shaquille O'Neal's marketing strategy is to be the biggest fish in any pond (see Exhibit 1.3). He and his agent developed a marketing concept they called "Team Shaq," in which they designed a Shaq logo and copyrighted the name "Shaq" and the phrase "Shaq Attaq."[7]

The "Spotlight on Real People" box on the next page discusses how people in the job market need to be marketed like "products."

**Exhibit 1.3**

Shaquille O'Neal is part of a marketing machine intended to promote "Team Shaq"—people marketing at its best.

## Marketing's Tools: The Marketing Mix

As Figure 1.3 demonstrates, the "...conception, pricing, promotion, and distribution..." in the definition of marketing means that whether it's a box of detergent, a sports medicine clinic, an alternative rock song, or a Roots sweatshirt, a product must be invented or developed, assigned value and meaning, and made available to interested consumers. These tools used by the marketing strategist to create **customer value** are called the **marketing mix** and are commonly known as *the four Ps*: product, price, promotion, and place. Together, the bundle of marketing mix elements represents an offered value to the consumer: what the customer will receive in an exchange. We will examine these components of the marketing mix in detail later in this book. For now, let's briefly look at each element of the four Ps to gain some insight into its meaning and role in the marketing mix.

**customer value** What the customer gets in the purchase, use, and ownership of a product relative to the costs and sacrifices incurred.

**marketing mix** A combination of the product itself, the price of the product, the place where it is made available, and the activities that introduce it to consumers, which creates a desired response among a set of predefined consumers.

**Figure 1.3** Marketing Mix Elements Create Value

## SPOTLIGHT ON REAL PEOPLE    TrueCareers

People are "products" that need to be marketed, and that's especially true in the job market. After watching the hassles their friends experienced while searching for entry-level jobs after graduating, 21-year-old undergraduates Rachel Bell and Sara Sutton had an idea. They believed that the Internet was the answer to matching up student job seekers with employers. For many, blanketing companies with letters and making hours of unproductive phone calls to surly company receptionists was a real dead end. So, Bell and Sutton put their last year of school on hold, swallowed hard, and started JobDirect (now called TrueCareers), an Internet-based service that is now the largest database of entry-level student jobs on the Web.

The service is free to students, but companies—including IBM, Xerox, and Lotus—pay a fee to access the résumé database. These clients can search for résumés fitting spe-

cific criteria, such as students who speak French and have at least a B average.

Although all of the jobs in the TrueCareers database are currently located in the U.S., students from Canada and other countries around the world are able to use the database free of charge, providing they are willing and able to accept a job in the United States.

The largest Canadian site for job postings and career information is Workopolis.com, a joint venture between The Globe and Mail and Torstar Corporation (**www.workopolis. com**). However, Monster.ca is challenging Workopolis.com for Canadian market supremacy. Other sites include CACEE WorkWeb (**www.cacee.com**) and the Canadian government site for Human Resources Development Canada (**www.hrdc-drhc.gc.ca**).

1. What is TrueCareers' market?
2. What benefits does a service such as TrueCareers provide to these customers?
3. How does this chapter's concept of "people marketing" fit in with what TrueCareers does?
4. Compare the Workopolis.com and Monster.ca Web sites. What is the positioning of each site? How could each be improved to meet the needs of its target market?

**TrueCareers**
www.truecareers.com

**price** The seller's assignment of value to a product.

**market** All of the customers and potential customers who share a common need that can be satisfied by a specific product, who have the resources to exchange for it, who are willing to make the exchange, and who have the authority to make the exchange.

**place** The availability of the product to the customer at the desired time and location. Also known as channels of distribution.

**Roots**
www.roots.com

**PRODUCT** The product is a good, service, idea, place, person—whatever is offered for exchange. Notice, therefore, that the concept of product as defined in marketing is broader than its usage in everyday language, where it primarily signifies a tangible good. This aspect of the marketing mix includes the design and packaging of a good, as well as its physical features and any associated services, such as free delivery. Disney takes great pains to offer its customers a superior product in its theme parks. The parks are designed for families to have fun (e.g., rides, entertainment, shopping, eating) and immerse themselves in their vacation (e.g., guests are offered a Disney charge card upon arrival so they do not have to carry cash).

**PRICE Price** is the seller's assessment of the value of a product, what they would like to receive from the buyer in exchange for the product. The decision about how much to charge for something is not simple. For example, jeans that cost $30 have a different image than those that cost $80. Procter & Gamble (P&G), which used to determine its prices based on what a product actually cost to develop plus a profit, now does research on what consumers in different countries can afford and develops products that it can offer at lower prices when the **market** is unwilling to buy the regular-priced ones. For example, in Brazil, P&G launched Pampers Uni, a less expensive version of its Pampers brand of diapers to expand the number of tiny customers in that country who sported its brand on their bottoms.[8] Mike's Hard Lemonade is priced competitively with imported beers. This helps maintain an image that it's a premium product and that consumers of the product are sophisticated and are not cheap.

**PLACE Place** is the availability of the product to the customer at the desired time and location. As we'll see in Chapter 10, this *P* is also known as the *channels of distribution*, which are the firms that work together to get a product from a producer to a consumer. For consumer goods like Roots clothing products, this channel includes retailers such as Sears, as well as their own Roots retail outlets and the Roots Web site.

PROMOTION **Promotion** refers to the marketing communication activities undertaken to inform consumers or organizations about goods, services, or ideas, and to encourage potential customers to buy these goods, services, or ideas. Communication activities can take many forms, including personal selling, advertising, in-store displays, coupons, billboards, and public relations. Mike's Hard Lemonade's communication strategy supports the brand image by developing and supporting the "personalities" of Mike and the lemonade. Cute stories about Mike and lemons were included on the packaging, and the product was brought to consumers' attention with print advertising, in-store displays, and on-shelf signage. After Mike's initial success, television advertising was created that showed "lemons being hurt real bad in the making of this product" and investigators trying to determine "who has been hurting the lemons." These quirky light-hearted ads helped make Mike's the leading brand in the Canadian cooler market. They also have a hip Internet site that further supports the brand's personality.

**promotion** The coordination of communication efforts by a marketer to influence consumers or organizations about goods, services, or ideas.

**Mike's Hard Lemonade**
www.mikeshardlemonade
.com

## HOW ARE MARKETING DECISIONS MADE?

"Marketing is a process of planning and executing…" This part of the definition of marketing suggests that marketing is a series of steps and decisions that entail both careful thought (planning) and action (executing). When it's done right, marketing is a strategic decision process in which marketing managers determine the market strategies that will help the organization meet its long-term objectives. To do this, marketers develop and implement a *marketing plan*.

## Marketing Planning

The overall objective of the marketing plan (and marketing in general) is to achieve objectives—individual, organizational, and societal—by creating superior customer value, for exchange with customers in one or more target market segments, with a sustainable strategy. Consistent with the marketing concept, this suggests that organizational objectives are best met by creating superior value for customers—that is, creating products that satisfy the needs and wants of consumers better than available alternatives. Because consumers have different needs and wants and different ideas on how best to satisfy them, marketers need to decide which consumers they are going to try to satisfy and which they are not.

You should notice something about our discussion up to this point—marketing is primarily an *analytical* task, focused on identifying and producing valued products, but doing this in a sustainable way that allows the organization to achieve long-term objectives. To accomplish this, marketers engage in marketing planning, a process of identifying and analyzing alternative ways of competing in the marketplace. To see how much thinking and analysis goes into marketing decisions, consider some of the many factors a firm like Levi Strauss has to think about when planning and developing its marketing strategy:

• What jeans styles will our core customers of young people be looking for in three to five years?

• What are our competitors doing to attract and keep our customers? How are we positioned competitively in the mind of the consumer?

• Which customer groups that don't currently buy a lot of blue jeans might we target for Levi's products?

• How will new developments in computerized production technologies affect the denim manufacturing process?

• Will the current trend for many companies to institute "Casual Fridays," when employees can wear jeans to work, affect long-term demand for Levi's products?

• What will be the impact on our brand's image if we decide to sell our jeans through discount stores such as Wal-Mart?

**Levi Strauss & Co.**
www.levistrauss.com

- Is television advertising (an expensive marketing communications tool) the right way to communicate with our target market, or is there a better way?

- How will consumers' growing awareness about the use of child labour in Third World countries affect their attitudes toward manufacturers that locate plants overseas?

Answers to these and other questions provide the foundation for developing an organization's marketing plan. It supports management's decisions for setting specific marketing objectives and determining what strategies the organization will develop to meet these objectives.

## Finding and Reaching a Target Market Segment

**market segment** A distinct group of customers within a larger market, who are similar to one another in some way and whose needs differ from other customers in the larger market.

The most critical decision marketers make is in the selection of the specific target market segment(s) on which they will focus their customer value creation efforts. A **market segment** is a distinct group of customers within a larger market who have similar needs, wants, preferences, and behaviours, who seek similar product solutions, and whose needs differ from other customers in the larger market. Parents with young children, for example, typically seek different entertainment products than teenagers and young adults. Depending on its goals and resources, a company may choose to focus on one or more market segments. The chosen market segment(s) become the organization's **target market(s)** toward which it directs its marketing efforts. Because different target markets have different and sometimes conflicting needs, wants, and preferences, marketers typically have to choose among alternative segments on which to focus. This is one of Jacqui Cohen's dilemmas at Army & Navy department stores—how to attract new consumers without turning off other consumers at the same time. Similarly, Canadian fashion designer Linda Lundstrom (and her company, Linda Lundstrom Ltd.) doesn't make clothes for everyone. First, she designs clothing only for women. Lundstrom further narrows her market by focusing on the needs of women with less-than-perfect figures. She also gears her line toward working women who need clothes that can wear and travel well. Her most successful item is an extremely warm winter coat that combines comfort and function with a style based on First Nations artist Norval Morriseau's traditional patterns.

**target markets** The market segment(s) on which an organization focuses its marketing plan and toward which it directs its marketing efforts.

**mass market** All possible customers in a market, regardless of the differences in their specific needs and wants.

Some firms choose to reach as many customers as possible by offering their products to a **mass market**, which consists of all possible customers in a market, regardless of the differences in their specific needs and wants. This strategy, however, is not tenable in the long run—usually competitors of mass marketers, or even the mass marketers themselves, bring alternative products to market that have greater appeal to a subset of the people in the mass market (such as Barq's root beer), eroding the market share of the mass market product.

**SEGMENTING THE MARKET** As will be discussed in more detail in Chapter 3, market segmentation is a process of dividing the overall market into groups of consumers who have similar needs and wants (seek similar benefits) or have similar purchase or consumption behaviours (buy or use products similarly) that are different from consumers in other groups.

Consumers can be grouped by characteristics such as sex, age, income, place of residence, or even hobbies and leisure activities, if these characteristics reflect differences in underlying needs, wants, or behaviours. One way that Levi Strauss slices up the market is in terms of age segments—this makes sense, since different age groups have different clothing wants and may wear jeans for different purposes. Business-to-business markets are sometimes divided into segments using characteristics such as type of business, decision-making criteria, size, or sales volume, if these characteristics reflect differences in the needs, wants, or behaviours of organizations.

**SELECTING A TARGET MARKET NATIONALLY AND GLOBALLY** Marketers weigh each of the segments in terms of profitability potential against the organization's resources and ability to satisfy the needs of the segments. On the basis of this analysis, the organization decides whether it will focus on a single segment or several segments. For example, Hewitt (see

Exhibit 1.4) is an outsourcing company that has decided to focus exclusively on the needs of the human resources (HR) professional. As the ad for Hewitt illustrates, it offers tailored solutions in HR areas such as talent, benefits, payroll, health care, and retirement.

Many companies know that they must look for potential target markets beyond their own geographical borders to compete in today's world economy. Modern marketers are busy meeting the needs of people all around the world, especially when the demand for products at home flattens.

Expanding internationally is desirable, for example, to the Mattel Corporation, as you can see in Exhibit 1.5. The average North American girl owns eight Barbies, making it the best-selling toy ever. The domestic market is starting to become saturated, so Mattel is diversifying to offset the company's reliance on North American Barbie sales. Europe has nearly twice as many children as North America; and numbers in Mexico, South America, Japan, and Southeast Asia are even greater. Mattel now manufactures 75 percent of its toys in plants around the world, including Indonesia, Malaysia, China, Mexico, and Italy.[9]

One trend for multinational companies is to focus on selling products to developing countries, a trend some refer to as B2-4B—"business to four billion"—which refers to the approximate number of potential customers in these markets. Hewlett Packard (HP), for example, believes that much of the firm's future growth could come from developing countries. In 2001, the company began its plans to sell, lease, or donate $1 billion (U.S.) in goods and services to governments, development agencies, and not-for-profit groups in these areas. In fact, to satisfy the needs of this market, HP is developing low-power or solar-powered devices that will connect to the Net wirelessly or via satellites. But Hewlett Packard's Third-World efforts are not just philanthropic. It believes that this kind of investment will allow HP to tap into the huge potential markets that will develop in these countries.[10]

Throughout the text we will emphasize marketers' need to think globally—even if they only act locally. Smart marketers know that whether in Third World countries or developed countries, long-term success means finding customers wherever they are, from Montreal to Manila.

**DEVELOPING AND POSITIONING THE OFFERING** After choosing the target market(s), marketers need to develop an offering that appeals to the needs, wants, and preferences of that target market better than alternatives provided by competitors.

To do this, marketers make a set of decisions about the product itself, its price, the place it is available for purchase, and the activities that introduce it to consumers. These decisions, collectively called the marketing mix decisions, establish the **market position** of the product offering, create superior customer value, and create a desired response among members of the target market. Just as a radio DJ puts together a collection of separate songs (a musical mix) to create a certain mood, the idea of a mix in this context reminds us that no *single* marketing activity is sufficient to accomplish the organization's objectives, and that consistency among the decisions is critical to the overall marketing (or music) program.

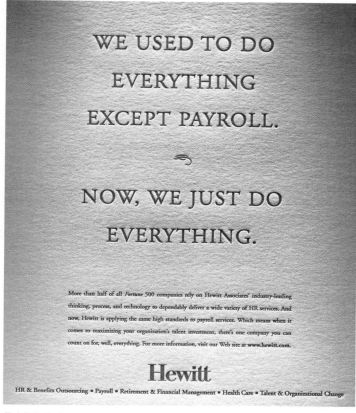

**Exhibit 1.4**
Hewitt targets HR professionals.

**Mattel Corporation**
www.mattel.com

**market position**   The way in which the target market perceives the offering in comparison to competitors' brands.

**Exhibit 1.5**

Mattel is exporting the Barbie craze to consumers around the world.

## Marketing As a Process: Final Thoughts

The idea of marketing being a process has taken on new importance today. It tells us that successful marketing exchanges occur continuously over time. The concept of **relationship marketing** sees marketing as a process of building long-term relationships, not only with key customers but also with suppliers, distributors, employees, and other **stakeholders**, who are integral to the value creation process. Managing customer, supplier, distributor, and other relationships is so critical to the success of most organizations that a fifth *P*—people—is often considered part of the "marketing mix." Part of Toyota's tremendous success in North America can be attributed to how it builds relationships with its customers, the communities in which its plants are located, its suppliers, and its dealers. Toyota considers the needs of all these stakeholders before making decisions on launching new products.

## WHEN DID MARKETING BEGIN? THE EVOLUTION OF A CONCEPT

Now that we have an idea of how the marketing process works, let's take a step back and see how this process of understanding needs first and *then* satisfying them has developed over time. Although it may sound like common sense, the notion that businesses and other organizations succeed when they satisfy customers' needs is a recent one. Let's look at how the marketing discipline has developed from a product orientation to a New Era orientation. This evolution has certainly not been universal—you can still find many examples of companies today that have the mindset associated with each of these orientations.

## The Product Orientation

Organizations that focus on the most efficient production and distribution of products, and not whether these products best satisfy consumers' needs, have a **product orientation**. Some of today's technology-oriented companies have a product orientation—they make technologically "neat" products without much thought to consumer needs and wants. The

**relationship marketing** A marketing philosophy that focuses on building long-term relationships with customers, suppliers, distributors, and other key stakeholders to satisfy mutual needs.

**stakeholders** Individuals or organizations who affect, or are affected by, the activities of a firm.

**product orientation** Management philosophy that emphasizes the most efficient ways to produce and distribute products.

Marketing in Action Case at the end of this chapter demonstrates that Miele, the German maker of domestic appliances, used to have an internal product orientation, before it switched to a marketing orientation.

Firms that focus on a product orientation tend to view the market as a homogeneous group that will be satisfied with the basic function of a product. Sometimes this view is too narrow. For example, sales of Procter & Gamble's Ivory Soap declined because P&G viewed the brand as plain old soap, not as a cleansing product that could provide other benefits as well. Ivory Soap lost business to newer deodorant and "beauty" soaps containing cold cream that appealed to different customer needs in this market.[11]

The Ivory Soap example demonstrates that firms that focus narrowly on the product learn an important lesson the hard way—customers do not buy products, they buy benefits. We will explore this concept in more detail in Chapter 7, Product Strategy.

## The Selling Orientation

When product availability exceeds **demand**, some businesses may engage in the "hard sell," in which salespeople aggressively push their products. During the Depression in the 1930s, firms shifted their focus from a production orientation to selling their goods any way they could. This **selling orientation** means that management views marketing as a selling function, or a way to move products out of warehouses so that inventories don't pile up.

This orientation began after World War II. During the war, Canada dramatically increased its industrial capacity to manufacture tanks, combat boots, parachutes, and countless other wartime goods. After the war, the peacetime economy boomed—Canadians had more disposable income, and manufacturers used the increased factory capacity to turn out an abundance of civilian favourites. Suddenly, people had lots of choices and a bounty of products, such as the car pictured in Exhibit 1.6, to choose from.

Consumers eagerly bought all the things they hadn't been able to get during the war years; but once these initial needs were satisfied, people became more selective. The race for consumers' hearts and pocketbooks was on. The selling orientation prevailed well into the 1950s. But consumers, as a rule, don't like to be pushed, and the hard sell approach gave marketing a bad image.

Companies that still follow a selling orientation tend to be successful at making one-time sales rather than building repeat business. In the end, such companies inevitably fail because their buyers do not come back.

## The Consumer Orientation

Grocery retailer Thrifty Foods enjoys a 25 percent market share on Vancouver Island by focusing on quality meats and produce, selection, value, and service. Over the past 23 years, president Alex Campbell has introduced unique services and programs for his customers, including home delivery, composting and recycling, and "kiddie-friendly" tills that offer Sesame Snaps and colouring books instead of candy.[12] Thrifty Foods has found that it pays to have a **consumer orientation**—being proactive and responsive in identifying and satisfying customers' needs and wants.

The effect of this consumer orientation, which began in the early 1950s, gave management a way to outdo the competition, and it elevated marketing's importance. Marketers researched market segments, assisted in tailoring products to the needs of different consumer groups, and did an even better job of

**demand**  Customers' desire for products coupled with the resources to obtain them.

**selling orientation**  A managerial view of marketing as a selling function, or a way to move products out of warehouses to reduce inventory.

**consumer orientation**  A management philosophy that focuses on being proactive and responsive in identifying and satisfying consumer needs and wants.

"... it's the '49 FORD by a landslide!"

FORD has "MAGIC ACTION" KING-SIZE BRAKES

FORD has "PICTURE WINDOW" VISIBILITY

FORD has "HYDRA-COIL" FRONT SPRINGS

FORD offers "MAGIC AIR" temperature control

FORD has the "MID SHIP" ride

FORD has SOFA-WIDE SEATS

FORD gives up to 10% greater gas economy

FORD offers two great engines 100 hp V-8 95hp Six

New  There's a Ford in your future

**Exhibit 1.6**

This ad for a 1949 Ford promotes images of the good life common in advertising during marketing's selling orientation era.

designing marketing messages than in the days of the selling orientation. The marketing concept was born.

## The New Era Orientation

Yet another fundamental change in marketing is occurring right now, as the goal of long-term growth continues. While the customer is still "number one," many of today's forward-thinking organizations are seeing their commitment to quality as more than simply satisfying consumers' needs. This **New Era orientation** to marketing means a devotion to excellence in designing and producing products that benefit the customer, *plus* the firm's employees, shareholders, and communities. New Era firms embrace the principles of the social marketing concept, seeking both economic and social profit.

One outgrowth of this new way of thinking is the focus on relationship marketing; another is the emphasis on social marketing, which includes efforts to promote consumers' health, safety, and well-being. New Era managers support such efforts as encouraging cultural diversity and ethical business practices, and helping the environment even as they pursue financial profitability. IKEA, for example, insists that their worldwide suppliers, including Canadian forest companies, provide solid wood materials in environmentally friendly ways.[13]

**New Era orientation** A management philosophy in which marketing decision making means a devotion to excellence in designing and producing products that benefit the customer plus the firm's employees, shareholders, and fellow citizens.

**IKEA**
www.ikea.ca

## MARKETING'S ROLE IN SOCIETY: ETHICAL BEHAVIOUR

Conflicts often arise in business when the goal to succeed in the marketplace provokes dishonest business practices. This is why colleges, universities, and corporations are teaching and reinforcing ethical behaviour as part of their curriculum and training.

## Ethical Behaviour Is Good Business

Companies usually find that stressing ethics and social responsibility is good business, at least in the long run. That is the reason why such companies as International Paper and Hewlett-Packard have very well-defined codes of conduct for their employees, which stress transparency, fairness, and integrity in dealings with stakeholders (e.g., customers, suppliers).

Others find out the hard way. For example, the Chrysler Corporation was accused of resetting the odometers of supposedly new cars because they had actually been driven by managers prior to sale. The company admitted the practice only after some managers tried to get out of paying speeding tickets by claiming that their speedometers didn't work because the cable was disconnected.[14] These actions caused the company great embarrassment, and it took years of hard work to restore the public's trust.

In contrast, Procter & Gamble voluntarily withdrew its Rely tampons from the market following reports of women who had suffered toxic shock syndrome (TSS). Although scientists did not claim a causal link between the usage of Rely and the onset of TSS, the company decided to undertake extensive advertising notifying women of the symptoms of TSS and asking them to return their boxes of Rely for a refund. The company took a $75 million loss and sacrificed an unusually successful new product that had already captured about one-quarter of the $1 billion sanitary product market.[15]

## Social and Ethical Criticisms of Marketing

Whether intentionally or not, some businesses do violate their bond of trust with consumers, and unfortunately the "dark side" of marketing is often the subject of criticism. In some cases, these actions are illegal, such as when a retailer adopts a "bait-and-switch" selling strategy, whereby consumers are lured into the store with promises of inexpensive products with the sole intent of getting them to switch to higher-priced goods.

In other cases, marketing practices have detrimental effects on society even though they are not illegal—just think of all the "spam" e-mail you get everyday. Some companies erect billboards for alcohol and tobacco products in low-income neighbourhoods where abuse of these products is a big problem; others sponsor commercials depicting groups of people in an unfavourable light to get the attention of a target market. Palmer Jarvis and KOKO Productions, for example, were the target of considerable outrage by children's advocates, sports associations, and the advertising industry in general when they placed an advertisement in *Marketing Magazine*, intended to be satirical and absurdist, that depicted a bloodied baseball bat with matted hair on it, and a caption of "disappointed coach." Let's consider some of the criticisms of marketing you may have heard and respond to them.

## Good or Bad Decision?

To promote an online game, SegaSoft created a fictional cult called the Cyber Diversion movement, which encourages the primal urge to kill. The firm developed a set of Web sites that were designed to look like they were put up by members of the cult. A company executive commented, "...there is some validity to the concept [that] you need an outlet for aggressive urges. If it becomes a movement, all the better. Starting a movement is a good way to market a product."[16] What do you think? Is encouraging violence, online or otherwise, an appropriate way to market a product?

1. *Marketers create artificial needs.* The marketing system has come under fire from both ends of the political spectrum. On the one hand, some members of the religious right believe that advertising contributes to the moral breakdown of society by presenting images of sinful pleasure. On the other hand, some leftists argue that the same deceitful promises of material pleasure function to buy off people who would otherwise be revolutionaries working to change the system.[17] They argue that the system creates demand that only its products can satisfy.

   *A Response*: A need is a basic motive, while a want represents one way that society has taught us the need can be satisfied. For example, while thirst is biologically based, we are taught to want Coca-Cola to satisfy that thirst rather than, say, water. Thus, the need is already there; marketers simply recommend ways to satisfy it. If the basic need is not there, no amount of slick marketing communication tactics is going to convince consumers to buy. The ad shown in Exhibit 1.7 was created by the American Association of Advertising Agencies, an industry group, to combat this perception.

2. *Marketing teaches us to value people for what they own rather than who they are.* Goods are arbitrarily linked to desirable qualities, so we learn that we can be popular, happy, and fulfilled only if we buy these products.

   *A Response*: Products meet existing needs, and advertising only helps to communicate their availability. Advertising is an important source of consumer information.[18] It is a service for which consumers are willing to pay because the information it provides reduces the time and effort needed to learn about the product.

3. *Marketers promise miracles.* Marketing leads consumers to believe that products have magical properties, that they will transform their lives. Marketers provide simplistic answers to complex problems.

   *A Response*: Marketers do not know enough about people to manipulate them. In testimony before the U.S. Federal Trade Commission, one executive observed that while people think that advertisers have an endless source of magical tricks and scientific techniques to manipulate people, in reality, the industry is successful when it tries to sell good products and unsuccessful when selling poor ones.[19]

## CAREERS IN MARKETING

Marketing was identified by *Canadian Business* as one of the "cool careers" on the Canadian business scene. This is not surprising because it is fun and challenging to work in a discipline that is directly concerned with understanding consumer

**Exhibit 1.7**

The American Association of Advertising Agencies tries to fight the perception that marketers make people buy things they don't want or need.

needs and satisfying them for the mutual benefit of consumers, businesses, shareholders, and society.

Business schools across the country are receiving increasing numbers of inquiries from prospective students about this important discipline. Marketers are currently in great demand, both in small and large Canadian organizations, providing future marketers with some great opportunities.[20]

Many students assume that the "typical" marketing job is in a large, consumer-oriented packaged goods company like Procter & Gamble. In fact, marketers work in other types of organizations, for example:

Service organizations (e.g., TELUS)
E-commerce organizations (e.g., Chapters Online)
Technology companies (e.g., IBM Canada)
Industrial equipment companies (e.g., Komatsu)
Retailers (e.g., Shoppers Drug Mart)
Agricultural companies (e.g., B.C. Hot House)
Not-for-profit organizations (e.g., The United Way)
Marketing research companies (e.g., Maritz Research)
Consulting companies (e.g., CGEY)
Advertising agencies (e.g., Publicis)

In smaller organizations, one person (perhaps the owner) may handle all of the marketing responsibilities. In larger organizations, several marketing specialists may work, along with other functional experts, on different aspects of marketing strategy.

What choices do you have in the marketing field once you graduate? Take a look below to discover the wide variety of exciting career choices that await you.

## Marketing Management

Most businesses hire individuals in the capacity of marketing managers, who report to the director of marketing (who in turn may report to a senior executive in marketing). Marketing managers work with the marketing mix elements to create sustainable strategies for chosen target markets.

## Marketing Research

In this chapter we have discussed how understanding consumer needs is the critical first step in segmenting, targeting, and positioning offerings in the marketplace. Marketing researchers make the understanding component possible by utilizing a variety of tools and techniques to understand customer needs and make recommendations. We will discuss marketing research in more detail in Chapter 4.

## Marketing Consulting

Marketing consultants work with clients to solve marketing problems. Clients face certain symptoms in their business (e.g., declining sales). This field is exciting because it is up to the consultant to diagnose, research, and solve the problem facing the client.

## Product and Brand Management

Many organizations have product or brand managers who are in charge of a particular product line (e.g., paper products at a consumer goods manufacturer) or a brand (e.g., Centrum vitamins). The challenge faced by these managers is to ensure the long-term vitality of their products and brands by creating an expanding pool of loyal customers.

## Sales

The modern sales professional is essentially a customer relationship manager, engaging in consultative selling to solve customers' problems. For example, Xerox Canada employs very talented and well-trained sales professionals who work with their key customers (e.g., a large bank) to help the customer compete better in the marketplace by reducing costs associated with paper needs or by helping the bank's various functions and departments share information (e.g., on customers) seamlessly. In this way, they create value for both Xerox as well as the customer.

## Advertising

Advertising is one of the marketing communication (promotion) tools used by a marketing strategist to achieve certain goals (e.g., creating awareness for a product). Marketing graduates who work in advertising work either on the advertising agency side or on the client side (thus facilitating relationships between the customer and agency). In either case, they are responsible for using the power of advertising to achieve marketing objectives.

# Real People, Real Decisions

▶ **How It Worked Out** at Army & Navy

Jacqui Cohen, president of Army & Navy, decided to re-establish the traditional positioning of Army & Navy as a place for young adults and young families to buy unique merchandise, find deals, and have an original retro-style destination shopping experience (Option 2).

The company invested $1 million to entice 18- to 25-year-olds and young parents into the store. Lanyon-Phillips Advertising created a humorous ad campaign, "You won't believe what's in store," that was irreverent, cheeky, campy, and fun, and emphasized the unique, bizarre, and cheap products at Army & Navy and the retro shopping experience. Print advertising, billboards, and transit shelter ads depicted items like: a $1 Virgin Mary night light ("she lights the way for millions"), Heinz beans ("cheap gas"), children's pacifiers ("for back-seat drivers"), and at Christmas, leopard underwear ("now we don our gay apparel").

The chain's original 1920s logo and orange and black colour scheme were revived to add to the retro feel of the brand. Flyers

were redone, focusing on sharp images and clear sell lines, with promotions taking effect on Saturday to entice young families to come to the store. Although the merchandising mix was not changed dramatically (learning from retailers such as Eaton's that failed when they tried to shift their inventory drastically), it did ensure that 30 percent of merchandise was directed at younger shoppers. Finally, it changed the address and front entrance of the downtown Vancouver store to 36 West Cordova and refered to it as its Gastown location.

The strategy worked well in three flagship stores—Vancouver, New Westminster, and Calgary—attracting new, younger customers, but it did not work well in the Prairies. Overall sales rose by five to ten percent with sales per customer increasing significantly. The company received several letters a week with positive comments about its innovative campaign. Based on this success, Cohen recently opened the first new Army & Navy store in 22 years in Langley, B.C.

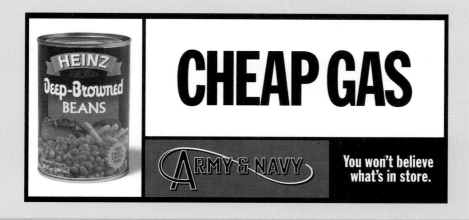

# CHAPTER SUMMARY

### 1. Define the marketing concept.

Marketing is the process of planning and executing the conception, pricing, promotion, and distribution of ideas, goods, and services to create exchanges that satisfy individual and organizational objectives. Organizations that seek to assure their long-term profitability by identifying and satisfying customers' needs and wants have adopted the marketing concept. Today, the societal marketing concept is being adopted by many firms that try to satisfy customers in a way that is also beneficial to society. Marketing activities are important to firms that provide goods and services to individual and business customers, as well as not-for-profit organizations and those that focus on sports, entertainment places, people, and ideas.

### 2. Describe what tools marketers use to create value for customers: the marketing mix.

The overall objective of marketing is to achieve success (individual, organizational, and societal) by creating superior customer value, for exchange with customers in one or more target market segments, with a sustainable strategy. This objective is consistent with the marketing concept. It suggests that marketing is primarily focused on achieving objectives through value creation. Because consumers have different ideas about what they need and want, marketers focus their value creation strategy on the needs and wants of a specific group of consumers—the target market.

Value is created through marketing mix decisions, also referred to as the four $P$s of marketing: product, price, place (channel of distribution), and promotion (marketing communications). Products can be goods, services, people, places, or ideas. The price is the assigned value or amount to be exchanged for the product. The place or channel of distribution gets the product to the customer. The organization communicates the value being created for the customer through its promotional efforts.

### 3. Outline the basics of marketing planning.

To create a competitive advantage for themselves in the marketplace, firms need to develop superior strategies. To do this, they identify market segments, select the target market(s) they want to serve, and create value for the chosen segment(s) by tailoring the marketing mix elements. Often, firms outline their marketing strategies and tactics in a document called the marketing plan.

### 4. Describe the evolution of the marketing concept.

Early in the twentieth century, companies followed a production orientation in which they focused on the most efficient ways to produce and distribute products. Beginning in the 1930s, some firms adopted a sales orientation that encouraged salespeople to aggressively sell products to customers. In the 1950s, organizations adopted a customer orientation that focused on understanding customer needs and then satisfying those needs. This led to the development of the marketing concept.

Today, many firms are moving toward a New Era orientation that includes not only a commitment to customers, but also concern for both economic and social profit. Outgrowths of this orientation are relationship marketing, which focuses on building long-term relationships with customers, and social marketing, which advocates social changes and promotes worthy causes.

### 5. Explain marketing's role within an organization.

Although marketing is the only function *directly* concerned with understanding customer needs and satisfying them, marketing decisions cannot be made in isolation from an organization's other functions. Marketing, finance, manufacturing, research and development, human resources, and other functional areas must work together to achieve the organization's goals.

# CHAPTER REVIEW

## Marketing Concepts: Testing Your Knowledge

1. Briefly explain what marketing is.
2. What is the marketing concept? How is it different from the social marketing concept?
3. How does marketing facilitate exchange?
4. What is customer value?
5. Define these terms: consumer goods, services, and industrial products.
6. What are the elements of the marketing mix? What role do they play in creating value for the customer?
7. Explain the concept of market segmentation. Why can't a firm be successful in the long-term by practising mass marketing?
8. What are target markets? How do marketers select and reach target markets?
9. Trace the evolution of the marketing concept.
10. What are some criticisms of marketing and how would you respond to them?

## Marketing Concepts: Discussing Choices and Issues

1. The marketing concept focuses on the ability of marketing to satisfy customer needs. As a student, how does marketing satisfy your needs? What areas of your life are affected by marketing? What areas of your life (if any) are not affected by marketing?
2. Do you think students should study marketing even if they are not planning a career in marketing or business? Explain your reasoning.
3. In this chapter, a number of criticisms of marketing were discussed. Have you heard these criticisms before? What other criticisms of marketing have you heard? Do you agree or disagree with these criticisms, and why?

## Marketing Practice: Applying What You've Learned

1. An old friend of yours has been making and selling leather handbags and bookbags to acquaintances and friends for some time and is now thinking about opening a shop in your town. But he is worried about whether he'll have enough customers who want handcrafted bags to keep a business going. Knowing that you are a marketing student, he asks you for some advice. What can you tell him about market segments, target markets, product, price, marketing communications, and distribution strategies that will help him get his business off the ground?
2. Assume that you are employed by your city's chamber of commerce. A major focus of the chamber is to get industries to move to your city. As a former marketing student, you know that there are issues involving product, price, marketing communications, and even distribution that can attract business. Next week, you have an opportunity to speak to the members of the chamber, and your topic will be "Marketing a City." Develop an outline for that presentation.
3. As a marketing professional, you have been asked to write a short piece for a local business newsletter about the state of marketing today. You think the best way to address this topic is to review how the marketing concept has evolved and to discuss the New Era orientation of marketing. Write the short article you will submit to the editor of the newsletter.
4. You and your friends sometimes discuss the various courses you are taking. One of your friends says to you, "Marketing's nothing but selling stuff. Anybody can do that without taking a course." Another friend says, "Yeah, all marketers do is write ads." As a role-playing exercise, present your arguments against these statements to your class.

## Marketing Mini-Project: Learning by Doing

The purpose of this mini-project is to develop an understanding of the importance of marketing to different organizations.

1. Working as a team with two or three other students in your class, select an organization in your community that practises marketing. It may be a manufacturer, service provider, retailer, not-for-profit organization—almost any organization will do. Schedule a visit with someone in the organization who is involved in the marketing activities. Ask that person to give your group a tour of the facilities and explain the organization's marketing activities.

2. Divide the following topics among your team, and ask each person to be responsible for developing a set of questions to ask during the interview to learn about the company's program:
   - What customer segments the company targets
   - How it determines needs and wants
   - What products it offers, including features, benefits, and goals for customer satisfaction
   - What its pricing strategies are, including any discounting policies
   - What marketing communication strategies it uses, and what these emphasize to position the product(s)
   - How it distributes products, and whether it has encountered any problems
   - How marketing planning is done and who does it
   - Whether social responsibility is part of the marketing program and, if so, in what ways

3. Develop a team report of your findings. In each section of the report, share what you learned that is new or surprising to you compared to what you expected (based on your reading of Chapter 1).

4. Develop a team presentation for your class that summarizes your findings. Conclude your presentation with comments on what your team believes the company was doing well and where they could make improvements.

## Real People, Real Surfers: Exploring the Web

The New Era orientation means that a firm like Levi Strauss is devoted to excellence in designing and producing products that benefit customers as well as the firm's employees, shareholders, and fellow citizens. Many firms share this on their Internet Web pages. Visit the Web site for Levi Strauss (**www.levistrauss.com**). Then visit the Web site for one of their competitors such as Lee Jeans (**www.leejeans.com**) or Wrangler jeans (**www.wrangler.com**). Follow the links in the sites to learn as much as you can about the company. You might first check the site map to see what links are provided on the site. Look for answers to the following questions.

1. What evidence do you find on the firms' Web sites that each is a New Era firm?

2. Which company has the better Web site? What makes it better? Based on your visit to the Web sites, what do you think is the major purpose of each company's site? To promote their products? To sell on the Web? To develop a brand image? Something else?

3. How do the companies use their Web sites for promoting their products? Is the Web site a unique form of marketing communications or just an extension of their normal advertising?

4. What market segments do you think each firm is targeting with its Web site? What features of the Web sites gave you this idea?

5. Do the Web sites provide an opportunity for the firm to gather information about customers so that they can customize contact with them?

6. Are there any features of the Web site that will cause consumers to come back again and again?

7. What are your major criticisms of each of the Web sites? What would you do to improve each site from a marketing perspective?

Life is tough for manufacturers in the developed world these days as competitors from countries with lower wage rates entice customers with lower prices. However, the German manufacturer of high-quality domestic appliances, Miele, has thrived for the last 100 years by breaking all the rules. Miele, which makes washing machines, vacuum cleaners, coffee makers, ovens, kitchen fittings, and commercial catering equipment, competes by providing customers with high-quality goods manufactured to exacting standards. It steadfastly refuses to move down market and compete on price.

Miele makes its goods in Germany, a country with a high wage structure. Not only does Miele assemble its own goods, it makes all the parts for its machines in-house, rather than outsourcing production to suppliers. For example, it makes 4 million electric motors a year for all its products. This type of control over the manufacturing process comes with a higher cost structure for Miele. This does not worry the owners of the business because their products are sought after by consumers in the marketplace, even though they command a price premium of up to 70 percent over their competitors.

Miele sells 90 percent of its products in Europe, with the rest being sold in North America, mainly in the United States. Although this company has been very successful to date, some analysts are beginning to question whether Miele's marketing approach will work in the long run. Besides the ever-present threat of low-priced competitors, there is the increasingly cost-conscious consumer to think about. Also, sales of domestic appliances in Europe are barely growing.

However, Miele does not seem worried about these threats. It relentlessly pursues efficiencies in production and product development by investing 12 percent of its revenues in these areas, a number much higher than its competitors. Even though it used to be a product-oriented company, these days it relies on its marketing research to better understand and serve the needs of its customers. For example, research revealed that Greek consumers cook with a lot more oil than German consumers. Miele now coats its ovens destined for Greece with special coatings to make it easier to remove oil splashes.

Miele's overall approach is one of confidence. It believes that its superior marketing practices will enable it to thrive for the next 100 years!

Source: Based on *Financial Times*, February 14, 2003.

## Things to Think About

1. Why do you think Miele is so successful in the marketplace? Can you answer by analyzing its marketing mix?

2. What threats does Miele face in the next few years?

3. Do you think Miele's strategy will be successful? Why or why not?

4. What alternatives does Miele have to compete in the marketplace?

5. If you owned Miele, what actions would you take to ensure that your firm thrives for the next 100 years?

## Montreal Sandwich—Part 1

Many new businesses offer special promotions (for example, a low introductory price or savings coupons) to entice customers to try their goods or services. Others do not buck the trend, and stay fairly close to what their competitors are doing. This video case is about an entrepreneur who took a totally different route by gambling on a concept not proven in Canada.

Frederick started Lina's Sandwiches, an upscale sandwich store, with an investment of around $400 000. The store is located in Place Ville Marie, in the heart of Montreal. Twenty-five thousand professionals work there during the daytime, and Frederick wants them to think nothing of spending $10 for a sandwich at lunch.

A native of Montreal, Frederick lived for a while in Monaco. While he has a business degree, he has no formal business experience. His mother has always taught him to think positively. That attitude will come in handy as he competes for lunch dollars with a popular eating establishment, Movenpick, right across from his location.

Lina's Sandwiches is popular in Paris, where customers enjoy luxury sandwiches in a nice atmosphere. But can a European concept be successful in Montreal, where regular sandwiches sell for around $5? By the end of his first day Frederick sells 50 sandwiches. To be profitable, he has to sell 250 sandwiches a day. However, he has not done any advertising, and his store has opened right after the busy Christmas season.

When we get an update on his business, we notice that Frederick has lowered his prices by about 15%, has added a catering service, and sells 200 sandwiches a day.

## Questions

1. Marketing is a disciplined process used to solve business problems. How can your knowledge of marketing help Frederick compete in the marketplace?
2. What suggestions do you have that would help to change consumers' perceptions so they would willingly spend around $10 for a luxury sandwich?
3. Can you provide examples of other entrepreneurs who have completely changed consumer perceptions and habits? How did they achieve their success?
4. Of all the marketing mix elements discussed in Chapter 1 (product, price, marketing communications, channel of distribution), which one do you think holds the key to Frederick's success? Why?

Source: This case was prepared by Ajay Sirsi and is based on "Montreal Sandwich," *Venture* #893.

# CHAPTER 2
## Making Strategic Marketing Decisions

### CHAPTER OBJECTIVES

WHEN YOU HAVE COMPLETED YOUR STUDY OF THIS CHAPTER, YOU SHOULD BE ABLE TO

1. Explain how businesses develop plans at different levels within the organization.

2. Describe the steps in the marketing planning process.

3. Outline how the marketing plan is related to other functional plans (e.g., sales, production, finance) within the organization.

4. Explain how strategic marketing mix decisions are made in international markets.

5. Explain how firms practise ethical and socially responsible behaviour in the marketplace.

# Real People, Real Decisions

## Meet **Henrik Kaas,** a Decision Maker at Sony Nordic

Henrik Kaas is the CEO of Sony Nordic, headquartered in Copenhagen. His profile demonstrates the need for firms to carefully plan their entry into a foreign market, and the seemingly minor things that can derail marketing projects. After graduating with an MBA from the Copenhagen Business School in 1993, Henrik went to work as a Marketing Manager with GTE Sylvania Lighting. In 1998 he joined Sony Nordic as their Marketing Director, a post he held for two years. He was then promoted to the post of Deputy Managing Director of Sony Nordic, as well as Managing Director of Sony Denmark.

A few years ago, Sony released the Sony Memory Stick, a new product that would allow integration of all the company's electronics products. Consumers could connect the Memory Stick to a Sony Digital camera, then connect the Memory Stick to a Sony VAIO computer, and download the images. They could also download music to the Memory Stick on a computer, connect the Memory Stick to a Sony Walkman, and play the downloaded songs.

As Deputy Managing Director of Sony Nordic, Henrik was responsible for the company's activities in Denmark, Norway, Sweden, Finland, and the Baltic countries of Estonia, Latvia, and Lithuania. Henrik knew connectivity was a great concept, but one that's hard to explain unless someone actually demonstrates how it works. Consumers would have to be given hands-on lessons.

To introduce Sony connectivity products, Sony Nordic created the Sony Experience Tour for its "Go Create" campaign. This Tour was part promotion, part educational event: A specially outfitted bus with workstations featuring VAIO laptops, digital cameras, and networked Walkmans would travel around the Nordic countries to teach consumers about the power of connectivity. The bus also provided online connections via satellite to the Sony Experience Web site. By visiting the site, while using the Memory Stick, users could "go create." They could upload pictures, produce slide shows, and use a slide builder for mailing images to friends and family. Henrik estimated that 15 000 to 20 000 people would take the Tour during the summer, so he knew it had to be well planned.

The tour aimed to reach people who spoke numerous languages. Danish, Swedish, and Norwegian are all fairly similar languages, though the pronunciation and some words are different. Finnish and the three Baltic languages are different from the other three. However, the target market group in all of these countries generally spoke English as a second language. For this reason, Sony Nordic decided to produce the Web site in English.

The Sony Experience tour crew included staff from a Danish agency as well as local staff who were a mix of Sony salespeople and freelancers. All were fluent in their native language and English. The plan was to station the local staff in each country outside the bus to hand out leaflets and entice passersby into the bus. The Danish staff would be waiting inside the bus to explain the Sony products.

As soon as the crew made its first stop in Oslo, they realized they had a serious language problem. The staff in the bus did not feel that they had communicated well enough with the Norwegian visitors who came in to learn more about Sony products. The Danes tried to speak English, but the visitors preferred to receive information in their native language. Unfortunately, some visitors gave up and left the bus. Obviously, the Tour needed retooling. Henrik considered his options.

## Option 1. *Place locals inside the bus and Danish staff outside the bus.*

Stop the Tour for a while and place the local, native-speaking employees inside the bus, and the Danish event staff outside to hand out the leaflets. However, this option would require training the local staff about Sony products and delaying the Tour, which had been planned months ahead. Sony had chosen some sites at yearly music festivals, where dates were fixed and fees already paid to place the bus in these venues.

## Option 2. *Use only native-speaking staff.*

Using only native-speaking staff would solve the language problem. However, the new staff would need training and days of touring would be lost. The whole crew would have to change with each new country. Each new crew would have to "start over" in learning how to communicate Sony's products to the public.

Now, join Henrik and the decision team at Sony Nordic. Which option would you choose, and why? Also, to enable you to think strategically like a marketer, how should Sony Nordic deal with cultural differences when introducing new products? Create a list of guidelines and procedures that Sony should follow when entering a foreign market. The material in this chapter will give you the necessary tools to answer this question.

**Sony**
www.sony.com

# "PLAN WELL AND PROSPER"

Whether a firm is a not-for-profit organization like the United Way, a family-based retailer like Army & Navy, or a major manufacturer like Sony, planning for the future is a key to prosperity. Success in the competitive world of business is not accidental; businesses that succeed do so because they are capable of developing and implementing superior strategies in the marketplace. Often, businesses that fail meet their fate because of improper planning.

All firms operate in a dynamic environment. In today's world of business, consumer interests, technologies, the competition, and the economy are changing faster than ever. This makes good planning, which enables a firm to meet the challenges of this dynamic environment and to control its own destiny, more important than ever.

In this chapter, we'll look at the different steps in creating and implementing plans within a business organization. First we'll see how managers make the decisions that guide the entire organization. Then, we'll examine the marketing planning process and the stages in that process that lead to the development and implementation of a marketing plan. Finally, we will discuss the relationship between the marketing planning process and other plans developed within the business, called functional plans.

In successful firms, both large and small, business planning is an ongoing process of making decisions that guide the firm both in the short term and for the long haul. Planning identifies and builds on a firm's strengths and helps managers at all levels make informed decisions in a changing business environment. Planning means that an organization develops objectives before it takes action. In large firms, such as IBM, Sony, and L'Oreal, which operate in many markets, planning is a complex process involving many people from different areas of the company's operations. In a small business like Mac's Diner, however, planning is quite different; Mac himself is chief cook, occasional dishwasher, and the sole company planner. With mid-size firms, the planning process falls somewhere in between, depending on the size of the firm and the complexity of its operations.

We all know, in general, what planning is—we plan a vacation or a great Saturday night party or how we are going to get work completed. When businesses plan, the process is more complex. Business planning usually occurs on an annual basis at three levels—strategic, marketing, and operational. Figure 2.1 outlines this process. **Strategic planning** is the managerial decision process that matches the organization's resources (e.g. manufacturing facilities, financial assets, and skilled workforce) and capabilities to its market opportunities for long-term growth. These decisions focus on the firm's ability to respond to changes and opportunities in its environment. In a strategic plan, the top management team (i.e., the chief executive officer, or CEO, president, and other top executives) defines the firm's purpose and specifies what the firm hopes to achieve over the next few years, increasingly in consultation with a cross-section of employees who bring varied

**strategic planning** A managerial decision process that matches an organization's resources and capabilities to its market opportunities for long-term growth and survival.

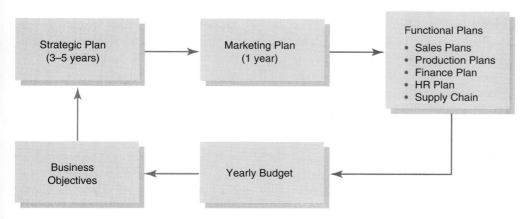

**Figure 2.1** Annual Planning at Different Levels Within a Business Organization

perspectives and knowledge to the process. For example, a firm's strategic plan may set a goal of increasing the firm's total revenues by 10 or even 20 percent in the next five years.

Strategic plans are usually developed for a period of three to five years and take a long-term view of the strategic health of the business. In large firms, strategic planning can actually occur at two different levels. First, there is overall corporate strategic planning, which determines the organization's different business and product pursuits. Second, the individual business units do strategic planning for their products. Strategic planning at Disney, for example, involves an assessment of resources and capabilities for starting new businesses. In addition to making movies and running theme parks, Disney is now in the cruise ship business and operates a number of Disney vacation resorts. Disney's corporate planning expanded its theme park business to Europe and Japan—separate business units. At Disney there are separate strategic plans for each of the different Disney businesses.

Given its high-level, long-term emphasis, a strategic plan is not a document that can be readily implemented. Therefore, as shown in Figure 2.1, firms develop a one-year plan, called the marketing plan, which takes its direction from the strategic plan. There are two main differences between a strategic plan and a marketing plan. The first is time horizon. While the strategic plan is developed for a period of three to five years, the marketing plan is developed for a period of one year. The second difference is that the marketing plan contains details regarding the marketing mix elements (product strategy, pricing strategy, channel of distribution strategy, marketing communication strategy), while the strategic plan does not contain this detail.

Perhaps you are beginning to see the central role played by the marketing planning process. The development of the marketing plan enables the business to set priorities regarding markets it wants to compete in (market segments), customers it wants to serve (target customers), and how it plans to serve those customers (marketing mix strategy). Once these priorities are set, the business develops a set of functional plans such as a sales plan, production plan, finance plan, supply chain plan, and a human resource plan. Collectively, some businesses call these plans the operating plan.

Based upon the requirements of each functional plan, the business is now in a position to allocate resources for the year by setting a budget. The business also sets some objectives it wants to achieve and this closes the loop shown in Figure 2.1.

As an example of the three levels of planning, consider how planning might occur in a company that manufactures bicycles. In the strategic plan, the firm has a corporate goal of increasing revenues by 15 percent over the next five years by developing new bicycles for a new market—racing enthusiasts. The marketing director, a middle manager, is responsible for marketing planning. One of her objectives is to gain 20 percent of the racing bike market by successfully introducing three new models during the coming year. Cross-functional planning is necessary for the new bike models—she must work with the finance and manufacturing departments to analyze product manufacturing capabilities and product profitability. The director of marketing communications, who works under the marketing director, will develop plans to promote the new bikes to potential customers, while the sales manager will develop a plan for the company's sales force to sell the bikes to its customers through the retail channel.

So far, we have a general understanding of the three levels of planning. Now we'll discuss in more detail strategic planning and the important role that marketing plays in it.

## STRATEGIC PLANNING: GUIDING THE BUSINESS

Marketers don't work and plan in isolation. Before we talk about the marketing planning process, therefore, we need to understand how firms develop strategic plans. In this section, we'll take a closer look at the four key stages in top-level strategic planning: defining the organization's business mission, evaluating the environment, setting organizational objectives, and planning the business portfolio.

# Defining the Organization's Business Mission

In the first stage of strategic planning, a firm's top executives define the mission of the organization, top management's vision of why the firm exists, how it is different from other firms, and the place in the market it wants to take. Decision making in the strategic planning stage revolves around such "soul-searching" questions as: What business are we in? What customers should we serve? What kinds of value and products can we create for them? How should we develop the firm's capabilities and focus its efforts? In many firms, the answers to questions like these become the lead items in the organization's strategic plan. They become part of a **mission statement**, a formal statement that describes the organization's overall purpose and what it hopes to achieve in terms of its customers, products, and resources. Figure 2.2 on the next page shows examples of mission statements.

Robert Goizueta headed the Coca-Cola Company for 17 years. During that time, sales more than quadrupled, going from $4 billion to $18 billion. It seems like he knew what he was doing. When Goizueta took on that job, one of his first actions was to create a mission statement for the company. It began, "Our challenge will be to enhance and protect the Coca-Cola trademark, giving shareholders an above-average return and entering new businesses only if they can perform at a rate substantially above inflation." [1]

By focusing all company efforts on building brand value, satisfying customers, and increasing profitability, that mission statement led Coke into two decades of phenomenal worldwide growth. The ideal mission statement is not too broad, too narrow, nor too short-sighted. A mission that is too broad will not provide adequate focus for the organization. It doesn't do much good to claim: "We are in the business of making high-quality products"; yet it's hard to find a firm that doesn't make this claim. A mission statement that is too narrow may inhibit managers' ability to visualize possible growth opportunities. Imagine the disastrous consequences that would happen to McDonald's if its mission statement read: "We are in the hamburger business."

The term *marketing myopia* is often used to describe firms that develop short-sighted visions of who they are. [2] For example, in the 1980s, Kodak faced intense competition from Japanese film and camera companies, which had developed electronic cameras capable of storing images digitally on compact disks. The future of filmless photography came a giant step closer—an exciting advancement but not the greatest news for Kodak, which viewed itself as being in the film business. Abandoning its product-oriented, myopic mission, Kodak redefined itself as being in the "imaging" business—a consumer-oriented mission—with a focus on products that process and convert images both on film and in the form of electronic data. [3] This broader view led to the development of new products for its core business and caused Kodak to venture into electronic publishing, medical and graphics arts imaging, printing, and digital scanning. However, given its long-reliance on a product-centric focus, its competitors are ahead of the game. Do you think Kodak can successfully redefine itself?

Kodak is not alone in its efforts to redefine itself. As Exhibit 2.1 on page 35 shows, Philip Morris, once simply a tobacco products company, has redefined itself strategically as a consumer products company, offering many of the products we consume on a regular basis.

## Evaluating the Environment: SWOT Analysis

The second step in strategic planning is an assessment of an organization's external and internal environments. **SWOT analysis** is a tool often used by managers and other strategic planners in this task. SWOT analysis seeks to identify meaningful strengths (S) and weaknesses (W) in the organization's internal environment, and opportunities (O) and threats (T) coming from outside the organization, the external environment. A SWOT analysis enables a firm to capitalize on opportunities and minimize threats, because it can develop strategies that successfully match what the firm does best with profitable new market opportunities.

**Coca-Cola**
www.coca-cola.com

**Kodak**
www.kodak.com

- *AT&T:* We aspire to be the most admired and valuable company in the world. Our goal is to enrich our customers' personal lives and to make their businesses more successful by bringing to market exciting and useful communications services, building shareowner value in the process. (www.att.com/factbook/co_mission.html)

- *Sierra Club:* To explore, enjoy, and protect the wild places of the Earth; to practice and promote the responsible use of the Earth's ecosystems and resources; to educate and enlist humanity to protect and restore the quality of the natural and human environment; and to use all lawful means to carry out these objectives. (www.sierraclub.org/planet/199512/steward.html)

- *MADD:* The mission of Mothers Against Drunk Driving is to stop drunk driving and to support the victims of this violent crime. (www.charweb.org/organizations/madd/mission.htm)

- *First National Bank of Bowie:* Our mission is to be a profitable, sound, responsive, locally owned community bank that provides ultimate protection for depositors' funds. Our goals are to grow and create shareholder value. (www.fnbbowie.com/keepmiss.htm)

- *Blackhawk Controls Corporation:* The aim of Blackhawk Controls is to provide motion solutions to industry. This includes AC and DC drives, servos, steppers, controllers, and complete systems. We specialize in single and multiple axes. We have designed applications for web converting, plastics, profile and sheet lines, wire, boxboard, print presses, bindery lines, and woodworking machinery. (www.blackhawkcontrols.com/mission/htm)

- *Huff Realty, Inc.:* Jim Huff Realty is a company dedicated to excellence; using innovative real estate marketing skills and state-of-the-art technology to provide the highest-quality services to our clients and customers; above all, preserving a belief in people. (www.huff.com/info/mission/html)

- *The Quaker Oats Company:* To meet the needs of consumers through innovative marketing and manufacturing of healthful, good-tasting products that contribute to a healthy lifestyle and consumer well-being around the world, yielding above-average returns over time for our shareholders. (www.quakeroats.com/vis_mis.htm)

- *Pfizer Inc.:* Over the next five years, we will achieve and sustain our place as the world's premier research-based health care company. Our continuing success as a business will benefit patients and our customers, our shareholders, our families, and the communities in which we operate around the world. (www.pfizer.com/pfizerinc/about/vision/mission.html)

- *First Union Corporation:* Our strategic priorities are to provide our customers unparalleled service, convenience and responsiveness; balance earnings power through geographic and product diversity; provide the most innovative financing solutions and a broad array of products; increase the production of our specialty businesses; maximize operating efficiency; and emphasize capital strength and loan quality with growth in fee income, deposits, and loans. (www.firstunion.com/profile/strprior/html)

- *Spina Bifida Association of Saskatchewan:* Our mission is to improve the quality of life of all individuals with spina bifida and/or hydrocephalus, and their families, through awareness, education, and research. (firebar.sasknet.sk.ca/~sbass/mission.html)

**Figure 2.2** Examples of Organizational Mission Statements

**external environment** The uncontrollable elements outside of an organization that may affect its performance either positively or negatively. These include demographic/social/cultural factors, economic factors, competitive factors, regulatory factors, and technological factors.

The **external environment** consists of those uncontrollable elements outside of the organization that may affect it either positively or negatively. The external environment includes five major categories. In Table 2.1 you can see the impact of these external factors on Scotts Canada Ltd., a supplier of fertilizers to consumers who want to grow a beautiful garden. Opportunities and threats can come from any part of the external environment. Sometimes trends or currently unserved customer needs provide opportunities for growth, while others signal possible danger or threats down the road.

For entrepreneur Shabazz Fuller, a changing fashion trend provided a "phat" opportunity. In 1991, Fuller was an unlicensed street vendor, hawking T-shirts in Harlem, New York, and designing flashy outfits for local rap performers. When black urban culture took root among mainstream youth across America, Fuller and his partner saw an opportunity and turned their T-shirt business into a $5 million success called Shabazz Brothers Urbanwear. The spread of hip-hop presented an opportunity for major clothing manufacturers like Fila USA and Tommy Hilfiger who have also cashed in with urbanwear designs.[4] We'll talk more about environments in Chapter 14, when we discuss how to develop marketing plans.

The **internal environment** is all of the controllable elements inside an organization that influence how well the organization operates. Internal strengths and weaknesses often reside in the firm's current strategy and performance. How superior is the current value created by the firm's products? What is the relative market share of these products? What has been their financial performance? Internal strengths and weaknesses also reside in the resources, technology, intellectual capital, and other assets of the firm. For example, firms need to have appropriate technical skills to compete in their industry. Their employees need to have appropriate skills, abilities, and training to produce the firm's products. A firm's physical facilities can be an important strength or weakness, as can its level of financial stability, its relationships with suppliers and channel members, its corporate reputation, and its ownership of strong brands in the marketplace.

Internal strengths may also lie in the organization of the firm—its structure, culture, and systems (how it gets work done). Some firms, for example, have a positive work climate that encourages creativity, innovation, and teamwork. Other firms have a "chilly" climate, characterized by negativity, work-to-rule, and in-fighting among employees—which can seriously affect product quality and relationships with customers, suppliers, distributors, and other stakeholders. Finally the beliefs, values, and preferences of senior management in an organization can be a strength or weakness, as these senior people provide leadership, vision, and direction for the activities of the organization.

Marketers use SWOT analysis to help them make strategic and tactical decisions. Internal strengths and external opportunities provide rationale to support a particular course of action. Internal weaknesses and external threats provide reasons why a particular course of action might not be appropriate. For example, a major new product introduction—the A380, a 555-passenger jetliner—by a tough competitor (Airbus) could end Boeing's dominance in the commercial jet market. Although weaknesses and threats could have negative impact on a proposed strategy, it should be recognized that some weaknesses and threats can

**Exhibit 2.1**

Philip Morris, once simply a tobacco products company, now sees itself as a consumer products company with a variety of product offerings. Its annual report reflects that shift in strategic orientation.

**internal environment** The controllable elements inside an organization, including its people, its facilities, and how it does things that influence the operations of the organization.

**Table 2.1** The External Environment Facing the Firm

| External Environmental Factor | How It Affects Scotts Canada Ltd. |
| --- | --- |
| Demographic/Social/Cultural | As consumers age, they have more disposable income. Also gardening as a hobby is popular socially and culturally, Scotts can capitalize on this trend by showing consumers how its products can help build a beautiful garden. |
| Economic | Gardening is "affordable luxury," according to Scotts. When times are tough, people turn to their gardens to beautify their living space. Also, an attractive garden increases the "curb value" of the house. |
| Competitive | Scotts competes with such firms as Nu-Gro to satisfy consumers' needs. Scotts has a patented process whereby each fertilizer particle has Nitrogen, Phosphorous, and Potassium (their competitors do not). |
| Regulatory | The city of Toronto has banned the use of chemicals on lawns. Scotts is in an excellent shape to capitalize on this external factor by showcasing the use of fertilizers, instead of harmful chemicals, to grow a lawn. |
| Technological | Scotts has to be aware of research advances in universities and laboratories worldwide so they manufacture cutting-edge products that do not harm the environment. Scotts has secured the global marketing rights from the Ministry of Agriculture and Food in Canada to produce and distribute a biological weed control product (a fungus that kills weeds and then dies). |

be mitigated or overcome with a good strategic plan. Boeing could counter the competitive threat by planning to introduce a really innovative jetliner of its own. The key to SWOT analysis is not get bogged down in analysis paralysis. Firms face hundreds, if not thousands, of internal and external environmental considerations that shape and have an impact on their business. You will want to identify the top six to ten issues that might have the greatest implications for the marketing decisions you have to make. Ask yourself: Does this fact or piece of information have a major implication for a decision I have to make? If not, it's probably not worth documenting in a SWOT analysis.

## Planning for Growth: The Business Portfolio

In small companies that offer a single good or service, the firm's business strategy is simple. But many large firms realize that relying on only one product can be risky, so they have become multi-product firms with self-contained divisions organized around products or brands. These businesses or **strategic business units (SBUs)** are individual units within the firm, each having separate missions, business objectives, resources, managers, and competitors. For companies with a number of different SBUs, strategic planning means making decisions about how to best allocate resources among these different businesses to ensure growth for the total organization.

As illustrated in Figure 2.3, each SBU has its own strategic focus within the firm's overall strategic plan, and each has its own target market and strategies for reaching its goals. Just like an independent business, each SBU is a separate profit centre within the larger corporation—each SBU is responsible for its own costs, revenues, and profits.

Large corporations often have many divisions or SBUs. For example, Harley-Davidson is a firm with several SBUs. While mostly known for its "hogs," the company also owns the Holiday Rambler Corporation, which makes motor homes, and the Utilimaster Corporation, a subsidiary of Holiday Rambler, which manufactures parcel delivery vans, truck bodies, and specialty vehicles. As is often the case, Harley's SBUs produce very different products—it's hard to confuse a "hog" with a squat delivery van. Just as the collection of different stocks an investor owns is called a portfolio, the different products owned by a larger firm is called its **business portfolio**. Having a diversified portfolio of products with different revenue-generating and revenue-using characteristics reduces the firm's dependence on one product or one group of customers.

**strategic business units (SBUs)** Individual units within the firm that operate like separate businesses, with each having its own mission, business objectives, resources, managers, and competitors.

**business portfolio** The group of different products or brands owned by an organization and characterized by different income-generating and growth capabilities.

**Figure 2.3** The Role of Strategic Business Units

As Figure 2.1 shows, taking guidance from the strategic plan, the marketing function develops a marketing plan. We turn to this topic next.

## THE MARKETING PLANNING PROCESS

Solid planning means that a firm has a viable product at a price consumers are willing to pay, the means to get that product to the place consumers want it, and a way to communicate (promote) the product to the right consumers. The marketing planning process culminates in the development of a formal document called the **marketing plan**. Although we will discuss the process of developing a marketing plan in great detail in Chapter 14, let us briefly examine the marketing plan template shown in Figure 2.4 on the next page.

### Creating a Competitive Advantage: Marketing's Strategic Focus

It is important to understand that the underlying goal of *all* marketing strategies and plans is to create a **competitive advantage** for the firm—to take what the company does really well and outperform the competition, thus providing customers with a benefit the competition cannot provide. A competitive advantage gives consumers a reason to choose one product over another again and again.

The marketing planning process, as demonstrated by the marketing plan template, begins

**marketing plan** A document that describes the marketing environment, outlines the marketing objectives and strategy, and identifies who will be responsible for carrying out each part of the marketing strategy.

**competitive advantage** The ability of a firm to outperform the competition, providing customers with a benefit the competition cannot.

## Good or Bad Decision?

Successful marketing strategies depend on understanding a firm's environment, and that means learning as much as you can about the competition. For example, former Staples Inc. chairman, Thomas G. Stemberg, had his wife Dola apply for a job with rival Office Depot Inc.'s delivery-order centre to confirm rumours that Office Depot was starting its own delivery service. The Boehringer Mannheim Corp. filed suit when Johnson & Johnson's Life Scan Inc. employees were caught eavesdropping on a sales meeting to learn about a new Boehringer product. How far should a company be allowed to go to learn about its competitors?

**Figure 2.4** Marketing Plan Template

with a thorough analysis of the external environment facing the firm. This includes the current market situation to ascertain marketplace attractiveness, competitor analysis, analysis of the macro environment (such as cultural or technological trends), and analysis of customer needs and trends. Taken together, this external analysis provides the firm with a set of opportunities and threats.

Next, the business examines the external opportunities and threats vis-à-vis its internal strengths and weaknesses to conduct the SWOT analysis we discussed earlier. Based on the SWOT analysis, the business develops a set of financial and marketing objectives.

Marketing objectives normally include one or more sales objectives. After all, without sales, there are no profits; and without profits, there is no business. Some examples of sales objectives are: "To increase sales of our deluxe model toy by 15 percent during the next 12 months"; "To increase our toy market share by five percent each year for the next three years"; "To sell one million toys during the holiday season."

If a firm has decided that its growth strategy is to focus on product development—new or improved products for existing customers—it will develop product objectives. Because it is more profitable to retain customers than it is to replace them, firms often set objectives for improvements in quality or service to develop customer loyalty. In the breakfast cereal market, where consumers are more fickle than loyal, firms like Kellogg and General Mills may set objectives for developing new brands to suit the tastes of everyone—children, teens, and adults—or they may set goals for a new product to retain customers who are being lured away by a competitor's new honey-coated, fruit-and-fibre cereal. In other cases, a firm may decide to modify a product by taking advantage of trends, as when Frito-Lay developed its line of "lite" snacks.

In some instances, firms find that their best opportunities for growth are stated in the form of market objectives. These goals can involve entering new markets or increasing product usage in served markets, through using either market development strategies (existing products sold to new customers) or diversification strategies (new products for new customers). Manufacturers of recreational vehicles (motor homes and travel trailers),

for example, used a market development strategy in targeting baby boomers (see Exhibit 2.2). Joining together in a "Go RVing Coalition," they spent US$15 million on advertising aimed at this under-50 market in a three-year period.[5]

Once the marketing and other objectives are developed, the business develops detailed strategies using the marketing mix elements of product, price, channel of distribution, and marketing communications. Tactical plans to implement the strategies are developed next. Without tactical plans, strategies do not get implemented. Finally, the business outlines the financial benefits of developing the marketing plan and details on how the marketing plan efforts will be controlled (for example, what goals will be achieved by

**Exhibit 2.2**

The RV industry believes that baby boomers can be its next big market.

what time periods and any corrective actions that will be taken if the marketing plan is not on target).

## Marketing Planning to Functional Plans

As shown in Figure 2.1, the marketing plan sets a common foundation for the development of functional plans such as sales, HR, and production. Each function develops its own plans to implement the marketing strategies outlined in the marketing plan. Before you read further, what do you notice about the planning process so far?

What you should see is that all plans, regardless of level, dovetail into one another. In other words, if the process outlined in Figure 2.1 is working properly, all departments (functions) within an organization are following the guidelines set out by the high-level strategic plan, but at their own level of detail. It is in this way that the entire organization works together as one enterprise, each function thinking and acting toward the common good of the business by focusing on the customer.

## Setting the Budget and Business Objectives

In the final stages of the planning process, top management sets a yearly budget based on marketing and functional plans and sets objectives the business hopes to achieve. These are specific accomplishments or outcomes that an organization hopes to achieve by a specific time.

Organizational objectives, therefore, are a direct outgrowth of the mission statement and broadly identify what the firm hopes to accomplish within the general time frame of the firm's long-range strategic business plan. For example, to turn around the hard times in the 1980s and assure its future for the 1990s and beyond, Harley-Davidson's managers set objectives calling for a new emphasis on quality, the redesign of its touring bikes, and investing in marketing communications to soften Harley's "Hell's Angels" image and attract new customers.

Organizational objectives can be as varied as the organizations that develop them. They may relate to revenue/sales, profitability, the firm's standing in the market, return on investment (ROI), productivity, innovation, use of the firm's resources, product development/introduction, customer relations/satisfaction, or even social responsibility. Often objectives are quantitative—they state the specific levels of measurable business accomplishments that are to be achieved by the organization as a whole. For example, a firm might have as an objective a 10 percent increase in profitability by increasing productivity, by reducing costs, or by divesting itself of an unprofitable division. Or it might meet this objective by developing new products, investing in new technologies, or entering new markets.

Campbell Soup was hovering near the bottom of the food industry when David W. Johnson became president and CEO of the company. Johnson saw Campbell as a firm that had lost its direction and focus, and his first act was to develop a set of measurable business objectives focusing on growth. Johnson jettisoned business divisions that didn't fit in with Campbell's core products and undertook a large-scale restructuring of the company into divisions that unified and coordinated business activities. As a result, Campbell exceeded its growth goals while launching 122 new products.[6] In the process, it transformed itself from a soup company to a food company.

## Strategic Marketing Mix Decisions in International Markets

Marketers operating in two or more countries have a crucial decision to make: How necessary is it to develop a customized marketing mix for each country? As the ad in Exhibit 2.3 on page 41 shows, Xerox has chosen to communicate a standardized message in other countries (the ad appears in a Spanish magazine).

The choice between standardization and localization can be difficult and complex. For example, as seen in Exhibit 2.4 on page 42, Wal-Mart has similar signs and store layout in

# SPOTLIGHT ON REAL PEOPLE     Aliah, Inc.

Big companies and consulting firms work hard and spend hard to transform knowledge into strategy. An entrepreneur named Aly Abulleil goes a step farther—he develops strategic planning software that captures emotions as well.[7]

As a young planner with an Egyptian oil company, Abulleil worked on the mathematical concepts of game theory, which explores how conflicts in decision making can be resolved. After entering a Ph.D. engineering program at the University of Pittsburgh, he began to build a business, called Aliah, Inc., to help middle management make decisions. His first client was Timken, a large manufacturer of ball bearings. To combat a production problem the company was having, Abulleil analyzed the choices engineers were making. He broke every issue down into a series of questions, each with only two alternatives. The engineers not only had to choose an option, they had to indicate how strongly they felt about their choice, which incorporated the intensity of managers' emotions. This approach was quite different from other planning programs.

The business was running on a shoestring, but his staff stuck with him—partly because they could see how the planning method worked in their own lives. For example, his technical chief used it to solve problems in his church, and his general manager relied on the software to help junior high students set personal priorities. In 1996, everything changed: IBM adopted the software as a planning tool, and soon other major firms like Boeing and Lubrizol were using it to develop strategy.

1. How does Aliah help managers in the strategic planning process?
2. What role should emotions or intuition (versus rational, objective analysis) play in this process?
3. How can Aliah best convey its different approach so that the company can increase its own market share among products and services used to facilitate strategic planning? Are there other potential customers besides corporate planners who might be convinced to use the software?

its Japanese stores, but Japanese shoppers are confused about the term "Rollback" yet understand the price discounts offered by the retailer. For a discussion on Wal-Mart's strategy in Japan, please see the case at the end of this chapter.

**STANDARDIZATION VERSUS LOCALIZATION** Advocates of standardization argue that the world has become so small and tastes so homogeneous that basic needs and wants are the same everywhere.[8] A focus on the similarities among cultures certainly is appealing. After all, if no changes in a firm's marketing strategy had to be made to compete in foreign countries, it would realize large economies of scale, because it could spread the costs of product development and promotional materials over many markets. For example, Reebok created a new centralized product development centre to develop shoe designs that can easily cross borders.[9] Widespread, consistent exposure also helps create a global brand by forging a strong, unified image all over the world—Coca-Cola signs are visible on billboards in London and on metal roofs deep in the forests of Thailand.

In contrast, those in favour of localization feel that the world is not *that* small, and products and promotional messages should be tailored to local environments. These marketers feel that each culture is unique and that each country has a *national character*—a distinctive set of behavioural and personality characteristics.[10] Snapple failed in Japan because consumers there didn't like the drink's cloudy appearance. Similarly, Frito-Lay Inc. stopped selling Ruffles potato chips (too salty) and Cheetos (the Japanese didn't appreciate having their fingers turn orange after eating a handful).[11]

**PRODUCT DECISIONS** A firm seeking to sell a product in a foreign market has three choices. Sell the same product in the new market, modify it for the market, or develop a brand-new product for the foreign market. Let's take a closer look at each option.

- A *straight extension strategy* retains the same product for domestic and foreign markets. Coca-Cola sells the same formula in every country, and Gillette offers the same razor blades everywhere.

- A *product adaptation strategy* recognizes that in many cases people in different cultures do have strong and different product preferences. Sometimes these differences can be subtle, yet important. That explains why Kellogg's, which markets the identical version of its Corn Flakes and Rice Krispies brands in North America and Europe, had to remove the green "loops" from Froot Loops after research showed that Europeans felt they were too artificial looking.[12]

- In other cases, products must be adapted because varying living conditions or customs require different designs. When the Electrolux appliance company began selling refrigerators in Europe, it found that Northern Europeans want large refrigerators because they shop once a week in supermarkets, whereas Southern Europeans want them small because they shop daily in open-air markets. Northerners like freezers on the bottom, southerners on the top. And the British are avid purchasers of frozen foods, so they insist on a unit with 60 percent freezer space.[13]

- A *product invention strategy* means that a company develops a new product as it expands to foreign markets. Ford's "world cars," including the Focus model, are being sold around the globe. In some cases, a product invention strategy takes the form of *backward invention*. The firm may find it needs to offer a less complex product than it sells elsewhere, such as a manually operated sewing machine or a hand-powered clothes washer to people without access to a reliable source of electricity.

**Exhibit 2.3**

As this Spanish Xerox ad shows, Xerox has decided to communicate standard messages in other countries.

In India, Coca-Cola bought a local brand called Thums Up, after finding that this Coke imitator was outselling Coke four to one. Coca-Cola abandoned the Indian market in 1977, when the government ordered the company to turn over its secret formula. By the time it returned in 1993, Thums Up had become so entrenched that Coke decided in this rare case that it was better to market a local imitator than its own brand.[14]

**Kellogg's**
www.kelloggs.com

**MARKETING COMMUNICATIONS (PROMOTION) DECISIONS** The marketer must also decide whether it's necessary to change product promotions in a foreign market. Some firms endorse the idea that the same message will appeal to everyone around the world. The advertising director for the Unisys Corporation, a company that specializes in computers, explained the decision to launch a standardized global campaign: "Now they are seeing the same message, the same company, the same look wherever they go. That really stretches my advertising dollars."[15]

Unisys's decision to adopt a global message illustrates one key to the success of a standardized strategy: It is more likely to work if there are not unique cultural factors affecting the purchase. Computer buyers tend to have more in common than, say, perfume buyers. This "one world, one message" strategy also has a greater chance of success if the firm's target customers live in cosmopolitan urban areas where they regularly see images from different countries. The Swedish ad for Diesel jeans in Exhibit 2.5 includes imagery from North Korea to appeal to these "global consumers." For such a campaign to succeed, the

**Exhibit 2.4**

Wal-Mart's experience in Japan highlights the role of standardization versus localization.

message should focus on basic concepts, such as romance or family ties, because these are likely to be understood everywhere.

Fans of a localization strategy, on the other hand, feel that cultural differences translate into market differences, which may in turn call for different advertising strategies. When Tim Hortons moved into the U.S. market, for example, it faced a completely undeveloped "morning market" in that country for coffee and baked goods. Many U.S. customers were grabbing a cup of coffee at a local gas station on their way to work. Tim Hortons' strategy became one of creating a morning market by using an advertising tag line: "Morning people. Where do they come from?" This strategy contrasted to their focus on lunch menu items, such as sandwiches and chili, in the Canadian market.[16]

**PRICE DECISIONS** Costs associated with transportation, tariffs, and differences in currency exchange rates often make the product more expensive for a company to make or sell in foreign markets compared to its home country. Aside from cost factors, sometimes a higher price is charged in international markets because consumers there value the uniqueness of the product. Kokanee beer, for example, is sold for $1 more per six-pack than its American competitors, because American consumers place a higher value on a product that is Canadian.

**grey market** The importing of products by an unauthorized party, who then sells them for a fraction of the price.

One danger of pricing too high is that competitors will find ways to offer the product at a lower price, even if this is done illegally. A **grey market** exists when an unauthorized party imports products and then sells them for a fraction of the price. Goods such as watches, cameras, and perfumes often move through the grey market—Seiko estimates that one out of every four of its watches brought into the United States is unauthorized.[17]

**Exhibit 2.5**

Some marketing communications, such as this ad for Diesel jeans, are not tailored to specific foreign markets.

A company can also run into trouble if it tries to price a product too low to establish it in a new market. Some countries outlaw a practice called **dumping**, in which a company tries to get a toehold in a foreign market by pricing its products lower than they are offered at home—often removing excess supply from home markets and keeping prices up there. In one case, Eastman Kodak accused Japanese rival Fuji Photo Film of selling colour photographic paper in the United States for as little as a quarter of what it charges in Japan.[18]

**DISTRIBUTION DECISIONS** Getting the product to foreign consumers is half the battle. Marketers used to dealing with a handful of large wholesalers or retailers may have to rely instead on thousands of small stores, or they may run into problems finding a way to package, refrigerate, or store goods for long periods of time in less developed countries.

Sometimes similar distribution arrangements across countries are possible and present an advantage for companies. McCain Foods, for instance, found entering the South American market was made easier because of existing distribution arrangements with McDonald's restaurants in markets like North America. McDonald's started its expansion in the late 1990s into Brazil, Chile, Uruguay, Paraguay, and Argentina by building close to 400 McDonald's outlets. McCain, a supplier for McDonald's restaurants in North America, was asked to supply the 25 000 tonnes of frozen fries a year needed to supply the South American restaurants. To fulfill that need and keep up with the McDonald's expansion plans in the region, which meant opening a new restaurant about every four days until the year 2000, McCain built a plant in Argentina. Having established production and distribution in the region, McCain then began to explore other distribution arrangements for its products, namely the fast-growing frozen food grocery segment in South America. It is estimated that Argentina, Brazil, and Chile have the fastest-growing frozen food markets in the Western hemisphere.[19]

Establishing a reliable distribution system is essential if the marketer is to succeed in an international market. Establishing a reliable system might be especially difficult in developing countries where thousands of individual distributors (some who transport goods to remote rural areas on ox carts or bicycles) must be persuaded to take on the product. It's also essential in developed countries, where competition for shelf space may be fierce. For example, the British product Virgin Cola entered the United States market in 1998 and the Canadian market in 1999 after its successful launch in the United Kingdom in 1994. Although the product had also been successful in other European markets before coming to North America, it has not yet made a big impact in North America, partly because distribution is a key to success in the North American beverage business. With Pepsi and Coca-Cola controlling so much of the distribution in North America, new entrants like Virgin have a difficult time getting their product distributed in this market.

# ETHICAL AND SOCIALLY RESPONSIBLE BEHAVIOUR IN THE MARKETPLACE

Many consumers today are concerned with the ethical practices of companies. As a result, astute marketers recognize that long-term profitability depends on making quality products while acting in an ethical and socially responsible manner. Marketing is *still* concerned with the firm's "bottom line," but now many managers also consider **social profit**, which is the net benefit both the firm and society receive from a firm's ethical practices and socially responsible behaviour.

Creating social profit is so important to The Body Shop Canada that the first line of their mission statement reads, "We dedicate our business to the pursuit of social and environmental change."[20] Evidence of this commitment to social profit can be seen in The Body Shop's long-standing environmental activism, their stand against using animals in product testing, and their community service activities, including campaigns for fair international trade and activities to fight violence against women. Exhibit 2.6 shows Ben & Jerry's Statement of Mission. As you can see, the ice-cream maker is very concerned about

**dumping** Pricing products lower in a foreign market than they are offered in the home market.

**social profit** The benefit an organization and society receive from the organization's ethical practices, community service, efforts to promote cultural diversity, and concern for the natural environment.

**The Body Shop Canada**
www.thebodyshop.ca

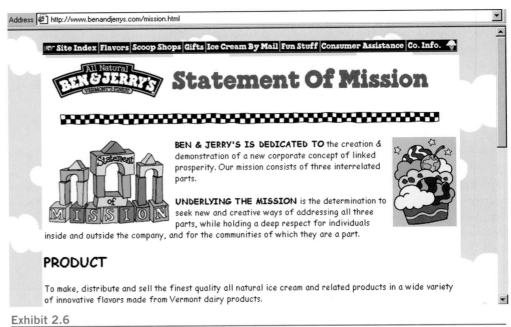

**Exhibit 2.6**

Ben & Jerry's Ice Cream is a New Era firm that proudly displays its focus on improving the quality of life of employees and the community.

customers, employees, and the community. We call efforts to do business *right* and do it *well* the *New Era of marketing*.

In this section, we will look at organizations like Ben & Jerry's and The Body Shop Canada that practise this philosophy by examining how these firms do it right with their focus on ethics and social responsibility.

## Doing It Right: Ethical Behaviour in the Marketplace

Business ethics is the first step toward creating social profit. But what does ethical business behaviour mean to New Era firms and to their marketing strategies? Ethics are rules of conduct—how most people in a culture judge what is right and what is wrong. **Business ethics** are basic values that guide a firm's behaviour, and these beliefs govern the decisions managers make about what goes into their products, how they are advertised and sold, and how they are disposed of.

In the New Era of marketing, we are witnessing greater concern about business decisions based solely on short-term profits. It has been suggested that business operates in an "ethics era"—a period in which both executives and consumers are becoming concerned about the downside of "business as usual."[21] A report from the Canadian Democracy and Corporate Accountability Commission has revealed that 74 percent of Canadian shareholders believe that business executives should "embrace a broader social ethic" in their corporate responsibilities.[22]

The emphasis on ethical business practices means that sometimes firms must make decisions that hurt them in the short term. Despite robust sales of a video game called Night Trap made by Sega, executives at Toys 'R' Us pulled the product from store shelves. This costly action was taken after the store chain received complaints from parents, who objected to their children playing a game in which scantily dressed sorority sisters fight off zombies who try to suck out their blood with a giant syringe.

Notions of right and wrong differ between organizations and cultures. Some businesses, for example, believe it is acceptable for salespeople to use any means to persuade customers to buy, even giving them partly true or even false information, while other firms feel that anything less than total honesty with customers is wrong. Because each culture has its own

**business ethics** Rules of conduct for an organization.

set of values, beliefs, and customs, ethical business behaviour varies in different parts of the world. Transparency International, an organization dedicated to fighting corruption in business around the world, created an International Corruption Perceptions Index, which highlights the differences in the perceptions of corrupt business practices around the world. Out of the 91 countries ranked in their recent Index, Finland was identified as number one, the country perceived to have the least corrupt business practices, and Canada ranked as number seven, ahead of both the U.K. (number 13) and the U.S. (number 16).

**Transparency International**
www.transparency.org

To reduce the confusion about what is right and wrong in international and domestic business operations, many firms develop their own **code of ethics**, or written standards of behaviour, to which everyone in the organization must subscribe. These documents eliminate confusion about what the firm considers to be ethically acceptable behaviour for employees. For example, Dow's Code of Business Conduct (available through its Web site in 15 different languages) includes ethical principles and policies to deal with issues such as bribery, political contributions, equal employment opportunity, and environment, health and safety.

**code of ethics** Written standards of behaviour to which everyone in the organization must subscribe.

Regarding questionable payments, the Code states:

> It is against Dow policy to make unlawful, improper, or other kinds of questionable payments to customers, government employees, or other third parties. We sell our products on the merits of price, quality, and service. We do not seek business obtained through deviation from this principle. We will not offer expensive gifts, bribes, or any other kind of payment or benefit to representatives of customers, suppliers, competitors, government, or governmental agencies. This applies to any individual or organization at any level, whether domestic or foreign.

**Dow**
www.dow.com

Professional associations also often establish codes of ethics to guide the behaviour of members. For instance, to help members of the marketing profession in North America and elsewhere adhere to ethical behaviour in their marketing efforts, the American Marketing Association (AMA), the largest professional marketing association in the world, has developed its own Code of Ethics, which is shown in Figure 2.5. In Canada, the Professional Marketing Research Society, the professional organization for the marketing research community, has its own set of ethical standards that all members must adhere to.

**Professional Marketing Research Society**
www.pmrs-aprm.com

**THE HIGH COSTS OF UNETHICAL MARKETPLACE BEHAVIOUR** Ethical business is good business. New Era marketers understand that unethical practices can wind up costing dearly in the long run both to the firm's finances and to its reputation. Recently, Boeing's CEO, Phil Condit, resigned because of its unethical behaviour regarding obtaining information about a competitor's bid to supply the U.S. Department of Defense. As a result, Boeing has been barred from competing on other bids and its reputation is tarnished.

**CONSUMERISM: FIGHTING BACK** Organized activities that bring about social and political change are not new to the Canadian scene. Women's right to vote, child labour laws, universal medicare, minimum wage, and equal employment opportunities have all resulted from social movements in which citizens, public and private organizations, and business work to change society. **Consumerism** is the social movement directed at protecting consumers from harmful business practices.

**consumerism** A social movement that attempts to protect consumers from harmful business practices.

The modern consumerism movement in Canada began in the late 1940s, when the Consumers' Association of Canada (CAC) was established. The mission of the CAC is to inform and educate consumers, and also to advocate on their behalf.[23] Since its inception, the CAC has been active in helping to establish protective legislation for consumers, related to labelling and packaging, bans on the use of certain pesticides, and improved quality standards for agricultural and manufactured goods. Recent activities of the CAC have focused on fighting the practice of negative-option marketing by the cable industry, in which consumers were automatically charged for services that they did not sign up for unless they contacted the cable company to cancel, and conducting a national consumer survey regarding Canadians' perceptions of the quality of goods and services.

**Consumers' Association of Canada (CAC)**
www.consumer.ca

Members of the American Marketing Association are committed to ethical, professional conduct. They have joined together in subscribing to this Code of Ethics embracing the following topics:

**Responsibilities of the Marketer**
Marketers must accept responsibility for the consequences of their activities and make every effort to ensure that their decisions, recommendations, and actions function to identify, serve, and satisfy all relevant publics: customers, organizations, and society.

Marketers' professional conduct must be guided by:
1. The basic rule of professional ethics: not knowingly to do harm;
2. The adherence to all applicable laws and regulations;
3. The accurate representation of their education, training and experience; and
4. The active support, practice, and promotion of this Code of Ethics.

**Honesty and Fairness**
Marketers shall uphold and advance the integrity, honor, and dignity of the marketing profession by:
1. Being honest in serving consumers, clients, employees, suppliers, distributors, and the public;
2. Not knowingly participating in conflict of interest without prior notice to all parties involved; and
3. Establishing equitable fee schedules including the payment or receipt of usual, customary, and/or legal compensation for marketing exchanges.

**Rights and Duties of Parties in the Marketing Exchange Process**
Participants in the marketing exchange process should be able to expect that:
1. Products and services offered are safe and fit for their intended uses;
2. Communications about offered products and services are not deceptive;
3. All parties intend to discharge their obligations, financial and otherwise, in good faith; and
4. Appropriate internal methods exist for equitable adjustment and/or redress of grievances concerning purchases.

It is understood that the above would include, but is not limited to, the following responsibilities of the marketer:
In the area of product development and management,
- disclosure of all substantial risks associated with product or service usage;
- identification of any product component substitution that might materially change the product of impact on the buyer's purchase decision;

- identification of extra cost-added features.

In the area of promotions,
- avoidance of false and misleading advertising;
- rejection of high pressure manipulations, or misleading sales tactics;
- avoidance of sales promotions that use deception or manipulation.

In the area of distribution,
- not manipulating the availability of a product for purpose of exploitation;
- not using coercion in the marketing channel;
- not exerting undue influence over the reseller's choice to handle a product.

In the area of pricing,
- not engaging in price fixing;
- not practicing predatory pricing;
- disclosing the full price associated with any purchase.

In the area of marketing research,
- prohibiting selling or fundraising under the guise of conducting research;
- maintaining research integrity by avoiding misrepresentation and omission of pertinent research data;
- treating outside clients and suppliers fairly.

**Organizational Relationships**
Marketers should be aware of how their behavior may influence or impact on the behavior of others in organizational relationships. They should not demand, encourage, or apply coercion to obtain unethical behavior in their relationships with others, such as employees, suppliers, or customers.
1. Apply confidentiality and anonymity in professional relationships with regard to privileged information;
2. Meet their obligations and responsibilities in contracts and mutual agreements in a timely manner;
3. Avoid taking the work of others, in whole, or in part, and represent this work as their own or directly benefit from it without compensation or consent of the originator or owner;
4. Avoid manipulation to take advantage of situations to maximize personal welfare in a way that unfairly deprives or damages the organization of others.

Any AMA member found to be in violation of any provision of this Code of Ethics may have his or her Association membership suspended or revoked.

**Figure 2.5** AMA Code of Ethics

The CAC outlines seven Consumer Rights, which it argues that both government legislation and ethical businesses should recognize and provide:

- *The Right to Safety*: Consumers should be confident that products are not dangerous when used as intended.
- *The Right to Be Informed*: Businesses should provide consumers with adequate information to make intelligent product choices. This right means that product information provided by advertising, packaging, and salespeople should be honest and complete.

- *The Right to Be Heard*: Consumers should have the means to complain or express their displeasure to obtain redress or retribution from companies. Government agencies and industry self-regulatory groups should respond to every customer complaint.

- *The Right to Redress*: Consumers should be provided with the opportunity to take action if their needs are not met in the marketplace.

- *The Right to Choose*: Consumers should be able to choose from a variety of products. No one business should be allowed to control the price, quality, or availability of goods and services.

- *The Right to a Healthy Environment*: Consumers have the right to expect that government and businesses will make choices that ensure a healthy environment.

- *The Right to a Consumer Education*: Consumers have a right to expect that they will be provided with the skills necessary to make educated choices in the marketplace.

The Consumers Council of Canada, another consumer organization that strives to improve the marketplace for Canadian consumers, has suggested an eighth consumer right to be protected: The right to privacy, an increasingly important right in the age of information technology.[24]

Consumers continue to have a vigorous interest in consumer-related issues, and New Era marketers are responding by voluntarily making changes to prevent both consumer anger and government intervention. New Era marketers avoid both the financial losses and loss of reputation that consumerism activities may cause by having their customers' best interests in mind from the start.

## Ethics in the Marketing Mix

As we've seen previously, marketing mix strategies are crucial to a firm's success in achieving its objectives. Marketing managers are responsible for determining the most ethical way to price, package, communicate, and distribute their offerings to reach profit and market share objectives. Let's examine how ethical considerations can influence marketing mix decisions.

**MAKING A PRODUCT SAFE**  In product strategies, a key ethical decision concerns product safety. It may be tempting to cut costs on design, safety testing, and production to be able to rush a new product to market or to beat competitors on price. However, responsible companies realize that product safety needs to be a priority. They do everything to ensure that their product meets safety standards when it goes to market, and they react swiftly if a product is found to be unsafe after it is on the market. In any month in Canada, there are several product recalls: Manufacturers recognize safety problems with their products and ask consumers to return them. You can log on to the CBC Web site to check out the latest product recalls.

**PRICING THE PRODUCT FAIRLY**  The potential for unethical pricing strategies is so great that many shady pricing practices are illegal. For example, firms that compete in a market in which there are only a few other firms are not allowed to decide in advance on a common price for their product. This practice, called **price fixing**, eliminates price competition, which otherwise would keep prices down. Another pricing strategy is *price discrimination*, charging lower prices to larger customers. This is acceptable only if it reflects real cost savings for the manufacturer or is necessary to meet competitors' pricing.

A pricing strategy that is unethical but not illegal is *price gouging*—raising the price of a product to take advantage of its popularity. When Chrysler introduced its PT Cruiser, some consumers paid up to US$10 000 over the sticker price to get the car.

New Era firms price their products fairly—and they have been known to cut their prices in times of need. When a hurricane hit the southern United States in 1992, many local firms selling building materials raised their prices, knowing that residents would pay anything to protect what was left of their possessions. Home Depot, however, did just the opposite. The

**CBC**
www.cbc.ca/consumer/
market/recalls/index.html

**price fixing**  An illegal business practice in which firms decide in advance on a common price for their product.

stores sold materials for restoring walls and roofs at cost. In the process, Home Depot gained the loyalty of many consumers throughout North America who heard the story.[25]

During an eastern Canadian ice storm in 1998, some Ontario and Quebec businesses didn't just lower prices; they gave away products for free. St. Viateur Bagel Shop in Montreal, for example, gave away their famous bagels to people without power, and IGA stores gave away baked goods to those in need.[26]

**PROMOTING THE PRODUCT ETHICALLY** Marketing management's decisions on how to promote the firm's products are likely to draw the most criticism from consumers. To promote ethical behaviour on the part of advertisers and to provide consumers with a forum for expressing complaints about advertising, the Canadian advertising industry follows a process of self-regulation through Advertising Standards Canada (ASC). The Canadian Code of Advertising Standards, which ASC administers, has specific guidelines regarding unfair or deceptive advertising to ensure the accuracy and appropriateness of claims. For example, ASC heard a complaint against Gone Hollywood Video, of Burnaby, BC, regarding a newspaper ad that the organization had run to recruit franchisees. The ads promised "100% success rate" and claimed that franchisees could "Earn Jurassic Profits." Gone Hollywood Video was unable to substantiate the claims made in the ad, so the complaint against them was upheld.[27]

ASC also enforces guidelines with respect to appropriate gender portrayal in ads. These Gender Portrayal Guidelines state that advertising should not include sexual exploitation and should always portray women and men as equals. Although these guidelines were originally intended to fight negative portrayals of women in advertising, increasingly complaints by consumers have related to the portrayal of men. Just prior to its demise, a complaint was lodged against Eaton's, and the company agreed to stop showing an ad that ASC found to sexually objectify men. The ad depicted a glamorous woman going off to work, while her husband remained behind, shackled to the kitchen. Although Eaton's claimed that the ad was meant to fight gender myths by using humour, ASC reinforced the Gender Portrayal Guidelines, which state that the use of humour "should not serve as an excuse to stereotype women or men or portray behaviour that is not acceptable today." (**www.adstandards .com**)

**GETTING THE PRODUCT WHERE IT BELONGS** Channels of distribution decisions can also create ethical dilemmas. For example, because their size gives them bargaining power in the channel of distribution, many large retail chains are forcing manufacturers to pay a **slotting allowance**, a fee paid in exchange for agreeing to place the manufacturer's products on the retailer's valuable shelf space. While the retailers claim that such fees pay the cost of adding products to their inventory, many manufacturers feel slotting fees are unethical. Certainly the practice prevents smaller manufacturers who cannot afford the slotting allowances from reaching consumers.

## DOING IT RIGHT: A FOCUS ON SOCIAL RESPONSIBILITY

We've learned how New Era firms gain social profit by practising business ethics when making marketing mix decisions. The second part of social profit is **social responsibility**, a management process in which organizations engage in activities that have a positive effect on society and promote the public good. These activities include environmental stewardship, cause marketing, and encouraging cultural diversity. Firms like Ben & Jerry's that believe in social responsibility represent a business value system that goes beyond the short-term bottom line. Instead, they consider the short- and long-term effects of decisions on the company, its employees, consumers, the community, and the world at large.

### Serving the Environment

When New Era firms make socially responsible business decisions that also protect the environment, they assume a position of **environmental stewardship**. The Body Shop

**Advertising Standards Canada**
www.adstandards.com

**slotting allowance** A fee paid by a manufacturer to a retailer in exchange for agreeing to place products on the retailer's shelves.

**social responsibility** A management practice in which organizations seek to engage in activities that have a positive effect on society and promote the public good.

**environmental stewardship** A position taken by an organization to protect or enhance the natural environment as it conducts its business activities.

Canada practises this through "sustainability" strategies, the development of products that use resources sparingly to sustain those resources for future generations. Toyota has developed a hybrid car, the Toyota Prius, which combines a gasoline engine with a powerful electric motor, as depicted in Exhibit 2.7.

The term **green marketing** describes efforts by firms to choose packages, product designs, and other aspects of the marketing mix that are earth friendly but still profitable.

**green marketing**  A marketing strategy that supports environmental stewardship by creating an environmentally founded differential benefit in the minds of consumers.

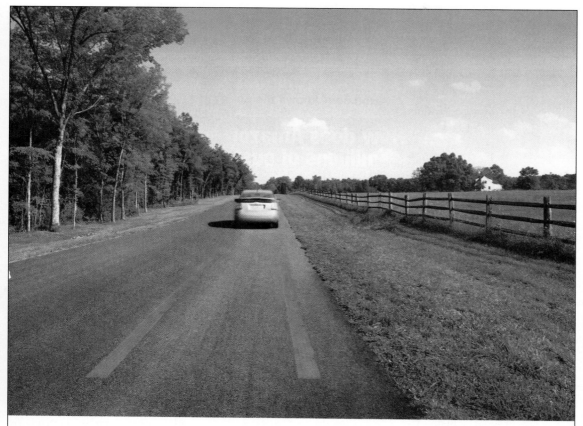

# Introducing
# high performance technology that's also good
# for the environment. Now you can burn more rubber and less gas. Toyota's revolutionary new

Hybrid Synergy Drive® combines a gasoline engine with a powerful electric motor that never needs to be plugged in.

The result? Super-efficient, super-charged performance.

For example, Hybrid Synergy Drive will inject a V6 SUV with the power and torque of a V8. Remarkably, the SUV will also achieve the average fuel efficiency of a compact car with a fraction of conventional emissions.

This groundbreaking yet affordable technology has already hit the roads in the all-new Prius. And soon, Hybrid Synergy Drive will be available in more and more Toyota products – including SUVs.

One day, all cars may be quicker off the mark. And slower to leave a mark.

**toyota.com/tomorrow**  ©2003

TODAY    TOMORROW    **TOYOTA**

**Exhibit 2.7**

Toyota's hybrid car is an example of the company's environmental stewardship.

**Environmental Choice Program**
www.environmentalchoice.com

**Sonoco Products Co.**
www.sonoco.com

The Canadian government, through Environment Canada, encourages Canadian companies to practise green marketing through such programs as the EcoLogo. This program promotes stringent, environmentally friendly guidelines for industries, ranging from automotive products to office supplies. If a business meets the guidelines, it may use the EcoLogo on its product to signal its environmental soundness to consumers. Companies that have been granted the right to use the EcoLogo include Frigidaire Canada, which manufactures energy-efficient dishwashers and washing machines, and Fuji Graphics Systems, which has developed photo processing systems that are gentle to the environment.[28]

Green marketing practices can indeed be successful for a firm's bottom line. For example, Electrolux found that profits from its solar-powered lawn mowers, chain saws lubricated with vegetable oil, and water-conserving washing machines actually were 3.8 percent higher than profits from the company's conventional products.[29]

Here's how some other firms are "turning green":

- Sonoco Products Co., one of the world's largest packaging companies with operations in five Canadian provinces, began its "We make it, we take it back" program in 1990. The company takes its used boxes back from customers, who don't have to worry about disposing of them. Sonoco benefits because it uses recycled packaging for more than two-thirds of its raw materials.[30]

- As depicted in Exhibit 2.9, Shell Canada Limited is concerned about sustainable development. It has developed an environmental fund to provide grants to community-driven environmental projects.

## Serving Society: Cause Marketing

**cause marketing** A marketing strategy in which an organization serves its community by promoting and supporting a worthy cause or by allying itself with a not-for-profit organization to tackle a social problem.

**Cause marketing** is a strategy of joining forces with a not-for-profit organization to tackle a social problem. In the past, this practice usually meant running a short-term promotion and then donating profits to a charity. But consumers often saw these programs as gimmicky and insincere, especially when there was no apparent connection between the company and the cause. As a result, sales increased during the promotion, but there were no long-term benefits to either the sponsoring firm or the cause it was trying to help.

Today, New Era firms have abandoned this one-shot approach and instead make a long-term commitment to tackle a social problem, such as illiteracy or child abuse.[31] Avon Canada's Flame Crusade against Breast Cancer is one example of cause marketing. Since its inception in 1993, the program has raised over $5.2 million for breast cancer research through the sales of such products as the Flame pin (see Exhibit 2.8).[32] Avon hopes that its long-term involvement with breast cancer awareness will result in both health benefits for women and increased good will for the company—a "win-win" situation.

## Serving the Community: Promoting Cultural Diversity

**cultural diversity** A management practice that actively seeks to include people of different sexes, races, ethnic groups, religions, and sexual preferences in an organization's employees, customers, suppliers, and distribution channel partners.

In a country as culturally diverse as Canada, promotion of **cultural diversity** is not only the right thing to do, it's also important to the long-term financial health of the organization. When firms adopt cultural diversity programs, they make sure that marketing policies and hiring practices give people an equal chance to work for the company and buy its products.

Warner-Lambert Canada, manufacturer of such brands as Listerine, Trident, and Dentyne, embraces cultural diversity; as one company document states, "The more our organization reflects the consumer population, the more it will be in sync with what customers want, need, and are looking for."[33]

The diversity philosophy also extends to the disabled. Smart marketers view the disabled as both customers and valued employees. Hertz, for example, offers cars that disabled people can drive at nearly 800 Hertz rental locations and has worked to equip shuttle buses and vans with lifts to transport these customers.[34]

**Exhibit 2.8**

Avon Flame: a successful cause marketing program that female customers appreciate.

## Sustainable Development – we're committed to the long journey

Shell Canada is in the business of meeting today's energy needs in a socially and environmentally responsible way, while always keeping the long term in mind.

So it's not surprising that Shell's journey to sustainable development (SD) began more than a decade ago. Shell's commitment to SD – the integration of economic, environmental and social considerations in our everyday business was formalized 14 years ago. Our first sustainable development policy was adopted in 1990 and our first SD report was published shortly after – one of the first in the world.

Through environmental assessment studies, cutting-edge technology, extensive stakeholder engagement and public consultation, Shell is an industry leader in pursuing business based on the principles of sustainable development.

Our support of the Canadian Environment Awards, the Shell Conservation Internship Program and the Shell Environmental Fund helps demonstrate our long-term commitment to SD.

Established in 1990, the Shell Environmental Fund (SEF) awards grants to community-driven environmental projects. This year the SEF celebrates a milestone of over $10 million in grants to more than 3,500 Canadian projects.

While the road to SD is long, Shell is dedicated to help build a sustainable future.

For more information, visit Shell Canada's Web site at www.shell.ca.

**Exhibit 2.9**

Profits and principles at Shell Canada Limited.

We've seen that New Era firms create social profit by adhering to ethical business practices. Social profit is also created when firms practise social responsibility by being concerned about the environment, promoting diversity, and serving their communities through cause marketing.

# Real People, Real Decisions

## ▶ How It Worked Out at Sony Nordic

Henrik chose Option 1. The Danish-speaking crew was moved outside to distribute the leaflets and the local freelancers were given an intensive training course on the products and the Web site. As a result of these changes, the Sony Experience Tour was a great success. Far exceeding expectations, a total of 60 000 visitors entered the Sony Experience bus and had hands-on experience with all the latest Sony connectivity products. Some 30 000 visitors went to the Web site, including 6000 people who uploaded pictures and produced slide shows.

Even with extensive knowledge of local markets, it can be difficult to predict customers' behaviour. From your research you've probably discovered that there are greater differences among consumers in neighbouring countries than you may have thought. Henrik realized that the spoken language of the Tour should be local, even if English is widely spoken in Nordic

countries, and even if the Sony Experience Web site is in English, the language of the Internet.

Henrik learned a valuable lesson: when a company is trying to reach consumers in international markets, localization is key to success. He now believes it is important to think globally, but act locally. Henrik is a great example of what it takes to succeed in marketing (and in business, for that matter)—the ability to constantly learn from one's experiences. In fact, Henrik's self-described management style is "To set the target and fix the framework." By this he means that the process used to achieve a goal is key to success. If the process is right, the outcome will be right as well. Finally, Henrik's parting advice to students is "Treat others as you would like them to treat you." Sound words to live by, indeed.

## Key Terms

business ethics, p. 44

business portfolio, p. 36

cause marketing, p. 50

code of ethics, p. 45

competitive advantage, p. 37

consumerism, p. 45

cultural diversity, p. 50

dumping, p. 43

environmental stewardship, p. 48

external environment, p. 34

grey market, p. 42

green marketing, p. 49

internal environment, p. 35

marketing plan, p. 37

mission statement, p. 33

price fixing, p. 47

slotting allowance, p. 48

social profit, p. 43

social responsibility, p. 48

strategic business units (SBUs), p. 36

strategic planning, p. 31

SWOT analysis, p. 33

# CHAPTER SUMMARY

1. **Explain how businesses develop plans at different levels within the organization.**

   Planning in most business organizations occurs mainly at two levels: Strategic and functional. Strategic plans are high-level plans that envision where the business is going within the next 3 to 5 years. Mission statements guide the formation of strategic plans, which are developed for the entire business, or for individual strategic business units (SBUs) within the organization.

   Given their high-level nature, strategic plans cannot be implemented directly. For this reason, firms develop a one-year plan, which takes its direction from the strategic plan, called the marketing plan. From this, the different functions such as production, sales, finance, human resources, etc. develop their own plans. In this way, the entire organization is working toward a common goal.

2. **Describe the steps in the marketing planning process.**

   Marketing planning begins with an evaluation of the external and internal environments facing the business. Marketing managers then set quantitative and qualitative market objectives, such as desired levels of sales, development of new or improved products, or growth in new or existing markets. Next, marketing mangers select the target market(s) the organization will go after and decide what marketing mix strategies they will use. Tactical plans are developed to implement the strategies and mechanisms to control the marketing plan are put in place. Therefore, the marketing planning process ends with the development of a formal, written document—the marketing plan.

3. **Outline how the marketing plan is related to other functional plans (e.g., sales, production, finance) within the organization.**

   The marketing plan provides a common foundation for the development of other functional plans. The marketing plan outlines what markets and customers the business will pursue and what marketing strategies will accomplish the established objectives. Based on this, each function knows what it needs to do to contribute toward the successful implementation of the marketing strategies. Therefore, the sales function knows what sales targets need to be achieved; the production function knows what needs to be produced by when; the HR function knows what human resources will be required, and so on.

4. **Explain how strategic marketing mix decisions are made in international markets.**

Firms competing in the international marketplace have strategic decisions they need to make regarding the deployment of the marketing mix elements. The main question they have to ask is this—should we standardize our strategies across international markets, or should we customize? These decisions are not easy because a number of factors influence the decisions such as laws in foreign countries, consumer preferences, and availability of resources and channels of distribution.

5. **Explain how firms practise ethical and socially responsible behaviour in the marketplace.**

Many consumers today are concerned with the ethical practices of companies. As a result, astute marketers recognize that long-term profitability depends on making quality products while acting in an ethical and socially responsible manner. Marketing is *still* concerned with the firm's "bottom line," but now many managers also consider social profit, which is the net benefit both the firm and society receive from a firm's ethical practices and socially responsible behaviour.

The second part of social profit is social responsibility, a management process in which organizations engage in activities that have a positive effect on society and promote the public good. These activities include environmental stewardship, cause marketing, and encouraging cultural diversity. Firms like Ben & Jerry's that believe in social responsibility represent a business value system that goes beyond the short-term bottom line. Instead, they consider the short- and long-term effects of decisions on the company, its employees, consumers, the community, and the world at large.

# CHAPTER REVIEW

## Marketing Concepts: Testing Your Knowledge

1. What are the different levels of planning within a business organization?
2. What is a mission statement? Why is a mission statement important to an organization?
3. What is a SWOT analysis? What role does it play in the planning process?
4. What is a business portfolio? Why do firms develop SBUs?
5. Why is marketing planning important to a firm?
6. What are the elements of a sound marketing plan?
7. What does it mean for a firm to have a competitive advantage? What factors give a firm a competitive advantage in the marketplace?
8. What are marketing objectives? What types of marketing objectives do firms normally include in marketing planning?
9. How are marketing plans related to other functional plans within a business?
10. Explain the tradeoffs involved in marketing mix decisions when firms enter international markets. Provide concrete examples.
11. What is social profit? What are the two main components of social profit?

## Marketing Concepts: Discussing Choices and Issues

1. What do you think about the different levels of planning in business organizations? What are the benefits of such an approach? Do you see any drawbacks?
2. Do you agree with the idea that marketing is a firm's most essential functional area, or do you think a firm's success depends equally on all of its functional areas? Explain your reasoning.
3. Do you think firms should concentrate on developing products that are better in some way than competitors' products, or should each firm focus on making the best product it can

without regard to competing products? As a consumer, which approach is more likely to produce products that satisfy you the most?

4. Most planning, whether by businesses or by not-for-profit organizations, involves strategies for growth. But is growth always the right direction? Can you think of some organizations that should have contraction rather than expansion as their goal? Do you know of any organizations that have planned to get smaller rather than larger to be successful?

## Marketing Practice: Applying What You've Learned

1. Assume that you are the marketing director for a local micro-brewery and that your boss, the company president, has decided to develop a mission statement to add to this year's annual report. He's admitted that he doesn't know much about developing a mission statement and has asked you to help guide him in this process. Write a memo outlining what exactly a mission statement is, why firms develop such statements, how firms use missions statements, and your thoughts on what the firm's mission statement might be.

2. As a marketing student, you know that large firms often organize their operations into a number of strategic business units (SBUs). A college or university might develop a similar structure where different academic units are seen as separate businesses. Working with four to six classmates, consider how your college or university might divide its total academic units into separate SBUs. What would be the problems with implementing such a plan? What would be the advantages and disadvantages for students and for faculty? Present your analysis of university SBUs to your class.

3. Assume you are the new marketing assistant in a small metropolitan hospital whose market consists of the residents in the city district and the students and faculty of a large nearby college or university. You have been asked for ideas that the organization might use in promotional activities to draw clients who might otherwise choose a larger facility across town. Develop a list of the consumer segments in the hospital's market (for example, elderly, children, college or university athletes, international students), and for each segment, identify possible features and benefits the hospital might emphasize in its promotions to attract that segment.

4. Pick two firms that both operate in foreign markets, but use different strategies to compete. In your opinion, which strategy is superior? Why? Base your answer on a thorough analysis of the marketing mix variables.

5. Do you think firms practising new era marketing are doing it for the financial benefit? What do you think is the future of new era marketing? What is the next big idea that will emerge from this concept?

## Marketing Mini-Project: Learning by Doing

The purpose of this mini-project is to gain an understanding of marketing planning through actual experience.

1. Select one of the following for your marketing planning project:
   * Yourself (in your search for a career)
   * Your college or university
   * A specific department in your college or university

2. Next, develop the following elements of the marketing planning process:
   * A mission statement
   * A SWOT analysis
   * Objectives
   * A description of the target market(s)
   * A brief outline of the marketing mix strategies—product, pricing, distribution, and marketing communications strategies—that satisfy the objectives and address the target market

3. Prepare a formal, but brief, marketing plan using the template provided in this chapter as a guide.

# Real People, Real Surfers: Exploring the Web

Visit the home pages of one or more of the firms whose mission statements are given in Figure 2.2. Follow the links to find out about the company's products, pricing, distribution, and marketing communications strategies. Do a Web search for other information about the company. Based on your findings, answer the following questions.

1. What is the organization's "business"? What is the overall purpose of the organization? What does the organization hope to achieve?

2. What customers does the organization want to serve?

3. What elements of the Web page specifically reflect the business of the organization? How is the Web page designed to attract the organization's customers?

4. Do you think the marketing strategies and other activities of the organization are consistent with its mission? Why do you feel this way?

Develop a report based on your findings and conclusions about the organization. Present your report to your class.

Managers at the Seiyu supermarket chain in Japan, which is 38 percent owned by Wal-Mart Stores, start their day with a ritual just as their counterparts do in Bentonville, Arkansas, where Wal-Mart is head-quartered. "Give me an S!" their Japanese manager shouts. "S!" comes the reply. The group spells "S-E-I-Y-U." Finally, the manager asks: "Who is number 1?" Their reply: "Customers!"

While it may appear that Wal-Mart has simply replicated its North American strategy in Japan, nothing could be farther from the truth. The Wal-Mart story in Japan is one of market entry strategy, product positioning, learning about cultural differences, and making strategic choices.

Unlike Toys "R" Us or Costco that opened stores under the corporate name in Japan, Wal-Mart decided to buy a part of Seiyu and use its name to compete instead of the Wal-Mart name and logo. Wal-Mart felt that it could not only take advantage of Seiyu's well-known, but struggling, brand, but also use a local partner to navigate through Japan's complex supplier network.

Many analysts feel Wal-Mart will not succeed in Japan for several reasons. One, the Japanese market is dominated by powerful manufacturers and wholesalers, who keep prices high. How will a discounter like Wal-Mart, which relies on low prices, succeed? Two, Japanese consumers are very different from North American consumers. They are very finicky and are set in their buying habits. Three, the entire Japanese corporate culture is unlike that of North America. Many Japanese corporations are very hierarchical, with rigid boundaries between senior managers and juniors. At Wal-Mart, on the other hand, managers interact in a very informal way with colleagues, lavishing them with praise for a job well done, something that is new to the Japanese way of thinking.

At the present, Wal-Mart has been concentrating its attention on managing stores based on sales information, rather than manager's hunches. To do this, it has invested heavily in product scanners and databases that provide managers with accurate information about inventory, sales, and prices.

Wal-Mart has been sensitive to local cultural issues. In the process of modernizing stores, it has added small fish markets in the stores where consumers can buy fresh fish. In North America, Wal-Mart relies on consumers to know that it practises "everyday low prices". However, Japanese consumers rely on weekly circulars informing them of specials. Initially, Wal-Mart refused to use these promotional materials. However, consumers complained, so Wal-Mart returned to the Japanese practice of using circulars.

Although some North American tactics do not translate well in Japan (for example, consumers did not know the meaning of the term "rollback"), others appear to be working well. Wal-Mart uses strict training methods it uses in North America in Japan. For example, it is teaching managers to be more assertive and to be more at ease when interacting in public. Japanese mangers, in a training session, had to dance in front of the class for being late or forgetting to turn off their cellphones!

Source: Adapted from Ken Belson, "Wal-Mart Hopes It Won't Be Lost in Translation," *The New York Times*, December 14, 2003, Section 3, pages 1, 12.

## Things to Think About

1. What factors do you think Wal-Mart would have taken into account to make strategic choices in the Japanese market?

2. Evaluate Wal-Mart's decision to enter the Japanese market with a partner, instead of opening its own stores.

3. Do you think Wal-Mart will be successful in Japan? Why or why not?

4. If you were working for Wal-Mart in Japan, what steps would you take next to ensure successful entry into the Japanese market?

## Caribbean Beer—Part 1

This video case is about two sisters, Alysha and Paula Harrison, who decide to become entrepreneurs by brewing (under license) a popular Caribbean beer called Banks, and an energy drink called Malta. As the case opens we see Alysha and Paula at Toronto's annual Caribana parade, a perfect place to promote their beer.

Bankrolled by their father to the tune of one million dollars, the two sisters, with no previous brewing experience, embark on their venture. As shown in the video, they face problems usually faced by startups: misbehaving machinery, stubborn customers, and employee turnover. To complicate matters, Paula announces that she is pregnant, and exits the scene to take maternity leave. Alysha is left to run the entire operation on her own.

We see in the video that being financed by your family has its advantages and disadvantages. While the two sisters would like to operate independently, their lack of business acumen hinders them, and they have to lean on their father for advice and help.

Grace, a major distributor of Caribbean foods, agrees to have the sisters brew Malta, the energy drink. Although this appears to be wonderful news, Grace is a tough customer who refuses to pay in advance and refuses to sign a two-year deal. Alysha manages to secure a deal to supply Grace for a three-month period at a time. This is very typical in channels of distribution—the big player, closer to the end consumer, has more power.

From the start, the business faces an uphill battle. Production costs are higher than expected and this eats into profit margins. Vanya Richardson, the young brewmaster, quits, and the job of brewing falls on Dan and Daryl, who were previously working in operations. A Toronto distributor refuses to pay delivery costs for an order worth thousands of dollars. Alysha and Paula are learning lessons they never anticipated when they were in school!

## Questions

1. In this chapter we discuss the different plans successful businesses develop. Do you think a small startup should also develop plans at three levels: strategic, marketing, and operational? Why or why not?

2. Develop a mission statement for Alysha and Paula's business. Compare your statement with two other breweries: Molson and Big Rock. Which mission statement do you think provides the best direction for the business?

3. What do you think the two sisters could have done to prevent some of the problems they faced in their business?

4. The two sisters decide to sell their beer in the United States, with Alysha managing the operations in Canada and Paula being responsible for marketing in the US. What is your opinion of such an arrangement? Will it work? What are some advantages and disadvantages of having two functions (operations and marketing) located in different places?

Source: This case was prepared by Ajay Sirsi and is based on "Caribbean Beer," *Venture* #889.

# PART II

Societal Success • Business Success • Customer Success • Part I • Part II • Part III • Part IV

# Preparing for Marketing Strategies

**You learned in Part I that successful businesses accurately understand customers' needs.** Perhaps two questions were left unanswered in your mind: What tools do firms use to understand customer needs? Among the myriad needs in the marketplace, how does a business choose which needs to serve? In this part you will learn all about marketing research tools to understand customer needs. You will also learn about market segmentation and the buying behaviour of customers and consumers: fundamental concepts, without which a firm cannot develop superior marketing strategies.

# CHAPTER 3
## Market Segmentation and Positioning

## CHAPTER OBJECTIVES

WHEN YOU HAVE COMPLETED YOUR STUDY OF THIS CHAPTER, YOU SHOULD BE ABLE TO

1. Understand the five steps of developing a target marketing strategy.

2. Define the terms segmentation, target marketing, and positioning.

3. Segment consumer and business-to-business markets.

4. Explain how marketers evaluate and select potential market segments.

5. Understand how a firm develops and implements a positioning strategy.

6. Describe how a positioning strategy can be defended.

# Real People, Real Decisions

## Meet **Candace Fochuk-Barey,** a Decision Maker at Ford Motor Company of Canada

As Marketing Manager, Special Markets at the Ford Motor Company of Canada, Candace Fochuk-Barey is responsible for overseeing the positioning of Ford brands and services to specific target markets. Currently one of Ford's priority special markets is women, especially those 24 to 54 years old. While many automotive marketing activities have traditionally targeted men, recently Ford has been proactive in targeting women, recognizing that women represent a large and potentially profitable target segment for car and truck sales. To facilitate the effective targeting of Ford products to Canadian women, Fochuk-Barey participates in various new product launch teams at Ford and was instrumental in founding the Ford of Canada's Women's Council and the Canadian Chapter of the Women's Automotive Association International.

Fochuk-Barey, who has a degree from McMaster University, began her career at Ford in 1979 and has held a variety of positions since then in general marketing, vehicle sales, and customer service. She is also active in her community, helping to organize the Canadian Woman Entrepreneur of the Year Awards and sitting on the Career Assessment and Planning advisory board of the YWCA of Toronto.

In the late 1990s, management at Ford Canada realized that the company was not getting a large share of the women's market. Ford had captured almost 23 percent of the Canadian car market by 1998, but it had less than 15 percent share of the total car sales to women. Candace Fochuk-Barey's research of the market highlighted the importance of women consumers to Ford: Women influence 80 percent of all vehicle purchases. If Ford did not do a better job of understanding and targeting women, it was going to have a hard time improving the overall share of the market.

Fochuk-Barey identified some characteristics of the women car buyer segment. Of those women who are involved in vehicle purchases, 44 percent are between the ages of 25 and 54 and half of them do not have a spouse. These characteristics had some important implications for Ford's target marketing activities. For example, communicating with these consumers by showing a happy nuclear family in ads, which Ford had done in the past, was probably not connecting with a large part of this segment. Research also showed that women take more time than men to search for information before making a car purchase (six to nine months, compared to less than three months for men), and that women like to purchase from a company that they feel cares about customers and their community. With respect to the actual product, women car buyers are looking for a reliable car that is durable, offers good value, is easy to handle, and has a good warranty.

With these characteristics of the segment in mind, Fochuk-Barey formulated some marketing activities designed specifically for better serving the needs of women: Ford offered its dealers a course on "Service—Responding to a Woman's Perspective"; recruited more women as salespeople; began sponsoring the Run for the Cure, a national fundraiser for breast cancer research; and ran seminars for women on such topics as car maintenance and car seat safety.

After achieving some success with these initial targeting efforts, Fochuk-Barey wanted to expand Ford's focus on women customers. She felt there was an opportunity to target a specific vehicle—the Ford Windstar—to women. The Windstar made sense for a couple of reasons. First, one-third of all trucks sold in Canada were sold to women, and the majority of these vehicles were minivans. So women, especially mothers, were interested in minivan products. Second, the Windstar made sense from an internal point of view. Ford wanted to improve its performance in the minivan product category since it ranked fifth out of the five largest automakers in that market. The Windstar had achieved a five-star safety rating, the top safety rating for any minivan. This was a potential selling point to mothers who were concerned for the safety of their children.

Fochuk-Barey recognized that there were potential risks for Ford in focusing the marketing efforts for one vehicle so strongly on one target group. Were women a large enough group to make the product profitable? Would Ford alienate some male customers for the product by focusing its efforts so strongly on women? Fochuk-Barey considered two options.

**Option 1.** The first option was to identify women, and mothers specifically, as the primary target market for the Windstar. This would involve changing every aspect of the marketing for the Windstar, starting with the design of the vehicle through to the ads and sales efforts, to meet the needs of mothers. With this option, it would be the first time that women would be considered the primary target segment for a Ford car or truck.

**Option 2.** The second option was to target the Windstar to women, but with a less substantial effort. Women would be just one of the target markets for the product, so the design of the vehicle would not be changed to specifically meet the needs of mothers. Instead, the target marketing efforts would primarily be reflected in advertising decisions.

Now, put yourself in Candace Fochuk-Barey's shoes: Which option would you choose, and why?

Sources: Lesley Daw, "Female-friendly Ford," *Marketing Magazine,* 17 August 1998: 2–22; Liza Finlay, "Mom power," *Marketing Magazine,* 19/26 July 1999; personal interview with Candace Fochuk-Barey.

# THE CONCEPT OF SEGMENTATION

The goal of the marketer is to satisfy needs, but in our complex society, it is naive to assume that everyone's needs are the same. Candace Fochuk-Barey and her colleagues at Ford Canada know that different types of consumers have different priorities when it comes to buying a car. So when Ford designs and markets its cars, it needs to consider the different needs that exist in the marketplace. Understanding these needs is especially complex today, because technological and cultural advances have created a condition of market fragmentation. **Market fragmentation** occurs when people's diverse interests and backgrounds have divided them into different groups with distinct needs and wants. Because of this diversity, the same product or service will not appeal to everyone.

Consider, for example, the effects of fragmentation in the fast-food industry. When a McDonald's hamburger was still a novelty (with under a million sold), people were happy to order just a plain hamburger, fries, and drink. Today's consumers would be very unhappy if salads, chicken, or wraps disappeared from the menu. But how many menu items do McDonald's, Harvey's, or Pizza Hut need to offer? Why is it that kids insist on a Happy Meal, whereas their parents prefer to grab a pita at Wendy's or a veggie burger at Harvey's?

At one time, it was sufficient to divide the sports shoe market into athletes versus non-athletes. Today, a walk through any sporting goods store will reveal that the athlete market has fragmented in many directions, and includes shoes designed for jogging, basketball, tennis, cycling, cross-training, and skateboarding. Some manufacturers of athletic footwear geared to young boarders, such as Vans (Exhibit 3.1), Airwalk, and DC, chalked up annual sales gains of 20 to 50 percent in the past few years. Known to their peers as shredders, riders, or skaters, the youth who wear these shoes can be seen riding skateboards down the handrails and steps of city parks, riding rails or doing jumps on snowboards, stunt bikes, or wakeboards. Over the next few years, sports marketers expect the skateboard and snowboard populations to double and wakeboarders to soar sixfold. To cash in on this trend, PepsiCo Inc.'s Mountain Dew began to feature snowboarding in its advertisements and was rewarded with a hefty increase in sales.[1]

Instead of trying to sell the same thing to all customers, marketers often select a **target marketing strategy**, in which they divide the total market into different segments based on customer characteristics, select one or more segments, and develop products to meet the needs of those specific segments. The five-step process of segmentation, targeting, and positioning is illustrated in Figure 3.1. Understanding customers will be discussed in Chapters 4, 5, and 6. The creation of marketing mix programs is discussed in Chapters 7 through 13. Our focus here is on segmentation, targeting, and positioning.

**Segmentation** is the process of dividing a larger market into subgroups, where within groups people have fairly homogeneous needs and wants and where between groups people have sufficiently different needs and wants that they would be interested in very different product solutions or marketing programs. Because consumers have different needs and wants and the same marketing program is unlikely to appeal to all consumers, marketers identify the key groups in a market, choose which group(s) to focus on (target), decide how they want their brand to compete and be known by these consumers (positioning), and design marketing programs (make marketing mix decisions) to create product offers that uniquely appeal to the chosen target groups. There are very few, if any, products with universal appeal. Even for products as popular as cola soft drinks, some consumers prefer

**Ford Motor Company of Canada**
www.ford.ca

**market fragmentation** Creation of many consumer groups due to a diversity of distinct needs and wants in modern society.

**target marketing strategy** Dividing the total market into different segments based on customer characteristics, selecting one or more segments, and developing products to meet the needs of those specific segments.

**segmentation** The process of dividing a larger market into smaller pieces, based on one or more meaningful, shared characteristics.

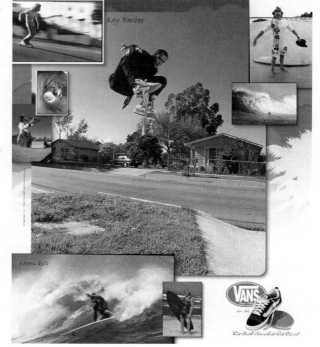

**Exhibit 3.1**
Young shredders are the focus of many marketers.

| 1. Select Markets | 2. Market Segmentation | 3. Market Targeting | 4. Market Positioning | 5. Create and Execute Marketing Mix Programs |
|---|---|---|---|---|
| a. Define your market<br>b. Understand customers: needs and wants; benefits, features, and attributes sought; and purchase and consumption behaviour | a. Identify groups: geographic, behavioural, pyschographic, and demographic segmentation<br>b. Describe (profile) the groups: who, what, when, where, why | a. Evaluate segment attractiviness: size, growth; strategic fit, competitive or comparative advantage; level of competition, defendability<br>b. Decide which one(s) to target | Decide how you want to compete, be differentiated, and be known for value creation in the minds of consumers | |

**Figure 3.1** Steps in the Target Marketing Process

**Thermohair Inc.**
www.thermohair.com

Coca-Cola® over Pepsi, some prefer Pepsi over Coke®, some prefer diet colas, some prefer flavoured colas (e.g., Dr. Pepper, Vanilla Coke®; Exhibit 3.2), some prefer caffeine enhanced colas like Jolt, and others prefer non-soft drink beverages. Theresa Bergeron, President of Thermohair Inc., (Exhibit 3.3; also see CBC Video Case "Mohair Socks," p. 208), has developed a product line of specialty socks made of kid (baby goat) mohair. Not everyone would be interested in a $25 pair of durable, warm, comfortable socks, but people involved in outdoor recreational sports like hiking and camping might be.

## Selecting and Segmenting a Market

One of the challenges in developing marketing strategy is determining what market you are in and what market you should be segmenting. For example, in Chapter 2, we saw that Kodak redefined itself from being in the film business to being in the imaging business—leading Kodak to venture into new markets. Take the brand Gatorade, for example. As the brand manager, would you want to be segmenting the beverage market, the sports drink market, or the performance sports drink market? Deciding what "market" you are competing in has significant implications for the segments you might identify. You must also consider the geographic scope of the market—are you segmenting the beverage market in North America, Canada, or one or more provinces? The decision of how to define the markets you are competing in is typically done at the executive (strategic planning) level of an organization. As an entrepreneur or consultant, you may need to make this decision yourself—based on your experience, your understanding of the consumer, competitive, and technological environments, and your understanding of the mission, strategic directions, and competencies of your organization.

**CRITERIA FOR IDENTIFYING MARKET SEGMENTS** Before discussing how to segment a market, let's review the criteria for a successful segmentation scheme. There is no right or wrong way to segment a market but some segmentation schemes are more useful than others for identifying market opportunities and being able to position products that

**Exhibit 3.2**

Coca-Cola® developed Vanilla Coke® to appeal to a flavoured-cola market segment.

uniquely appeal to a well-defined group of consumers or customers—the term used to describe organizational or business-to-business buyers.

A viable segmentation scheme should satisfy the requirements outlined in Figure 3.2.

1. Members of the segment must be similar to each other in their product needs and wants such that the same marketing programs (product offers) would be appealing to most members of the group.

2. At the same time, consumers in each segment should be sufficiently different from consumers in other segments that different marketing programs or product offers would be appealing to the different segments. Segment differences need to be actionable—that is, they require different product, pricing, distribution, and/or communication strategies to create a product offer that appeals to each segment. Without real differences in consumer needs and wants, firms might as well use a mass-marketing strategy. For example, it's a waste of time to develop two separate lines of skin care products for working and non-working women, if both segments have the same needs and wants with respect to skin care.

3. The segment must be large enough now and in the future to warrant targeting. What is large enough is a judgment call, and usually depends on the size of the company doing the segmentation scheme. Large organizations like Procter & Gamble may be interested only in market segments with sales potential in the millions of dollars. A smaller company may be interested in segments with sales potential in the tens or hundreds of thousands of dollars. In considering the B.C. market, for example, the Beef Information Centre evaluated the Chinese Canadian community as a possible segment. Chinese Canadians spend more money on food than any other ethnic group, and if just 25 percent of the close to 300 000 Chinese Canadians in British Columbia ate one more beef meal a month, sales of beef in British Columbia would increase by 77 000 kilograms per year. This analysis led the organization to target the Chinese Canadian segment in Vancouver through magazine ads like the one in Exhibit 3.4, recipes distributed at grocery stores, and the sponsorship of a Chinese cooking show on TV.[2]

4. The segment must represent a measurable market—that is, people in the segment have purchasing power: the authority, willingness, and ability to make a purchase decision. Children, for example, may not have the authority to make a purchase. Religious or cultural beliefs may impact willingness to buy (such as beef-based hamburgers in India). Low-income consumers may not have the ability to buy.

5. Finally, the segment must be reachable. Marketers must be able to identify consumers or organizational customers in the segment and communicate the product offer to them in a cost effective manner. It is easy to select television programs or magazines that will efficiently reach older consumers, consumers with specific levels of education, certain ethnic groups, or residents of major cities, because the media they prefer are easy to identify. It is unlikely, however, that marketing communications can reach only left-handed blonde people with tattoos who listen to hip-hop. Therefore, it may not make sense to target that segment.

**THERMOHAIR**®

**The ultimate in luxury for your feet!**
We use only the first cut of the finest kid mohair, renowned for its softness, warmth, durability and absorbency. Special knit loops cushion your step. Ideal for walking, hiking, sports, and casual wear.
$54.00 for each gift box of two pair
Call Toll Free 1-877-766-4247
Fax (613) 989-3328 Phone (613) 989-1340

**Exhibit 3.3**

Thermohair Inc. focuses on a narrow segment interested in warm, comfortable, durable socks that are made for cold weather (they even have a rib-free line for people with circulation problems).

- Similar Enough within the Group
- Different Enough between the Groups
- Large Enough
- Measurable Market
- Reachable

**Figure 3.2** Criteria for Effective Segmentation Schemes

**Exhibit 3.4**

Chinese Canadian consumers were identified as a large segment for the Beef Information Centre of British Columbia.

## THE PROCESS OF SEGMENTATION

**segmentation variables** Bases for dividing the total market into fairly homogenous groups, each with different needs and preferences.

Segmentation is the central tenet or cornerstone of marketing strategy. Not all consumers or business market customers want the same things and marketers have to decide which consumers or customers they are going to focus on to create an appealing product-offer. Several **segmentation variables**, or bases for segmentation, can be used to group consumers into actionable segments. For example, consider the sports shoe industry. Some sports, such as running, are more popular in some provinces than others, so marketers consider geography. Not everyone is willing or able to pay $150 for the latest running shoe, so marketers consider disposable and discretionary income. Men may be more likely to participate in some sports, such as basketball, whereas women may be likely than men to want the latest aerobics styles, so marketers also consider gender. Not all age groups are going to be equally interested in buying specialized athletic shoes, and some kids may be more inclined to "extreme" sports than others. As this example shows, the larger consumer "pie" can be sliced into smaller pieces in a number of ways, including geographic, demographic, psychological, and behavioural differences. These segmentation variables are used to identify the groups, and then create descriptions or profiles of the groups. So, just how do marketers segment a population? The process is similar for organizational (business to business) markets and we will discuss some of the differences shortly.

### Behavioural Segmentation

**behavioural segmentation** Technique that divides consumers into segments on the basis of how they act toward, feel about, or use a product or service.

Savvy marketers realize that if the objective is to create groups that want very different product offers, it makes sense to try to group them by the similarity of their needs, wants, and preferences, the benefits they seek, the features and attributes they desire, or their purchasing or consumption behaviour. This approach to segmentation is called **behavioural segmentation** and marketers such as Club Med (Exhibit 3.5) and McDonald's have found it a useful place to start because it identifies groups that require distinct marketing programs. Recent research by Digital Consumer Projects in New York suggests online individual behaviour matters more than the demographics of an individual, finding seven behavioural segments that include "surfers," "loiterers," and "quickies."[3]

Behavioural segmentation divides consumers on the basis of how they act toward, feel about, or use a product or service. **Benefit segmentation** or value segmentation is a powerful behavioural segmentation approach where consumers are grouped by the benefits they seek in a product category. For example, Peachtree Network, a company that operated online grocery stores across Canada, originally segmented its market into three benefit segments: busy people, people with mobility difficulties, and people who liked and were motivated to use the technology behind the service.[4] In many industries, consumers seek different types of benefits from products and can be grouped accordingly. For example, the following benefit-based groups might be identified (among others) as restaurant industry segments: convenience seekers, fun seekers, health-oriented, fine-dining experience seekers, novelty seekers, cost-oriented, family-oriented, image- or status-oriented, or culture seekers. Each of us may fall into more than one of these benefit-seeking categories at different times or in different contexts, but restaurant owners know that different consumers seek different benefits from a restaurant and select restaurants based on the benefits they wish to receive at a particular time. That is why restaurants are usually clearly positioned to appeal to one or more of these benefit segment groups. Think of all the restaurants you know: what benefit(s) do they primarily focus on delivering? The advantage of segmenting by benefits is that the resulting groups are usually seeking very different product solutions, which makes the segmentation scheme very actionable in terms of designing appropriate marketing programs.

Another common approach to behavioural segmentation is **product usage segmentation**. In this approach, groups are identified based on how they use a product or how much they use a product. Baking soda, for example, is marketed to a variety of end-use segments including: deodorizing fridges, sinks, or rugs; cooking; and teeth brushing. Airlines often identify consumer and business traveler segments, which is a proxy for describing the frequency of product use (light users versus heavy users) and how they use the service. Many marketers (particularly those in business-to-business markets) abide by a rule of thumb called the **80/20 rule**: 20 percent of purchasers account for 80 percent of the product's sales (this ratio is just an approximation). Therefore, it often makes more sense to focus on the smaller number of people who are heavy users of a product rather than on the larger number who are just casual users. Kraft Foods began an advertising campaign to remind its core users to not "skip the zip," after its research showed that indeed 20 percent of households account for 80 percent of the usage of Miracle Whip. These heavy users consume about 8 kilograms of Miracle Whip a year.[5]

Some marketers find it useful to divide the market into users and non-users of a good or service so they can reward current users (as Air Canada does with frequent flyer miles) or try to win over new ones. For example, Prudential segments the insurance market in terms of whether people are currently Prudential policy owners or non-owners. When the company deals with current policy owners, it focuses on making it easier for them to buy additional policies when they decide they're ready to do so; when communicating with non-owners, it uses a different focus to persuade them to take the plunge and buy that first policy. Indeed, two-thirds of Prudential's new insurance policies sales are to existing policyholders.[6] The user/non-user segmentation approach, however, has two major limitations:

**Exhibit 3.5**

Club Med offers different products to segments seeking diverse vacation experiences.

**benefit segmentation** A segmentation approach that groups consumers or customers based on the benefits or value they seek in buying and using products.

**product usage segmentation** A segmentation approach that groups consumers or business customers based on the amount of a product purchased or consumed or how the product is used.

**80/20 rule** A marketing rule of thumb that 20% of purchasers account for 80% of a product's sales.

Non-users are often not clearly identifiable and reachable, thus failing to satisfy the fifth criterion for identifying market segments outlined above and current users may not be a very homogeneous group, which is the first criterion (see Figure 3.2 on page 65) and may not reflect the users desired by the marketing organization.

**usage occasions** Indicator used in one type of market segmentation based on when consumers use a product most.

Another way to segment a market based on behaviour is to look at **usage occasions**, or the context in which consumers use the product most. Many products are associated with specific occasions, including time of day, holidays, whether for a business function or casual situation. Greeting cards, for example, are a product associated with specific occasions. Carlton cards, Canada's leading greeting card marketer, experiences peak demand related to four special occasions: Christmas, Valentine's Day, Mother's Day, and Easter.[7] In addition to meeting the demand for these occasions with specialized cards, advertising, and in-store promotions, Carlton also engages in marketing efforts designed to encourage the giving of cards on other occasions, such as Earth Day. Similarly, ski resorts like Mont Tremblant, that experience heavy demand during vacation periods, might offer great bargains during the off-season to tempt vacationers who would otherwise just visit the resort during Christmas vacation.

Being strongly associated with an occasion can be a mixed blessing for a product. On the one hand, sales can be almost guaranteed at that time (think about how many people cook a whole turkey on Thanksgiving); on the other hand, a product can become locked into an occasion. Ocean Spray is working hard to expand cranberry consumption beyond the holiday season. By introducing new cranberry foods like Craisins (dried cranberry snacks), spritzers, and cranberry-based beverages, the company has tripled sales over a 10-year period.[8] This strategy reflects a desire to make cranberries more of an "everyday" product.

**Ocean Spray**
www.oceanspray.com

## Segmenting by Psychographics

Consumers and customers often make purchase decisions that reflect or support their attitudes, values, interests, opinions, emotions, personality, and lifestyles. Collectively these concepts are referred to as psychographics and they will be discussed further in Chapter 5. **Psychographic segmentation** groups consumers by these and other variables related to an individual's psychology, mental state, or self and is concerned with the motivation for consumers to buy products. As we will see in Chapter 5, marketers not only seek to understand how consumers behave but also how they think and feel about products, what motivates them, how they learn, and how they make purchase decisions.

**psychographic segmentation** A segmentation approach that groups people based on their attitudes, beliefs, values, lifestyles, or other psychological orientations.

Grouping consumers by their psychological orientation to a purchase often results in a useful segmentation scheme that meets the criteria of Figure 3.2 as differences in these psychological considerations usually reflect differences in needs and wants and are precursors to purchase and consumption behaviour. For example, Covenant House, a charitable organization that helps homeless people, recognized that donors care more about the cause and believe their donations will make a difference. With this understanding, Taxi Advertising and Design of Toronto developed a series of highly effective (and award-winning) campaign elements targeting new donors. One showed black and white images of homeless people sitting alone on the ground in a transit shelter, replaced by images of young children in the same position, with the tag line, "How old do they have to be before you give a damn?" A print element illustrating donation importance is shown in Exhibit 3.6.

Lifestyles are a powerful segmentation variable because they capture a number of behavioural, psychographic, and demographic characteristics that reflect how different groups of people live, what they care about, and how they behave. Think about your high-school experience. Were there cliques or groups of students like Jocks, Nerds, Preppies, Stoners, and others who hung out together, dressed similarly, had similar attitudes and values, and behaved similarly? You could probably describe each of those groups in some detail. That's what marketers do. Some advertising agencies and manufacturers develop their own psychographic classifications of consumers, identifying lifestyle segments like Yuppies (young urban professionals), Dinks (dual income, no kids), Shredders (boarders), Granolas (earthy, environmentally concerned, peaceniks), and others. Products are communicated to people in these segments by showing how the brand supports or is consistent with a particular lifestyle. Beer marketers, for example, often use lifestyle advertising to demonstrate what your life (or at least social life) would be like if you adopted their particular brand. Similarly, car marketers like Toyota, Mazda, Volvo, Saturn, or Mercedes try to show you what kind of people drive (or should want to drive) their cars. The Ducane Grill ad in Exhibit 3.7 appeals to those whose lifestyle includes outdoor grilling at home.

Other marketers choose to subscribe to larger services that divide the

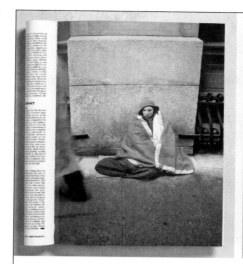

An actual peel-off sticker was placed on this magazine ad.

When readers peeled the sticker off, a message was revealed.

**Exhibit 3.6**

Removable stickers of homeless children in this Covenant House public service announcement demonstrates that donations make a difference: "Your donation gets kids off the street."

population into segments and sell pieces of this information to clients for specific strategic applications. The most well known of these systems is **VALS™ (Values and Lifestyles)** developed by SRI International. VALS divides people into eight groups, which are determined by both psychological characteristics, such as willingness to take risks, and "resources," which include such factors as income, education, energy levels, and eagerness to buy. As shown in Figure 3.3, three self-orientations are key to the system. Consumers with a principle orientation base decisions on abstract, idealized criteria rather than on feelings or a desire for societal approval. People with a status orientation strive for a clear social position and make decisions based on the perceived opinions of a valued social group. Action-oriented individuals are motivated by a desire to make an impact on the physical world or to affect others and resist social controls on their behaviour.

The VALS system helps identify consumers who are most likely to be interested in certain types of products, services, or experiences. For example, people who tend to fall into the experiencer category are likely to agree with statements like "I like a lot of excitement in my life" and "I like to try new things." VALS helped Isuzu market its Rodeo sport utility vehicle by focusing on experiencers, many of whom believe it is fun to break rules in ways that do not endanger others. The car was positioned as a vehicle that lets a driver break the rules by going off-road, and sales increased significantly.[9]

VALS is one of the most comprehensive psychographic systems available, but because its conclusions are based on residents of the United States, many Canadian firms prefer to use Canadian psychographic systems, such as the one developed by the Environics Research Group. Like VALS, Environics segments people on the basis of attitudes, values, and lifestyles. The 12 "tribes" identified by Environics range from the Rational Traditionalists (who are motivated by financial independence, security, and stability, and whose key values include respect for authority, duty, and delayed gratification) to the Social Hedonists (who are motivated by experience seeking, and who value hedonism, immediate gratification, and sexual permissiveness).[10] While the Rational Traditionalists may be a good target market for certain financial and insurance services, the Social Hedonists would probably be a prime target for *Tribe Magazine* and such leisure activities as snowboarding. Another Canadian-based lifestyle scheme is the Goldfarb segments (Figure 3.4 on page 72) that identify six groups of Canadian adults: structured, discontented, fearful, resentful, assured, caring.

**VALS™ (Values and Lifestyles)** Psychographic system that divides people into eight segments.

**SRI International**
www.future.sri.com

**Environics Research Group**
www.environics.net

**Exhibit 3.7**

Lifestyle marketing means appealing to consumer groups that have a preference for certain activities. This ad for the superior Ducane grill appeals to those whose lifestyle includes outdoor grilling at home—like they remember as a child.

**demographics** Variables that describe objective characteristics of a population or group.

**Statistics Canada**
www.statcan.ca

**Jones Soda**
www.jonessoda.com

## Segmenting by Demographics

**Demographics** are vital for identifying the best potential customers for a product or service because objective characteristics like a person's sex or age are (usually) easy to identify, and information about the demographics of a consumer market are easily obtained from government sources like Statistics Canada. Demographics are extremely useful in the development of profiles or descriptions of market segments because demographic variables help identify people in segments so they can be reached with a marketer's communication strategy. Communications media publish demographic information about their viewers, listeners, or readers to help marketers decide which media are best for reaching which audiences.

However, with a few notable exceptions, demographic variables like age, sex, income, family structure, social class, ethnicity, and education do not usually provide a good starting point or main basis for segmentation because demographic-based segmentation schemes usually do not meet the criteria that the people within each group are similar enough that the same marketing programs (product offers) would be appealing to most members of that group (first criterion, Figure 3.2 on page 65). For example, one might be tempted to segment the music market by age, suggesting that teenagers may listen to different music than people in their 20s, 40s, or 60s. While teenagers may be more likely than other age groups to listen to grunge or hip-hop music, not all teens like and listen to this style of music, and there are people in their 20s, 30s, 40s, and perhaps even older, who do. By creating age segments we are suggesting that most people in a particular age category have similar needs, wants, preferences, and buying behaviour with respect to music and that they would likely purchase the same or similarly positioned artists or brands, which are different from the artists or brands that consumers in other segments would likely purchase. If you thought this were true, then age would be an appropriate basis for segmenting the music market. However, it might make sense to segment the music market by psychographic variables such as values, attitudes, interests, opinions, or lifestyles, and then use age and other demographic variables to describe each of the psychographic groups created. This is a subtle, but important point for creating useful segmentation schemes—demographics are extremely useful for describing market segments and for directing communication messages, but are generally limited as the primary basis for segmentation. As Peter van Stolk, the Vancouver-based founder of Jones Soda (Exhibit 3.8 on page 73), told the Beverage Forum in Manhattan, "It's not about demographics. It's psychographics. You didn't grow up with the computer and crack and AIDS. Our consumers did."[11]

There are some notable exceptions where demographic variables are related to differences in needs, wants, preferences, and purchase behaviour and it would make sense to use these variables as the main basis for segmentation.

**SEX** It makes sense to segment the clothing, fashion, footwear, or fragrance industries by sex, for example, because physiological and socialization differences between men and women can result in different needs, wants, and preferences. However, men and women may also seek different benefits, features, or attributes so, in many cases, starting with benefit segmentation would result in a similar segmentation scheme as if starting with sex. Socialization by sex starts at a very early age and markets need to be responsive to consumer preferences; even diapers come in pink for girls and blue for boys. As proof that consumers take these differences seriously, market researchers report that most parents refuse to put male infants in pink diapers.[12] Ford Canada recognizes that women and men may have different needs when it comes to purchasing and servicing cars and trucks, which is why the company is now focusing efforts on trying to better understand and serve the needs of Canadian women. Volvo has created a concept car designed by women for women.[13] Similarly, companies such as Home Depot Canada, Marriott Hotels, and Mr. Lube, which have traditionally focused on marketing to men, have started developing products and messages specifically targeting Canadian women.[14] The publishers of *What* magazine focuses on a segment of co-gender lifestyles of Canadian youth, but *Fuel*, a new entry by Youth Culture (which also publishes *Verve* for girls), is focused on male teens—its research finding that boys and girls liked, and wanted to learn and read about different things (Exhibit 3.9). Its biggest hurdle has been convincing advertisers that boys shop, and develop brand loyalty, just for different products.[15]

**AGE** Consumers in different age groups have very different needs and wants with respect to product categories. Members of a generation tend to share the same outlook and spending priorities and these outlooks and priorities change as people age (what you spend your discretionary money on is likely different than what your parents spend their discretionary money on). However, unless brands specifically reflect these differences in product category needs and wants (such as we saw with *What* and *Fuel* magazines), age is less useful for identifying differences in brand preferences than for identifying differences in product category preferences.

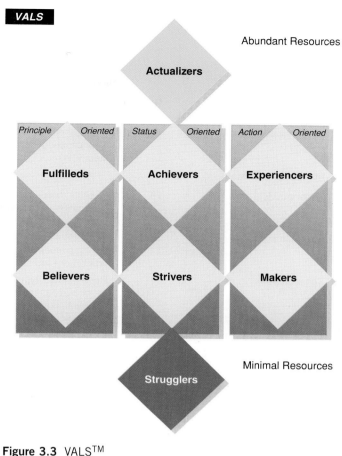

**Figure 3.3** VALS™

Source: SRI International, Menlo Park, CA

Canadian demographer David Foot has identified several segments of Canadian consumers based on age. These include the Baby Boom (those people born in 1947–1966), The Baby Bust (those born in 1967–1979), the Baby Boom Echo (those born in 1980–1995), and the Millennium Busters (those born in 1996–2010).[16] While each of these groups of consumers presents needs that some marketers are interested in, the largest demographic segment in Canada, the **baby boomers**, accounts for about one-third of the Canadian population and is, therefore, a segment of prime importance to many marketers. Several companies have achieved success by monitoring the changing needs of this group of consumers. Coca-Cola, for example, can attribute part of its success in North America to the fact that boomers drank a lot of pop when they were young. Coke has now modified its marketing efforts to keep up with the changing tastes of the boomers. It changed its product line to include juice and bottled water to cater to the concerns that aging boomers have for their health.[17]

**baby boomers** The largest age segment in Canada, it includes people who were born between 1947 and 1966.

The President's Choice private label products, sold through Loblaws and affiliated stores, also appeal to the needs of the baby boom segment (Exhibit 3.11 on page 74). These products include the Decadent chocolate chip cookie, which offers indulgence, low-fat foods that are "Too Good to Be True" and help boomers stay healthy, and ready-made frozen meals that offer a meal solution for time-starved boomers.[18]

The baby boom echo comprises the children of the baby boomers. The largest members of the baby boom echo are now youth and teens, who represent a lucrative group of consumers. The youth market in Canada is estimated to be worth over $13.5 billion, and teens are the second fastest growing segment in Canada.[19] These consumers tend to spend their

| Segment | Percent of | Characteristics |
|---|---|---|
| **Traditionalists** | | |
| Day-to-Day Watchers | 24 | Represent the status quo; don't like the fast pace; motivated by familiarity, loyalty, and security; influenced by quality, brand name, and authority figures. |
| Old-Fashioned Puritans | 18 | Prefer simpler times; express conservative values; motivated by price and quality; influenced by value-oriented messages; motivated by sales and other forms of discounts. |
| Responsible Survivors | 12 | Frugal shoppers who look for best price; have money but do not like to spend it; motivated by price; shop at low-end stores; heavy television viewers, so it is a good medium to reach them with. |
| **Non-traditionalists** | | |
| Joiner Activists | 16 | Idealists; liberal-minded; careful decision makers; willing to spend; motivated by information, therefore receptive to advertising messages; rational appeals have influence (quality, service, dependability, etc.). |
| Bold Achievers | 15 | Aggressive and confident individuals; success- and responsibility-oriented; innovators who lead in attitude and purchase decision; motivated by status, prestige, and success; products purchased reflect success; want higher-priced goods and exclusivity. |
| Self-indulgents | 14 | Resent authority; motivated by self-gratification, therefore often buy impulsively (even on major purchases); price not a factor; want easy road to success; messages should stress gratification as source of motivation. |

**Figure 3.4** Goldfarb Segments

Source: Lifestyle Segments in Canada from *Canadian Marketing in Action*, Sixth Edition, p. 98 by Keith Tuckwell. Reprinted by permission of Pearson Education Canada Inc.

**Moosehead**
www.moosehead.ca

**Molson**
www.molson.com

**Labatt**
www.labatt.ca

money on items such as clothing, personal grooming, entertainment, sports, and eating out. Montreal-based La Senza has successfully targeted teen and tween (aged 8 to 12) girls with La Senza Girl stores (Exhibit 3.12 on page 76), and banks such as the Royal Bank and CIBC have savings programs and debit cards specifically aimed at kids.[20] VanCity Credit Union recently targeted youth with a banking service "Not for the majority," offering free banking service to anyone under the age of 25. The campaign is backed with a combination of street marketing, Web promotions, contests, special events, and a text messaging campaign targeting 5000 youth in Vancouver who had been given cell phones by research company Digital Youth, in exchange for volunteering to receive promotional messages and advertising.

The older part of the baby boom echo, those people born in the early- to mid-1980s, are now in colleges and universities, or have joined the workforce, and are starting to make major purchases on their own. This college age group is an important target group for companies like DirectProtect, which sells insurance to students, and brewers such as Moosehead, Molson, and Labatt, who realize that many of the heavy users of their products can be found on campuses across Canada.

Older consumers, most of whom are the parents of the baby boomers, are another age segment of interest to Canadian marketers. Twenty-two percent of the Canadian population is 55 years of age or older.[21] Since many people are now retiring younger than age 65, these consumers are enjoying increased leisure time, making them an ideal target for travel and other leisure products. Health is also a major concern for these consumers; some of them may be experiencing failing health, and others are simply interested in maintaining good health as they age. The Healthwatch service provided by Shoppers Drug Mart, which provides advice from pharmacists, a database of individualized health information, and a health magazine, is a good example of a service targeted to the needs of these consumers.

FAMILY STRUCTURE Because family needs and expenditures change over time, one way to segment consumers is to consider the stage of the family life cycle they occupy (this will be discussed further in Chapter 5). Not surprisingly, consumers in different life cycle segments (such as teens, young adults, married with children, empty nesters) are unlikely to need the same products, or at least in the same quantities.[22] For example, many food companies cater to the needs of people who live alone by providing single portion frozen and

**Exhibit 3.8**

Jones Soda targets psychographic segments.

prepared foods, but also offer "jumbo" packs for those people who live in larger households.

As we age and move into new life situations, different product categories ascend and descend in importance to us. Young singles and newlyweds are the most likely to exercise, to go to bars, concerts, and movies, and to consume alcohol. Young families are heavy users of disposable diapers and toys and games for children. They are also interested in household appliances, furniture, and such vehicles as minivans. Older couples and singles are more likely to use maintenance services, and older people are a prime market for retirement communities and golf products. Condominiums that are built in Canadian cities are often designed with different family structures in mind. Some target single divorced men and women; others go after young families and include amenities such as on-site day care; and still others target vacation home buyers.[23] Canadian department stores also consider family life cycle by specifically targeting brides- and grooms-to-be with wedding registry services.

**INCOME AND SOCIAL CLASS** The distribution of wealth is of great interest to marketers, because it determines which groups have the greatest buying power: Many marketers are interested in capturing the hearts and wallets of high-income consumers. In Canada, the average family income is about $58 000, but 13.5 percent of the population has a household income above $100 000.[24] These high-income consumers are a good target market for such luxury products as expensive jewellery, as well as financial services of brokers and investment products. The Wealthy Boomer Inc. is a Canadian company that targets high-income baby boom consumers with its magazine, *The Wealthy Boomer*. At the same time, other marketers target average- and lower-income consumers—the majority of Canadian consumers. The Hudson's Bay Company successfully targets these income groups with its Bay and Zellers department stores.

Sometimes, it is possible for a company to appeal to both average- and higher-income consumers. Leon's Furniture, a company that has successfully appealed to average-income consumers in the past, decided to expand its customer base in 2000 by appealing to a more affluent target market. The company revised its product line to include more upscale furniture and renovated

**Wealthy Boomer Inc.**
www.thewealthyboomer.com

**Exhibit 3.9**

*Fuel* magazine targets a segment of young males.

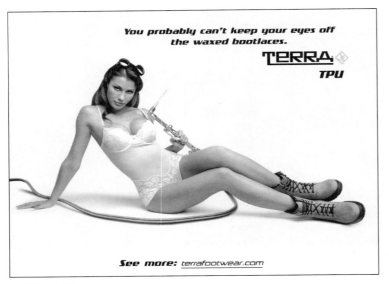

**Exhibit 3.10**

Terra Footwear: an example of a controversial ad.

**CHUM Limited**
www.chumlimited.com

**Dinawo Sportswear and Casuals**
www.dinawo.com

**Exhibit 3.11**

Loblaws targets baby boomers with President's Choice products.

stores to appeal to a higher-end market. The challenge for the company, though, was trying to convince the new target consumers that Leon's actually was upscale. In a series of TV ads, a high-income couple is shown having success shopping at Leon's, but they are wearing a fake nose and glasses disguise so that their friends won't see them shopping there. The campaign was a success with the new upscale market, and was also a hit with the current, average-income consumers.[25]

**ETHNICITY** As will be discussed further in Chapter 5, many Canadian marketers are adopting a multicultural approach to their marketing activities in recognition of the ethnic diversity of the Canadian population. Ethnicity can have a strong impact on a consumer's preferences for products and services, such as magazines or television shows, foods, apparel, and choice of leisure activities.

French Canadian consumers, who account for 20 to 30 percent of Canadians, are the second largest ethnic market in Canada (after those people of British origin) and are, therefore, an important segment for marketers.[26] Most French Canadian consumers live in Quebec, but there are also large segments of French Canadian consumers in New Brunswick and Ontario. As will be discussed further in Chapter 5, national marketers often decide to specifically target the French Canadian market through the development of different products to suit the needs of this group and the use of French language advertising. For example, MusiquePlus and MusiMax are the French language music video TV stations owned by CHUM, the same company that operates MuchMusic and MuchMoreMusic in the English Canadian market. While MusiquePlus and MusiMax show many of the same videos as on the English stations, French music and programming is featured to appeal to the music tastes of the French Canadian consumers. As the vice president of sales for CHUM Specialty Television, observes, "They are not MuchMusic and MuchMoreMusic in French. They have an identity of their own with a more regional than national focus."[27] So when Procter & Gamble was looking for a French Canadian spokesperson for Cover Girl cosmetics, it chose Genevieve Borne, a MusiquePlus VJ, because of her appeal to female French Canadian teens.

Over one million people in Canada are of Aboriginal origin, they are located in various regions throughout the country, and 42 percent live off reserve.[28] The Aboriginal population is growing at four times the rate of any other segment, half of the Aboriginal people in Canada are under the age of 25, the income of Aboriginal consumers is rising faster than that of other Canadians, and there are more than 20 000 Aboriginal-owned business.[29] One company that targets Aboriginal consumers is Dinawo Sportswear and Casuals, a native-owned clothing business located on the Six Nations Reserve in Ontario, that produces clothing incorporating native art and symbols.[30] The banking sector in Canada has also been proactive in targeting both Aboriginal consumers and business owners. All of the major Canadian banks operate branches in Aboriginal communities with services targeted to meet their needs, as the ad for the Royal Bank in Exhibit 3.13 shows.[31] The Aboriginal Peoples Television Network (APTN) and *Spirit* magazine are examples of media targeting Aboriginal peoples. A key challenge in marketing to Aboriginal peoples is to recognize the ethnic diversity within this group: Inuit, Metis, First Nations (such as Cree, Maliseet, Dene, Ojibway, Mohawk, Haida), which have significantly different languages, history, traditions, and environments that influence current thinking, attitudes, and behaviours. As this segment has traditionally been misunderstood and under researched, it is particularly important to conduct research (see Chapter 4) to understand these consumers.

Other than people of British, French, and Aboriginal origins, the three largest ethnic groups in Canada are German, Italian, and Chinese. Of these three, the fastest growing is the Chinese Canadian community.[32] Tropicana Products Ltd. considers the Chinese Canadian community to be one of the most important target markets for its orange juice product. It communicates with this target with Chinese language print ads placed in Chinese Canadian newspapers and promotions such as coupons for 68 cents (both 6 and 8 are considered to signify prosperity in the Chinese culture). The company is careful to avoid the use of the number four (which means death) in any of its pricing and advertising.[33]

Other large ethnic groups in Canada include the South Asian community, which accounts for 2.4 percent of the population, and the Black community, which is 2 percent of the Canadian population.[34] Bell Canada provides customer service representatives who speak Hindi, Punjabi, Urdu, and Tamil to better serve its South Asian customers.[35] To reach the over 351 000 people in Canada of Jewish origin, companies such as Baskin-Robbins offer kosher food products, Hallmark offers cards and festive products targeted to Jewish holidays, and the Liquor Control Board of Ontario offers 80 different types of kosher wines.[36]

Targeting ethnic groups is especially important in urban centres in Canada. In Toronto and Vancouver, visible minorities make up over 30 percent of the total population. In Ottawa, Montreal, Edmonton, and Calgary, they make up between 10 and 12 percent of the population.[37] The composition of ethnic markets is different across these cities, however. For example, in Montreal, 30 percent of the visible minority population, the single largest group, is Black; whereas in Vancouver and Toronto the largest ethnic group is Chinese.[38] Targeting ethnic markets is accomplished through the use of ethnic media, such as *Sing Tao Daily*, a newspaper for Chinese Canadians, or *The Weekly Gleaner*, a Caribbean Newspaper, and such television stations as CFMT-TV (see Exhibit 3.14) which targets a variety of ethnic groups including Italian, Portuguese, Greek, and South Asian. Other methods of reaching these markets include sponsorships of ethnic cultural and community events, such as Bell Canada's sponsorship of the Chinese New Year Festival at the SkyDome in Toronto.

**GEOGRAPHY** People's preferences for products and services often depend on which region of the country they live in. For example, a recent study of how upper-income

 **Good or Bad Decision?**

Terra Footwear, a supplier of footwear to the Canadian military, law enforcement agencies, and construction industries, recently had to pull a controversial communications campaign it had developed for workboots (Exhibit 3.10). The theme of the campaign was sexy images featuring female models in lingerie, in suggestive poses, wearing Terra workboots, with humorous tag lines. The Web site featured a steaming video commercial of topless dancers wearing the boots. According to Robert Worrall, Terra Footwear Vice President, the intent was to present the product in a lighthearted and humorous manner. The Manitoba Federation of Labour, which has more than 95 000 members, threatened a boycott against Terra over the ads. The women's committee of the Canadian Auto Workers, one of the largest trade unions in Canada, soon followed and union leaders began organizing demonstrations at stores where Terra products are sold. They also put pressure on Terra Footwear by calling MPs to demand that they pressure the firm to pull its ads or cancel Terra's contracts to supply boots to the Canadian military. Mark Krausewitz, marketing manager for Terra, said that the reaction was unexpected and that "essentially there was a large group of people who did not see the humour in our spots".[39] Some industry observers thought the campaign short-sighted considering that Terra has a popular line of women's workboots. Shari Graydon, formerly head of Media Watch, an organization that monitors the depiction of women in media, argues that media images have social consequences and play a role in "normalizing sexual harassment in the workplace." However, Toronto writer David Menzies argues that it is only advertising, it works, it wasn't pornographic, and why should "a small gaggle of humorless harpies ruin things for the rest of us"? He further adds that there has been no outcry over the well-endowed "boy-toy" currently being exploited by those Calvin Klein briefs billboards.[40] What do you think? Should marketers be allowed to use highly sexual appeals? What if the appeal was specifically targeting young people—such as with many of the Calvin Klein ads?

**Terra Footwear**
www.terrafootwear.com

**Exhibit 3.12**

La Senza Girl stores targets teens and tweens.

**geodemography** Segmentation technique that combines geography with demographics.

people across Canada spend their money showed significant regional differences. Compared to the average Canadian, those upper-income people living in Edmonton were more likely to spend their money on skiwear and snowmobile suits, those in Saskatoon were more likely to purchase home exercise equipment, those in Montreal were more likely to purchase leather and fur coats and jackets, those in Halifax were more likely to purchase art goods and decorative ware, those in St. John's were more likely to buy snow blowers, and those in the north were more likely to purchase outboard motor boats.[41] Similarly, a study of snacking behaviour found that Maritimers consume more potato chips than consumers in other regions (almost double the national average), and Quebec consumers eat less than half of the average amount of corn chips that consumers in other regions do.[42]

Recognition of these kinds of regional differences can lead marketers to focus efforts on one or more regions, or to have different marketing strategies in different regions. When marketers want to segment regional markets even more precisely, they sometimes combine geography with demographics by using a technique called **geodemography**. A basic assumption of geodemography is that "birds of a feather flock together": People who live near one another share similar characteristics. Sophisticated statistical techniques identify geographic areas that share the same preferences for household items, magazines, and other products. This allows marketers to construct segments consisting of households with a common pattern of preferences, so that a company can hone in on those customers who are most likely to be interested in its specific offerings—in some cases so precisely that families living on one block will be included in a segment whereas those on the next block will not.

One Canadian geodemographic system, PSYTE, is a large database developed by Compusearch Micromarketing Data and Systems. This system classifies Canadian consumers into 60 clusters, based on postal code and demographic information. The resulting clusters include Boomers and Teens, Conservative Homebodies, Young City Singles, Brie and Chablis, and Suburban Nesters.[43] The PSYTE system is used by Canada Post in its GeoPost Plus program, which allows marketers to target direct mail to clusters of consumers that match their target segment. For example, the Boomers and Teens segment is described as "late middle-aged consumers who are university and college educated with children over the age of six. Mostly double income families who live in their own homes." The cluster Young City Singles are "young singles and some couples who rent predominantly newer, downtown apartments and other dwellings." Using a geodemographic system like GeoPost Plus, a marketer of home improvement products like outdoor paint and fencing can identify precisely which postal codes will be the best prospects for direct mail advertising for their product, while avoiding other postal codes where residents aren't likely to be interested.

## SEGMENTING BUSINESS MARKETS

We've reviewed the segmentation variables marketers use to divide up the consumer market, but how about all the business-to-business or industrial marketers? Segmentation also helps them to divide up business and organizational customers. Though the specific variables may differ, the underlying logic of dividing the larger market into manageable pieces that share relevant characteristics is the same.[44] Although industrial markets tend to be smaller (in numbers of customers) and more concentrated, it is still important to segment these markets because no company has unlimited resources for developing and selling products and segmentation enables these companies to focus on the best opportunities and develop products that uniquely meet the needs of their customers.

## COMPANY-SPECIFIC BEHAVIOUR OR CHARACTERISTICS

Just as it is fruitful to consider the behaviour of individual consumers when devising a segmentation scheme, it is fruitful to consider how businesses and other organizations behave when devising segmentation schemes for industrial or business-to-business segmentation. Organizational buying behaviour will be the focus of Chapter 6. For now, it is important to recognize that organizations, through the people within them, act and behave in ways that are both similar to, and different from consumers and the way they behave and operate is influenced by the types of products and services it both sells and needs. Consequently, one way to segment organizations is by the unique ways each operates.

Organization buying and consumption behaviour is influenced by the production technology used; the type of purchases made; the business customer's degree of technical, financial, or operations expertise; how they make purchase decisions and who is involved in those decisions; whether the prospect is a current user or non-user of the product; and the frequency or size of the transactions. These **operating variables** are all useful bases of segmentation. For example, Grand & Toy (Exhibit 3.15) recognized the differences in the buying behaviour of large and small businesses when it launched The Stockroom, an Internet-based office

## Partners in Your Future

Original art by Natalie Rostad

$R$oyal Bank Financial Group has long been a leading provider of services to Aboriginal communities through our specialized products, educational programs, career opportunities and initiatives to assist Aboriginal economic development. We have specialized teams all across Canada that understand the financial requirements of Aboriginal peoples.

Our Aboriginal Banking initiatives reflect the bank's commitment to all of its customers - understanding their financial services requirements, offering flexible solutions, and treating clients as they want to be treated. We are committed to ensuring your financial and banking requirements are being met. Royal Bank will continue to be "Partners in Your Future".

**ROYAL BANK**

**Exhibit 3.13**
Aboriginal consumers are an important segment for the Royal Bank.

**operating variables** The production technology used, the business customer's degree of technical, financial, or operations expertise, and whether the prospect is a current user or non-user of the product.

**The Stockroom**
www.thestockroom.ca
**Grand & Toy**
www.grandandtoy.com

# BRINGING YOU THE WORLD AT HOME

**ROGERS** MEDIA

Contact Melanie Farrell at (416) 260-3619
mfarrell@rci.rogers.com

cfmt
international

**Exhibit 3.14**
The CFMT TV station appeals to consumer segments from a variety of ethnic backgrounds.

**Exhibit 3.15**

Grand & Toy targets behaviour-based business segments.

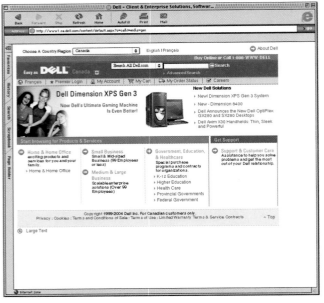

**Exhibit 3.16**

Dell Canada focuses on four main product-use segments.

**industrial psychographics** The application of psychographics to the business-to-business context.

**Dell Canada**
www.dell.ca

**Strategis**
www.strategis.gc.ca

supplies store that targets small businesses. While the Grand & Toy Web site is geared to the needs of large businesses (offering benefits like large volume discounts), The Stockroom site caters to small businesses with its products and pricing policies. The general manager of The Stockroom describes the company's approach this way, " . . . we felt it was important to take a very aggressive, focused stance, purely aimed at the small business segment." [45]

Business marketers also must consider how different customers will use their products or services. They must focus on identifying different end-use applications for these offerings. The personal computer industry is a good example of how firms can segment a market based on end use. Some major PC manufacturers, such as Dell, have divided the market into four segments: corporate, small business, government, and home or home-office (Exhibit 3.16)—each with its own computer use profile. IBM segments its mainframe market into user "verticals" different applications (such as health care or manufacturing) for which the mainframe computers might be used.

## Industrial Psychographics

Being concerned with psychology, thinking, feeling, and other mental states, the concept of psychographics relates only indirectly to organizations; but it is does relate to the people who run and work in those organizations. **Industrial psychographics**, the application of psychographics to the business-to-business context, has mainly been applied to understanding buyers (purchasing agents or multiple people in a buying centre) in order to help salespeople better understand their one-on-one relationships with clients. It may also be fruitful to segment business markets by the mission, goals, and values of an organization and its management team since purchase and consumption decisions and behaviours are likely to be consistent with those missions, goals, and values. This is the thinking of Steve Munden, director of research at the Toronto-based marketing firm Warrillow and Co. Munden is developing a psychographic profile of generation Xers who own small- and medium-sized businesses. These entrepreneurs are people in their mid 20s to 30s who are increasingly leaving the workforce to take control of their lives and find financial independence. Munden thinks a psychographic profile of these entrepreneurs will help his clients better target these business organizations—as the beliefs, values, and orientation of these entrepreneurs are expected to play a large role in their company's purchase decisions. [46]

**ORGANIZATIONAL DEMOGRAPHICS** Demographic data help business marketers understand the needs and characteristics of their potential customers. For example, a manufacturer of work uniforms needs to know which industries currently provide uniforms for employees. For each industry that uses uniforms, from chemical processing to pest control, a marketer needs to know how many companies are potential customers, the number of employees in each company, what types of uniforms are needed, and so on. That information enables the manufacturer to offer its services to the prospects that are most likely to be interested in outfitting employees in its protective clothing.

Many industries use the North American Industry Classification System (NAICS), which will be further discussed in Chapter 6, to obtain information about the size and number of companies operating in a particular industry. Other government information sources, such as Statistics Canada and Strategis, provide valuable business demographic information.

## DEVELOPING PROFILES

Once marketers have divided a market into segments that meet the criteria of Figure 3.2, the next task is to develop a brief **segment profile** or description of each segment, with sufficient depth to be able to understand the segment so it can be evaluated and either be targeted or rejected.

One useful template for developing these profiles is illustrated in Figure 3.5. A rich profile would normally include a description of: 1) who is in the segment (using demographics, psychographics, and geographic variables); 2) what people or organizations in this segment want (benefits, features, and attributes) and why (needs, motivations); 3) when and where they expect to buy and use the product; 4) how they typically buy the product (such as, purchase decision process, influences, sources of information, media preferences); and 5) how they typically use the product (consumption behaviour). In addition marketers try to estimate the size of each segment and its expected growth rate. For the purposes of selecting market segments to target, these profiles are usually created based on experience

**segment profile** A description of the "typical" customer in a segment.

**Who are they?**
- What are their demographic characteristics?
- What are their psychographic characteristics?
- What are the geodemographic characteristics?
- How price sensitive are they?

**What do they want and why?**
- What are the benefits, features, attributes, or characteristics sought by consumers in this segment?
- What do they need and want?
- What motivates the purchase and consumption decision?

**When do they buy and use it?**
- What triggers the purchase decision?
- What is the context in which they buy the product?
- How often do they buy the product?
- What time of day, part of the week, or month, or year is it purchased?
- What time of day, part of the week, or month, or year is it used or consumed?

**Where do they buy and use it?**
- What stores or other distribution channels do they use?
- Where are they when they use the product?

**How do they buy and use it?**
- How do they decide what to buy? (Decision-making process used)
- What or who influences the purchase decision?
- What media do they use/access in making the decision?
- Is it a thinking (cognitive) or feeling (emotional) decision?
- Is it a high involvement (important or risky) decision or a low involvement (not important or risky)
- How do they use or consume the product?
- How much of it do they use?

**Segment Size**
- What is the market potential?
- What is the expected growth rate of the segment?

**Figure 3.5** A Framework for Creating Rich Segment Profiles and judgment. Sophisticated marketers, however, use market research and analytic tools such as Cluster Analysis to verify profile assumptions or to more scientifically identify the segments and their characteristics. This is discussed further in Appendix 4A. The profiles of the segment(s) chosen for targeting (see below) are developed in much more detail and provide, in part, the basis for making marketing mix decisions.

To estimate the size and growth of a segment, marketers try to forecast each segment's **market potential**. This is the maximum demand expected among consumers or customers in that segment for a particular product. To determine market potential, the firm must identify the number of consumers or customers in the segment and how much they spend in the product category. Then it must determine the sales potential for its product if it targets this segment—how many consumers or customers would buy this product during the forecast period and with what frequency or quantity. This number is the total dollar potential. The firm then projects its market share—what percentage share of the market is likely to buy their particular brand(s). Multiplying total dollar potential by market share gives the likely actual dollar amount the firm might make. Forecasting is an advanced topic that you will likely learn more about in senior level courses. For the initial, brief profiles, an estimate of the relative size of each segment is expected. This would be based on experience, observation, analysis, and/or market research.

## Market Targeting

Once marketers have divided a market into actionable segments and have developed a brief profile of each segment, they need to evaluate the attractiveness of each potential segment and decide which one or more of these groups they will target with marketing programs. The consumer or customer group(s) selected are the firm's **target market(s)**.

SoyaWorld, a Canadian soy beverage marketer, has attained 60 percent of the dairy alternative market by carefully considering specific target markets. Soy beverages make up the fastest-growing beverage category in Canada, and SoyaWorld has identified three main targets in the total market: the mainstream dairy market, the Asian market, and the organic market. For the mainstream dairy segment, SoyaWorld introduced So Good, a soy beverage with an improved taste that comes in several flavours. Since the product was being promoted as an alternative to milk, So Good was packaged to look like milk and was placed in the dairy cases of major supermarkets. Billboards, TV, and magazine ads, such as the one shown in Exhibit 3.17, were all used to reach the mainstream market. SoyaWorld targets Asian consumers with its Sunrise brand, a product that has a more traditional soy taste. For the organic target segment, it offers So Nice, a soy beverage, and Rice Choice, a fortified rice beverage. To reach the organic and Asian segments, the SoyaWorld products are distributed through specialty retailers, such as Chinese grocery stores and health food stores, in addition to selected larger grocery stores.[47] In this section, we'll review how marketers like SoyaWorld assess the customer groups in the market, and what selection strategies they use for effective targeting.

**TARGET MARKET SELECTION** There are three basic criteria for deciding which market segments are attractive to an organization: segment size and growth, the external decision environment, and the internal decision environment (see SWOT analysis in Chapter 2). Figure 3.6 summarizes these criteria.

**market potential** The maximum demand expected among consumers in a segment for a product or service.

**target market** A group that a marketing organization focuses on when developing marketing programs.

**SoyaWorld Inc.**
www.soyaworld.com

**Exhibit 3.17**
SoyaWorld targets the mainstream dairy market with the So Good soy beverage.

1.  *Segment Size and Growth.* When choosing market segments to target, one consideration is the size and growth of the segment. The segment must be "the right size"—large enough to be profitable now and in the future, but small enough that an organization can compete effectively in it. It is a lot easier to compete in a high growth segment than in a low or declining growth segment because in a high growth segment, new customers do not have to be taken away from existing competitors.

2.  *External Environment.* While segment size and growth is part of the external environment, marketers tend to give that issue special attention because of its strategic importance. There are, however, other external environment considerations when choosing market segments. One is the level of competition. Large and high growth segments are highly attractive to other competitors and a smaller organization may not have the resources to compete effectively against them. It may make sense for smaller companies, with more limited resources, to focus on smaller segments (market niches) and not compete directly with larger competitors. This was the strategy of Sun Microsystems when they focused on the computer segment of engineering and scientific workstations in the early 1990s. As a small company they were able to dominate a very small, but high growth, niche and grow with that niche to become a dominant player in the overall computer market. Similarly, when Toyota introduced the Echo subcompact car into the Canadian market, the target segment was described demographically as "60/40 male/female, 40% married, median age 32, 48% university educated with an average household income $42 000." In addition, the segment displayed the following psychographic traits: idealistic, experimental, independent, educated, urban, and not brand loyal.[48] This is likely a fairly small segment, even on a national level, and it suggests that even large companies may decide to focus on small segments if they can create unique value there better than competitors. It may be more profitable to be a "big fish in a small pond" and being that "big fish" may discourage other competitors from entering the market segment.

    Related to the extent and level of competition is the industry structure. A local monopoly (or near monopoly) like Roger's Cable may choose to focus on large, less well-defined segments because there are no direct competitors (other than satellite TV services) focusing their strategies on more narrow segments. Where there is extensive competition, different competitors will focus on increasingly narrow market segments, making it difficult for others to compete effectively in multiple segments.

    A segment with many substitute products may limit the price and hence profits in that segment. Segments where there are few buyers or buyers with otherwise strong bargaining positions might also be unattractive as these buyers can keep prices down and play one supplier off another. Segments with strong suppliers (large, concentrated, or with few competitors or substitutes) may similarly be unattractive. Finally, as we will see in Chapter 8, segment attractiveness is also related to the stage of the product life cycle—where mature and declining markets are less attractive than new and growing ones.

3.  *Internal Environment.* The marketer must also be able to adequately serve the needs of the segment and have the expertise and resources to do so better than the competition. Some years ago, Exxon made the mistake of trying to enter the office products business, a growing segment. The company's expertise at selling petroleum products did not transfer to copying machines, and the effort was unsuccessful. Four Seasons Hotels, on the other hand, was recently able to transfer its expertise in exceptional accommodation services aimed at a tightly defined, luxury lifestyle audience, to an entirely new market sector, residential properties.[49] The attractiveness of a segment depends on a company's ability to create value in that segment and defend their strategy in that segment. This requires an assessment of the strengths and weaknesses of the organization relative to the needs of the consumers and competition in that segment (see SWOT analysis in Chapter 2).

**Figure 3.6** Criteria for Choosing Target Market Segments

# TARGETING STRATEGY
## Undifferentiated Marketing

A company like Wal-Mart that selects an **undifferentiated (or mass) targeting strategy** is appealing to a broad spectrum of people. If successful, this type of operation can be very efficient, especially because production, research, and promotion costs benefit from economies of scale—it's cheaper to develop one product or one advertising campaign than to choose several targets and create separate products or messages for each. But the company must be willing to bet that people have similar needs, or that any differences among

**undifferentiated (mass) targeting strategy** Appealing to a broad spectrum of people.

them will be so trivial that they will not matter, so that the same product and message will appeal to many customers. This is the approach Henry Ford used in offering the Model-T Ford—"in any colour, so long as it was black". Today it is difficult to create a single product or offering that has very broad appeal. Consumers expect choices, there are many distribution channels from which to purchase products, and there are many focused-communication outlets that let marketers cost-effectively communicate to increasingly narrow target markets. Companies with new-to-the-world innovations are the ones who most commonly practise undifferentiated marketing, but segments in these markets quickly develop as competitors enter these markets with differentiated products and consumers become more knowledgeable and demanding about the product category. When competitors are using a differentiated strategy it makes it difficult for the original innovator to continue using an undifferentiated strategy.

## Differentiated Marketing

**differentiated targeting strategy** Developing one or more products for each of several distinct customer groups and making sure these offerings are kept separate in the marketplace.

A company that chooses a **differentiated targeting strategy** develops one or more products for each of several distinct customer groups and makes sure these offerings are kept separate in the marketplace. A differentiated strategy is called for when consumers are choosing among well-known brands, when each has a distinctive image in the marketplace, and when it's possible to identify one or more segments that have distinct needs for different types of products. Most large organizations follow a differentiation strategy. The cosmetics company L'Oréal uses a differentiated targeting strategy. The company has the resources to offer several product lines at a variety of prices. It targets the luxury market with such brands as Lancôme and Helena Rubinstein, whereas less expensive offerings such as Elsève and L'Oréal target large department stores and discounters.[50] Even within product lines, Procter & Gamble has multiple laundry detergent products focused on different laundry detergent segments.

## Concentrated Marketing

**concentrated targeting strategy** Focusing a firm's efforts on offering one or more products to a single segment.

**niche marketing** A type of concentrated targeting strategy where the market segment chosen is relatively small.

When a firm focuses its efforts on offering one or more products to a single segment, it is using a **concentrated targeting strategy**. A concentrated strategy is often useful for smaller firms that do not have the resources or the desire to be all things to all people. For example, the cosmetics company Hard Candy, shown in Exhibit 3.18, markets its funky line of nail polish and other products only to twentysomething women (or to those who wish they still were). **Niche marketing** is a type of concentrated targeting strategy where the market segment chosen is relatively small. Jones Soda, for example, focuses on the alternative soft drink niche by offering a series of soft drink products for people who want a premium beverage that stands out, is individualized, expresses personality, and makes a fashion statement. Niche marketing is becoming the norm in many markets as it allows many competitors to each make unique appeals and be the product of choice for some group of consumers.

## Customized Marketing

**custom marketing strategy** Approach that tailors specific products and the messages about them to individual customers.

Ideally, marketers should be able to define segments so precisely that they can offer products and services that exactly meet the needs of every individual or firm. **Custom marketing strategy**, also called a micro-marketing strategy, is when specific products and the messages about them are tailored to individual customers or locations. An individualized strategy is often used in business markets by companies, such as aircraft manufacturer Bombardier, to make sure the individual needs of its few customers who spend a lot of money are met. In consumer markets, this level of concentration shows up in personal or professional services, by doctors, lawyers, and hair stylists, for example. In most consumer markets, individualized marketing strategies are neither practical nor possible when products are mass-produced. However, advances in technology, coupled with the new emphasis on building solid relationships with customers, have enabled **mass customization**. Clothing manufacturers like Levi Strauss and Suited For Sun, for example, use digital imaging technology to do body scans of customers than enable the creation of perfectly fitting jeans, swimwear, or other clothing products. Calgary-based Critical Mass has worked with Nike to develop NIKEiD, an interactive part of the Nike Web site, where consumers can design and purchase their own running shoes.[51] Dell Computers uses the Internet to enable custom built computers where customers choose among various options and Dell makes the computer to order. Individualized communication has also been enabled by Internet and e-mail technologies. Online retailers, such as HMV.com, for example, are able to send customized messages to users regarding the status of their orders, upcoming promotions that may be of interest based on the products they have bought in the past, and announcements of new releases. We will return to the issue of customization in Chapter 13 when we review new advances in the management philosophy of customer relationship management.

**Exhibit 3.18**

Hard Candy uses a concentrated targeting strategy as the company targets twentysomething women.

# POSITIONING

The final, crucial stage of the target marketing process is providing consumers in a targeted market segment with a product or service that meets their unique needs and expectations. **Positioning** means developing a marketing strategy to differentiate a firm from its competitors in the minds of target consumers or customers. A **brand concept** is how a firm wants to be positioned—how it wants to be known by its target market as being different from, and better than, its competitors. WestJet, for example, wants to be known as the airline brand that provides the best value—low prices and good service from friendly, personable staff (Exhibit 3.19A). BC Ethic, the apparel manufacturer known for repopularizing the retro, button-down bowling shirt style worn by *Seinfeld's* Kramer,[52] positions its shirts as being "cool" and supports that positioning by offering customized embroidered shirts free to music artists like Barenaked Ladies and Cypress Hill (Exhibit 3.19B).

While much of marketing communication strategy involves establishing a brand's positioning in the minds of its customers, sometimes the intended positioning is not achieved. **Brand image** is the perceived positioning of a product by consumers. Canadian consumers, for example, perceived Knorr soups, sauces, and marinades, as being "refined, polished, and sophisticated"—but Unilever wanted its Knorr brand to be more accessible and work as an everyday solution. The company developed its "A Little Bit More" campaign to reinforce the idea that Knorr products have more interesting ingredients than competitors and offer numerous opportunities for everyday culinary creativity. The phrase "A little bit more" in Knorr's communication strategy is its slogan or tag line—which usually communicates the unique selling proposition or key point of differentiation underlying a brand's positioning. We will see other examples of this shortly.

**mass customization** Approach that modifies a basic product or service to meet the needs of an individual.

**NIKEiD**
www.Nike.com/nike_id

**positioning** Developing a marketing strategy aimed at influencing how a particular market segment perceives a product or service as being differentiated in comparison to the competition.

**brand concept** How the marketer wants the brand to be positioned.

**brand image** How consumers perceive the positioning of the brand.

## SPOTLIGHT ON REAL PEOPLE    Pita Boys

Understanding their consumer segment's characteristics and the practice of target marketing have led to success for two young entrepreneurs, Stephen Vail and David Fullerton, founders of the Pita Boys restaurants in Halifax. Although the four Pita Boys restaurants attract 18- to 45-year-old consumers, the focus of marketing efforts has been on the younger end of that range, namely university and college students. While the older customers are professionals, who view the meat and vegetable pita offerings at Pita Boys as a healthy lunch alternative, the younger customers are students, who not only like the food but also respond to the Pita Boys advertisements that appear in student and entertainment newspapers. The ads are simple (black and white) but feature creative, memorable slogans such as "We serve drunks," "Crazy, Dancin' Pita Rollin Machines," and "Because Size Does Matter." Sponsorship of movie premieres and concerts has also been effective at reaching the student market. As Fullerton says, "The student market is easy. I know people that age, and I know what it feels like to be them."

The success of the targeting activities of the Pita Boys restaurants has grabbed the attention of much larger, more experienced marketers. Coca-Cola, for example, pays for ads on a local Halifax radio station, which feature both Coke and the Pita Boys, simply because it wants to be associated with the popular restaurants. Two beer companies are also involved in marketing activities with the Pita Boys to enhance their own profiles among students, even though the restaurants do not serve beer.[53]

1. What dimensions, in addition to age, can be used to segment the market for Pita Boys restaurants?
2. The Pita Boys restaurants currently use a concentrated targeting strategy. Evaluate the pros and cons of the company switching to a differentiated targeting strategy.

## POSITIONING STRATEGIES

There are numerous frameworks or typologies that summarize key marketing and positioning strategies and they all have different perspectives on how products can be differentiated. One of these suggests that firms can focus on one or more of the following strategies: product leadership, customer intimacy, or operational excellence.[54] Product leadership is a strategy of competing by continuously bringing innovative and useful new products or technologies to market. Adopted by companies such as 3M, Apple, and Nike, it is concerned with product innovation, quality, performance superiority, and other forms of functional value (see Chapter 1). Positioning consistent with a product leadership strategy focuses on dimensions such as the following:

- Quality (e.g., Ford: "Quality is Job 1"; Gillette: "The best a man can get")
- Reliability or Durability (e.g., Timex: "it takes a lick'n and keeps on tick'n")
- Key features or attributes (e.g., Honda Civic: "Better gas mileage. A Civic responsibility")
- Innovation (e.g., Lexus: "The Relentless Pursuit of Excellence"; GE: "Progress is our most important product")
- Performance (e.g., BMW: "The ultimate driving machine"; Apple: "The Power to Do Your Best")
- Outcomes (e.g., Buckley's: "It tastes awful. And it works"; Exhibit 3.20)

Customer intimacy, or micro-marketing, is a strategy concerned with creating tailored solutions for narrowly defined market segments. Companies such as Kraft, Nordstrom, Marriott, and Levi Strauss aim to excel at providing superior customer experiences and/or personalized or customized interactions through outstanding service quality, customer support, flexibility, and customization. Concerned with the creation of experiential or emotional value, customer intimacy positioning strategies focus on dimensions such as the following:

- Sensory experience (e.g., KFC: "Finger Lick'n Good"; A&W: "That frosty mug sensation")

**Exhibit 3.19**

WestJet competes with a value positioning while BC Ethic wants to be "cool."

- Excitement, Adventure (e.g., Nike: "Just Do It"; Pontiac: "We drive excitement"; Club Med: "Do it now, do it fast, and do everything at the same time")
- Fun or Pleasure (e.g., McDonald's: "I'm lovin' it"; Lay's "Betcha can't eat just one")
- Emotion (e.g., Harlequin: "Live the emotion"; Hallmark: "When You Care Enough to Send the Very Best")
- Social value (e.g., DeBeer's: "Diamonds are forever"; AT&T: "Reach out and touch someone")
- Responsiveness, customized, personalized (e.g., Burger King: "Have it your way"; Speedy Muffler: "At Speedy you're a somebody")
- Safety or security (e.g., Allstate: "You're in good hands with Allstate"; Michelin: "Because so much is riding on your tires")
- Novelty, knowledge, or fantasy (e.g., Disney Online: "Where the magic comes to you"; Microsoft: "Where do you want to go today?")

Operational excellence is a strategy focused on cost effectiveness, efficiency, and customer convenience. Companies such as Zellers, WestJet Airlines, Dell, and IKEA (Exhibit 3.21) are tenacious at lowering costs and customer prices while making it more convenient to do business with them. Concerned with the creation of cost-sacrifice value, operational excellence positioning strategies focus on dimensions such as the following:

- Price (e.g., Zellers: "The lowest price is the law"; Buy.com: "Canada's Low Price Internet Superstore")
- Value (e.g., IKEA: "Swedish for common sense")
- Convenience (e.g., 7-11: "Oh thank heaven"; American Express: "Don't leave home without it")

**Q.** Do I have to?

**A.** Do you want relief so you can feel better?

**It tastes awful. And it works.**

**Exhibit 3.20**

Buckley's cough syrup is positioned on the outcome "it works," consistent with a product leadership strategy.

- Personal investment (time, effort, energy) (e.g., Yellow Pages: "Let your fingers do the walking")
- Risk (e.g., Levi's Jeans: "Have you ever had a bad time in Levi's?"; Listerine Mouthwash: "Even your best friends won't tell you")

Another common positioning strategy is concerned with symbolic-expressive value—differentiating your brand by the psychological meaning associated with it. Some products (luxury goods for example) appeal to consumer's self-concepts and self-worth—that is, they make us feel good about ourselves. Other products (such as music or comfort foods among many others) have personal meaning—associations with people or events that only have meaning to a particular consumer (such as an association with Tide because Mom used it). Products can also provide a means of self-expression. Products such as Calvin Klein fragrances, Roots clothes, a Volkswagen Beetle, or Body Shop lotions allow consumers to reflect or express their personalities, tastes, and values. Still other products focus on social meaning—how others see us. Products such as BMW cars, Birks jewellery, and Lee Valley Tools are purchased because of their prestige, status, or image. Brands can also be positioned on one or more of these four symbolic meaning dimensions. For example:

- Self identity/concept/worth (e.g., L'Oréal: "Because I'm worth it")
- Personal meaning: (e.g., Kodak: "Share Moments. Share Life")
- Self-expression (e.g., Cannon: "Express Yourself")
- Social meaning (e.g., Grey Poupon: "Pardon me. Do you have any Grey Poupon?"; Rolls-Royce: "Trusted to deliver excellence")

There are many other ways to differentiate products and establish a brand's position in the marketplace. These include:

- Product class: The Mazda Miata is a sporty convertible.
- Competition: The Pepsi Challenge claims "More people prefer the taste of Pepsi over Coke." (This is an example of head-to-head competitive positioning, other organizations try to *associate* their brand with the market leader.)
- Occasions: Wrigley's gum is an alternative at times when smoking is not permitted.
- Users: Sunny Delight is the "Goodness kids go for."

## Developing Positioning Strategies

Different positioning strategies require different organizational strengths (capabilities), focus, and resource allocation and they are often associated with different organizational cultures (Table 3.1). This makes it difficult to be the industry leader in more than one of these areas. Companies also focus on differentiating themselves on only a few dimensions to make it easier for consumers to learn the intended brand concept. Positioning strategies, like target markets, are chosen based on internal environment factors like organizational strengths, competencies, resources, and culture and external environment factors like consumer behaviour and the strength and

**Exhibit 3.21**

IKEA promotes a value positioning, consistent with an operational excellence strategy.

**Table 3.1** Positioning Strategy Implementation

|  | Product Leadership | Customer Intimacy | Operational Excellence | Symbolism / Meaning |
|---|---|---|---|---|
| Strategy | Innovate, bring new products to market quickly that have superior features, functions, performance or outcomes | Develop exceptional customer experiences and tailored, customized solutions | Provide the best value by reducing costs, lowering prices, and by making it easy to do business with you | Develop superior symbolism or meaning for your product that creates psychological attachment to your brand |
| Structure | Flat, organic, flexible | Decentralized, empowerment close to customer contact | Strong centralized decisions focused on process or system improvements | Centralized decision making to control corporate and brand image, strong brand management structure |
| Culture | Entrepreneurial, creative, rewards innovation | Customer oriented, flexible, rewards customer satisfaction and loyalty | Bureaucratic, run by accountants, cost savings are rewarded. | Culture reflects and supports brand positioning. Brand management is rewarded. |
| Resource | Research & Development | Customer Research | Procurement | Marketing Communications |
| Focus | New Product Development, Production, Distribution | Service Quality, Customer Support, Flexible Manufacturing | Distribution, Scale Efficiencies, Manufacturing Efficiencies | Product Quality, Brand Management, Customer Research |

positioning of competitive brands. Four key steps to developing positioning strategies are: analyze competitors' positions, identify sustainable competitive advantage, implement the strategy with marketing mix decisions, and evaluate and modify the strategy if necessary.

ANALYZE COMPETITORS' POSITIONS Marketers typically start by understanding how their competitors are perceived by the target market. Aside from direct competitors in the product category, marketers consider whether there are other products or services that provide the same benefits that people in the segment are seeking. For example, when a company such as Coca-Cola develops a new drink, it must consider not only archrival Pepsi, but also how to compete against many alternative soft drinks and other beverages. The surprise success of Jolt Cola, which is fortified with caffeine, led Coca-Cola to develop Surge to target students, athletes, and people who don't like the taste of coffee but who need to "Feed the Rush."[55]

IDENTIFY SUSTAINABLE COMPETITIVE ADVANTAGE Central to positioning decisions is whether an organization is able to support and defend that positioning. The first element is whether the organization can actually create and communicate the value proposition suggested by its desired positioning: Does it have the skills, abilities, and resources to create an offer (a set of marketing mix decisions) that will be perceived as being superior by members of the target market on the differentiation dimensions reflected in the positioning strategy, and if so, can it communicate this effectively to the target market, and can it continue to do this until its goals are met as an organization? This is an issue of a company being able to sustain its basis for value creating differentiation, in the minds of its target customers.

The second element of competitive advantage is whether the positioning strategy can be defended against competitors. There are three main ways to defend a positioning strategy. The first is to continuously innovate to keep ahead of competitors. This is the approach typically followed by organizations adopting a product leadership strategy. The second approach is to hide in a small enough niche market that competitors are not likely to enter—either because the market is not big enough to warrant attention, or because there are significant first mover advantages in that market, such that followers into the market are at serious disadvantage. The third is to protect current source(s) of competitive advantage by erecting barriers to competition. Some of these barriers include:

- Marketing expertise: companies that are market oriented and customer driven can protect a customer intimacy positioning by being closer to and more understanding of customer needs, wants, and behaviours; by being more flexible; and by being more responsive to customers.

- Customer loyalty: competitors find it difficult to get loyal customers to switch brands. Companies who have develop loyal customers can protect their positioning by maintaining high levels of customer satisfaction. Some strategy experts argue that relationships are the only true source of sustainable competitive advantage as other barriers can eventually be eroded.

- Monopolization of a scare resource: retailers restrict competition by gaining exclusive access to retail locations. Other organizations secure exclusive supply or distribution contracts to limit the ability of competitors to enter markets.

- Proprietary technology: patents, copyrights, and other mechanisms that protect intellectual property can help protect current sources of competitive advantage.

- Culture-based expertise: companies that develop core competencies or specialized knowledge in applications, manufacturing, new product development or other value creating activities within organizations can protect a positioning strategy based on that expertise if it permeates an organization's culture in a way that is difficult to emulate. Cultures take a long time to develop and it is very difficult for competitors to emulate culture-based expertise.

- Legislation or regulatory approval: cell phone companies and cable companies are partially protected from competition by the Canadian Radio and Television Commission and the need for regulatory approval to set up cell networks or cable networks.

- Capital requirements: high market entry costs, such the cost of specialized equipment, technology, or setting up a salesforce or distribution channel, can be a barrier to competitors, particularly in small market niches that may only support one or two competitors.

**IMPLEMENT THE POSITIONING STRATEGY WITH MARKETING MIX DECISIONS** The success of a target marketing strategy hinges on a marketer's ability to identify and select an appropriate market segment or market segments. Then the marketer must devise a marketing mix that will effectively target the segment's members, by positioning the product to appeal to that segment. As this discussion suggests, market segmentation and positioning, together, are the two most important concepts in marketing. Segmentation and positioning decisions are also the most difficult for marketers to make.

Montreal-based G.I. Energy Drinks developed the following strategy when it introduced the Guru energy drink. The company segmented the market in terms of age and psychographics, and then targeted a segment of 16- to 24-year-olds, whose profiles indicated they were into "new-age" beverages that would give them a feeling of energy without unhealthy additives. The company reached these consumers by selling its drinks at raves in Montreal and Toronto (see Exhibit 3.22), advertising in club culture magazines, and sponsoring events like snowboarding demonstrations. A company spokesperson describes the Guru positioning strategy this way: "We really feel the best way to reach people is through trial and onsite promotions.... We want to provide the consumer with a drink that will enhance the activity they are already participating in."[56]

We previously discussed some of the challenges in segmentation. The four main positioning challenges are: 1) vague positioning where companies do not clearly articulate their main point(s) of differentiation; 2) confused positioning, where the positioning strategy keeps changing (like McDonald's) making it difficult for consumers or customers to understand what the brand is supposed to mean to them; 3) off-target positioning where

Exhibit 3.22
Many Canadian energy drinks, such as Generator and Guru, reach target segments by being sold at raves.

companies do not differentiate themselves on dimensions important to consumers or customers; and 4) over positioning, where companies position themselves too narrowly, either appealing to too small a market segment or being unable to change or adapt their positioning with changing market conditions.

**EVALUATE THE TARGET MARKET'S RESPONSES AND MODIFY THE STRATEGY** The target marketing process is ongoing. Over time the firm may find that it needs to change the segments it targets, and the needs or wants of people in these chosen segments may change as well. Marketers need to monitor these changes and adjust their positioning strategies when necessary. Sometimes marketers redo a product's position to respond to marketplace changes.

An example of such a makeover, a strategy called **repositioning**, was undertaken by Adults Only Video, a Canadian video chain that specializes in the sale and rental of pornographic movies. The company decided to reposition itself to appeal to couples aged 25 to 54. The company's traditional target market was males 18 to 25, but increased competition for this segment from Internet providers caused the company to reassess its position. The management at Adults Only Video described its repositioning as a move from a "sleazy" image to a "softer" one. The repositioning was accomplished by changing the product mix in the stores (to include products like candles, books, and magazines) and changing its advertising strategy to include female voice-overs in its radio ads and the placement of print ads in mainstream newspapers. The company also ran a large promotion, the "Millionaire Kiss-off," in which couples could win $1 million by breaking the world's record for the longest kiss.[57]

The Campbell Company of Canada is trying to reposition itself from being a soup company to being a food company. Its Power2Cook campaign uses traditional advertising, direct marketing, and a re-tooled Web site to teach young and busy cooks, male and female, how to prepare tasty meals using Campbell products.

**repositioning** Redoing a product's position to respond to marketplace changes.

**Campbell's Power2Cook**
www.power2cook.ca

## Bringing a Product to Life: The Brand Personality

Brands, like people, can be described in terms of personality traits. These descriptions might include words like cheap, elegant, sexy, bold, or wimpy. A positioning strategy often

## SPOTLIGHT ON REAL PEOPLE · Girl Guides Go Groovy

The world is ever changing. Businesses are constantly predicting and reacting, and sometimes a call for change must to be turned into complete repositioning for company survival. This predicament is exactly what the Girl Guides of Canada encountered in 2002 after experiencing steady decline in membership. The organization was formed in 1910 and remains the largest organization for girls and women in Canada, but its concepts and activities had been stuck in the 90s. The Guides hired Tony Ritchie, principal strategist at Ritchie-Bridges Strategy who admitted, "It's as simple and complex as saying we need a complete brand transformation." The Guides also hired Cossette Communications Marketing to handle its creative, media, and public relations, and Youthography out of Toronto to redesign the Girl Guides Web site. The Guides replaced the old brown uniforms with brightly coloured cargo pants and fleeces, 'You go girl' was incorporated as the theme in pro-motional materials, and the rebranding strategy that Girl Guides were "fun, bold, energetic, popular, and real" was pushed as well. To keep up with technology, the Web site was revamped to be used not just as a corporate information mechanism but also as a communication tool, and as a fun place for current and potential guides and volunteers to surf. The world famous cookies were changed too. The cookie boxes have a fresh up-to-date look that reinforces the fun, bold, energetic, and 'you go girl' themes. The focus of all of this change and energy is ultimately a revived and healthier organization. There is still a long way to go but the Girl Guides know that the organization and its overall concepts must change and adapt to the outside environment in order to survive and prosper.

Source: The Girl Guides Go GROOVY, Sarah Dobson, *Marketing Magazine Online*. April 28, 2003.

1. What obstacles will the Girl Guides and other companies face in the midst of repositioning? What can companies do to deal with these challenges?
2. How do you think an organization as geographically spread out as the Girl Guides of Canada could best unite its efforts to change? What would be the best way to communicate within the organization?

**brand personality** A distinctive image that captures a product or service's character and benefits.

tries to create a **brand personality** for a product or service—a distinctive image that captures its character and benefits. When the Mark Anthony Group was developing a name for its lemonade-based alcohol product, it did research with consumers to determine what name would communicate the right brand personality. The "person" it chose for its hard lemonade, "Mike," is described as a "fun, party, happy-go-lucky guy who is infatuated with lemons."[58]

After 124 years of positioning itself as the brand that "kills the germs that cause bad breath," Listerine lost market leadership in the 1980s to Scope and private label brands, in part because the brand was perceived as being cold, old-fashioned, authoritarian, serious, and stuffy—much like Margaret Thatcher, the British Prime Minister at the time.[59] In the 1990s Listerine tried many times to reposition its brand but it could not shake its authoritarian brand personality and consumers closed their ears to bad-breath lectures. In the late 1990s Listerine research identified that consumers were now much more aware of plaque, tartar, and gingivitis and that a shift to healthier gums positioning could be compelling and ownable. Research also found that the use of Listerine reduces gingivitis better than brushing and flossing alone and the challenge was then to develop a new brand personality that was both lighthearted and powerful. By developing a parody of a comic book action hero that fights the evil gingivitis, Listerine was able to transform its image and is now perceived by consumers as powerful, larger than life, immortal, and unfailing (Exhibit 3.23). Listerine's dollar share went from 38 percent in 1999 to 45 percent in early 2002, strong growth for a mature brand in a mature market.

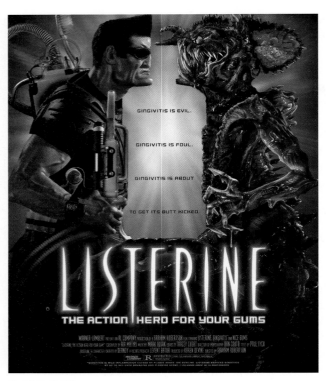

**Exhibit 3.23**

Listerine was able to change its brand personality using its action-hero campaign and significantly regained market share.

Products as people? Marketing researchers find that most consumers have no trouble describing what a product would be like "if it came to life." People often give clear, detailed descriptions, including what colour hair the product would have, the type of house it would live in, and even whether it would be thin, overweight, or somewhere in between.[60] If you don't believe us, try doing this yourself.

## PERCEPTUAL AND POSITIONING MAPPING

Creating a brand personality as part of a positioning strategy is one way of developing an identity for the product that the target market will prefer over competing brands. How do marketers determine where their product actually stands in the minds of consumers? One solution is to ask consumers what characteristics are important and how competing alternatives would rate on these attributes. Marketers use this information to construct a **perceptual map**, a picture of where products or brands are "located" in consumers' minds.

**perceptual map** A picture of where products or brands are "located" in consumers' minds.

For example, suppose you want to construct a perceptual map of women's magazines as perceived by Canadian women to give you some guidance while developing an idea for a new magazine. After interviewing a sample of female readers, you determine questions women ask when selecting a magazine: Is it "service oriented," emphasizing family, home, and personal issues or is it "fashion forward," oriented toward personal appearance and fashion? Is it for "upscale" women, who are older and established in their careers or for relatively "downscale" women, who are younger and just starting out in their careers?

The perceptual map in Figure 3.7 illustrates how these ratings might look for certain major women's magazines. It depicts the aggregate or average perception of how brands are perceived by multiple consumers on the dimensions of upscale/downscale and service/fashion, and it should be recognized that no individual consumer may hold these average perceptions. The shaded areas in Figure 3.7 represent two segments of consumers who seek the benefits and attributes offered by the set of magazines encircled. These are only two of many dimensions on which consumers compare magazines and marketers typically produce a series of positioning maps in order to understand how their and other

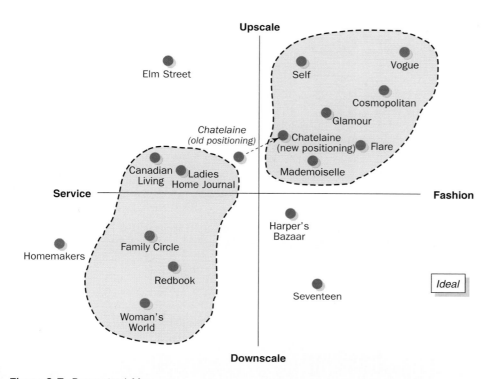

**Figure 3.7** Perceptual Map

brands are perceived by consumers. Other dimensions on which to position magazines might include cost (high/low), age appropriateness (young/old), sex appropriateness (mainly for men/mainly for women), and content (serious/frivolous)—among other possible dimensions.

The map also provides some guidance as to where your new women's magazine might be positioned. You might decide to compete directly with either the cluster of "service magazines" in the middle left or the fashion magazines in the upper right. In this case, you would have to determine what benefits your new magazine might offer that these existing magazines do not. *Chatelaine*, for example, repositioned itself in 1999 from a service-type magazine to a more urban, contemporary, youth, and fashion-oriented publication. This repositioning moved *Chatelaine* further away from its nearest Canadian competitor, *Canadian Living*.

To introduce a new magazine, you might try to locate an unserved area in this perceptual map. *Elm Street*, a relatively new entrant to the Canadian women's magazine scene, has tried to position itself for the upscale woman who is interested in articles on a broad range of topics, a part of the market that it felt was unserved. An unserved area of the map either represents an unserved segment and hence a potential opportunity for marketers, or it represents a positioning that is not in demand by a segment of consumers. According to Figure 3.7 (see "ideal") there may be room for a magazine targeted to downscale "cutting-edge" fashion, perhaps for younger women.

Positioning maps are similar to perceptual maps, except that they may include factual as well as perceptual information. By including factual information in the map, marketers can illustrate how brands compete in a marketplace. Figures 3.8 and 3.9 illustrate multiple positioning maps for a subset of Canadian universities with medical or doctoral programs, based on research conducted by *Maclean's* magazine (Table 3.2).[61] National reputation, a perceptual dimension included in the *Maclean's* ratings, is assessed by guidance councillors, recruiters, and university officials from across the country. The other information collected is factual.

**Chatelaine**
www.chatelaine.com

**Table 3.2** *Maclean's* Rating of Universities with Medical/Doctoral Programs (2002)

|  | U of T | Queens | McGill | UWO | UBC | U of A |
|---|---|---|---|---|---|---|
| **Average Entering Grade (%)** | 85.7 | 87.3 | 86.1 | 85.1 | 86.6 | 84.0 |
| **1st Yr Classes by Tenured Faculty** | 70.9 | 53.2 | 42.9 | 72.6 | 38.7 | 46.9 |
| **% of Classes Sized 51-100** | 44.7 | 34.1 | 35.8 | 17.6 | 39.8 | 33.4 |
| **Operating Budget per Student** | 9884 | 7861 | 7529 | 8246 | 6981 | 8669 |
| **National Reputation (Rank)** | 2 | 4 | 3 | 10 | 7 | 5 |
| **Average Tuition** | 4875 | 4828 | 5156 | 4870 | 2883 | 4491 |

Source: Reprinted with permission from *Maclean's* magazine.

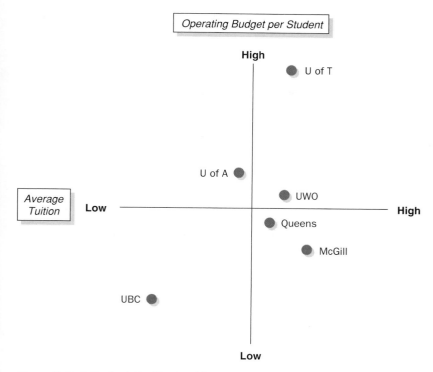

**Figure 3.8** A Factual Positioning Map

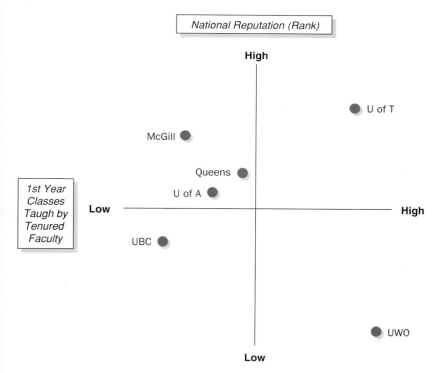

**Figure 3.9** A Factual and Perceptual Positioning Map

# Real People, Real Decisions

## ▶ How It Worked Out at Ford Motor Company

Candace Fochuk-Barey and her colleagues chose Option 1: They decided to target the Ford Windstar van primarily to mothers. In addition to researching the needs of mothers, the company put together an internal design team, which was made up of 30 female employees who were also moms. The redesigned Windstar included such "mom friendly" features as sleeping baby lights (that don't come on and wake the baby when the van doors are opened), a personal audio system for children riding in the back, a conversation mirror (so that mothers driving can see the road and their kids riding in the back), a storage area for diapers under the radio, a larger fuel tank so that the driver would have to fill up less frequently, and smart locks so

kids can't be locked in.

The design team also became an integral part of the advertising for the new van. That the redesigned Windstar was a success for Ford clearly illustrates the power of understanding the needs of a particular segment and addressing those needs through a targeted marketing strategy.

Fochuk-Barey has continued to target other Ford products and services to women. For example, Ford runs a Web site (www.ford4women.com), which encourages women to learn more about car ownership, and Ford offers free seminars "Car Smarts—Seminars for Women" at dealerships across the country.

# CHAPTER SUMMARY

## 1. Understand the five steps of developing a target marketing strategy.

The first step, select and understand markets, involves specifying the market that you are going to segment including its geographic scope. Then you need to sufficiently understand consumers or customers in this market to be able to identify groups. The second step, market segmentation, involves dividing a large market into a set of smaller markets that share important, actionable, characteristics, the developing profiles of the segments that describe them in sufficient detail to be able to choose among them. The third step is targeting, in which marketers select one or more of these groups to serve as their target market. The fourth step, called positioning, is developing a clear image of to communicate to members of the target market of how a brand is different and better than its competitors. The fifth step is developing marketing mix recommendations that create the offer for consumers or customers in the chosen segment(s) with the desired positioning.

## 2. Define the terms segmentation, target marketing, and positioning.

Segmentation is the process of dividing a larger market into smaller pieces, based on one or more meaningful, shared characteristics. Target marketing is dividing the total market into different segments based on customer characteristics, selecting one or more segments, and developing products to meet the needs of those specific segments. Positioning is how a particular market segment perceives a product or service as being differentiated in comparison to the competition.

## 3. Segment consumer and business-to-business markets.

Marketers frequently find it useful to segment consumer markets based on how consumers behave toward the product, for example, benefits or value sought, their brand loyalty, usage rates (heavy, moderate, or light), usage occasions, and product type purchased. A second dimension, psychographics, uses measures of psychological and social characteristics to identify people with shared preferences or traits. Demographic characteristics including age, gender, family life cycle, social class, ethnic identity, or place of residence may be a viable basis for segmentation but are critical elements in developing profiles of the segments. Categories similar to those in the consumer market are used for segmenting business markets. Business demographics include industry or company size, North American Industry Classification (NAICS) codes, and geographic location. Business markets may also be segmented based on operating variables and end-use applications. The recommended process is to start with a behavioural basis to see if groups can be identified by "what they want" or "how they use" a product. The other bases can then be used to develop the segment profiles more fully.

## 4. Explain how marketers evaluate and select potential market segments.

An effective segmentation scheme is one that meets the criteria of: groups similar enough within that members would want similar product solutions; different enough between that they would want different product solutions; large enough to warrant targeting; measurable; and reachable. To choose one or more segments to target, marketers examine each segment and evaluate its potential for success as a target market based on an assessment of its size and growth, other external environment factors like level of competition, and internal environment factors like the organization's ability to create unique value for the segment. The firm may choose an undifferentiated, differentiated, concentrated, or custom strategy, based on the company's characteristics and the nature of the market.

## 5. Understand how a firm develops and implements a positioning strategy.

After they have selected the target market(s) and overall strategy, marketers must determine how they wish the brand to be perceived by consumers relative to the competition: Should the brand be positioned like, against, or away from the competition? Brand concept is how the marketer wants its brand to be positioned; brand image is how consumers perceive the positioning of the brand. Through positioning, a brand personality is developed. Brand

## Key Terms

**80/20 rule**, p. 67

**baby boomers**, p. 71

**behavioural segmentation**, p. 66

**benefit segmentation**, p. 67

**brand concept**, p. 83

**brand image**, p. 83

**brand personality**, p. 90

**concentrated targeting strategy**, p. 82

**custom marketing strategy**, p. 82

**demographics**, p. 70

**differentiated targeting strategy**, p. 82

**geodemography**, p. 76

**industrial psychographics**, p. 78

**market fragmentation**, p. 63

**market potential**, p. 80

**mass customization**, p. 83

**niche marketing**, p. 82

**operating variables**, p. 77

**perceptual map**, p. 91

**positioning**, p. 83

**product usage segmentation**, p. 67

**psychographic segmentation**, p. 68

**repositioning**, p. 89

**segment profile**, p. 79

**segmentation**, p. 63

**segmentation variables**, p. 66

**target market**, p. 80

**target marketing strategy**, p. 63

**undifferentiated targeting strategy**, p. 81

**usage occasions**, p. 68

**VALS™ (Values and Lifestyles)**, p. 69

positions can be compared using such research techniques as perceptual mapping. In developing and implementing the positioning strategy, firms analyze the competitors' positions, determine the competitive advantage offered by their product, tailor the marketing mix in accordance with the positioning strategy, and evaluate responses to the marketing mix selected. Marketers must continually monitor changes in the market that might indicate a need to reposition the product.

**6. Describe how a positioning strategy can be defended.**

There are three main ways to defend a positioning strategy. The first is to continuously innovate to keep ahead of competitors. The second approach is to hide in a small enough niche market that competitors are not likely to enter—either because the market is not big enough to warrant their attention, or because there are significant first mover advantages in that market, such that followers into the market are at serious disadvantage. The third is to protect current source(s) of competitive advantage by erecting barriers to competition, such as: marketing expertise (closer to the customer or more responsive); customer loyalty, control of a scare resource; or proprietary technology.

# CHAPTER REVIEW

## Marketing Concepts: Testing Your Knowledge

1. What is market segmentation and why is it an important strategy in today's marketplace?
2. Explain consumer psychographic segmentation.
3. How can consumer behaviour be used for segmenting consumer markets?
4. List and explain the major demographic characteristics frequently used in segmenting markets.
5. What are the major dimensions used for segmenting business markets?
6. List the criteria used for determining whether a segment may be a good candidate for targeting.
7. Explain undifferentiated, differentiated, concentrated, customized, and mass-customization marketing strategies.
8. What is product positioning? Describe process marketers use to create product positions.
9. Describe the various ways positioning strategies may be defended.
10. What are positioning and perceptual maps and how are they used by marketers?

## Marketing Concepts: Discussing Choices and Issues

1. Some critics of marketing have suggested that market segmentation and target marketing lead to an unnecessary proliferation of product choices, which wastes valuable resources. These critics suggest that if marketers didn't create so many different product choices, there would be more resources to feed the hungry, house the homeless, and provide for the needs of people around the globe. Are the results of segmentation and target marketing harmful or beneficial to society as a whole? Should these criticisms be of concern to firms? How should New Era firms respond to these criticisms?
2. Retailers like Canada Safeway and Zellers have membership programs that ask customers to provide personal and sometimes financial information. The purchases the customer makes are then captured by the checkout scanner when the membership or loyalty card is presented. Explain how this data could be used to identify market segments and develop detailed segment profiles.
3. Some firms have been criticized for targeting unwholesome products to certain segments of the market—the elderly, ethnic subcultures, and the disabled. What other groups deserve special concern? Should a firm use different criteria in targeting such groups? Should the government oversee and control such marketing activities?
4. What are some ways in which a small business could defend its positioning against larger competitors?

## Marketing Practice: Applying What You've Learned

1. Assume that you have been hired to develop a marketing plan for a small regional brewery. In the past, the brewery produced and sold a single beer to the entire market—a mass-marketing strategy. As you begin your work for the firm, you feel that the firm could be more successful if it developed a target marketing strategy. The owner of the firm, however, is not convinced. Write a memo to the owner outlining:

   a. the basic reasons for target marketing.

   b. the specific advantages of a target marketing strategy for the brewery.

2. Assume that you are the director of marketing for a company that markets personal computers to business and organizational customers. You feel that if your market is segmented, you will be able to satisfy your customers' needs more efficiently and effectively. You must first decide what bases to use for segmenting the market.

   a. Develop a list of the potential segmentation variables you might use.

   b. Include your thoughts on how useful each might be to your marketing strategy.

   c. Develop a segmentation scheme for this market and develop a rich profile of at least one segment.

3. As the marketing director for a company that is planning to enter the business market for photocopy machines, you are attempting to develop an overall marketing strategy. You have considered the possibility of using mass-marketing, concentrated marketing, differentiated marketing, and custom marketing strategies.

   a. Write a report explaining what each type of strategy would mean for your marketing plan in terms of product, price, promotion, and distribution channel.

   b. Evaluate the desirability of each type of strategy.

   c. What are your final recommendations for the best type of strategy?

4. You are an account executive for a marketing consulting firm, and your newest client is an educational institution—the one you are currently attending. With a group of classmates, develop an outline of your ideas for positioning the institution, including the following:

   a. Who are your competitors?

   b. What are the competitors' positions?

   c. What target markets are most attractive for your client?

   d. How will you position your client for those segments relative to the competition?

   Present your results to your class.

## Marketing Mini-Project: Learning by Doing

This mini-project will help you develop a better understanding of how target-marketing decisions are made. The project focuses on the market for automobiles.

1. Gather ideas about different dimensions useful for segmenting the automobile market. You may use your own ideas and those mentioned in the Real People, Real Decisions case on Ford Motor Company of Canada. You probably will also want to examine advertising and other marketing communications developed by different automobile manufacturers; read articles in newspapers and magazines; look at Internet automobile sellers; and talk with salespeople at local automobile dealerships about different types of consumers and the cars that they buy.

2. Based on the dimensions for market segmentation you have identified, develop a questionnaire and conduct a survey of consumers. You will have to decide which questions should be asked and which consumers should be surveyed.

3. Analyze the data from your research and identify the different potential segments.

4. Develop segment profiles that describe each potential segment.

5. Generate several ideas for how the marketing strategy might be different for each segment based on the profiles.

6. Develop a presentation (or write a report) outlining your ideas, your research, your findings, and your marketing strategy recommendations.

## Real People, Real Surfers: Exploring the Web

In this chapter, you learned about psychographic segmentation systems, such as VALS and the Environics "tribes." To learn more about these systems, visit the SRI (the creators of VALS) Web site (www.future.sri.com) and the Environics Web site (www.environics.net). When you follow the VALS links, you will discover that SRI has also developed three other segmentation systems: Geo-VALS, Japan-VALS, and iVALS.

1. Based on the Environics site, describe all of the Environics tribes. For each tribe, identify what companies might be interested in targeting them. What tribe do you identify with?

2. From the information on the SRI Web site, describe Geo-VALS, Japan-VALS, and iVALS. What are some ways these segmentation systems might be used by organizations?

3. You can determine your own VALS type by taking the survey on the SRI Web site. Although the segments are based on people who live in the United States, the questions are also relevant for Canadians. When taking the survey, simply omit the zip code question. After you determine which segment you belong to, assess whether you think this VALS type accurately portrays you.

4. What is your opinion of the SRI and Environics Web sites? Whom do you think the companies are targeting with the sites? Do you think the sites are an effective way to promote products to potential customers? What suggestions do you have for improving the Web sites?

Write a report of your findings.

Marketers invest considerable time, effort, and money attracting customers, but large and small organizations alike have found that some customers are simply not worth having. Some customers can actually cost you money—taking more resources to service and satisfy them than the profit generated on their purchases. Consultant Ian Gordon suggests that organizations should "fire" the customers they lose money on.[62] These are the customers who set up accounts with shipping companies and never ship anything, buy only when products are on sale, or complain about everything, looking for concessions and other "make-goods." It is particularly hard for new businesses to turn away business, but not all business is worth it.

It is not hard to find out who these 25 to 30 percent of customers are. Many companies have a mountain of customer information gathered from scanners and smart cash registers, credit card summaries, call centres, and customer feedback programs that can be mined with simple software tools to identify the most profitable and least profitable customers. Clearnet, for example, tries to assess the value of every customer. It steeply discounts the sales of cell phones to attract a long-term stream of monthly phone usage. If a customer is not generating sufficient revenue to warrant Clearnet's investment in the phone, Clearnet first tries to get them to use it more and then tries to reduce the cost of servicing the customer by reducing service levels. As a last resort, it will cut off the phone service, buy back the phone for what the customer paid for it, and politely suggest that another service provider would better meet that customer's needs. In the airline industry, WestJet has cut unprofitable routes while Air Canada is mandated to keep basic service levels, even if it loses money on them.

Canadian financial institutions also try to segment their market and focus on distinct profitable segments. CIBC recognizes that its most profitable customers are not those who pay bills and make withdraws, but those who have investable assets and complex financial needs. To please these customers CIBC has created a new look and feel based on emotions, soft lighting, and store greeters. The branches also have a separate discrete area, where the bank's top clients meet with their personal advisors. Less "desirable" customers have seen service fee increases.

The Bank of Montreal also uses research and Customer Relationship Management (CRM) software to help them develop highly detailed segment profiles—helping them to group customers by their profitability, and focus attention on retaining the most profitable customers. Credit Unions target other segments. North Shore Credit Union, (North Vancouver) is generating a reputation as a customer service leader, and its campaign to build customer intimacy has made it Canada's fastest growing credit union. NSCU positions itself as being more caring and more customer and community focused than traditional banks. Vancouver City Credit Union (VanCity), positions itself as a financial institution that not only cares about its members, but also the natural environment and key social issues. It was the first to start an ethics-based mutual fund and recently ran advertisements showing support for same-sex relationships. It wants to attract similarly environmentally and socially minded customers and turns away some customers whose businesses are not consistent with the values of the other credit union members.

Identifying market segments and choosing target markets is central to marketing strategy. However there are some controversial and potentially discriminatory practices when it comes to serving the needs and wants of some customers and not others.

This case was written by Dr. Brock Smith with the assistance of Ms. Karen Osberg drawing on the following sources: "Firing Your Customer," *Venture* Episode #710, January 26, 1999; "Cutting Through All the Hype About CRM," Lesley Young, *Marketing Magazine Online,* February 12, 2001.

## Things to Think About

1. Is it acceptable for organizations to "fire" customers or not do business with those in less desirable segments?

2. Is it acceptable for companies to identify their most profitable customers and focus the efforts on retaining those customers or should customers be treated equally?

3. What is the downside for a financial institution of measuring the current profitability of customers and then developing strategies to retain these customers while discouraging customer that are not profitable.

4. If a company did really want to "fire" a customer so they no longer did business together, how might this been done most effectively? What risks are involved for a company doing this?

5. In what industries would it make most sense for government regulation that ensures all customers receive some basic level of service?

# CBC ⬤ VIDEO CASE

## Cobra Cars

It's no secret that entrepreneurs encounter all kinds of dilemmas. But when a brand new and extremely expensive and specialty business is run by an inexperienced son and a busy father these dilemmas can get quite complex. Leonard Skok and his son Allan were determined to build a specialty car empire under the brand Superformance Canada, that would sell factory-built replicas of the 1965 Shelby Cobra and the 1957 Roadster to car enthusiasts across Canada. Allan, straight out of business school, was put in charge of sales and given the task of selling a minimum of 24 of the $85 000 luxury cars per year. Starting in Ontario, Allan showcased the cars on Bay Street in Toronto, at the Toronto Indy car race, and at vintage auto shows, and got good public relations coverage in the Ontario media. But after the first year, when only 12 cars had been sold, it became obvious that not just anyone could afford life in the fast lane and would pay $85 000 for a replica sports car. Allan found that the serious customers were quite demanding and hard to please. Expenses, such as flying customers to Toronto to test drive the cars, were adding up and engine troubles were affecting test drives.

Determined to keep going, and financed through Leonard Skok's other business of buying used cars in Canada and selling them in the United States, Allan refined his sales pitch and closing techniques while his father kept pushing him with the hard numbers of what they needed to sell in order to stay afloat and reach the goal of expanding into the Vancouver market.

Shortly into the second year, Allan sold four cars in a week and prospects were looking up. The next challenge was to keep to the delivery schedule without compromising quality control. After receiving the parts from the South African manufacturer, each car would take a week to assemble and Allan knew that positive or negative word-of-mouth from these well-connected customers could make or break the company. Sales still have not reached the break-even point and Allan has not been able to attract the financing needed to expand the business. Superformance Canada is still alive, building, and selling specialty cars, but its dreams for expansion are currently on hold.

## Questions

1. How would you segment the automobile market?
2. Develop a detailed profile of the market segment(s) Allan should be targeting.
3. What competencies does a small company need to develop to defend a position in a niche market like this one?

---

Source: This case was prepared by Brock Smith and is based on *Venture*, "Cobra Cars," #851.

**Superformance Canada**
www.superformance.ca

# CHAPTER 4
## Marketing Research

## CHAPTER OBJECTIVES

WHEN YOU HAVE COMPLETED YOUR STUDY OF THIS CHAPTER, YOU SHOULD BE ABLE TO

1. Understand the role of the marketing information system and the marketing decision support system in marketing decision making.

2. Describe the marketing research process.

3. Understand the differences among exploratory, descriptive, and causal research, and describe some research techniques available to marketers.

4. Describe the different types of data collection methods and types of samples that researchers use.

5. Understand the growing use of online research.

# Real People, Real Decisions

## Meet **Dr. Marshall Rice,** a Decision Maker at SurveySite

Dr. Marshall Rice is the founder of SurveySite, the Internet's leading provider of online market research. Located in Toronto, SurveySite conducts Web-based research for local, national, and international clients, including Microsoft, Ford Motor Company, Canadian Tire, The World Bank, Dell Computer Corporation, and Telus. Rice and his team at SurveySite use such research methods as online surveys and Web-based consumer panels to help clients better understand their Internet customers. Their research is used to support many different types of marketing decisions, including the look and design of a company's Web site, which products and services to offer to customers, how to provide better customer service, and what prices to charge for a company's products.

Rice has a BA from the University of Manitoba and a Masters and Ph.D. in communications from the University of Illinois. In addition to his duties at SurveySite, he is a professor of marketing at the Schulich School of Business at York University in Toronto.

Marshall Rice was considering how to expand SurveySite's business. The company had traditionally focused on providing survey-based research on the Web, but Rice was interested in looking at different methodologies that could be adapted to the Internet environment. One product he considered offering to his customers was an online focus group, which would combine some elements of traditional focus groups (such as group discussion) with the flexibility of the Internet environment. He wanted to draw on the Internet chat room idea by inviting the group participants to a Web site that would allow them to participate in focus group discussions on their own time over a specified period, say three to five days. Like traditional focus groups, the online focus group would be led by a trained moderator, who would monitor the online discussion and keep participants on track.

Rice decided to conduct his own marketing research to determine whether his existing clients would be interested in online focus groups and, if they were, what features they would like to see. To conduct this exploratory research, he interviewed a small sample of his most important clients. During these interviews, respondents told him that one problem with traditional focus groups is that customers from only limited geographic regions and time zones can participate in the groups; this is a concern for companies like Microsoft, who have customers around the world. Conducting groups online would allow participants in different geographic areas to be involved in the same groups.

Another benefit that some clients mentioned was the ability to get results quickly. Because the participants in the online focus groups would be typing in their responses on their computers, the client would have the transcript from the focus group immediately after the group ended. Clients also liked the idea that they could observe the focus group while it was happening and "talk" to the moderator privately by typing in questions that they hadn't thought of before the focus group. Additionally, several clients mentioned that the anonymity of the online environment might encourage responses from individuals who may be shy in a group, and that this anonymity could also encourage all respondents to be more honest. Finally, several clients thought that the online environment may get rid of one of the most annoying problems in "live" focus groups: the domination of the group by one or two loud, opinionated members. Those people who tried to dominate a group online could be more effectively dealt with by the moderator (perhaps through a private e-mail).

Not all of the clients were completely sold on the online focus group idea, though. Some clients were concerned that the anonymity provided by the online environment would detract from the reliability of the information. How could the researchers be sure that the person recruited for the group was actually the only one involved in typing in responses? Other clients were concerned with the inability to see nonverbal communication from the participants (such as facial expressions and body language) or to hear intonation, both of which can indicate a person's feelings and reactions better than simply words.

As Rice reviewed the responses of his clients, he began to wonder whether the online focus group product was worth introducing. Even traditional focus groups were losing some of their appeal for companies. If companies were not sold on the focus group concept generally, they would certainly not be interested in online groups. Rice was also considering the cost of organizational changes that would be necessary to support the introduction of the new product. Focus groups required people who could be moderators and analyze qualitative data. There would have to be some retraining of existing SurveySite employees and some new people hired to be able to offer this new technique.

In making his decision, Rice considered two options.

**Option 1** was to develop and introduce an online focus group product.

**Option 2** was to abandon the online focus group product idea for now and continue to focus the efforts of SurveySite on survey research techniques online. As a follow-up to the exploratory interviews with existing clients, plan to conduct more extensive research with both existing and potential clients to better determine the potential for online focus groups.

Now, join Marshall Rice and the SurveySite team. Which option would you choose, and why?

# INFORMATION FOR DECISION MAKING

In Chapter 1 we talked about how marketing is a decision process in which marketing managers determine the strategies that will help the organization meet its long-term objectives. In Chapter 2 we said that successful planning means that managers made good decisions for guiding the organization. But how do marketers make good decisions? How do they go about developing marketing objectives, selecting a target market, positioning—or repositioning—their product, and developing product, price, promotion, and place strategies? The answer is information. To make good decisions, marketers must have information that is accurate, up-to-date, and relevant. The Tetley Tea Company knows this first hand. Since the company entered the Canadian tea market in the mid-1980s, it has done continuous market research with tea-drinking consumers to better understand their attitudes and motivations as well as their view of competitive products. The company's research efforts have certainly paid off. Since the product was introduced, the brand has gone from last place in the market to first, a feat the company attributes directly to having good consumer information.[1] In this chapter we will talk about some of the tools that marketers use to get the information they need.

**SurveySite**
www.surveysite.com

## The Marketing Information System

Firms develop a **marketing information system (MIS)** to meet the information needs of marketing managers. The MIS is a process that first determines what information managers need and then gathers, sorts, analyzes, stores, and distributes relevant and timely marketing information to system users. The MIS system includes three important components: (1) data, (2) computer hardware and software to analyze the data and create reports, and (3) MIS experts who actually manage the process to generate and distribute the needed information.

**marketing information system (MIS)** Procedure developed by a firm to continuously gather, sort, analyze, store, and distribute relevant and timely marketing information to its managers.

Where do the data come from? Information to feed the system comes from several major sources: internal company data, marketing intelligence data on competition and other elements in the firm's business environment, information gathered through marketing research, and acquired databases.

These data are stored and accessed through computer hardware and software. Based on an understanding of managers' needs, MIS personnel generate a series of regular reports for various decision makers. Frito-Lay's MIS, for example, generates daily sales data by product line and by region that its managers use to evaluate the market share of different Frito-Lay products compared to each other and to competing snack foods in each region.[2] Imperial Tobacco Canada's MIS includes asking 2000 adult smokers a month to provide information on their brand usage, brand switching, reasons for brand switching, new product awareness, and purchase location. Each year the company measures awareness, consumption behaviour, and loyalty for every brand in the Canadian market, converting this to brand and benefit segmentation. Figure 4.1 shows the elements of an MIS.

**INTERNAL DATA SYSTEM** The internal data system uses a variety of information from within the company to produce reports on the results of sales and marketing activities. Internal data include a firm's internal records of sales—information such as which customers buy which products in what quantities and at what intervals, what items are in stock, and which ones are back-ordered because they are out of stock, when items were shipped to the customer, and what items have been returned because they are defective.

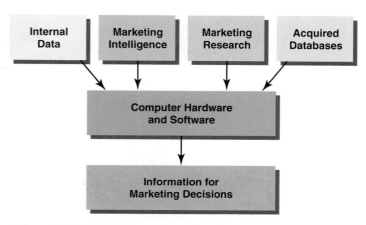

**Figure 4.1** The Marketing Information System

A firm's marketing information system (MIS) stores and analyzes data from a variety of sources and turns the data into information useful for marketing decision making.

**intranet** An internal corporate communication network that uses Internet technology to link company departments, employees, and databases.

Often an MIS allows salespeople and sales managers in the field to access the internal records using laptop computers through a company **intranet**. An intranet is an internal corporate communication network that uses Internet technology to link company departments, employees, and databases. Intranets are secured so that only authorized employees have access. When the MIS is made available to salespeople and sales managers, they can serve their customers better by having immediate access to information on pricing, inventory levels, production schedules, shipping dates, and the customer's sales history. But, equally important because salespeople and sales managers are the ones in daily direct contact with customers, their reports which are entered directly into the system via the company intranet can provide an important source of information on changes in sales patterns or new sales opportunities.

From the internal data, marketing managers can get daily or weekly sales data by brand or product line. They can also get monthly sales reports to measure progress toward sales goals and market share objectives. Marketing managers of retailers like Wal-Mart and Zellers, for example, use up-to-the-minute sales information obtained from store cash registers around the country so they can detect problems with products, promotions, and even the firm's distribution system (Exhibit 4.1).

**marketing intelligence** A method by which marketers get information about everyday happenings in the marketing environment.

MARKETING INTELLIGENCE As we discussed in Chapter 2, to make good decisions marketers need to have information about the marketing environment. Thus, a second important element of the MIS is the **marketing intelligence** system, a method by which marketers get information about everyday happenings in the marketing environment. Although the name *intelligence* may suggest cloak-and-dagger spy activities, in reality nearly all the information companies need about their environment including the competitive environment is available by monitoring everyday sources: newspapers, trade publications, or simple observations of the marketplace. Marketing intelligence is an ongoing process that allows firms to monitor conditions that affect demand for existing products or create demand for new products. St. John's-based Cable Atlantic estimates that their marketing research budget is four to five times higher than the national average because the company considers marketing intelligence to be so critical to marketing decision making. The company also conducts large market research studies, using techniques such as phone surveys,

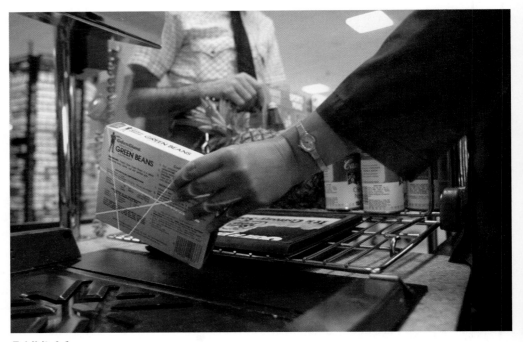

**Exhibit 4.1**

Retailers like Zellers and Wal-Mart use scanner data to help make marketing decisions.

about every 12 months to keep up with trends and events affecting consumer demand. The marketing intelligence activities have produced bottom-line results. Cable Atlantic has achieved a cable penetration rate among its customers that is 10 percent higher than the national average.[3] Because salespeople are the ones "in the trenches" every day, talking with customers, distributors, and prospective customers, they can be an invaluable source of marketing intelligence.

In recent years, the World Wide Web has become a major source of marketing intelligence. Tremendous amounts of information are available on company Web pages (including those of competitors), through news sources from around the globe, through government reports, and on trade association sites. The ease of accessing and searching the Web and individual sites makes the Internet an even more attractive source of marketing intelligence. Industry Canada, for example, offers a variety of online tools and resources to help Canadian businesses be more effective in market intelligence, including ebiz.enable, an online service that helps Canadian businesses track key industry information and trends (Exhibit 4.2).

Sometimes companies engage in specific activities to gain intelligence. For example, retailers often hire "mystery shoppers" (see Spotlight on Real People, page 118) to visit their stores (and those of their competitors) posing as customers to see how people are treated—imagine being paid to shop for a living! Other information may come from purchasing competitors' products and from attending trade shows.

Marketing managers may use marketing intelligence data to forecast the future so that they will be on top of developing trends. Indeed, some marketing researchers, known as *futurists*, specialize in predicting consumer trends to come. They try to forecast changes in lifestyles that will affect the wants and needs of customers in the coming years. Futurists try to imagine different **scenarios**, or possible future situations, that might occur and assign a level of probability to each. A scenario can be shaped by a number of key outcomes. For example, deregulation laws could shape the future of the Canadian banking, airline, energy, or dairy industries. In those cases the futurist might develop different scenarios for different levels of deregulation, including forecasts assuming no deregulation, moderate deregulation, and complete deregulation. Each scenario allows marketers to consider the impact of different marketing strategies and come up with plans based on which outcomes it considers most likely to happen. No one can predict the future—especially sudden, momentous events that change our lives like large-scale terrorist attacks—but it's better to make an educated guess than no guess at all and be caught totally unprepared. Most large organizations are involved in scenario planning. At Siemens, for example, a multidisciplinary team called FutureScape is spread all over the world, and its members work on FutureScape scenarios alongside their normal work, interacting mostly on the company's intranet, although members occasionally meet in person for workshops.[4] At Nokia, hundreds of people throughout the organization focus on building scenarios and investigating the link between business concepts and possible futures in which they will work.[5] Of course, collecting marketing intelligence is just the beginning. An effective MIS must include procedures to ensure that the intelligence data are translated and combined with internal data and other marketing information to create useful reports for marketing managers.

**Innovation in Canada**
www.innovationstrategy.gc.ca/gol/innovation/interface.nsf/engdocBasic/2.2.html

**Strategis**
http://strategis.ic.gc.ca

**ebiz.enable**
http://strategis.gc.ca/epic/internet/inee-ef.nsf/en/h_ee00499e.html

**scenarios** Possible future situations that futurists use to assess the likely impact of alternative marketing strategies.

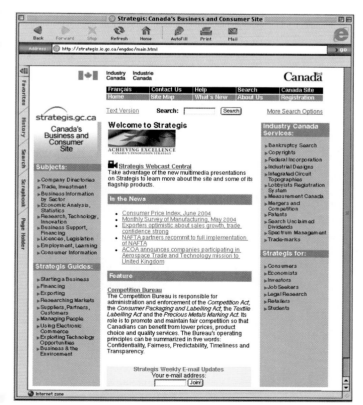

**Exhibit 4.2**

Industry Canada's Strategis Web site offers data and tools for market intelligence.

One prominent futurist company, BrainReserve, tracks themes that show up in movies and other mass media. BrainReserve has predicted such trends as cocooning (staying home), cashing out (quitting the rat race), down-aging (acting youthful), and the surge of demand for such products as fresh food and four-wheel-drive cars.[6] Although many marketers disagree with these predictions, others eagerly retain the services of these futurists to help them prepare for the years ahead.

**MARKETING RESEARCH** A third type of information that is a part of a company MIS is data gathered through marketing research. Whether their business is selling cool stuff to teens or coolant to factories, firms succeed by knowing what customers want, when they want it, where they want it—and what competing firms are doing about it. In other words, the better a firm is at obtaining valid marketing information, the more successful it will be. The process of collecting, analyzing, and interpreting data about customers, competitors, and the business environment to make a specific marketing decision is called **marketing research**. Although marketing intelligence information is collected continuously to keep managers abreast of happenings in the marketplace, marketing research is called for when unique information is needed for specific decisions. Virtually all companies rely on some form of marketing research, though the amount and type of research vary dramatically (Exhibit 4.3).

In general, marketing research data available in an MIS includes **secondary research**, syndicated research reports, and primary research (custom research) reports. Secondary research is research produced by another organization or individual, for another purpose than the problem at hand, which may also address some information needs of an MIS. One type of secondary data is published material. This includes general business sources such as guides, directories, indexes, and statistical data and articles and reports published by popular and business press, such as *The Globe and Mail Report on Business* and the *Financial Post* (Exhibit 4.4). Much of this information is now available on the Internet. Some useful secondary data sources are found in Table 4.1.

Published material also includes government sources such reports generated by Statistics Canada, or reports produced by Industry Canada. One data source used by many Canadian marketers is Statistics Canada's *Market Research Handbook*, which contains such demographic information as population size, average household income, and family structure for all

**marketing research** The process of collecting, analyzing, and interpreting data about customers, competitors, and the business environment in order to make a specific marketing decision.

**secondary research** Research collected for a purpose other than the decision at hand.

### Table 4.1 Some Useful Secondary Data Sources

**Blue Book of Canadian Business** (www.cbr.ca) includes profiles of Canada's top-performing companies (public, private, crown, and cooperatives), including executive biographies; sales, assets, net income, and stock trading volume, and can be a very useful resource for business-to-business marketing activities.

**Carlson On-Line Services** (www.fin-info.com). Find companies trading on the stock exchanges.

**CompuServe** (www.compuserve.com) provides full-text articles from more than 450 business and trade publications.

**Dun & Bradstreet Canada** (www.dnb.ca/marketspectrum) provides customized market information to businesses by combining their database of market information with the information their customers have already collected.

**TradeMap** (www.exportsource.ca/trademap_e.cfm) is an online database of trade statistics that provides detailed export and import profiles and trends for more than 5300 products in 200 countries and territories.

**Strategy Magazine Online** (www.strategymag.com) contains articles on marketing in Canada and has a search engine that searches the archives of the magazine.

**Marketing Magazine Online** (www.marketingmag.ca) contains articles on marketing practices, campaigns, and people in Canada and has a search engine that searches the archives of the magazine.

**Marketing Tools** (www.marketingtools.com), run by American Demographics magazine, lets users search for marketing books and articles.

provinces and 45 major cities across the country.[7] Because this information is available in many libraries across the country, it is an especially cost-effective resource for small businesses that are trying to better understand their markets. Industry Canada's Strategis Web site is a valuable source of Canadian industry information. Trade associations also conduct research on behalf of their members and produce industry reports, such as the *Directory of Chains* published by *Canadian Grocer*.

Another type of secondary data is computerized databases. Your college or university library likely has online directories, full-text databases, and special purpose databases that allow you to access information produced from a variety of information sources. These may include:

- Lexis/Nexis: A very large database containing the full text of over 200 newspapers and many other materials such as newsletters, trade journals, legal cases, reference works, and a few academic journals. Covers topics in all areas but is strongest in the areas of business, management, government, political science, law, current events, patents, and medicine.

- Hoovers Company Profiles: Corporate profiles and financial information on publicly traded companies.

- Standard & Poor's NetAdvantage: Lists public and private companies trading on U.S. stock exchanges. Includes company name, location, address, executive biographies, SIC codes, and sales information.

- ABI Inform / Proquest: Full text article search capability covering more than 6000 academic and popular press business journals worldwide.

- Canadian Newsstand: Full text article search covering major Canadian newspapers and magazines.

- Predicasts PROMT: Summary and full text information about products and markets from nearly 1000 business and trade journals, industry newsletters, newspapers, market research studies, news releases, and investment and brokerage firm reports.

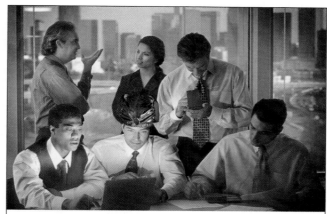

**Exhibit 4.3**

Companies like Dun & Bradstreet Canada provide customized market research for businesses.

Syndicated research firms collect fairly general data on a regular basis and sell the information to many firms. Nielsen Media Research, for example, tracks television viewership and program ratings across Canada. D~code is a syndicated research firm that focuses on understanding the Nexus generation (18- to 34-year-olds) in Canada. Other firms focus on tracking sales and brand attitude information in specific industries. As valuable as it may be, **syndicated research** doesn't provide all of the answers to marketing questions because the information collected typically is broad but shallow; it gives good insights about general trends such as who is watching what TV shows or what brand of perfume is hot this year. Often firms need to undertake custom marketing research, especially when they need to know more about *why* these trends have surfaced.

**Primary research** is research conducted for a single firm to provide answers to specific questions. Sometimes marketing managers need more specific information, such as immediate feedback on a proposed change in pricing strategy or consumers' perceptions of a new advertising campaign. Marketers might also use specific information to identify opportunities for new products or to provide data about the quality of their existing

**Statistics Canada**
www.statcan.ca

**D~code**
www.d-code.com

**syndicated research** Research by firms that collect data on a regular basis and sell the reports to multiple firms.

**primary research** Research conducted by or for a single firm to provide information for a specific marketing decision.

**Exhibit 4.4**

*Marketing Magazine* is a useful source of information about Canadian marketing and communications practices, campaigns, and people.

products, who uses them, and how (Exhibit 4.5). Most of the research conducted by market research companies such as SurveySite is customized research that provides this type of specific information. For example, SurveySite helped Hewlett-Packard determine a name for their new scanning product by performing an online survey with over 4000 respondents.[8]

Marketers may use marketing research to identify opportunities for new products, to promote existing ones, or to provide data about the quality of their products, who uses them, and how. Sometimes a company will even do research to counter a competitor's claim. For example, Procter & Gamble (P&G) challenged rival Revlon's claim that its ColorStay line of cosmetics won't rub off. P&G researchers wanted to answer a specific question: Was ColorStay's claim true? That kind of question can't be answered by buying a syndicated report, so Procter & Gamble commissioned 270 women to provide the specific information needed to support its case against Revlon. The women rubbed their cheeks against their shirts while wearing ColorStay and reported that, in fact, most of the shirts did get stained. But Revlon countered that P&G's test was flawed because the women may have been encouraged to rub too hard. Revlon did their own test on 293 women who were told to use "the pressure they use when caressing someone else's face." This time the women found few stains. To avoid further controversy Revlon now says that ColorStay won't rub off under "normal circumstances."[9] Aren't you relieved?

**ACQUIRED DATABASES** A large amount of information that can be useful in marketing decision making is available in the form of external databases. Firms may acquire databases from any number of sources. For example, some companies are willing to sell their customer database to non-competing firms. Privacy legislation in Canada will restrict this particular practice, however, as information provided to an organization can only be used by that organization for the expressed purpose for which respondents have given consent.

## Marketing Decision Support Systems

As we have discussed, a firm's MIS generates regular reports to decision makers on what is going on in the internal and external environment. But sometimes these reports are inadequate. Different managers may want different information and in some cases the problem that must be addressed is too vague or unusual to be easily answered by the MIS process. As a result many firms beef up their MIS with a **marketing decision support system (MDSS)**. An MDSS includes analysis and interactive software that allows managers, even those who are not computer experts, to access MIS data and conduct their own analyses, often over the company intranet. Figure 4.2 shows the elements of an MDSS.

Typically an MDSS includes both basic and sophisticated statistical software and modeling tools. Such software allows managers to examine complex relationships among factors in the marketplace and allows them to examine possible or preconceived ideas about relationships in the data—by asking "what-if" questions. For example, media modeling software allows marketers to see what would happen if they made certain decisions about where to place their advertising versus other possibilities. A manager may be able to use sales data and a model to find out how many consumers stay with his brand and how many switch, thus developing projections of brand share over time. Table 4.2 presents some examples of the different questions that might be considered by an MIS versus an MDSS. Appendix 4.A provides an introduction to the basic and advanced analytic tools used by marketers. These are

**marketing decision support system (MDSS)** The data, analysis software, and interactive software that allow managers to conduct analyses and find the information they need.

just some of the analytic tools available to marketers and they should suggest to you that there can be significant "science" behind making marketing decisions.

## Searching for Gold: Data Mining

As we have discussed, most MIS systems include internal customer transaction databases and many include acquired databases. Often these databases are extremely large. To take advantage of the massive amount of data now available, sophisticated analysis techniques called **data mining** are becoming a priority for many firms. Data mining is a process in which analysts sift through massive amounts of data (often measured in terabytes—much larger than kilobytes or even gigabytes) to identify unique patterns of behaviour among different customer groups.

American Express, for example, uses data mining to understand shopping patterns. By mining the data, the company can identify customer segments whose shopping patterns indicate they may respond to different types of offers. If its data show that some of its female cardholders buy a lot of clothes at Holt Renfrew, American Express might offer these women a discount if they also buy shoes at the store and whip out their Amex card to pay for them.[10]

Data mining uses supercomputers that run sophisticated programs so different databases can be combined to understand relationships among buying decisions, exposure to marketing messages, and in-store promotions. These operations are so complex that often companies need to build a *data warehouse* (sometimes costing more than $10 million!) simply to store the data and process it.[11]

Data mining has four important applications for marketers.[12]

• *Customer acquisition:* Many firms work hard to include demographic and other information about customers in their database. For example, a number of supermarkets like

**Exhibit 4.5**

Automakers such as Ford conduct extensive market research on consumers' car preferences.

**data mining** Sophisticated analysis techniques to take advantage of the massive amount of transaction information now available.

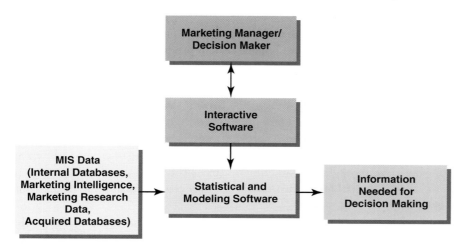

**Figure 4.2** The Marketing Decision Support System

Although an MIS provides many reports managers need for decision-making, it doesn't answer all their information needs. The marketing decision support system (MDSS) is an enhancement to the MIS that makes it easy for marketing managers to access the MIS system and find answers to their questions.

**Table 4.2 Examples of Questions That Might Be Answered by an MIS and an MDSS**

| Questions Answered with an MIS | Questions Answered with an MDSS |
|---|---|
| What were our company sales of each product during the last month and the last year? | Have our sales declines simply reflected changes in overall industry sales or is there some portion of the decline that cannot be explained by industry changes? |
| What changes are happening in sales in our industry and what are the demographic characteristics of consumers whose purchase patterns are changing the most? | Are the same trends seen in our different product categories? Are the changes in consumer trends very similar among all of our products? What are the demographic characteristics of consumers who seem to be the most and the least loyal? |
| What are the best media for reaching a large proportion of heavy, medium, or light users of our product? | If we change our media schedule by adding or deleting certain media buys, will we reach fewer users of our product? |

Canada Safeway offer weekly special price discounts for store "members." And, of course, the membership application form requires that customers indicate their age, family size, address, and so on. With this information the firm can determine which of its current customers respond best to specific offers and then send the same offers to noncustomers who share the same characteristics.

- *Customer retention:* The firm can identify big-spending customers and then target them for special offers and inducements other customers won't receive. Banks such as CIBC and credit card companies like MasterCard identify their most profitable customers and have developed programs to ensure those people are completely satisfied.

- *Customer abandonment:* Strange as it may sound, sometimes a firm wants customers to take their business elsewhere because they actually cost the firm too much to service them. A department store may use data mining to identify unprofitable customers—those who are not spending enough or who return most of what they buy. For example, data mining has allowed Federal Express to identify customers as "the good, the bad, and the ugly."[13] As a result, FedEx's strategy is to keep the "good" consumers as profitable customers and make "bad" customers (those who cost the company more than they generate in revenues) more profitable by charging them higher shipping rates. For the "ugly" customers who spend very little, FedEx is saving money by no longer trying to attract their business. Cell phone companies like Clearnet offer to buy back handsets from customers who are not using them enough to generate a profit to the service provider.

- *Market basket analysis:* The firm can develop focused promotional strategies based on its records of which customers have bought certain products. Sears, for example, analyzes which of its customers have recently bought power tools like table saws or routers and targets them to receive mailings and phone calls about accessories.

So far, we have looked at the MIS and the MDSS, the overall systems that provide the information marketers need to make good decisions. We've seen how the data included in the MIS and MDSS include internal records, marketing intelligence data gathered by monitoring everyday sources, acquired databases, and information gathered to address specific marketing decisions through the marketing research process. In the rest of the chapter we'll look at the steps that marketers must take when they conduct marketing research.

## THE STEPS IN THE MARKETING RESEARCH PROCESS

The collection and interpretation of strategic information is hardly a one-shot deal that managers engage in "just out of curiosity." Ideally, marketing research is an ongoing *process*, a series of steps marketers take to learn about the marketplace. Whether a company conducts the research itself or hires another firm to do it, the goal is the same—to help managers make informed marketing decisions. Figure 4.3 shows the steps in the research process, and we'll go over each of these now.

## Defining the Problem

Defining the research problem as precisely as possible allows marketers to search for the right answers to the right questions. Sometimes marketers cannot determine exactly what the problem is because they're focusing on symptoms, such as declining sales, and not on the underlying problem that's causing sales to drop. For example, a drop in sales of a sunscreen may be due to a new competitor, lack of cooperation from distributors, or even a fashion trend promoting a deep tan.

Defining the problem has four components:

1. Specify the management decision.

The most important stage of the research process is figuring out what marketing (or other) decisions need to be made with the information being sought. For example, is the key decision "what market segments should I target?" or is the key decision "how should I price this product?" The research needed for making the first decision won't be useful for making the second decision or vice versa—and generally, you can only focus on one key decision in any given piece of research because different decisions require different research questions, samples, and methods. Specifying the relative importance of the decision is also useful as it helps guide the scope of the research activity and how much time, effort, and resources should be allocated to the project.

2. Specify the research objectives or research questions.

What questions will the research attempt to answer? Once the key decision is identified, you need to ask yourself "what general questions do I need to answer to make that decision?" For example, if the key decision is "what market segments should I target?" some key questions (among others) that need to be answered are:

What are the key alternative market segments?

What are the profiles and size of these segments?

What brands are currently targeted at each segment?

How is our brand positioned (or how might it be positioned) relative to competitors?

What are sources of competitive advantage that will allow us to defend our desired positioning?

Often the importance of a research question surfaces during exploratory research. For example, Mercedes-Benz regularly monitors drivers' perceptions of its cars, partly through feedback from dealers. When the company started getting reports from its dealers that people were viewing the cars as being deserved only after they become "successful," it developed the "ice cream" television ad shown in Exhibit 4.6. It attempts to dispel the attitude that consumers should wait until their big promotion to indulge themselves.[14] Often marketers want to know how much of a product they are likely to sell. There are many approaches to developing a sales forecast. Some of the common approaches are described in Appendix 4.B at the end of this chapter.

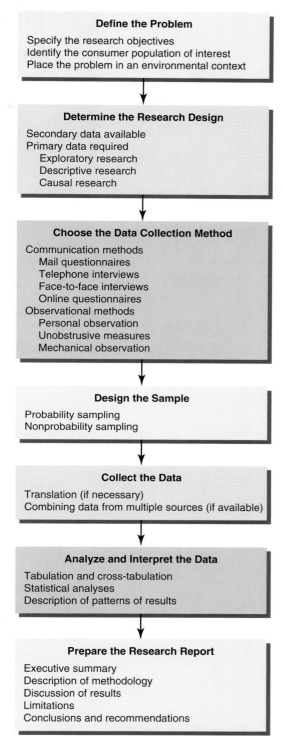

**Figure 4.3** Steps in the Marketing Research Process

The marketing research process includes a series of steps that begins with defining the problem or the information needed and ends with the finished research report for managers.

**Exhibit 4.6**

Mercedes-Benz tried to project a more "everyday" image by running ads such as this one featuring Raymond, a man who put off trying ice cream until his big promotion.

**Mercedes-Benz**
www.mercedes-benz.ca

3. Identify the information needs.

Once researchers specify the research questions or objectives, they need to specify what specifically needs to be learned or known, and from whom—indicating the population or group of interest. For example, to answer the research question "what are the profiles of each segment?" we would want to know specific information like:

What are the benefits sought by each identified segment?
What are the demographic characteristics of each segment? (e.g., sex, age, income)
What are the psychographic characteristics of each segment? (e.g., lifestyle, interests, values)
What is the media use behaviours for each segment? (e.g., magazines and newspapers read, radio stations listened to, TV programs watched)

These information needs are not the questions you would see in a questionnaire or interview guide but they inform those questions and give a researcher rationale for including or not including specific questions on a questionnaire. If the question does not address an information need, it is not required on the questionnaire. Information needs also inform methodology or the research technique as different types of information can be gathered from different sources or by using different techniques.

4. Place the problem in an environmental context.

The problem definition should also specify the factors in the firm's internal and external business environment that might be causing or influencing the situation. Placing the problem in the context of the firm's environment helps researchers structure the research, determine the specific types of questions to ask, and identify factors they will need to take into account when interpreting results. Environmental conditions also provide a valuable perspective. For example, when the economy is tight and sales of luxury cars are generally declining, the population to be studied might be narrowed down to a select group of consumers who are still willing and able to indulge in a luxury vehicle. Alternatively, consumers may be moving away from glitzy status-conscious materialism, so that the research question comes down to how promotional strategies can convey honest and basic values that go beyond "snob appeal."

## Determining the Research Design

**research design** A plan that specifies what information marketers will collect and what type of study they will do.

Once marketers have isolated specific problems, the second step of the research process is to decide on a "plan of attack." This plan is the **research design**, which specifies what information marketers will collect and what type of study they will do. All marketing prob-

**Figure 4.4** Marketing Research Design Techniques

For some research problems, the secondary research may provide the information needed. At other times, one of the primary research methods may be needed.

lems do not call for the same techniques, even though marketers can solve some problems effectively with a number of alternate techniques, and diversity in approaches can often provide greater insight and greater confidence in the results. Figure 4.4 summarizes many of the techniques used by market researchers.

**SECONDARY VERSUS PRIMARY RESEARCH** The very first question to ask in determining the research design is whether or not the information required for making a decision already exists—either inside the organization or from external secondary sources. For example, a coffee producer who needs to know the differences in coffee consumption among different demographic and geographic segments of the market may find that the information needed is available from a study conducted by the Canadian Coffee Association for its members or even from Agriculture and Agri-Food Canada. The use of secondary data can save time and money because the expense of designing and implementing a study has already been paid. However, secondary data, having been created for another purpose, may not be current enough or relevant enough for a particular marketing decision. Another key limitation of secondary data is that the methodology used to collect it is often not reported and users do not know whether there were any flaws or limitations in the research design. The advantage of primary data is that it is designed specifically to meet the needs of the organization. However, collecting primary data can be a difficult, expensive, and time-consuming process.

**EXPLORATORY RESEARCH** Marketers use **exploratory research** to generate topics for future, more rigorous studies, ideas for new strategies and opportunities, or just to get a better handle on a problem they are experiencing with a product. Because the studies are usually small in scale and less costly to conduct than other techniques, marketers can use exploratory research to test their hunches about what's going on without too much risk. Exploratory studies often involve in-depth probing of a few consumers who fit the profile of the "typical" customer. Researchers may interview consumers, salespeople, or other employees about products, services, ads, or stores. They may simply "hang out" and watch what people do when choosing among competing brands in a store aisle. Or they may locate places where the consumers of interest hang out and ask questions in these settings. As Exhibit 4.7 shows, some researchers find that many young people are too suspicious or skeptical in traditional research settings, so they may interview young people waiting in lines to buy concert tickets or in clubs.[15] Pantene and Sony, for example, have reached over 500 000 Canadian teens by sponsoring high school video dance parties and then providing incentives for the teens to visit the company Web sites to provide product feedback and answer buying behaviour questions.[16]

**Canadian Coffee Association**
www.coffeeassoc.com
**Agriculture and Agri-Food Canada**
www.agr.gc.ca

exploratory research Technique that marketers use to generate insights for future, more rigorous studies.

**Exhibit 4.7**

Video dance parties help marketers collect data from young people on their own turf.

Most exploratory research provides *qualitative data*, detailed verbal or visual information (for example, videotapes of people preparing dinner at home) about consumers' attitudes, feelings, and buying behaviours that is summarized in words rather than numbers. Researchers for a manufacturer of Swiss chocolate, for example, interviewed consumers and found that many chocolate lovers hide secret stashes around their houses. The company used the results of this exploratory research to develop an advertising campaign built around the theme: "The True Confessions of Chocaholics."[17]

Exploratory research can take many forms. **Consumer interviews** are one-on-one discussions in which an individual shares his or her thoughts in person with a researcher.

**consumer interviews** One-on-one discussions between a consumer and a researcher.

**focus group** A product-oriented discussion among a small group of consumers led by a trained moderator.

In addition to interviewing actual users of their product, some marketers find it useful to interview people who may not themselves be consumers, but who may know a lot about the consumers. One Canadian ad agency working on an ad campaign for scotch interviewed bartenders to gain additional insight into scotch drinkers. Another agency in England, working on an ad for a shoe company, talked to people who shined shoes and to prostitutes who had clients with foot fetishes.[18]

The **focus group** is the technique marketing researchers most often use for collecting exploratory data. Focus groups usually consist of eight to twelve recruited consumers, who sit together to discuss a product, ad, or some other marketing topic introduced by a discussion leader or moderator. Ontario energy and energy service provider Direct Energy, for example, used focus groups in a repositioning process that resulted in the company wanting to be known for its people and ideas rather than just for its products, technology, or dependability. The ad depicted in Exhibit 4.8 used talking appliances to encourage consumers to pay more attention to the needs of their home that would save them money, time, and inconvenience.[19] Typically, the moderator tapes these group discussions, which may be held at special interviewing facilities that allow for observation ("spying") by the client, who watches from behind a one-way mirror. Focus groups don't *always* run smoothly, particularly if one or two opinionated members dominate the session or if "professional" focus group participants get by screening criteria intended to ensure the participants fit the intended participant profile (Exhibit 4.9).

Researchers screen focus group participants in advance to meet criteria that will make their opinions relevant. For example, participants may be recruited, not because they use the company's brand, but because they use a competitor's product. General Motors used focus groups to discover what features of competitors' cars appealed to drivers so that these could be incorporated into its own designs. One result was that GM followed Saab's example by putting fuses in the glove box.[20] As will be discussed in more detail later in this chapter, Web-based research companies like SurveySite are able to conduct focus groups with people around the country or around the world by setting up interactive sessions online.

Many researchers use **projective techniques** to get at people's underlying feelings, especially when they feel that people will be unable or unwilling to express their true reactions. A projective test asks the participant to respond to some ambiguous object, often by telling a story about it. For example, Georgia-Pacific—the manufacturer of Brawny® paper towels—was locked in a struggle with ScotTowels for the number-two market position behind Bounty. The company decided to re-examine its brand identity, personified by a character named the Brawny Man, a giant man holding a peavey, a heavy wooden lever used by lumbermen to handle logs (Exhibit 4.10). Managers believed Brawny was a bit old-fashioned. Women in focus groups were asked questions such as, "What kind of woman would he go out with?" and "What is his home life like?" Then they were asked to imagine how he would act in different situations. Responses were reassuring—the women saw Brawny as a knight in shining armour who would get them out of difficult situations—a good spokesper-

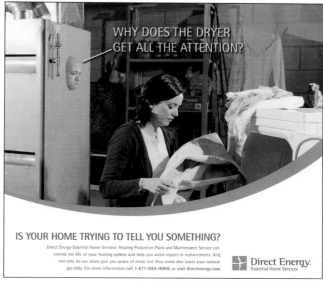

**Exhibit 4.8**

Direct Energy used focus group results to develop these ads aimed at repositioning the company as a source of energy ideas.

son for a product that's supposed to be reliable and able to get the job done. Brawny Man kept his job.[21]

The **case study** is a comprehensive examination of a particular firm or organization. In business-to-business marketing research in which the customers are other firms, for example, researchers may try to learn how one company makes its purchases. Their goal is to identify the key decision makers, to learn what criteria they emphasize when choosing between suppliers, and perhaps to learn something about any conflicts and rivalries among these decision makers that may influence their choices.

An **ethnography** is a detailed report on observations of people in their own homes or communities. Although a true ethnography, as conducted by anthropologists, can involve living with a group for months or years, marketing researchers usually devise shortcuts to get the information they need. True North Communications, for example, has devised an ethnographic research technique called "Mind and Mood," in

**Exhibit 4.9**

Focus groups are typically run with six to ten participants.

which consumer interviews are conducted in a few hours in the respondent's home. As one advertising professional who uses the technique says, "You actually go into people's homes to talk to them. You meet them where they're most comfortable, see what they've got on their walls, what kind of furnishings they have, and you can get a sense of what's important to them."[22]

When the Ontario Ministry of Health was creating an anti-smoking campaign, ethnographic interviews were conducted with teenagers to understand their motivations for smoking as well as what was important to them. The researchers determined that a health message (such as the traditional "If you smoke, you will get cancer") was not going to convince teens to give up smoking. Instead the ads needed to touch on important issues for that age group. The final ads used messages such as "Smoking cigarettes will make you ugly" and showed images like a girl aging as she smoked.[23]

**projective techniques** Tests that marketers use to explore people's underlying feelings about a product, especially appropriate when consumers are unable or unwilling to express their true reactions.

**case study** A comprehensive examination of a particular firm or organization.

**ethnography** A detailed report on observations of people in their own homes or communities.

**Exhibit 4.10**

Projective techniques help consumers express their image of the Brawny Man—the personification of Brawny® paper towels.

**descriptive research** Tool that probes more systematically into the problem and bases its conclusions on large numbers of observations.

**cross-sectional design** Type of descriptive technique that involves the systematic collection of quantitative information at one point in time.

**DESCRIPTIVE RESEARCH** We've seen that marketers have many tools at their disposal, including focus groups and ethnographic techniques, to help them better define a problem or opportunity. These are usually modest studies involving a small number of people. In some situations, this information is all that the marketer needs to make decisions; but very often, the next step after exploratory research is to conduct **descriptive research**, which probes more systematically into the problem and bases its conclusions on larger numbers of observations. These observations typically are quantitative data that take the form of averages, percentages, or other statistics summarizing results from a large set of measurements. Quantitative data can be as simple as the number of large-screen TVs sold in a month in Future Shop locations in different regions of the country, or as complex as statistical analyses of responses to a survey mailed to thousands of consumers. In each case, analyses are conducted to answer a specific question in contrast to the "fishing expedition" that may occur in exploratory research.

The most common descriptive technique is **cross-sectional design**. This involves the systematic collection of quantitative information, such as responses to a survey or data from store register receipts, from one or more samples of respondents at one point in time. The data may be collected on more than one occasion but generally not from the same pool of respondents. Lever Pond's did a cross-sectional survey of dermatologists to determine which soap they recommend to their patients for mildness. Since 87 percent of the respondents recommended the Lever Pond's brand Dove, and only 13 percent recommended the competitive brand, the company turned the results of its survey directly into an advertising campaign. Outdoor billboards that showed the results of the survey were used in major centres across Canada.[24]

## SPOTLIGHT ON REAL PEOPLE    Gateway to Excellence

Marketers have many sophisticated research tools at their disposal, and one of the most effective is a form of observation that's about as low-tech as you can get: Go shopping. Many businesses hire "mystery shoppers" to visit stores, hotels, and restaurants. Posing as regular customers, they report back on how they were treated, how employees described products to them, the cleanliness of the facilities, or even what other shoppers say in casual conversation about the choices available. This "customer viewpoint" information is invaluable to managers who want to improve service levels and sales. Colleen Stech, manager of the

Greater Nanaimo Chamber of Commerce's Gateway to Excellence program, has sent out a team of secret shoppers to Nanaimo businesses to find out how well they look after their customers. The Gateway team has been able to pass on valuable information to businesses from a neutral, outside source, about just how these businesses are doing. The Chamber has rewarded those that have demonstrated excellent customer service. Stech notes that one of the leading causes of poor employee morale is lack of training and offers an optional training program for the Nanaimo businesses that need to work on customer service.[25]

1. This chapter describes several ways to conduct marketing research. How would you classify the research technique used by mystery shoppers?
2. What are the advantages of mystery shoppers over other forms of marketing research?
3. What are the disadvantages or limitations about making decision based on reports of mystery shoppers?

In contrast to the one-shot study, a **longitudinal design** tracks the responses of the same sample of respondents over time. Market researchers often create *consumer panels* to gather this kind of information; a sample of respondents representative of a larger market agrees to provide information about purchases on a weekly or monthly basis. When 3M wanted to find out how it should market its Buf-Puf Sponge facial scrub pads, the company recruited a teen advisory board by running ads in *Seventeen*, *Sassy*, and *'Teen*. 3M periodically consults these consumer panel members about their use of personal care products and their concerns about appearance.[26]

**longitudinal design** Technique that tracks the responses of the same sample of respondents over time.

CAUSAL RESEARCH It's a fact that purchases of both diapers and beer peak between 5:00 p.m. and 7:00 p.m. Can we say that purchasing one of these products caused shoppers to purchase the other as well—and, if so, which caused which? Or is the answer simply that this happens to be the time that young fathers stop at the store on their way home from work for brew and Pampers?[27]

The descriptive techniques we've examined do a good job of providing valuable information about *what* is happening in the marketplace, but they can't tell us *why*. Sometimes marketers need to know if something they've done has brought about some change in behaviour. For example, does the layout and design of a store affect the amount people buy? This question can't be answered through simple observation.

For example, managers at a grocery chain notice from their sales data across a number of stores that purchases of produce are higher in those stores that are designed to resemble farmers' markets with free-flowing layouts and "stalls," where produce is displayed. Can we say that design of these stores caused the increased sales, or is the answer simply that these stores happen to be located in areas where people buy more produce no matter what the store looks like?

**Causal research** refers to techniques that attempt to understand cause-and-effect relationships. In causal research, marketers want to know if a change in something (for example, layout used in a store) is responsible for a change in something else (for example, an increase in produce sales). They call the factors that might cause such a change *independent variables* and the outcomes *dependent variables*. In this example, the layout of the store is an independent variable and sales data for produce are a dependent variable.

**causal research** Techniques that attempt to understand cause-and-effect relationships.

To rule out alternative explanations, researchers must carefully design **experiments** that test specified relationships among variables in a controlled environment. Because this approach tries to eliminate competing explanations for the outcome, respondents may be brought to a *laboratory* where the researcher can be sure that they are reacting to precisely what they should be and nothing else. For example, a study testing whether the layout in a grocery store influences the likelihood that shoppers will buy more produce might bring a group of people into a testing facility, where they are shown a "virtual store" on a computer screen and are asked to fill a grocery cart as they click through the "aisles" (Exhibit 4.11) The experiment might vary the interior of the store as a market style layout or a more typical grid layout to see if this affects whether people put more produce into their carts.

**experiments** Techniques that test prespecified relationships among variables in a controlled environment.

Although a laboratory allows researchers to exert careful control over what test subjects see and do, marketers don't always have the luxury of conducting this kind of "pure" research. It is possible to conduct *field studies* in the real world, as long as care is taken to be sure that the variables are carefully controlled.

For example, the grocery chain could choose two grocery stores for which the demographics

## Good or Bad Decision?

Sometimes telemarketers portray themselves as marketing researchers to get consumers to listen to their sales pitches. They ask consumers to answer a "survey" and then follow up with a sales offer. This practice, called sugging, is a concern of legitimate market researchers, who often find their own information gathering affected by the negative consumer reaction to this practice. The Canadian Marketing Association has taken a strong stance in its Code of Ethics against sugging, but many telemarketers continue using this technique, presumably because it is so effective. Do you think it is appropriate for telemarketers to engage in sugging?[28]

**Exhibit 4.11**

Some marketing research firms such as Decision Insight are developing sophisticated in-store simulations that allow respondents to navigate around a "virtual store" to select merchandise. Clients can use this technique to conduct marketing research on such issues as package designs, pricing changes, and optimal placement of merchandise.

of the people who shop there are known to be the same. Then the company could vary the layouts in the stores, using the market style design in one store and the traditional design in the other, and record produce purchases made over a six-month period. If a lot more produce was bought in the first store than in the second (and the company was sure that nothing else was different between the two stores, such as discounted prices on produce offered by a competitor of one of the stores during the same time), the company might conclude that the presence of a market style layout in the store does indeed result in increased produce sales.

## Choose the Method for Collecting Data

When the researcher decides to conduct descriptive research, the next step in the marketing research process is to figure out just how to collect it. The two main primary data collection methods can be broadly described as interactive and passive.

**INTERACTIVE METHODS** Interactive methods involve some kind of interview or other direct contact with respondents who answer questions. These responses are then combined with those of other respondents to arrive at some general conclusions. The most common interactive instrument is a **survey**, a questionnaire asking participants about their beliefs or behaviours. For example, when Bayer wanted to determine how to improve the health care products it offers, including the Aspirin brand, it mailed out surveys to 10 000 health care professionals across Canada including doctors and pharmacists.[29] Surveys can be administered on the phone, in person, through the mail, by fax, or over the Internet.

Surveys or questionnaires differ in their degree of structure. With a totally unstructured questionnaire, the researcher loosely determines the questions in advance. Questions may evolve from what the respondent says to previous questions. At the other extreme the researcher uses a completely structured questionnaire. She asks every respondent the exact same questions and each participant responds to the same set of fixed choices. You have probably experienced this kind of questionnaire, where you might have had to respond to a statement by saying if you "strongly agree," somewhat agree," and so on. Moderately struc-

**survey** A questionnaire that asks participants about their beliefs or behaviours.

tured questionnaires ask each respondent the same questions but the respondent is allowed to answer the questions in his own words.

Surveys can be administered in a variety of ways, each of which has its pros and cons. These are summarized in Table 4.3.

**Mail Surveys** *Mail surveys,* such as the one done by Bayer, are easy to administer and offer a high degree of anonymity to respondents. On the downside, because the questionnaire is printed and mailed, researchers have little flexibility in the types of questions they can ask and little control over the circumstances under which the respondent is answering them. Mail surveys also take a long time to get back to the company and are likely to have a much lower response rate than other types of surveys because people tend to ignore them.

**Telephone Surveys** *Telephone surveys* usually consist of a brief phone conversation in which an interviewer reads a short list of questions to the respondent. One problem with this approach is that the growth of *telemarketing,* the sale of products and services over the phone, has eroded the willingness of many consumers to participate in phone surveys—especially when those telemarketers have pretended to be conducting marketing research (see Good or Bad Decision? on page 119). Another drawback of telephone surveys is that the respondent may not feel comfortable speaking directly to an interviewer, especially if the survey is about a sensitive subject. Finally, increasing numbers of people use answering machines and caller identification to screen calls, further reducing the response rate.

**Table 4.3** Advantages and Disadvantages of Data Collection Methods

| Date Collection Method | Advantages | Disadvantages |
|---|---|---|
| Mail Questionnaires | Respondents feel anonymous<br>Low cost<br>Good for ongoing research | May take a long time for questionnaires to be returned<br>Low rate of response and many may not return questionnaires<br>Inflexible questionnaire<br>Length of questionnaire limited by respondent interest in the topic<br>Unclear if respondents understand the questions |
| Telephone Interviews | Fast<br>High flexibility in questioning<br>Low cost<br>Limited interviewer bias | Decreasing levels of respondent cooperation<br>Limited questionnaire length<br>High likelihood of respondent misunderstanding<br>Respondents cannot view materials<br>Cannot survey households without phones<br>Consumers screen calls with answering machines and caller ID |
| Face-to-Face Interviews | Flexibility of questioning<br>Can use long questionnaires<br>Can determine if respondents have trouble understanding questions<br>Can use visuals or other materials | High cost<br>Interviewer bias a problem<br>Take a lot of time |
| Online Questionnaires | Instantaneous data collection and analysis<br>Questioning very flexible<br>Low cost<br>No interviewer bias<br>Lack of geographic restrictions | Unclear who is responding<br>No assurance respondents are being honest<br>Limited questionnaire length<br>Unable to determine respondent understanding of question<br>Self-selected samples |

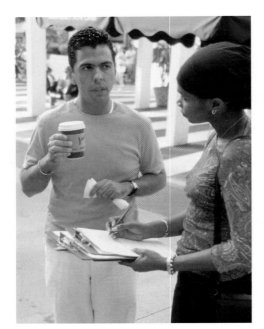

**Exhibit 4.12**

Mall intercepts are a common way to collect data from shoppers.

**Face-to-Face Surveys** *Face-to-face surveys*, in which a live interviewer asks questions of a respondent by, for example, going door-to-door, used to be a common way to collect data. However, this practice has declined markedly in recent years due to escalating costs and security concerns—people just aren't willing to open their doors to strangers anymore. More typically, today's face-to-face interviews occur in a "mall-intercept" study (Exhibit 4.12) in which researchers recruit shoppers in malls or other public areas. Mall-intercepts offer good opportunities to get feedback about marketing issues like new package designs or styles or even reactions to new foods or fragrances. However, because only certain groups of the population frequently shop at malls, a mall-intercept study does not provide the researcher with a representative sample of the population unless the population of interest is mall shoppers. In addition to the mall-intercept being more expensive than mail or phone surveys, respondents may be reluctant to answer questions of a personal nature in a face-to-face context. Rather than relying on face-to-face surveys, Staples Business Depot Canada decided to use automated kiosks in its stores to survey consumers about their satisfaction with the company. Because of the anonymity that the kiosk affords respondents, the company estimates that two out of three people take part in the kiosk surveys, compared with one out of three who are asked to do a face-to-face survey.[30]

**Online Surveys** *Online surveys*, such as those administered by SurveySite, are growing in popularity, as more consumers and businesses are getting hooked up to the Internet. The Carrier Corporation, which makes air conditioners, found respondents more willing to answer questions about its products via computer, perhaps because it's more interesting to take a survey this way.[31] Online surveys are a quick and cost-effective way to collect data. Unlike mail and phone surveys, online surveys can generate a large number of responses very quickly. However, it must be remembered that, like the people who visit malls, people who use the Internet are not representative of the total population. Online surveys are, therefore, useful only for those companies whose population of interest is people who are online. An additional concern about online surveys relates to the quality of responses the firm will receive—particularly because no one can be really sure who is typing in the responses.[32]

All these interactive techniques require a response from the consumer, whether in the form of a verbal response to an interview question, a checkmark placed on a piece of paper, or a mouse click on a computer screen.

**PASSIVE METHODS** Other forms of data collection use a *passive instrument* in which the consumer's behaviours are simply recorded—often without his or her knowledge. Researchers do this through personal observation, unobtrusive measures, and mechanical observation.

**Rocky Mountaineer Railtours**
www.rockymountaineer.com

**Personal Observation** With *personal observation*, consumers in public settings are watched to understand how they react to marketing activities (Exhibit 4.13). After Frito-Lay found that shoppers spend twice as much time in the coffee aisle as in the snack foods section, it began to advertise its chips near the coffee cans.[33] Researchers for Rocky Mountaineer rail tours observed their customers' behaviour as they were travelling through the Canadian Rockies by train. They noticed that these travellers seemed to like the experience of the train trip itself as much as the beautiful scenery they were seeing. This led the company to change the theme of their advertising from just talking about the mountain scenery to talking about the train service experience. One of the ads claimed: "No one ever wrote a folk song about a minivan," and the overall slogan for the new ads was "The only way to see the Canadian Rockies." The company saw a 23 percent increase in its bookings as a result of the ads.[34]

Some companies have successfully used observation in combination with other methods, such as consumer interviews, in an effort to improve the quality of information gathered.

To examine how consumers make milk brand decisions, researchers in Atlantic Canada observed over 200 consumers in 12 stores and followed up with brief interviews. In the interviews, consumers claimed that they bought a certain brand, even though the researcher knew from observation that they had bought a different one. Similarly, in interviews most consumers claimed that they checked the expiry date on the milk cartons, whereas observation showed that hardly anyone did so. All of this information allowed the researchers to conclude that milk is a low-involvement purchasing decision with weak loyalty levels. The consumers were not deliberately lying in the interviews; they simply did not pay that much attention to their milk buying behaviour.[35] As this example shows, sometimes it is wise to use multiple research methods when performing marketing research.

**Unobtrusive Measures** Researchers also use *unobtrusive measures* to check traces of physical evidence that remain after some action has been taken, when they suspect that people will probably alter their behaviour if they know they are being observed. For example, instead of asking a person to report on the alcohol products currently in his or her home, the researcher might go to the house and perform a "pantry check," recording the bottles found there. The Vancouver Police Department (VPD) developed a campaign called "Bait Cars" (Exhibit 4.14) that included radio ads targeted towards a younger listening audience. These ads aired throughout the day to serve as deterrents to thieves who were thinking about stealing cars. The VPD started running more ads on the radio station the BEAT when anecdotal testaments from police and evidence from the stolen Bait Cars indicated that many thieves regularly tuned into the BEAT. Another measure taken by the VPD included placing transit shelter ads in areas where significant numbers of stolen cars were abandoned, the rationale being that thieves steal cars from all over town, but abandon them closer to where they live.[36]

**Exhibit 4.13**

Producers of children's toys use observation to test new toy designs.

Some companies and their research firms sift through garbage, searching for clues about family consumption habits (Exhibit 4.15). The "garbologists" can tell, for example, which soft drink accompanied what kind of food. As one garbologist noted, "The people in this study don't know that we are studying their garbage so the information is totally objective."[37] Garbology is also conducted in business dumpsters to find competitive information—although many marketers question the ethics of doing so.

**Mechanical Observation** *Mechanical observation* relies on non-human devices to record behaviour. For example, some grocery stores use infrared sensors in their ceilings to track the movements of shopping carts.[38] Another application of mechanical observation is people meters, operated by such companies as Nielsen Media Research and BBM Bureau of Measurement. These boxes are attached to the television sets of selected viewers to record patterns of television watching. These "television ratings" are how the networks determine how much to charge advertisers for commercials and which shows to cancel or renew. Nielsen also uses observation on the Internet to determine which Web sites are most popular on a daily and weekly basis. The Nielsen Web usage data can be viewed at the Nielsen NetRatings site.

**Nielsen NetRatings**
www.nielsen-netratings.com

**Exhibit 4.14**

The Vancouver Police Department used unobtrusive measures to find out what radio stations car thieves listen to in the Bait Car campaign.

**Exhibit 4.15**

"Garbologists" search for clues about consumption activities, an unobtrusive measure.

**validity** The extent to which research actually measures what it was intended to measure.

**reliability** The extent to which research measurement techniques are free of errors.

# Data Quality: Garbage In, Garbage Out

A firm can gather data in many ways, including focus groups, ethnographies, observational studies, and controlled experiments. But how much faith should it place in what it finds?

A research project is only as good as the information it collects. All too often, marketers who have commissioned a study assume that because they have a massive report full of impressive-looking numbers and tables, they must have the "truth." Unfortunately, there are times when this "truth" is really just one person's interpretation of the facts. At other times, the data used to generate recommendations are flawed. As the expression goes, "Garbage in, garbage out."[39] Typically, three factors influence the quality of research results—validity, reliability, and representativeness.

**VALIDITY Validity** is the extent to which the research actually measures what it was intended to measure. This was part of the problem underlying the famous New Coke fiasco in the 1980s, in which Coca-Cola underestimated people's loyalty to its flagship soft drink after it replaced "Old Coke" with a new, sweeter formula. The company assumed that blind taste testers' preferences for one anonymous cola over another were a valid measure of consumers' preferences for a cola brand. Coke found out the hard way that only measuring taste is not the same as measuring people's deep allegiances to their favourite soft drink, and sales eventually recovered after the company brought back the old version as "Coca-Cola Classic."[40]

**RELIABILITY Reliability** is the extent to which the research measurement techniques are free of errors. Sometimes, for example, the way a researcher asks a question creates an error by biasing people's responses. Imagine that an interviewer working for Trojans condoms stopped male college students on campus and asked them if they used contraceptive products. Do you think their answers might change if they were asked the same questions on an anonymous survey they received in the mail? Most likely they would be different, because people are reluctant to disclose what they actually do when their responses are not anonymous. Researchers try to maximize reliability by thinking of several different ways to ask the same questions, by asking these questions on several occasions, or by using several analysts to interpret the responses.

Reliability is a problem when the researchers can't be sure the consumer population they're studying even understands what is being asked. For example, children are difficult subjects for market researchers, because they tend to be undependable reporters of their own behaviour, have poor recall, and often do not understand abstract questions.[41] In many cases, the children cannot explain why they prefer one item over another (or they're not willing to share these secrets with grown-ups).[42] For these reasons, researchers have had to be especially creative in designing studies involving younger consumers. In the example shown in Figure 4.5 (called a *completion test*), boys are told to write in the empty balloon what they think the boy in the drawing will answer when the girl asks, "What program do you want to watch next?" Reliability is increased because the children can respond to pictures depicting a familiar situation in their own words.

REPRESENTATIVENESS **Representativeness** is the extent to which consumers in the study are similar to a larger group in which the organization has an interest. This criterion for evaluating research underscores the importance of **sampling**, the process of selecting respondents for a study. The issue then becomes how large or small the sample should be and how these people are chosen. We'll talk more about sampling in the next section.

## Design the Sample

Once the researcher has defined the problem, decided on a research design, and determined how to collect the data, the next step is to decide from whom to obtain the needed data. Of course, the researcher *could* collect the information from every single customer or prospective customer, but this would be extremely expensive and time consuming, if possible at all. Instead, researchers collect most of their data from a small proportion or *sample* of the population of interest. Based on the answers of this sample, researchers hope to generalize to the larger population. Whether such inferences are accurate or inaccurate depends on the type and quality of the study sample. There are two main types of samples: probability and non-probability samples.

**Figure 4.5** A Completion Test Designed for Children

It can be especially difficult to get accurate information from children. Researchers often use visuals such as this completion test to encourage children to express their feelings.

Source: James McNeal, "Child's play," *Marketing Tools*, January-February 1998:20.

PROBABILITY SAMPLING With a **probability sample**, each member of the population has some known chance of being included in the sample. Using a probability sample ensures researchers that the sample is representative of the population and that inferences about the population made from the sample are justified. For example, if a larger percentage of males than females in a probability sample say they prefer action movies to "chick flicks," one can infer with confidence that a larger percentage of males than females in the general population also would rather see a character get sliced and diced.

The most basic type of probability sample is a *simple random sample* in which every member of a population has a known and equal chance of being included in the study. For example, if we simply take the names of all 40 students in your class and put them in a hat and draw one out, each member of your class has a 1 in 40 chance of being included in the sample. In most studies the population from which the sample will be drawn is too large for a hat so marketers generate a random sample from a list of members of the population using a computer program.

Sometimes researchers use a *systematic sampling procedure* to select members of a population in which they select the *n*th member of a population after a random start. For example, if we want a sample of 10 members of your class, we might begin with the second person on the role and select every fourth name after that, that is, the second, the sixth, the tenth, the fourteenth, and so on. Researchers know that studies that use systematic samples are just as accurate as with simple random samples. Unless a list of members of the population of interest is already in a computer data file, it's a lot simpler to create a systematic sample.

Another type of probability sample is a *stratified sample* in which a researcher divides the population into segments that are related to the study's topic. For example, imagine that you are interested in studying what movies are most liked by members of a population. You know from previous studies that men and women in the population differ in their attitudes toward different types of movies—men like action flicks and women like romances. To create a stratified sample, you would first divide the population into male and female segments. Then respondents from each of the two segments would be selected randomly in proportion to their percentage of the population. In this way, you have created a sample that is proportionate to the population on a characteristic that you know will make a difference in the study results.

**representativeness** The extent to which consumers in a study are similar to a larger group in which the organization has an interest.

**sampling** The process of selecting respondents who statistically represent a larger population of interest.

**probability sample** A sample in which each member of the population has some known chance of being included in the sample.

Cluster sampling also divides a population into groups, but in this approach the groups are representative microcosms a population, in that each reflects the characteristics of the population as a whole. In cluster sampling the population is divided into mutually exclusive and collectively exhaustive subpopulations and then a subset of the groups are chosen using a probability sampling technique like a simple random sample. Respondents are then chosen within the groups using another probability sampling technique. Cluster sampling is quiet cost effective because you only have to create a sampling frame (list of potential respondents) for the cluster groups chosen. Political pollsters use cluster sampling in order to make national assessments of party popularity based on the responses of a few hundred voters.

**NONPROBABILITY SAMPLING** Sometimes researchers do not feel the time and effort required to develop a probability sample are justified, perhaps because they need an answer quickly or they just want to get a general sense of how people feel about a topic. They may choose a **nonprobability sample**, which entails the use of personal judgment in selecting respondents—in some cases just asking whomever they can find! With a nonprobability sample, some members of the population have no chance at all of being included in the sample. Thus, there is no way to ensure that the sample is representative of the population. Results from nonprobability studies can be generally suggestive of what is going on in the real world but not necessarily definitive.

> **nonprobability sample** A sample in which personal judgment is used in selecting respondents.

A *convenience sample* is a nonprobability sample composed of individuals who just happen to be available when and where the data are being collected. For example, if you simply stand in front of the student union and ask students who walk by to complete your questionnaire, that would be a convenience sample. In our SurveySite case, Marshall Rice conducted interviews with a convenience sample of some of his best customers when he did his exploratory research.

In some cases firms even use their own employees as a convenience sample or as "guinea pigs." When Gap Inc. was developing the concept for its chain of Old Navy stores, the company gave employees who fit the desired Old Navy customer profile $200 apiece and set them loose on a shopping spree (Exhibit 4.16). The employees were then interviewed about what they had bought so these products would be on Old Navy's shelves when the stores opened (nice work if you can get it!). [43]

A *quota sample* is the division of the total population into categories by age, income, marital status, or other demographic. The researcher draws a portion (quota) of names from those categories relevant to the study, ignoring those who belong to other categories, until a predetermined quota of potential respondents is met. A quota sample is much like the stratified sample except that with a quota sample, individual members of the sample are selected through personal judgment as they are in a convenience sample.

## Collecting The Data

At this point the researcher has determined the nature of the problem that needs to be addressed. He or she has decided on a research design that will specify how to investigate the problem and what kinds of information (data) will be needed to do so. Once these decisions have been made, the next task is to actually collect the data.

Although collecting data may seem like a simple process, researchers are well aware of its critical importance to the accuracy of research. When interviewers are involved, researchers know that

**Exhibit 4.16**

Gap Inc. used a convenience sample of its own employees to help develop Old Navy's merchandizing strategy.

the quality of research results is only as good as the poorest interviewer collecting the data. Careless interviewers may not read questions exactly as written or they may not record respondent answers correctly. So marketers must train and supervise interviewers to make sure they follow the research procedures exactly as outlined. In this section we'll talk about some of the problems in gathering data and some solutions.

Many people are concerned about potential violations of privacy, as firms continue to gather detailed data about their personal lives. The Blockbuster Entertainment Corp., for example, encountered a firestorm of criticism when it was accused of trying to sell information detailing customers' video rental habits.[44] Critics charged that people's movie preferences (whether for action movies, pornography, or cartoons) were their own business. Data gatherers need to ensure that the information collected will be used only for the stated purpose and that respondents are aware of their right to refuse to provide information.

On January 1, 2004 the Canadian government enacted a new privacy law (the Personal Information Protection and Electronic Documents Act or PIPEDA) intended to balance consumer rights against business needs. The key underlying principles of the act are outlined in Table 4.4.[45] Complicating matters, however, is that the provinces of Alberta and British Columbia have their own consumer privacy laws which have not been deemed "substantially similar" to the PIPEDA—making it unclear to which law organizations in those provinces should adhere.

**GATHERING DATA INTERNATIONALLY** Conducting market research in other countries is important for Canadian firms operating in international markets. However, market conditions and consumer preferences vary widely in different parts of the world, and there are big differences in the sophistication of market research operations and the amount of data available to global marketers.

**Table 4.4** Canada's New Privacy Law

**Accountability:** All organizations must have a privacy officer or representative who will ensure that the organization is compliant with the new law.

**Expressed Purpose:** Information may only be used for the expressed purpose for which consumers have given their consent. New consent must be acquired if you want to use the information for another purpose.

**Consent:** Information can only be used after gaining informed consent from consumers. For sensitive information (e.g., financial information) consumers must actively express consent (opt-in) while for non-sensitive information (e.g., phone numbers or addresses) consumers must be able to easily opt-out of providing consent for its use.

**Third Party Use:** You can only make customer information available to others if you have consent of the customer and you keep a record of having received that consent.

**Accuracy:** Organizations are required to keep personal information on consumers as accurate, complete, and up-to-date as possible.

**Need:** Information collected can only be retained if it is being used for the purpose collected. Information collected from people who are no longer customers must be destroyed.

**Safeguards:** Reasonable safeguards must be in place to ensure against unauthorized access or alteration of records.

**Openness:** Organizations must be prepared to publicize their information handling practices through all points of contact with customers. Organizations should have privacy policies and their staff must be trained in these policies.

**Individual Access:** Consumers have the right to know what information has been collected about them, their records must be made available upon request, and they may request erroneous information be corrected.

**Compliance:** Organizations must have a formal inquiry and complaint-handling mechanism to investigate if a consumer challenges an organization's compliance with the new law. Consumers may also challenge compliance with Federal privacy commission.

For these reasons, choosing an appropriate data collection method is difficult. In some countries, many people do not have phones, or low literacy rates may interfere with mail surveys. Local customs can be a problem as well. Offering money for interviews, a common practice in Canada, is considered rude in Latin American countries.[46] Focus groups are virtually impossible in Saudi Arabia, where gatherings of four or more people except for family or religious events are banned. Interviews are also difficult there since it is illegal to stop strangers on the street or knock on the door of someone's house.[47] Cultural differences also affect responses to survey items. Both Danish and British consumers, for example, agree that it is important to eat breakfast, but the Danish sample may be thinking of fruit and yoghurt, whereas the British sample is thinking of toast and tea. Sometimes these problems can be overcome by involving local researchers in decisions about the research design, but, even so, care must be taken to ensure that they fully understand the study's objectives and can relate what they find to the culture of the sponsoring company.

Language differences can also pose challenges for international marketing research. When SurveySite conducted an online survey for Microsoft across 13 countries, for example, the study had to be translated into seven different languages.[48] To ensure that surveys using many languages are translated properly, researchers often use a process called *back-translation*, which requires two steps. First, a questionnaire is translated into the second language by a native speaker of that language. Second, this new version is translated back into the original language to ensure that the correct meanings survive the process. Even with precautions such as these, however, researchers must interpret data obtained from other cultures with care.

**SINGLE SOURCE DATA** One research issue that marketers have been trying to solve for years is knowing what impact each piece of their marketing mix is having on their total marketing strategy. Short of moving in with a family for a few months, marketers had no way to determine the effect of multiple promotional activities. Today, though, sophisticated technology allows researchers to gather data from actual store transactions that they can then trace to different components of the marketing mix.

The term **single-source data** refers to information that is integrated from multiple sources. In single-source systems, data on purchasing behaviour and advertising exposure are measured for members of a consumer panel using electronic television meters, retail scanners, and split-cable technology in which different customers on a television cable system can be exposed to different ads. Because single-source systems can measure the impact of a number of different marketing activities in combination, they allow marketers to monitor the impact of many marketing communications on a particular customer group over time. For example, a firm that sells laundry detergent might use single-source systems to answer the following questions:

**single-source data** Information that is integrated from multiple sources, to monitor the impact of marketing communications on a particular customer group over time.

- Which consumer segments are more likely to be brand loyal and what segments frequently switch brands of laundry detergent?
- Are coupons or price-off packs more likely to increase sales?
- Does increased advertising exposure influence brand switching?
- What is the total effect of increased advertising and the use of coupons?

A great deal of single-source data come from checkout scanners in stores. In addition to speeding up your checkout time, scanners store a record of just how many bags of munchies you bought and what brands you chose. Combined with records from the store's other customers (and buyers at other locations), this is a potential pot of gold for firms willing to invest in the research needed to track all those millions of transactions.

For retailers who can specifically identify individual consumers, perhaps because they have a loyalty card that links their purchases with demographic information, the data from scanners are especially useful. For example, Shoppers Drug Mart tracks the purchases of regular customers who show an Optimum card when they get to the register (Exhibit 4.17). Using this information, Shoppers Drug Mart can more effectively make merchandizing decisions and tailor special offers, including coupons, to these customers. So heavy consumers of diapers, for example, might be sent cents-off coupons for baby food or children's Tylenol.

Purchases made online are also continuously recorded, and the identity (username) of the consumer (as well as their virtual address) is always recorded along with their purchases. Thus, companies such as Chapters.indigo.ca can track the purchase habits of each consumer and use that information to tailor communication messages to individuals. If a consumer has ordered several gardening books, for example, they could be sent an e-mail when a new gardening book comes out and offered a special deal if they purchase the book. We'll be studying this style of database marketing in more detail in Chapter 15.

**Exhibit 4.17**

Shoppers Drug Mart's Optimum card allows the company to match demographic and financial data of consumers with their shopping behaviour.

## Analyze and Interpret the Data

Once marketing researchers have collected the data, what's next? It's like a spin on the old "if a tree falls in the woods" question: "If results exist but there's no one to interpret them, do they have a meaning?" Well, let's leave the philosophers out of it and just say that marketers would answer "no." Data need analysis for them to have meaning.

To understand the important role of data analysis, let's take a look at a hypothetical research example. In our example, a company that markets frozen foods wishes to better understand consumers' preference for varying levels of fat content in their diets. They have conducted a descriptive research study in which they collected primary data via telephone interviews. Because they recognize that gender is related to dietary preferences, they have used a stratified sample that includes 175 males and 175 females.

Typically, marketers first tabulate the data as shown in Table 4.5—that is, they arrange the data in a table or other summary form so they can get a broad picture of the overall responses. The data in this table show that 43 percent of the sample prefers a low-fat meal. In addition there may be a desire to cross-classify or cross-tabulate the answers to questions by other variables. *Cross-tabulation* means that the data are examined by subgroups, in this case males and females separately, to see how results vary between categories. The cross-tabulation in Table 4.5 shows that 59 percent of females versus only 27 percent of males prefer a meal with low fat content. In addition, researchers may wish to apply additional statistical tests, such as those described in Appendix A of this chapter—which you'll learn more about in subsequent courses.

Based on the analysis, the researcher must then interpret or draw conclusions from the results and make recommendations. For example, the study results shown in Table 4.5 may lead to the conclusion that females are more likely than males to be concerned about a low-fat diet. The researcher might then make a recommendation to a firm that it should target females in the introduction of a new line of low-fat foods.

## Prepare the Research Report

The final step in the marketing research process is to prepare a report of the research results. In general, a research report must clearly and concisely tell the readers—top management, clients, creative departments, and many others—what they need to know in a way that they can easily understand. In general, a research report will include these sections:

- An executive summary of the report that covers the high points of the total report
- An understandable description of the research methodology
- A complete discussion of the results of the study, including the tabulations, cross-tabulations, and additional statistical analyses

**Table 4.5** Examples of Data Tabulation and Cross-Tabulation Tables

**Fat Content Preference**
**(Number and percentages of responses)**

| Questionnaire Response | Number of Responses | Percentage of Responses |
|---|---|---|
| Do you prefer a meal with high fat content, medium fat content, or low fat content? | | |
| High fat | 21 | 6 |
| Medium fat | 179 | 51 |
| Low fat | 150 | 43 |
| Total | 350 | 100 |

**Fat Content Preference by Gender**
**(Number and percentages of responses)**

| Questionnaire Response | Number Females | Percentage of Females | Number Males | Percentage of Males | Total Number | Total Percentage |
|---|---|---|---|---|---|---|
| Do you prefer a meal with high fat content, medium fat content, or low fat content? | | | | | | |
| High fat | 4 | 2 | 17 | 10 | 21 | 6 |
| Medium fat | 68 | 39 | 111 | 64 | 179 | 51 |
| Low fat | 103 | 59 | 47 | 27 | 150 | 43 |
| Total | 175 | 100 | 175 | 100 | 350 | 100 |

- Limitations of the study (no study is perfect)
- Conclusions drawn from the results and the recommendations for managerial action based on the results.

## ONLINE RESEARCH

The growth of the Internet is rewriting some of the rules of the marketing research process. As more and more people have access to the Web, many companies are using services like those provided by SurveySite—it's fast, it's relatively cheap, and it lends itself well to forms of research from simple questionnaires to online focus groups.

The Web is revolutionizing the way many companies collect data and use them to guide their strategic decisions. There are two major types of online research. One type is information gathered by tracking consumers while they are surfing. The second type is information gathered through questionnaires on Web sites, through e-mail, or from moderated focus groups conducted in chat rooms—such as the one illustrated in Exhibit 4.18.

## Online Tracking

The Internet offers an unprecedented ability to track consumers as they search for information—we'll talk more about this process in the next chapter. Marketers can better understand where people go to look when they want to learn about products and services—and which advertisements they stop to browse along the way. How can marketers do this? One way is by the use of "cookies." **Cookies** are text files inserted by a Web site sponsor into a user's hard drive when the user connects with the site. Cookies remember details of a visit to a Web site, typically tracking which pages the user visits. Some sites request or require that visitors "register" on the site by answering questions about themselves and their likes and dislikes. In such cases, cookies also allow the site to access these details about the customer.

**cookies** Text files inserted by a Web site sponsor into a Web surfer's hard drive that allow the site to track the surfer's moves.

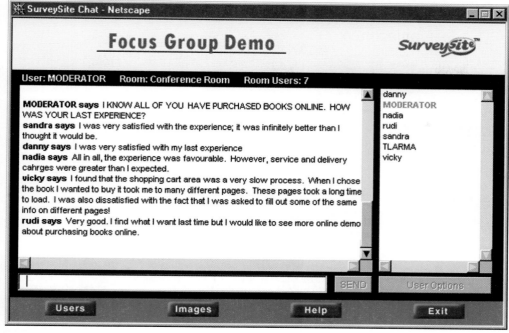

**Exhibit 4.18**

SurveySite online focus groups help clients understand consumers' buying behaviour on the Internet.

This technology allows Web sites to customize services, such as when Indigo Books and Music or Advanced Amazon.Com recommends new books to users based on what books they have ordered in the past (Exhibit 4.19). Most consumers have no idea that cookies allow Web sites to gather and store all this information. You can block cookies or curb them, although this can make life difficult if you are trying to log on to many sites such as online newspapers or travel agencies that require this information to admit you.

Who owns your cookies? This information generated from tracking consumers' online journeys has become a product as well—companies sell this consumer data to other companies that are trying to target prospects. But consumers have become increasingly concerned about the sharing of these data. In a study of 10 000 Web users, 84 percent objected to the reselling of their information to other companies. Although Internet users can delete cookie files manually or install anticookie software on their computers, there are many people who feel there is a need for privacy regulation and for cookie regulation in order to limit potential abuses.

**amazon.com**
www.amazon.com
**Indigo Books and Music**
www.chapters.indigo.ca

## Online Testing, Questionnaires, and Focus Groups

The Internet offers a faster, less expensive alternative to traditional communication data collection methods. There are several ways that companies are using the Internet to get feedback from consumers including new-product development, estimating market response, and exploratory research.

**NEW-PRODUCT DEVELOPMENT** Procter & Gamble spent more than five years testing products such as Febreze, Dryel, and Fit Fruit & Vegetable Wash the old-fashioned way before launching nationally. Using online tests, the Crest MultiCare Flex & Clean toothbrush was launched in less than a year. General Motors and Nissan are two automakers that now gather online consumer reactions to upcoming products. Such research allows manufacturers to learn what consumers want in future vehicles.[49] Experts predicted that as much as 25 percent of all consumer market research would be online by 2002[50] (Exhibit 4.20).

**Procter & Gamble**
www.pg.com

**Exhibit 4.19**

Amazon.com uses sophisticated software called "collaborative filtering" to keep track of shoppers' book choices and recommend new books based on past patterns.

**ESTIMATING MARKET RESPONSE** Both Mercury Records and Virgin Records have used online research to test music for performers including Bon Jovi and the Spice Girls.[51] In a typical test, respondents listen to the songs and then click on buttons to indicate how much they like or dislike the music.

**EXPLORATORY RESEARCH** Conducting focus groups online has mushroomed in popularity in recent years. For example, Procter & Gamble's Web site includes a Try & Buy New Products section that sells P&G products still being test-marketed and directs consumers to

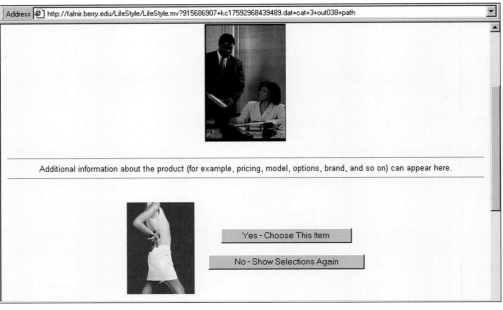

**Exhibit 4.20**

Some online research firms collect consumers' responses to a variety of proposed new product styles before the items are actually produced. This study by Mind/Share, Inc. tested clothing styles for a major manufacturer.

virtual, real-time focus groups.[52] Of course, with online groups it is impossible to observe body language, facial expressions, and vocal inflection. But marketers continue to develop new ways to talk to consumers in virtual space, including software that allows online focus group participants to indicate nonverbal responses. For example, an online participant can register an expression of disgust by clicking on the command to "roll eyes."[53]

Many marketing research companies are running, not walking, to the Web to conduct studies for clients. Why? For one thing, replacing traditional mail consumer panels with Internet panels allows marketers to collect the same amount of data in a weekend that used to take six to eight weeks. And consumers can complete surveys when it is convenient— even at 3 a.m. There are other advantages: Even large studies can be conducted at low costs. International borders are not a problem either as Internet use is very high in many countries and it's easy to recruit respondents. Web-based interviews eliminate interviewer bias or errors in data entry.[54]

However, no data collection method is perfect and online research is no exception— though many of the criticisms of online techniques also apply to off-line techniques. One potential problem is the representativeness of the respondents. Although the number of Internet users continues to grow, many segments of the consumer population, mainly the poor and elderly, do not have equal access to the Internet. Also, in many studies (just as with mail surveys or mall intercepts) there is a *self-selection bias* in the sample: Respondents have agreed to receive invitations to take part in online studies, which means they tend to be the kind of people who like to participate in surveys. As with other kinds of research such as live focus groups, it's not unusual to encounter "professional respondents"—people who just enjoy taking part in studies (and getting paid for it). Online firms such as Harris Interactive address this problem by monitoring their participants and regulating how often they are allowed to participate in different studies over a period of time.

There are other disadvantages of online research. Hackers can actually try to influence research results. Even more dangerous may be competitors who can learn about a firm's marketing plans, products, advertising, and so forth by intercepting information used in research. One company, E-Poll, uses a methodology to prevent some of these problems.[55] To preview TV pilots, commercials, and ad campaigns, E-Poll sends respondents a CD-ROM.

# Real People, Real Decisions

▶ ## How It Worked Out at SurveySite

Marshall Rice decided to pursue Option 1 and introduce an online focus group product right away. Based on his exploratory research and his own experience, he felt that the focus group technique could be successfully adapted to the Internet environment and would provide clients with a value-added product. He also felt that timing was important. SurveySite operates in the online environment, where decisions need to be made quickly. SurveySite couldn't afford to take a wait-and-see attitude, because that would allow competitors to develop the product first.

Instead of developing just one type of focus group, Rice and the team at SurveySite developed two different versions. The Online Focus Group was developed as a direct alternative to live, face-to-face groups. These groups of eight to ten people get together in a chat room for about 90 minutes of moderated discussion. The second product is unique to the Internet environment: FocusSite is a two-day focus group, which is held with 25 or more participants. Respondents participate in the discussion on their own schedule several times during the two days, which allows companies to gather extensive amounts of information about their customers, while providing the respondents with flexibility.

Both products have been very successful for SurveySite. Companies have used the online focus groups to better understand customer motivations and to gauge customer reaction to specific marketing tactics, such as Web sites and Internet banner ads. You can view a demonstration of the online focus group by visiting the SurveySite Web site at **www.surveysite.com**.

The CD guides respondents to a secure area on the E-Poll site, which requires them to enter a password before they can watch the research content and answer the questionnaire.[56]

Despite the potential drawbacks, online research has a bright future. Indeed, it has the potential to take off even faster as a result of the 2001 terrorist attacks, since many people are more hesitant to answer questions from strangers, drive to focus group facilities, or open mail surveys from sources they don't recognize. Firms such as SurveySite are on the cutting edge of an exciting new industry.

# CHAPTER SUMMARY

**1. Understand the role of the marketing information system and the marketing decision support system in marketing decision making.**

A marketing information system (MIS) is composed of internal data, marketing intelligence, marketing research data, acquired databases, and computer hardware and software. Firms use an MIS to gather, sort, analyze, store, and distribute information needed by managers for marketing decision making. The marketing decision support system (MDSS) allows managers to use analysis software and interactive software to access MIS data and to conduct analyses and find the information they need.

**2. Describe the marketing research process.**

The research process begins by defining the problem and determining the research design or type of study. Next, researchers choose the data collection method, that is, whether there is secondary data available or if primary research with a communication study or through observation is necessary. Then researchers determine what type of sample is to be used for the study and then collect the data. The final steps in the research are to analyze and interpret the data and prepare a research report.

**3. Understand the differences among exploratory, descriptive, and causal research, and describe some research techniques available to marketers.**

Exploratory research typically uses qualitative data collected by individual interviews, focus groups, or observational methods such as ethnography. Descriptive research includes cross-sectional and longitudinal studies. Causal research goes a step further by designing controlled experiments in order to understand cause-and-effect relationships between marketing independent variables, such as price changes, and dependent variables, such as sales.

**4. Describe the different types of data collection methods and types of samples that researchers use.**

Researchers may choose to collect data using mail questionnaires, telephone interviews, face-to-face interviews, or online questionnaires. A study may utilize a probability sample such as a simple random or stratified sample in which inferences can be made to a population based on the sample results. Nonprobability sampling methods include a convenience sample and a quota sample. The research tries to ensure that the data are valid, reliable, and representative. Validity is the extent to which the research actually measures what it was intended to measure. Reliability is the extent to which the research measurement techniques are free of errors. Representativeness is the extent to which consumers in the study are similar to a larger group in which the organization has an interest.

**5. Understand the growing use of online research.**

Marketers increasingly are using the Internet for online research. Online tracking uses cookies to record where consumers go on a Web site. Consumers have become increasingly concerned about privacy and how this information is used and made available to other Internet companies. The Internet also provides an attractive alternative to traditional communication data collection methods because of its speed and low cost. Many firms use the Internet to conduct online focus groups.

# CHAPTER REVIEW

## Marketing Concepts: Testing Your Knowledge

1. What is a marketing information system (MIS)? What types of information are included in a marketing information system? How does a marketing decision support system (MDSS) allow marketers to easily get the information they need?

2. What are the steps in the marketing research process? Why is defining the problem to be researched so important?

3. What is the goal of exploratory research? What techniques are used to gather data in exploratory research?

4. What is descriptive research? What techniques are used in descriptive research?

5. What is causal research?

6. What are some advantages and disadvantages of telephone interviews, mail questionnaires, face-to-face interviews, and online interviews? What unique data collection problems exist in foreign markets?

7. How do probability and nonprobability samples differ? What are some types of probability samples? What are some types of nonprobability samples?

8. What are single-source data? What are some ways that marketers use single-source data?

9. What is meant by reliability, validity, and representativeness of research results?

10. What are online tracking studies? What are some strengths and weaknesses of Internet focus groups?

## Marketing Concepts: Discussing Choices and Issues

1. Do you think marketers should be allowed to conduct market research with young children? Why or why not?

2. Some marketers attempt to disguise themselves as marketing researchers when their real intent is to sell something to the consumer. What is the impact of this practice on legitimate researchers? What do you think might be done about this practice?

3. Are you willing to divulge personal information to marketing researchers? How much are you willing to tell, or where would you draw the line?

4. What is your overall attitude toward marketing research? Do you think it is a beneficial activity from a consumer's perspective? Or do you think it merely gives marketers new insights on how to convince consumers to buy something they really don't want or need?

5. Sometimes firms use data mining to identify and abandon customers who are not profitable because they don't spend enough to justify the service needed or because they return a large proportion of the items they buy. What do you think of such practices? Is it ethical for firms to prune out these customers?

6. Many consumers are concerned about online tracking studies and their privacy. Do consumers have the right to "own" data about themselves? Should governments limit the use of the Internet for data collection?

7. One unobtrusive measure mentioned in the chapter involved going through consumers' or competitors' garbage. Do you think marketers should have the right to do this? Is it ethical?

## Marketing Practice: Applying What You've Learned

1. Your firm is planning to begin marketing a consumer product in several global markets. You have been given the responsibility of developing plans for marketing research to be conducted in Eastern Europe, Western Europe, and China. In a role-playing situation, present the difficulties you expect to encounter, if any, in conducting research in each of these areas.

2. As an account executive with a marketing research firm, you are responsible for deciding on the type of research to be used in various studies conducted for your clients. For each of the following client questions, list your choices.

    a. What do consumers like and dislike about shampoo?

    b. What are the best media vehicles for a local insurance broker to use for its advertising?

    c. How much label information on cereal boxes do consumers read before they make a purchase?

    d. Are consumers more likely to buy brands that are labelled as environmentally friendly?

    e. How do women determine if a particular perfume is right for them?

    f. What types of people read the local newspaper?

    g. How frequently do consumers switch brands of soft drinks?

    h. How will an increase in the price of a brand of laundry detergent affect sales?

    i. How do the different members of a family participate in the purchase of a new car?

3. Your marketing research firm is planning to conduct surveys to gather information for a number of clients. Your boss has asked you and a few other new employees to do some preliminary work. He has asked each of you to choose three of the topics that will be included in the project and to prepare an analysis of the advantages and disadvantages of mail surveys, telephone surveys, face-to-face surveys, or observation for each.

    a. the amount of alcoholic beverages consumed in a city

    b. young adults' use of illegal drugs

    c. why a local convenience store has been losing customers

    d. how heavily the company should invest in manufacturing and marketing home fax machines

    e. the amount of money people spend on lottery tickets

    f. reader recall of magazine advertisements

    g. what local doctors would like to see changed in the hospitals in the city

    h. consumers' attitudes toward several sports celebrities

## Marketing Mini-Project: Learning by Doing

The purpose of this mini-project is to familiarize you with research techniques used by marketers and to help you apply these techniques to managerial decision-making.

1. With a group of three other students in your class, select a small retail business or fast-food restaurant to use as a "client" for your project. Be sure to get the manager's permission before conducting your research. Then choose a topic from among the following possibilities to develop a study problem:

    • Employee-customer interactions
    • The busiest periods of customer activity
    • Customer perceptions of service
    • Customer likes and dislikes about offerings
    • Customer likes and dislikes about the environment in the place of business
    • The benefits customers perceive to be important
    • The age groups that frequent the place of business
    • The buying habits of a particular age group
    • How customer complaints are handled

2. Develop a plan for the research:

    a. Define the problem as you will study it.

    b. Choose the type of research you will use.

    c. Select the techniques you will use to gather data.

    d. Develop the mode and format for data collection.

3. Conduct the research.

4. Write a report or develop a class presentation that includes four parts.

    a. Introduction: a brief overview of the business and the problem studied.

    b. Methodology: the type of research used, the techniques used to gather data (and why they were chosen), the instruments and procedures used, the number of respondents, duration of the study, and other details that would allow someone to replicate your study.

c. Results: a compilation of the results (perhaps in table form) and the conclusions drawn.

d. Recommendations: a list of recommendations for actions management might take based on the conclusions drawn from the study.

## Real People, Real Surfers: Exploring the Web

Monitoring changes in demographics and other consumer trends is an important part of the marketing intelligence included in an MIS. Today, much of this information is gathered by government research and is available on the Internet.

Statistics Canada provides tabled data for Canadian cities at its site, **www.statcan.ca**. Using both Statistics Canada data and any other data you can find on the Internet, develop a report on a Canadian city of your choice that answers the following questions.

1. What is the total population of the city?

2. Describe the population of the area in terms of age, income, education, ethnic background, marital status, occupation, and housing.

3. How does the city compare to the demographic characteristics of the entire Canadian population?

4. What is your opinion of the different Web sites you used? How useful are they to marketers? How easy were they to navigate? Was there information that you wanted that was not available? Was there more or less information from the sites than you anticipated? Explain.

# MARKETING IN ACTION CASE

## Chapter 4 Pet Food Express

Donna Boyd and Tom Earl were designing a business they would start when they finished their business studies in three months. They were enthusiastic about the possibilities for their idea: a pet food delivery service (tentatively named Pet Food Express) for a medium-sized city in Ontario. They knew no similar service was available in the city, and that most pet owners shopped for pet food either at grocery or pet stores. As dog and cat owners themselves, they felt there was a real need for this service: It would provide convenience to pet owners by offering a selection of popular pet foods that could be ordered over the phone or via e-mail. The delivery aspect of the service would provide real benefits for people who like to shop in bulk for their pet food, but who don't like the hassle of transporting the food. Tom and Donna also thought that they would be able to offer better discounts than stores because they wouldn't incur the large overhead that stores do. They also anticipated that the service would especially appeal to pet owners who were seniors and those who did not have a vehicle of their own.

To assess demand for their idea, Donna and Tom decided to conduct some market research. They decided to do a phone survey with people randomly chosen from the local phone directory. They designed the following questionnaire.

Hello, my name is _____ and I am conducting a survey. May I have a moment of your time to ask you a few questions?

1. Do you own a dog or a cat? Yes____ No____
2. Do you have more than one pet? Yes____ No____
3. Do you do the purchasing of the pet food? Yes____ No____ (If no, may I please speak with the person who does the purchasing?)
4. Do you buy canned or dry food for your pet? Canned____ Dry____
5. What brand of pet food do you buy?

If they purchase dry food ask this:

6. Which one of these size/price combinations do you prefer? a) 10 lb. bag for $15, b) 20 lb. bag for $25, c) 40 lb. bag for $40
7. What do you find most unappealing about buying a large quantity of pet food?
8. On a scale of 1–5, with 1 being Not at all Important and 5 being Very Important, how important are the following to you when you purchase your pet food? Brand____ Price____ Size of Package____ Nutrition____ Quality____ Selection____ Store____ Location____ Pet's Preference____ Delivery Service____
9. At which store do you buy the bulk of your pet food?
10. How often do you prefer buying your pet food? Weekly____ Biweekly____ Monthly____ Other____
11. If a delivery service for your pet food were available, would it appeal to you? Yes____ No____
12. What radio station do you normally listen to?
13. Which of the following age groups do you belong to? Less than 18____ 18–25____ 25–45____ 45–64____ 65 and over____
14. Which of the following groups would your total household income fall under? Less than $20 000____ $20 000–$45 000____ $45 000–$60 000____ over $60 000____
15. Do you ever purchase products over the Internet? Yes____ No____

## Things to Think About

1. Evaluate Tom and Donna's proposed research technique (telephone survey). Develop a more comprehensive market research plan based on the first two stages of the marketing research process.
2. What changes would you make to the questionnaire? Rewrite it, incorporating your changes.
3. What other sources of information would be useful to them as they develop their business idea?

# Clinical Trial Ethics in Market Research

Drug companies are under constant pressure to innovate and develop new cures. However, there are many steps that biotechnology and drug companies must take in order to ensure that new drugs are safe and that the side effects are known. Human "guinea pigs" have taken on a new role and a new presence in drug testing. Participants are sometimes eager to test drugs—either because it is a relatively easy way to earn money, or because patients see the new and unproven drugs as a last hope for a cure to, or relief from, their condition. However, this quick cash and chancy shot at a cure comes with a price—and that price may not be well understood by the participants.

Many drug-testing participants are not properly informed of all known side effects (nor of the ones that are currently not known—and hence the need for testing). One Canadian cancer patient, for example, was not aware that the medication he was testing had been linked to over 400 deaths in China. Not only is there inadequate informed consent from participants, but some drug companies do not record problems or negative test results because of the pressure to get their drugs approved and prevent million-dollar projects from failing.

Health Canada should be very concerned with these problems, but instead it has taken a more business-oriented stance by continuing to promote Canada to biotech companies south of the border as a good place to do clinical trials: "Think Clinical Trials, Think Innovation. Think Canada." Canadian laws are much more lax than those in the United States and Health Canada plays on such leniency, by advertising tax breaks and a "no fuss" market entry for international biotech companies. Although studies may be approved faster in Canada than in the United States, in this country, unlike the United States, there is no governing body that keeps tabs on ethics boards or that ensures laws are being respected and studies executed correctly. The one organization that makes decisions on whether drugs can be tested in Canada is so overworked it often passes drugs in a matter of minutes.

Many people who are aware of this drug-testing problem agree that something needs to be done before harmful or even fatal drugs are tested by unknowing citizens. National standards need to be created and enforced, the Canadian board that approves drugs for testing needs to be expanded and given adequate time to investigate, and all data drawn out from research needs to be published and made available to the public.

Consider Health Canada's position on this issue.

## Questions

1. What arguments support their position and what arguments counter their position?
2. Should the drug testing industry be regulated, and if so, who should regulate it?
3. Consider product testing in general. How would you strike a balance between the need to protect the safety of those testing products and the safety of those buying the products?

Source: This case was prepared by Brock Smith and is based on *Marketplace,* "Clinical Trials," #22019.

## DESCRIPTIVE STATISTICS

As the name suggests, descriptive statistics are statistical tools used to describe data. Many marketing reports only use descriptive statistics as these are the easiest to interpret and they answer many marketing questions.

*Frequency distributions* are used when marketers need to answer questions about a single variable, such as: what percentage of visitors comes to Victoria, B.C., to attend a convention or conference; or how much money do visitors spend on accommodation? A frequency distribution is a count of the different values associate with a variable (a question in a questionnaire). Table 4.A1 is an example of a frequency distribution. It reports information collected by Tourism Victoria, the destination marketing organization responsible for attracting tourists to Victoria. Frequency distributions could also be represented in chart form, such as a bar chart.

In this frequency distribution, the frequency of answers to each response category is reported, as is the percent—the ratio of the frequency vs. total observations or cases, including missing values. The valid percent is what marketers usually interpret as this value is the frequency divided by the valid number of cases (the ones without missing values). Cumulative percent adds the valid percentages of each successive category.

Marketers report measures of *central tendency*, or the midpoint of a frequency distribution, in order to understand and make comparisons of how respondents typically answered a question. Common measures of central tendency include the mean, median, and mode. The mean, the arithmetic average, is the most common measure of the midpoint of a frequency distribution and is appropriate when data is interval or ratio scaled. The mode is the value that occurs most frequently—representing the highest peak in the frequency distribution—and is used when data is categorical. The median is the middle value when data is arranged in ascending or descending order—it is the value where 50 percent of cases are below that value and 50 percent are above. It is the best measure of central tendency for ordinal data or when there are extreme values (outliers) in interval or ratio data that would make the mean too high or low to be a good indicator of the midpoint of a frequency distribution.

## BIVARIATE STATISTICS

Bivariate statistics compare the distributions of two variables to see if they are related in some way. A *cross-tabulation* reports the joint frequency distribution of two categorical variables in a single contingency table as in Table 4.A2. It helps us to understand how one variable, such as tourist expenditure relates to another variable such as country of origin.

Some researchers prefer contingency tables that only include the percentage of cases in each cell, for ease of interpretation, while others prefer to see the frequencies or both the frequencies and percentages. The question of whether or not there is a relationship between the two variables in a cross-tab analysis can be assessed using statistics such as the chi-square statistic, which tests the null hypothesis that there is no relationship between the two variables. Hypothesis testing would be discussed further in a market research course. Cross-tabulation is widely used in marketing research because managers find it easy to interpret and understanding how two variables relate can provide useful insight to inform marketing decisions. For example, it might be very helpful for Tourism Victoria

**Table 4.A1** Reasons for Visiting Victoria

|  |  | Frequency | Percent | Valid Percent | Cumulative Percent |
|---|---|---|---|---|---|
| Valid | Vacation/Pleasure | 263 | 51.9 | 52.2 | 52.2 |
|  | Visiting Friends/Family | 86 | 17.0 | 17.1 | 69.2 |
|  | Business & Pleasure | 48 | 9.5 | 9.5 | 78.8 |
|  | Business Only | 57 | 11.2 | 11.3 | 90.1 |
|  | Convention/Conference | 13 | 2.6 | 2.6 | 92.7 |
|  | Sporting Event | 9 | 1.8 | 1.8 | 94.4 |
|  | Other | 28 | 5.5 | 5.6 | 100.0 |
|  | Total | 504 | 99.4 | 100.0 |  |
| Missing | System | 3 | 0.6 |  |  |
| Total |  | 507 | 100.0 |  |  |

**Table 4.A2** Tourist Expenditure by Country of Origin

| | | Country | | | |
|---|---|---|---|---|---|
| | | **CAN** | **INT'L** | **USA** | **Total** |
| categorical | 0–$100 | 377 | 33 | 162 | 572 |
| expenditure | $101–$200 | 257 | 41 | 160 | 458 |
| per party | $201–$500 | 218 | 28 | 222 | 468 |
| | More than $500 | 60 | 3 | 54 | 117 |
| Total | | 912 | 105 | 598 | 1615 |

to know that U.S. visitors spend more, proportionately, than other visitors when it is deciding where to target its advertising dollars.

A second common bivariate statistic is the *Pearson correlation coefficient* (also called simple correlation, or just correlation). Correlation is the strength of the linear association between two interval or ratio scaled variables—that is, as the values of one variable increases, what happens to the values of the other variable? Correlation does not imply causation—it just indicates, on a range from –1 to +1, the strength of the association between the two variables, where zero is no relationship at all. Marketers find correlation analysis useful because it helps them to understand whether relationships exist between variables of interest, such as: whether sales increase as more money is spent on advertising, or whether spending on a customer loyalty program, like Air Miles, is correlated with an increase in customer loyalty. In Table 4.A3, Tourism Victoria learns that there is a small, positive correlation of 0.12 between Overall Visitor Satisfaction and Total Number of Activities the respondent participated in. We do not know if greater activity results in greater satisfaction or whether greater satisfaction results in greater activity, but we do know that there is a relationship between these variables (the significant value "Sig" is less than 0.05, indicating that the likelihood of there being no relationship between these variables is very low). This might be useful to help Tourism Victoria decide whether or not to encourage the development of more attractions or other things to do in

Victoria, or whether or not to develop information sources on what there is to do in Victoria.

There are many other statistical tools used by marketers. A t-test is a bivariate tool used to assess whether the mean of a variable is equal or different for two groups. Cereal marketers, for example, might like to know whether boys under the age of 13 eat more of their cereal than girls under the age of 13, when making packaging decisions and promotion decisions.

## MULTIVARIATE STATISTICS

Multivariate statistics refer to analytic tools that involve more than two variables. Each of these tools have different data requirements (the type of scale used to capture the data). The common types of scales and the statistics or analysis that are permissible with each type of data are summarized in Table 4.A4. This is an issue that would be addressed in detail in a course on market research. For now, you should be aware that most of the tools require at least interval scale data. Interval scale data is where the response categories to a question on a questionnaire represent equal increments, such as with the Centigrade temperature scale ($10°C$ is $5°C$ colder than $15°C$ and $5°C$ warmer than $5°C$, or where equality is assumed such as in a Likert scale (e.g., Strongly Agree, 1, 2, 3, 4, 5, Strongly Disagree).

*One-way analysis of variance* determines whether the mean (average) response to a question is statistically different in three or more groups. Tourism Victoria, for

**Table 4.A3** Correlation Between Satisfaction and Number of Activities

**Correlations**

| | | Q3SATISF | ACTIVTOT |
|---|---|---|---|
| Overall Satisfaction | Pearson Correlation | 1 | 0.120** |
| | Sig. (2-tailed) | . | 0.000 |
| | N | 1871 | 1698 |
| Number of Activities | Pearson Correlation | 0.120** | 1 |
| | Sig. (2-tailed) | 0.000 | . |
| | N | 1698 | 1871 |

**Correlation is significant at the 0.01 level (2-tailed).

**Table 4.A4** Common Scales

| Scale | Basic Characteristics | Common Examples | Marketing Examples | Permissible Statistics | |
|-------|----------------------|-----------------|--------------------|------------------------|---|
| | | | | Descriptive | Inferential |
| Nominal | Numbers identify and classify objects | Social Security numbers, numbering of football players | Brand numbers, store types, sex classification | Percentages, mode | Chi-square binomial test |
| Ordinal | Numbers indicate the relative positions of the objects but not the magnitude of differences between them | Quality rankings, rankings of teams in a tournament | Preference rankings, market position, social class | Percentile, median | Rank-order correlation, Friedman ANOVA |
| Internal | Differences between objects can be compared; zero point is arbitrary | Temperature (Fahrenheit, Centigrade) | Attitudes, opinions, index numbers | Range, mean, standard deviation | Product-moment correlations, t-test, ANOVA, regression, factor analysis |
| Ratio | Zero point is fixed; ratios of scale values can be computed | Length, weight | Age, income, costs, sales, market shares | Geometric mean, harmonic mean | Coefficient of variation |

Source: Malhotra, Naresh, *Marketing Research: An Applied Orientation,* 4th Edition, © 2004. Reprinted by permission of Pearson Education Inc. Upper Saddle River, NJ.

example, finds it useful to know that people who come to Victoria via the Victoria Clipper catamaran passenger service spend more money while visiting Victoria than visitors who come by air or come in their cars via BC Ferries. The null hypothesis being tested with one-way ANOVA is that the mean values of the groups with respect to a variable of interest are equal. This is usually rejected, and the alternative hypothesis that at least two of the groups differ is accepted, if the significant value is less than 0.05 (corresponding to a 95% confidence interval). The data on transit methods, for example, demonstrates that at least two of the BC Ferries, Clipper Navigation, and air travel visitor groups to Victoria differ in expenditure per party. Something called a post-hoc test is required to determine which of the groups differ from each other.

*Discriminant analysis* determines which variables are the most important for differentiating (determining the differences between) two or more groups. One-way analysis of variance tells us if the means of the groups differ with respect to a variable, but discriminant analysis tells us which of these differences are the most important. If marketers knew, for example, what are the most important differences in the profiles of different market segments, they could use that information to target those segments more effectively.

*Cluster analysis* is an analytic tool that groups respondents by the commonality or consistency of their answers to questions. Cluster analysis identifies groups where the people in the group are of maximum similarity to each other, based on their answers to the questions, and of

maximum difference from people in other groups—two of the criteria for effective segmentation schemes discussed in Chapter 3. If questions have been asked about benefits and features sought, purchase and consumption behaviour, and response to marketing mix variables (like price sensitivity) then cluster analysis will identify actionable, behaviour-based market segments—another objective of a good segmentation scheme. To help develop a rich profile of these clusters or segments, marketers capture demographic and psychographic information from respondents and describe the segments using frequency distributions, means, correlations, and cross-tab analysis, and determine how the segments are similar or different using one-way analysis of variance and discriminant analysis.

*Regression analysis* is a powerful tool for analyzing relationships between a metric (interval or ratio scale) variable and one or more other variables (called independent variables), when the focal variable of interest is considered dependent on the others. It is used to determine whether a relationship exists between the dependent variable and one or more of the independent variables. Marketers, for example, might want to know if there is a relationship between sales and advertising expenditure, pricing, or distribution intensity. It can also be used to determine the strength of this relationship and the structure or form of the relationship—in the way of an equation. It is most often used to predict values of the dependent variable. Marketers for example, would like to predict sales volumes or market share (see the discussion on forecasting in Appendix 4.B). It can also be used to determine the unique effects or impact of one variable (such as price) when others (such as level of competitor advertising) are taken into account.

*Multidimensional scaling* (MDS) is a sophisticated analytic tool that creates perceptual maps like the ones illustrated in Chapter 3. It takes data related to consumer preferences or their perceptions of the similarity of brands or other stimuli and represents the geometric relationships among the brands in a multidimensional space. Market researchers infer the underlying dimensions respondents use to form their similarity perceptions or preferences by interpreting groupings of brands on the map—identify what those brands have in common that would cause respondents to consider them similar. MDS is used to determine 1) the number and nature of the dimensions used by consumers in comparing brands, 2) the positioning of current brands on these dimensions, and 3) the positioning of consumers' ideal brands on these dimensions.[57]

Sales forecasting is one of the most important and difficult challenges for marketers. It is important because key decisions such as amount of product to produce, the size of plant to build, the number of employees to hire, and the amount of financing required, is based on a sales forecast. It is difficult because a lot of factors influence demand for a product. In some industries like fashion, computers, and consumer electronics, these factors are either highly dynamic or difficult to identify. In these contexts, forecast accuracy of plus or minus 70 percent might be considered good. In stable, mature industries past demand is often a good indication of future demand and forecast accuracy in the plus or minus 5 percent range might be achievable. While forecasts can be for any future time period, most organizations try to predict sales one to three years into the future. There are numerous approaches to sales forecasting and these can generally be grouped into subjective (qualitative) and objective (quantitative) approaches. Sophisticated sales organizations use multiple approaches to make their forecasts and some of these are described below.

*Subjective methods* are based on perceptions or opinions.

- Users' Expectations: Asking customers how much of a product they expect to buy in the forecast period. This approach works well in stable industries where there are not a lot of customers.

- Sales Rep Composite: Sales reps are asked to estimate demand in their territory based on their understanding of customer buying intentions, and then the individual estimates are added together to generate the forecast. This approach requires an established sales force, but can be quite accurate as an overestimate by one sales rep are often made up for by underestimate of another. Most sales organizations, however, find that their sales reps tend to be overly optimistic, and based on experience with their sales force, discount their composite forecast between 5 and 15 percent.

- Executive Opinion: Senior managers are asked their opinion about future sales. This approach can be effective if the executives are close to their customers, and have a strong understanding of industry dynamics and market factors.

- Goal Based: Some marketers set their forecast at the level needed to achieve their marketing goals or objectives. This approach is often used by small start-up organizations that simply want to achieve some level of profitability. The problems with this approach are that

the goal may be too optimistic and may not be reflective of actual demand, or the goal may be set too low, inviting competitors to meet the excess demand.

*Objective methods* are based on some sort of modeling approach and the use of quantitative analytic tools or statistics.

- Time Series: In this approach the sales data from previous years are used to predict sales in future years (trend analysis). A moving average takes the average sales of the previous five years as the forecast for each successive year. Exponential smoothing gives greater weight to the most recent years. These approaches can be effective in stable industries if future sales are expected to be a lot like prior sales.

- Market-Factor: A common and simple approach is to forecast derivation sales based on an understanding of the factors that influence demand. A market-build-up approach would use market research to find out the typical demand per person in a target market and this figure would be multiplied by the size of the target market to establish the forecast. For example, the demand for Gatorade in Canada might be determined by multiplying the average beverage consumption of Canadians (available from Statistics Canada) by the number of Canadians who are physically active (also available from Statistics Canada) by the number of Canadians for fit the profile of Gatorade consumers (determined by primary research). As discussed in Appendix A, regression analysis is an analytic tool that allows market researchers to predict sales as a dependent variable using a set of independent variables (demand factors) thought to be determinants of sales.

- Test Markets: Test market data can also be used to develop a sales forecast. Test market locations are chosen to be representative of the overall population of interest. By changing levels of price, advertising, shelf location, and other marketing mix decisions for different, equivalent groups, marketers can develop models that will optimize those decisions to maximize sales.

- Conjoint Analysis: Conjoint analysis is an analytic tool that uses consumer preference and attribute rating data of a relatively small subset of product concepts or brands to estimate demand for any combination of the attributes. It is only appropriate for those product categories, like computers, where consumers make purchase decisions by making trade-offs among levels of key attributes (e.g., processor speed, memory, hard drive capacity).

- Base Modeling: Base modeling techniques estimate demand for new to the world innovations by comparing key attributes of the innovation to previous innovations and basing the forecast on the known demand curves of those prior innovations.

# CHAPTER 5
## Consumer Buying Behaviour

## CHAPTER OBJECTIVES

WHEN YOU HAVE COMPLETED YOUR STUDY OF THIS CHAPTER, YOU SHOULD BE ABLE TO

1. Explain why understanding consumer behaviour is important to organizations.

2. Explain the prepurchase, purchase, and postpurchase activities consumers engage in when making decisions.

3. Describe how internal factors influence consumers' decision-making processes.

4. Describe how situational factors at the time and place of purchase may influence consumer behaviour.

5. Describe how consumers' relationships with other people influence their decision-making processes.

6. Understand how the Internet offers consumers opportunities for peer-to-peer marketing.

# Real People, Real Decisions

## Meet **Michel Bendayan,** a Decision Maker at Mega Bloks

Michel Bendayan is an International Sales and Marketing director for Mega Bloks, the publicly-traded, Montreal-based company that is the second largest construction toy manufacturer in the world after Lego. Mega Bloks is a worldwide organization employing over 3000 people, and selling a line of 75 to 100 Mega Bloks items in four sizes in 100 countries. Sales of Mega Bloks have grown exponentially in the past five years and Mega Bloks is now the world market share leader in the preschool construction toy segment.

Michel Bendayan has been a Director of International Sales and Marketing since 2003, and recently took over responsibility for Asia, Australia, and Africa in addition to his previous focus on Eastern Europe and the Middle East. Before joining Mega Bloks in 1998, Bendayan worked for Hasbro Canada as assistant product manager for the Parker Brothers and Milton Bradley brands, and prior to that he completed a BCom degree from McGill University in 1994.

As International Sales and Marketing director, Bendayan determines international marketing strategy and product launch tactics. His role includes identifying new distributors, working on getting product listings, understanding retail and consumer preferences and trends, and working with retailers to grow the sales of Mega Bloks products.

Soon after taking over the Asia portfolio, Bendayan learned that Mega Bloks' sales in Japan were weak. The Japanese toy market is the second largest in the world, after the United States, and construction toys represent a much smaller proportion of that market than in either the United States or Europe, suggesting to Bendayan that there was an opportunity to increase Mega Bloks' sales in Japan. For the previous five years Mega Bloks had worked with three different Japanese distributors, but had only marginal sales success. Bendayan didn't know if the problem was with the distributors, the product line, or both.

One thing he had learned in the European market was the European consumers and distributors were quite different from those in North America. Focus group research had found that European consumers liked simple, compact, box packaging (similar to that of Lego or Playmobile) that showed a picture of the product or the product in use, and had little writing. In North America, most consumers were influenced either by the flashiness of the packaging—bolder colours, graphic call-outs, and bold text that highlighted product benefits—or the size of the packaging, bigger or more interesting being better. Consequently Mega Bloks packaged their North American products in either bulk bags or shaped theme packaging such as a set of Bloks that came in a dump truck or in a container shaped like a bear. North American consumers tend to like detailed information on the packaging that explains who the product is for and how it is used, but such detailed text makes European packaging very cluttered as it has to be presented in multiple languages. European distributors considered Mega Bloks to be a premium foreign brand while in North America it is positioned as a high quality but value brand.

Conducting similar research, Bendayan found that Japanese consumers were even more quality oriented than the Europeans and would reject toys with the slightest scratches or dented boxes. Japanese consumers demand the use of Japanese script on the packaging, and while North American products are often considered prestigious, Japanese consumers want a Japanese look and feel to the packaging. Because Japanese households have even less space then European households, and rooms often have multiple uses, consumers demand efficient and utilitarian packaging—wanting to be able to easily put toys back in their boxes or containers and put them out of sight. Japanese consumers are also much more conscious of and involved with pop-culture characters (e.g., Power Rangers). Differences were also found with Japanese retailers who were much more varied (e.g., hypermarkets, supermarkets, convenience stores), fragmented (lots of different channels), and much more relationship oriented. Although there are fewer specialty toy stores, many Japanese toy manufacturers are among the largest toy companies in the world.

With a desire to develop a strong long-term brand in the Japanese market, Bendayan and his colleagues considered three distribution alternatives and three product line alternatives:

Distribution alternative one (D1) was to continue to work through small distributors. Even though the previous distributors did not understand the product line well and lacked focus and commitment to the product lines, Bendayan thought there might be some better small distributors and it might be easier to get the interest and attention of smaller distributors than the larger ones who already had strategic relationships with the large Japanese toy manufacturers. On the other hand, these small distributors were often small because they did not have access to as many channels and were not embedded in a large corporate network.

Distribution alternative two (D2) was to sell direct. Bendayan thought that the Japanese market was potentially big enough for Mega Bloks to consider developing their own sales and distribution company in Japan. Bendayan thought that such an investment could pay off in the long run as it would be closer to the customer and would not be reliant on others. The risk, however, was that no one in the Mega Bloks organization knew a lot about Japanese business practices or Japanese consumers and it would take months, or even years, to establish the key retail relationships needed for the sales reps to be effective.

Distribution alternative three (D3) was to partner with a large Japanese manufacturer or distributor. This alternative was attractive as a strategic partner could offer local expertise, knowledge of the Japanese consumer, and access to a large distribution network. The downside was that Mega Bloks would be a much smaller organization and may not get the attention needed and all the "help" would come at the expense of significantly higher margins demanded by the partner organization.

With respect to the product line, Bendayan considered three alternatives.

Production line alternative one (P1) was to sell the existing U.S. or European product lines. It would be easiest and fastest to sell the current lines without any customization, and the European lines had already been customized to reflect space issues. While international brands were popular in Japan, Bendayan did not know if this would be true for children's toys. He didn't know if Japanese consumer preferences would accept the brand without modification; it might be perceived as too "western."

Production line alternative two (P2) was to sell existing product lines but customize the packaging for the Japanese market. The easiest customization option was to change the packaging to portray a Japanese image, but retain the current product lines that were the most popular sellers in Europe and North America. This approach had worked well in Europe where European consumers responded well to new, cleaner package designs, and packing that facilitated storage such as bags or plastic boxes.

Production line alternative three (P3) was to develop an entirely new product line for the Japanese market. This option would be the most expensive and would take a year or more to implement. The key advantage would be that a new product line could be designed to specifically appeal to Japanese consumers. Such a new line would also have stronger appeal to Japanese distributors. The downside was that minimum order quantities and sales would need to be achieved to justify the production costs. If standard products were sold, it would not matter as much if sales targets were missed.

Now, join the Mega Bloks decision team. Which options would you choose, and why?

## UNDERSTANDING CUSTOMERS

Compelling new products, clever packaging, and creative advertising surround us, clamouring for our attention—and our money. But consumers don't all respond in the same way to marketing activities. Each consumer is a unique person, with unique reasons for choosing one product over another. Recall that the focus of the marketing concept is to satisfy consumers' wants and needs. These wants and needs can be satisfied only to the extent that marketers understand why and how people buy products. D~Code, for example, is a Canadian research firm that helps Canadian marketers understand 18- to 34-year-old "Nexus" consumers by answering such questions as: what are the attitudes and lifestyles of Nexus consumers, why do they prefer certain products, which ads do they respond to, and how do they purchase products? UThink, another Canadian marketing research and strategy firm offers similar services to help marketers understand 13- to 29-year-olds. **Consumer behaviour** is the process individuals or groups go through to select, purchase, and use goods, services, ideas, or experiences. Marketers recognize that consumer behaviour is an ongoing process—it is more than what happens at the moment a consumer hands over money and, in turn, receives a good or service.

**consumer behaviour** The process individuals or groups go through to select, purchase, and use goods, services, ideas, or experiences to satisfy their needs and desires.

Although it seems as if some purchases are made spontaneously (and we may regret our rashness later), in reality we make most buying decisions only after we have undergone a series of steps—problem recognition, information search, evaluation of alternatives, product choice, and postpurchase evaluation—summarized in Figure 5.1.

Traditionally, researchers have tried to understand how consumers make decisions by assuming that people carefully collect information about competing products, determine which products possess the characteristics or product attributes important to their needs, weigh the pluses and minuses of each alternative, and arrive at a satisfactory decision. But how accurate is this picture of the decision-making process?

Although it does seem that people undergo these steps when making an important purchase, is it realistic to assume that they do this for everything they buy? Researchers now realize that consumers actually possess a set of decision approaches, ranging from painstaking analysis to pure whim, depending on the importance of what is being bought and how much effort the person is willing to put into the decision.[1] Researchers have found it convenient to think in terms of an "effort" continuum, which is anchored on one end by

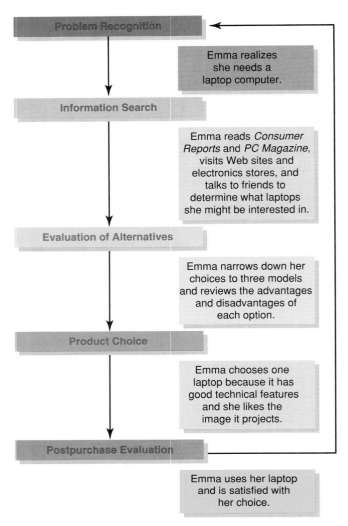

**Figure 5.1** The Consumer Decision-Making Process

**involvement** The relative importance of perceived consequences of the purchase to a consumer.

**perceived risk** The belief that use of a product has potentially negative consequences, either financial, physical, or social.

*habitual (or routine) decision making* (such as deciding to purchase a can of pop) and at the other end by *extended problem solving* (such as deciding to purchase a computer). Many decisions fall somewhere in the middle and are characterized by *limited problem solving*, which means that consumers do work to make a decision, but most likely rely on simple rules of thumb instead of learning about and considering all the ins and outs of every product alternative. Some Internet marketers believe that the Internet can reduce the effort needed to make product decisions by offering so many products and services in one place.

*Involvement* determines the extent of effort a person puts into deciding what to buy. **Involvement** is the importance of the perceived consequences of the purchase to the person. As a rule, we are more involved in the decision-making process for products that we perceive as being important, pleasurable, or risky in some way. **Perceived risk** may be present if the product is expensive, complex, and hard to understand, or if the purchase of the wrong product could result in embarrassment or social rejection. For instance, some people perceive clothing purchases as risky because they feel a wrong choice could lead to negative social consequences. Perceived risk can also be a factor in the buying process for certain products. A study of condom buying among Canadian university students, for example, found that 66 percent of men and 60 percent of women reported being embarrassed when buying condoms and, therefore, do not buy them. As one researcher put it, "Approaching the cashier is the moment of truth. There is also the worry that a 'price check on a 12-pack of Durex condoms' will be announced to the entire store."[2] Marketers will sometimes refer to high or low involvement products, but this is misleading. Products are not high or low involvement—decisions are. What is a high involvement decision for one consumer may be a low involvement decision for another (Exhibit 5.1). Bill Gates, for example, probably doesn't spend a lot of time thinking about what type of television to buy. When marketers say a car is a high involvement product, they really mean it is a high involvement decision for most consumers.

When perceived risk is low, as in buying a pack of gum, the consumer feels *low involvement* in the decision-making process—the consumer is not overly concerned about which option he or she chooses because it is not especially important or risky. In low-involvement situations, the consumer's decision is often a response to environmental cues, such as deciding to try a new type of chewing gum because it is prominently displayed at a store checkout counter. Under these circumstances, managers must concentrate on how products are displayed at the time of purchase to influence the decision maker. For example, a chewing gum marketer may decide to spend more money to be sure its gum stands out at a checkout display or to change the colour of the gum wrapper to a bright pink to be sure it gets noticed among the other gums.

For *high-involvement* purchases, such as a house, car, computer, or interview suit, the consumer is more likely to carefully process all of the available information and to have thought about the decision well before buying the item. The consequences of the purchase are important and risky, especially because a bad decision can result in significant financial losses, aggravation, decreased performance, or embarrassment. So for high-involvement products, managers must start to reduce perceived risk by educating the consumer about why their product is the best choice well in advance of the time that the consumer is ready to make a decision. To understand what goes on during each of the steps in the decision-making process, in the next section we'll follow the fortunes of one consumer, a student named Emma, who is in the market for a new notebook computer. This is a high involvement purchase decision for her because of the cost of the product and because the performance of the computer will have an important impact on her own performance in courses and, perhaps, in future jobs.

## Problem Recognition

**Problem recognition** occurs whenever the consumer sees a significant difference between their current state of affairs and some desired or ideal state. The consumer needs to solve a *problem*, which may be small or large, simple or complex (Exhibit 5.2). Emma has a problem. She needs to have a computer for writing papers, doing research on the Internet, and sending e-mail, but the computers provided on campus are always busy when she needs a computer the most, such as at the end of term. Emma also wants her computer to be portable so that she can use it to take notes in classes and take it to the library while she researches her assignments. Thinking about the future, Emma realizes that, in her job, she will probably have a lot of work to do after hours. Having a notebook computer will allow her to do the work in the comfort of her own apartment.

Do marketing decisions have a role in buyers' problem recognition? Although most problem recognition occurs spontaneously, marketers can develop creative advertising messages that stimulate consumers to recognize that their current state—that old car—just doesn't equal a shiny, new convertible. Figure 5.2 provides examples of marketing activities for problem recognition and the other stages of the consumer decision process.

## Information Search

Once Emma recognizes her computer problem, she needs adequate information to resolve it. During the **information search** part of the decision-making process, the consumer checks their memory and surveys the environment to identify what options exist to solve the problem. Marketing communication helps consumers in this task and many advertisements are focused on generating awareness about brands. BMW Group Canada, for example, wanted to create awareness and interest in the new Mini but wanted to do so in keeping with the brand's character of an individualistic, high performance, premium vehicle that is fun to drive. The company used a public relations campaign that featured a caged Mini that could be seen by pedestrians and passing traffic en route to autoshows across Canada. The sign on the cage read: "Please do not feed, tease, or annoy the Mini." For her information search, Emma might rely on ads she has seen for notebook computers, recommendations from friends, and additional research she might do by reading *Consumer Reports* and *PC Magazine*, or by signing onto Web sites for companies, such as Dell Computers Canada and Apple Canada. She also might visit some electronics stores, like the Future Shop, where she can discuss her purchase with salespeople and try out some computers.

Increasingly, consumers are using Internet search engines, portals, or "shopping bots" for information search. Search engines are sites such as Google, AltaVista, and Webcrawler that find information on the Web by searching sites for keywords (Exhibit 5.3). Other sites such as Expedia simplify searches because they organize information from a lot of separate Web sites according to common themes.

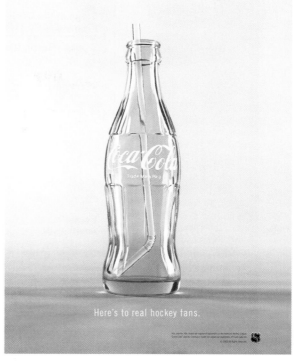

**Exhibit 5.1**

Soft drink purchase decisions are low involvement for most consumers. By linking its brand to hockey, Coke® is trying to make it more involving to Canadian consumers.

**problem recognition** The process that occurs whenever the consumer sees a significant difference between his or her current state of affairs and some desired or ideal state. This recognition initiates the decision-making process.

**information search** The process whereby a consumer searches for appropriate information needed to make a reasonable decision.

**Dell Computers Canada**
www.dell.ca

**Apple Canada**
www.apple.com/ca

**Google**
www.google.ca

**AltaVista**
www.ca.altavista.com

**Webcrawler**
www.webcrawler.com

**Expedia**
www.expedia.ca

| Stage in the Decision Process | Marketing Strategy | Example |
|---|---|---|
| Problem Recognition | Encourage consumers to see that existing state does not equal desired state | TV commercials showing the excitement of owning a new car |
| Information Search | Provide information when and where consumers are likely to search | Targeted advertising on TV programs with high target market viewership |
| | | Sales training that ensures knowledgeable salespeople |
| | | Make new car brochures available in dealer showrooms |
| | | Design exciting, easy to navigate, and informative Web sites |
| Evaluation of Alternatives | Understand the criteria consumers use in comparing brands and communicate own brand superiority | Conduct research to identify most important evaluative criteria |
| | | Create advertising that includes reliable data on superiority of a brand (e.g., kilometres per litre, safety, comfort) |
| Product Choice | Understand choice heuristics used by consumers and provide communication that encourages brand decision | Advertise "Made in Canada" (country of origin) |
| | | Stress long history of the brand (brand loyalty) |
| Postpurchase Evaluation | Encourage accurate consumer expectations | Provide honest advertising and sales presentations |

**Figure 5.2** Marketers' Responses to Decision Process Stages

When they understand the stages of the consumer decision process, marketers can develop strategies to lead consumers to a choice that pleases both the consumer and the marketer.

Some portals, such as Spanish-language YupiMSN.com, focus on specific customer segments. This unique portal makes it easy for readers to access Spanish-language Web sites that provide information on education, entertainment, sports, politics, music, and local and international news. Having recognized the enormous and rapidly growing Spanish-speaking market, Bill Gates' Microsoft empire acquired the once independent Yupi.com as part of its global expansion. And with the strength and prestige of Microsoft, YupiMSN.com has created a major link among all Spanish-speaking countries worldwide.

Robots, also called "shopbots" or "intelligent agents" are software programs used by some Web sites that find Internet retailers selling a particular product. The programs troll the Web for information, and then "report" it back to the host site. Some of these sites also provide information on competitors' prices and may even ask customers to rate the various retailers that they have listed to provide recommendations for other consumers on which sellers are good and which are less than desirable. We should note, however, that some sites do not wish to compete on price and don't give bots access. Emma, in her search for a personal computer, could visit ComputersCanada.com to quickly search computer prices across Canada. The role of marketers during the information search phase of the decision process is to

**Exhibit 5.2**

Marketers like Pfizer Canada help consumers recognize needs and wants. Launching Viagra with the "Good Morning" campaign got consumers to wonder why this fellow was so happy.

make sure information about their brand is available when and where consumers look. Most computer manufacturers make sure information about their newest models is on the Web, is advertised frequently in dealer flyers and magazines, and, of course, is available in dealer showrooms.

Information search is often an ongoing process and this stage may be more extensive and intensive for some consumers than others. It ends with the identification of alternatives for consideration, called the **consideration set**.

## Evaluation of Alternatives

Once consumers have identified the set of products they are interested in, they narrow down their choices by deciding which of all the possibilities are feasible and evaluating the remaining alternatives. Emma might want a top-of-the-line notebook, like a Dell Inspiron, but realizes that her student budget doesn't allow for such a purchase. As she looks around, she decides that the notebooks she likes in her price range are the Apple iBook, the Compaq Presario, and the Gateway Solo. She has narrowed down her options by considering only affordable notebooks.

Now, Emma has to choose. It's time for her to look more systematically at each of the three possibilities and identify the important characteristics, or **evaluative criteria**, she will use to decide among them. These may be the power of the computer, its weight, the size of the monitor, the battery life, the warranty offered, or even the computer's design or colour options. During her evaluation, Emma learns of a new Apple product—the iMac—which seems to her to have a lot of the features of a notebook. Judging from the ad in Exhibit 5.4, it appears it would work well with the iPod she got for her birthday.

Marketers often play a role in educating consumers about *which* product characteristics should be used as evaluative criteria—usually, they emphasize the dimensions in which their product excels. Where Compaq Presario might focus on price because it is one of the least expensive notebook computers available, Apple is educating consumers about the value of compatibility and owning a family of products.

## Product Choice

But how do consumers like Emma actually apply their evaluative criteria? Some consumers use **heuristics** (mental shortcuts) to simplify the evaluation process—taking the advice of someone else, buying the cheapest brand or the most expensive brand (assuming that price reflects quality), or buying the one that "feels" right (has the greatest emotional appeal). Perhaps the most common heuristic is just buying the brand a consumer always buys—either through habit or through **brand loyalty**. Consumers are brand loyal when they make repeat brand purchases because they believe that brand is superior, have such strong preferences that they will pay more, or search harder to find that brand, and they feel that it's not worth the effort to consider competing options. The creation of brand loyalty is a prized goal for marketers. People form preferences for a favourite brand and then may literally never change their minds in the course of a lifetime, making it extremely difficult for rivals to persuade them to switch.

Other consumers put more thought into their purchase decision and have key criteria that absolutely have to be met. Emma, for example, is only considering laptop or notebook computers and is not willing to consider a desktop model. In doing so, she is applying a non-compensatory evaluation strategy—where a consumer is unwilling to make trade-offs on product attributes such as getting a faster processor, more memory, and a larger hard drive for a lower price on a desktop computer. A compensatory strategy is where consumers are willing to

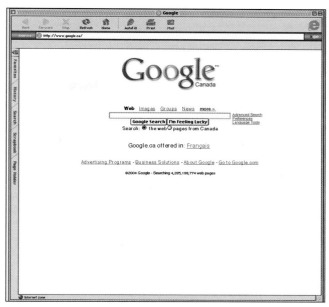

**Exhibit 5.3**
Google is a popular search engine for Web surfers.

**consideration set** The set of alternative brands the consumer is considering for the decision process.

**evaluative criteria** The dimensions that consumers use to compare competing product alternatives.

**Computers Canada.com**
www.computers-canada.com
**CNET.com**
www.CNET.com

**heuristics** A mental rule of thumb that leads to a speedy decision by simplifying the process.

**brand loyalty** A pattern of repeat product purchases, accompanied by an underlying positive attitude toward the brand, which is based on the belief that the brand makes products superior to its competition.

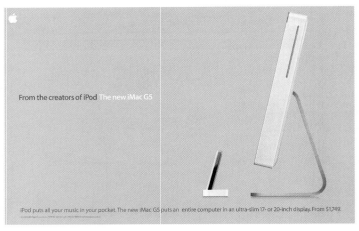

From the creators of iPod The new iMac G5

iPod puts all your music in your pocket. The new iMac G5 puts an entire computer in an ultra-slim 17- or 20-inch display. From $1,749.

**Exhibit 5.4**

One role of marketing communication is to make consumers aware of evaluative criteria.

make trade-offs to get the best overall deal (value) for their needs. There are different types of compensatory and non-compensatory strategies and many consumers use a mix of these strategies, even within the same decision process. These are summarized in Figure 5.3.

Emma has spent several weeks thinking about the alternatives, and she's finally ready to take the plunge and buy! After agonizing over her choice, she decides that, even though the Gateway and Dell laptops were rated highly by *Consumer Reports,* the Apple iBook just feels right. It meets all the basic technical criteria and it appeals to her sense of individuality. The iBook is the lightest of all the options and will easily fit in her backpack. She signs onto the Apple Canada Web site and buys her notebook computer. A few days later the computer arrives at her door. In the end, Emma used a mix of decision strategies (lexigraphic, conjunctive, and heuristics) to make her purchase decision.

## Postpurchase Evaluation

In the last stage of decision making, the consumer evaluates the quality of the decision made. After mulling over the alternatives and picking one, they evaluate just how good a choice it was. Everyone has experienced **cognitive dissonance** (regret or buyer's remorse) after making a purchase, and (hopefully) we have all been pleased with something we've bought. Marketers pay particular attention to cognitive dissonance, as they want consumers to have enduring positive attitudes towards the brands they have purchased so they become loyal consumers—reducing the cost of marketing in the future and reducing the likelihood of the consumer switching to another brand. Cognitive dissonance is greatest when decisions are important and there are other viable brands in the consideration set. Through marketing communication strategies that reaffirm to the consumer what a good decision they made, marketers try to reduce or minimize cognitive dissonance.

The evaluation of the product results in a level of **consumer satisfaction/ dissatisfaction**, which is determined by the overall feelings, or attitude, a person has about a product after purchasing it. In this case, fortunately, Emma's feelings couldn't be better. Her computer is reliable and easy to use, and its light weight means that she can easily carry it to her classes.

Just how do consumers decide if they are satisfied with their purchases? One answer would be, "That's easy. The product is either wonderful, or it isn't." However, it's a little more complicated than that. When consumers buy a product, they have some *expectations* of product quality. How well a product or service meets or exceeds these expectations determines customer satisfaction. In other words, consumers assess product quality by comparing what they have bought to a *performance standard* created by a mixture of information from marketing communications, informal information sources such as friends and family, and their own experience with the product category.

So, even though Emma's new iBook is not as powerful as some of the other options she considered, she's happy with her purchase because it meets or exceeds her expectations. Emma has completed the consumer decision-making process by recognizing a problem, conducting an information search to resolve it, identifying the feasible alternatives, making a product choice, and then evaluating the quality of her decision.

## OTHER DECISION PROCESSES

Emma's computer purchase was an example of high involvement, extended problem-solving decision that typically follows the process outlined in Figure 5.1. But marketers

**cognitive dissonance** The regret or remorse buyers may feel after making a purchase.

**consumer satisfaction/dissatisfaction** The overall feelings or attitude a person has about a product after purchasing it.

| | Decision Rule | Marketing Implications |
|---|---|---|
| Compensatory | Simple Additive: Sum the scores of each brand rating on each attribute, chose the brand with the highest overall score. | Develop brands with strong overall value. Help consumers compare brands to make the overall value choice. |
| | Weighted Additive: Give weights to each criteria, for each brand multiple the rating and the weight, sum the scores and chose the brand with the highest overall score. | Understand the criteria weights and design products that excel on those criteria. Position your product on the key criteria. Try to change the weights of criteria to make them more or less important in the minds of customers—such as Intel did with the Intel Inside campaign. |
| Non-Compensatory | Lexicographic: Rank the decision criteria; evaluate the brands on the most important criteria. Chose the brand with the highest rating on the most important criteria. If there is a tie, go on to the next most important criteria until a brand is chosen. | Understand the top three or four most important criteria for your target market and continuously innovate to lead on those criteria. If you are not the leader, try to change consumer attitudes about the importance of the criteria or try to get them to adopt a different evaluative strategy. |
| | Elimination by Aspects: Rank the decision criteria, and determine minimal acceptable levels for each criterion. Keep in the evoked set, brands that meet the minimum level of the most important criteria. Go on to the next most important criteria until there is only one brand in the consideration set and chose that brand. | Understand the most important criteria for your target market and continuously innovate to be close to the leaders on the top criterion. Try to establish a criterion in the minds of consumers where your competitors are not able to compete effectively. Demonstrate that your brand exceeds typical minimum standards on key criteria. |
| | Conjunctive: Determine minimal acceptable levels for each criterion. Keep in your evoked set brands that meet or exceed the minimal level on all criteria. If there is a tie, add criteria or raise the minimum standards. | Understand the criteria and minimum levels. Continuously innovate to meet minimum levels on all criteria. Innovate to develop features or functions not provided by competitors. Try to establish these features or functions as criteria in the evaluation process. |
| Heuristics (Illustrative Examples) | Habit: Buy the brand you bought last time. | Make your brand available; develop strong brand recognition; remind consumers that this is their brand. |
| | Price: Buy the cheapest or most expensive brand. | Innovate to keep a low cost structure and position your brand as the value leader—or position your brand as a premium brand and support the quality inference through marketing communications. |
| | Affect: Buy the brand that "feels" right. | Develop strong emotional connections to your brand through packaging and marketing communications. |
| | Recommendation: Buy the brand that someone says is best. | Market to the opinion leaders and market mavens (see page 171). Provide incentives or recognition for referrals. |

**Figure 5.3** Product Decision Strategies

know that not all consumer decisions are well researched and thought through. Some people make emotional or affective (feeling-based) decisions like buying a car because it looks good, or buying a new dress because it's cute. For example, Toyota Canada has recently tried to differentiate the company based on emotion—remaking their image from boring high quality cars to fun, hip, and sporty high quality cars. Other people make impulse decisions, acting without giving a lot of thought to the decision—grabbing a chocolate bar at a grocery check-out counter or deciding to play a video game after walking past an arcade.

A framework developed by the Foote, Cone, and Belding advertising agency offers a useful way of looking at these different consumer decision processes.[3] The FCB grid (Figure 5.4) identifies thinking (cognition) and feeling (affect) as two primary approaches to consumer decision-making, for both high and low involvement decisions. The four quadrants of the resulting 2x2 matrix represent four common decision approaches: informative decisions, affective decisions, habitual or responsive decisions, and self-satisfaction or impulse decisions. These approaches differ in the order in which consumers learn about brands (evaluate brands and establish beliefs), feel about brands (emotional response or attachment), and act to purchase brands. The extended problem-solving model of Figure 5.1 is represented in quadrant 1. In quadrant 2, consumers have emotional responses or attachments to brands and then learn enough about them to decide whether or not to buy them. In quadrants 3 and 4, consumers act first, then evaluate or interpret (feelings) the outcomes. While the FCB model has been criticized for being simplistic, not accounting for consumer experience, and not accounting well for negative emotions, many marketers find it useful to include in segment profiles because of its strategy implications. Informative decisions (quadrant 1), for example, are aided by marketers: providing specific and detailed information; providing product demonstrations; and making direct comparisons to alternatives. Other communication strategy implications will be discussed in Chapter 12.

## WHAT INFLUENCES CONSUMER DECISIONS?

As well as understanding the mechanics of the consumer decision-making process, marketers try to ascertain what influences in consumers' lives affect this process. There are three main categories: internal, situational, and social influences. In Emma's case, for exam-

| | Thinking | | Feeling | |
|---|---|---|---|---|
| **High Involvement** | Informative | | Affective | |
| | Extended Problem Solving | Evaluation–Belief (learn) | Emotional Decision Making | Feeling |
| | Examples: Cars, Computers, High-end bikes | Feeling | Examples: Jewellery, Cosmetics, Fashion, Apparel, Motorcycles | Evaluation–Belief |
| | | Action | | Action |
| **Low Involvement** | Habitual | | Self-Satisfaction (Reaction) | |
| | Routine Problem Solving | Evaluation–Belief | Impulse Decisions | Action |
| | | Action | | Feeling |
| | Examples: Food, Household Items, Beverages | Feeling | Examples: Candy, Snacks, Liquor, Cigarettes | Evaluation–Belief |

**Figure 5.4** The FCB Grid

ple, the evaluative criteria she used to compare notebook computers and her feelings about each computer may have been influenced by such internal factors as her desire to be unique, such situational factors as her satisfaction with the information and service provided on the Apple Canada Web site, and such social influences as her prediction that her friends would be impressed when they saw her taking notes in class on a new notebook computer. Figure 5.5 shows the influences in the decision-making process and emphasizes that all of these factors work together to affect the ultimate choice each person makes. Let's consider how each of these three types of influence works, starting with internal factors.

**Figure 5.5** Influences on Consumer Decision Making

A number of different factors in consumers' lives influence the consumer decision-making process. Marketers need to understand these influences and which ones are important in the purchase process to make effective marketing decisions.

## Internal Influences on Consumer Decisions

People associate the textures of fabrics and other surfaces with product qualities, and some marketers are exploring how touch can be used in packaging to arouse consumer interest. Some new plastic containers for household beauty items incorporate "soft touch" resins that provide a soft, friction-like resistance when held. Focus group members who tested one such package for Clairol's new Daily Defense shampoo described the sensations as "almost sexy" and were actually reluctant to let go of the containers![4] That's a powerful impact for a piece of plastic. Now we will examine how internal factors relating to the way people absorb and interpret information influence the decision-making process.

**PERCEPTION Perception** is the process by which people select, organize, and interpret information from the outside world. We receive information in the form of *sensations*, the immediate response of our sensory receptors—eyes, ears, nose, mouth, and fingers—to such basic stimuli as light, colour, and sound. Our impressions about products often are based on their physical qualities. We try to make sense of the sensations we receive by interpreting them in light of our past experiences. For example, Emma chose the Apple notebook computer partly because of its distinctive design, which she associates with style and individuality.

The perception process has important implications for marketers because, as consumers absorb and make sense of the vast quantities of information competing for their attention, it is likely that they won't notice any one marketing message. And, if they do notice it, there's no guarantee that the meaning they give it will be quite the same one the marketer intended. The issues that marketers need to understand during this process include exposure, perceptual selection, and interpretation.

**Exposure** The stimulus must be within range of people's sensory receptors to be noticed. For example, the lettering on a billboard must be big enough for a passing motorist to read easily, or the message will be lost. Many people believe (falsely) that even messages they can't see will persuade them to buy advertised products. Claims about subliminal advertising involving messages hidden in ice cubes, among other places, have been surfacing since the 1950s. Although many consumers believe in subliminal advertising and are convinced this technique can get them to buy things they do not really want, there is little evidence of its use or even evidence that this technique would work even if it were used. Images that can be perceived are so effective that marketers really do not even consider subliminal effects. The Pepsi ad shown in Exhibit 5.5 is effective because the characters in the ice cubes are clearly visible.

**perception** The process by which people select, organize, and interpret information from the outside world.

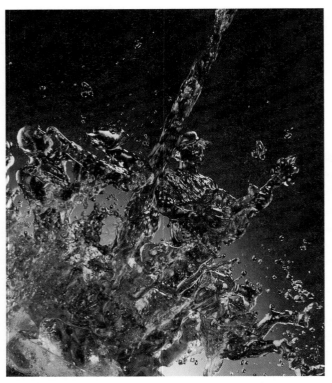

**Exhibit 5.5**

This Pepsi ad pokes fun at the idea of subliminal advertising—the images in the ice and splashes are not subliminal at all.

**Benetton**
www.benetton.com

**motivation** An internal state that drives us to satisfy needs by activating goal-oriented behaviour.

**hierarchy of needs** An approach that categorizes motives according to five levels of importance, the more basic needs being on the bottom of the hierarchy and the higher needs at the top.

**Perceptual Selection** Consumers choose to pay attention to some stimuli but not to others. Consumers are more likely to be aware of messages that speak to their current needs. A newspaper ad for a fast-food restaurant that would go unnoticed after lunch may grab your attention if you sneak a glance at the paper during a class that ends at lunchtime.

**Interpretation** Meaning is assigned to the stimulus. This meaning is influenced by prior associations the person has learned. The Benetton ad shown in Exhibit 5.6 is a great example of how these assumptions alter our interpretations. Although the ad shows two men handcuffed to each other, some people assumed that the black man was cuffed to the white man, and the company was the target of many complaints about racism after the ad appeared.

**MOTIVATION** **Motivation** is an internal state that drives us to satisfy needs. Once we activate a need, a state of tension exists that *drives* the consumer toward some *goal* that will reduce this tension by eliminating the need. For example, Emma began to experience a gap between her present state—having to rely on the computers on campus—and a desired state—having a computer that allows her to work at home and on campus. The need for a new notebook computer is activated, which motivates Emma to test and learn about different models, to talk with friends about their experiences with notebook computers, and finally to buy a new notebook computer.

Psychologist Abraham Maslow developed an influential approach to motivation.[5] Maslow formulated a **hierarchy of needs**, which categorizes motives according to five levels of importance, the more basic needs being on the bottom of the hierarchy and the higher needs at the top. The hierarchy suggests that before a person can meet needs in a given level, they must first (at least partially) meet the needs in the levels

UNITED COLORS OF BENETTON.

**Exhibit 5.6**

People's prior assumptions coloured their interpretations of this controversial ad.

**Figure 5.6** Maslow's Hierarchy of Needs and Related Advertising Slogans

below. As illustrated in Figure 5.6, this approach shows individuals starting at the lowest level with basic needs for food, clothing, and shelter and then progressing to higher levels to satisfy more complex needs, such as the need to be accepted by others or to feel good about themselves. Ultimately, people can reach the highest-level needs and they will be motivated to attain such goals as spiritual fulfillment. As the figure shows, if marketers understand the particular level of needs that is relevant to consumers in their target market, they can tailor their products and messages to point out how these needs can be satisfied. In 1969 Clayton Alderfer proposed a revision to Maslow's need hierarchy based on empirical evidence that the middle levels of Maslow's hierarchy overlap. Alderfer proposed three levels: Existence (concern with basic material existence requirements), Relatedness (desire we have for maintaining interpersonal relationships), and Growth (intrinsic desire for personal development). He also recognized that more than one need may be motivational at the same time and that if higher order needs are not satisfied, people will compensate with satisfying more lower order needs.[6]

**LEARNING** **Learning** is a change in behaviour after gaining information or experience. Learning about products can occur deliberately, as when we set out to gather information about different CD players before buying one brand. We also learn even when we are not trying. Consumers recognize many brand names and can hum many product jingles, for example, even for products they do not use. Psychologists who study learning have advanced several theories to explain the learning process and, because a major goal for marketers is to "teach" consumers to prefer their products, these perspectives are important. In this section, we'll briefly review the most important perspectives on how people learn.

**Behavioural Learning** **Behavioural learning theories** assume that learning takes place as the result of connections that form between events perceived by the individual. In one type of behavioural learning, **classical conditioning**, a person perceives two stimuli at about the same time. After a while, the person transfers his or her response from one stimulus to the other. For example, an ad shows a product and a breathtakingly beautiful scene, so that (the marketer hopes) you will transfer the positive feelings you get from looking at the scene to the advertised product. Another common form of behavioural learning is called **operant conditioning**, which occurs when people learn that their actions result in rewards or punishments. This feedback influences how they will respond in similar situations in the future. Just as a rat in a maze learns the route to a piece of cheese, consumers who receive a reward,

**learning** A relatively permanent change in behaviour caused by acquired information or experience.

**behavioural learning theories** Theories of learning that focus on how consumer behaviour is changed by external events or stimuli.

**classical conditioning** Learning that occurs when a stimulus eliciting a response is paired with another stimulus that initially does not elicit a response on its own but will cause a similar response over time because of its association with the first stimulus.

**operant conditioning** Learning that occurs as the result of rewards or punishments.

**Exhibit 5.7**

Premiums such as this one provide consumers with another reason to choose one brand over the other.

**stimulus generalization** Behaviour caused by a reaction to one stimulus that occurs in the presence of other similar stimuli.

**cognitive learning theory** A theory of learning that stresses the importance of internal mental processes and that views people as problem solvers, who actively use information from the world around them to master their environment.

**attitude** A learned predisposition to respond favourably or unfavourably to stimuli based on relatively enduring evaluations of people, objects, and issues.

**personality** The psychological characteristics that consistently influence the way a person responds to situations in the environment.

such as a prize in the bottom of a box of cereal, will be more likely to buy that brand again. The feedback acts as a *reinforcement* for the behaviour. Behaviour modification is similar to operant conditioning, only the reward is offered up-front to encourage the desired behaviour, such as the *Time* magazine incentive in Exhibit 5.7.

The learned associations in classical and operant conditioning also have a tendency to transfer to other similar stimuli in a process called **stimulus generalization**. This means that the good or bad feelings associated with a product will "rub off" on other products that resemble it. For example, some marketers create *product line extensions*, in which new products share the name of an established brand so that people's good feelings about the current product will transfer to the new one. Dole, which is associated with fruit, was able to introduce refrigerated juices and juice bars; Sun Maid branched out from raisins to raisin bread.

**Cognitive Learning** In contrast to behavioural theories of learning, **cognitive learning theory** views people as problem solvers who do more than passively react to associations between stimuli. Supporters of this viewpoint stress the role of creativity and insight during the learning process. One type of cognitive learning theory is *observational learning* (also called *vicarious learning*), which occurs when people watch the actions of others and note what happens to them as a result. They store these observations in memory and, at some later point, use the information to guide their own behaviour, especially when they admire or identify with these people in some way. Many promotional strategies, such as the ad in Exhibit 5.8, centre on endorsements by movie stars, athletes, and music idols whose fans have observed their successes.

**ATTITUDES** An **attitude** is a lasting evaluation of a person, object, or issue.[7] Consumers have attitudes toward very product-specific behaviours, such as using Crest toothpaste rather than Colgate, as well as toward more general consumption-related behaviours, such as how often to brush one's teeth.

A person's attitude has three components: affect, cognition, and behaviour. In a marketing context, *affect* is the overall feeling a person has about a product. *Cognition* is the beliefs and knowledge the person has about the product. *Behaviour* is what happens when the person takes action by buying or using the product.

Depending on the nature of the product, one of these three components—feeling, knowing, or doing—will be the dominant influence in creating an attitude toward a product. Affect is usually dominant for expressive products that we use to say something about ourselves (such as perfume), in which the way the product makes us feel determines our attitude toward it. Cognition may be more important for complex products, such as computers, which require us to process technical information. Behaviour often determines attitudes for commonly purchased, low-involvement items, such as chewing gum, for which we often form an attitude based simply on how the product tastes or performs.

**PERSONALITY Personality** is the set of unique psychological characteristics that consistently influences the way a person responds to situations in the environment. One adventure-seeking consumer may always be on the lookout for new experiences and cutting-edge products while another is happiest in familiar surroundings, using the same brands repeatedly. To appeal to thrill seekers who like to break the rules, Isuzu positioned its Rodeo sport utility vehicle as a car that lets a driver break the rules. Advertising was created to support this idea by showing kids jumping in mud puddles, running with scissors, and colouring out of the lines.[8] For marketers, identifying differences in personality contribute value to crafting marketing strategies. Some specific characteristics, called personality traits, relevant to marketing strategies include innovativeness, self-confidence, and sociability.

**Innovativeness** Innovativeness is the degree to which a person likes to try new things. Cutting-edge products, such as radical new hairstyles and fashions, might appeal to innovative people.

**Self-confidence** Self-confidence is the degree to which a person has a positive evaluation of his or her abilities, including the ability to make good product decisions. People who don't have much self-confidence are good candidates for services of image consultants, who assist in making the right choices.

**Sociability** Sociability is the degree to which a person enjoys social interaction. A sociable person might, for example, respond to entertainment-related products that claim to bring people together or make parties more fun.[9]

The notion that consumers buy products that are extensions of their personality traits makes sense. Marketers try to create *brand personalities* to appeal to different types of consumers. The ad for Benjamin Moore paints in Exhibit 5.9, for example, positions their brand of paint as a way of expressing personality and style.

How we feel about our own personalities strongly influences our purchasing decisions. We may buy a certain type of clothing or drink a particular brand of beer because we think it makes a statement about who we are. A person's **self-concept** is his or her attitude toward the self. The self-concept is composed of a mixture of beliefs about one's abilities, observations of one's own behaviour, and feelings (usually both positive and negative) about one's personal attributes, such as body type or facial features. The extent to which a person's self-concept is positive or negative can influence the products he or she buys.

In developing a new line of snack cakes, Sara Lee found that consumers who had a negative self-concept preferred portioned snack items because they felt they lacked the self-control to regulate how much they ate.[10] On the more positive side, *self-esteem advertising* attempts to stimulate positive feelings about the self.[11] This technique is used by Kellogg's to position Special K cereal as a lifestyle choice. Kellogg's attempts to counter negative self-esteem by making consumers feel good about themselves and feel good about the product, while promoting a healthy lifestyle. This message has recently been adapted to position Special K as part of a low carb lifestyle (Exhibit 5.10).

**AGE GROUPS** As we discussed in Chapter 3, a person's age is an important determinant of the product categories he or she wants. Many of us feel we have more in common with those of our own age because we share a common set of experiences and memories about cultural events, whether these involve World War II or Edgefest. Indeed, marketers of products from cookies to cars are banking on *nostalgia* to draw in customers, as people are attracted to products and services that remind them of past experiences. Winnipeg-based K-Tel International has successfully introduced several products that appeal to consumer nostalgia. Its online music store offers 1970s music classics from K.C. and the Sunshine Band and ABBA. Because of

You should see what's underneath.
The calcium in milk keeps bones strong and helps prevent osteoporosis.

**got milk?**

**Exhibit 5.8**

Canadian actor Kim Cattrall is one of many celebrities to endorse milk, helping consumers learn observationally.

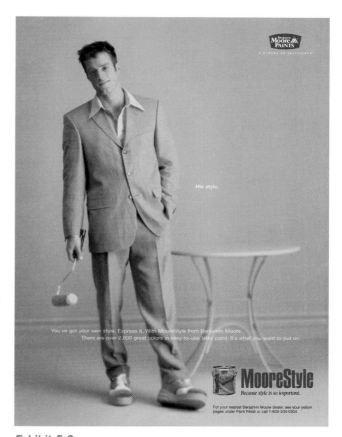

His style.

You've got your own style. Express it. With MooreStyle from Benjamin Moore. There are over 2,000 great colors in easy-to-use latex paint. It's what you want to put on.

**MooreStyle**
Because style is so important.

For your nearest Benjamin Moore dealer, see your yellow pages under Paint Retail or call 1-800-304-0304.

**Exhibit 5.9**

Personality and style can influence product choice.

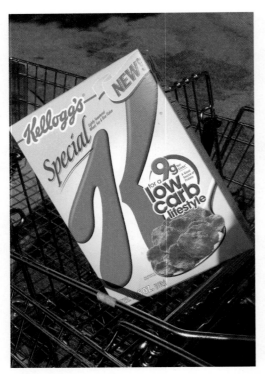

**Exhibit 5.10**

Promotion of healthy living and lifestyles is one way Kellogg's links positive consumer attitudes about themselves with positive attitudes towards the Special K brand.

**self-concept** An individual's self-image that is composed of a mixture of beliefs, observations, and feelings about personal attributes.

**family life cycle** A means of characterizing consumers based on the different family stages they pass through as they grow older.

**K-Tel International**
www.ktel.com

**Teencanadaonline.com**
www.teencanadaonline.com

**lifestyle** The pattern of living that determines how people choose to spend their time, money, and energy and that reflects their values, tastes, and preferences.

numerous calls from nostalgic consumers, the company also recently reintroduced one of its most successful products from the 1970s: the Patty Stacker, a plastic tube that helps consumers make perfect hamburger patties.[12] Many marketing strategies appeal to a specific age group, such as children, Nexus consumers, the middle-aged, or the elderly. As we age, our needs change. The young adult, who spends a lot of time in bars, clothing stores, or perhaps backpacking across Europe, grows into the newlywed, who focuses on setting up house—and perhaps anticipates the time when a baby's diapers and toys will fill it up. Canadian demographer David Foot has a series of books that look at the marketing and business implications of past and future demographic changes in North America—look for the most recent one in your school's library (Exhibit 5.11).

Young people are among the most enthusiastic users of the Internet and Canadians are among the highest Internet users in the world. According to one study, 62 percent of teenagers say they log on from home for 4.2 hours a week while 46 percent spend 2.3 hours a week using a computer outside the home.[13] For many teenagers, this activity has replaced "old-fashioned fun" such as watching the tube or hanging out at the mall. North American teens spend over $1 billion online each year so many firms are working hard to develop Web sites to capture their interest. Teencanadaonline.com is one site that offers teens a variety of online experiences. What do teens do online? Approximately three out of four do research and nearly two out of three use it for e-mail, while far less use the Internet for finding or buying products. For marketers, this means that the Internet may be a great way to get information about their goods and services to teens but not so good for sales. E-tailers are expecting teens to buy more online as they get older and have more discretionary income.

And so the process goes, until a person reaches old age, at which time his or her priorities may shift from saving for the kids' education to buying a retirement home. Therefore, our purchase preferences depend on our current position in the **family life cycle**—the life stages people typically pass through as they grow older. Marketers who understand the family life cycle can anticipate product needs. Campbell's soup, for example, understands that parents of "tweens" are very busy taking their kids to soccer, ballet, swimming, skating, and other lessons, often while working full time. Campbell's recently launched a new product aimed at mothers on the go. It is important to note that dramatic cultural changes affecting people's living arrangements have forced marketers to change their concept of the traditional family life cycle. This updated view takes into account single-parent families, childless couples, and homosexual relationships and considers the unique needs of each living situation when developing new products and communicating with these consumers.

**PSYCHOGRAPHICS** As discussed in Chapter 3, psychographics describe the activities, attitudes, interests, opinions, and lifestyles of consumers and these can have a great bearing on purchase decisions. A **lifestyle** is a pattern of tastes as expressed in a person's preferences for activities such as sports, interests such as music, and opinions on politics and religion. *Lifestyle marketing* is a strategy that recognizes that people can be grouped into common market segments based on similarities in lifestyle preferences.[14] Consumers often choose products, services, and activities that are associated with a certain lifestyle. As the D~Code researchers found out, there are some unique lifestyles that characterize Nexus consumers and lead to product preferences. Beer and car marketers often use lifestyle advertising to show consumers how particular brands fit with the way you live (or might like to live). Unilever Canada is now promoting its Becel margarine brand as part of a healthy living lifestyle. Television, print, and in-store advertising, sales promotions, mini-

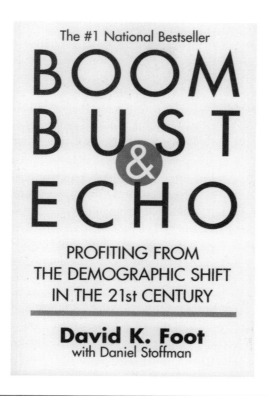

The #1 National Bestseller

# BOOM BUST & ECHO

### PROFITING FROM THE DEMOGRAPHIC SHIFT IN THE 21st CENTURY

## David K. Foot
with Daniel Stoffman

**Exhibit 5.11**

*Boom, Bust, and Echo* is a popular series of books that examines the marketing and business implications of demographic changes.

magazines, and a healthy-living Web site all focus on how Canadian consumers can improve their health.

## Situational Influences on Consumer Decisions

We've seen that such internal factors as how people perceive marketing messages, their motivation to acquire products, and their unique personalities influence the decisions they will make. In addition, when and where consumers shop influences their purchase choices. Important cues include people's physical surroundings, as well as the number and type of other consumers present in that situation. Dimensions of the physical environment, such as decor, smells, the "feel" of natural fabrics like wool versus synthetic ones like polyester, and even temperature, can significantly influence consumption. One study found that pumping certain odours into a casino actually increased the amount of money patrons fed into slot machines.[15]

**THE PHYSICAL ENVIRONMENT** It's no secret that people's moods and behaviours are strongly influenced by their physical surroundings. Despite all their efforts to pre-sell consumers through advertising, marketers know that the store environment influences many purchases. For example, consumers decide on about two of every three supermarket product purchases in the aisles. Therefore, the messages they receive at the time and their feelings about being in the store are important influences on their decisions.[16]

Two dimensions, *arousal* and *pleasure*, determine if a shopper will react positively or negatively to a store environment. In other words, the person's surroundings can be either dull or exciting (arousing), and either pleasant or not. Just because the environment is arousing doesn't necessarily mean it will be pleasant—we've all been in crowded, hot stores that are anything but. Maintaining an upbeat feeling in a pleasant context is one factor behind the success of theme parks such as Disney World, which try to provide consistent doses of carefully calculated stimulation to patrons.[17]

**Becel Heart Healthy Steps**
www.becelhearthealthysteps
.com

**Exhibit 5.12**

The Rainforest Cafe is a themed environment that integrates shopping and eating.

**West Edmonton Mall**
www.westedmall.com

The importance of these surroundings explains why many retailers are combining two favourite consumer activities, shopping and eating, into elaborate *themed environments.* Eating out is an important form of out-of-home entertainment for many consumers, and innovative firms are scrambling to offer customers a chance to eat, buy, and be entertained all at once. The West Edmonton Mall, the largest shopping and entertainment complex in the world, provides its customers with a themed environment including over 800 stores, 110 restaurants, 26 movie theatres, a casino, and a large indoor amusement park. A lot of the appeal of these themed environments is that there are plenty of interesting things to look at while eating a meal or shopping. In addition to visual stimuli, other sensory cues can influence consumers—one reason why the Rainforest Cafes in Vancouver and Toronto offer simulated thunder and lightning storms in addition to rainforest scenery in their restaurants (Exhibit 5.12). Research supports the assertion that sounds and music can affect eating behaviour—one study found that diners who listened to loud, fast music ate more and faster than those who listened to classical music.[18]

Indeed, a growing recognition of the important role that is played by a store or restaurant's audio environment has created a new market niche; some companies are selling musical collections tailored to different activities. These include RCA Victor's "Classical Music for Home Improvements" and Sony Classics' "Cyber Classics," which are billed as music specifically for computer hackers to listen to while programming. Sony's "Extreme Classics," packaged just for bungee jumpers, is claimed to be the "loudest and most dangerous music ever written."[19]

*In-store displays* are a commonly used device to attract attention in the store environment. Although most displays consist of simple racks that dispense the product or related coupons, some include elaborate performances and scenery.[20] For example:

- Sunlight Detergent: A plastic mud puddle on the floor of the isle next to the Sunlight product, with the message "go ahead, get dirty." Consumers stop to look at and avoid stepping in what looks like brown liquid and are directed to the Sunlight product display.

- Quebec Frozen Food Association: A cardboard display showing a man peering around the corner plays the following message when a consumer is in front of it: "Psst! Yes, you. You've got to taste our frozen foods. They're so good. They're so fresh. And they're really practical."[21]

- Timex: A still-ticking watch sits in the bottom of a filled aquarium.

- Kellogg's Corn Flakes: A button with a picture of Cornelius the Rooster is placed within the reach of children near the corn flakes. When a child presses the button, they hear the rooster cock-a-doodle-do.

Advertisers also are being more aggressive about hitting consumers with their messages, wherever they may be. *Place-based media* is a growing specialized medium that targets consumers in airports, doctors' offices, campuses, or health clubs. Montreal-based Zoom Media targets the 18 to 34 age group with washroom ads, including ones that "speak" a taped message when someone stands in front of the ad.[22]

**TIME** Another important situational factor is how much time one has to make a decision. Time is one of consumers' most limited resources. We talk about "making time" or "spending time," and we are frequently reminded that "time is money." Many consumers believe they are more pressed for time than ever before.[23] This sense of time poverty makes consumers responsive to marketing innovations that allow them to save time, including such services as one-hour photo processing, bagged salads and other prepared foods in supermarkets, and ordering products on the Internet.[24] CDPlus is a Canadian company that sells music over the Internet. The company has been successful because consumers can log on to the CDPlus Web page, browse through thousands of titles, listen to selections from many of them, and order and pay for them—all without setting foot inside a store. This saves the customer time and the "store" is always open. Emma, our decision maker buying a notebook computer, appreciated the fact that she was able to save time by searching the Internet for product information and buying her computer online.

**CDPlus**
www.cdplus.com

## Social Influences on Consumer Decisions

Our discussion of consumers so far has focused on factors that influence us as individuals, such as the way we learn about products. Although we are all individuals, we are also members of many groups that, whether we realize it or not, influence our buying decisions. Families, friends, and classmates often influence our decisions, as do larger groups with which we identify, such as ethnic groups and political parties. Now let's consider how social influences such as culture, social class, and influential friends and acquaintances affect the consumer decision-making process.

CULTURE **Culture** is a society's personality. It is the values, beliefs, customs, and tastes, as well as the products and services produced or valued by a group of people. Cultural values are deeply held beliefs about right and wrong ways to live.[25] Canadian values include freedom and autonomy, mixed with a strong sense of community that is expressed through social institutions, such as our medical system.[26] Canadians also value education, and the bilingual and multicultural nature of Canada has made Canadians respectful of people's differences.

**culture** The values, beliefs, customs, and tastes that a group of people value.

A consumer's culture influences his or her buying decisions, and a renewed sense of nationalism has led many marketers to recognize the value of identifying their products specifically with Canada and Canadian cultural symbols.[27] For example, when Zellers introduced Martha Stewart products in Canada for the first time, ads showed Martha with a Mountie saying, "I think I'm going to like Canada." Post used a Canadian flag with a Shreddie in the middle instead of a maple leaf when the company introduced Maple Crunch Shreddies, and Molson used a moose in its ads to introduce Miller Lite beer to the Canadian market.[28] Another Molson product, Canadian, not only builds on national pride with its brand name, but also has consistently been promoted with culturally based, patriotic images and ads—such as the "I am Canadian" campaign that featured a young man ranting about how being Canadian is different than being American (Exhibit 5.13). The ad for Canoe.ca in Exhibit 5.14 also tries to appeal to the Canadian identity.

**Molson Canadian**
www.iam.ca
**Canoe Network**
www.canoe.ca

As the Canoe.ca ad shows, identifying and understanding differences between Canadian and American consumers is often an important issue for Canadian marketers, especially those working in U.S.-owned companies. U.S. management may favour using a U.S. marketing strategy in Canada, assuming that cultural differences are small and that Canadian consumers will respond the same way that American consumers do. In many ways, Canadian and American consumers are similar. However, as Lever Pond's found out in marketing its Degree deodorant product, Canadian consumers can be sometimes be quite different from their U.S. counterparts—its successful, humorous U.S. advertising campaign was not seen as funny by Canadian

**Exhibit 5.13**

Molson Canadian links its brand to Canadian culture.

WHAT COULD BE MORE CANADIAN
THAN SHOPPING BY CANOE?

www.canoe.ca
SHOP.CANOE.CA & MORE

In a country where cold weather and long line ups dampen more than our spirits, shopping on-line at **Shop.canoe.ca** just makes a lot of sense. It's smart shopping. **Shop.canoe.ca** offers convenient one-stop-shopping, with items such as clothing, books, CD's, giftware, computers, sporting goods and so much more. You can plan and make your purchases directly from a Canadian on-line retailer, 24 hours a day, 7 days a week, all from the comfort of your own home or office. Plus, all the stores listed on **Shop.canoe.ca** sell in Canadian dollars and ship to Canadian addresses which means no exchange rates, or duties to pay. So forget about shop 'til you drop and **Shop.canoe.ca**, instead at www.canoe.ca. Canada's Internet Network.

CANOE IS A QUEBECOR COMPANY.

**Exhibit 5.14**

The use of cultural symbols can be an effective way to connect with consumers.

consumers and had to be adapted to a more Canadian style of humour—self-deprecating and low-key. The "Stress" campaign that eventually ran in Canada showed stressful situations and a meter on the screen registering the stress levels. One ad showed a man in a bar, who is approached by a number of people who ask, "Remember me?": when a pregnant woman asks the question, the stress meter gives a maximum reading.[29]

Having spent considerable time in both cultures, author Elliott Ettenberg observes that Canadians are fort people and Americans are homesteaders. The Hudson's Bay Company helped settle Canada and the country was populated by people who wanted the security and safety of living in a fort. The British North America Act promised Canadians law, order, and good government—the essentials for a fort society to grow. Canadians strive to fit in, and prize collaboration, consensus, and compromise—also important virtues in a fort society. Ettenberg suggests that this has resulted in Canadian management being more fearful of change and being more controlling of expenditures. On the other hand, entrepreneurial homesteaders settled the United States—exploring, staking a claim to land, building a home, defending it by force, and then inviting friends and relatives to build nearby. The American constitution promises life, liberty, and the pursuit of happiness—the essentials for an entrepreneurial homesteader to succeed. Americans live to stand out and value leadership, insight, and action, resulting in management styles that are aggressive, focused on competitive advantage, and where quick decisions are made with little collaboration, committing full resources to experimental projects. You may not agree with Mr. Ettenberg, but it is one perspective that suggests why Canadian and American cultures differ in perspectives that could have implications for consumer decision-making.[30]

Many American multinational companies operating in Canada have chosen to create separate Canadian Web sites despite the fact that the Internet is a global medium. The reasons why companies such as Microsoft, Nabisco, Kellogg's, Kraft, and Pepsi-Cola have Canadian Web sites include: a need to serve consumers in both English and French; the existence of different products or models (as in the case of the Ford Motor Company); and the desire to cater to the unique needs of Canadian consumers. The manager of Microsoft's Canadian Web site argues "to properly service this environment, we feel it necessary to have a Web site representative of Canada's uniqueness."[31]

Canadian marketers also need to understand differences in culture between French Canadians and English Canadians and how these differences should impact marketing strategies. For instance, Bell Mobility found out that there were differences between French and English consumers with respect to their cell phone behaviour. English Canadians liked certain practical aspects of the cell phones while French Canadian consumers were much more interested in being able to use the phones in minor emergency situations. Bell had originally used the same campaign in both French and English Canada, with the only difference being language. But after the English campaign did poorly in Quebec, it hired a Quebec ad agency to do a uniquely French ad and consumers responded well to it.[32] Similarly, Wampole Canada launched maple-flavoured vitamin C tablets in Quebec only. The company has found that Quebec consumers prefer sweeter products and are more willing to try something new.[33] When Krispy Kreme entered the Quebec market it consulted with the Provincial language office to ensure they used the correct term—beignet (doughnut) instead of the less formal beigne (donut)—to be consistent with their English use of the term doughnut.[34] General Motors recently discovered the importance of understanding the French-Canadian culture when it learned from Quebec focus group participants that the name "Lacrosse" that it was considering for the Canadian version of a Buick sedan was slang among Quebec youth for masturbation.[35]

SUBCULTURES A **subculture** is a group, coexisting with other groups in a larger culture, whose members share a distinctive set of beliefs or characteristics. Each of us belongs to many subcultures including religious groups, ethnic groups, and regional groups, as well as those that form around media creations such as Trekkies (fans of *Star Trek*).

For Canadian marketers, some of the most important subcultures to consider are racial and ethnic groups, because Canada is such a diverse society. Many Canadian consumers identify strongly with their heritage and are influenced by products that appeal to this aspect of their identities. Additionally, the actual needs and wants of consumers in different subcultures may be very different. For example, research has found that 87 percent of Chinese Canadian homes have an automobile, compared to 72 percent of other Canadians. Seventy-one percent of Chinese Canadians prefer to buy new cars over used, and 81 percent pay with cash when purchasing a car.[36] These are some of the reasons why automakers, such as Ford Canada, have recognized the importance of the Chinese Canadian market. Several Canadian firms are now practicing **multicultural marketing** by successfully targeting consumers in several subcultures. For example, Burger King Canada has successfully targeted marketing efforts to Italian Canadians and Chinese Canadian consumers.[37] TELUS Mobility is targeting the Indian community in Canada (more than 900 000 people) by developing ads (Exhibit 5.15) that celebrate key religious festivals and using creative concepts that straddle the Indian and Canadian cultures (commonly observed behaviour within the targeted audience of people under 35) through "Hinglish," a colloquiel mix of Hindi and English.[38]

As briefly described in Chapter 3, marketers are only just beginning to recognize that men and women have different needs, beliefs, values, and approaches to purchase decisions. Female crash-test dummies, for example, only became standard in 2002 and life jackets designed for female physiology only became mass-produced in 2001. A study by the Television Bureau of Canada recently found that 70 percent of advertisements directed at women are virtually ignored, yet more women than men said advertising was important to them. When men complain about organizations, it is

**subculture** A group within a society whose members share a distinctive set of beliefs, characteristics, or common experiences.

**multicultural marketing** The practice of recognizing and targeting the distinctive needs and wants of one or more ethnic subcultures.

**Exhibit 5.15**
TELUS developed ads such as this one to appeal to the multicultural nature of its customers.

# Good or Bad Decision?

Marketers play an important role in helping consumers understand and act on their wants, but they can also influence expectations, and demonstrate attitudes and beliefs that not only reflect, but also help shape cultures and subcultures. Media and advertising, in particular, have been at the heart of arguments and discussions concerning the cause and influencers of eating disorders. Female models such as Kate Moss look emaciated and are underweight while male models are overly muscular and hairless (Exhibit 5.16). An intriguing new study among Fijian adolescent girls, published in the *British Journal of Psychiatry*,[43] has shown that prolonged exposure to television significantly increases disordered eating attitudes and behaviour. Significant increases of eating disorder behaviour such as self-induced vomiting to control weight were seen when compared to a control group and this behaviour was not associated with body mass index, indicating that the subjects' perceived rather than actual weight predicted purging behaviour. Can marketers and advertising campaigns be blamed for eating disorders and falsified body perceptions? Should marketers have greater responsibility for promoting a positive body image? Why or why not?

about inferior products or uninformed salespeople. When women complain, it is about bad treatment because of gender—being ignored or talked down to. Joanne Thomas Yaccato, author of *The 80% Minority: Reaching the Real World of Women Consumers*, suggests that corporate Canada does not understand the multi-dimensional nature of women's lives and have a disconnect around the importance corporate soul plays in their decision-making process. In the late 1990s, RBC Financial Group embarked on creating a "gender intelligent sales force" taking four years to train 1500 account managers on how to meet the financial needs of women. RBC saw a 10 percent increase in marketing share and a 29 percent increase in customer satisfaction with female entrepreneur clients.[39] International insurance company Axa developed a highly successful women-focused insurance brand in Quebec called Assurelle that included car insurance with free roadside assistance 24/7 anywhere in Canada or the United States—a program launched in a campaign with a platform "we treat you right."[40] Marketers are also focusing more on men. New men's magazines such as *Toro, Razor, Rev, Menz,* and *Umm* provide male-oriented content and enable marketers to specifically target men.[41]

In a country as large as Canada, regional subcultures also exist and influence consumer behaviour. For Tim Hortons, regional differences can be important in deciding what products to offer in their restaurants. Sugar pies, baked beans, and toast are available only in Quebec; Ontarians love fritters; and in some communities in British Columbia, chocolate croissants are a popular menu item.[42]

## SPOTLIGHT ON REAL PEOPLE  Monsterpin.com

Twenty-five-year-old business grad Dietrich Wedegaertner wants to help groups develop subcultures. His company, Monsterpin, creates on-line communities for groups and organizations wanting to more easily keep in touch with each other, share information, and interact. Starting with Web sites for students in Victoria and Vancouver, Wedegaertner plans to take his community concept to universities and colleges across the nation, and then expand into providing online community resources for other interest groups. While some trade can take place (e.g., textbook exchange, classifieds, and housing ads), the community's main function is to facilitate direct information exchange on relevant subjects, such as love and relationships, teacher and course evaluations ratings (similar to ratemyprofes-

sors.com), and class and course notes. Members have control over what content they see and about what content updates they will be notified about; they generate most of the content to ensure relevancy; the community establishes the rules and policies for what content is appropriate. By creating the forum for communities to develop, Wedegaertner hopes to increase student's sense of community with their peers, school, and college or university. This is a business, however, and while community membership is free, Monsterpin creates revenue by providing access to specific market segments for businesses interested in marketing to community members, or seeking information or feedback from community members.

1. Describe how the Monsterpin concept might help subcultures develop.
2. What decision-making process might consumers use in deciding whether to be a member of a Monsterpin online community? What internal and social influences might influence this decision?
3. What other communities do you think could benefit from having an online forum for interaction?

**SOCIAL CLASS Social class** is the overall rank of people in a society. People within the same social class work in similar occupations, have similar income levels, and usually share common tastes in clothing, decorating styles, and leisure activities. These people also share many political and religious beliefs, as well as ideas about valued activities and goals.[44]

Many products and stores are designed to appeal to people in a specific social class.[45] Working-class consumers tend to evaluate products in more utilitarian terms, such as sturdiness or comfort, rather than in style or fashionability. They are less likely to experiment with new products or styles, such as modern furniture or coloured appliances, because they tend to prefer predictability to novelty.[46]

Luxury goods often serve as **status symbols**, visible markers that provide a way for people to flaunt their membership in higher social classes (or at least to make others believe they do). Although ostentatious products fell out of favour in the 1990s, we are witnessing a resurgence of consumer interest in luxury goods. Companies such as Hermès International, LVMH Hennessy, Louis Vuitton, and Baccarat are enjoying sales gains of 13 to 16 percent, as affluent consumers are once again indulging their desires for the finer things in life (Exhibit 5.17).[47]

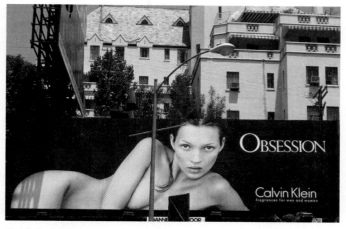

**Exhibit 5.16**

Calvin Klein, like many other fashion and clothing companies, uses provocative imagery to promote its products. Many people believe that media and advertising have been major influences on cultural and subcultural beliefs.

**social class**   The overall rank or social standing of groups of people within a society according to the value assigned to such factors as family background, education, occupation, and income.

**status symbols**   Products that consumers purchase to signal membership in a desirable social class.

## GROUP BEHAVIOUR

Anyone who has ever "gone along with the crowd" knows that people act differently in groups than they do on their own. There are several reasons for this. With more people in a group, it becomes less likely that any one member will be singled out for attention, and normal restraints on behaviour may be reduced. Decisions made by groups differ from those made by each individual. In many cases, group members show a greater willingness to consider riskier alternatives following group discussion than they would if each member made his or her own decision with no discussion.[48]

Even shopping behaviour changes when people do it in groups. For example, people who shop with at least one other person tend to make more unplanned purchases, buy more, and cover more areas of a store than those who go alone.[49] Group members may be convinced to buy something to gain the approval of the others, or they may simply be exposed to more products and stores by pooling information with the group. For these reasons, retailers are well advised to encourage group-shopping activities.

Most of us enjoy belonging to groups, and we may even derive comfort from knowing what others are thinking or doing as we try to make up our own minds. Group membership has entered cyberspace, as "netizens" around the world rapidly are forming virtual communities.[50] Communities such as Tripod and Geocities allow people to chat about their mutual interests, help one another with inquiries and suggestions, gain purchasing power, and, perhaps most importantly from a marketer's perspective, get suggestions for new products and services.

**Tripod**
www.tripod.com
**Geocities**
www.geocities.com

## Reference Groups

A **reference group** is a set of people a consumer wants to please or imitate. Unlike a larger culture, the "group" can be composed of one person, such as your spouse, or someone you've never met, such as a rock singer like Sarah McLachlan. The group can be small, such as your immediate family, or it could be a large organization, such as Greenpeace. The idea that reference groups can have a strong influence on consumer purchase decisions was the motivation behind a recent promotion by Coors. The beer company partnered with

**reference group**   An actual or imaginary individual or group that has a significant effect on an individual's evaluations, aspirations, or behaviour.

**Exhibit 5.17**
Louis Vuitton products are status symbols among affluent young women.

*Maxim* magazine targeting Canadian males 19 to 24 and the reference group was the other people at the party Coors was holding in Toronto with *Maxim*.

Consumers often change their behaviour to gain acceptance into a particular reference group. **Conformity** is at work when a person changes as a reaction to real or imagined group pressure. For example, someone preparing to go out to a club with a new group of friends may choose to wear clothing similar to what they think the others will be wearing to be sure of acceptance.

Home shopping parties, epitomized by the Tupperware party, capitalize on group pressures to boost sales.[51] A company representative makes a sales presentation to a group of people, who have gathered in the home of a friend or acquaintance. Participants model the behaviour of others who can provide them with information about how to use certain products, especially since the home party is likely to be attended by a relatively homogeneous group (e.g., neighbours or co-workers). Pressures to conform may be particularly intense and may escalate as more and more group members "cave in" (a process sometimes termed the *bandwagon effect*). Canadian companies such as Kids Only and Weekenders have no doubt benefited from the bandwagon effect by using home shopping parties to distribute their products.

**conformity** A change in beliefs or actions as a reaction to real or imagined group pressure.

Some of the strongest pressures to conform come from our **sex roles**: society's expectations of the appropriate attitudes, behaviours, and appearance for men and women. These assumptions about the proper roles of women and men, flattering or not, are deeply ingrained in marketing communications.[52] Many products take on masculine or feminine attributes, and consumers often associate them with one sex or the other.[53] For example, for many years, hardware stores were seen as "masculine," so much so that Home Hardware based in St. Jacobs, Ontario, had the advertising slogan, "Home of the Handyman." But at the end of the 1990s, Home Hardware replaced its slogan of 25 years when it was realized that the company had equal numbers of male and female customers in their stores. Their new slogan, "Help is close to home," avoided any sex role references.[54]

**sex roles** Society's expectations about the appropriate attitudes, behaviours, and appearance for men and women.

## Opinion Leaders

**opinion leader** A person who is frequently able to influence others' attitudes or behaviours by virtue of his or her active interest and expertise in one or more product categories.

Some individuals are particularly likely to influence others' product decisions. An **opinion leader** is a person who influences others' attitudes or behaviours.[55] Opinion leaders are valuable information sources, because they are usually knowledgeable about a product category and, unlike commercial endorsers who are paid to represent the interests of just one company, they have no "axe to grind." In addition, opinion leaders often are among the first to buy new products, so they absorb much of the risk. This experience reduces uncertainty for others who are not as courageous. And, although company-sponsored communications tend to focus exclusively on the positive aspects of a product, this hands-on experience makes opinion leaders more likely to impart *both* positive and negative information about product performance.

Think about the people you know on campus who may be opinion leaders when it comes to setting trends in fashion or being the first to get a new CD. One study identified a group of male students who were opinion leaders for fashion products on campus. These men shared some important characteristics[56]:

- They were socially active.
- They appeared conscious and narcissistic.

- They were involved in rock culture.
- They were heavy readers of magazines, including *Playboy* and *Sports Illustrated*.
- They were likely to own more clothing in a broader range of styles than other students.

Related to the concept of opinion leaders are market mavens—people who are very knowledgeable about a product category such as cars, computers, or fashion and are sought by others for advice. They may not have direct experience with a particular brand, but provide general buying advice to those who ask them.

## PEER-TO-PEER E-COMMERCE

One of the most exciting aspects of the new digital world is that consumers can interact directly with other people who live around the block or around the world. Peer-to-peer, or as it is more commonly referred to, **consumer-to-consumer (C2C) e-commerce** refers to online communications and purchases that occur among individuals without directly involving the manufacturer or retailer. Picture a small group of local collectors who meet once a month at a local diner to discuss their shared interests over coffee. Now multiply that group by thousands, and include people from all over the world who are united through the Internet by a shared passion for sports memorabilia, Harley-Davidson motorcycles, or refrigerator magnets—all are participating in C2C e-commerce.

Yes, group membership has entered cyberspace in a big way, as "netizens" around the world are forming virtual communities of consumption. These are groups of people who meet online and share their enthusiasm for a product, recording artist, art form, celebrity, and so on. These groups allow consumers to remain anonymous while they form around an incredibly diverse set of interests—everything from Barbie dolls to fine wine. Marketers who target these online communities know that members are more likely to buy products that other group members find of value.

It has been estimated that over 40 million people worldwide participate in virtual communities. These loyal consumers help one another evaluate the quality of choices in the marketplace.

Companies such as Warner Bros. also are actively promoting virtual communities related to their products. The company noticed that many fans of Bugs Bunny, Batman, and the Tasmanian Devil were including images and sound clips on their personal Web pages and then selling ad space on those pages. Instead of suing its fans, Warner created an online community called ACME City that builds homepages for registered members.[57] Let's look at some specific types of brand communities that are shaking up the ways businesses operate.

## Virtual Communities

Virtual communities come in different forms including multi-user dungeons; rooms, rings, and lists; boards; auction sites; product rating sites; and protest sites.

**MULTI-USER DUNGEONS** Originally, these communities were environments where players of fantasy games met. Now they refer to any cyber environment in which people socially interact through role and game playing. In a game called EverQuest, more than 50 000 people around the globe pay to roam around a fantasyland in cyberspace. This game combines the stunning graphics of advanced gaming with the social scene of a chat room. Players create a character as a virtual alter ego, which may be a wise elf or a backstabbing rogue. If a character is powerful enough, it can sell on eBay for $1000 or more! Players can travel around this cyberworld in groups of six. In many cases they settle into a regular group and spend two to three hours each night online with the same people. One couple even held a virtual wedding while playing. The bride reported, "We only had one death, a guest who was killed by the guards. It was a lot of fun."[58]

Realizing that the average online player logs 17 hours per week, firms such as Sony, Microsoft, and Sega are building virtual worlds to get a piece of the action. As one game

**consumer-to-consumer (C2C) e-commerce** Communications and purchases that occur among individuals without directly involving the manufacturer or retailer.

**EverQuest**
http://eqlive.station.sony.com/

company executive put it, "This is not a genre of game but a breakthrough new medium. It provides a completely new social, collaborative, shared experience. We're basically in the Internet community business."[59] This new medium opens up many possibilities for marketers, since participants often render judgments on a variety of topics such as hot new bands or movies that can influence the opinions of other participants.

**ROOMS, RINGS, AND LISTS** These virtual communities include Internet relay chat (IRC), otherwise known as chat rooms. Rings are organizations of related homepages and lists are groups of people on a single e-mail list who share information. For example, ICQ maintains rings devoted to many topics such as music, electronics, and genealogy. Clubzone.com is a Vancouver-based online community targeting club goers. Ryze.com is a North American networking community of professionals.

**BOARDS** Boards are online communities organized around interest-specific electronic bulletin boards. Active members read and post messages sorted by date and subject. There are boards devoted to musical groups, movies, wine, cigars, cars, comic strips, and even fast-food restaurants. Ponder the case of Widespread Panic. The band has never had a music video on MTV or cracked the Billboard Top 200. But it's one of the top 40 touring bands in the United States. How did it get to be so successful? Simple—the group built a virtual community of fans. Fans send messages to its recording studio and hardcore followers can find out vital information, such as what band members ate for lunch.[60]

**AUCTION SITES** Auction sites let consumers buy, sell, and barter with each other. The best-known auction site is eBay, where you can buy anything from a rare Beatles poster to an antique iron. At one point, an eBay member even tried to sell a human kidney ("You can choose either kidney…. Of course, only one is for sale, as I need the other one to live"). Bidding went to over $5.7 million before the company ended the auction.[61]

**PRODUCT RATING SITES** Sites such as Deja.com give people a forum for their opinions and let them rate products.[62] One product-rating site called Epinions.com even rates and rewards product reviewers. Anyone can sign up to give advice on products that fit into the site's 12 categories, and shoppers can rate the reviews on a scale from not useful to very useful. Reviewers earn royalties of between $1 to $3 for every 10 times their review is read. When recommendations result in a sale, the company earns a referral fee from merchants. One of the site's founders observes that the site relies on a "web of trust," and he claims, "It mimics the way word of mouth works in the real world."[63]

**PROTEST SITES** Protest sites let consumers "vent" by sharing negative experiences they have had with companies. In some cases these protest sites pose a public relations problem for companies, so companies try to eliminate them. Dunkin' Donuts bought a site from a disgruntled customer who created the Web page to complain after he could not get skim milk for his coffee.[64] And sometimes these sites spread untrue information about corporations. For example, rumours began spreading on newsgroups that Procter & Gamble's Febreze cleaning product killed dogs. In a pre-emptive move to minimize problems before they started, P&G registered numerous Web site names so no one else could—including febrezekillspet.com, febrezesucks.com, and ihateprocterandgamble.com.[65] P&G now maintains a page on its Web site dedicated to fighting rumours.[66]

**Procter & Gamble Rumours**
www.pg.com/company/
who_we_are/
trademark_pgrumor.jhtml

In the last part of this chapter, we've seen how other people, such as friends or even casual acquaintances, influence our purchase decisions. We've considered how our preferences are shaped by our group memberships, by our desire to please or be accepted by others, even by the way we think we're "supposed" to act as men or women. We've explored why some people are more influential than others in affecting our product preferences. In addition to the influences exerted on each of us by virtue of being members of a culture, a social class, and several subcultures, it's easy to see that group affiliations exert a powerful pull on us as we make marketplace decisions. It's clear that people truly are "social animals," and to understand consumer behaviour we need to consider internal factors such as personality, situational factors such as the amount of time available to decide, and social factors such as group identity to get a handle on what we *thought* was the relatively simple business of making a decision.

# Real People, Real Decisions

### ▶ **How It Worked Out** at Mega Bloks

Michel Bendayan and other senior Mega Bloks managers decided to re-enter the Japanese market using a large strategic partner (alternative D3). They approached Bandai, the largest toy manufacturer in Japan and one of the top toy manufacturers worldwide. Bandai was well known for its character-licensed toys, which included lines of Power Rangers, Masked Riders, Ultraman, and Anpanman products. Bandai, however, did not make construction toys, so even though the company is much larger than Mega Bloks, the partnership held some advantages for Bandai. The Bandai-Mega Bloks partnership was the largest distribution deal Mega Bloks had ever done. Because the consumers were thought to be highly character oriented, because Bandai had experience and licenses for key Japanese characters, and because there were concerns that the western culture themes of the current Mega Bloks might not be desired by Japanese consumers, Bendayan and his colleagues decided to jointly develop two new product lines with Bandai (alternative P3). Using many of the same components as North American products, the preschool line featured Anpanman characters and was sold in tubs and resealable bags for ease of clean up and storage. The other line targeted boys 5 to 8 with more action oriented characters and themes, and was offered in more standard boxes. The intent was to develop a foundation of Japanese-themed products that would be the base from which top selling world lines could be added.

The preschool line exceeded sales expectations but the product targeted at 5- to 8- year-olds did not. Bendayan thought that this might have mostly been the result of the licensed characters being "old"—they get refreshed every year and manufacturers have to hit a much faster production cycle than in North America to keep abreast of the trends, but it might also have been because there were fewer buckets and resealable bags in the line. There was also some consumer concerns about the preschool line—Bandai had thought that the small sized building blocks would be suitable for 3- to 5-year-olds, but feedback suggested the bricks were too small for this age group. Similar blocks were targeted to 5- to 7-year-olds in North America. Thus while Bandai understood the general Japanese toy market, it did not fully understand the construction toy market. This joint learning has fuelled the development of a new line of construction blocks targeting 5- to 8-year-old Japanese boys.

# CHAPTER SUMMARY

### 1. Explain why understanding consumer behaviour is important to organizations.

The marketing concept focuses on satisfying consumers' wants and needs. For organizations to succeed at this, they need to understand the processes that occur before, during, and after the selection of goods or services.

### 2. Explain the prepurchase, purchase, and postpurchase activities consumers engage in when making decisions.

Consumer decisions differ greatly, ranging from habitual, almost mindless, repeat (low-involvement) purchases to complex, extended problem-solving activities for important, risky (high-involvement) decisions. First, consumers recognize that there is a problem to be solved. The search for information in memory and in the marketplace reduces the risk of making a wrong choice. The set of alternatives, those that will be actively considered, are judged based on various dimensions or evaluative criteria. Consumers may simplify the process by using mental shortcuts or heuristics. Following the purchase, consumer perceptions of product quality lead to satisfaction or dissatisfaction.

### 3. Describe how internal factors influence consumers' decision-making processes.

A number of internal factors influence consumer decisions. Perception is how consumers select, organize, and interpret stimuli. Consumers must first be exposed to the marketing communications. To prevent sensory overload, consumers practise perceptual selectivity; that is, they are selective in their attention by focusing on stimuli. Consumers differ in interpretation of stimuli, because the meaning assigned is based on individuals' prior experiences or beliefs. Marketers should understand that consumers act because they are motivated to achieve goals, which may depend on which level of needs is currently satisfied. Learning is a change in behaviour that results from information or experience. Behavioural learning results from external events such as rewards, punishments, or the previous pairing of stimuli. Behavioural learning may result in stimulus generalization in which attitudes toward a brand or company may be transferred to other products, such as product line extensions. Cognitive learning refers to internal mental activity and includes observational learning in which behaviour results from imitation of the observed behaviour of socially attractive others.

An attitude is a lasting evaluation of a person, object, or issue. There are three components to attitudes: affective, cognitive, and behavioural. Marketers design products consistent with consumer attitudes or seek to change attitudes, frequently focusing on one of the three components.

Marketing strategy should also consider consumers' psychological makeup or personality. Personality traits, such as innovativeness, self-confidence, and sociability may be used to develop market segments. Marketers seek to understand a consumer's self-concept to develop product attributes that match some aspect of the consumer's self.

Both the age of consumers and their family life cycle classification are strongly related to consumption preferences. Consumer behaviour may also differ based on lifestyles, thus creating different marketing segmentation opportunities. Similarly, the use of psychographics in which people are grouped according to activities, interests, and opinions may explain reasons for purchasing products.

### 4. Describe how situational factors at the time and place of purchase may influence consumer behaviour.

The physical and social environments at the time of purchase create differences in consumer behaviour. Retailers often create themed environments and in-store displays to influence customers to make purchases. Time (or the lack of it) influences which products are selected and characteristics of the decision process.

5. **Describe how consumers' relationships with other people influence their decision-making processes.**

Consumers' overall priorities for products and activities are determined by the culture of the society in which they live. Consumer decisions may be influenced by cultural values, or the enduring beliefs of the culture. In Canada, differences between French Canadian and English Canadian consumers often influence marketing strategies. Consumers within the same culture may also be members of different religious, ethnic, or regional subcultures. Many Canadian companies practise multicultural marketing by targeting their marketing strategies to consumers from various ethnic subcultures.

Social class and reference groups are other types of social influence that have an impact on product and store choices. One way social influences are felt is in the expectations of society regarding the proper roles for men and women, which have led to many sex-typed products. Consumers are motivated to please or imitate people they know or whom they respect. Purchases often result from conformity to real or imagined group pressure. Opinion leaders are especially influential people.

6. **Understand how the Internet offers consumers opportunities for peer-to-peer marketing.**

Peer-to-peer or consumer-to-consumer (C2C) e-commerce includes marketing communication and purchases between individuals. C2C activities include virtual brand communities, auction sites, product rating sites, and protest sites.

# CHAPTER REVIEW

## Marketing Concepts: Testing Your Knowledge

1. What is consumer behaviour? Why is it important for marketers to understand consumer behaviour?

2. How does the decision process differ under conditions of high involvement and low involvement? What are the steps in the decision process and what activities occur in each?

3. What is perception? For marketers, what are the implications of each component of the perceptual process?

4. How are consumers motivated to buy certain products over others? How has Maslow's hierarchy of needs contributed to an understanding of consumer behaviour?

5. What behavioural and cognitive learning theories are important to marketers? How do these perspectives differ when applied to consumer behaviour?

6. How do the three components of attitudes account for consumer decision making and purchasing behaviour?

7. What is personality? How is consumer behaviour influenced by an individual's personality and self-concept?

8. Why is self-concept such an important personal influence on purchasing behaviour? How do age and the family life cycle influence consumers? What is the significance of lifestyles in understanding consumer behaviour and purchasing decisions?

9. Why is an understanding of social influences such as culture and subculture important to marketers? What is the significance of social class to marketers? What are reference groups, and how do they influence consumers?

10. What are the situational influences on consumer purchasing behaviour? How does each affect purchasing decisions?

11. What is peer-to-peer e-commerce? How do consumers communicate and purchase using the Internet?

## Marketing Concepts: Discussing Choices and Issues

1. Some consumer advocates have criticized marketing messages that link products to idealized people and situations and encourage the belief that the products will change consumers' lives in the portrayed direction. Do you agree or disagree? Explain your reasoning?

2. This chapter raised the question, "Do we buy what we are?" What answer would you give based on your experience? Provide examples that support your opinion.

3. A number of current demographic or cultural trends are important to marketers. What are some important trends that may affect marketing of the following products?

   a. housing

   b. home health care

   c. newspapers

   d. education

   e. travel and tourism

4. Affect, cognition, and behaviour are three components that can be used by marketers to shape people's attitudes about products. Identify the product categories you think are most likely to be affected by each component and discuss the merits of trying to change people's attitudes about them.

5. Culture is not static. What values, beliefs, and customs of Canadian culture do you see changing? How are these changes affecting marketing? What products will be affected by these changes?

6. Consumers often buy products because they feel pressure from reference groups to conform. Does conformity exert a positive or negative influence on consumers? How do consumer demographics, psychographics, and lifestyles affect their readiness to conform? With what types of products is conformity more likely to occur?

## Marketing Practice: Applying What You've Learned

1. Assume that you are the director of marketing for a chain of camping and outdoor gear stores. Your firm is expanding and it is your job to develop general recommendations for store design. Prepare a summary of your recommendations for store design elements that you believe will provide the best shopping environment for your customers.

2. Assume that you are an account executive with an advertising agency. Your current client is a firm that makes swimwear. You know that swimwear purchases are often influenced by a variety of social or "other people" factors. Write a report that lists these social influences, explain why each is important, and outline how you might use these influences in developing an advertising campaign.

3. This chapter indicated that consumers go through a series of steps (from problem recognition to postpurchase evaluation) as they make purchases. Write a detailed report describing what you would do in each of these steps when deciding to purchase one of the following products:

   a. an automobile

   b. a suit

   c. a vacation

4. Sometimes advertising or other marketing activities cause problem recognition to occur by showing consumers how much better off they would be with a new product or by pointing out problems with products they already own. For the following product categories, what are some ways in which marketers might try to stimulate problem recognition?

   a. cell phone

   b. toothpaste

   c. vitamins

   d. fast food

5. You work for a firm that markets frozen foods and are concerned about the effects of current consumer trends, including the increasingly diverse ethnic make-up of the population, changing roles of men and women, increased concern for time and for the environment, and decreased emphasis on owning status goods. Others in your firm do not understand or care about these changes. They believe that the firm should continue to do business just as it always has. Develop a role-playing exercise with a classmate to discuss these two different points of view for your class. Each of you should include the importance of each of these trends to your firm and your suggestions for marketing strategies to address these trends.

## Marketing Mini-Project: Learning by Doing

The purpose of this mini-project is to increase your understanding of the roles of personal, social, and situational factors in consumer behaviour.

1. With several other members of your class, select one of the following product categories (or some other product of your choice):
   a. perfume
   b. computers
   c. women's or men's shoes
   d. automobiles

2. Visit three stores or locations where the product may be purchased. (Try to select three that are very different from each other.) Observe and make notes on all the elements of each retail environment.

3. At each of the three locations, observe people purchasing the product. Make notes about their characteristics (e.g., age and sex) and their actions in the store in relation to the product.

4. Prepare a report for your class describing the situational variables and individual consumer differences you discovered and how they relate to the purchase of the product.

5. Present your findings to your class.

## Real People, Real Surfers: Exploring the Web

Visit the Web site for D~Code (**www.d-code.com**). Answer the following questions about the information at the site.

1. What research methods that D~Code uses to understand Nexus consumers are described on the site? What do you think are the advantages and disadvantages of using these methods to understand consumer behaviour?

2. What information about Nexus consumer behaviour is described on the site?

3. Identify five Canadian companies that you think would be interested in information on Nexus consumers. How might these companies use information about Nexus consumers in designing their marketing strategies?

## Chapter 5 Kraft Foods: Obesity Initiative

According to the World Health Organization, obesity has reached epidemic proportions globally with more than 300 million adults clinically obese and 1 billion adults overweight. An estimated 1.5 million visits for obesity were made to Canadian office-based physicians in the 12 months ending June 2003. Almost half of Canadian adults are overweight and the most recent statistics show that the percentage is growing. While poor nutrition, lack of information and education, and inactivity are partially to blame, consumers and health officials are also focusing blame on fast food companies and companies that make fatty prepared foods. Just like the bevy of lawsuits against tobacco companies for not informing consumers about the risks of smoking, fast food retailers and food manufacturers may find themselves in the "fat seat" and held responsible for growing waistlines.

In response to the obesity epidemic some companies, like McDonald's, are trying to alter their menus to include more healthy food options, others are completely ignoring the issue. A few companies like Kraft, McCain, Tim Hortons, and Frito-Lay have embraced this issue and are working out ways to help solve the problem.

Kraft Foods, in particular, has a history of giving back to communities, offering help, and using their resources for the greater good. Kraft Canada donates an average of 900 000 kilograms of food annually to Canada's food banks, and helps bring quality perishable nutritious food to thousands of people in need every day. To address the continent's current weight issue, Kraft Foods has launched an extensive global obesity initiative developed in council with international health advisers.

Kraft Foods Obesity Initiative will focus on four key areas. The first key area is product nutrition. Kraft will put a cap on the portion size of single-serve packages, offer guidelines for the nutritional characteristics of all products, and will plan an effort to improve existing products and provide alternative choices where appropriate. Kraft has already put their plan to action by replacing the trans-fatty ingredients in Oreo's with more health conscious ingredients. The second key area Kraft has promised to focus on is its marketing practices. Kraft has eliminated all in-school marketing and has shifted its marketing focus to encourage appropriate eating habits and active lifestyles. Kraft has also recognized consumer information as another key area of concentration. Nutrition labels will now be included on all products worldwide as will activity-related information. Kraft's Web site will be revamped to include information about healthy, active lifestyles and eating choices. Finally Kraft has identified advocacy and dialogue as its last key area of interest. Kraft will support public policies to engage schools and communities in helping to improve fitness and nutrition. Kraft will work to increase dialogue with key stakeholders to help guide the company's continuing response to the obesity issue.

Kraft has decided to attack the worldwide obesity issue head on. Kraft is using its resources and power to influence society and competitors for the better. By taking on this initiative Kraft is also showing its consumers that it is socially responsible and cares.

Sources: Based on www.imshealthcanada.com/htmen/3_1_36.htm; www.cbc.ca/news/bigpicture/obesity/statistics.html; Lesley Young, "In the Fat Seat," *Marketing Magazine Online*, 11 August 2003.

## Things to Think About

1. Do you think that the initiative Kraft is spearheading is a good idea? Do you think it will help them or hinder them in the long run? How?

2. Do you think that Kraft will alienate its core customers? Or are they more likely to enhance brand loyalty and attract new customers?

3. Do you think consumers will put their money where their mouths are? Will consumers say they want to be healthy but continue to trade-off nutrition for taste?

4. How do you think Kraft's competitors will react to the Obesity Initiative? What would you do?

Funerals are a billion-dollar business in Canada and the industry is expected to grow significantly in the next 25 years as the baby boomer generation ages. For most consumers, funerals represent the third largest purchase that they will make. Yet most consumers find the product upsetting and the purchase process emotionally draining. Darryl Roberts, a former funeral home director and author of the exposé *Profits of Death*, suggests that guilt is a very large part of the industry and how sales reps get customers to spend more than they had intended. Even when the deceased has left written instructions for a simple service, sales reps can make bereaved family members feel bad about not giving their loved one a proper send-off and shame them into buying more expensive caskets, flower arrangements, or other associated goods and services.

Service Corporation International (SCI) is an American corporation that is buying up independent funeral homes in Canada and marketing them under the "Family Funeral Care" brand name. Jon Beneken, vice-president of SCI Canada, says that SCI is not trying to fool people into thinking that they are still dealing with a family-run funeral home, but rather that the brand name implies that SCI services are for families. He further argues that SCI sales reps are not trying to up-sell customers, but are merely helping customers understand their decisions and choices.

SCI, however, is accountable to shareholders and has strong incentives to maximize profits. The SCI sales training manual mentions that "our growth and future will only be strengthened through sales." Many SCI sales reps are paid on straight commission, and they are well trained to maximize a sale. Norm and Rene Cook, former SCI funeral home employees, learned how to jack up the bottom line by going directly to the most expensive casket, pointing out all of the features, and then simply saying "Don't you think this is the casket that your father deserves?" and waiting for a reply. Then Norm and Rene would take the customer down the price list until they were embarrassed to go any lower.

This was the experience Gail Fraser had when she went to an SCI-owned funeral home to make arrangements for her mother's funeral. She experienced a lot of pressure to spend more money—making her "feel bad." When the employee showed her the cardboard box her mother had ordered, Fraser thought "it was the last attempt to shame me into providing something more fitting for my mother."

SCI claims zero tolerance for this type of behaviour but it appears to happen frequently. Independent funeral homes visited by CBC investigators were more likely to recommend more economical packages in the $2500 range, with savings of 30 percent or more over SCI-owned homes, whereas one SCI home recommended an $11 000 solution.

The advice given to consumers is buyer beware. Some SCI funeral homes marked up caskets 800 percent over the wholesale cost. Memorial societies are now forming to help consumers navigate this marketplace. The Memorial Society of BC charges $10 for registering funeral service requests, and a society representative will go to the funeral homes with family members when they are finalizing the arrangements.

## Questions:

1. Other industries such as cosmetics, weight loss, infertility, and weddings use emotional appeals to sell products to consumers. At what point would you consider emotional-based appeals to be unethical?

2. Until consumers become more proactive in shopping for funeral services, funeral homes can get away with extremely high mark-ups. What limits the ability of consumers to be more proactive in seeking better value in this context?

3. If you were going to start a funeral home business, what assumptions about consumer behaviour would you make?

4. Is this an industry that should be regulated by the government? Why or why not?

Source: This case was prepared by Brock Smith and is based on "Funeral Homes," *Marketplace* #21010.

# CHAPTER 6
## Organizational Buying Behaviour

## CHAPTER OBJECTIVES

WHEN YOU HAVE COMPLETED YOUR STUDY OF THIS CHAPTER, YOU SHOULD BE ABLE TO

1. Describe the general characteristics of business-to-business markets and business buying practices.

2. Explain how marketers classify business and organizational markets.

3. Explain the business buying situation and describe business buyers.

4. Summarize the main stages in the business buying decision process.

5. Explain how e-commerce is dramatically changing business-to-business marketing.

# Real People, Real Decisions

## Meet **Marion Lay,** a Decision Maker at 2010 LegaciesNow

Marion Lay is President and CEO of 2010 LegaciesNow, a not-for-profit society that works with non-governmental organizations and all three levels of government to create effective sports, recreation, volunteer, literacy, and arts programs throughout British Columbia and Canada. 2010 LegaciesNow works with government agencies, Bid and Games sponsors, and other community stakeholders to ensure that sports, arts, and culture legacies result from Canada hosting the 2010 Winter Olympic Games.

Lay, a bronze medallist in swimming at the 1968 Olympics in Mexico City, was previously interim chair of the 2010 Vancouver–Whistler bid committee until Jack Poole and John Furlong took the lead roles just prior to the 2002 Winter Games in Salt Lake City, Utah. Following her career as a swimmer, Lay earned a Master's degree in the Sociology of Sport from the University of California at Haywood and embarked on a consulting career in the area of women in sport. She was recognized and honoured by the International Olympic Committee (IOC) with a trophy award for women in sport in the Americas. As an executive member of the Canadian Olympic Committee, she was approached by tourism industry leaders in Vancouver to assist the initial Bid Committee to help Vancouver win the right to represent Canada in the international competition. Marion and the Vancouver Bid Team crafted a winning positioning for the Vancouver–Whistler bid drawing on: a planned legacy platform; the notion that Vancouver was the most liveable city to which the IOC had not been; and the fact the Whistler was rated as the top mountain resort in North America and one of the top in the world. The Canadian Olympic Committee agreed that Vancouver–Whistler was the Canadian city and ski resort it would want to showcase to the world.

Lay and her team began planning the international bid competition the same way she started planning the Canadian competition—by determining who the key decision makers were and developing a profile of their interests, values, voting history, and people they trusted. Lay thought it particularly important to determine if the Canadian bid team knew someone the decision makers trusted in order to get an introduction and perhaps an ally. In positioning the bid in the early stages, the bid team had two options.

**Option 1.** The traditional approach, used by many of the international competitors, involved the bid team identifying and heavily lobbying the key decision makers and their influencers. The technical merits of the bid (i.e., the site, infrastructure, transportation, and security plan), although important, would play less of a role than the marketing effort to showcase the venue, the Olympic spirit of the host country, and the ability to stage a world-class promotional campaign—in essence, develop strong emotional appeal for the bid. In the past, some countries crossed an ethical boundary and were known to have bestowed generous gifts (e.g., trips, large screen televisions, University entrance and scholarships for children) on IOC members to secure their favour. The Vancouver–Whistler Bid team knew that Canadians would not want to win that way and that Canadians also don't know how to play that game well. Additionally, if the IOC was serious about cleaning up its image following the Salt Lake scandals, the team determined that a "clean," ethical bid from Canada could be a winner. Thus, for Canada, the traditional approach would entail developing a solid "technical package" and then "selling" the merits of the bid through personal contacts, backed by a strong promotional campaign. This is the approach that was successful for Calgary in winning the 1988 Winter Olympic Games. There were problems with this approach: the IOC members were mainly European and Canada was relatively unknown to them and there were complex political relationships and implications surrounding the decision that could transcend any rational bid decision process.

**Option 2.** The alternative approach for the team was to position the Vancouver Bid as highly ethical. An ultra-ethical Canadian bid was in a position to help the IOC improve its reputation and make the Olympic product better. Canada could build on its "Dudley Do Right" reputation and its strong track record in peace keeping, social issues, and sustainability to position it as the best choice for the IOC to demonstrate that the games would not be awarded based on questionable practices and political influence. The bid would also have a strong "technical package," but would have less showmanship and more substance relating to environmental stewardship and social sustainability. This approach would rely on IOC members to choose Canada because it was the right thing to do, because Canada would do what was promised, and because Canada knows how to be a good host. This approach would involve some risk: millions of dollars were already invested in the bid, and with the potential impact of billions of dollars on the line, there would be great pressure to secure votes by any means possible. To take the ethical high ground, Canada would have to practise an ethical bid process that could be undermined by one slip up by one member of the team.

Now join the 2010 Winter Olympic bid team. Which option would you choose and why?

# BUSINESS MARKETS: BUYING AND SELLING WHEN STAKES ARE HIGH

You might think most marketers spend their days dreaming up the best way to promote cutting-edge Web browsers or funky shoes. Not so. Many marketers know that the "real action" is more likely to be found in lead pipes, office supplies, safety shoes, meat lockers, or machine tools. In fact, some of the most interesting and most lucrative jobs for young marketers are in industries you probably have never heard of.

An individual consumer may decide to buy two or three T-shirts at one time, each emblazoned with a different design. Large companies such as Canadian Tire, Petro-Canada, Pepsi-Cola, and McDonald's buy hundreds, even thousands, of employee uniforms embroidered with their corporate logos in a single order. Like an end consumer, a business buyer makes decisions—with an important difference. The purchase may be worth millions of dollars, and both the buyer and seller have a lot at stake in making a wise decision.

In this chapter, we'll look at the big picture of the business marketplace, in which the fortunes of business buyers and sellers can hang in the balance of a single transaction. Then we'll examine how marketers categorize businesses and organizations to develop effective business marketing strategies. Finally, we'll look at business buying behaviour and the business buying decision process.

To begin, consider these transactions: Bombardier (owners of de Havilland, Canadair, Lear, and Short PLC) makes business jets such as the one in Exhibit 6.1 to sell to corporate customers. Procter & Gamble sells cases of Tide to RC Distributors, a Northern Ontario wholesaler. The Stratford Festival buys costumes, sets, and programs. Ford Motor Company plans to purchase 350 000 Hewlett-Packard computer systems for employee home use. BC Gas buys advice from Anderson Consulting. The Winnipeg Public Library buys a Canon copier. Home Depot buys drywall from the Canadian Gypsum Company.

All of these market activities have one thing in common—they are part of **business-to-business marketing**. This is the marketing of goods and services that businesses and other organizational customers buy for some purpose other than personal consumption. Firms may resell these goods and services or may use them to produce still other goods and services to sell to other businesses or to support their own operations. Business-to-business customers include manufacturers, wholesalers, retailers, and a variety of other organizations such as hospitals, colleges and universities, and government agencies. Another name for business-to-business markets is organizational markets.

Business customers create vast opportunities for marketers. When measured in dollars, the market for business and organizational goods and services is *four* times larger than the consumer market.[1]

To put the size and complexity of business markets into perspective, let's consider a single product—a pair of jeans. A consumer may browse through several racks of jeans and ultimately purchase a single pair, but the store at which the consumer shops has purchased many pairs of jeans in different sizes, styles, and brands from different manufacturers. Each of these manufacturers purchases fabrics, zippers, buttons, and thread from other manufacturers that, in turn, purchase the raw materials to make these components. In addition, all of the firms in this chain need to purchase equipment, electricity, labour, computer systems, office supplies, packing materials, and countless other goods and services. So, even a single purchase of the latest style of Diesel jeans is the culmination of a series of buying and selling activities among many organizations—many people have been keeping busy while you're out shopping.

**business-to-business marketing** The marketing of goods and services that business and organizational customers need to produce other goods and services for resale or to support their operations.

**Exhibit 6.1**

Bombardier is a Canadian firm that builds business jets for corporations and individuals.

# Characteristics that Make a Difference in Business Markets

In theory, the same basic marketing principles hold in both consumer and business markets—firms identify customer needs and develop a marketing mix to satisfy those needs. For example, imagine the company that made the desks and chairs in your classroom. Just like a firm that markets consumer goods, the classroom furniture company first must create an important competitive advantage for its target market of colleges and universities. Next the firm develops a marketing mix strategy beginning with a product—classroom furniture that will withstand years of use by thousands of students while providing a level of comfort required of a good learning environment (and you thought those hard-backed chairs were intended just to keep you awake during class). The firm must offer the furniture at prices the schools will pay and must develop a sales force or other marketing communication strategy to make sure your school (and hundreds of others) consider—and hopefully choose—its products when furnishing classrooms. Although marketing to business customers does have a lot in common with consumer marketing, there are differences that make this basic process more complex.[2] Figure 6.1 looks at some of these differences and they are reviewed in the following sections.

MULTIPLE BUYERS In business markets, products often have to do more than satisfy an individual's needs. They must meet the requirements of everyone involved in the company's purchase decision. If you decide to buy a new chair for your room or apartment, you are the only one who has to be satisfied. For your classroom, the furniture must satisfy students, faculty members, administrators, campus planners, and the purchasing department. Instead of simply deciding on an appropriate price for the product, business-to-business marketers frequently must submit written quotes stating their prices and then hope a competitor doesn't submit a lower quote.

NUMBER OF CUSTOMERS Compared to consumers, organizational customers are few and far between. In Canada, there are about 10 million consumer households but fewer than 50 000 businesses and organizations. Unless your name is Bronfman or Gates, each organizational buyer has more to spend than you do as an individual consumer. Business marketers

**Organizational Markets**

- Purchases made for some purpose other than personal consumption
- Purchases made by someone other than the user of the product
- Decisions frequently made by several people
- Purchases made according to precise technical specifications based on product expertise
- Purchases made after careful weighing of alternatives
- Purchases made based on rational criteria
- Purchasers often engage in lengthy decision process
- Interdependencies between buyers and sellers; long-term relationships
- Purchases may involve competitive bidding, price negotiations, and complex financial arrangements
- Products frequently purchased directly from producer
- Purchases frequently involve high risk and high cost
- Limited number of large buyers
- Buyers often geographically concentrated in certain areas
- Products: often complex; classified based on how organizational customers use them
- Demand derived from demand for other goods and services, generally inelastic in the short run, subject to fluctuations, and may be joined to the demand for other goods and services
- Promotion emphasizes personal selling

**Consumer Markets**

- Purchases for individual or household consumption
- Purchases usually made by ultimate user of the product
- Decisions usually made by individuals
- Purchases often made based on brand reputation or personal recommendations with little or no product expertise
- Purchases frequently made on impulse
- Purchases made based on emotional responses to products or promotions
- Individual purchasers often make quick decisions
- Buyers engage in limited-term or one-time-only relationships with many different sellers
- Most purchases made at "list price" with cash or credit cards
- Products usually purchased from someone other than producer of the product
- Most purchases are low risk and low cost
- Many individual or household customers
- Buyers generally dispersed throughout total population
- Products: consumer goods and services for individual use
- Demand based on consumer needs and preferences, is generally price elastic, steady over time, and independent of demand for other products
- Promotion emphasizes advertising

**Figure 6.1** Differences between Organizational and Consumer Markets have a narrow customer base and a small number of buyers. Kodak's business division, which markets sophisticated medical products to hospitals and other medical groups, has a limited number of potential customers compared with its consumer film division.

SIZE OF PURCHASES Business-to-business products can dwarf consumer purchases, both in the quantity of items ordered and in the price of individual purchases. A company that supplies uniforms to other businesses, for example, buys hundreds of large drums of laundry detergent each year in contrast to a consumer household that buys one box of detergent every few weeks. Organizations purchase some products (e.g., highly sophisticated pieces of manufacturing equipment, computer-based marketing information systems) that can cost into the millions of dollars. For example, the Nortel Networks

**Exhibit 6.2**
Telecommunications switches made by Nortel Networks are usually considered large purchases by organizations.

telecommunications switch shown in Exhibit 6.2 sells for about $80 000. Recognizing such differences in the size of purchases allows marketers to meet business customers' needs. Although it makes perfect sense to use mass-media advertising to sell laundry detergent to consumers, selling thousands of dollars worth of laundry detergent or a million-dollar computer is best handled by a strong personal sales force.

GEOGRAPHIC CONCENTRATION Another difference between business markets and consumer markets is geographic concentration—many business customers are located in a small geographic area rather than spread out across the country. Consumers buy and use products like toothpaste and televisions whether they live in the heart of Toronto or in a small fishing village on Prince Edward Island. This is not true for business-to-business customers, who may be exclusively located in a single region of the country (Exhibit 6.3). In Canada, much of the industrial buying power is concentrated in Toronto, Montreal, and Calgary, where major Canadian corporations have their head offices.

## Business-to-Business Demand

Demand in business markets differs from consumer demand. Most demand for business-to-business products is derived, inelastic, fluctuating, and joint. Understanding these differences

**Exhibit 6.3**
Customers for Caterpillar heavy equipment are geographically concentrated.

in business-to-business demand is important for marketers in forecasting sales and in planning effective marketing strategies.

DERIVED DEMAND Consumer demand is a direct connection between a need and the satisfaction of that need. Business customers don't purchase goods and services to satisfy their own needs. Business-to-business demand is **derived demand**, because a business's demand for goods and services comes either directly or indirectly from consumers' demand. For example, the demand for building products such as Canadian Gypsum's drywall or even the Jacuzzi Whirlpool tubs shown in Exhibit 6.4 is derived from the demand for new homes. Retailers buy goods to resell in response to consumer demand while other organizations and firms buy products that are used to produce still more goods and services that consumer markets demand.

**derived demand** The demand for business or organizational products that is derived from demand for consumer goods or services.

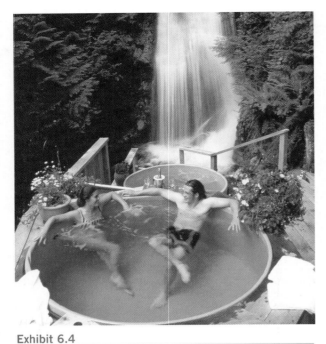

**Exhibit 6.4**

For Jacuzzi, demand for tubs goes up and down with the economy and the number of new homes being built.

**inelastic demand** The demand for products does not change because of increases or decreases in price.

**acceleration principle (multiplier effect)** A marketing phenomenon in which a small percentage change in consumer demand can create a large percentage change in business-to-business demand.

```
┌─────────────────────────────────────┐
│        Demand for education          │
└─────────────────────────────────────┘
                   ↓
┌─────────────────────────────────────┐
│   Derived demand for textbooks       │
└─────────────────────────────────────┘
                   ↓
┌─────────────────────────────────────┐
│     Derived demand for paper         │
└─────────────────────────────────────┘
                   ↓
┌─────────────────────────────────────┐
│      Derived demand for pulp         │
└─────────────────────────────────────┘
                   ↓
┌─────────────────────────────────────┐
│ Derived demand for forestry products │
└─────────────────────────────────────┘
```

**Figure 6.2** Derived Demand

Consider Figure 6.2. Demand for forestry products comes from the demand for pulp to make paper used to make textbooks. The demand for textbooks comes from the demand for education. As a result of derived demand, the success of one company may depend on another company in a different industry. The derived nature of business demand means that marketers must be constantly alert to changes in consumer trends that ultimately will have an effect on business-to-business sales.

**INELASTIC DEMAND** The demand for business or organizational products is generally *inelastic*. **Inelastic demand** means that, regardless of whether the price of a business-to-business product goes up or down, customers will still buy the same quantity. (The notion of price elasticity in discussed further in Chapter 9.) We see inelastic demand in business-to-business markets because an individual business product is usually one of the many parts and materials that go into producing the consumer product. It is not unusual for a large increase in price for a single business product to have little effect on the price of the final consumer product. For example, the BMW in Exhibit 6.5 sells for about $50 000. To produce the car, BMW purchases thousands of different parts. If the price of tires, batteries, or stereos goes up—or down—BMW will still buy enough to meet consumer demand for its cars. As you might imagine, increasing the price of a $50 000 car by $30 or $40 or even $100 won't change consumer demand.

Business-to-business demand isn't always inelastic. Sometimes producing a consumer good or service relies on only one or a few materials or component parts. If the price of the part increases, demand may become elastic if the manufacturer of the consumer good passes the increase on to the consumer. Steel, for example, is a large component of automobiles. If the price of steel goes up, automobile manufacturers will pay a lot more for a necessary component of their product. An increase in the price of steel can drive up the price of automobiles so much that consumer demand for drops, decreasing the demand for steel.

**FLUCTUATING DEMAND** Considering that demand comes from the end consumer, even small changes can create large increases or decreases in business demand. The **acceleration principle** (also called the multiplier effect) explains how a small percentage change in consumer demand can create a large percentage change in total industrial or business demand. Consider, for example, a five percent increase in consumer demand for air travel. If the airlines are already filling their flights, they may decide to buy new planes to meet the increased consumer demand. For Boeing or Bombardier Aerospace, the orders for new planes may double or even triple the normal demand.

A product's *life expectancy* is another reason for fluctuating demand. Business customers tend to purchase certain products (e.g., large machinery) infrequently, perhaps only every 10 or 20 years. Thus, demand for such products fluctuates; it may be very high one year when customers' machines are wearing out but low the following year because the old machinery is working fine.

Changes in a company's inventory policies can also create demand fluctuations. Consider a firm that has historically kept a 30-day supply of parts. Operations managers may decide to keep a 14-day supply of parts to reduce costs. Demand for the part will first go down because the manager will be placing a smaller order (for 14 days) and then level off at that 14-day quantity.

**Exhibit 6.5**
The final sticker price of the BMW convertible depends on the price BMW has to pay for thousands of parts.

**JOINT DEMAND** **Joint demand** is the result of two or more goods being necessary to create a product. For example, General Motors requires tires, batteries, and spark plugs. If the supply of one of these products decreases, General Motors will be unable to manufacture as many automobiles and will not buy as many of the other items. Therefore, the sale of B.F. Goodrich tires to General Motors partly depends on the availability of batteries and spark plugs, even though the tire manufacturer has nothing to do with these products.

> **joint demand** The demand for two or more goods that are used together to create a product.

## CLASSIFYING BUSINESS-TO-BUSINESS MARKETS

Many firms buy products in business markets so that they can produce other goods in turn. Many of the Canadian Gypsum Company's customers are contractors who build homes and

---

### SPOTLIGHT ON REAL PEOPLE — AdFarm Marketing

Agriculture is big business. Kim McConnell is CEO of AdFarm, a Canadian based North American advertising firm specializing in agricultural products. AdFarm has taken the idea of understanding customers and target markets to the next level. Where "other agencies speak to agriculture," says Creative director Glenn Dawes, "we embody it." The AdFarm office is decorated in farm décor. The reception hall is rimmed with steel walls making it resemble a grain silo. Papier mâché cows poke their heads over imitation "stalls." In the centre of the room, a scarecrow overlooks a mini grain field and, in a corner, there are dancing papier mâché pigs. The "creative room" is a Winnipeg designer's airy metallic take on a collapsing Prairie barn. AdFarm staff blend into the décor wearing wool shirts, workboots, and jeans.

Employees at AdFarm take turns overlooking company-rented farms in Calgary and Fargo (North Dakota) to help them understand their market and their customers' customers even better. AdFarm recognizes farmers have a minimal "bullshit" meter and agri-chemical and product companies appreciate it when they can work with an agency that understands their industry. AdFarm is reaping the benefits: It's the largest agency in North America focusing solely on agriculture with billings topping $70 million and has set its sights on the global market. The secret to AdFarm's success? McConnell admits, "In agriculture, clients need more than good creativity. They need knowledge in business and that's our advantage."

Source: Based on Norma Ramage, "Crazy About Ag Marketing," *Marketing Magazine Online*, 25 August 2003.

1. What can other marketers learn from AdFarm in terms of understanding their customers?
2. Is AdFarm's competitive advantage sustainable? How easy would it be for others to copy it?
3. What challenges may AdFarm encounter as it tries to spread its market reach globally?

offices and sell them to families and organizations. Other business-to-business customers resell, rent, or lease goods and services. Still others, such as the Red Cross, provincial governments, and local churches, serve the public in some way. As Figure 6.3 shows, these distinctions lead to broad categories: producers, resellers, and organizations. For business marketers, the classification of firms is significant because it identifies firms that purchase similar products and that have similar buying practices. This identification helps marketers develop strategies that effectively target different organizational customers.

**North American Industry Classification System (NAICS)** The numerical coding system that the United States, Canada, and Mexico use to classify firms into detailed categories according to their business activities and shared characteristics.

One tool that firms use is the **North American Industry Classification System (NAICS)**. This is a numerical coding system for classifying industries, and was developed jointly by the United States, Canada, and Mexico. NAICS replaced the U.S. Standard Industrial Classification (SIC) system in 1997 so that the North American Free Trade Agreement (NAFTA) member nations could compare economic and financial statistics.[3] Like the SIC system, the NAICS is used to collect and report data on business activity such as the number of firms, the total dollar amount of sales, the number of employees, and the growth rate for industries—broken down by geographic region. These reports have become an essential tool for classifying business-to-business customers. Many firms use them to assess potential markets and to determine how well they are doing compared to their industry group as a whole.

The NAICS uses a different six-digit numerical code for each industry. At its inception, the system included 20 major sectors identified by two-digit numbers, shown in Figure 6.4. The major sectors are further broken down into subsectors (three digits), industry groups (four digits), industries common to Canada, the United States, and Mexico (five digits), and specific country industries (six digits—"0" for Canada). The system is updated every five years to allow classifications to keep up with changes in the economy.

To use the NAICS to find new customers, a marketer might first determine the NAICS groups of current customers and then evaluate the sales potential of the overall NAICS groups or particular segments based on the number of employees of firms in the groups. For example, a firm that supplies employee uniforms could evaluate the sales potential of firms having 150 and 1000 employees in an NAICS category and set its sights on attractive firms in that category. In other cases, a firm might choose to target firms in a cross-section of categories, as Sprint did in its "Real Solutions" campaign which was aimed at all companies that employ 100 to 500 people.[4] Now we will take a closer look at the four major categories into which organizations fall.

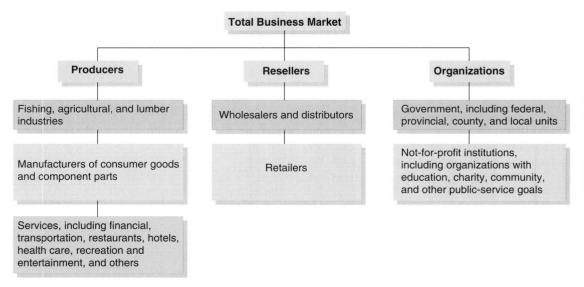

**Figure 6.3** The Business Marketplace

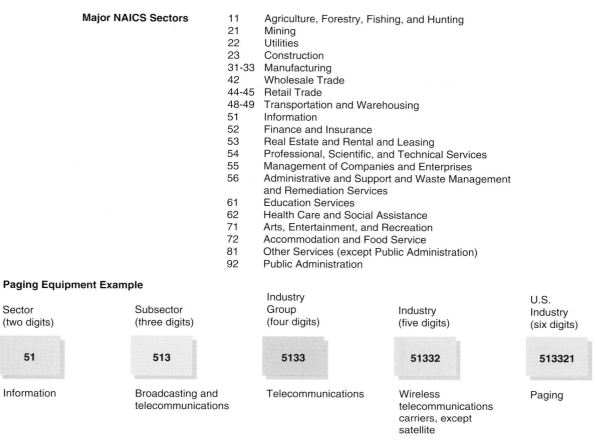

**Figure 6.4** North American Industrial Classification System (NAICS)

## Producers

**Producers** purchase goods for use in the production of other goods and services that are, in turn, sold to make a profit (Exhibit 6.6). Producers are customers for a vast number of products from raw materials to goods manufactured by other producers. For example, DuPont buys resins and uses them to manufacture insulation material for sleeping bags. Ontario mould maker Protoplast buys aluminum ingots, which it turns into industrial moulds. Auto manufacturers, such as Ford, buy a variety of component parts—from transmissions to carpet—for use in the cars they ship to consumers. Service producers buy linens, furniture, and food to create the quality accommodations and meals their guests expect.

**producers** The individuals or organizations that purchase products for use in the production of other goods and services.

## Resellers

**Resellers** buy finished goods for the purpose of reselling, renting, or leasing to other businesses. Resellers include retailers and wholesalers. Bestfoods, for example, sells its food products to the distribution arms of giant resellers such as Loblaws, IGA, and Westfair, who then distribute the food to their retail stores. Although resellers do not produce goods, they do provide their customers with the time, place, and possession utility we talked about in Chapter 1 by making the goods available to consumers when and where they want them.

**resellers** The individuals or organizations that buy finished goods for the purpose of reselling, renting, or leasing to others to make a profit and to maintain their business operations.

## Governments

**Government markets** make up the largest single business or organizational market in Canada. The Canadian government market includes more than 6000 government agencies and organizations, more than 740 municipal and local governments, 10 provincial govern-

**government markets** Federal, provincial, and local governments that buy goods and services to carry out public objectives and to support their operations.

**Exhibit 6.6**

Gowling Lafleur Henderson LLP (Gowlings), one of Canada's largest law firms, is a producer of legal services. This ad was part of a campaign to help differentiate the firm in the minds of business customers.

**competitive bids** A business buying process in which two or more suppliers submit proposals (including price and associated data) for a proposed purchase and the firm providing the better offer gets the bid.

**MERX**
www.merx.com

**not-for-profit institutions** Organizations with charitable, educational, community, and other public service goals that buy goods and services to support their functions and to attract and serve their members.

ments, 3 territorial governments, and a federal government that collectively spent more than $371 billion in 1998.[5] The federal government alone has more than 225 separate institutions[6] that typically procure (through a tendering process) $5 to $6 billion worth of goods and services each year.[7]

Governments are just about the only customers for certain products such as snowplows, garbage trucks, transit buses, and light rapid trains like the one illustrated in Exhibit 6.7. Many government expenditures are for more familiar and less expensive items, such as printer toner, pens, and Post-it Notes. The Vancouver–Whistler 2010 Olympic organizing committee, for example, will be spending more than $20 million to set up offices and the athletes village—buying products ranging from office equipment to beds and pillows.

For business marketers, selling goods and services to governments is different from selling to producer or reseller markets. Taking a prospective buyer to lunch may be standard practice in the corporate world, but in government markets, this practice may be in conflict with ethical (and legal) standards for government personnel. Because governments make purchases with taxpayer money, laws require them to adhere to strict regulations. Generally, government buyers must develop detailed specifications and obtain **competitive bids** for even the simplest purchases. With competitive bids, potential suppliers must submit detailed proposals including price and associated data for a proposed purchase. The firm making the best offer gets the bid. Government agencies are often required by law to accept the lowest bid from a qualified vendor.

Governments regularly publish information on upcoming bidding opportunities to let possible vendors know about purchases they are about to make. In Canada, the federal government's tendering process is managed by a private company called MERX, which offers a Web site for searching and submitting tenders for government procurement opportunities with a value of $25 000 or more. MERX also gives companies access to thousands of other procurement opportunities from provincial and municipal governments as well as hundreds of colleges, universities, hospitals, and school boards across Canada.

## Not-for-profit Institutions

**Not-for-profit institutions** are organizations (e.g., hospitals, churches, colleges, universities, museums, nursing homes) that operate for charitable, educational, community, and other public service goals and buy goods and services to support these functions. The institutional market also includes charitable and cause-related organizations, such as the Salvation Army and the Red Cross. Not-for-profit institutions tend to operate on low budgets and, in all but the largest ones, non-professional part-time buyers who have other duties—or are volunteers—normally make the purchases. These customers often rely on marketers to provide more advice and assistance before and after the sale than professional business buyers require.

## THE NATURE OF BUSINESS BUYING

So far we've talked about how business-to-business markets are different from consumer markets and about the different types of customers that make up business markets. In this section, we'll discuss some of the important characteristics of business buying.

To be successful in business-to-business markets means developing marketing strategies that meet the needs of organizational customers better than the competition. To do this, marketers must understand business buying behaviour. Armed with this knowledge, marketers are able to participate in the buyer's decision process from the start. Take a firm that sells equipment to hospitals. Understanding that physicians (rather than buyers) who practise at the hospital often initiate decisions to purchase new equipment means that the firm's salespeople will make sure the physicians know about new technologies and improved equipment. In this section, we'll first look at the different types of buying situations found in business markets. Then we'll examine the role of professional purchasers and buying centres in business buying.

**Exhibit 6.7**

Governments are the only customers for certain products.

## The Buying Situation

Like end consumers, business buyers spend more time and effort on certain purchases than on others. Devoting such effort to a purchase decision often depends on the complexity of the product and how often the decision has to be made. A **buy class** identifies the degree of effort required of the firm's personnel to collect information and make a purchase decision. These classes are straight rebuys, modified rebuys, and new-task buys.

**STRAIGHT REBUY** Buyers, when a purchase has low risk, often rely on strategies to simplify the process, such as using a fixed set of trusted suppliers for routine purchases.[8] Products like computer paper, shipping cartons, and cleaning compounds are low risk. Being successful in such markets means keeping prices down and developing selling policies to keep the buying process as simple as possible. A **straight rebuy** is the purchase of items that a business-to-business customer regularly needs. The buyer has purchased the same items many times before and routinely reorders them when supplies are low, often from the same suppliers. Reordering takes little time. Buyers typically maintain a list of approved vendors that have demonstrated their ability to meet the firm's criteria for pricing, quality, service, and delivery (Exhibit 6.8).

Because straight rebuys can mean steady income for a firm, many business marketers go to great lengths to cultivate and maintain relationships with customers that will lead to straight rebuys. Salespeople, for example, regularly call on these customers to personally handle orders and to see if there are additional products the customer needs; they may also attempt to obtain long-term contracts. Rebuys keep a supplier's sales volume up and selling costs down.

**MODIFIED REBUY** Straight rebuy situations do not last forever. A **modified rebuy** occurs when a firm wants to shop around for suppliers with better prices, quality, or delivery times. A modified rebuy can also occur when an organization has new needs for products it already buys. A buyer who has purchased many copying machines in the past, for example, may have to evaluate several lines of equipment, such as the document centre in Exhibit 6.9 on page 193, if the firm has a new need for digitized office equipment.

**NEW-TASK BUYING** A first-time purchase is a **new-task buy**, often characterized by uncertainty and risk. New-task buys require the most effort because the buyer has no previous experience on which to base a decision. Companies like Vancouver-based FatPort are selling Wi-Fi network hubs to pubs, laundry mats, independent hotels, and other small businesses, helping them become wireless Internet service providers. This technology allows different devices and people to communicate with each other through radio frequencies. Most small business owners have little experience with wireless communication technology, making this a new-task purchase decision that comes with some risk and a lot of uncertainty. In new-task buying situations, buyers not only lack experience with the product, but

**buy class** One of three classifications of business buying situations that characterize the degree of time and effort required to make a decision in a buying situation.

**straight rebuy** A buying situation in which business buyers make routine purchases that require minimal decision making.

**modified rebuy** A buying situation classification that business buyers use to categorize a previously made purchase that involves some change and that requires limited decision making.

**new-task buy** A new business-to-business purchase that is complex or risky and that requires extensive decision making.

**FatPort**
www.fatport.com

**FedEx offers the broadest range of shipping solutions.**
Overnighting a box to Biloxi? Use FedEx Express. Sending a tube to Tuba City? Try FedEx Ground. A package to Pakistan? FedEx Express International. A pallet to Palo Alto? FedEx Express Domestic Freight. How about two tons of tuna to Taiwan? FedEx International Freight can handle it. With real-time tracking, delivery confirmation and a money-back guarantee. Need more information? Visit **fedex.com** or call 1-800-Go-FedEx.
**Be absolutely sure.®**

**FedEx**

**Exhibit 6.8**

Delivery and shipping services are a straight rebuy decision for most businesses.

are also unfamiliar with firms that supply the product. Supplier choice is therefore critical and buyers will gather much information about quality, pricing, delivery, and service from several potential suppliers.

For suppliers, new-task buying represents both a challenge and an opportunity. Although a new-task buy can be significant in itself, many times the chosen supplier gains the added advantage of becoming an "in" supplier for more routine purchases that will follow. A growing business that needs an advertising agency for the first time, for example, may seek exhaustive information from several firms before selecting one and will continue to use the chosen agency's services for future projects without exploring other alternatives. Marketers know that to get the order in a new-task buy situation, they must develop a close working relationship with the business buyer. Such relationships mean that buyers can count on business marketers to help develop product specifications and terms for the purchase that are in the best interests of the customer's organization and its needs.

## The Professional Buyer

Just as it is important for marketers of consumer goods and services to understand their customers, it is essential that business-to-business marketers understand who handles the buying for business customers. Trained professional buyers typically carry out buying in business-to-business markets and are often called *purchasing agents*, *procurement officers*, or *directors of materials management*. Unlike consumers who may spend only a few hours a month making purchase decisions, professional purchasers do it all day, every day.

Professional buyers have a lot of responsibility. They spend the company's money and buy the products that keep it running. These buyers tend to focus on economic factors beyond the initial price of the product, including transportation and delivery charges, accessory products or supplies, maintenance, and other ongoing costs. They select suppliers, negotiate for the lowest prices, and are responsible for selecting quality products and ensuring their timely delivery. Their purchases can range in price and significance from paper clips to multimillion-dollar computer systems.

Sometimes business buyers, like consumers, make decisions based on emotions, brand loyalty, long-term relationships established with particular salespeople, or aesthetic concerns. Even age, income, education, personality, and attitudes can affect a buyer's decisions. Marketing communications play a crucial role in the buyer's decision process. For example, most buyers depend on vendors' salespeople to keep them informed of new products.

A key factor in many purchase decisions is whether the buyer perceives the purchase to be risky.[9] Some buyers are more risk averse than others. Successful business marketers try to develop strategies that help the buyer avoid risk. These include providing samples of a new product for a business customer or placing a new piece of equipment in the customer's facility to try for a few weeks.

**centralized purchasing** A business buying practice in which an organization's purchasing department does the buying for all of the company.

Big firms with many facilities in different locations often practise **centralized purchasing**. This means that, even when others in the organization participate in the decision of what to buy, one department does all the buying for the company.[10] With centralized purchasing, a firm has more buying power and can get the best prices. Wal-Mart can offer its customers lower prices than other stores (see Exhibit 6.10), because its centralized purchasing department buys large quantities of items and can demand volume discounts from suppliers. For sellers such as Kraft Foods, centralized purchasing means they only need to make a single sale to have their peanut butter in IGA locations across the country.

The professional buyers who work in centralized purchasing offices often become experts at the ins and outs of certain types of products, and each may have a specialized role in the purchasing function. In the buying departments of retail chains, for example, an individual buyer (and several assistant buyers) may be responsible for buying only women's sleepwear or junior tops or children's size 2 to 6X. This specializing leads to greater expertise in the buyer's specific area.

## The Buying Centre

Whether or not a firm's buying is a centralized process and whether or not the purchase situation calls for a modified or new-task buying situation, several people may need to work together to reach a decision. Depending on what they need to purchase, these participants may be production workers, supervisors, engineers, secretaries, shipping clerks, or financial officers. In a small organization, everyone may have a voice in the decision. The group of people in the organization who participate in the decision-making process is the **buying centre**.

**THE FLUID NATURE OF THE BUYING CENTRE** Although the term *buying centre* may conjure up an image of offices buzzing with purchasing activity, it usually is a cross-functional team of decision makers. Generally, the members of a buying centre have some expertise or interest in the particular decision and they are able, as a group, to make the best decision.

Hospitals, for example, frequently make purchase decisions through a large buying centre. When making a decision to purchase disposable oxygen masks, for example, one or

### Rule the jobs.
Canon gives you complete control over your jobs from beginning to end. With the most robust finishing capabilities that include saddle stitching, tab support, document inserts, cover inserts, booklet making and z-folding. The list goes on and on.

### Rule the volumes.
Whatever your volume needs are, we have the solutions to not only meet them, but to surpass them. You choose from 350,000 up to 2,000,000 pages/month.

### Rule your world.
When you combine the throughput, volume and finishing capabilities that Canon offers you, the possibilities are endless. They're scalable to cover your entire world's jobs and volumes.

### It's your decision.
Finally there is a better choice for all your production needs. With up to 2,000,000 pages/month and full finishing capabilities you now have complete control over your high volume world.

imageRUNNER 7200   imageRUNNER 8500   imageRUNNER 105   imageRUNNER 110

1 800 OK CANON   **Canon** KNOW HOW™   www.canon.ca

**Exhibit 6.9**
Changing technology makes purchasing for the digitized office a modified rebuy.

**buying centre** The group of people in an organization who influence and participate in purchasing decisions.

**Exhibit 6.10**
Centralized purchasing is one way Wal-Mart keeps "dropping" prices for its customers.

more physicians, the director of nurses, and purchasing agents may work together to determine quantities and select the best products and suppliers. A separate decision regarding the types of pharmaceutical supplies to stock might need a different group to advise the purchasing agent. This means that marketers must continually identify which employees are involved in every purchase and develop relationships with them all.

**ROLES IN THE BUYING CENTRE** Buying centre participants have unique roles in the decision process. In some cases, the purchasing agent or professional buyer who makes the purchase may also make the decision. In other cases, the buyer's chief role is to gather information for users of the product or a top manager who will ultimately make the decision.

For suppliers, the buying centre concept complicates the marketing process. A salesperson, for example, may have to provide different types of information to satisfy the interests of all participants. For example, a customer's engineers may want to know about the technical specifications of the product, whereas managers who will oversee the use of the product are interested in the safety of the product or in what types of in-service training the supplier is willing to provide. The salesperson also has to determine who has the most influence on the decision, who plays the key role of decision maker, and who actually makes the purchase. Consider again the hospital purchase of oxygen masks. The purchasing department's major concerns likely centre on price and delivery schedules, the nursing staff may be interested in packaging that is easy to open, and the physicians may be concerned with product design and that there will be few, if any, faulty masks. The salesperson must convince everyone that his or her product will satisfy their needs better than that of the competition.

Depending on the complexity of the purchase and the size of the buying centre, a participant may assume one, several, or all of the six roles shown in Figure 6.5. Let's review them.

The *initiator* begins the buying process by first recognizing that the firm needs to make a purchase. A production employee, for example, may notice that a piece of equipment is not working properly and notify a supervisor. At other times, the initiator may suggest purchasing a new product because it will improve the firm's operations. Depending on the initiator's position in the organization and the type of purchase, the initiator may or may not influence the actual purchase decision. For marketers, it is important to make sure individuals who might initiate a purchase are aware of improved products they offer.

The *user* is the member of the buying centre who needs the purchased product. The user's role in the buying centre varies. For example, an administrative assistant may give his or her input on the features needed in a new copier that the assistant will be "chained to" for several hours a day. Marketers need to inform users of their products about ease of use and other user benefits their products provide over those of competitors.

| Role | Potential Player | Responsibility |
|---|---|---|
| Initiator | Production employees, sales manager, almost anyone | Recognizes that a purchase needs to be made |
| User | Production employees, secretaries, almost anyone | Individual(s) who will ultimately use the product |
| Gatekeeper | Buyer/purchasing agent | Controls flow of information to others in the organization |
| Influencer | Engineers, quality control experts, technical specialists, outside consultants | Affects decision by giving advice and sharing expertise |
| Decider | Purchasing agent, managers, CEO | Makes the final purchase decision |
| Buyer | Purchasing agent | Executes the purchase decision |

**Figure 6.5** Roles in the Buying Centre

The *gatekeeper* is the member who controls the flow of information to other members. Typically, the gatekeeper is the purchasing agent who gathers information and materials from salespeople, schedules sales presentations, and controls suppliers' access to other participants in the buying process. For salespeople, developing and maintaining strong personal relationships with gatekeepers is critical to being able to offer their products to the buying centre.

An *influencer* affects the buying decision by dispensing advice or sharing expertise. By virtue of their expertise, engineers, quality control specialists, and other technical experts in the firm generally have a great deal of influence in purchasing equipment, materials, and component parts used in production. The influencers may or may not wind up using the product. Marketers need to identify key influencers in the buying centre and work to convince them of their product's superiority.

The *decider* is the member of the buying centre who makes the final decision. This person usually has the greatest power within the buying centre and often has power within the organization to authorize spending the company's money. For a routine purchase, the decider may be the purchasing agent. If the purchase is complex, a manager or CEO may be the decider. The decider is key to a marketer's success and deserves a great deal of attention in the selling process.

The *buyer* is the person who has responsibility for executing the purchase. Although the buyer often has a role in identifying and evaluating alternative suppliers, this person's primary function is handling the details of the purchase. The buyer obtains competing bids, negotiates contracts, and arranges delivery dates and payment plans. Once a firm makes the purchase decision, marketers turn their attention to negotiating the details of the purchase with the buyer. Successful marketers are well aware that providing exemplary service in this stage of the purchase can be key to future sales.

## THE BUSINESS BUYING DECISION PROCESS

We have seen a number of players in the business buying process, beginning with an initiator and ending with a buyer. To make matters more challenging to marketers, members of the buying team go through several stages in the decision-making process. The business buying decision process, as Figure 6.6 shows, is a series of steps similar to those in the consumer decision process (discussed in Chapter 5). The business buying process is more complex than the consumer decision-making process, however, and each step can mushroom into several additional steps.

## Problem Recognition

As in consumer buying, the first step in the business buying decision process occurs when someone sees that a purchase can solve a problem. For straight rebuy purchases, this step may be a result of the firm running out of paper, pens, or garbage bags. In these cases, the buyer places the order and the decision-making process ends. Recognition of the need for modified rebuy purchases often comes from wanting to replace outdated equipment, from changes in technology, or from an ad, brochure, or other form of marketing communication that offers the customer a better product at a lower price. The need for new-task purchases often arises because the firm wants to enhance its operations in some way or a smart salesperson tells the business customer about a new product that will increase the efficiency of the firm's operations.

**INFORMATION SEARCH** In the second step of the decision process for purchases other than straight rebuys, the buying centre searches for information about products and suppliers. Members of the buying centre may individually or

**Figure 6.6** Steps in the Business Buying Decision Process

collectively refer to reports in trade magazines and journals, seek advice from outside consultants, and pay close attention to marketing communication from different manufacturers and other suppliers. As in consumer marketing, marketers ensure that information is available when and where business customers want it—by placing ads in trade magazines, mailing brochures and other printed material to prospects, and having a well-trained, enthusiastic sales force regularly calling on customers.

DEVELOPING PRODUCT SPECIFICATIONS Business buyers often develop product specifications, written descriptions laying out their exact product requirements—quality, size, weight, colour, features, quantities, warranty, service terms, and delivery and training requirements for the purchase. When the product needs are complex or technical, engineers and other experts are key players in identifying specific product characteristics and determining whether standardized, off-the-shelf or customized, made-to-order goods and services will do.

OBTAINING PROPOSALS Once the product specifications are in hand, the buyer's next step is to obtain written or verbal proposals, or *bids*, from one or more potential suppliers. For standardized or branded products in which there are few, if any, differences in the products of different suppliers, this may be as simple as an informal request for pricing information, including discounts, shipping charges, and confirmation of delivery dates. At other times, the request is a formal written *request for proposal* or *request for quotation*, which requires suppliers to develop detailed proposals or price quotations for supplying the product.

## Evaluation of Alternatives

When evaluating alternatives, the buying centre assesses the proposals. Total spending for goods and services can have a major impact on the firm's profitability, so all other things being equal, price is the primary consideration. Pricing evaluations take into account discount policies for certain quantities, returned goods policies, the cost of repair and maintenance services, terms of payment, and the cost of financing large purchases. For capital equipment, cost criteria also include the life expectancy of the purchase, the expected resale value, and disposal costs for old equipment. In some cases, the buying centre may negotiate with the preferred supplier to match the lowest bidder. Although a bidder often is selected because it offers the lowest price, the buying decision may be based on other factors. For example, American Express wins bids for its travel agency business by offering extra services such as a corporate credit card and monthly reports that detail the company's total travel expenses.

The more complex and costly the purchase, the more time spent searching for the best supplier—and the more marketers must do to win the order. For example, marketers often make formal presentations and product demonstrations to the buying centre group. In the case of installations and large equipment, marketers sometimes arrange for buyers to speak with or even visit other customers to see for themselves how the product performs.

## Product and Supplier Selection

Once buyers have assessed all proposals, they make a purchase decision—the selection of the best product and supplier to meet the firm's needs. Although price is usually a factor, in firms that have adopted a total quality management approach (discussed in Chapter 2), the quality, reliability, and durability of materials and component parts are paramount. Reliability and durability rank high for equipment and systems that keep the firm's operations running smoothly without interruption. For some purchases, warranties, repair service, and regular maintenance after the sale are important.

A supplier's ability to make on-time deliveries is the critical factor in the selection process for firms that have adopted an inventory management system called **just in time (JIT)**. JIT systems reduce inventory and stock to very low levels (or even zero) and ensure

**American Express**
http://home3
.americanexpress.com/
canada/en/homepage/
default.asp

**just in time (JIT)** Inventory management and purchasing processes that manufacturers and resellers use to reduce inventory to very low levels and ensure that deliveries from suppliers arrive only when needed.

a constant supply through precisely timed deliveries just when needed (Exhibit 6.11). For both manufacturers and resellers, the choice of supplier may come down to one whose location is nearest. To win a large customer, a supplier organization may even have to be willing to set up production facilities close to the customer to guarantee JIT delivery.[11]

**Exhibit 6.11**
Toyota was an early adopter of the JIT system as space is at a premium in Japan and operations are constantly being challenged to run smoother.

One of the most important functions of a buyer is deciding how many suppliers can best serve the firm's needs. Sometimes one supplier is more beneficial to the organization than multiple suppliers. **Single sourcing**, in which a buyer and seller work quite closely, is particularly important for a firm that needs frequent deliveries or specialized products. But reliance on a single source means that the firm is at the mercy of the chosen supplier to deliver the needed goods or services without interruption. **Multiple sourcing** is buying a product from several suppliers. With multiple sourcing, suppliers are more likely to remain price competitive. And if one supplier has problems with delivery, the firm has others to fall back on.

Using one (or a few) suppliers rather than many has advantages. A firm that buys from a single supplier becomes a large customer with a lot of clout when it comes to negotiating prices and contract terms. Having one (or a few) suppliers also lowers the firm's administrative costs because it has fewer invoices to pay, fewer purchase orders to put into the system, and fewer salespeople to see.

Sometimes supplier selection is based on **reciprocity**, which means that a buyer and seller agree to be each other's customers by saying essentially, "I'll buy from you and you buy from me." For example, a firm that supplies parts to a company that manufactures trucks would agree to buy trucks from only that firm. Consumer and Corporate Affairs Canada frowns on reciprocal agreements and often determines that such agreements between large firms are illegal because they limit free competition—new suppliers simply don't have a chance against the preferred suppliers. In other countries, reciprocity is a common and, often, expected practice in business-to-business marketing.

With **outsourcing**, firms obtain outside vendors to provide goods or services that might otherwise be supplied in-house. For example, the federal government could have managed its own electronic tendering system but found it more cost effective and efficient to outsource this service to MERX.

Another type of buyer-seller partnership is **reverse marketing**. Instead of sellers trying to identify potential customers and then "pitching" their products, buyers try to find suppliers capable of producing specific products they need and then attempt to "sell" the idea to the suppliers. The seller works to satisfy the buying firm's needs while assuring themselves of product quality, sufficient supply, and reasonable terms.

**single sourcing**  The business practice of buying a particular product from only one supplier.

**multiple sourcing**  The business practice of buying a particular product from many suppliers.

**reciprocity**  A trading partnership in which two firms agree to buy from one another.

**outsourcing**  The business buying process of obtaining outside vendors to provide goods or services that otherwise might be supplied in-house.

**reverse marketing**  A business practice in which a buyer firm shapes a supplier's products and operations to satisfy its needs.

## Postpurchase Evaluation

Just as consumers evaluate purchases, an organizational buyer assesses whether the performance of the product and the supplier is living up to expectations. The buyer surveys the users to determine their satisfaction with the product as well as with the installation, delivery, and service provided by the supplier. By reviewing supplier performance, a firm decides whether to keep or drop the supplier. Many suppliers recognize the importance of conducting their own performance reviews on a regular basis. Measuring up to a customer's expectations can mean winning or losing a big account.

## Good or Bad Decision?

Canadian Schools are in a quandary.[12] Funding cutbacks have crippled school budgets forcing many to seek corporate sponsorships and exclusive contracts for vending machine rights. Marketers want to establish brand loyalty and teens are both a coveted and, when in schools, a captive audience. The Peel District School Board in Ontario has received $5.5 million in the first three years of an exclusive 10-year contract with Coca-Cola. The York Region District will receive $3.5 million plus to put toward scholarships for a five-year contract with Pepsi products. The Calgary Board of Education recently announced that public schools, classrooms, and programs can now be named for corporate donors.

Concerned parents claim that, while schools are preaching nutrition in the classroom, they are pushing junk food in the hallways. Advocates argue that kids are going to buy junk food anyway, so some of the money may as well go to support education. This issue is heating up. The principal of Pitt River Middle School in Coquitlam, B.C., tried to replace the fast-food mall in her school last September with fresh sandwiches, bagels, fruit, and milk, but the school district insisted the school return to selling fast foods, in order to "maintain buying efficiencies."

A number of marketers, however, are taking it upon themselves to be more socially responsible. Kraft Foods recently announced it would stop all in-school marketing and promotions for a range of products including Oscar Mayer meats, Oreos, and Kool-Aid. The soft drink industry announced it would voluntarily withdraw its carbonated drinks from Canadian elementary and middle schools by the beginning of the next school year. Concerned consumers see this as a token gesture because many elementary schools don't allow soft drink vending machines on their premises and the big money is in high schools.

Do you think schools or school boards should be seeking corporate sponsorships or distribution contracts? Should the fast-food industry be allowed to self-regulate on this issue or should a provincial or national policy be set? Do you think Kraft Foods' strategy will be effective in the long run if others do not follow its lead?

## ELECTRONIC BUSINESS-TO-BUSINESS COMMERCE

The Internet has brought about the most important changes in organizational buying behaviour in recent years. Electronic commerce, or e-commerce, is the buying and selling of products electronically via the Internet. We see e-commerce in consumer markets—sites such as Chapters.Indigo.com or Futureshop.com that sell consumer goods (to be discussed further in Chapter 11). In this chapter we are concerned with e-commerce in business markets. **Business-to-business (B2B) e-commerce** refers to the Internet exchanges between two or more businesses or organizations. B2B e-commerce includes exchanges of information, products, services, and payments (Exhibit 6.12). It's not as glitzy as consumer e-commerce, but it has changed the way businesses operate.

For several decades, firms have used electronic data interchange (EDI) systems to communicate with business partners. EDI allows for limited communication through the exchange of computer data between two companies. But EDI is expensive and transmits only rigidly formatted electronic documents such as purchase orders and invoices.

Today, many firms have replaced their EDI systems with Internet tools that allow electronic transfer of all kinds of data—even engineering drawings—as well as EDI-type exchanges. Ford, General Motors, and DaimlerChrysler, for example, established a huge automotive-parts exchange on the Internet linking 60 000 suppliers around the world to bid on more than US$240 billion worth of auto-part purchases.[13] For sellers, too, e-commerce provides remarkable advantages. Boeing, for example, received orders for $100 million in spare parts in the first year that its Web site was in operation.[14] The Internet also allows businesses to reach new markets. Saskatoon-based Point2.com, for example, is able to coordinate the sale of used mining equipment that would otherwise have been discarded because of the cost of an individual seller finding a buyer for their specialized equipment.[15]

Using the Internet for e-commerce allows business marketers to link directly to suppliers, factories, distributors, and customers, radically reducing the time necessary for order and delivery of goods, tracking sales, and getting feedback from customers. Forester Research forecasts that by 2005, 18 percent of all business-to-business trade in Canada will be done online, representing $250 billion of Canada's $1.3 trillion dollar B2B market.[16] John Roth, former President and CEO of Nortel Networks Corp., Canada's largest information technology company, suggested that "the Internet changes everything—everyone (big or small) can now become a global competitor and supplier."[17] One implication of this

**business-to-business (B2B) e-commerce** Internet exchanges between two or more businesses or organizations.

**Nortel Networks**
www.nortelnetworks.com

is that all firms, big and small, will need to have an international orientation as well as a source of competitive advantage to compete successfully. This is what Victoria-based WorldBid.com hopes to facilitate. Worldbid.com is the largest source of international trade leads, requests for quotation, and tender opportunities from companies and government organizations around the world. Over 230 000 businesses have registered to help increase sales, reduce supplier costs, and find new business contacts.[18]

In the simplest form of B2B e-commerce, the Internet provides an online catalogue of products and services that businesses need. Companies find that their Internet site is important for delivering online technical support, product information, order status information, and customer service to corporate customers (Exhibit 6.13).

## Intranets, Extranets, Private Exchanges, and Buying Groups

Although the Internet is the primary means of e-commerce, some companies have used similar computer technology to develop more secure means of conducting business. **Intranets** are in-house computer connections an organization creates to distribute information internally. City workers in Mississauga, Ontario, for example, use the intranet "WebBoard" to communicate all official announcements, new policies, technology implementations, staff appointments, and most recently, smog alerts.[19] Intranets are more secure than Internet connections, because they are protected by electronic firewalls that prevent access by unauthorized users.

When the intranet is opened to authorized external users, it is called an *extranet*. With extranets, marketers allow suppliers, distributors, and other authorized users to access data that the company makes available. Toronto-based 3Com Canada Inc., for example, uses extranet technology as a way to connect to branch offices, keep in touch with partners, and offer employees better ways of getting their jobs done.[20]

In addition to saving companies money, extranets allow business partners to collaborate on projects (such as product design) and to build better relationships. Hewlett-Packard and Procter & Gamble, for example, swap marketing plans and review ad campaigns with their advertising agencies through extranets. Extranets are also used by public service organizations to coordinate their resources and ability to serve the public. Ontario hospitals, for example, have an emergency patient referral system called CritiCall that allows admitting clerks, hospital administrators, and even physicians to track beds, emergency department status, and other medical resources. This allows the direction of patients to facilities that can help them quickly.[21]

Some of the most interesting online activity in the B2B world is taking place on **private exchanges**. These are systems that link a specially invited group of suppliers and partners over the Web. A private exchange allows companies to collaborate with suppliers they trust—without sharing sensitive information with others.

Wal-Mart, IBM, and Hewlett-Packard are among the giant firms already operating private exchanges. IBM Canada, for example, created AirWeb—a B2B e-market that allows IBM's 20 000 employees to book corporate travel online 24/7. AirWeb was created in partnership with American Express and is supported by Air Canada, Hertz, Delta Hotels, and 17 other American Express partners.[22] Many other companies are getting on board as well. For example, the director of inventory control for Ace Hardware can click his mouse and instantly get an up-to-the minute listing of the screwdrivers, hammers, and other products his suppliers have in stock. In addition, suppliers he has invited to participate in his private

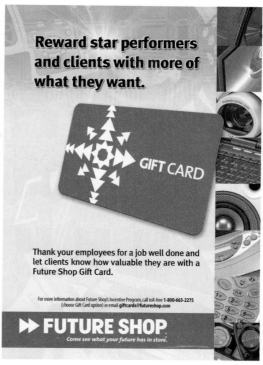

**Exhibit 6.12**
While Future Shop mainly focuses on business-to-consumer marketing, this ad shows it also caters to B2B customers.

**Worldbid.com**
www.worldbid.com

**intranet** An internal corporate communication network that uses Internet technology to link company departments, employees, and databases.

**private exchanges** Systems that link an invited group of suppliers and partners over the Web.

**B2B** It's not a fashion.
**It's a revolution.**

B2B is more than the latest craze, it's the new way to do business. Only eXcelon allows you to create a truly collaborative environment between you and your business partners. Making it possible to manage all your business content, not just transaction data. Integrating your business processes with those of your partners, into a single, unified workflow. Enabling all your partners to participate regardless of size, communication language or level of technical skill. Providing seamless connections to your existing enterprise systems. Leveraging partnerships is the promise of B2B. eXcelon makes it a reality. **www.exln.com**.

**eXceLon™**

eXcelon Corporation   25 Mall Road   Burlington, MA 01803   USA   1-800-962-9620

**Exhibit 6.13**

The popularity of online systems to connect buyers and sellers fuels demand for sophisticated software systems to manage these linkages.

**buying group** The coordination of purchasing among member organizations to realize economies of scale and other efficiencies.

**Onvia, Inc.**
www.onvia.com

exchange (and only those suppliers) can submit bids when he sees that Ace stores are running low on hammers. In the "old days" before this process, it would take 7 to 10 days to purchase more hammers, and Ace's suppliers could only guess how many they should have on hand to supply the chain at any given time. The system benefits everyone because Ace keeps tighter controls on its inventories and its suppliers have a more accurate picture of the store's needs so they can get rid of unneeded inventory and streamline their costs.

IBM estimates that it saved almost $400 million worldwide in 2000 by relying on private exchange systems. Small wonder that one research firm estimates the world's biggest firms will soon spend between $50 million to $100 million to build private exchanges.[23]

**Buying groups** reflect a cooperative purchasing effort among organizations that individually may be too small to command volume discounts or enjoy other economies of scale. By pooling their purchases with other companies, buying group members can cut overall procurement costs by as much as 10 percent.[24]

Gold Leaf Office Products Ltd. is a Canadian buying group that has 11 member companies, with combined annual sales of about $180 million. In addition to handling their bulk buying, the staff at Gold Leaf's office publishes catalogues for members, prints advertising flyers, and runs a group-wide private brand of supplies—all of better quality and at a lower cost to the firms than they could manage on their own. Onvia, Inc., founded in Vancouver in 1996 and now operating out of Seattle, combines the purchasing power of more than 400 000 small business owners and gives them access to the goods and services of about 700 manufacturers and 25 wholesale distributors at reduced prices.[25]

## Security Issues

There are several security issues with B2B e-commerce (Exhibit 6.14). You may be concerned about someone obtaining your credit card number and charging even more to your account than you do, but companies have even greater worries. When hackers break into company sites, they can destroy company records and steal trade secrets. Both B2C and B2B e-commerce companies worry about *authentication* and ensuring that transactions are secure. Authentication means making sure that only authorized individuals are allowed to access a site and place an order. Maintaining security also requires firms to keep the information transferred as part of a transaction, such as a credit card number, out of criminals' hands.

Well meaning but careless employees can create security problems as well. They can give out unauthorized access to company computer systems by not keeping their passwords into the system a secret. For example, hackers guess at passwords that are easy—nicknames, birth dates, hobbies, a spouse's name. To increase security of their Internet sites and transactions, most companies now have safeguards in place—firewalls and encryption devices, to name the most common two.

**Exhibit 6.14**

Internet Security is a major problem for B2B marketers.

# Real People, Real Decisions

## How It Worked Out for the 2010 Winter Olympic Bid Team

Marion Lay, the first Board of Directors, and the bid management team set the initial course to position the 2010 Winter Games international bid as an ultra-ethical bid and this positioning was carried through in the later stages of the process by John Furlong (President of the Vancouver–Whistler bid committee) and Jack Poole (Chairman and CEO). This positioning was consistent with Canada's international image and leadership in anti-doping and other initiatives to make the games "clean" and "fair." To pull it off, Lay and, subsequently, Furlong had to recruit people to the bid team that shared these values and had the conviction to stick to their values in the face of intense pressure to win at all costs. Following the selection of Beijing over Toronto and other cities for the 2008 summer games, Lay and Furlong brought in key people from the Toronto bid team who had developed profiles of and strong relationships with, key IOC members. A "soft sell" approach was used to get peo-

ple the IOC members trusted to present the merits of the Canadian bid and why it would be good for the IOC to align itself with a highly ethical and environmentally and socially sustainable bid, from a country known for playing fair.

Canada won the right to host the 2010 Winter Olympic Games by just three votes. The South Korean bid team put together a technically solid bid, had developed a highly persuasive promotional campaign backed by large corporate sponsors, and had implemented a personal influence strategy to secure votes. After Austria was eliminated, however, much of the European vote swung to Canada as being the best bid and the right thing to do to clean up the image of the IOC. This result, although closer than expected, validated the positioning strategy that was initially developed by Marion Lay and her team.

# CHAPTER SUMMARY

**1. Describe the general characteristics of business-to-business markets and business buying practices.**

Business-to-business markets include business and organizational customers that buy goods and services for purposes other than personal consumption. Business and organizational customers are usually few in number, may be geographically concentrated, and often purchase higher-priced products in larger quantities. Business demand is derived from the demand for another good or service, is generally not affected by price increases or decreases, is subject to great fluctuations, and may be tied to the demand and availability of some other good.

**2. Explain how marketers classify business and organizational markets.**

Business customers include producers, resellers, governments, and not-for-profit organizations. Producers purchase materials, parts, and various goods and services needed to produce other goods and services to be sold at a profit. Resellers purchase finished goods to resell at a profit, as well as other goods and services to maintain their operations. Governments and other not-for-profit organizations purchase the goods and services necessary to fulfill their objectives. The North American Industry Classification System (NAICS), a numerical coding system developed by NAFTA countries, is the most widely used classification system for business and organizational markets.

**3. Explain the business buying situation and describe business buyers.**

The business buy class identifies the degree and effort required to make a business buying decision. Purchase situations can be straight rebuy, modified rebuy, and new-task buying. Business buying is usually handled by trained professional buyers. A buying centre is a group of people who work together to make a buying decision. The roles in the buying centre are initiator, user, gatekeeper, influencer, decider, and buyer. The most important recent change in business buying is the growth of e-commerce, in which firms buy and sell products using the Internet, intranets, or extranets.

**4. Summarize the main stages in the business buying decision process.**

The stages in the business buying decision process are similar to, but more complex than, the steps in consumer decision making. These steps include problem recognition, information search during which buyers develop product specifications and obtain proposals from prospective sellers, proposal evaluation, supplier selection, and formal evaluation of the performance of the product and the supplier. A firm's purchasing options include single or multiple sourcing. In outsourcing, firms obtain outside vendors to provide goods or services that otherwise might be supplied in-house. Other business buying activities are reciprocity and reverse marketing.

**5. Explain how e-commerce is dramatically changing business-to-business marketing.**

Every company, large or small, can now become a global competitor and supplier. This means that all firms need to have an international orientation and some source of competitive advantage. The Internet allows business marketers to link directly to suppliers, factories, distributors, and customers, radically reducing the time necessary for the order and delivery of goods, for tracking sales, and for getting feedback from customers. It also means companies can get access to a worldwide supply of goods and services, putting pressure on both pricing and quality.

# CHAPTER REVIEW

## Marketing Concepts: Testing Your Knowledge

1. What are some general characteristics of business-to-business markets? What is one primary difference between business customers and consumers?

2. How is business-to-business demand different from consumer demand? What are some of the factors that cause business demand to fluctuate?

3. How are business-to-business markets generally classified? What types of purchases do the major types of organizations make?

4. What is the NAICS? What purpose does it serve? Of what use is it to business marketers?

5. Describe the three buy class situations.

6. What is the role of electronic commerce in business-to-business marketing?

7. What are the characteristics of business buyers?

8. What is a buying centre? What are the roles of the various people in a buying centre?

9. What are buying groups, and how is the Internet facilitating rapid growth in these groups?

10. What are the stages in the business buying decision process? What happens in each stage?

11. What is single sourcing? Multiple sourcing? Outsourcing? Explain how reciprocity and reverse marketing operate in business-to-business markets.

## Marketing Concepts: Discussing Choices and Issues

1. Do you agree with the idea that business-to-business marketing is more important to a country's economy than consumer marketing? Which one do you think provides better career opportunities for new college and university graduates? Explain your answers.

2. A number of business buying practices may be criticized as being unfair to one or more suppliers. What are the benefits of reciprocity to business firms? Is anyone hurt by reciprocity?

3. The practice of buying business products based on sealed competitive bids is popular among all types of business buyers. What are the advantages and disadvantages of this practice to buyers? What are the advantages and disadvantages to sellers? Should companies always give the business to the lowest bidder? Why or why not?

4. When firms engage in outsourcing, they relinquish control over how goods and services are produced. What are the advantages of outsourcing to a firm? What are some of the hazards of outsourcing? What can firms do to make sure that outsourcing is beneficial to both them and the outsourcing firm?

## Marketing Practice: Applying What You've Learned

1. You are looking for a part-time job and being considered by a small, weekly newspaper. Knowing that you are a marketing student, the editor has asked you to provide a sample article that explains business demand in a way that will be interesting to the owners of small local shops and other businesses. Write that article and circulate it among three classmates, asking each to provide brief written comments and suggestions.

2. You've just been hired by a small consulting company that services small- to medium-sized firms. One of the company's clients produces custom-imprinted T-shirts for local sports teams and other groups and is thinking about switching to a JIT inventory control system. The client, who has 10 employees, currently buys the T-shirts in bulk and keeps large quantities of stock imprints and other supplies on hand. Your boss has asked you to prepare a list of issues the owner has to consider. Prepare the list and discuss each point with a classmate who assumes the client's role.

3. As a new director of materials management for a textile firm that manufactures sheets and towels, you are hoping to simplify the buying process where possible, thus reducing costs for the firm. You have first examined each purchase and classified it as a straight rebuy, a modified rebuy, or a new-task purchase. Your next job is to outline the procedures or steps in the purchasing process for each type of purchase. Indicate the type of purchase and outline the steps that must be taken in the purchase of each of the following items.

   a. computer paper

   b. textile dyes for this year's fashion colours

   c. new sewing robotics

   d. new software to control the weaving processes

## Marketing Mini-Project: Learning by Doing

The purpose of this mini-project is to gain knowledge about one business-to-business market using the NAICS codes and other government information.

1. Select an industry of interest to you and use the NAICS information found on the Internet (**www.statcan.ca/english/Subjects/Standard/standard_classifications.htm**) or in your library.

   a. What are the codes for each of the following classifications?

      NAICS Sector (two digits)

      NAICS Subsector (three digits)

      NAICS Industry Group (four digits)

      NAICS Industry (five digits)

      Canadian Industry (six digits)

   b. What types of products are or are not included in this industry?

2. Find out what information Industry Canada has on your industry. Go to the Strategis Web site (**http://strategis.ic.gc.ca/sc_mrkti/tdst/engdoc/tr_homep.html**) to review Canadian industry statistics. Note that Strategis still uses SIC codes instead of NAICS codes, so you will have to look up your industry again using the "Search For SIC Code" button on the page.

   Statistics Canada is the country's national statistical agency with a mandate to collect, compile, analyze, abstract, and publish statistical information on virtually every aspect of the nation's society and economy. Go to the Statistics Canada Web site (**www.statcan.ca/english/search**) and enter the name of your industry into the search engine. What information does Statistics Canada have on your industry?

3. Canadian Industry Norms & Key Business Ratios is a CD-ROM resource available in many libraries, that has data useful for analyzing trends and assessing the strengths and weaknesses of the agriculture, mining, construction, transportation, wholesaling, utilities, retailing, finance, insurance, real estate, and services industries. Information on specific companies is also available. See what information is available on one of these industries.

4. The Blue Book of Canadian Business provides detailed profiles of leading Canadian companies (public, private, crown, and cooperatives) in terms of sales, assets, net income, and stock trading volume. The Canadian Key Business Directory profiles the top 20 000 public and private companies. Look up one of the companies in your industry and find their net sales, gross profits, and income before tax.

## Real People, Real Surfers: Exploring the Web

Mega Bloks (see Chapter 5) isn't the only company that makes construction toy products. Visit Mega Bloks' Web site (**www.megabloks.com**) and that of their main competitor, Lego (**www.lego.com**), and other specialty toy producers such as Rokenbok (**www.rokenbok.com**) or K'nex (**www.knex.com**).

Based on your experience, answer the following questions.

1. In general, how do the Web sites compare? Which are easier to navigate, and why? Which are more innovative and attractive, and why?

2. Evaluate each site from the perspective of a toy store buyer. What features in each site would be useful? What information is available that a buyer might need? Which site would be most useful for a buyer? Why?

3. Evaluate each site from the perspective of a parent. What features in each site would be useful? What information is available that a parent might need? Which site would be most useful for a parent? Why?

Venture 4th provides office space, secretarial services, technology services, and marketing, accounting, and other business expertise for start-up ventures in Halifax, Nova Scotia. The brain trust of four commerce graduates (Sean O'Connor, Sarah Brown, Rick Styles, and Paul Rainer), Venture 4th currently has six clients, ranging from a fledgling e-tail business to a profitable specialty food importer.

Ever since Venture 4th opened its doors two years ago, office technology has been a major headache. The four partners started their service business on a shoestring budget—using their own computers and desktop printers, purchasing an inexpensive fax machine and scanner, and renting a low-end photocopier for general use. (Clients with special computer and high-speed Internet access needs provided those resources for themselves.) Unable to afford a more elegant Ethernet solution, the company ran a "sneaker net" system, where users brought disks to a central computer to use the laser printer, colour inkjet printer, and scanner. This system was adequate for the first year, when there were only two clients. With greater demand on the resources, however, and differences in computer speeds, software versions, and printer drivers, the system was driving everyone crazy—particularly Rick Styles, who was responsible for keeping this hodgepodge of equipment operating. The issue came to a head when the e-tail client said he couldn't continue to run his business out of the Venture 4th office space without more reasonable office technology support.

When this was discussed at the weekly partners' meeting, Sarah Brown, the partner primarily responsible for new business development, indicated that she thought she could land two more clients and another $40 000 a year revenue if the company had more modern and higher-capacity office equipment linked in a network solution. With this to motivate them, the Venture 4th team began to investigate the purchase of an Ethernet office network linked to high-speed Internet access and a digital imaging system comprising an integrated network printer, copier, scanner, and fax machine.

It took Styles three weeks to do a preliminary investigation of the options. He called Copies Plus, from which Venture 4th was renting its Rocket copier, and Iain Carver, their small business representative, came the following day to do a needs analysis. Based on current and projected printing and copying volume, Carver recommended a digital imaging system that could make at least 10 000 copies a month. This ruled out the "all in one" desktop solutions Styles had been looking at the last time he was in Future Shop. Carver recommended the Rocket 3000E system, left a brochure, and promised to follow up with a price quote. During the visit, Carver "tuned up" the rental unit and left some samples of a new brand of laser printer paper that Copies Plus was carrying.

The next day, a Xena representative called, asked for Styles, and made an appointment for the following week to discuss Xena document solutions. The rep, Peter Smith, having overheard Sarah Brown talking about their need for a new copier one evening at a downtown bar, had approached her with a funny "pick-up" line, engaged her with polite conversation, and then returned (to her relief) to his friends. Later he approached one of Brown's friends and found out where she worked. When he met with Styles, he marvelled at his ability to keep the current system running and promised to return with a system recommendation and prices.

About a week after Styles had received a faxed Rocket quote and a couriered envelope with Smith's recommendation and pricing for a Xena 33DT system, Sean O'Connor mentioned that he had seen a Cambon digital imaging system in the law firm used by Venture 4th. O'Connor had been quite impressed with the system and had talked with one of the secretaries about it while waiting to see the firm's lawyer. The secretary said that the system had been in place for about a year and had made a big difference in the law firm's ability to produce and manage the receipt of thousands of documents. This recommendation prompted Styles to call a Cambon distributor, who faxed him the specifications of the Cambon DC330.

At Venture 4th, strategic decisions and those involving more than $10 000 had to have unanimous approval by the partners. Therefore, Styles invited Carver, Smith, and a representative from the Cambon distributor to the partners' meeting to present the merits of their systems. At the end of each presentation, Styles asked the reps whether the presented price was the best they could do. In a "Regis" parody, Paul Rainer followed this with, "Is that your final answer?" Only the rep from the Cambon distributor responded with a last-minute price reduction, taking $200 off the price of the system.

The Rocket system had the fastest copying—35 pages per minute versus 33 for the Cambon and 32 for the Xena—and it was rated for the greatest volume—20 000 to 60 000 copies per month versus 10 000 for the other two. While the Rocket system was the least expensive at $14 500, its printing technology was not PostScript compatible without adding an optional $1500 feature. PostScript compatibility is important for desktop publishing applications—which some of Venture 4th's clients might want.

The Xena system, priced at $19 200, came with a PostScript printing capability but did not have a stapling feature. Xena had a strong reputation for product quality and support, and its history of copying innovation impressed the partners.

The rep from the Cambon distributor arrived late but did a credible job explaining the benefits of his system. The Cambon system, priced at $18 100 (after the $200 reduction) had been awarded a "recommended buy" by the U.S.-based Buyers Laboratory, a product testing and rating organization. Although the Cambon product took longer to warm up than the others, it had the highest printing resolution at 1200 X 600 dpi (dots per inch) versus 600 X 600 for the other two and the greatest paper capacity at 3500 sheets compared to 2000 sheets for the others. The Xena rep, presenting before the Cambon rep, had explained that there were more important factors than dpi for print quality and that the Xena system had the crispest image.

At the end of the partners' meeting, Styles summarized the advantages and disadvantages of each system. The partners agreed that they should purchase one of the systems. O'Connor liked the Cambon solution best, having been impressed on his visit to the law firm, and noted that the Cambon distributor had lowered his price once and might do so again if pressed. Brown liked the idea of saving some money by buying the Rocket, then upgrading later if anyone wanted to get the PostScript option. Styles and Rainer leaned toward the Xena solution, considering company's reputation; they also noted that the rep from the Cambon distributor came late and questioned what kind of support they might get from him. The partners decided that they should all go to see each of the systems in action.

The next day, Styles called the reps and arranged a visit to one of their installations. When they visited the company with a Rocket system, the paper had just jammed on the system and a technician had to be called. The staff that used the system said that this didn't happen very often and that they were generally happy with the system. Both the Xena and Cambon solutions were working when the Venture 4th partners came to see them, and the staff who used the systems raved about the products.

A few days later, Styles called the three reps to say that he and his partners were going to make a purchase decision at 4:00 that afternoon. He told them that if they wanted to reconsider their pricing and submit a lower quote, they could do so before 3:00. At 1:00, the Rocket rep faxed in a new price of $14 000 and a one-year option to buy the PostScript upgrade at $1300. At 2:00, the Cambon rep faxed in a new price of $17 900 and offered free installation and three hours of staff training. Styles called the Rocket rep back, confirmed that his price included installation, and got a verbal commitment to three hours of staff training. At 2:45, Styles called Smith at Xena and was told that the original price of $19 200 was the best he could do and that the price included installation and three hours of training. At 4:15, during the partner deliberations, the Xena rep called back. He told Styles that Xena was going to announce a price reduction on the 332DC system the next day and that his manager had authorized a $500 price reduction for Venture 4th. Armed with this new information, Styles went back into the partner meeting to get a consensus decision.

Source: This case was written by Professor Brock Smith of the University of Victoria.

## Things to Think About

1. If you were a partner of Venture 4th, which system would purchase, and why?

2. How does this purchase process compare with the model illustrated in Figure 6.6?

3. Where was the most time spent in this purchase process? Why?

4. Assuming that this decision process is typical, what are the implications for sales and marketing organizations?

## Mohair Socks

Theresa Bergeron was once a champion angora goat breeder. Now, she is an entrepreneur and the president of Thermohair Inc., a thriving international mohair sock business that she operates from South Mountain, Ontario. She sells high-end socks made from mohair (the fleece of baby angora goats) that wholesale for about $15 and retail for around $30. They are a popular item among hikers and outdoor enthusiasts. While the business is profitable, Bergeron faces the dual challenges of sourcing a sufficient supply of quality mohair and distributing her product more extensively. Bergeron has been hit hard by the restructuring of the mohair market; her regular suppliers are either retiring or cutting back production, and the South African mohair producers are buying up virtually all other sources of the fibre.

Bergeron is experiencing a paradoxical dilemma. She continues to work hard to find new store owners interested in her product and to build sales with current distributors—to the point where she does half-a-million dollars in annual sales. But now the problem is getting her hands on materials to make the socks. She knows it is crucial to get a hold of the materials before retailers give up on her, change their minds, or order another kind of sock.

In the past, Bergeron sourced mohair fibre from Texas and other parts of the world. She then shipped it to England to be spun into yarn, sent the yarn to a company in Georgetown, Ontario, to knit the socks, and then shipped the socks to her home in South Mountain where her family sorted and labelled the product. To stay on top of this type of supply chain, Bergeron needs to stay aware of international competition for raw fibre, manage fluctuating currency exchanges, account for long lead times in supply acquisition and production, and ensure that the yarn manufacturer maintains quality control so that the knitter can use the yarn. Even world weather patterns have an impact on her business—a drought in South Africa can result in the death of goats, which can then lead to a world shortage of mohair and skyrocketing costs.

Many of Bergeron's traditional suppliers now use their own fibre to make mohair products. After considerable search, she finally finds a new supplier from South Africa that claims to provide the quality and quantity of fibre needed to make her socks. She orders a sample to see if it will pass the quality level test needed by her yarn maker. In the end, Teresa's mohair sock connection comes through. The South African mohair is not only cheaper, but it has the same high quality as the mohair from her previous and unpredictable suppliers. Her supply crisis solved, at least temporarily, she now turns her attention to increasing distribution and sales.

## Questions

1. As a retail buyer, what would you look for in a sock supplier? How long would you wait for Bergeron to fix her supply problem?
2. What are some of the challenges in buying your supply from producers all over the world?
3. What organizational buying behaviour concepts are most pertinent to Bergeron's situation?

Source: This case was prepared by Brock Smith and is based on *Venture*, "The Goat Lady of South Mountain," # 871.

# PART III

Part III

Part II

Societal Success

Business Success

Customer Success

Part IV

Part I

# Developing Marketing Strategies

**You learned in Part II that the process of market segmentation enables a business to choose the target markets it wants to serve.** But how exactly does it "serve" these markets? By developing superior marketing strategies that enable it to be a superior competitor in the marketplace. You will learn in this part that marketing strategies are developed using a combination of product, pricing, marketing communications (promotion), and channel of distribution (place) strategies.

*OPTION 1*     *OPTION 2*     *OPTION 3*

# CHAPTER 7
# Product Strategy

## CHAPTER OBJECTIVES

WHEN YOU HAVE COMPLETED YOUR STUDY OF THIS CHAPTER, YOU SHOULD BE ABLE TO

1. Explain how the layers of a product lead to competitive advantage.

2. Explain the good–service continuum and its importance.

3. Explain the key differences between goods and services.

4. Describe how firms develop new products.

5. Discuss the importance of innovations.

6. Explain the process of product adoption and the diffusion of innovations.

# Real People, Real Decisions

## Meet **Dee Dee Gordon,** a Decision Maker at Lambesis

Dee Dee Gordon is co-president of Look-Look, Inc., a youth culture research and marketing solutions company. Prior to this, she was the head of research at Lambesis advertising agency, at which she and colleague Sharon Lee developed the *L Report*, a document to track youth trends.

A few years ago, the Cosmar division of Renaissance Cosmetics, Inc., launched a product called Nail Fetish, a small collection of artificial nails and decals targeted to teenage girls. To build on this product, the company's Dana fragrance division decided to market a perfume called Fetish to the same audience. Dana's goal was to sell $8 million of the fragrance in its first year. Reaching this goal would not be easy—the women's mass fragrance market had been experiencing steadily declining sales, and the category was dominated by heavyweights like Coty and Revlon. The company retained advertising agency Lambesis to help it research the best way to capture the hearts and pocketbooks of this young audience.

Lambesis started by asking teenage girls what they wanted in a fragrance. Although respondents said they preferred expensive boutique brands like MAC, a different picture emerged when the girls were asked to empty their handbags—in reality, they were buying mostly cheap drugstore brands. Feedback compiled via the *L Report* underscored the importance of status symbols for this group and emphasized the importance these girls attach to displaying valued possessions on their dressers. They valued objects that were so cool that they could be used to hold things or be reused in some way.

Dee Dee Gordon saw an opportunity to create a new, mass-market fragrance, targeted to teenage girls, that would be prestigious and cool enough to motivate the girls to keep the bottle and show it off to their friends. The product positioning strategy became "Fetish is cool, hip, and fun; it's the only beauty brand that really understands me." Research showed that girls in this age group were fascinated by futur-

istic bottle designs and interesting packaging such as the Orbitz beverage bottle or the CK One perfume holder.

The company focused on creating a design that would express this new attitude. As inspiration, its designers used findings from the initial research that asked girls to empty their purses. It modeled the bottle after other items found in these bags, such as beepers and pagers, toys like Hello Kitty, and accessories like hair barrettes. A set of eight package concepts was developed, and a series of focus groups among girls ages 14 to 17 was conducted to get reactions. Based on the responses, the company narrowed its package choice down to three options (shown at the beginning of this chapter).

**Option 1.** The girls liked this concept because it could be clipped to their clothing or bags. The girls also said they would enjoy collecting the different-coloured fragrance bottles.

**Option 2.** Overall, the girls disliked the vial, but they did like the stand because it could also be used to hold pens and pencils.

**Option 3.** The girls liked the functionality of this design. Many said they would wear the cap as a hair accessory. Others said they were concerned the elastic band would break when worn in the hair. Some girls had concerns about the perfume spilling once the cap was removed.

Now, put yourself in Dee Dee's shoes: Which option would you choose and why? To get a handle on this product problem, it may be helpful to try to understand the mind-set of teenage girls. If possible, interview some 12- to 15-year-old girls about what they look for in a perfume. Ask them how they display their bottles and other personal care products. How do they carry these around, or do they? What kinds of statements are these girls trying to make through their fragrance choices?

# BUILD A BETTER MOUSETRAP...

"Build a better mousetrap and the world will beat a path to your door." Although we've all heard that adage, the truth is: Just because a product is better, there is no guarantee it will succeed. For decades, the Woodstream Company built wood mousetraps. Then the company decided to build a better one. Woodstream's product development people researched mouse eating, crawling, and resting habits; built prototypes of different mousetraps to come up with the best possible design; and tested them in homes. Finally, the company unveiled the sleek-looking "Little Champ," a black plastic miniature inverted bathtub with a hole (see Exhibit 7.1). When the mouse went in and ate the bait, a spring snapped upward, and the mouse was history.[1]

Sounds like a great new product (if you're not a mouse), but the "Little Champ" failed. Woodstream studied mouse habits, *not* consumer preferences. The company later discovered that husbands set the trap at night, but wives were left to dispose of the trap holding the dead mouse in the morning. Unfortunately, wives thought the "Little Champ" looked too expensive to throw away, so they felt they should empty the trap for reuse. This was a task most women weren't willing to do—they wanted a trap they could happily throw away.

Woodstream's failure underscores the importance of creating products that provide benefits people seek. It also tells us that any number of products, from low-tech cheese to high-tech traps, potentially deliver these benefits. In this case, cheese and a shoebox could trap a mouse as well as a high-tech trap. So, in developing new products, marketers need to take a close look at whether the products successfully satisfy consumers' needs better than the alternatives.

As defined in Chapter 1, a product is anything tangible or intangible that, through the exchange process, satisfies consumer or business customer needs. Products can be physical goods, services, ideas, people, or places. A good may be a sweatshirt, pack of cookies, digital camera, house, tractor, or pair of jeans. A **good** is a tangible product, something that we can see, touch, smell, hear, taste, or possess. In contrast, intangible products—services, ideas, people, places—are products that we can't always see, touch, taste, smell, or possess. Banking services, a concert, convincing people to recycle or vote for a particular political candidate, and getting people to visit a particular province on their next vacation are all examples of intangible products.

Marketers think of the product as more than just a *thing* that comes in a package. They view a product as a *bundle* of attributes, including packaging, brand name, benefits, and supporting features in addition to a physical good. In this chapter, we'll first examine what a

**goods** Tangible products we can see, touch, smell, hear, or taste.

**Exhibit 7.1**

A better mousetrap? Only if it satisfies customer needs.

product is, and how thinking about the different layers of a product helps a marketer build an edge in the marketplace. Then we'll look at the differences between goods and services and the implications this has for marketing strategy. Finally, we will examine new products—how marketers develop new products, and how markets accept them.

## Layers of the Product Concept

A product is *everything* that a customer receives in an exchange. As Figure 7.1 shows, the product has four distinct layers—the core, functional, augmented, and potential product. These layers are very useful because they teach us how to build a competitive edge in the marketplace. Let us see how.

The *core product* refers to product features or attributes: Dove soap has moisturizing cream. The *functional product* refers to how the product performs or functions: How easy is it to use Dove, how foamy is it, etc. The *augmented product* refers to the augmentations (i.e., additions) the marketer attaches to the basic product: Dove's packaging, logo, brand name, customer satisfaction guarantees, etc. Finally, the *potential product* refers to the solution the customer gets from the offering: Because Dove does not dry skin, its regular use helps prevents wrinkles and promotes younger looking skin.

How does this knowledge of product layers build a competitive advantage? The answer is simple—consumers do not buy product features, they buy the benefits offered by the product. So, Dove should not focus on the fact that its soap contains moisturizing cream; instead, it should focus its marketing communications efforts on the benefits the brand provides to consumers. It is this potential product that consumers can relate to and that can build a relationship with the brand. Also, the potential product is difficult for competitors to successfully imitate because Dove has claimed it first.

In Table 7.1 we identify several core products. Can you identify the potential product in each case? (The answers can be obtained in Table 7.3 at the end of the chapter, but no peeking!)

## The Goods–Services Continuum

In reality, most products are a *combination* of goods and services. The purchase of a "pure good" like a car still has service components, such as bringing it to the dealer for maintenance work. The purchase of a "pure service" like a makeover at a department store has product components, for example, lotions, powders, and lipsticks the cosmetologist uses to create the "new you."

The goods–services continuum in Figure 7.2 shows that some products are dominated by either tangible or intangible characteristics—for instance, salt versus teaching—whereas others tend to include a mixture of goods and services—such as flying in an airplane. A product's placement on this continuum gives some guidance as to which marketing issues are likely to be most relevant. As the product approaches the tangible pole of this continuum, there is fairly little emphasis on service; the physical product itself is the focal point, and people will choose one over others based on the product's function or image. To com-

**Figure 7.1** Product Layers

**Table 7.1** Can you identify the potential product for each core product?

| Core Product | Potential Product |
| --- | --- |
| Industrial gloves | ? |
| Shopping mall | ? |
| Medical diagnostic equipment (e.g. CAT scan) | ? |
| Coffee | ? |

pete, the marketer will try to differentiate based on services. So, car manufacturers may try to differentiate goods by providing a unique service dimension (e.g., the dealership experience).

As the product gets near the intangible pole, the physical product shrinks in importance, and the service encounter plays a key role in shaping the service experience. Marketers of these products try to make their offerings more tangible. Scarborough General Hospital, for example, provides all patients with a chart explaining precisely when and exactly what is going to happen to them during their stay in the hospital. This minimizes patient frustration by shaping their expectations (we discuss this further in the next chapter, as well as in Chapter 15).

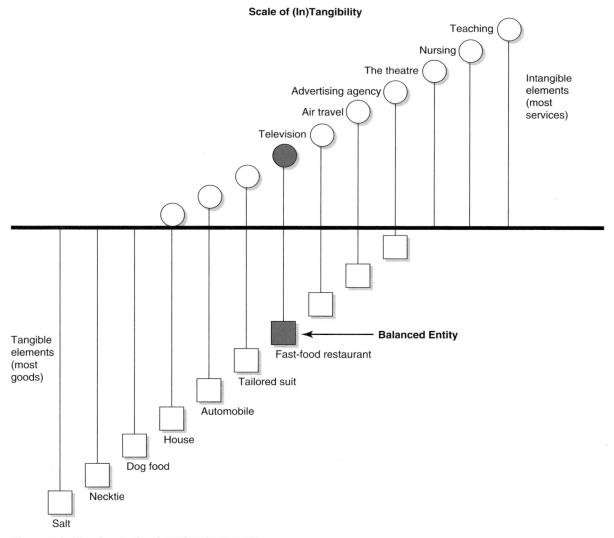

**Figure 7.2** The Goods–Services Continuum

In the middle of the continuum, however, both goods and services contribute substantially to the quality of the product, because these products rely on people to satisfactorily operate equipment that will deliver quality service. Let's consider each of these three positions as we move from products dominated by tangibles to those dominated by intangibles.

**GOOD-DOMINATED PRODUCTS** Many tangible products are accompanied by supporting services, even if this means only that the company maintains a toll-free telephone line or Web site for questions or provides a 30-day warranty against defects. Including a service with the purchase of a physical good is termed **embodying**.[2] This is a popular option in the computer industry, especially for companies that are trying to break into international markets saturated with cheap products but with insufficient guidance in their use. As millions of people buy computers and other hardware, they are apt to find it difficult to navigate the maze of set-up instructions, and next to impossible to cope with machines that unexpectedly crash. Indeed, one survey by *PC Magazine* found that 28 percent of its readers needed technical support in the first year of owning a personal computer. What's more, in grading manufacturers' service performance, they gave two-thirds of them Cs and Ds. Companies with the resources to do so find that embodying follow-up service is a potent marketing tool when competing with "clone" manufacturers. As an executive at Compaq (now owned by Hewlett Packard) observed, "The bad guys give us an opportunity to differentiate."[3]

**embodying** The inclusion of a service with a purchase of a physical good.

**EQUIPMENT- OR FACILITY-DRIVEN SERVICES** As Figure 7.2 shows, some products require a mixture of tangible and intangible elements. Many hospitals and restaurants fall in the middle of the continuum because they rely on expensive equipment or facilities and skilled personnel to deliver a product.

*Facility-driven services*, such as automatic car washes, amusement parks, museums, movie theatres, health clubs, and zoos, must be concerned with these three important factors:[4]

- *Operational factors:* Technologies must move customers smoothly through the service: Clear signs and other guidelines must show customers how to use the service. In particular, firms need to minimize waiting times. Marketers have developed a number of tricks to give impatient customers the illusion that they aren't waiting too long. One hotel chain, responding to complaints about the long wait for elevators, installed mirrors in the lobby: People's tendency to examine their appearance occupied them until the elevators arrived, and protests declined.[5] Burger King's research showed that multiple lines create stress in customers—especially if one moves faster than the others—so it shifted to single lines in which customers at the head of the line order at the next available register.[6]

- *Location factors:* These are especially important for frequently purchased services, such as dry cleaning, that are obtained at a fixed location. Fast food restaurants, such as Subway, try to have several restaurants, all in convenient locations, to satisfy customers' need for convenience.

- *Environmental factors:* Service managers who operate a storefront service requiring people to come to their location realize they must create an attractive environment to lure customers. That's why sports venues such as the Saddledome in Calgary offer plush luxury suites, where wealthy patrons can watch sports events in style. The Calgary Flames, like many Canadian sports franchises, tries to provide all fans with a fun, exciting environment when they attend their games by including such features as between-period contests, promotions, and other fun events.[7]

One trend is for services to adopt a more retail-like philosophy, borrowing techniques from clothing stores or restaurants to create a pleasant environment. Banks, for example, are creating signature looks for branches through the use of lighting, colour, and art. When ING Direct, a Netherlands-based bank, opened in Canada, it didn't open any traditional bank branches. The company, which specializes in Web- and telephone-based banking transactions, decided to open cafés instead of branches, where banking services were sold along with Starbucks and other brands of coffee.[8]

**ING Direct**
www.ingdirect.ca

**PEOPLE-BASED SERVICES** At the intangible end of the continuum are people-based services. In the Great American Backrub store, for instance, customers sit in a specially designed chair and, for $7.95, get a massage that lasts exactly eight minutes (no appointment necessary). The owner of the store explained, "To get Americans to buy massages, I realized you had to solve three problems. You had to come up with something that was quick, inexpensive, and most important, you had to find a way to do it without asking people to take their clothes off."[9]

Because people have less and less time to perform various tasks, the importance of people-based services is increasing. Personal concierge services, such as Toronto-based Orderly Lives, is a growing industry, because they help consumers meet obligations despite time pressures by doing almost anything for them, from organizing a party to doing the grocery shopping to planning a vacation.[10] Self-improvement services such as those offered by personal shoppers, wardrobe consultants and personal trainers also are popular and, in some cities, even professional dog walkers do a brisk business.

## What Are the Key Differences between Services and Goods?

**Services** are acts, efforts, or performances exchanged from producer to user without ownership rights. Like other intangibles, a service satisfies needs by providing pleasure, information, or convenience. About 75 percent of the Canadian population is employed in the services sector in such industries as banking, insurance, professional services, hospitality, transportation (see Exhibit 7.2), education, health care, hotels, restaurants, and recreational services.[11]

Services come in many forms, from those done *to* you, such as a massage or a teeth cleaning, to those done *for* you, such as having your CD player repaired, getting a new paint job on your car, or having an organization like Charity.ca ensure that your money gets to the charity of your choice. Regardless of whether they affect our bodies or our possessions, *all* services share four characteristics that make them distinct from goods: intangibility, perishability, variability, and inseparability.

**INTANGIBILITY** Service intangibility means that customers can't see, touch, or smell good service. Unlike the purchase of a good, they cannot inspect or handle services before they purchase them. Because they're buying something that isn't there, consumers look for reassuring signs before purchasing, and marketers must ensure that these signs are available when consumers look for them. That's why the service provider's appearance and the "look" of the facility can make or break a service business. When we talk about how customers decide if a service is giving them what they want, marketers overcome the problem of intangibility by providing physical cues to reassure the buyer. These cues include uniforms, brand logos, and carefully designed Web sites.

**PERISHABILITY** Service perishability means that a firm can't store its services—it's a case of use it or lose it. When rooms go unoccupied at a ski resort, there is no way to make up for the lost opportunity to exchange a product for money. Marketers try to avoid these problems by using the marketing mix to encourage demand for the service during times when it would otherwise be low. **Capacity management** is the process by which organizations adjust their services in an attempt to match demand. In the summer, for example, Whistler combats its perishability problem by opening its lifts to mountain bikers, who tear down the sunny slopes.

**VARIABILITY** Service variability is the inevitable differences in a service provider's performances from one day to the next: An NHL goalie may be "hot" one game and ice cold the next. Even the same service performed by the same individual for the same customer can vary. It's rare that you get exactly the same cut from a hair stylist.

It is difficult to standardize services, because service providers and customers vary. Your experience in courses is an example. A university or college can standardize its offerings to some degree—course calendars, course content, and classrooms are fairly controllable.

**services** Intangible products that are exchanged directly from the producer to the customer.

**capacity management** The process by which organizations adjust their offerings in an attempt to match demand.

There's A to B.
And then there's *A to Z*.

**Welcome to Executive First.
A world of difference.**

The concept is perfectly simple: master the most excellent service on earth, and take it to the air. To that end, our Executive First® instructors collaborated with the Paris-based International Concierge Institute, the Institut de tourisme et d'hôtellerie du Québec, and the Hotel Mandarin in Geneva, Switzerland. Training that translates into refined, intuitive service from our in-flight personnel. They'll make sure you're comfortable, pour your wine and plate your delicious new Executive First meals with panache. An exceptional level of service. And now even more room to sit back, relax, and marvel at how one simple concept makes all the difference in the world.

*More choice, more ease, more value.*

Henry Chow
*Instructor—in-flight service training, Vancouver*

aircanada.com

**AIR CANADA**

**Exhibit 7.2**

Almost 75 percent of the Canadian population works in the service sector.

**service encounter**   The actual interaction between the customer and the service provider.

**disintermediation**   The process of eliminating interaction between customers and service providers.

Professors, however, vary in their training, life experiences, and personalities, so there is little hope of being able to make teaching uniform (not that this would necessarily be desirable anyway). And because students with different backgrounds and interests vary in their needs, the lecture that one finds fascinating might put another to sleep.

Firms handle this aspect of services by standardizing their processes as much as possible. McDonald's, for example, has a Hamburger University outside Chicago where managers and franchisees are taught different aspects of the restaurant process, including the correct arm motion to use when salting french fries!

**INSEPARABILITY** Although a firm can manufacture goods before sale, a service can take place only at the time the service provider performs an act on either the customer or the customer's possession. In some cases, the service can be sold before delivery, such as a ticket to a concert months before the event.

Still, the expertise, skill, and personality of a provider, or the quality of a firm's facilities and equipment, cannot be detached from the offering itself. The central role played by employees in making or breaking a service underscores the importance of the **service encounter**, or the interaction between the customer and the service provider.[12] The most expertly cooked meal is ruined if a surly or incompetent waiter brings it to the table. Our interactions with service providers can range from the most superficial, such as buying a movie ticket, to telling a psychiatrist (or bartender) our most intimate secrets. In each case, though, the quality of the service encounter can play a big role in determining how we feel about the service we receive.

To minimize the potentially negative effects of bad service encounters and to save on labour costs, some service businesses are experimenting with **disintermediation**, which eliminates the need for customers to interact with people. Examples are self-service gas stations, Internet banking, and ABM machines. Even salad and dessert bars reduce reliance on a server. A recent *Economist* article suggested that pilots eventually will be made redundant as advances in aviation technology become incorporated into new products.[13]

## DEVELOPING NEW PRODUCTS

Building on our knowledge of the nature of a product, we'll now examine how firms go about developing new products. Product development doesn't simply mean creating totally new products never before on the market. Many companies do that; but for many other firms, product development is a continuous process of looking for ways to make an existing product better or finding just the right shade of green for this year's bath fashions.

Not all new products are important. Consider what happened when a man named Lonnie Johnson walked into the slick conference room of Larami Corporation. He smiled mischievously at the assembled executives. Then he opened his pink, battered Samsonite suitcase and took out a gizmo that looked a bit like a phaser from *Star Trek*. Holding out this combination of a hand-held pump apparatus, PVC tubing, Plexiglas, and plastic pop bottles, Johnson aimed and fired. A giant stream of water shot across the room. Within a year, the Super Soaker (see Exhibit 7.3) had become one of the most successful water toys in retail history.[14]

The successful introduction of new products is getting tougher for entrepreneurs to accomplish. Even for large corporations, successful new product introductions are becoming more and more difficult. First, the costs of research and development are often so huge that firms must limit the number of new products in development. The fast pace of technological change means that products are outdated faster than ever, giving firms less time to recover their research and development costs. And, with so many products competing for limited shelf space, retailers often charge manufacturers exorbitant fees to stock a new product, increasing manufacturers' costs even more.[15] Firms must reduce the time it takes to get good products to market and increase the speed of adoption to quickly recover these costs.

**Exhibit 7.3**

Entrepreneur Lonnie Johnson with his invention, the Super Soaker.

New product development occurs in three phases, as Figure 7.3 shows. In the *visionary phase*, a firm generates and screens ideas to identify those that will work best for it. The *planning and development phase* means turning those ideas into a product. The *test and improve phase* means trying out marketing strategies in test markets to improve the marketing plan and product, if needed, before full commercial launch.

## The Visionary Phase

In the visionary phase of product development, marketers generate new product ideas, screen new product concepts, and complete a business analysis. Marketers use a variety of sources to come up with great new product ideas that provide important customer benefits and are compatible with the company's mission. Ideas can come from employees,

| Phase of Development | Outcome |
|---|---|
| **Visionary** | |
| • Idea generation. | Identify product ideas that will provide important customer benefits compatible with company mission. |
| • Product concept screening. | Estimate potential technical and commercial success of product ideas. |
| • Perform business analysis. | Estimate potential for profit. What is the potential demand, what expenditures will be required, and what is the cost of marketing the product? |
| **Planning and Development** | |
| • Begin commercial development. | Develop a marketing plan. |
| • Begin technical development. | Design the product and the manufacturing and production process. |
| **Test and Improve** | |
| • Test complete marketing plan. | Develop evidence of potential success in the real market. |
| • Marketing mix adjustments. | Make improvements in marketing mix as needed. |
| • Launch product. | Implement full-scale marketing plan. |

**Figure 7.3** Phases in New Product Development

customers, as well as salespeople, service providers, and others who have direct customer contact. Often firms use such marketing research activities as focus groups for new product *idea generation*. For example, a company like CanWest Global Communications that operates TV stations might hold focus group discussions to get ideas about types of programs not currently available.

Although ideas for products initially come from a variety of sources, it is up to marketers to expand these ideas into more complete product concepts. Product concepts describe what features the product should have and the benefits those features will provide for consumers. The second step in developing new products is screening product concepts. In *screening*, marketers and researchers examine the chances that the product concept might achieve technical and commercial success, thereby weeding out concepts that have little chance of success. Estimating *technical success* is assessing whether the new product is technologically feasible—is it possible to build this product? Estimating *commercial success* is deciding whether anyone is likely to buy the product. The marketing graveyard is littered with products that sounded interesting but that failed to catch on, including jalapeño pop, aerosol mustard, microwavable ice cream, aerosol toothpaste, and edible deodorant.[16,17]

The marketers of Fit® (see Exhibit 7.4) had to first determine that producing a fruit and vegetable wash product would be possible—technical success. Researchers then had to interview consumers to see if they thought a fruit and vegetable cleaning product was something that they would purchase.

Once a product concept passes the screening stage, marketers conduct a *business analysis*. Even if they have evidence that there is a market for the product, they still must find out if the product can be a profitable contribution to the organization's product mix. How much potential demand is there for the product? Does the firm have the resources that will be required for successful development and introduction of the product?

The business analysis for a new product begins with assessing how the new product will fit into the firm's total product mix. Will the new product increase sales, or will it cannibalize sales of existing products? Are there possible synergies between the new product and the company's existing offerings that may improve visibility and the image of both? What is the probable customer demand for the new product? An equally important part of the business analysis is estimating the marketing costs necessary to stimulate demand and achieve desired distribution levels. This estimation may include the costs of training a sales force, recruiting distributors, advertising, conducting sales promotions, and communicating through press releases and direct mail.

## Planning and Development

If it survives the scrutiny of a business analysis, a new product concept then undergoes commercial and technical development. *Commercial development* means putting together a marketing plan that builds on the initial projections made during product screening and business analysis. Forecasts are adjusted to fit more precise information about the market and how customers will respond to the product. Marketers also plan pricing, advertising, and distribution strategies. Prospective customers are again involved in the planning and development process—the better a firm understands how customers will react to a new product, the better its chances of commercial success.

In *technical development*, a firm's engineers work with marketers to refine the design and production process. Those involved in the technical development process must, for example, determine which parts of a finished good the company will make and which ones will be bought from other suppliers. If goods are to be manufactured, the company may have to buy new production equipment or modify existing machinery. Someone has to develop work instructions for

**Exhibit 7.4**

Marketers must make sure that consumers will buy unique product concepts such as Fit®, or risk heavy losses.

## SPOTLIGHT ON REAL PEOPLE — Industrial Research Assistance Program

Succeeding in the competitive world of business is tough, especially if you are a small- or medium-sized Canadian company. It is for this reason that the Industrial Research Assistance Program (IRAP) was created. Operating under the auspices of the National Research Council Canada, IRAP's goal is to help small- and medium-sized (SME's) Canadian companies realize their full potential by turning knowledge and innovation into strategic opportunities, jobs, and prosperity for all Canadians.

Canadian SME's with under 500 employees and industrial associations desiring to enhance their technological capability are eligible for IRAP's portfolio of services: (1) technology and business advisory services, (2) financial assistance for R&D activities, (3) networking opportunities, and (4) partnerships.[18]

1. Go to IRAP's Web site (**http://irap-pari.nrc-cnrc.gc.ca**) and look at the companies IRAP has assisted. What type of assistance do you think is most valuable for a small- or medium-sized business?
2. How can IRAP most effectively reach young entrepreneurs developing Internet-based businesses?

employees and train them to produce the product. In developing service processes, technical development includes such decisions as which activities will occur within sight of customers and whether parts of the service can be automated to make delivery more efficient.

Technical development sometimes requires applying for a patent. Because patents legally prevent competitors from producing or selling the invention, a patent can reduce or eliminate competition in a market for many years, allowing a firm "breathing room" to recoup investments in technical development. For example, for many years, G.D. Searle Pharmaceuticals (now owned by Monsanto) held the patent for its NutraSweet brand of artificial sweetener. This exclusive right to make and sell the product allowed the company to reap huge profits, because no other company had a similar product. Now that the patent has expired, Searle faces competition in this market.

## Testing and Improving the Product

The final phase of new product development includes test marketing, making final adjustments to the marketing mix, and commercial launch. In **test marketing**, the firm tries out the complete marketing plan—the distribution, advertising, sales promotion—but in a small geographic area that is similar to the larger market it hopes to enter. Test marketing can be conducted in an area as small as one city or as large as a country. For example, Vancouver has become a popular test market for innovative products, because Vancouverites have a reputation for being interested in new and unconventional things.

Kera Vision, a U.S. optical company, chose Vancouver as a test market for Intacs, a product that attaches to the eye to reshape the cornea and improve vision.[19] LG Electronics, a Korean appliance manufacturer, used all of Canada as a test market for the North American launch of its "smart" appliances, including an Internet fridge, which allows users to surf the Web, send e-mail, or watch TV on a monitor built into the fridge, and a washing machine that automatically measures the detergent, determines water level, and sets the speed.[20]

There are pluses and minuses to test marketing. On the negative side, test marketing is extremely expensive. It can cost over a million dollars to conduct a test market even in a single city. A test market also gives the competition a free look at the new product, its introductory price, and the intended marketing communications strategy—and an opportunity to foil the test market by increasing their own promotion or get to the market first with a competitive product.

**test marketing** Testing the complete marketing plan in a small geographic area that is similar to the larger market the firm hopes to enter.

Because of the problems with test marketing, marketers sometimes conduct *simulated test markets*. Simulated test markets imitate the introduction of a product into the marketplace using computer software. These simulations allow the company to test the impact of price cuts, new packaging, or even where on store shelves to feature the product. The process entails gathering basic research data on consumer perceptions of the product concept, the physical product, the advertising, and other promotional activity. The test market simulation model uses that information to predict the product's success much less expensively (and more discreetly) than a traditional test market. As this simulated test market technology improves, traditional test markets may become a thing of the past.

On the positive side, by offering a new product in a limited area of the market, marketers can evaluate and improve the marketing program. Sometimes, test marketing uncovers a need to improve the product itself; sometimes, it indicates product failure, allowing the firm to save millions of dollars by "pulling the plug."[21]

The last step in new product development is the *product launch*. Launching a new product requires full-scale production, distribution, advertising, sales promotion—the works. For this reason, full-scale introduction of a new product cannot happen overnight. A launch requires planning and careful preparation. Marketers must implement trade promotion plans, which offer special incentives to encourage dealers, retailers, or other members of the channel to stock the new product so that customers will find it on store shelves the very first time they look. They must also develop consumer promotions, such as coupons. Marketers may arrange to have point-of-purchase displays designed, built, and delivered to retail outlets. If the new product is especially complex, customer service employees must receive extensive training and preparation.

As launch time nears, preparations gain a sense of urgency. Sales managers explain special incentive programs to salespeople. Soon, the media announce to prospective customers why they should buy and where they can find the new product. All elements of the marketing program—ideally—come into play like a well-tuned orchestra.

## IT'S "NEW AND IMPROVED!" UNDERSTANDING THE IMPORTANCE OF INNOVATIONS

**innovation** A product that consumers perceive to be new and different from existing products.

"New and improved!" What exactly do we mean when we use the term *new product*? From a marketing standpoint, a new product or an **innovation** is anything that customers *perceive* as new and different. Innovations may be a cutting-edge style such as body piercing, a fad such as Beanie Babies, a new communications technology such as wireless communication, or a new product such as M3 players. It may be a completely new product that provides benefits never available before, or it may simply be an existing product with a new style, in a different colour, or with some new feature. If an innovation is successful, it spreads through the population. First, it is bought and used by only a few people, and then more and more consumers adopt it.

Not all innovations are successful. Take, for instance, the Nehru jacket shown in Exhibit 7.5. In the 1960s, men's fashion designers felt men were ready for a dramatic and exciting change. Enter the Nehru jacket, fashioned after the traditional clothing worn by leaders of Indian society and named after a former prime minister of India. The suit was 100 percent polyester, a popular fabric in the 1960s. The problem was that polyester was also hot and uncomfortable and never seemed to fit the body just right. Whether it was the fabric or the look, men overwhelmingly rejected the Nehru style. Manufacturers and retailers lost millions of dollars, because they introduced the suit without first understanding their customers—just because fashion designers thought it was a great idea to radically change the way men dressed didn't mean the average guy would agree. Years later, it was rumoured that there were warehouses in which thousands of unsold Nehru jackets were still being stored. Let the buyer beware—they may resurface.

**Exhibit 7.5**

The Nehru suit of the 1960s: Not all innovations are successful.

Understanding innovations can be critical to the success of firms for at least two reasons. First, technology is advancing at a dizzying pace. Products are introduced and become obsolete faster than ever before. In many industries, firms are busy developing another new-and-better product before the last new-and-better product even hits store shelves. Nowhere is this more obvious than with personal computers, for which a steady change in technology makes consumers want a better, faster machine before the dust even settles on the old one. One company, Gateway, offers consumers a purchase plan that gives them the option of trading the machine in for a newer model every two years to make sure customers have what they want—and that they get it from Gateway.

Another reason why understanding new products is important is the high cost of developing them and the even higher cost of new products that fail. In the pharmaceutical industry, the cost of bringing each new drug to market is between $200 and $500 million.[22] Even the most successful firms can't afford many product failures with that kind of price tag.

Marketers must understand what it takes to develop a new product successfully; they must do their homework and learn what it is about existing products consumers find less than satisfactory and what exactly it will take to do a better job satisfying customer needs. Savvy marketers know they'll waste a lot of investment money if they don't.

Finally, new product development is an important contribution to society. We would never suggest that *everything* new is good, but many new products allow us to live longer, happier lives of better quality than before (see Table 7.2). Although there are some who disagree, most of us feel that our lives are better because of telephones, televisions, CD players, microwave ovens, and computers—except when these items break down. We're not saying that firms create new products because they want to make our lives better—businesses create new products that make our lives better because that's how they make profits and keep their shareholders happy.

**Table 7.2  Innovations That Have Changed Our Lives**

| Products that have changed how we play | | | Products that have changed our homes | |
|---|---|---|---|---|
| 1900 | Kodak Brownie camera | | 1907 | Vacuum cleaner |
| 1948 | Polaroid camera | | 1918 | Frigidaire refrigerator |
| 1976 | JVC videorecorder | | 1928 | Home air conditioner |
| 1982 | Philips/Sony CD player | | 1942 | Permacel duct tape |
| **Products that have changed how we work** | | | 1946 | Tupperware |
| 1900 | Paper clip | | 1967 | Amana microwave oven |
| 1959 | Xerox photocopier | | **Products that have changed the way we communicate** | |
| 1966 | Xerox fax machine | | 1921 | RCA radio |
| 1971 | Intel microprocessor | | 1935 | RCA television |
| 1980 | 3M Post-it Notes | | 1939 | The paperback book |
| 1984 | Apple Macintosh | | 1991 | World Wide Web |
| **Products that have changed how we travel** | | | **Products that have changed our clothing** | |
| 1903 | Harley-Davidson motorcycle | | 1913 | Zipper |
| 1908 | Ford Model T | | 1914 | Bra |
| 1936 | DC-3 | | 1936 | Bass penny loafer |
| 1950s | Skateboard | | 1939 | Nylons |
| 1957 | Boeing 707 | | 1954 | Velcro |
| **Products that have changed our health and grooming** | | | 1959 | Lycra |
| 1903 | Safety razors | | 1961 | P&G Pampers |
| 1921 | Johnson & Johnson Band-Aid | | | |
| 1928 | Penicillin | | | |
| 1931 | Tampax tampon | | | |
| 1960 | Searle birth control pill | | | |
| 1988 | Eli Lilly Prozac | | | |

Source: Adapted from Christine Chen and Tim Carvell, "Products of the Century," *Fortune*, November 22, 1999, pp. 133–136.

# Types of Innovations

Innovations differ in their degree of newness, and this helps to determine how quickly the products will be adopted by many members of a target market. Because innovations that are more novel require greater effort and more changes in behaviour, they are slower to spread throughout a population than new products that are similar to what is already available.

Marketers classify innovations into three categories based on their degree of newness; however, it is better to think of these three types as ranges along a continuum. The three types of innovations are based on the amount of disruption or change they bring to people's lives. For example, when the first automobiles were produced, they caused tremendous changes in the lives of their owners, far greater changes than when auto manufacturers introduced "new and improved" autos with automatic transmissions, air conditioning, and driving directions provided via satellite.

**continuous innovation** A modification of an existing product that sets one brand apart from its competitors.

**knock-off** A new product that copies with slight modification the design of an original product.

CONTINUOUS INNOVATIONS A **continuous innovation** is a modification to an existing product, such as MasterCard's ability to handle business expenses (see Exhibit 7.6). This type of modification can set one brand apart from its competitors. Roots has used continuous innovation in many of its product lines, adding a new style of leather jacket or a new neckline for a shirt. Most product innovations are continuous innovations. The term *continuous* tells us that the changes are evolutionary rather than revolutionary. Small changes reposition the product or allow a manufacturer to offer new product options.

With a continuous innovation, the consumer doesn't have to learn anything new to use the innovation. From a marketing perspective, this means that it is far easier to convince consumers to adopt the innovation. A typewriter company, for example, many years ago modified the shape of its product to make it more "user friendly" to secretaries. One simple change was curving the tops of the keys, as we see on today's computer keyboards, because secretaries complained that flat surfaces were hard to use with long fingernails. Today, computer manufacturers have gone a step further by building ergonomic keyboards that are less likely to cause painful wrist ailments.

How different does a new product have to be from existing products? It is said that "imitation is the sincerest form of flattery," and decisions regarding how much (if at all) one's product should resemble those of competitors often are at the centre of marketing strategy development. Sometimes, marketers feel that the best strategy is to follow the competition. For example, the packaging of "me-too" or look-alike products, such as store brand versions of national brands, can create instant market success, because consumers assume that similar packaging means similar products.

A **knock-off** is a new product that copies with slight modification the design of an original product. Firms deliberately create knock-offs of clothing, jewellery, or other items, often with the intent to sell to a larger or different market. For example, companies may copy the haute couture clothing styles of top designers and sell them at lower prices to the mass market. It is difficult to legally protect a design (as opposed to a technological invention), because it can

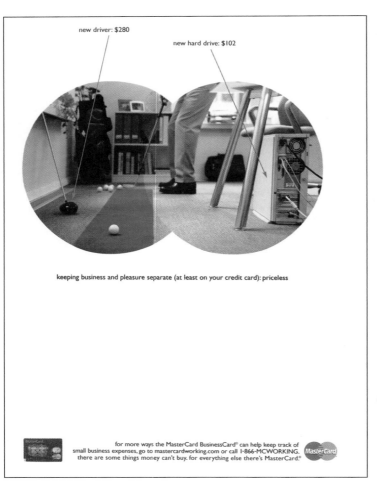

new driver: $280

new hard drive: $102

keeping business and pleasure separate (at least on your credit card): priceless

for more ways the MasterCard BusinessCard® can help keep track of small business expenses, go to mastercardworking.com or call 1-866-MCWORKING. there are some things money can't buy. for everything else there's MasterCard.®

**Exhibit 7.6**

The introduction of the ability to keep track of small business expenses is an example of continuous innovation.

be argued that even a very slight change—different buttons or a slightly wider collar on a dress or shirt—means the knock-off is not an exact copy. However, industry pressure is building for legal protection of designs. Manufacturers argue that a design element, say, a distinctive curve on a car bumper, is as important to the integrity of the car as a mechanical innovation.[23]

**DYNAMICALLY CONTINUOUS INNOVATIONS** A **dynamically continuous innovation** is a pronounced modification to an existing product that requires a modest amount of learning or change in behaviour to use it. The history of audio equipment is a series of dynamically continuous innovations. For many years, consumers enjoyed listening to their favourite songs on record players. Then in the 1960s, that same music became available on a continuous-play eight-track tape, requiring the purchase of an eight-track tape player. Then came cassette tapes, requiring a cassette player. In the 1980s, consumers could hear songs digitally mastered on compact disks; that required the purchase of a new CD player. In the 1990s, recording technology moved one more step forward with digital video disk (DVD) technology. Now, consumers download music into receivers and take their custom mix of music everywhere. Even though each of these changes required learning how to operate new equipment, consumers were willing to buy the new products because of the improvements in music reproduction, the core product benefit.

> **dynamically continuous innovation** A change in an existing product that requires a moderate amount of learning or behaviour change.

**DISCONTINUOUS INNOVATIONS** A **discontinuous innovation** creates major changes in the way we live. To use a discontinuous innovation, consumers must engage in a great amount of learning, because no similar product has ever been on the market. Such major inventions as the airplane, car, and television have radically changed lifestyles. Another discontinuous innovation, the personal computer, is changing the way we shop and is allowing more and more firms' employees to work out of their homes.

> **discontinuous innovation** A totally new product that creates major changes in the way we live.

Recognizing the degree of newness of innovations is important in developing marketing strategies. For example, if marketers know that consumers may resist adopting a new and radically different product, they may offer consumers free product trial or place heavier emphasis on a personal selling strategy to convince consumers that the new product offers benefits worth the hassle. Business-to-business marketers of technology products such as software, for instance, often provide in-service training for employees of their customers who invest in new products.

## ADOPTION AND DIFFUSION PROCESSES

We've presented the steps marketers take to develop new products from generating ideas to launch, and we have examined the importance of understanding innovations. Now, we'll look at what happens after that new product hits the market—how an innovation spreads throughout a population.

New products do not satisfy customer needs until the customer uses them. **Product adoption** is the process by which a consumer or business customer begins to buy and use a new good, service, or an idea. The term **diffusion** describes how the use of a product spreads throughout a population.

> **product adoption** The process by which a consumer or business customer begins to buy and use a new good, service, or an idea.

> **diffusion** The process by which the use of a product spreads throughout a population.

After months or even years spent developing a new product, a firm faces the challenge of getting consumers to buy and use the product—and to do so quickly—so that it can recover the costs of product development and launch. To accomplish this, marketers must understand the product adoption process. In this section, we'll discuss the stages in this process. We'll also see how consumers and businesses differ in their eagerness to adopt new products and how the characteristics of a product affect its adoption rate—an important consideration for the introduction of new products.

## Stages in a Customer's Adoption of a New Product

Whether the innovation is a new type of retail store or a better mousetrap, individuals and organizations pass through six stages in the adoption process. Figure 7.4 shows how a per-

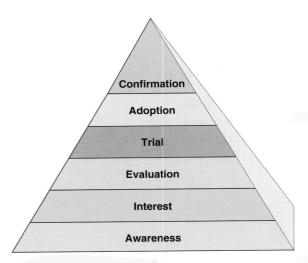

**Figure 7.4** Adoption Pyramid

son goes from being unaware of an innovation through the stages of awareness, interest, evaluation, trial, adoption, and confirmation. At every stage, people drop out of the process, so the proportion of consumers who wind up using the innovation on a consistent basis is a fraction of those who are exposed to it.

**AWARENESS** Learning that the innovation exists is the first step in the adoption process. To make consumers aware of a new product, marketers often conduct a massive advertising campaign, or media blitz. Car companies use this approach to communicate to consumers that a new model has been introduced. This strategy works for new products when consumers see a new product as something they want and need and just can't live without.

**INTEREST** For some of the people who become aware of a new product, a second stage in the adoption process is *interest*—a prospective adopter begins to see how a new product could satisfy an existing or newly realized need. Interest also means that consumers look for and are open to information about the innovation.

Marketers often design teaser advertisements to give prospective customers just enough information about the new product to make them curious and stimulate their interest. A recent ad for the telecommunications company Telus had billboards across Canadian cities featuring a very adorable pig. The billboards created a buzz, with people wondering whom the ads were for and what product it represented. It turned out that the ads were for new camera cell phones by Telus. Despite the marketers' best efforts, though, some consumers drop out of the process at this point.

The concept of different layers of a product discussed at the beginning of this chapter provides an excellent guide for marketers at this stage. Remember, we said that consumers do not buy product features (attributes), they buy product benefits. Therefore, smart marketers stress the product's benefits at this stage to generate interest. For example, when Goodyear introduced a new tire, the Aquatread, it stressed the fact that the tire would help drivers with superior traction in wet conditions.

**EVALUATION** In the evaluation stage, a prospect weighs the costs and benefits of the new product. For complex, risky, or expensive products, people think about the innovation a great deal before trying it. For instance, a firm will carefully evaluate buying a $6000 video conferencing system before purchase.[24] Marketers for such products help prospective customers see how such products can benefit them—holding video conferences means a company doesn't have to pay travel costs for employees to attend central location meetings.

However, little evaluation may occur with an impulse purchase. For example, consumers may do very little thinking before buying a chewing gum such as Trident Advantage, shown in Exhibit 7.7. For these products, marketers design the product and packaging to be eye-catching and appealing to get consumers to notice the product quickly.

Some potential adopters will evaluate an innovation positively enough to move on to the trial stage. Those who do not think the new product will provide adequate benefits drop out.

**TRIAL** The next stage in the adoption process is *trial*—the potential adopters will actually experience or use the product

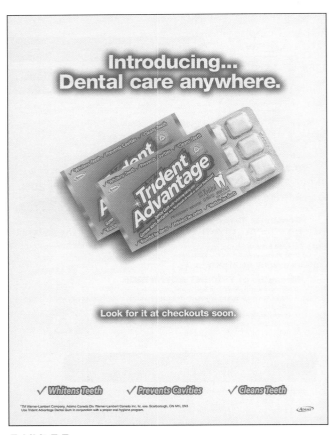

**Exhibit 7.7**

Consumers aren't likely to spend much time evaluating new impulse products like chewing gum before buying them.

for the first time. Often marketers stimulate trial by providing opportunities for consumers to sample the product. For example, when Barq's Root Beer (see Exhibit 7.8) was introduced into the Canadian market, the company used a sampling team, the Barq's Brigades, to give consumers free samples in stores and at sporting events to ensure that people tried the product.[25] Based on the trial experience, some potential buyers move on to adoption of the new product.

**ADOPTION** At the *adoption* stage, a prospect chooses a product. If the product is a consumer or business-to-business good, this means buying the product and learning how to use and maintain it. If the product is an idea, this means that the individual agrees with the new idea. For example, consumers who have adopted the idea that recycling helps protect our natural resources will carefully sort and recycle their glass, aluminum, plastic, and paper products.

This does not mean that all individuals or organizations that first choose an innovation are permanent customers, although many firms make this mistake. Some potential customers, even after initial adoption, do not go on to the final stage of confirmation. Marketers need to provide follow-up contacts and communications with adopters to ensure that they are satisfied and remain loyal to the new product over time.

**CONFIRMATION** With initial adoption of an innovation, a customer weighs expected versus actual benefits and costs. Favourable experiences contribute to new customers becoming loyal adopters, as their initially positive opinions result in *confirmation*. Nothing lasts forever, however. Even loyal customers may decide that a new product is not meeting expectations and reject it. Some marketers feel that *reselling* the customer in the confirmation stage is important. They provide advertisements, sales presentations, and other communications to reinforce a customer's choice.

## The Diffusion of Innovations

Diffusion describes how the use of a product spreads throughout a population. Marketers would prefer that their entire target market immediately adopt a new product; but this does not happen. Consumers and business customers differ in how eager or willing they are to try something new, lengthening the diffusion process by months or even years. Based on adopters' roles in the diffusion process, experts have classified them into five different categories.

**ADOPTER CATEGORIES** Some people like to try new products. Others are so reluctant, you'd think they're afraid of anything new. As Figure 7.5 shows, there are five categories of adopters: innovators, early adopters, early majority, late majority, and laggards.[26] To understand how these differ, we'll study the adoption of one product—the microwave oven.

**Innovators** are roughly the first 2.5 percent of adopters. This segment is extremely adventurous and willing to take risks with new products. Innovators are typically well educated, younger, better off financially than others in the population, and worldly. Innovators who were into new technology knew all about microwave ovens

**Exhibit 7.8**
When Barq's® was introduced in Canada, sampling teams (the Barq's® Brigades) conducted product sampling events to drive product trial.

**innovators** The first segment (roughly 2.5 percent) of a population to adopt a new product.

## Good or Bad Decision?

When a new product is hot, it's hot—but the burning desire to get hold of it can make it too hot to handle. Athletic shoe manufacturers compete fiercely to produce dynamically continuous innovations that kids want. For example, Nike, Reebok, and other manufacturers introduce new models every year, and with each new version, the products become more and more desirable to young kids. News of one new model's arrival date in stores sometimes causes a frenzy. Students go so far as to skip school—with permission from their parents—to be the first in line to buy the latest shoe. Do you think marketers should feel good or bad about kids being so anxious to buy their new products?

before other people were aware they existed. Because innovators pride themselves on trying new products, they probably purchased microwaves when they were first introduced to the market in the mid-1970s.

**Early adopters**, approximately 13.5 percent of adopters, buy product innovations early in the diffusion process, but not as early as innovators. Unlike innovators, early adopters have greater concern for social acceptance. Typically, they are heavy media users and often are heavy users of a new product category. Others in the population often look to early adopters for their opinions on various topics, making them key to a new product's success. For this reason, marketers often target early adopters in developing advertising and other communications efforts. For example, early adopters of the Bioré pore-cleaning strips (see Exhibit 7.9) were young, 18- to 34-year-old women who were heavy readers of fashion magazines. Bioré targeted this group with heavy advertising for the strips in fashion magazines and by giving out free samples at the Lilith Fair Tour.[27] After reading articles in *Consumer Reports* and other sources of information on new products, early adopters of the microwave made their first purchase in the late 1970s.

The **early majority**, about 34 percent of adopters, avoid being either first or last to try an innovation. They are typically middle-class consumers and are deliberate and cautious. Early majority consumers have slightly above-average education and income levels. When the early majority adopts a product, it is no longer considered new or different—it is, in essence, already established. Early majority microwave owners made their purchase in the early and mid-1980s, by which time there were 10 to 15 brands of microwaves sold by a wide variety of retailers.

**Late majority** adopters, about 34 percent of the population, are older, more conservative, and typically have lower-than-average levels of education and income. The late majority adopters avoid trying a new product until it is no longer risky. By that time, the product has become an economic necessity, or there is pressure from peer groups to adopt. Late majority homes did not have a microwave until their friends began asking, "How can you survive without a microwave?" By that time, the price of the ovens had gone down, and the innovators, early adopters, and even many of the early majority were purchasing a second or even a third microwave. To attract late majority buyers, marketers may offer lower-priced models of a product.

**Laggards**, about 16 percent of adopters, are the last in a population to adopt a new product. Laggards are typically lower in social class than other adopter categories and are bound by tradition. By the time laggards adopt a product, it may already be superseded by other innovations.

By understanding these adopter categories, marketers are better able to develop strategies to speed the diffusion or widespread use of their products. For example, early in the diffusion process, marketers may put greater emphasis on advertising in special-interest magazines to attract innovators and early adopters. Later they may lower the product's price or come out with lower-priced models with fewer features to attract the late majority. We'll discuss the strategies for new and existing products in the next chapter.

**PRODUCT FACTORS AFFECTING THE RATE OF ADOPTION** If you could predict which new products will succeed and which will fail, you'd quickly be in high demand as a consultant by companies worldwide. That's because companies make large investments in new products; but failures are all too frequent. Estimates of new product success rates range from 46 to 65 percent.[28] Much research is devoted to making us smarter about new product successes and failures.

**early adopters** Those who adopt an innovation early in the diffusion process but later than the innovators.

**early majority** Those whose adoption of a new product signals a general acceptance of the innovation.

**late majority** The adopters who are willing to try new products when there is little or no risk associated with the purchase, when the purchase becomes an economic necessity, or when there is social pressure to purchase.

**laggards** The last consumers to adopt an innovation.

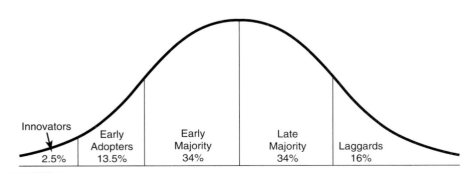

**Figure 7.5** Categories of Adopters

Researchers have identified five characteristics of innovations that affect the rate of adoption. Figure 7.6 summarizes these factors: relative advantage, compatibility, complexity, trialability, and observability.[29] Whether a new product has each of these characteristics affects the speed of diffusion. As we've discussed, it took many years for the microwave to diffuse or spread throughout the Canadian population—from the mid-1970s to the early 1990s.[30] Examining these five factors helps understand both why the new product was not adopted during its early years and why adoption sped up later.

*Relative advantage* is the degree to which a consumer perceives that a new product provides superior benefits. In the case of the microwave oven, consumers in the 1960s and early 1970s did not feel that the product provided important benefits that would improve their lives. But by the late 1970s, that perception had changed, primarily because more women had entered the workforce. The 1960s' woman had all day to prepare the evening meal—she didn't have a need for the microwave. But in the late 1970s, when many women left home for work at 8:00 a.m. and returned home at 6:00 p.m., an appliance that would "magically" defrost a frozen chicken and cook it for dinner in 30 minutes provided a genuine advantage.

*Compatibility* is the extent to which a new product is consistent with existing cultural values, customs, and practices. Did consumers see the microwave oven as being compatible with existing ways of doing things? No. Cooking on paper plates? If you put a paper plate in a conventional oven, you'd likely get a visit from the fire department. By anticipating compatibility issues early in the new product development stage, marketing strategies can address such problems in planning communications programs, or there may be opportunities for altering product designs to overcome some consumer objections.

*Complexity* is the degree to which consumers find a new product or its use difficult to understand. Many microwave users today haven't a clue about how a microwave oven cooks

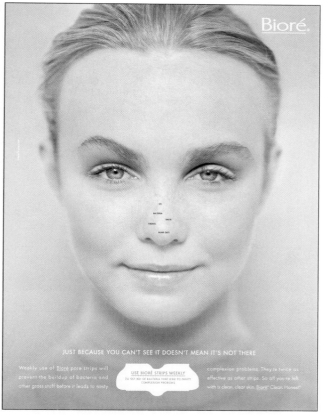

**Exhibit 7.9**

Most consumers were willing to try clean pore strips only after early adopters made recommendations.

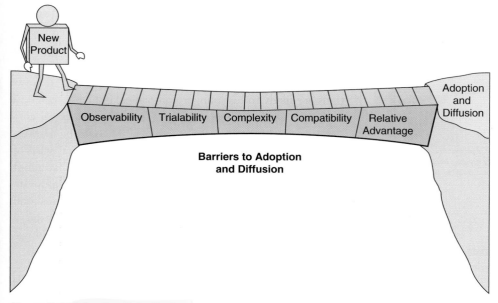

**Figure 7.6** Adoption Rate Factors

**Exhibit 7.10**
The observability of in-line skating helped to increase the rate of adoption of in-line skates.

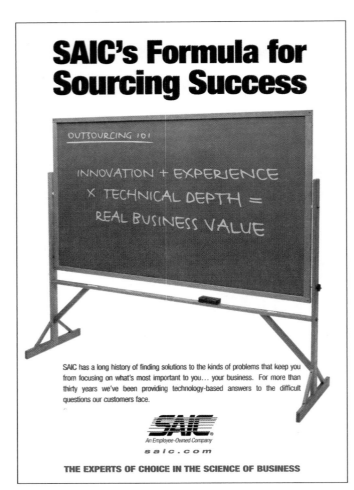

**Exhibit 7.11**
SAIC positions itself as the sourcing expert.

food. But when the product was introduced, consumers asked and marketers answered—microwaves cause molecules to move and rub together, creating friction, which produces heat—cooked pot roast. But that explanation was complex and confusing for consumers of the 1960s.

*Trialability* is the ease of sampling a new product and its benefits. Marketers took a very important step in the 1970s to speed up adoption of the microwave oven—product trial. Just about every store that sold microwaves invited shoppers to visit the store and see and sample an entire meal cooked in the microwave.

*Observability* is how visible a new product and its benefits are to others who might adopt it. The ideal innovation is easy to see. For example, in-line skates gained instant attention, because walkers, runners, and bikers saw bladers (see Exhibit 7.10) zip by them on bike and jogging paths. The microwave was moderately observable. Only close friends and acquaintances who visited someone's home could see whether the household had a microwave. Although marketers can't do much about the observability of new products—consumers are likely to keep their mattresses away from public viewing no matter what marketers do—they do recognize that marketing strategies for new products that are not observable face difficult challenges. They must develop a marketing mix that convinces consumers to invest in the product, even though no one else will know.

## Organizational Differences Affect Adoption

Just as there are differences among consumers in their eagerness to adopt new products, businesses and other organizations are not alike in their willingness to buy and use new industrial products.[31] Firms that welcome product innovations are likely to be younger companies, in highly technical industries, with younger managers and entrepreneurial corporate cultures. Early adopter firms are likely to be market-share leaders that adopt new innovations and try new ways of doing things to maintain their leadership. Firms that adopt new products only when they recognize they must innovate to keep up are in the early majority. Late majority firms tend to be oriented toward the status quo and often have large financial investments in existing production technology. Laggard firms are probably already losing money.

Business-to-business products, like consumer products, can possess characteristics that will increase their likelihood of adoption. Organizations are likely to adopt an innovation that helps them increase gross margins and profits. It is unlikely that firms would have adopted new products like voice mail unless they provided a way to increase profits by reducing labour costs. Organizational innovations are attractive when they are consistent with a firm's ways of doing business. Cost is also a factor in the new products firms will adopt. Firms are more likely to accept a new product if they perceive the improvement to be large in relation to the investment they will have to make.

For example, SAIC (see Exhibit 7.11) positions itself as the outsourcing expert for technical solutions. It tells customers that they can focus on running their business, while SAIC focuses on other issues, such as back office functions. This enables businesses to save money in the long run by not having to do all functions in-house.

**Table 7.3** A Focus on Potential Products Provides Competitive Advantage

| Core Product | Potential Product | Competitive Advantage |
|---|---|---|
| Industrial gloves | Safety | All industrial gloves are the same. But a focus on teaching workers how to use gloves to be safe enables manufacturers to differentiate. |
| Shopping mall | Entertainment destination | Do you agree with the statement: "A shopping mall is nothing but a large warehouse for retail stores?" Will this thinking provide a competitive edge? |
| Medical diagnostic equipment (e.g., CT scan) | Patient satisfaction, hospital efficiency | Most machines offer the same functionality. Successful sales professionals focus on the benefit to the customer (the hospital). |
| Coffee | Café culture | Who would have thought before Starbucks that we would cheerfully fork over almost $5 for a drink called a latte? |

# Real People, Real Decisions

## How It Worked Out at Lambesis

Dee Dee and her colleagues decided to merge the strongest features of options 1 and 2. The final design appears in the advertisement developed for the fragrance (shown here). In the first month following the Fetish product launch, the fragrance sold 500 percent faster than any other product in Dana's history. Based on this promising early start, the company increased its sales goals by 50 percent.

The option chosen by Dee Dee fits with her motto: "Don't be afraid to innovate." No wonder she has chosen this motto—she considers Mary Kay Ash and her mother her heroes. Mary Kay Ash started with $5000 and built Mary Kay Inc., a billion dollar cosmetics company. She famously said, "If your mind can conceive it, and if you can believe it, you can achieve it." Dee Dee regrets not finishing college and makes up for this by reading biographies (so she can learn from other people's experiences) and continuing her "can do" attitude.

**Exhibit 7.12**

This ad for Fetish shows the design option that was selected by Lambesis for the new perfume.

# CHAPTER SUMMARY

### 1. Explain how the layers of a product lead to competitive advantage.

A product may be anything tangible or intangible that satisfies consumer or business-to-business customer needs. Products include goods, services, ideas, people, and places. The core product refers to product features or attributes. The functional product refers to how the product functions or performs. The augmented product refers to the augmentations (additions) the marketer does to the basic product (e.g., packaging or customer warranties). Finally, the potential product refers to the solution the customer seeks from the product.

The layers of a product enable a firm to build competitive advantage in this way—firms recognize (sometimes reluctantly) that customers do not buy product features; they buy product benefits. By emphasizing benefits instead of features, the firm is in a position to differentiate itself from its competitors. See Table 7.3 for differences between core and potential products.

### 2. Explain the good–service continuum and its importance.

Although some products are pure goods (e.g., salt) and others are pure services (e.g., a haircut), most products fall along a continuum of goods and services. That is, most products have characteristics of goods and services. This is important to remember because a marketer with a product that has a higher percentage of tangibility (a good) will try to differentiate the offering by including services. On the other hand, a marketer with a product that has a higher percentage of intangibility (a service) will try to "tangibilize" the offering as much as possible.

### 3. Explain the key differences between goods and services.

All services share four characteristics that make them distinct from goods: intangibility, perishability, inseparability, and variability. Services are intangible (they cannot be touched). Therefore, marketers must use other means such as marketing communications to communicate the service experience to the customer (e.g., an ad can show the pleasure one may experience spending a week soaking in the sun on an island). Services, unlike goods, cannot be stored. Therefore, marketers must utilize their capacity wisely, or else the service (e.g., an unsold hotel room) is gone forever.

Services cannot be separated from their point of production (unlike a good, which may be manufactured thousands of kilometres away from its point of consumption). This means that the service encounter between customer and service provider is crucial to measure and manage. Finally, services are variable because they rely on human "production." Therefore, such firms as McDonald's leave nothing to chance—all elements of the service delivery are standardized.

### 4. Describe how firms develop new products.

New product development includes a visionary phase and a planning and development phase followed by testing and improvement. In the visionary phase, marketers generate new product ideas, assess their potential technical and commercial success, and conduct a business analysis to estimate the profitability of the new product. Planning and development includes developing a marketing program, planning how the product will be manufactured (if it is a good), and possibly obtaining a patent. The effectiveness of the new product may then be assessed in an actual or a simulated test market. Finally, the product is launched, and the entire marketing plan is implemented.

### 5. Discuss the importance of innovations.

Innovations are anything consumers perceive to be new. Understanding new products is important to companies because of the fast pace of technological advancement, the high cost to companies for developing new products, and the contributions to society that new products can make. Marketers classify innovations by their degree of newness. A *continuous innovation* is a modification of an existing product, a *dynamically continuous innovation* provides a greater change in a product, and a *discontinuous innovation* is a new product that creates major changes in people's lives.

6. **Explain the process of product adoption and the diffusion of innovations.**

Product adoption is the process by which an individual begins to buy and use a new product, whereas the diffusion of innovations is how a new product spreads throughout a population. The stages in the adoption process are awareness, interest, trial, adoption, and confirmation. To better understand the diffusion process, marketers classify consumers according to their readiness to adopt new products as innovators, early adopters, early majority, late majority, and laggards.

Five product characteristics that have an important effect on how quickly (or if) a new product will be adopted by consumers are relative advantage, compatibility, product complexity, trialability, and observability. Similar to individual consumers, organizations differ in their readiness to adopt new products based on characteristics of the organization, its management, and characteristics of the innovation.

# CHAPTER REVIEW

## Marketing Concepts: Testing Your Knowledge

1. What is a product (hint: the term product is used differently in marketing than in everyday language)?
2. What is meant by the core product, the functional product, the augmented product, and the potential product?
3. Explain how understanding the layers of a product leads a marketer to build competitive advantage.
4. Explain the good–service continuum and its importance.
5. What are some key characteristics of services that distinguish them from goods? Why is this understanding important?
6. What is a new product? Why is understanding new products so important to marketers?
7. List and explain the steps in developing new products.
8. Explain the different types of innovations based on their degree of newness.
9. List and explain the stages in an individual's adoption of an innovation.
10. List and explain the categories of adopters.
11. Describe the product factors that affect the speed of adoption for (a) consumers and (b) business organizations.

## Marketing Concepts: Discussing Choices and Issues

1. This chapter discussed the core product, functional product, augmented product, and potential product. Does this mean that marketers are simply trying to make products that are really the same seem different? When marketers understand these four layers of the product and develop products with this concept in mind, what are the benefits to consumers? What are the benefits to marketers?
2. Can you provide examples of core versus potential products? How easy or hard was it for you to come up with these examples? Do you find your thinking about product strategy (and building competitive advantage, in general) has changed as a result of learning these concepts?
3. Some people argue that there is no such a thing as a tangible good; everything is a service (that is, an experience). What do you think? What are some advantages and disadvantages of such thinking?
4. The phrase "new and improved" has been used so many times that, for many people, it is meaningless. Why has this occurred? What challenge does this present to marketers?
5. Discontinuous innovations are totally new products—something seldom seen in the marketplace. What are some examples of discontinuous innovations introduced in the past 50 years? What do you think the future holds for new products: will they be continuous or discontinuous innovations?

6. This chapter explained that knock-offs are slightly modified copies of original product designs. Should knock-offs be illegal? Who is hurt by knock-offs? Is the marketing of knock-offs good or bad for consumers in the short run? In the long run?

7. It is not necessarily true that all new products benefit consumers or society. What are some new products that have made our lives better? What are some new products that have actually been harmful to consumers or to society? Should there be a way to monitor new products that are introduced to the marketplace?

## Marketing Practice: Applying What You've Learned

1. Assume that a firm marketing a new low-calorie, fat-free chocolate candy bar has recently hired you. Because of your knowledge of new product adoption, you know that consumers go through a series of stages in adopting a new product—awareness, interest, and so on. You also realize that it is important for marketers to "help" customers move from one stage to the next. Develop your recommendations for marketing activities that would be appropriate for each stage in the adoption process.

2. As a member of a new product team with your company, you are working with engineers in developing the world's first practical, battery-powered automobile. You know that different product characteristics (relative advantage, compatibility, and so on) influence the speed of adoption of the product. Considering such product characteristics, make a list of suggestions for the engineers (or for the marketing department) that will speed the adoption of the new product when it is introduced.

3. Assume that you are employed in the marketing department of the firm in the preceding example. How would you use your knowledge of goods and services to communicate the benefits of this car? Can you think in terms of core versus potential products when you provide your answer?

4. Firms go to great lengths to develop new product ideas. Sometimes new ideas come from brainstorming, in which groups of individuals get together and try to think of as many different, novel, creative—and hopefully profitable—ideas for a new product as possible. With a group of other students, participate in brainstorming for new product ideas for one of the following (or some other product of your choice).

    a. an exercise machine

    b. computer software

    c. a new type of college or university

    Then, with your class, screen one or more of the ideas for possible further product development.

## Marketing Mini-Project: Learning by Doing

What product characteristics do consumers think are important in a new product? What types of service components do they demand? And most important, how do marketers know how to develop successful new products? This mini-project is designed to let you experience making some of these decisions.

1. Create (in your mind) a new product item (a good or service) that might be of interest to students like you. Develop a written description and possibly a drawing of this new product.

2. Show this new product description to a number of your fellow students who might be potential users of the product. Ask them to tell you what they think of the product. Some of the questions you might ask them are:

    a. What is your overall opinion of the new product?

    b. What basic benefits would you expect to receive from the product?

    c. What about the physical characteristics of the product? What do you like? Dislike? What would you add? Delete? Change?

    d. What do you like (or would you like) in the way of product packaging? (If the product is a service, think how you would communicate its existence and benefits.)

    e. What sort of services would you expect to receive with the product?

f. Do you think you would try the product? How could marketers influence you to buy the product?

3. Develop a report based on what you found. Include your recommendations for changes in the product and your feelings about the potential success of the new product.

## Real People, Real Surfers: Exploring the Web

Visit the Web site for three fashion retailers: Roots (**www.roots.com**), the Gap (**www.gap.com**), and Le Chateau (**www.lechateau.ca**). After you have visited the company Web sites, explore the Internet for additional information on each firm. Based on your experience on the Internet, answer the following questions:

1. Describe the number and variety of consumer and business-to-business products each company produces.

2. Is an emphasis on product development evident in the description of the companies from their Web sites?

3. Does the Web site provide opportunities for consumers to purchase products? To provide input about existing products? To offer new product ideas?

4. What can you find out about each firm's new product development process? How does the process lead to extraordinary new products?

5. What is your evaluation of each Web site? Does the Web site focus more on the company's products or on some other aspect of the company? Does it provide easy access to important information about the company's products? What visitors would be attracted to the Web site? Is the Web site designed in such a way to encourage visitors to return to the site?

Throughout its history, Boeing has been a very successful company. When it introduced its first product, the 707, it did not even know if a market existed for the product. It went ahead anyway, and the bold gamble paid off. The 707 became wildly popular, enabling Boeing to focus on new product innovations.

The 737, initially developed for the U.S. Armed Forces, was targeted at the commercial market. Boeing's timing was just right. During the 1970s air travel was becoming a reality for many people. Before then, travelling by air was reserved only for the privileged few. The Boeing 737 was a boon for airlines. It enabled them to pack many passengers on one flight, thus apportioning costs such as landing fees, salaries, and fuel over a broader range of passengers.

For decades Boeing has enjoyed near monopoly in commercial aviation. But that has changed. Airbus, a European maker of commercial and defence airplanes, has overtaken Boeing in sales numbers. Airbus has also introduced a slate of new models over the years, but perhaps nothing will come close to the ultimate battle shaping up between these two corporations.

The difference lies in product strategy and assumptions about the future. Airbus has bet that, in the future, airlines are going to succeed by packing as many passengers as possible into an aircraft. In response, it is building the A380, a monster airplane that will fly 555 passengers at one time. Airbus has already secured several concrete orders for this plane.

Boeing, on the other hand, has bet on the opposite, claiming that airlines will succeed by moving people faster between two airports. In response, it is introducing the 7E7, an airplane that will move passengers from point to point faster than ever.

But this is not the end of the story. Boeing has made several missteps. It totally underestimated Airbus' resolve to build the A380. Boeing also toyed with other new product ideas, none of which got under way. For example, Boeing thought about developing the Sonic Cruiser, capable of travelling near the speed of sound. While Boeing dithered, Airbus made strategic gains by making a commitment to the A380.

In the meantime, Boeing has tried to diversify its product line by entering the defence market and bought McDonnell Douglas. However, Boeing has been embroiled in scandals involving defence contracts. In response, Boeing's CEO at the time resigned.

Source: Adapted from articles in *Business Week* and *The New Yorker*.

## Things to Think About

1. Describe the core, functional, augmented, and potential products for Boeing and Airbus.

2. What type of innovation (continuous, dynamically continuous, or discontinuous) is the A380? What implications does this have for the future marketing of the A380?

3. Why do you think Boeing has suffered the missteps listed in the case? Why do successful companies suffer this fate?

4. Whose strategy for commercial aviation do you think is superior? Why?

5. If you were a member of Boeing's board of directors, what questions would you have asked the former CEO? What questions would you want to ask the new CEO?

# Earthbuddies—Part 1

This video and its sequel (featured in the next chapter) spans eight years in the life of an entrepreneur. Fresh out of business school, Anton starts a business with four partners, selling the Earthbuddy toy: a head made out of sawdust and grass seed that grows green grass "hair" once it is watered.

The concept is not new; there are other "grass heads" on the marketplace. Yet, because of strong selling skills, Anton and his partners secure orders from large retailers—K-Mart, Canadian Tire, and Zellers—making $400 000 in profit in just four months.

Then, the partners hit the big time: K-Mart's American parent has promised to place an order for 500 000 Earthbuddies, a contract with a potential for $500 000 in profit! This dream hinges on two key factors: K-Mart actually placing the order and Anton's ability to deliver on time.

Here is the frightening part: to make the delivery deadline, the entrepreneurs cannot wait for the purchase order; they have to start production right away. What happens if K-Mart does not come through? It could mean the end of the business as their cost to make the products will be half a million dollars. The team decides to take the risk.

The challenge lies in making 16 000 Earthbuddies a day. One hundred forty new workers have to be trained overnight, and lining up reliable suppliers proves to be a problem as they run out of materials, such as sawdust or pantyhose, constantly.

## Questions

1. Would you say the Earthbuddy is a continuous innovation, a dynamically continuous innovation, a discontinuous innovation, or none of the above? Provide reasons for your answer.
2. This video highlights many key factors that need to be considered when developing new products. Make a list of these factors and outline how you would handle them if you were in Anton's shoes.
3. In spite of heavy competition from other "grass heads" in the marketplace, Earthbuddy secured the biggest retail clients. What factors do you think accounted for its success?

Source: This case was prepared by Ajay Sirsi and is based on "Earthbuddies," *Venture* #819.

# CHAPTER 8
## Product Management

## CHAPTER OBJECTIVES

WHEN YOU HAVE COMPLETED YOUR STUDY OF THIS CHAPTER, YOU SHOULD BE ABLE TO

1.  Explain the different product objectives and strategies a firm may choose.

2.  Explain how firms manage products throughout the product life cycle.

3.  Discuss how branding creates product identity and describe different types of branding strategies.

4.  Describe how organizations are structured for new and existing product management.

# Real People, Real Decisions

## Meet **Julie Desrosier,** a Decision Maker at One of Canada's Largest Mutual Fund Companies

You will see at the end of Julie's profile why we have kept her company identity a secret!

Julie is an Advertising Manager within the Marketing Department at one of Canada's largest mutual fund companies. After graduating with a Bachelor of Arts degree from McGill University (with a major in Anthropology), Julie joined a company called AIM Funds Management Inc. as a Bilingual Client Relations Representative. After a year on the phones she felt comfortable enough in her knowledge of the industry and of clients to apply internally for an analyst position in the Marketing Research group. After two and a half years of conducting research and gaining in-depth knowledge and insights into the minds of her clients, competitors, and the industry in general, the opportunity arose to apply that knowledge to the position of Advertising Manager within the Marketing Department.

Julie was motivated to choose this career path mainly because of constantly evolving interests and a thirst for knowledge. She loves a good challenge and her career progression within the company has been based on her desire to keep learning and growing as both an employee and as a person in general. Coming from a social sciences background, the jump to working for a mutual fund company may not be obvious, as are her shifts from Client Relations to Marketing Research to Advertising. As Julie says, "The truth is, I didn't plan for it to turn out that way. I simply kept an open mind to new opportunities and was able to leverage and build upon the knowledge and experience I gained in each role."

A few years ago, Trimark Investments (a long-established, home-grown mutual funds company) was purchased by AIM Funds Management Inc., a fund company from the U.S. and a recent entrant to the Canadian mutual fund scene. As often happens when two companies (and brands) come together, the question of "what should we call ourselves?" came up almost immediately.

With the joining of the two companies, Julie and her colleagues were faced with a case of "opposites attract."

Trimark was a large, well-known, and well-established Canadian company that promoted a traditional, family-style environment for its employees. Its product offerings (mutual funds) were based on a "value" style of investing. AIM Funds was a small, youthful, and ambitious firm that had only been in Canada a short while and its product offerings were based on a "growth" style of investing.

From a product standpoint, it was a perfect match in terms of creating a well-rounded product offering. From a cultural standpoint, the match was a bit more awkward (e.g., large vs. small, established vs. youthful). In order to gain and maintain the confidence and trust of the financial advisors that sold the funds (and the end-investor that bought them), a decision needed to be made on how these two companies could be successfully integrated under a name that would not only fulfill both external and internal expectations, but would be representative of both brands.

The team considered three options.

**Option 1.** Keep AIM Funds Management as the company name. The advantage with this option was the fact that AIM was a larger, more established player in the mutual funds industry. The disadvantage was that AIM was not a well-established brand name in Canada.

**Option 2.** Keep Trimark Investments as the company name. Keeping the Trimark name would ensure that the brand resonated with Canadian clients and consumers. The disadvantage with this option was that the merged company name would not reflect AIM's youthful sense of energy (an important consideration in financial services).

**Option 3.** Choose a new name. The challenge in brand decisions is choosing a name that will provide the firm with a competitive advantage in the marketplace.

Now, join Julie and her colleagues. Which option would you choose and why?

# CREATING AND NURTURING PRODUCTS

What makes one product fail and another enjoy great success? What is the difference between a product and a brand? Do all products enjoy brand status? It's worth repeating what we said in Chapter 2: Firms that plan well succeed. Product planning plays a big role in the firm's *marketing plans*. The strategies outlined in the product plan tell how the firm expects to develop a product that will meet marketing objectives. In Chapter 7, we discussed what a product really is and how new products are developed and introduced into the marketplace. In this chapter, we'll finish the product part of the story by discussing how companies manage products and examine the steps in product planning (Figure 8.1). This will include developing product objectives and the strategies required to successfully market products as they evolve over time. We'll also discuss branding, one of the most important decisions product planners make, and examine how firms organize for effective product and brand management.

**Figure 8.1** Steps in Managing Products

# USING PRODUCT OBJECTIVES TO DECIDE ON A PRODUCT STRATEGY

When marketers develop product strategies, they are making decisions about product benefits, features, styling, branding, labelling, logos, and packaging. But what do they want to accomplish? Clearly stated product objectives provide focus and direction. Product objectives should support the broader marketing objectives of the business unit in addition to supporting the overall mission of the firm. For example, if the objectives of the firm focus on a certain return on investment, its marketing objectives may then focus on market share and/or unit or dollar sales volume necessary for the firm to attain that return on investment. Product objectives need to specify how product decisions will support or contribute to reaching a desired market share or level of sales. (You will find more on the relationship between marketing objectives and marketing strategies in Chapter 14 on developing and implementing marketing plans.)

To be effective, product-related objectives must be measurable, clear and unambiguous, and feasible, and must specify a time frame. Consider, for example, how a frozen-entrée manufacturer might state its product objectives:

- "In the upcoming fiscal year, modify the product's fat content to reflect the trend toward low fat foods."

- "Introduce three new items to the product line to take advantage of increased consumer interest in ethnic foods."

- "During the coming fiscal year, improve the chicken entrées to the extent that consumers will rate them better tasting than the competition."

The frozen entrée manufacturer might use a matrix, like the one shown in Figure 8.2 to guide product objectives.

As shown in Figure 8.2, the firm can follow one of four strategies, depending on whether the products or markets are current or new. A good way for a firm to use the grid is to ensure it has a good balance between the four quadrants. A focus on only one or two quadrants suggests that the firm may be vulnerable to marketplace forces.

Planners must keep in touch with consumers or business customers, so that their objectives accurately respond to customer needs. Equally important in developing product objectives is an up-to-date knowledge of competitive product innovations. Above all, product objectives should consider the *long-term implications* of product decisions. Planners who sacrifice the long-term health of the organization to reach short-term sales or financial goals are being irresponsible. Product planners may focus on one or more individual products at

|  | Current Markets | New Markets |
|---|---|---|
| **Current Products** | **Market Penetration**<br>The frozen entrée manufacturer may entice consumers to buy more of its products | **Market Development**<br>The frozen entrée manufacturer may expand internationally |
| **New Products** | **Product Development**<br>The frozen entrée manufacturer may develop a new line of fat-free products aimed at current consumers | **Diversification**<br>The frozen entrée manufacturer may introduce a new line of products aimed at a new market: the ethnic consumer |

**Figure 8.2** A Product–Market Grid to Guide Product Decisions

a time, or they may look at a group of product offerings as a whole. In this section, we examine these different strategies.

## Objectives and Strategies for Individual Products

**Volkswagen**
www.volkswagen.com

The Volkswagen Beetle is an interesting story of a product that triumphed over great obstacles. When the product was first introduced in North America in the 1960s, dealers complained that the car was too ugly to sell. Many of those dealers were soon kicking themselves; dealers who did accept the challenge sold over 21 million Beetles to true believers who adored the car's simple engineering and funky image. The Beetle was a tremendously successful product in the 1960s and 1970s despite its poor image. In the late 1990s, Volkswagen decided to capitalize on baby boomers' warm memories of the Beetle by introducing a "concept car" model reminiscent of the original (Exhibit 8.1).

Some product strategies, including those used in introducing the new VW Beetle, focus on a single new product. However, strategies for individual products may be quite different for new products, for regional products, and for mature products.

For new products, the objectives relate to successful *introduction*. Warner-Lambert Canada worked hard to introduce Dentyne Ice gum to youth across Canada.[1] After a firm has experienced considerable success with a product in a local or regional market, however, it may consider it time to grow the business by introducing the product nationally. Big Rock Brewery, a Calgary microbrewery, used its success in the Alberta beer market to introduce its beer into Ontario and British Columbia.[2]

For mature products, product objectives may focus on breathing new life into a product long taken for granted while holding onto the traditional brand personality. In the case of Cracker Jacks, for instance, this means keeping consumer perceptions of the product positive. The images of Sailor Jack and his dog Bingo have been updated at least four times since the original design of 1893.[3]

## Objectives and Strategies for Multiple Products

Although a small firm might focus on one product, a larger company usually markets a mix of related products. This means that some strategic decisions affect two or more products at once. Thus, the firm must think in terms of its entire *portfolio* of products. Product planning means developing *product line*

**Exhibit 8.1**

Volkswagen created customer excitement with its new Beetle.

and *product mix* strategies that encompass multiple offerings. Figure 8.3 illustrates these concepts, using some Procter & Gamble products as examples.

**PRODUCT LINE STRATEGIES** A **product line** is a firm's total product offering designed to satisfy a single need or desire of a group of target customers. For example, Procter & Gamble's line of fabric and home-care products includes four different types of laundry soap: Tide, Cheer, Gain, and Ivory Snow. To do an even better job of meeting varying consumer needs, each of the brands comes in several different formulations. For example, in addition to regular Tide, there is Tide with bleach and Ultra Tide. The number of separate items offered within the same category determines the length of the product line.

When a firm has a large number of variations in its product line, it is said to carry a *full line*. With a full-line strategy, it is possible to please many customer segments, thus increasing total sales potential. A company that adopts a *limited-line strategy* markets a smaller number of product variations. Sometimes, having a limited product line can improve the image of a firm, because it is perceived to be a specialist and has a clear, specific position in the market. Rolls-Royce, for example, makes only expensive, custom-built automobiles and, for years, has maintained a unique position in the automobile industry.

In developing product strategies, organizations may decide to extend their product lines by adding more brands or models. Bombardier Inc., the manufacturer of Sea-Doos and Ski-Doos, extended their recreational product line with the introduction of their ATV Traxter (Exhibit 8.2).

When a company stretches its product line, it must decide on the best direction in which to go. If a firm's current product line includes middle- and lower-end items, an *upward line stretch* would add new items—those with a higher price, better quality, or more features. Folgers and Maxwell House took this route by adding such new coffee varieties as Gourmet Supreme, Columbian Supreme, French Roast, and Italian Espresso Roast.

Conversely, a *downward line stretch* completes a line by adding items at the lower end. Here the firm must be careful that the lower-end items don't blur the images of higher-priced, upper-end offerings. A firm like Godiva may not want to run the risk of cheapening its image, for example, by creating a new, less expensive chocolate bar to compete with products like Mr. Big and Sweet Marie.

**Procter & Gamble**
www.pg.com

**product line** A firm's total product offering designed to satisfy a single need or desire of target customers.

**Bombardier Inc.**
www.bombardier.com

| | | Width of Product Mix → | | |
|---|---|---|---|---|
| **Paper Products** | **Fabric and Home-Care Products** | **Health Care Products** | **Beauty Care Products** | **Food and Beverage Products** |
| Pampers | Bounce | Metamucil | Cover Girl | Crisco |
| Always | Cascade | Pepto Bismol | Max Factor | Folgers |
| Tampax | Ivory Liquid | Crest | Old Spice | Pringles |
| Bounty | Downy | Scope | Secret | Sunny Delight |
| Royale | Swiffer | Vicks | Head & Shoulders | |
| | Mr. Clean | | Pantene | |
| | COMET | | Pert | |
| | Spic and Span | | Vidal Sassoon | |
| | Tide | | Camay | |
| | Cheer | | Clearasil | |
| | Gain | | Noxema | |
| | Ivory Snow | | Coast | |
| | Dryel | | Ivory soap | |
| | Febreze | | Zest | |
| | | | Oil of Olay | |

*Length of Product Line* (vertical axis label on left)

**Figure 8.3** Product Line Length and Product Mix Width

**Exhibit 8.2**

Bombardier added the Traxter ATV to its recreational product line, which already included Ski-Doo and Sea-Doo.

In some cases, a firm may decide that its existing product line is meeting the needs of only a small portion of the market and that there is more than one opportunity for growth. Then the product strategy may call for a *two-way stretch*, that is, adding items at both the upper and lower ends. Marriott Hotels, for example, has added Fairfield Inns and Courtyard at the lower end and Marriott Marquis Hotels and the Ritz Carlton at the upper end.

A *filling-out* strategy may mean adding sizes or styles not previously available in a product category. Quebec's Lassonde did this when it was the first juice company in North America to use aseptic plastic bottles for its Fruite drinks. It also introduced the first refrigerated vegetable juice in North America, Vegetable Delight.[4] Sometimes the best strategy may be to *contract a product line*, particularly when some of the items are not profitable. For example, when sales for the once-popular Oldsmobile brand slowed, GM dropped the brand from its line in 2004.

As we have seen, there are many ways a firm can modify its product line to meet the competition or take advantage of new opportunities in the marketplace. To further explore these strategic decisions, we return to Procter & Gamble. What does P&G do if the objective is to increase market share in the fabric-care market? One possibility would be to expand its line of laundry detergents. If the line extension meets a perceived consumer need not being addressed currently, this would be a good strategic move. But, whenever a product line or a product family is extended, there is the danger of **cannibalization**, which occurs when sales of an existing brand are eaten up by the new item, as the firm's current customers switch to the new product. This explains why P&G has created a whole new product line with its Dryel product to achieve growth in fabric care. The Dryel product (Exhibit 8.3) is not cannibalizing sales from detergents such as Tide and Ivory Snow.[5]

**PRODUCT MIX STRATEGIES** Product planning can go beyond a single product item or a product line to entire groups of products. A firm's **product mix** is its entire range of products. For example, in addition to a deep line of shaving products, Gillette makes toiletries such as Dry Idea and Right Guard deodorant, Paper Mate and Flair writing instruments, Oral B toothbrushes, Braun small appliances, and Duracell batteries.

In developing a product mix strategy, planners usually consider the *width of the product mix,* the number of product lines produced by the firm. By developing several different product lines, firms can reduce the risk associated with "putting all their eggs in one basket." Normally, firms develop a mix of product lines that have some similarities, for example, products that can share distribution channels or manufacturing facilities. Sometimes, firms expand into new product lines to take advantage of a strong brand reputation with an existing target market. As you can see in Exhibit 8.4, Victorinox®, the makers of the popular Swiss Army™ knife, has extended its product into apparel and watches.

**cannibalization** The loss of sales of an existing product when a new item in a product line or product family is introduced.

**product mix** The total set of all products a firm offers for sale.

## MARKETING THROUGHOUT THE PRODUCT LIFE CYCLE

The zipper, a Canadian invention, is an example of a humble, low-tech product that has managed to live an exceptionally long life. Although the zipper was invented in the 1800s, it was not used in men's clothing until the 1930s. These "hookless fasteners," as they were once called, were originally intended for use on high-buttoned shoes. It took time for them to be used in men's trousers, because competitors argued that this "newfangled gadget" could result in serious injuries. In 1936, the Prince of Wales adopted the zipper and was the first monarch to "sit on a throne bezippered."

Like the zipper, many products have very long lives. The **product life cycle** is a useful way to look at how product features change over the life of a product. In Chapter 7, we discussed how marketers introduce new products; but launching a product is only the beginning. Product marketing strategies must evolve as they continue through the product life cycle (Exhibit 8.5 on page 249).

The concept of the product life cycle does not relate to a single brand but to the generic product *category*. Thus, we talk about the life cycle of personal computers, not Compaq computers, of automobiles, not the Focus. Some individual brands have short life expectancies: Who remembers the Bricklin car or Evening in Paris perfume? Others seem almost immortal: Think of such brands as Campbell's Soup, Ivory Soap, or American Express.

## The Introduction Stage

We can divide the life of a product into four separate stages. The first stage of the product life cycle, shown in Figure 8.4, is **introduction**—customers get their first chance to purchase the good or service. During this early stage, a single company usually produces the product. If the product is accepted and profitable, competitors will follow with their own versions.

During the introduction stage, the goal is to get first-time buyers to try the product. Sales (hopefully) increase at a steady but slow pace. As shown in Figure 8.5, the company does not make a profit during this stage, due to research and development (R&D) costs and heavy spending for advertising and other promotion.

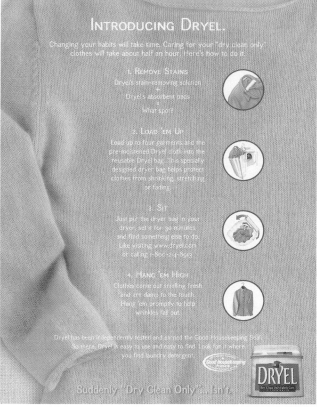

**Exhibit 8.3**

By introducing a new product line with Dryel, Procter & Gamble was able to meet new customer demands and avoid cannibalizing laundry detergent brands.

**product life cycle** Concept that explains how products go through four distinct stages from birth to death: introduction, growth, maturity, and decline.

**introduction** The first stage of the product life cycle, in which slow growth follows the introduction of a new product in the marketplace.

**Figure 8.4** The Product Life Cycle

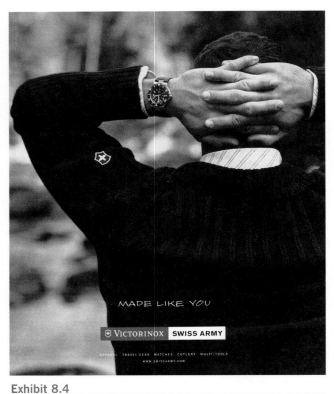

**Exhibit 8.4**

Victorinox® has extended its product into apparel and watches.

Pricing may be high to recover the R&D costs (demand permitting) or low to attract large numbers of consumers. The Hitachi advertisement in Exhibit 8.5 is designed to appeal to consumers who are willing to pay for the latest technological advances.

For a new product to be successful, consumers must first know about it and believe that it is something they need. Thus, marketing during the introduction stage often focuses on informing consumers about the product, how to use it, and its benefits.

How long does the introduction stage last? For the microwave oven, it was several years. How long the introduction stage lasts depends on a number of factors, including marketplace acceptance and producer willingness to support the product during its start-up. In the case of the microwave, sales in countries such as Japan were much stronger, because the companies supported the product through its long introduction stage.

Not all products make it past the introduction stage. In fact, the failure rate for new products has been cited to be as high as 90 percent.[6] One of the most noted examples of products that never got past the introduction stage is the Ford Edsel automobile. Introduced in 1957 and named after the only son of Ford's founder, the Edsel was designed to compete with such cars as the Chrysler New Yorker. It boasted high horsepower, tail fins, three-tone paint jobs, wraparound windshields, a "horse-collar" grille, and a push-button gearshift. The problem was that consumers didn't like the Edsel. Only 110 847 Edsels were made before Ford abandoned the car, making the word *Edsel* synonymous with product failure.[7]

| Characteristic | Introduction | Growth | Maturity | Decline |
|---|---|---|---|---|
| **Product** | Single company produces single product | New competitors enter the market creating new variations of the product | New features added; sales are mostly replacement products | Number of variations reduced |
| **Goals** | Get first-time buyers to try the product | Encourage brand loyalty | Attract new users | Remain profitable; decide whether to keep or phase product out |
| **Sales** | Increase at a steady but slow pace | Rapid increase | Peak, then level off, often decline | Continue to decline |
| **Profits** | Negative | Increase and peak | Profit margins narrow | Declining |
| **Pricing** | High: recover R&D costs Low: attract large numbers of customers | May need to reduce because of increased competition | Price to maintain market share | May reduce if can remain profitable |
| **Marketing Communications** | Informing customers | Heavy advertising to counter new competition | Reminder advertising | Decreased to maintain profitability |

**Figure 8.5** Marketing Strategies through the Product Life Cycle

## The Growth Stage

The second stage in the product life cycle, the **growth stage**, sees a rapid increase in sales while profits increase and peak. Marketing's goal here is to encourage brand loyalty by convincing the market that this brand is superior to others in the category. In this stage, marketing strategies may include the introduction of product variations to attract market segments and grow market share. When competitors appear, marketers must use heavy advertising and other types of promotion. Price competition may develop, driving profits down. Some firms may seek to capture a particular segment of the market by positioning their product to appeal to a certain group.

## The Maturity Stage

The **maturity stage** of the product life cycle is usually the longest. Sales peak and then begin to level off and even decline while profit margins narrow. Competition grows intense when remaining competitors fight for a piece of a shrinking pie. Because most customers have already accepted the product, sales are often to replace a worn-out item or to take advantage of product improvements. For example, almost everyone owns a television, so companies typically sell new TVs to consumers whose sets have broken down. During the maturity stage, firms try to sell their product through all suitable retailers, because product availability is crucial in a very competitive market. Consumers will not go far to find one brand when others are closer at hand.

To remain competitive and maintain market share during the maturity stage, firms may tinker with the marketing mix, coming out with new versions of the product that include new features. For example, television manufacturers try to invigorate sales with flat-screen TVs. Warner-Lambert Canada introduced Listerine oral care strips, the first product extension of Listerine mouthwash (Exhibit 8.6). The strips offer the same breath freshening benefit of the original Listerine, but are small and dissolve in the mouth, thereby making the Listerine product portable and offering consumers a new benefit.[8]

Attracting new users of the product is another strategy used in the maturity stage. As we saw in Figure 8.2 market development means introducing an existing product to a market that doesn't currently use it. Many Canadian firms are finding new markets for their products in countries around the world. To find new users for their products, firms in the Canadian wine industry, for example, have been actively pursuing markets in Pacific Rim countries such as Korea and China.

## The Decline Stage

The **decline stage** of the product life cycle is characterized by a decrease in product category sales. This is often because new technology has made the product obsolete, as when computers caused the decline of the typewriter. Although a single firm may still be profitable, the market as a whole begins to shrink, profits decline, and suppliers pull out. In this stage, there are usually many competitors with no one having a distinct advantage.

A firm's major product decision in the decline stage is whether to keep the product. Once the product is no longer profitable, it drains resources from the firm—resources that could help develop newer products. If the decision is to drop the product, elimination can

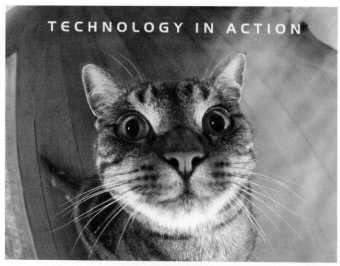

**Exhibit 8.5**

This Hitachi ad is targeted at a business-to-business audience using consumer techniques to bring attention to the company's latest innovations.

**growth stage** The second stage in the product life cycle, during which the product is accepted and sales rapidly increase.

**maturity stage** The third and longest stage in the product life cycle, in which sales peak and profit margins narrow.

**decline stage** The final stage in the product life cycle, in which sales decrease as customer needs change.

**Exhibit 8.6**

By introducing Listerine in a new format to meet customer needs for convenience, Warner-Lambert Canada gave a mature product new life.

**brand** A name, term, symbol, or any other unique element of a product, which identifies one firm's product(s) and sets them apart from the competition.

be handled in two ways: Phase it out by cutting production in stages and letting existing stocks run out, or drop the product immediately. If the established market leader anticipates that there will be some residual demand for the product for a long time, it may make sense to keep the product on the market. The idea is to sell a limited quantity of the product with little or no support from sales, merchandising, advertising, and distribution, and let it "wither on the vine." Some classic products have been able to hang on with little or no marketing support. For example, the Pilot stapler (Exhibit 8.7) has been on the market for over 70 years: Despite sleeker and less costly competitors, the Pilot maintains its reputation as *the* heavy-duty stapler.[9]

## CREATING PRODUCT IDENTITY: BRANDING DECISIONS

Knowing the stage of their product in the product life cycle helps marketers successfully manage the product. Equally important is giving that product an identity: Branding is an extremely important element of product strategies. In this section, we examine what a brand is, the importance of branding and how firms make branding decisions.

### What's in a Name (or a Symbol)?

How do you identify your favourite brand? By its name? By the logo (how the name appears)? By the packaging? By some graphic image or symbol, such as Canadian Tire's red triangle and green maple leaf? A **brand** is a name, term, symbol, or any other unique element of a product, which identifies one firm's product(s) and sets it apart from the competition. Consumers easily recognize the Coca-Cola logo, the pink Energizer bunny (a *trade character*), and the triangular blue Nabisco logo (a *brand mark*) in the corner of the box. Branding provides the recognition factor products need to succeed in regional, national, or international markets.

**CHOOSING A BRAND NAME, MARK, OR CHARACTER** There are several important considerations in selecting a brand name, brand mark, or trade character. It must have a positive connotation and be memorable. Consider Toro's experience when it introduced a lightweight snow thrower called the "Snow Pup." Sales were disappointing, because "pup" conveyed a small, cuddly animal, not a desirable image for a snow thrower. Renamed the "Snow Master," its sales went up markedly.[10]

A brand name is probably the most used and most recognized form of branding. Kool-Aid, a word that most kids know, has been used to maintain a long-term relationship with consumers. Kool-Aid now markets iced tea versions of its beverages to appeal to adult tastes (Exhibit 8.8).

A good brand name can position a product by conveying a certain image or personality (Molson Canadian) or describing how it works (Drano), or else it may be ambiguous, such as Exxon, Ajax, and Lotus. Brand names sometimes need to change over time. For example, Kentucky Fried Chicken became KFC when "fried" went out of style, the Canadian Imperial Bank of Commerce became CIBC to avoid the use of "imperial," and for similar reasons the Hudson's Bay Company became HBC.[11]

How does a firm select a good brand name? Good brand designers say there are four "easy" tests: *easy to say,*

**Exhibit 8.7**

The venerable Pilot stapler may be in decline, but it's not dead. Loyal fans have kept this niche product on the market.

## SPOTLIGHT ON REAL PEOPLE    The Body Blocker Company

Lila Lewandoski and Shashi Behl decided, while studying together at the University of Saskatchewan, that they wanted to be business partners. They now operate The Body Blocker Group, a company that makes and sells UV-protective clothing for kids and adults. The idea for their clothes came from Lewandoski's concern about sun damage to her skin after working for many summers as a lifeguard. After researching the physics of ultraviolet rays and checking out the other manufacturers of UV-protective clothing, the pair developed a business plan, including the product strategy for the company. Their business plan was so strong that it won an award from the Canadian Youth Business Foundation and secured a business loan, which allowed them to develop a prototype for their clothing: a high-necked, knee- and elbow-length, one-piece suit for children.

To test their product, Lewandoski and Behl did "market research" for an entire summer at a wading pool in Calgary by talking with parents and allowing kids to try on the suits. They studied the response to the suits and found out that kids did not like the high neck and that people wanted a sportier, more colourful suit. With the results of this research, Behl and Lewandoski revised the product in line with the quality objectives of their company. Behl describes the overall product quality objective of the company this way: "We aim to create tough, long-lasting clothes."

The two entrepreneurs have worked with a fashion designer to refine their product line even further. Now they have kids' suits available in purple or blue with stripes in multiple colours. They have also added other products to their line—shirts, hats, skirts, and sarongs for adults; hats and dresses for kids. Their product mix has also been expanded to include sunscreen products and a laundry product for swimsuits.[12]

1. In what stage of the product life cycle is UV-protective clothing?
2. Visit The Body Blocker Web site (**www.bodyblocker.com**). Would you say that the entrepreneurs are creating a unique brand identity for their product on the Web site? What suggestions would you make for the development of an even stronger brand identity?
3. What are some other potential product line and product mix expansion strategies for The Body Blocker company?

*easy to spell*, *easy to read*, and *easy to remember*. Consider P&G's Tide, Cheer, Gain, Downy, and Ivory Snow. And the name should also "fit" four ways: *fit the target market*, *fit the product's benefits*, *fit the customer's culture*, and *fit legal requirements*. When the Mutual Life Assurance Company of Canada decided to change its brand name, it chose a very non-traditional name for the insurance market: Clarica. A multimillion-dollar advertising campaign supported the name change, but the name was criticized by many marketers for, among other things, sounding more like skin cleanser than an insurance company. Clarica responded with the humorous ad in Exhibit 8.9, which it hoped would further increase the awareness of its brand name.

When it comes to graphics for a brand symbol, name, or logo, the rule is: it must be recognizable and memorable. No matter how small or how large, the triangular Nabisco logo in the corner of the box is a familiar sight. And it should have visual impact. This means that from across a store or when you are quickly flipping the pages in a magazine, the brand will catch your attention. One product that made the wrong kind of visual impact with its brand name was a snack product called HITS. It was only on the shelves for a short time, because the manufacturer realized that when the packages were put end to end on store shelves, the logos produced an unintended effect: HitsHitsHitsHitsHits.[13]

Some marketers enhance brand recognition by creating a *trade character*, such as the Pillsbury Dough Boy, the Jolly Green Giant, or Mr. Clean. A&W uses the Root Bear to strengthen brand recognition (Exhibit 8.10 on page 253).

**TRADEMARKS** The legal term for a brand name, brand mark, or trade character is **trademark**. Marketers can legally register brands as trademarks to make their use by competitors illegal in Canada. However, it is possible for a firm to have protection for a brand even if it has not legally registered it. Common law protection exists if the firm has used the name and established it over a period of time. Although a registered trademark prevents others from using it on a similar product, it may not bar its use for a product in a completely different type of business.

**Exhibit 8.8**

Kool-Aid has used its long-standing popularity with kids to make new iced tea products aimed at adults who drank Kool-Aid as kids.

**trademark**    The legal term for a brand name, brand mark, or trade character; a trademark legally registered by a government obtains protection for exclusive use in that country.

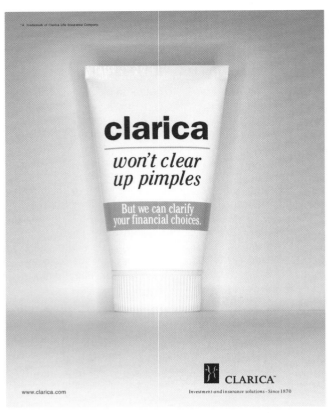

**Exhibit 8.9**

Clarica used this humorous ad to help make its brand name more memorable.

**brand equity** The value of a brand to an organization.

**brand extension** A new product sold with the same brand name as a strong existing brand.

**family brand** A brand that a group of individual products or individual brands share.

# The Importance of Branding

Marketers spend vast amounts of money on new product development, advertising, and promotions to develop strong brands. If successful, the investment creates **brand equity**, which is a brand's value to its organization. Brand equity means that a brand has high customer loyalty, perceived quality, and brand name awareness. For a firm, brand equity provides a competitive advantage, because it gives the brand the power to capture and hold onto a larger share of the market and to sell at prices with higher profit margins. Some of the most valuable brands in the world are BMW, Nike, Nokia, and IKEA.[14]

Research shows that the following factors make a brand successful[15]:

- The brand excels at delivering the benefits customers truly desire.
- The brand stays relevant.
- The pricing strategy is based on consumers' perceptions of value.
- The brand is properly positioned.
- The brand is consistent.
- The brand portfolio and hierarchy make sense.
- The brand makes use of and coordinates a full range of marketing activities to build equity.
- The brand's managers understand what the brand means to customers.
- The brand is given proper support, and that support is sustained over the long run.
- The company monitors sources of brand equity.

When brands possess strong brand equity, they provide important opportunities for a firm. A firm may leverage a brand's equity with **brand extensions**, new products sold with the same brand name, such as the Listerine oral care strips and Dentyne Ice mentioned earlier. If existing brand equity is high, the firm is able to sell the brand extension at a higher price than if it had given it a new brand, and the brand extension will attract new customers immediately. However, if the brand extension does not live up to the quality or attractiveness of the original brand, brand equity will suffer, reducing brand loyalty and sales.

# Branding Strategies

As marketing strategists know, brands are important to a marketing program's success, so decisions about branding strategies are a major part of product decision making. Marketers have to determine whether to create individual or family brands, national or private-label brands, or to co-brand.

**INDIVIDUAL BRANDS VERSUS FAMILY BRANDS** Part of developing a branding strategy is deciding whether to use a separate, unique brand for each product item—*an individual brand strategy*—or market multiple items under the same brand name—a **family brand**—an umbrella brand strategy. Individual brands may do a better job of communicating clearly and concisely what the consumer can expect from the product, whereas family brands allow a firm to develop a brand for an entire product line. Thus, the decision to use an individual or family branding strategy often depends on characteristics of the product and whether the company's overall product strategy calls for introduction of a single, unique product or for the development of a group of similar products. Pillsbury Canada uses family branding with its Green Giant, Pillsbury, Old El Paso, Underwood, and Accent family brands. Under the Old El Paso name are such Mexican foods as salsa and Nachips; under its Green Giant name are frozen and canned vegetables and other frozen products; and under the Pillsbury name are Pizza Pops, Toaster Strudel, and refrigerated baked goods.[16]

**NATIONAL AND STORE BRANDS** Retailers today are often in the driver's seat when it comes to deciding what brands to sell. In addition to choosing from producers' brands like those from Pillsbury Canada, called **national or manufacturer brands**, retailers decide whether to offer their own versions. **Store brands**, also called **private-label brands**, are the retail store's or chain's exclusive trade name. Loblaws, for example, sells its President's Choice private-label brand along with national brands.

Retailers choose a private-label branding strategy because they generally make a larger profit than on national brands. Private-label strategies are also important when retailers seek to maintain a consistent store image; for example, clothing retailers such as the Gap and Holt Renfrew protect their image by offering store brands.[17] The B.C. company Private Reserve Water produces private-label water for such companies as Holiday Inn Express, and several golf clubs, restaurants and catering companies across North America.

**LICENSING** Some firms choose to use **licensing** to brand their products. A licensing agreement typically means that one firm sells another firm the right to use a brand name for a specific purpose and for a specific period of time. Firms choose a licensing strategy for a variety of reasons: Sometimes it provides instant recognition and consumer interest in a new product; at other times licensing is important to positioning a product for a certain target market. For example, bourbon maker Jack Daniels licensed its name to T. Marzetti for producing Jack Daniels bourbon-flavoured mustard. Much better known, however, is the licensing of entertainment names. Movie producers license their properties to manufacturers of a seemingly infinite number of products: When Disney movies hit the screens, such licensed merchandise as figures, toys, and clothing are sold through stores and distributed through other retail outlets such as McDonald's.

**CO-BRANDING** Starbucks cafés in Chapters stores and McDonald's outlets in Wal-Mart stores are both examples of **co-branding**. Co-branding, which some call one of the "pre-eminent marketing strategies" today, joins two brands in partnership to market new or existing products.[18]

Co-branding ideally benefits both partners—in combination, the two brands can enjoy more recognition power than either would alone. Starbucks and Chapters products, for example, are complementary and appeal to the same target group, so by co-branding, both brands are strengthened.[19]

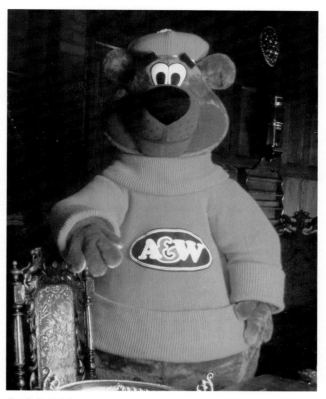

**Exhibit 8.10**
The A&W Root Bear is an example of a trade character.

**national or manufacturer brands** Brands that the manufacturer of the product owns.

**store or private-label brands** Brands that are owned and sold by a specific retailer or distributor.

**licensing** An agreement in which one firm sells another firm the right to use a brand name for a specific purpose and for a specific period of time.

**co-branding** An agreement between two brands to work together in marketing new or existing products.

# ORGANIZING FOR EFFECTIVE PRODUCT MANAGEMENT

Firms don't create great brands, people do. Like all elements of the marketing mix, the effectiveness of product strategies depends on marketing managers and the decisions they make. In this section, we discuss how firms organize for the management of existing products and for the development of new products.

# Good or Bad Decision?

Pharmaceutical marketers in Canada face a difficult challenge in trying to develop strong brand equity through advertising. Under the Food and Drugs Act, pharmaceutical advertisers can mention either their product's brand name or its use, but they cannot mention both in the same ad. Wyeth-Ayerst Canada decided to push these regulations to the limit with ads for their birth-control pill Alesse that aired on MuchMusic. The ads, titled "Lessons Learned," showed young women discussing lessons they had learned about relationships and men. Consistent with the regulations, the company did not mention the brand name in an ad that talks about contraception, but one woman in the ad says, "Less may be more for you," a phrase that sounds very much like "Alesse may be more for you." Do you think Wyeth-Ayerst Canada is adhering to the Food and Drugs Act legislation regarding pharmaceutical advertising? Health Canada is reviewing legislation with respect to pharmaceutical advertising, since the United States and other countries now allow pharmaceutical marketers to be more aggressive in their branding efforts. Do you think the existing Canadian legislation is fair? What should be the Canadian government's objectives in regulating advertising for pharmaceutical products?[20]

## Management of Existing Products

In small firms such as The Body Blocker Group, the marketing function may be handled by a single marketing manager, who is responsible for new product planning, advertising, making Web site decisions, marketing research, and just about everything else. The Body Blocker simply is not big enough—and doesn't need—a large marketing management team.

In larger firms with many products, a number of managers are responsible for different brands, product categories, or markets. Depending on the organization, product management may include brand managers, product category managers, and market managers.

**BRAND MANAGERS** Sometimes a firm has different brands within a single product category. For example, General Foods produces several brands of coffee, including Brim, Maxim, Maxwell House, International Coffees, Sanka, and Yuban. In such cases, a separate **brand manager** may be responsible for each brand.

**brand manager** A manager who is responsible for developing and implementing the marketing plan for a single brand.

Procter & Gamble brand managers once acted independently and were responsible for coordinating all marketing activities for a brand: positioning, identifying target markets, research, distribution, sales promotion, packaging, and evaluating the success of these decisions. Today, P&G's brand managers are more like team leaders. They still are responsible for positioning of brands and developing brand equity, but they are likely to work with sales, finance, and logistics staff members as a part of customer business teams working with major retail accounts.[21]

The brand management system has its problems. Acting independently, brand managers may fight for increases in short-term sales for their own brand. They may push too hard with coupons, cents-off packages, or other price incentives to a point where customers will refuse to buy the product without them. That can hurt long-term brand equity and profitability.

**PRODUCT CATEGORY MANAGERS** Some larger firms have such diverse product offerings that there is a need for extensive coordination. Eastman Kodak is best known for its cameras, film, and other photography supplies; however, it also markets X-ray film and equipment, health products like Bayer Aspirin, Phillips Milk of Magnesia, and Midol, household products such as Lysol and Minwax, and printers, optical disks, and photocopiers. In such cases, organizing for product management may include **product category managers**, who coordinate the mix of product lines within the more general product category and who consider the addition of new product lines. In recent years, both Procter & Gamble and Lever Brothers have consolidated brands under product category managers, who are responsible for profit and losses within the category.[22]

**product category manager** A manager who is responsible for developing and implementing the marketing plan for all of the brands and products within a product category.

**market manager** A manager who is responsible for developing and implementing the marketing plans for products sold to a specific customer group.

**MARKET MANAGERS** Some firms have developed a **market manager** structure, in which different managers focus on specific customer groups rather than on the products the company makes. This type of organization can be useful for firms that offer a variety of products serving the needs of a wide range of customers. For example, Raytheon (Exhibit 8.11), which specializes in consumer electronics products, special-mission aircraft, and business aviation, sells some products directly to consumer markets, others to manufacturers, and still others to government.[23]

# Organizing for New Product Development

In Chapter 7, we discussed the importance of new products to the long-term health of an organization. Because launching new products is so important, the management of launching them is, too. In some instances, one person handles new product development. However, in larger organizations, new product development almost always needs many people working under the new product manager.

**venture teams** Groups of people within an organization who work together focusing exclusively on the development of a new product.

The challenge in large companies is to get specialists in different areas to work together in **venture teams**, in which members focus exclusively on the new product development effort. The venture team may be located away from traditional company offices, perhaps in a separate building, called a *skunk works*. This odd term suggests that the group avoids opponents of change within the firm who might stop a project that challenges the status quo. Often having team members with different areas of knowledge, for example, design, engineering, and marketing, contributes to creativity and breakthrough ideas.

Whirlpool, the appliance company, can thank its venture team for winning $30 million in a nationwide save-energy refrigerator design contest sponsored by a group of electric utilities. The seven-person Whirlpool team developed a refrigerator that was 25 percent more energy efficient and did not use ozone-depleting chlorofluorocarbons.[24] Runner-up Frigidaire also used a team approach and discovered that the time they needed for new product development was cut in half.[25]

**Exhibit 8.11**

Firms such as Raytheon, that offer products to a wide variety of customers, need marketing managers to focus on different markets.

# Real People, Real Decisions

## How It Worked Out at Julie's Company

In the end, Option 3 was the winner and a new name was chosen: AIM Trimark Investments. As Julie says, "Decisions around branding are usually not made lightly or quickly. It took almost two years of research and consultation with both employees and clients to understand the meaning and value of both brands."

On the one hand, the Trimark brand had over 20 years of equity built into it. On the other hand, the AIM name represented something new, something "bigger" from a global perspective, and (although it was relatively new to Canada) it had managed to build a solid reputation among financial advisors. Both names resonated with clients and employees in different, but complementary, ways. Keeping both names seemed to be the best solution.

The result? AIM Trimark Investments has successfully positioned itself as a leader within the Canadian mutual funds industry. It currently has over 40 billion dollars in assets under management and has close to a 100 percent awareness level among clients (i.e., financial advisors). Regular surveys of both external and internal stakeholders (e.g., employees, financial advisors) reveal a strong corporate brand that invokes pride in its employees and an image as an industry leader among its clients.

Julie loves the challenge of working in a fast-paced, competitive (and often unpredictable) industry. "What I love most about my job—in addition to the people I work with—is that it allows me to be creative and strategic at the same time. It's also pretty neat to see an ad you worked on in a magazine you're reading or on TV during a commercial break," she says.

The most important thing Julie has learned is never underestimating the importance of communication. She believes communicating your knowledge and ideas is 49 percent content and 51 percent presentation. "The absolutely brilliant report that you spent six months preparing won't break through to key stakeholders if your presentation or communication skills are lacking. Worse case scenario is that your ideas will be dismissed because people simply did not 'get it'."

What advice does Julie have for students in preparing for a productive career?

The importance of keeping it BRIEF. Right from primary school, students are taught to write essays with the goal of achieving a minimum number of words. That is, we are taught to add a lot of filler to the things we write and the truth is, in the "real world" if you hand a 50-page report to an executive, you can pretty much bet on it being tossed into the recycling bin or into the back of a filing cabinet. The majority of executives expect an "executive summary" of any and all reports. If you can't summarize your main message or idea into one phrase, it could get missed (or worse, dismissed).

Keep an open mind. There is a ton of interesting opportunities out there you simply don't know about while you're in school. As you go through college/university, you often feel pressured to choose a particular career direction before graduating. If you allow yourself some room to explore you might be pleasantly surprised as to where you may end up.

Never underestimate the power of "people skills." Your ability (or inability) to interact in an appropriate way with the people you work with—and for—can make or break a successful career.

# CHAPTER SUMMARY

### 1. Explain the different product objectives and strategies a firm may choose.

Objectives for individual products may be related to introducing a new product, expanding the market of a regional product, or rejuvenating a mature product. For multiple products, firms may decide on a full- or a limited-line strategy. Companies often decide to extend their product line with an upward, downward, or two-way stretch, with a filling-out strategy, or they may decide to contract a product line. Firms that have multiple product lines may choose a wide product mix with many different lines or a narrow one with few.

### 2. Explain how firms manage products throughout the product life cycle.

The product life cycle explains how product categories go through four stages from birth to death. During the introduction stage, marketers seek to get buyers to try the product and may use high prices to recover research and development costs. During the growth stage, characterized by rapidly increasing sales, marketers may introduce new product variations. In the maturity stage, sales peak and level off. Marketers respond by adding desirable new product features or with market development strategies. During the decline stage, firms must decide whether to phase a product out slowly, to drop it immediately, or, if there is residual demand, to keep the product.

### 3. Discuss how branding creates product identity and describe different types of branding strategies.

A brand is a name, term, symbol, or other unique element of a product used to identify a firm's product. A brand should have a positive connotation and be recognizable and memorable. Brand names need to be easy to say, spell, read, and remember, and it should fit the target market, the product's benefits, the customer's culture, and legal requirements. To protect a brand legally, marketers obtain trademark protection. Brands are important, because they help maintain customer loyalty and because brand equity or value means a firm is able to attract new customers. Firms may develop individual brand strategies or market multiple items with a family or umbrella brand strategy. National or manufacturer brands are owned and sold by producers, whereas private-label or store brands carry the retail or chain store's trade name. Licensing means a firm sells another firm the right to use its brand name. In co-branding strategies, two brands form a partnership in marketing a new or existing product.

### 4. Describe how organizations are structured for new and existing product management.

To successfully manage existing products, the marketing organization may include brand managers, product category managers, and market managers. Large firms, however, often give new product responsibilities to new product managers or to venture teams, groups of specialists from different areas who work together for a single new product.

# CHAPTER REVIEW

## Marketing Concepts: Testing Your Knowledge

1. List and explain some popular objectives and strategies used for individual and multiple products.
2. Explain what is meant by a full-line strategy and a limited-line strategy. How might a firm stretch or expand its product line?
3. What is a product mix? What is meant by the width of a product mix?
4. How are products managed during the different phases of the product life cycle?
5. What is a brand? What are the characteristics of a good brand name? How do firms protect their brands?
6. List and explain some of the different branding strategies.

7. Describe some ways firms organize the marketing function to manage existing products. What are the ways firms organize for the development of new products?

## Marketing Concepts: Discussing Choices and Issues

1. Firms often take advantage of a popular, well-known brand by developing brand extensions, because they know that the brand equity of the original or parent brand will be transferred to the new product. However, the transfer can go the other way. If a new product is of poor quality, it can damage the reputation of the parent brand. A new product that is of superior quality can enhance the parent brand's reputation. What are some brand extensions that have either damaged or enhanced the parent brand equity?

## Marketing Practice: Applying What You've Learned

1. You may think of your college or university as an organization that offers a line of different educational products. Assume that you have been hired as a marketing consultant by your college or university to examine and make recommendations for extending its product line. Develop alternatives that the organization might consider:

   a. an upward line stretch

   b. a downward line stretch

   c. a two-way stretch

   d. filling-out strategy

   Describe how each might be accomplished. Evaluate each alternative.

2. Assume you are the vice-president of marketing for a firm that markets a large number of specialty food items, such as gourmet sauces, marinades, and relishes.

   a. Your firm is interested in improving its marketing management structure. You are considering several alternatives: a brand manager structure, having product line managers, or focusing on market managers. Outline the advantages and disadvantages of each type of organization. What is your recommendation?

   b. Your firm is also interested in aggressively pursuing the development of a number of new products. You have been asked to develop recommendations for organizing this new product development. Prepare a report that outlines your recommendations for organizing the new product development.

3. Assume you are working in the marketing department of a major manufacturer of athletic shoes. Your firm is introducing a new product, a line of disposable sports clothing. You wonder if it would be better to market the line of clothing with a new brand name or use the family brand name, which has already gained popularity with your existing products. Make a list of the advantages and disadvantages of each strategy. Develop your recommendation.

## Marketing Mini-Project: Learning by Doing

In any supermarket, you will find examples of all of the different types of brands discussed in this chapter: individual brands, family brands, national brands, store brands, and co-branded and licensed products. This mini-project is designed to give you a better understanding of branding as it exists in the marketplace.

1. Go to a supermarket in your community.

2. Select two product categories of interest to you, for example, ice cream, cereal, laundry detergent, soup, or paper products.

3. Make a list of the brands available in each product category. Identify what type of brand each is. Count the number of shelf facings (the number of product items at the front of each shelf) for each brand.

4. Arrange to talk with the store manager at a time that is convenient for him/her. Ask the manager to discuss:

   a. how the store decides which brands to carry.

   b. whether the store is more likely to carry a new brand that is an individual brand versus a family brand.

c. what causes a store to drop a brand.

d. the profitability of store or private-label brands versus national brands.

e. other aspects of branding that the store manager sees as important from a retail perspective.

5. Present a report to your class on what you learned about the brands in your two product categories.

## Real People, Real Surfers: Exploring the Web

As we discussed in this chapter companies protect their products by obtaining patents, copyrights, and legal protection for their brands with trademarks. The Canadian Intellectual Property Office oversees all of these forms of protection. Visit the Intellectual Property Office Web site at **http://strategis.ic.gc.ca/sc_mrksv/cipo/welcome/welcom-e.html**. Use the Internet site to answer the following questions.

1. What is a patent? What can be patented?
2. Who may apply for a patent? Can foreign individuals or companies obtain a Canadian patent? Explain.
3. What happens if someone infringes on a patent?
4. What is a copyright? Who owns a copyright?
5. What is copyright infringement? Give some examples.
6. What is a trademark?
7. Who may file a trademark application? Do firms have to register a trademark? Explain.
8. What are the benefits of trademark registration?
9. Can a person's name be registered as a trademark?
10. How long do trademarks, patents, and copyrights last?
11. How would you evaluate the Canadian Intellectual Property Office Web site? Was it easy to navigate? Was it useful? What recommendations do you have for improving the Web site?

Niall FitzGerald, the co-chairman of Unilever, the global consumer products giant, knows the importance of product mix. He constantly examines his product lines to ensure they are current. During the past five years he has bought such brands as Ben & Jerry's ice cream, SlimFast diet products, Bestfoods (maker of Hellmann's mayonnaise), and Knorr soups and sauces, while getting rid of Elizabeth Arden cosmetics.

In order to become more focused, lean, and competitive, Unilever has sold or eliminated 1200 brands, leaving it with 400. Under Mr. FitzGerald's watch, Unilever has transformed itself from a conglomerate that once owned shipping lines and ad agencies, to a consumer products company.

Niall believes that a company's portfolio can never reach a point of stability because the business environment is changing all the time. To keep his people motivated during times of change, he makes it very clear to them that change is no criticism of the past, but an absolute must for the future. To keep current, he spends time with retailers and young managers on his own, without their bosses present, asking about the company and how it can do better.

In spite of all the focused effort, Unilever has made mistakes. For example, as the Atkins diet craze took off in the United States, SlimFast marketers thought it was a fad. Even though SlimFast launched its own line of low-carbohydrate products, its sales fell 22 percent in 2003. To protect against such incidents and to keep brand managers current, at Unilever each manager has to earn their "marketer's license" and demonstrate that they have spent 200 hours talking with consumers, before they can talk about any marketing issue. Further, Niall insists that the language used inside the company is relevant to the consumer. Take "edible fats." "There's no consumer who wakes up in the morning and says, 'I think I have run out of edible fats.' It's margarine or it's spreads," says Niall.

Niall feels that to be a successful marketer you have to be prepared to fail and live with failure. His golden advice is to use the 40–70 rule: If you try to make a decision with 40 percent of what you need (information), you are in trouble. However, if you wait until you've got 70 percent, it's too late. "So be brave enough to take your decisions in the 40 percent to 70 percent zone," he says.

He himself is a living, breathing example of someone who has taken risks and failed spectacularly. In 1994, in an effort to win the laundry battle against Procter & Gamble, Unilever came up with a breakthrough called the Persil accelerator, which cleaned clothes. The problem was that if used improperly by the consumer, the product not only washed away dirt, but the clothes themselves. A competitor placed ads in newspapers with pictures of knickers with holes in them that had been washed with Persil.

Scientifically, the product was superior, but it had not been marketed right. Now, after a turnaround, the Persil business is healthier than it was before. Niall wasn't fired for his mistake, he was made chairman. This incident showcased to junior managers that it is OK to fail, as long as the failure is about taking risks based on creating more value for the consumer.

Five lessons from Niall about managing during change:

1. There are no tired brands, only tired brand managers.
2. Make sure the language used inside the company is relevant to the consumer.
3. When leading managers by example on the front lines, don't forget to step back and survey the big picture.
4. Be prepared to fail, and to live with failure.
5. When moving in a new direction, don't keep people who no longer fit the bill.

Source: Adapted from Deborah Ball, "Stocking a global pantry," *The Wall Street Journal*, 24 May, 2004, p. B1.

## Things to Think About

1. Why do you think Niall FitzGerald cast out Elizabeth Arden cosmetics from his brand stable? Provide your rationale based on concepts you have learned both in this chapter, as well as throughout the book.

2. If you were a brand manager at Unilever, you would not want to make the same mistake SlimFast did with underestimating the Atkins diet craze. Develop a model that will help you distinguish between a fad and a trend.

3. Compare two Unilever brands in two different product categories with a major competitor's brands. How are the brands positioned? What recommendations do you have on making the Unilever brands even stronger?

## Earthbuddies—Part 2

Since we last saw Anton and his partners (in the case at the end of the previous chapter), they have grown to a $103 million private toy company called Spinmaster. They have a hot new product line called Air Hogs—toys that move when pumped with air. Customers are desperate for their products.

The partners seem to know how to position their brand in the marketplace. For example, buyers from Wal-Mart want to place the Air Hogs car in the vehicle section, but Spinmaster feels it would get lost with the other products on the shelf. So, they suggest it should be placed in the hobby section. In fact, they want an entire Air Hogs section because they have developed a whole line of air pressure toys: cars, airplanes, and a top-secret item (a water rocket).

Spinmaster makes deals with large retailers as well as small specialty toy shops. In each case, they assign a "key account manager" to look after the customer's business. Toys 'R' Us, a large retailer, wants to build a relationship with Spinmaster. The catch is that they want first dibs on anything Spinmaster manufactures. Ultimately, the relationship with Toys 'R' Us appears to be successful, with the retailer showcasing the Air Hogs product mix in a separate catalogue.

The hits juts keep coming for Spinmaster: successful products include DMX Finger Bikes, The Wiggles, Catch a Bubble, and Astro Jacks. In addition, McDonald's has signed a deal with Spinmaster to make novelty food machines, such as the McFlurry maker.

## Questions

1. Earthbuddy to Spinmaster toys. What factors do you think enabled Anton and his partners to build a successful brand? Why have they succeeded in a crowded marketplace?
2. What is the identity of the Spinmaster brand? How would you compare its identity with Mattel or Fisher Price (famous toy brands)?
3. Do you think it is smart for Spinmaster to build relationships with all types of retailers, from large ones such as Toys 'R' Us and Wal-Mart, to small specialty retailers, to food retailers such as McDonald's? Do you see any problems for the brand with such a strategy?

Source: This case was prepared by Ajay Sirsi and is based on "Earthbuddies—The Sequel," *Venture* #819.

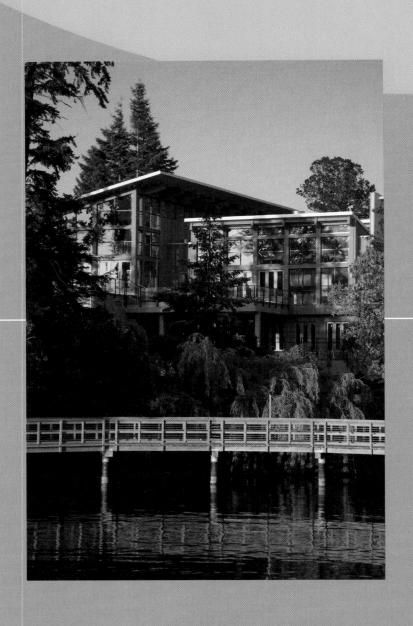

# CHAPTER 9
## Pricing Strategy

## CHAPTER OBJECTIVES

WHEN YOU HAVE COMPLETED YOUR STUDY OF THIS CHAPTER, YOU SHOULD BE ABLE TO

1. Explain the importance of pricing and how prices can take both monetary and non-monetary forms.

2. Understand the pricing objectives that marketers typically have in planning pricing strategies.

3. Understand the pricing strategies used to achieve different pricing objectives.

4. Apply pricing tactics to set price points.

5. Understand key implementation and legal issues with respect to pricing.

6. Understand some of the environmental factors that affect pricing strategies, including the Internet.

# Real People, Real Decisions

## Meet **Leanne Cadden,** a Decision Maker at Brentwood Bay Lodge and Spa

Leanne Cadden is an artist and an entrepreneur. As developer and manager of the art gallery at the Brentwood Bay Lodge and Spa, Cadden is responsible for all of the decisions involved in creating a high-end art gallery. The Brentwood Bay Lodge and Spa is a five-star luxury resort near Victoria, B.C. and is one of only three hotels in Canada to be awarded membership in the prestigious Small Luxury Hotels of the World.

During her BCom degree in Entrepreneurship at the University of Victoria, Cadden started her own art gallery and studio (**www.leannarto.com**) and was named "First Finalist" for "Victoria Young Entrepreneur of the Year" in 2003. The president of the Brentwood Bay Lodge was looking for an entrepreneurial apprentice to help with the start-up of the new resort and he wanted to create a fine art gallery as one of the resort's profit centres. Cadden, able to fill both roles, took the job because she saw an opportunity to learn from the entrepreneurs who were starting the resort, she would be given free reign to design an art gallery, and she would be responsible for the interior design of the $12 million project.

When Cadden started to build the fine art gallery, she needed to develop a revenue stream based on commission taken from the sales of artwork. The commission structure needed to attract high calibre and well-known artists to support a high-end positioning, but also needed to satisfy the owner's profit objectives. The challenge was to "sell" the image of the resort and its clientele to the artists and then to sell the top quality art of well-known artists to the hotel patrons and major art collectors.

Galleries take different commission percentages based on the level of service and money spent to promote the individual artists. Some establishments hang artwork on the walls and put up price tags and do not spend any money on promotions, advertising, or staffing. These galleries will take a commission of roughly 30 percent. The fine art gallery at Brentwood Bay Lodge and Spa (BBL) would commit a full-time staff member to sell the artwork, cover all overhead expenses, pay for all advertising and promotional materials including featuring each artist in six different publications, host a solo show for the artist (providing the room, food and beverages), host the most technologically advanced online gallery with secure online purchasing, and, most importantly, provide access to an elite clientele (resort guests) who wouldn't normally go to a traditional gallery. To cover these expenses, Cadden thought she would need to take a commission of 50 percent.

Not only did Cadden need to find an appropriate commission structure, but she also needed to factor in that the President of the resort had committed to donating 10 percent of all art gallery sales to a local charity as part of the resort's environmental commitment. Cadden had to decide whether that commitment would come from the gallery or the artists. She also had to decide whether all artists would be treated equally, with the same commission structure, or if the better artists, who sold their art at premium prices, would be offered a higher commission to entice them.

Cadden considered three options.

**Option 1.** A mixed commission structure where some artists would get 60 percent commission, others 50 percent, and BBL would pay the 10 percent to charity. The advantage of this commission structure was that the gallery could entice big names because of the commission flexibility. Many well-established artists have galleries falling at their feet to sell their work and can be picky about where they show. There is potential to sell over $100 000 of art per well-known artist. Many well-established artists command the rate they want and if they don't get it, they walk away. The disadvantage to this option was that some artists might feel of lesser importance than others, potentially creating hard feelings and hurt egos. A "no bargaining" policy with the commission structure would also save time and forgo the hassle of bartering for deals.

**Option 2.** All artists on the same commission structure at 50 percent (artist), 50 percent (BBL), and 10 percent (charity donation in BBL's name). The advantage of the 50/50 structure was that Brentwood Bay Lodge would receive the tax receipt for the charitable donation and would still have 40 percent of the sale to go towards operating and marketing costs of the art gallery department. This structure would also create a level playing field among the artists. The disadvantage of this option was that it might prove more difficult to score the big name artists who are used to commanding their own price. The industry standard for most galleries is a 60/40 split where the artist gets 60 percent of the selling price. The extra 10 percent would be the charitable donation.

**Option 3.** All artists on the same commission structure at 50 percent (artist), 40 percent (BBL), and 10 percent (charity donation given in artists' names). This alternative would be advantageous because the artists would get the tax benefit and would be pleased to have the donation in their names. The disadvantage was that the tax credit for such a donation is only about 17 percent, so less money would go to the artist than in option 1. Also, Brentwood Bay Lodge cares about its social reputation and would not get the positive press that would come with making the charitable donation. There would not be sufficient margin in BBL's 40 percent commission to make an additional charitable donation.

Now, join the Brentwood Bay Lodge and Spa team. Which option would you choose, and why?

# "YES, BUT WHAT DOES IT COST?"

That's certainly a top-of-mind issue for Leanne Cadden and the management team at the Brentwood Bay Lodge. In creating the luxury resort, they need to be concerned with both the cost of building and running the resort and the cost to the consumer. As manager of the art gallery, Cadden needs to set prices that make art products attractive to customers while also profitable for her organization.

What to charge for a product, whether it is a good, service, or idea, is a key strategic decision. In this chapter, we'll examine the set of decisions associated with the price element of the marketing mix, how those decisions are made, and the role of demand, costs, revenues, and the environment in the pricing decision process. We will start by discussing what price is, why pricing decisions are important, and the context in which pricing decisions are made. Then, after reviewing some "marketing math", we will examine pricing objectives, pricing strategies/strategies, price points and tactics, and implementation terms and conditions—which collectively are the key pricing decisions. These key decisions are illustrated in Figure 9.1. The chapter concludes with a discussion of environmental influences on pricing decisions.

**Figure 9.1** Key Pricing Strategy Decisions

## Monetary and Non-monetary Prices

"If you have to ask how much it is, you can't afford it!" We have all heard that, but how often do you buy something without asking the price? If we weren't concerned about price, we'd all drive dream cars, take trips to exotic places, and live like royalty. Most of us, however, need to consider a product's price before buying. **Price** is the value that customers give up, or exchange, to obtain a desired product. Payment may be in the form of money, goods, services, favours, votes, or anything else that has *value* to the other party.

As Chapter 1 explained, marketing is the process that creates exchanges of things of value. We usually think of this exchange as people trading money for a good or a service. Often, the monetary value of a product is called something other than price, sometimes to hide the idea that you are being charged a price or perhaps to assume an air of greater respectability. For example, colleges and universities charge *tuition* for an education, a lawyer or accountant charges a *professional fee*, and students who join a chapter of the American Marketing Association pay *dues*. No matter what it is called, it's still a price.

But in some marketplace practices, price can mean exchanges of non-monetary value. Long before societies minted coins, people exchanged one good or service for another. This practice of **bartering** was the basis for the economic development of Canada, with the Hudson's Bay Company trading goods to Northwest trappers for furs. Bartering still occurs today, and with advances in Internet technology, is increasing at more than 20 percent per year.[1] Canadian organizations such as Nation Wide Barter and Barter Plus Systems Inc. have established large barter networks, where organizations can exchange goods and services for barter credits. Someone who owns a home at a mountain ski resort, for example, may exchange a weekend for barter credits to spend in a restaurant or for car repairs. No money changes hands, but as the Canada Customs and Revenue Agency understands well, there is an exchange of value: Taxpayers are supposed to report as income the value of goods or services received in exchange for other goods or services.

Organizations that follow an operational excellence strategy (Chapter 3), or another cost-based differentiation strategy, focus on making the cost to the customer as low as possible. These also include non-monetary costs. When evaluating purchase alternatives, consumers take into account other economic costs such as **operating costs**, **switching costs**, and **opportunity costs**. Operating costs are those involved in using the product, such as toner in a printer. Switching costs are involved in moving from one brand to

**Brentwoood Bay Lodge**
www.brentwoodbaylodge
.com

**price** The value that customers give up, or exchange, to obtain a desired product.

**Nation Wide Barter**
www.nationwidebarter.com
**Barter Plus Systems Inc.**
www.barterplus.com

**bartering** The practice of exchanging a good or service for another good or service of like value.

**operating costs** Costs involved in using a product.

**switching costs** Costs involved in moving from one brand to another.

**opportunity cost** The value of something that is given up to obtain something else.

**Exhibit 9.1**

Health Canada tries to increase the perceived psychological cost of smoking.

another, such as getting new cheques printed if you switch banks. Opportunity costs are the benefits and value you give up, or miss out on, by engaging in one activity or buying one product and not another, such as the income you forgo while in school.

Sometimes the lowest priced product isn't the lowest cost product over time. The personal investment consumers make in buying and using products is also a cost. Convenience-store operators, such as Mac's or 7-Eleven, and Internet companies, such as Indigo.com, among other marketers, focus on minimizing the time, energy, and effort consumers have to expend to satisfy their needs and wants. As discussed in Chapter 5, consumers also experience psychological costs—such as stress, hassle, cognitive difficulty, and cognitive dissonance—when trying to buy and use products. (Have you ever tried to assemble a bike or gas barbecue?) Many marketers, auto-malls and courier companies, for example, focus on making it as easy as possible to buy and use their products. Psychological costs are particularly challenging when marketing ideas, such as not smoking. Health Canada uses shocking or disturbing images such as the one in Exhibit 9.1 to increase the perceived psychological cost of smoking. As one author put it, it's a lot more difficult to sell "brotherhood than soap."[2]

## The Importance of Pricing Decisions

How important are good pricing decisions? Pricing is probably the least understood and least appreciated element of the marketing mix. Marketers like to talk about advertising and other communication elements. It's fun to think about changing technology and how firms invest in new-product development. Even decisions about channels of distribution seem to be more exciting than setting the right price. Yet price has a major strategic impact on the firm—it determines the net value received by the customer in an exchange (benefits minus costs) versus the net value (profit) received by the firm.

The plight of U.S. airlines is a good example of how bad pricing decisions can hurt an entire industry. During the decade before 1992, companies in the airline industry engaged in a fierce price war. The per-mile fare was lowered nearly 25 percent (accounting for inflation of the dollar), while costs such as labour and fuel more than doubled.[3] As a result, from 1990 to 1992, the airlines lost over $10 billion, more than had been earned since the start of commercial air travel. Sometimes it's not advantageous for a firm to cut its prices.

Good pricing decisions are critical to a firm's success in the marketplace. For most organizations, the only source of profit is through the price charged for products. If customers are not willing to pay the price asked for a firm's product, the firm will not make a profit and will have failed its shareholders.

Even during the best economic times, most consumers rank "reasonable price" as the most important consideration in a purchase. In addition, reasonable prices count most when consumers decide where to shop.[4] Price is even more important during recessions, when consumers have less to spend and count their pennies carefully. Marketers try to come as close to reasonable as possible when deciding on a price.

Individual consumers aren't the only buyers who focus on price. As we saw in Chapter 6, purchasing agents for firms often put a high priority on getting the best price. At least one study has found that price may be second only to quality in these decisions. Buying professionals know that when all else is equal, getting a low price keeps costs down and helps make their firm's product competitive.[5]

# A Marketer's View of Costs

Before we can meaningfully discuss pricing objectives, strategies, price points, and terms and conditions, we need to understand the profit model and how marketers view costs. If you have taken an accounting course, you are likely familiar with the calculation for net income shown in Figure 9.2 and explained in more detail in the Appendix to this chapter. Marketers look at the financial world a bit differently in order to make marketing decisions (Figure 9.2). Marketers split the cost of goods sold (i.e., the total cost to make and sell the products that have been sold by an organization in a particular time period) into two components: fixed costs and variable costs.

**Fixed costs** are the costs incurred to make and sell the first unit of a product. They do *not* vary with the number of units produced and they have to be paid upfront, even if the organization does not sell any of the units produced. Fixed costs include rent, plant and equipment, utilities and overhead, advertising and other marketing communication expenses, the salaries of a firm's executives, managers, and employees, and any other costs that have to be paid upfront and do not change with the level of production.

**Variable costs** are the costs that change depending on the number of units produced. That is, they are the costs involved in making and selling one more unit of a product (other than the first). Variable costs for a manufacturer of bookcases like Palliser Furniture (Exhibit 9.2), for example, would include construction materials such as wood, nails, and glue; finishing materials like paint or varnish; packaging (boxes, shrinkwrap, etc); piecework labour (wages paid by the number of pieces finished or hourly wages allocated to the number of units produced); shipping; and sales commission (wages paid to sales staff based on the number of units sold).

In reality, calculating variable costs is often quite complex. For example, as the number of bookcases a factory produces increases or decreases, the variable costs may change. For example, if the company buys just enough lumber for one bookcase, the lumberyard will charge top dollar. If it buys enough for 100 bookcases, it will get a better deal. And if it buys enough for thousands of bookcases, it may cut variable costs even more. Even the cost of labour goes down with increased production, as manufacturers are likely to invest in labour-saving equipment that allows workers to produce bookcases faster. At some point diseconomies of scale will be reached, and using the bookcase example, the demand for the labour, lumber, or nails required to produce the bookcases may exceed the supply causing the average cost per bookcase to rise. Because variable costs are related to the number of units produced, marketers often use the average variable cost across a production range, or they use sensitivity analysis to calculate financial impacts of different production level scenarios.

Marketers split these costs up in order to make pricing decisions. At a minimum, the price charged must cover the variable costs—otherwise the company loses money on each transaction. The difference between the price charged by a manufacturer and their variable costs is their **contribution margin** (CM). It is called a contribution margin because these funds, in excess of the variable costs, contribute to paying off the fixed costs incurred upfront. The contribution margin for each unit sold times the number of units sold is the **total contribution** received by the organization. The total contribution less fixed costs is net profit before tax. Marketers know that they have to cover all of their fixed costs to stay in business. As we will see below, marketers sometimes use the concept of **total unit cost** (variable costs plus average fixed costs per unit) to ensure that prices cover all of the costs incurred.

**fixed costs** Costs of production that do not change with the number of units produced.

**variable costs** The costs of production (raw and processed materials, parts, and labour) that are tied to, and vary depending on, the number of units produced.

**contribution margin** The price an organization receives less its variable costs.

**total contribution** Contribution margin multiplied by the number of units sold.

**total unit cost** Variable costs plus average fixed costs per unit.

| Accounting View | Marketing View |
|---|---|
| Sales Revenue – Costs of Goods = Gross Margin | Sales Revenue – Variable Costs = Contribution Margin per Unit |
| Gross Margin – Operating Expenses = Net Income Before Taxes (Operating Income) | Contribution Margin × Units Sold = Total Contribution Margin |
| | Total Contribution Margin – Fixed Costs = Net Income Before Taxes (Operating Income) |

**Figure 9.2** Marketing Versus Accounting Views of Costs

**Exhibit 9.2**

Marketers like Palliser Furniture identify fixed costs and variable costs when making pricing decisions.

**break-even analysis** A method for determining the number of units that a firm must produce and sell at a given price to cover all its costs.

**Break-even analysis** is a technique marketers use to examine the relationship between cost and price and to determine what sales volume must be reached at a given price before the company breaks even. The break-even point is the point at which the company doesn't lose any money and doesn't make any profit; all costs are covered, but there isn't a penny extra. A break-even analysis allows marketers to identify how many units of a product they will have to sell at a given price to begin to be profitable.

Figure 9.3 demonstrates break-even analysis for a bookcase manufacturer like Palliser. The vertical axis represents the amount of costs and revenue in dollars, and the horizontal axis shows the quantity of goods produced and sold. In this break-even model, we assume that there is a given total fixed cost and that variable costs do not change with the quantity produced.

In this example, the total fixed costs (for the factory, the equipment, electricity) are $200 000, and the average variable costs (for materials and labour) are constant. The figure shows the total costs (variable costs plus fixed costs) and total revenues if varying quantities are produced and sold. The point at which the total revenue and total costs lines intersect is the *break-even point*. If sales are above the break-even point, the company makes a profit. Below that point, the firm suffers a loss.

To determine the break-even point, the firm first needs to calculate the *contribution per unit*, or the difference between the price the firm charges for a product (the revenue per unit) and the variable costs. This *contribution margin* is the amount the firm has after paying for the wood, nails, paint, and labour to contribute to meeting the fixed costs of production. For our example, assuming that the firm sells its bookcases for $100 each and that variable costs are $50 per unit, contribution per unit is $100 − $50 = $50. Using the fixed cost for the bookcase manufacturing of $200 000, we can now calculate the firm's break-even point in units of the product.

$$\text{Break-even point (in units)} = \frac{\text{total fixed cost}}{\text{contribution per unit to fixed costs}}$$

$$\text{Break-even point (in units)} = \frac{\$200\,000}{\$50} = 4000 \text{ units}$$

Thus, the firm must sell 4000 bookcases at $100 each to meet its fixed costs and to break even. In a similar way, we can calculate the break-even point in dollars. This shows us that to break even, the company must sell $400 000 worth of bookcases.

$$\text{Break-even point (in dollars)} = \frac{\text{total fixed cost}}{1 - \dfrac{\text{variable cost per unit}}{\text{price}}}$$

$$\text{Break-even point (in dollars)} = \frac{\$200\,000}{1 - \dfrac{\$50}{\$100}} = \frac{\$20\,000}{1 - 0.5} = \frac{\$20\,0000}{0.5} = \$400\,000$$

Now that we understand the profit model and how marketers view costs, we can discuss how marketers determine or set pricing objectives, strategies, price points, and terms and conditions.

# DEVELOPING PRICING OBJECTIVES

Pricing objectives must support the broader objectives of the firm, such as maximizing shareholder value, as well as its overall marketing objectives, such as increasing market share. Consider, for example, the different pricing decisions of the three major rivals in the breakfast cereal market.

From 1983 to 1988, major cereal producers increased net prices more than 6 percent per year for a total of 30 percent over the five-year period. Then came the low-priced supermarket brands, which, by 1994, had captured nine percent of the market. In response, the top two makers of ready-to-eat cereals announced very different pricing strategies. General Mills *cut* prices on three of its major brands in the large sizes in an effort to increase its market share. Kellogg's response, however, was a 2.6 percent price *increase* on its cereals; it planned to soften the impact with discount coupons, the idea being to hold customers and to increase profits with frequent price-oriented promotions.[6] Three years later, in 1996, Post announced it was "changing the way the entire cereal category works" with an across-the-board price rollback, and, at the same time, initiating a new advertising campaign.[7] Each of these pricing strategies had an objective: General Mills sought to increase market share, Kellogg tried to increase profits, and Post hoped to increase consumers' total consumption of cereal. Table 9.1 provides examples of different types of pricing objectives.

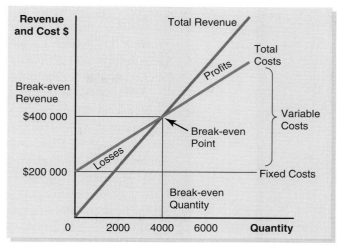

**Figure 9.3** Break-Even Analysis

## Profit Objectives

There are three main **profit objectives**: maximizing profits, achieving a target level of profit growth, or achieving a desired net profit margin (or a target return on investment). A profit objective is important to firms that believe that profit motivates shareholders and bankers to invest in a company. Coca-Cola recently announced a change in North American pricing strategy—to a premium pricing strategy designed to increases profits instead of a market share strategy that had achieved 8 percent annual sales growth but declining profits.[8]

**profit objective** Pricing products with a focus on a target level of profit growth or a desired net profit margin.

**Table 9.1** Pricing Objectives

| Type of Objective | Example |
| --- | --- |
| Sales or Market Share | Institute pricing strategy changes to support a 5 percent increase in sales. |
| Profit | During the first six months, set a price to yield a target profit of $200 000. <br> Or <br> Set prices to allow for an 8 percent profit margin on all goods sold. |
| Competitive Effect | Alter pricing strategy during first quarter of the year to increase sales during introduction of new product. <br> Or <br> Maintain low-end pricing policies to discourage new competitors from entering the market. |
| Customer Satisfaction | Simplify pricing structure to simplify decision process for customers. <br> Or <br> Alter price levels to match customer expectations. |
| Image Enhancement | Alter pricing policies to reflect the increased emphasis on the product's quality image. |

Although profits are an important consideration in pricing all goods and services, they are critical when the product is assumed to be a fad. Fad products can expect a rather short market life, making a profit objective essential to allow the firm to recover its investment in a short period of time. In such cases, the firm must harvest profits before customers lose interest and move on to the next electronic pet, troll doll, or cartoon idol.

Marketers who seek to achieve a target level of profit or target return on investment use the concept of break-even analysis in setting specific price objectives. Often a firm will set a *profit goal*, which is the dollar profit figure it desires to earn. The "break-even" point may be calculated with that dollar goal added to the fixed costs. This is not really a break-even point because it includes profits; but by adding the desired profit to fixed costs in the break-even equation, marketers can determine how many units would need to be sold at a particular contribution margin (price − variable costs) to achieve that level of profit. For example, if the bookcase manufacturer previously discussed feels it is necessary to realize a profit of $50 000, her calculations would be as follows:

$$\text{Break-even point (in units with target amount included)} = \frac{\text{total fixed cost} + \text{target profit}}{\text{contribution per unit to fixed costs}}$$

$$\text{Break-even point (in units)} = \frac{\$200\ 000 + \$50\ 000}{\$50} = 5000 \text{ units}$$

Sometimes the target return or profit goal is expressed as a *percentage of sales*. For example, a firm may say that it wants to make a profit of at least 10 percent on sales. In such cases, this profit is added to the variable cost in calculating the break-even point. In our example, the company wants to earn 10 percent of the selling price of the bookcase, or $10\% \times \$100 = \$10$ per unit. We add this $10 to the variable costs of $50 and calculate the new target amount as we calculated the break-even point before. The contribution per unit becomes:

$$\text{Contribution per unit} = \text{selling price} - (\text{variable costs} + \text{target profit})$$

$$= \$100 - (\$50 + \$10) = \$40$$

$$\text{Break-even point (in units)} = \frac{\text{total fixed cost}}{\text{contribution per unit to fixed costs}}$$

$$\text{Break-even point (in units)} = \frac{\$200\ 000}{\$40} = 5000 \text{ units}$$

**marginal analysis** A method that uses costs and demand to identify the price that will maximize profits.

Marketers who want to maximize profits sometimes use a technique called **marginal analysis** where demand is forecasted at different price levels and the profit expected in each price-demand scenario is calculated. Although the procedure is straightforward, it is often difficult to develop sufficiently accurate forecasts and variable costs can fluctuate with shortages, inclement weather, and other uncontrollable events.

## Sales or Market Share Objectives

**sales or market share objective** Pricing products to maximize sales or to attain a desired level of sales or market share.

A **sales or market share objective** involves setting prices at a level that will maximize sales, in either dollars or units, or will attain a desired level of sales or market share. Does setting a price to increase unit sales or market share (*sales objectives*) simply mean pricing the product lower than the competition? Sometimes this is the case. The telephone industry provides a good example: Suppliers such as Telus, Sprint, and AT&T constantly make rate adjustments to keep them ahead in the "telephone wars." Lowering prices is not always necessary to increase market share. If a company's product has an important competitive advantage over competitors' offerings, keeping the price at the same level as other firms do may satisfy sales objectives.

## Competitive Effect Objectives

**competitive effect objective** Pricing that is intended to have an effect on the marketing efforts of the competition.

A pricing plan with a **competitive effect objective** is intended to have a certain effect on the marketing efforts of the competition. Sometimes, a firm deliberately seeks to pre-empt or reduce the effectiveness of one or more competitors. Recently, Toys 'R' Us sought to cut into the Christmas toy sales of Wal-Mart. It launched an early-November program offering nearly $500 worth of price-off coupons. The move gave Wal-Mart too little time to react. This "Christmas surprise" enabled Toys 'R' Us to generate a significant portion of its holiday-time sales from one single price-off coupon program.[9] Price stability is another competitive effect objective. Retail gasoline companies like Shell, Esso, and Petro-Canada want to avoid price wars and closely match competitor pricing.

## Customer Satisfaction Objectives

Many customer-oriented firms believe that profits result from making customer satisfaction the primary objective. Firms that have **customer satisfaction (and retention) objectives** set prices to maximize the value to the customer, believing that by focusing solely on short-term profits, a company loses sight of keeping customers for the long term.

Events in the auto industry illustrate this difference between short-term and long-term pricing philosophies. Many people hate to buy a new car because they feel the dealers are untrustworthy hucksters and there is no way they can win in the auto marketplace. Not so with Saturn, where the objective is to satisfy customers. With Saturn's value pricing strategy, customers get one price and one price only—no haggling, no negotiation, and no "deals." As Exhibit 9.3 shows, customers can even go to Saturn's Web site to get detailed price information without needing a salesperson. This objective has worked for the company and is generating a new breed of car salesperson who uses low-pressure sales tactics and promises customer satisfaction and service after the sale.

The negative side of value pricing for car dealers is that it reduces margins, making each sale less profitable. Dealers must be convinced that customer-satisfying pricing will, in the long term, sell more cars and increase profits.

## Image Enhancement (Positioning) Objectives

Organizations that make pricing decisions based on **image enhancement (or positioning) objectives** recognize that consumers often use price to make inferences about the quality of a product. In fact, marketers know that price is often an important means of communicating not only quality but also image to prospective customers.

The image enhancement function of pricing is particularly important for prestige or luxury products like diamonds. While the high price tag on a Rolex watch or a Rolls-Royce car reflects the higher production costs, it is also vital to shaping an image of an extraordinary product with ownership limited to only wealthy consumers. The Burton Snowboard Company, like many other boarding companies, sets high prices on their products to communicate an elite image and uniqueness in the boarding subculture (Exhibit 9.4).

Another example of image pricing comes from Calgary-based Nevada Bob's Golf Inc., the world's largest chain of golf specialty retail stores. Backed by cross-Canada market research, it has begun moving its image upmarket—starting by taking "discount" out of the store brand name (it was "Nevada Bob's Discount Golf"). It now offers a broader and more upscale range of golf products, a more comfortable customer-friendly storefront, and improved customer service, while still offering a best-price guarantee.[10]

A low price is just as important in communicating a different image. Zellers' uses price to position the company as a value leader with its slogan, "The lowest price is the law." In other cases, such as for Timex watches, the desire is to communicate the image of a good-quality product that is reasonably priced.

**customer satisfaction objective** Pricing that is intended to maximize customer satisfaction and retention.

**Saturn**
www.saturn.com

**image enhancement objective** Pricing intended to establish a desired image or positioning to prospective customers.

**Nevada Bob's Pro Golf Shop**
www.nevadabobs.com

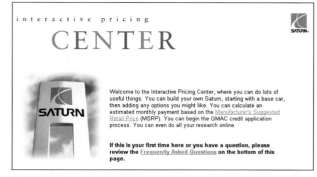

**Exhibit 9.3**

Saturn uses a pricing strategy designed to please customers: no "dealing," no hassle, no razzle-dazzle.

**Exhibit 9.4**

Pricing of Burton snowboards and clothing are consistent with a positioning objective.

## Flexibility of Price Objectives

It is important that pricing objectives be *flexible*. Often, it is necessary to develop pricing objectives (and strategies) tailored to different geographic areas and time periods. There may be varying levels of competition in different parts of the country, making it necessary to lower prices in the areas with the heaviest competition. Some geographic regions may have greater sales potential, making it wise for firms to develop pricing objectives aimed at obtaining a larger market share in those areas. Mortgage lenders may do this by offering lower rates in areas where new housing starts are booming.

Market conditions can change during the year, requiring price adjustments for seasonal and other reasons. Accommodation rental rates in Whistler, BC are much higher during the winter than during the summer; rates in Summerside, PEI, or Grand Bend, ON, are higher during the summer vacation months.

Pricing objectives are only one part of price planning. Before any prices can be set, marketers must understand the alternative pricing strategies available to achieve those objectives.

## PRICING STRATEGIES

An old Russian proverb says: "There are two kinds of fools in any market. One doesn't charge enough. The other charges too much."[11] This underscores the strategic decision behind pricing—how much value to offer the customer versus how much value to retain in terms of profit for the firm. Today's marketers may ponder the message. In modern business, there seldom is a one-and-only, now-and-forever, best pricing strategy; pricing today has more of the continuous decision-making character of a chess game. The organization must think two or three moves ahead. And no pricing decision is set in stone. Costs increase. Sales decline. The competition changes its prices. Price reductions can discourage new competitors or at least sabotage competitors' product introductions.

In the 1990s, for example, The Bay decided to shift toward a higher-price designer fashion image, abandoning its hard goods such as electronics and sporting goods. This strategy put them in direct competition with Eaton's, leaving Sears alone in the mid-price market. The Bay's pricing resulted in sagging sales and plummeting profits. A price war with Eaton's during the 1998 Christmas season caused both companies to lose millions of dollars. Eaton's eventually declared bankruptcy. The Bay, under the direction of president, Marc Chouinard, decided to return to a pricing strategy that focused on more moderate price points.[12] The Bay realized that having a successful pricing strategy is often a continuous process of evaluation and re-evaluation.

Marketers whose responsibility it is to develop pricing strategies will consider a number of alternative strategies and try to anticipate the outcomes. Below we discuss some of the more common pricing strategies associated with each price objective—these are summarized in Figure 9.4. You will notice in some cases that the same strategy can be used to achieve different objectives. In the discussion that follows we present each strategy only once, in the order they appear in Figure 9.4.

## Pricing Strategies to Achieve Profit Objectives

There are many pricing strategies consistent with profit-oriented price objectives. The three main sets of strategies are based on cost, demand, and experience.

**COST-BASED PRICING STRATEGIES** Cost-based strategies are typically associated with a target profit or return objectives. By understanding a product's cost structure, marketers can set prices to achieve a desired profit. Marketers use *cost-based strategies* because they are simple to calculate and are relatively safe, in that they ensure that the price will cover the costs the company incurs in producing and marketing the product.

Cost-based pricing methods, however, have drawbacks. They do not consider such factors as the nature of the target market, demand, competition, the product life cycle, and the product's image. In addition, although the calculations for setting the price may be simple and straightforward, it may be difficult to estimate costs accurately. Think about such firms as Nortel, Bombardier, and McCain, which produce many products. How do they allocate the costs for the plant, equipment, design engineers, maintenance, and marketing personnel, so that the pricing plan accurately reflects the cost of production for any particular product? For example, how do you allocate the salary of a marketing executive who deals with many different products? Should the cost be divided equally among all products? Should costs be based on the actual number of hours spent working on each product? Or should costs be assigned based on the revenues generated by each product? There is no one right answer. However, even with these limitations, cost-based pricing strategies are often a marketer's best choice.

**Cost-Plus Pricing** The most common cost-based approach to pricing a product is **cost-plus pricing**, in which a marketer totals the unit costs for the product and then adds an amount to cover desired profit.

The first step requires that the unit cost be estimated reasonably well and that the level of output does not change much. For this and the other examples, we will consider how a small manufacturer and a retailer price a line of jeans. As Table 9.2 shows, we will assume that the jeans manufacturer has a fixed cost of $2 000 000, to make 400 000 pairs of jeans, or $5 per pair. Variable costs for the jeans are $20 per pair, making the total cost $25 per pair.

The second step is to calculate the markup. There are two methods for calculating the markup percentage: markup on cost and the more popular markup on selling price. In *markup on cost pricing*, just as the name implies, a percentage of the cost is added to the cost to determine the selling price.

*Markup on cost:* For markup on cost, the calculation is:

$$\text{Price} = \text{total cost} + (\text{total cost} \times \text{markup percentage})$$

In our jeans example, if the manufacturer wants a profit of $2 000 000, what markup percentage would it use? The $2 000 000 is 20 percent of the $10 million total cost. To find the price, the calculation would be:

$$\text{Price} = \$25 + (\$25 \times 0.20) = \$25 + \$5 = \$30$$

(Note that in the calculations, the markup percentage is expressed as a decimal; that is, 20% = 0.20.)

*Markup on selling price:* As we noted, sometimes firms use a different calculation method—markup on selling price. Wholesalers and retailers more frequently use markup on selling price in pricing their products because the markup percentage becomes the seller's gross margin. For example, if a retailer knows it needs a 40 percent margin to cover overhead and profits, the retailer will calculate its price as a 40 percent markup on selling price.

Let's say a retailer buys the jeans from the manufacturer for $30 per pair. If the retailer requires a 40 percent markup on selling price, we would calculate the retailer's price as follows.

Profit Objectives
    Cost-Based
        Cost-Plus Pricing
        Price-Floor Pricing
    Demand Based
        Target Cost Pricing
        Yield Management
        Variable (Custom) Pricing
        Skimming (New products)
    Experience Based
        Experimental Pricing
        Judgment
Sales or Market Share Objectives
    Value Pricing (Everyday low pricing)
    Frequent Discounting
    Penetration Pricing (New products)
    Trial Pricing (New products)
Competitive Effect Objectives (stability)
    Price Leadership or Follower
    Premium Pricing
    Umbrella pricing (Pricing below the competition)
    Price Bundling
Customer Satisfaction Objectives
    Variable (Custom) Pricing
    Cost of Ownership Pricing
    Value Pricing (Everyday low pricing)
    Price Bundling
Image Enhancement / Positioning Objectives
    Premium Pricing
    Prestige/Image Pricing
Everyday Low Pricing

**Figure 9.4** Price Objectives and Strategies

**cost-plus pricing** A method of setting prices in which the seller totals all the unit costs for the product and then adds the desired profit per unit.

**Table 9.2** Markup on Cost: An Example for a Jeans Manufacturer

**Fixed Costs**

| | |
|---|---|
| Management and other nonproduction-related salaries | $750 000 |
| Rent | 600 000 |
| Insurance | 50 000 |
| Depreciation on equipment | 70 000 |
| Supplies | 30 000 |
| Advertising | 500 000 |
| Total fixed costs | $2 000 000 |
| Number of units (pairs of jeans) produced | 400 000 |
| Fixed costs per unit | $5.00 |

**Variable Costs**

| | |
|---|---|
| Cost of materials (fabric, zipper, thread, etc.) | $7.00 |
| Cost of production labour | 10.00 |
| Cost of utilities and supplies used in production process | 3.00 |
| Variable cost per unit (pair of jeans) | $20.00 |
| Total cost (fixed cost per unit plus variable cost per unit) | $25.00 |

**Markup on Cost**

Formula: Price = total cost + (total cost 3 markup percentage)

Price = $25.00 + ($25.00 × 0.20) = $25.00 + $5.00 = $30.00

$$\text{Price} = \frac{\text{cost}}{1 - \text{markup percentage}}$$

As we see in Table 9.3, the price of jeans with the markup on selling price is $50.00.

Just to compare the difference in the final prices of the two markup methods, Table 9.3 also shows what would happen if the retailer uses a markup on cost method. Using the same product cost and price with a 40 percent markup on cost would yield $42, a much lower price. The markup on selling price gives you the percentage of the selling price represented by the markup ($20 is 40 percent of the selling price of $50). The markup on cost gives you the percentage of the cost represented by the markup ($12 is 40 percent of the cost of $42). But what happens when costs go up? Do marketers increase their prices? If they do, consumers are likely to rebel. One solution is to keep the price constant but provide a bit less of the product. Frito-Lay, maker of salty snack foods, offset increasing production costs by cutting the contents by 6.7 to 7.5 percent per bag of Fritos, Cheetos, and potato chips.[13] To keep consumers from complaining that packages aren't full, a company may make the package ever-so-slightly smaller. In a similar move, Procter & Gamble once reduced the number of disposable diapers in its Luvs and Pampers packages by an average of 13 percent. Let the buyer beware!

**Table 9.3** Markup on Cost and Markup on Selling Price: An Example of a Retailers Pricing

| Mark-up on Selling Price | | Mark-up on Cost | |
|---|---|---|---|
| Retailer's cost for a pair of jeans | $30.00 | Retailer's cost for a pair of jeans | $30.00 |
| Markup percentage | 40% | Markup percentage | 40% |
| Formula: Price = $\dfrac{\text{cost}}{(1.00 - \text{markup percentage})}$ | | Formula: Price = total cost + (total cost × markup percentage) | |
| Price = $\dfrac{\$30.00}{(1.00 - .40)}$ = $\dfrac{\$30.00}{0.60}$ = $50.00 | | Price = $30.00 + ($30.00 × 0.40) = $30.00 + $12.00 = $42.00 | |

**Price-Floor Pricing** These cost-based pricing methods do not take into account any factors except costs and profits. But there are times when firms need to consider other factors, such as the advantage of having a plant operating at its peak capacity, which keeps a skilled workforce fully employed. **Price-floor pricing** is a method for calculating price that considers both costs and what can be done to ensure that a plant can operate at its capacity.

Price-floor pricing has limited use, usually when the state of the economy or other temporary market conditions make it impossible for a firm to sell enough units of its product at a price that covers fixed costs, variable costs, and profit goals to keep its plants operating at full capacity. In such circumstances, it may be possible to sell part of the units produced at a lower price, one that covers only the marginal costs of production. If the price-floor price can be set above the marginal costs, then the firm can use the difference to increase profits or to help cover its fixed costs.

For example, assume the jeans firm, operating at full capacity, can produce 400 000 pairs of jeans a year. The average variable costs per unit are $20; the price that covers fixed costs, variable costs, and a desired level of profits is $30 per pair. Due to a downturn in the economy, the firm finds that it can sell only 350 000 units at this price. Using price-floor pricing, the firm can sell the additional 50 000 pairs of jeans at a price as low as $20 and maintain full-capacity operations.

If it adopts this approach, the firm will not make anything on the additional units, but it will not lose anything either. If it sells the additional 50 000 pairs at $25, then it will not only cover the variable costs but will also increase its total profits—50 000 × $5 or $250 000—not a bad deal. But several risks accompany price-floor pricing. Selling the additional 50 000 pairs of jeans at a lower cost might cannibalize full-price sales, and if the lower price is offered to some retailers and not others, it might anger those not included and undermine customer loyalty.

Firms that produce their own national brands as well as manufacture private-label brands sold through various retailers and distributors may use price-floor pricing for the private-label end of the business. Thus, Frigidaire may sell 70 percent of its refrigerators under the Frigidaire name and the rest to Sears for sale under its own Kenmore brand name. The consumers in Exhibit 9.5 look at specifications to compare models of different prices.

Cost-based strategies are quite popular because they ensure that prices take into account an organization's costs. However, when firms base price strategies on cost, they are operating under the old production orientation and not a marketing orientation.

**DEMAND-BASED PRICING** **Demand-based pricing** is basing the selling price on an estimate of volume or quantity that a firm can sell at different prices. To use any of the pricing strategies based on demand, firms must research demand—they must learn what quantities of a product different target markets are willing to buy at different prices. Used pickup trucks in Alberta, for example, are in greater demand than in British Columbia, causing prices to be significantly higher in Alberta.

Often marketers use customer surveys in which consumers reveal whether they would buy a certain product and how much of it they would buy at various prices. More accurate estimates can be obtained by some type of field experiment. For instance, a firm might actually offer the product at different price levels in different test markets and map the results onto a demand curve.

The **demand curve**, which can be a curved or straight line, shows the quantity of a product that customers will buy in a market during a period of time at various prices if all other factors remain the same. Figure 9.5 shows demand curves for normal and prestige products. For most goods, the demand curve slopes downward and to the right (Normal goods, Figure 9.5). If prices decrease, customers will buy more. This is known as the *law of demand*. For example, if the price of bananas in the grocery store goes up, a customer will probably buy fewer of them. If the price increases too much, the customer will eat his or her cereal without bananas.

**price-floor pricing** A method for calculating price in which, to maintain full plant operating capacity, a portion of a firm's output may be sold at a price that covers only marginal costs of production.

**demand-based pricing** A price-setting method based on estimates of demand at different prices.

**demand curve** A plot of the quantity of a product that customers will buy in a market during a period of time at various prices if all other factors remain the same.

**Exhibit 9.5**

Price-floor pricing is a method for calculating price that considers both costs and what can be done to ensure that a plant can operate at its capacity.

There are situations, however, in which otherwise rational people desire a product more as it *increases* in price. For *prestige products*, such as luxury cars or jewellery or even some business diplomas and degrees, an increase in price may actually result in an *increase* in the quantity demanded, because consumers see the products as more valuable. The higher-price–higher-demand relationship has its limits, however. At some point price increases will make the product unattainable, and demand will begin to decrease, as shown by the backward direction taken by the top portion of the backward-bending curve under Prestige Products in Figure 9.5.

A strength of demand-based pricing strategies is that their use assures a firm that it will be able to sell what it produces at the determined price, because the price is based on

**Figure 9.5** Demand Curves for Normal and Prestige Products

research findings about customer demand rather than on the seller's costs. A major disadvantage is the difficulty of estimating demand accurately. Although sales forecasting is a topic covered in advanced marketing courses, it is important to know that estimating demand can be difficult. This is because the size of markets is often not known and needs to be estimated, the market share a firm might expect to capture needs to be estimated, and these projections need to take into consideration other factors that can affect demand, such as new competitors entering the market, the state of the economy, and changing consumer tastes. Dell Computers is one company that uses demand pricing (Exhibit 9.6).[14] Dell revises the price of its computers when necessary to offset decreasing sales. The computer company reviews its prices frequently (often a few times a month) in an attempt to keep tabs on customer thinking and give customers the value they want. Marginal analysis, as discussed briefly early in this chapter, is a technique that enables marketers to look at demand and costs at the same time; to assess profit under different forecasts.

Four specific demand-based pricing strategies are target cost pricing, yield management pricing, variable (custom) pricing, and skimming pricing. We'll talk about those next.

**Target Cost Pricing** Today firms are finding that they can be more successful if they match price with demand using a process called **target costing**. With target costing, a firm first determines the price at which customers would be willing to buy the product and then it works backwards to design the product in such a way that it can produce and sell the product at a profit. With target costing, a product's cost, and thus its price, are strongly tied to its design—70 to 80 percent of a product's costs are determined by its final design.

With target costing, firms first use marketing research to identify the quality and functionality needed to satisfy attractive market segments and what price they are willing to pay *before the product is designed*. As Table 9.4 shows, the next step is to determine what margins retailers and dealers require, as well as the profit margin the company requires. Based on this information, managers can calculate the target cost—the maximum it can cost the firm to manufacture the product. In addition, the company may break down this total target cost into different product functions or components, allocating more of the cost to product features consumers consider critical. If the firm can meet customer quality and functionality requirements, and control costs to meet the required price, it will manufacture the product. If not, it abandons the product.

One reason that target costing is practised more today is the global economy—competitor firms can bring "me too" products to market so quickly, usually within months, that there is little time to recover development costs much less to create brand loyalty. Success is tied to designing costs out of a product.

Camera maker Olympus Optical Company has adopted target costing. When Olympus began losing money in the mid 1980s, it first tried to introduce new products. A second initiative was to improve product quality. Its third initiative was to examine production costs. Olympus managers realized that success depended on their ability to manufacture products at a cost that would meet customers' requirements. Olympus determined that a baseline price for a compact camera in the Canadian market was $140. Considering import fees and

**target costing** A process in which firms identify the quality and functionality needed to satisfy customers and what price they are willing to pay *before the product is designed*; the product is manufactured only if the firm can control costs to meet the required price.

**Exhibit 9.6**

Dell uses a demand-based pricing strategy. The company regularly reviews sales performance and adjusts its prices accordingly.

**Table 9.4 Target Costing Using a Jeans Example**

Step 1: Determine the price customers are willing to pay for the jeans. $39.99

Step 2: Determine the markup required by the retailer. 40% = 0.40

Step 3: Calculate the maximum price the retailer will pay, the markup amount.

   Price to the Retailer = Selling price × (1.00 − markup percentage)

   Price to the Retailer = $39.99 × 0.60 = $23.99

Step 4: Determine the profit required by the firm. 15% = 0.15

Step 5: Calculate the target cost, the maximum cost of producing the jeans.

   Target Cost = Price to the Retailer × (1.00 − profit percentage)

   Target Cost = $23.99 × 0.85 = $20.39

the margins dealers required, Olympus determined a target cost for any new product. Initially only about 20 percent of proposed new models would meet the target costs on the first pass. But those that did quickly became the most popular—and profitable—compact cameras in the Canadian market.

**Yield-Management Pricing** **Yield management pricing** is another type of demand-based pricing strategy most commonly used by airlines, hotels, and cruise lines (Exhibit 9.8). With yield management pricing, firms charge different prices to different customers in order to manage capacity while maximizing revenues. Many service firms practise yield management pricing because they recognize that different customers have different sensitivities to price—some customers will pay top dollar for an airline ticket while others will travel only if there is a discount fare. The goal of yield management pricing is to accurately predict the proportion of customers who fall into each category and allocate the percentages of the airline's or hotel's capacity accordingly so that no product goes unsold.

For example, an airline may have two prices for seats: the full fare ($899) and the discount fare ($299). The airline must predict how many seats it can fill at full fare and how many can be sold at only the discounted fare. The airline begins months ahead of the date of the flight with a basic allocation of seats—perhaps it will place 25 percent in the full fare "bucket" and 75 percent in the discount fare "bucket." While the seats in the full fare bucket cannot be sold at the discounted price, the seats allocated for the discounted price can be sold at the full fare.

As flight time gets closer, the airline might make a series of adjustments to the allocation of seats in the hope of selling every seat on the plane at the highest price possible. If the Toronto Maple Leafs need to book the flight, chances are some of the discount seats will be sold at full fare, decreasing the number available at the discounted price. If, as the flight date nears, the number of full-fare ticket sales falls below the forecast, some of those seats will be moved to the discount bucket. This process continues until the day of the flight as the airline attempts to have every seat filled when the plane takes off. This is why you may be able to get a fantastic price on an airline ticket through discount travel agencies like Skyauction.com or Cheapticketscanada.com if you wait until the last minute to buy your ticket.

This strategy is similar to a price discrimination strategy where different segments are targeted for different pricing levels—such as the price difference between men's and women's hair cuts and men's and women's dry-cleaning.

**yield management pricing** A practice of charging different prices to different customers in order to manage capacity while maximizing revenues.

**Skyauction.com**
www.Skyauction.com

**Exhibit 9.7**

Hotels like Quebec City's Fairmont Le Chateau Frontenac use a yield management pricing strategy to maximize revenues.

**Variable Pricing** **Variable pricing**, or custom pricing, is a strategy of tailoring the price of a product to reflect variability in market demand and what different customers are willing to pay. The price of gasoline, for example, is often set higher during periods of peak demand—like long weekends. Variable pricing is common in business-to-business marketing contexts where prices are typically negotiated in new buy or modified re-buy situations like the digital imaging system purchase described in the Venture 4th case at the end of Chapter 6, or submitted as sealed bids (typical of government purchases). Coca-Cola has been experimenting with the concept of variable pricing in vending machines—with the price determined by the ambient temperature outside the machine—and a rationale that consumers may be willing to pay more for a cold Coke when it is hot outside.[15] Variable pricing could be considered a profit-oriented strategy as it ensures that products are sold at the highest price each customer is willing to pay. However, it could also be considered a customer satisfaction-based strategy as it also ensures customers get the best "deal" they are able to negotiate.

**variable pricing** A flexible pricing strategy that reflects what individual customers are willing to pay.

**Skimming Pricing** Skimming means taking the top or best part of something—like the cream that separates and rises to the top of non-homogenized milk, used for making ice cream and whipped cream. In pricing new products, one strategy is to set a **skimming price**, which means that the firm charges a high, premium price for its new product, expecting demand from the top spending, least price sensitive, target market. For example, when Top-Flite introduced its new Strata golf balls with a new dimple design and more solid core for better flight with metal clubs, the price was three times that of regular balls. Pro shops still couldn't keep them in stock.[16]

**skimming price** Charging a very high, premium price for a new product.

If a product is highly desirable and offers unique benefits, and early adopters are not price sensitive during the introductory stage of the product life cycle, a skimming pricing strategy allows a firm to quickly recover research, development, and promotion costs, resulting in earlier profitability than under other pricing strategies (Exhibit 9.8). For skimming pricing to be successful, however, there should be little chance that competitors can get into the market quickly. With highly complex, technical products, it may be quite a while before competitors can develop and test new products and get them into production. This is the case for patented pharmaceutical products that have a lock on the market for 25 years.

**experimental pricing** A strategy of experimenting with prices until the price that generates the highest profitability is found.

A skimming pricing strategy is most successful when the market consists of several customer segments with different levels of price sensitivity. There must be a substantial number of initial product customers who have very low price sensitivity. After a period of time, the price can go down, and a second segment of the market with a slightly higher level of price sensitivity will purchase, and so on. For example, hand calculators that once commanded $200 can now be bought for less than $2—accessible to almost everyone.

**judgment** A pricing strategy that draws on past experience of the marketer in setting appropriate prices.

**EXPERIENCE-BASED PRICING STRATEGIES** Because of the difficulty in forecasting demand for products at different prices, many marketers, and in particular retailers, use their own experience to set prices. **Experimental pricing** is when a marketer tries different levels of pricing to see what the demand is. Experimental pricing is often used in market pre-tests where different prices are used in different geographic markets to generate the data to create a demand curve at different price levels. It is also used, less formally, by retailers who try one price for a product, then make adjustments to the price to see what price level seems to generate the greatest profitability. This is also called trial-and-error pricing. Marketers also use **judgment**

**Exhibit 9.8**

Manufacturers of new- to-the-world, high-technology products like DVD recorders often use a skimming pricing strategy to recover research and development costs quickly.

in setting prices—drawing on past experience with similar products or their understanding of the market segment to set prices.

## Market Share Pricing Strategies

While variable pricing can result in maximizing profit, and satisfied customers, the negotiation process can be time consuming, and consumers have different levels of negotiating skills. This leaves some customers with cognitive dissonance, wondering if they got the best price.

**value pricing or everyday low pricing (EDLP)** A pricing strategy in which a firm sets prices that provide ultimate value to customers.

VALUE PRICING To address this issue, car manufacturers like Saturn, and retailers such as Zellers and Wal-Mart, practise **value pricing, or everyday low pricing (EDLP)**, which promises ultimate value to consumers—without having to negotiate or bargain for it (Exhibit 9.9). As discussed in Chapter 1, customer *value* is the benefits received by a customer relative to the costs and sacrifices necessary to obtain those benefits. This means that, in the customers' eyes, the product's price is justified by what they receive.[17]

Value-based pricing begins with customers, then considers the competition, and then determines the best pricing strategy. Smart marketers know that the firm that wins is not necessarily the one with the lowest prices but rather the one that delivers the most value.

This has been the strategy behind the success of WestJet Airlines. Modelled after Southwest Airlines, WestJet focuses on everyday low fares, short distances, and good customer service to attract budget-conscious leisure travellers throughout Canada. It started with understanding the target market—what it would take to get people out of their cars for short-haul trips—then the company made marketing mix decisions to deliver the value bundle sought by those customers: no-frills, direct flights, at rock-bottom prices, to and from under-utilized airports, using standard aircraft, serviced by personable staff, offering fun and lighthearted (perhaps even irreverent) customer interactions.

In practice, when marketers use EDLP strategies, consumers feel they get more for their money. Marketers hope that will make them see the price as reasonable and encourage them to remain loyal rather than snapping up whatever happens to be on sale. Deal-oriented consumers, however, have been conditioned to choose products because they are "on special" rather than because they are superior to others. The problem with "deals" or frequent price promotions is that consumers learn to wait for sales or stock up on products when they are on sale, thus making it difficult for companies to maintain "regular" margins and production volumes. Procter & Gamble tried to establish an EDLP strategy in the early 1990s for such products as Tide and Pampers, but abandoned this strategy in face of competitors continuing to offer sales, coupons, and other price promotions.[18]

**frequent discounting** A strategy of frequently using sale prices to increase sales volume.

FREQUENT DISCOUNTING The approach of using sales, coupons, and other discounts to stimulate sales is a **frequent discounting** strategy. Retailers like Future Shop who have weekly sale extravaganzas use this strategy to entice consumers into their stores where they may purchase both sale and non-sale items. The problem with frequent discounting is that it conditions consumers to wait for the sale price. If they can wait, consumers will not pay the "regular" price for a two-litre bottle of Coca-Cola, knowing that it goes on sale for 99 cents periodically and is in the $1.79 range regularly.

**penetration pricing** A pricing strategy in which a firm introduces a new product at a very low price to encourage more customers to purchase it.

PENETRATION PRICING Another market share-based strategy is **penetration pricing**. Penetration pricing, the opposite of skimming pricing, is when a new product is introduced at a very low price, as Intel did with its first Pentium processor chip.[19] Because rivals were way behind in developing competitive chips, Intel had used a skimming strategy for the 486 processor. However, when the Pentium 1 was introduced, Intel knew that Motorola was working with IBM and Apple to develop comparable chips, and it set a low price for the

**Exhibit 9.9**

Zellers is known for its everyday low pricing strategy.

Pentium 1 to sell more in a short period of time and derail Motorola's debut.[20] This strategy worked well for Intel. The low price encouraged demand and sales in the early stages of the product life cycle. If the marketing objective is to beef up market share, penetration pricing makes sense.

Another reason marketers use penetration pricing is to discourage competitors from entering the market. The firm first out with a new product has an important advantage. Experience has shown that a *pioneering brand* often is able to maintain dominant market share for the life of the product. Competitors looking at the market may feel that the potential for developing a profitable alternative is not good. Bayer aspirin and Hoover vacuum cleaners are examples of brands that were first to market, kept their leads for decades, and still dominate their fields. These pioneering brands don't need to do much talking to tell consumers who they are. Keeping prices low may even act as a *barrier to entry* to potential competitors, because the cost of developing and manufacturing a new similar product prevents a satisfactory return.

TRIAL PRICING With **trial pricing**, a new product carries a low price for a limited period of time to lower the risk for a customer, then the price is increased to "regular" levels.[21] In trial pricing, the idea is to win customer acceptance first and make profits later. A low-enough introductory price may be a preferred alternative to giving out free samples as the trial price will bring some positive contribution to the organization.

Telus, for example, is conducting a $65 million experiment to bring digital TV, movies on demand, Internet, e-mail, and phone service into homes for one monthly bill. After the trial offer, Telus will decide how widely the services will be offered and whether there is an opportunity to increase prices.[22] Microsoft introduced the Access database program at the short-term promotional price of $99, when the suggested retail price was $495. Trial pricing assumes that the strong benefits of using a product will create loyal customers, who will spread favourable word-of-mouth communications to other prospective users. Trial pricing also works for services. Health clubs and other service providers frequently offer trial memberships or special introductory prices. They hope that customers will try the service at a low price and be converted to a regular-price customer.

**trial pricing** Pricing a new product low for a limited period of time to lower the risk for a customer.

## Competitive Effect Pricing Strategies

Competitive-effect pricing strategies are those that are competitor focused. To achieve competitive effect objectives, a firm can adopt a price-leader–follower strategy, a premium pricing strategy, an umbrella pricing strategy, or adopt a price bundling strategy.

PRICE LEADERSHIP (FOLLOWER) Before Wal-Mart came to Canada, Zellers was clearly the price leader in discount stores. Other discount stores would price their products similar to Zellers.[23] A firm that chooses a **price leadership** strategy either is the industry leader or a firm that follows the industry leader by setting the same or similar prices. Usually, firms practise a price leadership strategy when they're in an oligopoly with relatively few producers—such as the Canadian petroleum industry or cell phone industry. In such an industry, it is in the best interest of all firms to minimize price competition for everyone to make a profit. Price leadership strategies are popular, because they provide an acceptable and legal way for firms to agree on prices without ever talking with each other.

Even when there isn't a single industry price leader, firms may adopt a parity pricing strategy—they try to keep their price about equal to key competitors' prices. Gasoline retailers attempt to maintain a parity pricing structure by responding quickly to competitive price moves; consumers often view this rapid response as *price fixing*. Numerous national and provincial investigations of gasoline prices have found no evidence of price fixing, and the petroleum companies are spending millions of dollars educating consumers about the cost structure of gasoline.[24,25]

PREMIUM PRICING Sometimes firms chose to price their products higher than competitive offerings. While this strategy helps to portray a premium or quality positioning, it also

**price leadership (follower)** The firm that sets price first in an industry; other major firms in the industry follow the leader by staying in line.

**Zellers**
www.hbc.com/zellers

helps firms achieve the competitive effect of market leadership and price stability. IBM computers, for example, are priced 10 percent to 15 percent higher than competitive offerings, in part because IBM's industry leadership allows them to, and it protects the pricing in the industry and enables competitors to compete on price entering a price war. For similar reasons, Microsoft computer peripherals, such as optical mice, are priced 10 percent to 20 percent higher than competitive products. Coca-Cola is counting on its market leadership position, brand equity, and customer loyalty to support a new premium pricing strategy, pricing Coke products above the competition, in an attempt to increase margins and profits.[26]

**UMBRELLA PRICING** The opposite of premium pricing is umbrella pricing or pricing below the competition. By using rock-bottom prices on popular CDs, electronics stores such as the Future Shop have been able to get shoppers into their stores, where many will buy the high-profit electronics equipment sold by the retailer. **Umbrella pricing** is a strategy of ducking under the competition's price by a standard percentage. Corel Corp., for example, consistently prices its office software suite at least 20 percent below that of Microsoft.

**PRICE BUNDLING Price bundling**, selling two or more goods or services as a single package for one price, can be a pricing strategy or tactic. As a strategy, it is an attempt to pre-empt competition and prevent consumers or customers from entering a discrete purchase decision for the product included with the one intended for purchase. Hewlett Packard bundles computer systems, for example, to include a system unit, a monitor, and a printer. By receiving the monitor or printer "free" with the system unit purchase, Hewlett Packard ends up not competing with Lexmark, Canon, or other computer peripheral manufacturers. Price bundling could also be used to achieve customer satisfaction objectives by including another product of value to the customer with their intended purchase. Malaysia Airlines, for example, bundles flights within Malaysia at a discount when international flights are purchased to Kuala Lumpur (Exhibit 9.10). We will discuss the tactical use of price bundling shortly.

**umbrella pricing**  A strategy of ducking under a competitor's price by a fixed percentage.

**price bundling**  Selling two or more goods or services as a single package for one price.

**cost of ownership**  A pricing strategy that considers the lifetime cost of using the product.

**Exhibit 9.10**

Price bundling often entices customers to spend more initially than if they bought only one product. This strategy is even used by airlines.

## Pricing Strategies to Achieve Customer Satisfaction Objectives

When firms develop pricing strategies that cater to the needs of customers, they are less concerned with short-term successes than with keeping customers for the long term. Firms truly dedicated to customer satisfaction look at the wants and needs of customers in developing pricing strategies. Three pricing strategies we have already discussed can be used to achieve customer satisfaction objectives: Variable pricing, value pricing, and price bundling. Another strategy to achieve customer satisfaction objectives is to consider total **cost of ownership**. The cost of ownership is the price consumers pay for a product, plus the cost of maintaining and using the product, less its resale (or salvage) value. Sanyo, for example, bases the price of its rechargeable batteries on customer cost-of-ownership (Exhibit 9.11)—comparing the cost of using regular batteries to the use of Sanyo's rechargeable ones and setting a price lower than the cost of multiple regular batteries.

## Pricing Strategies to Achieve Image Enhancement/Positioning Objectives

There are three common pricing strategies for achieving image enhancement (positioning) objectives. We have already discussed value pricing (everyday low pricing), which is used to support a value positioning strategy, in addition to being a way of increasing market share. We have also already discussed premium pricing as a competitive-effect based strategy, but premium pricing could also be used to support a premium positioning strategy where higher than competition pricing is intended to support inferences of higher quality or another basis of superiority. Related to premium pricing is **prestige pricing**, which is pricing a product significantly higher than competitive brands to make them status symbols (Exhibit 9.12). Rolex, for example, uses a prestige pricing strategy for their watches, which retail for $5000 to $10 000 (or more!). Prestige pricing is part of an exclusive positioning strategy, where only the very wealthy or privileged can purchase the brand.

## PRICE POINTS AND TACTICS

Once marketers have developed pricing strategies, the next step in price planning is to actually set prices by applying pricing tactics and to set the terms and conditions associated with that price. In practice, prices are set in the range determined by the product's costs, what customers are willing to pay, and the price of competitive or substitute products. However as seen in Figure 9.6, there are a number of considerations for setting prices within this range.

**Exhibit 9.11**

Sanyo bases its pricing on customer needs using a cost-of-ownership strategy.

## Pricing for Individual Products

How marketers present a product's price to the market can make a big difference in the attractiveness of the offering. Here are two tactics:

- With *two-part pricing*, two separate types of payments are required to purchase the product. For example, golf and tennis clubs charge yearly or monthly fees plus fees for each round of golf or tennis. Cellular phone and Internet service providers offer customers a set number of minutes usage for a monthly fee plus a per-minute rate for extra usage.

- *Payment pricing* makes products appear more attainable by breaking up the total price into smaller amounts payable over time. For example, many customers now opt to lease rather than buy a car. The monthly lease amount is an example of payment pricing, which tends to make people less sensitive to the total price of the car (Exhibit 9.13).[27]

**prestige pricing** A strategy where prices are set significantly higher than competing brands.

## Pricing for Multiple Products

A firm may sell several products that consumers typically buy together. When people buy a burger, pizza, or taco for lunch, they often purchase a drink, fries, or salad as well. Similarly, when someone buys a personal computer, a box of diskettes is usually not far behind. We have previously discussed price bundling as a pricing strategy. As a price tactic, price bundling is enhancing the perceived value of a purchase by combining two or more goods or services into a single offer, at a lower price than the individual items. A music buff, for example, can buy tickets to an entire concert series for a lower price than buying tickets to

**Exhibit 9.12**

Lee Valley tools uses prestige pricing to support a prestige image among woodworking and gardening hobbyists.

**captive pricing** A pricing tactic for two items that must be used together; one item is priced very low and the firm makes its profit on another, high-margin item essential to the operation of the first item.

**Pricing for individual products**
- Two-part pricing
- Payment pricing

**Pricing for multiple products**
- Price bundling
- Captive pricing

**Geographic pricing**
- F.O.B. pricing
- Zone pricing
- Uniform delivered pricing
- Freight absorption pricing

**Price discounts**
- Trade or functional discounts
- Quantity discounts
- Cash discounts
- Seasonal discounts

**Psychological pricing**
- Odd (even) number pricing
- Price lining

**Figure 9.6** Pricing Tactics

each concert separately. A movie ticket may include a drink and popcorn. Even an all-you-can-eat special at the local diner is an example of price bundling. Price bundling is an increasingly popular pricing tactic for consumer electronics, small and large appliances, and even automobiles where the tangible product is bundled with an extended warranty package. The tangible product is priced near cost while more significant margins are made on the extended warranty. The thinking behind price bundling as a tactic is whatever revenue a seller loses from the reduced prices, it makes up in increased total purchases.

**CAPTIVE PRICING** **Captive pricing** is a tactic a firm uses when it has two products that work only when used together. The firm sells one item at a very low price and then makes its profit on the second high-margin item. Computer printers are priced this way. The printer itself is sold at (or sometimes below) cost, but the ink required to use the printer is sold with very high margins. Gillette uses captive pricing to sell its shaving products. The Mach3 razor is sold for a relatively low price but the disposable blades sell for $1.50 or more per blade—and the typical user buys 30 blades a year. Although the blade and razor business generates only a third of corporate revenues for Gillette, the company's use of captive pricing tactics in this category delivers two-thirds of its profits (Exhibit 9.14).

## Geographic Pricing

Geographic pricing is a tactic that establishes how firms handle the cost of shipping products to customers near, far, and wide. Characteristics of the product, customers, and competition may make it advisable to charge all customers the same price, or it may make better sense to vary the prices charged to customers in different locations, regardless of the overall pricing strategy selected.

**F.O.B. PRICING** Often, pricing is stated as f.o.b. factory or f.o.b. delivered—f.o.b. stands for *free on board*, which means the supplier will pay to have the product loaded onto a truck or some other carrier. Also—and this is important—title passes to the buyer at the f.o.b. location. Thus, *f.o.b. factory* or **f.o.b. origin** means that the cost of transporting the product from the factory to the customer's location is the responsibility of the customer; **f.o.b. delivered** means that the seller pays both the cost of loading and transporting to the customer, which is included in the selling price.

The f.o.b. origin pricing creates many different prices, because the purchase price for each customer changes with shipping costs. But with f.o.b. delivered pricing, every customer pays the same price. Another option combines f.o.b. origin and f.o.b. delivered—sometimes, a seller's terms indicate that title to the product is transferred at the seller's location, but the seller will pay the freight. This plan is called *f.o.b. factory, freight prepaid.*

Sellers often prefer *f.o.b factory* pricing because of its simplicity. The marketer doesn't have to take into account the costs of shipping to different customers at varying distances from the factory. It also allows flexibility in how a product gets shipped, because pricing does not depend on a particular shipping method. In addition, the fact that the title is transferred before shipping shifts the risk of damage to the transit company and the customer.

**ZONE PRICING** Another geographic pricing tactic is **zone pricing**. Like f.o.b. factory pricing, zone pricing means that distant customers pay more than customers who are close to the factory. However, in zone pricing, there are a limited number of different prices charged, based on geographic zones established by the seller. All customers located in each zone pay the same transportation charge.

Zone pricing simplifies geographic cost differences, which is important in certain markets. It would be nearly impossible for Canada Post's Express courier service to charge one price if a package shipped from Winnipeg went to Toronto, a different price if it went to Mississauga, another if it went to Don Mills, Ontario. Therefore, Express Post charges different rates for shipping packages from any single location to different zones across the country.

**UNIFORM DELIVERED PRICING** With **uniform delivered pricing**, an average shipping cost is added to the price, no matter what the buyer's location or distance from the manufacturer's plant—within reason. Catalogue sales, home television shopping, e-commerce, and other types of non-store retail sales usually use uniform delivered pricing.

**FREIGHT ABSORPTION PRICING** **Freight absorption pricing** means the seller takes on part or all of the cost of shipping. This strategy is good for high-ticket items, when the cost of shipping is a negligible part of the sales price and the profit margin. Marketers are most likely to use freight absorption pricing in highly competitive markets or when such pricing allows them to enter new markets.

## Psychological Tactics

Marketers need to take into consideration consumer behaviour when making pricing decisions and this will be discussed further later in the chapter. As we saw in Chapter 5, part of understanding consumer behaviour is understanding consumer psychology. Two pricing tactics that draw on consumer psychology are odd (even) number pricing, and price lining.

**ODD (EVEN) NUMBER PRICING** We usually see prices reported in dollars and cents—$1.99, $5.98, $23.67, or even $599.99. Exhibit 9.15 shows this common practice. We see prices in even dollar amounts—$2, $10, or $600—far less often. The reason? Marketers have assumed that there is a psychological response to odd prices that differs from the responses to even prices. Research on the difference in perceptions of odd versus even prices has been inconclusive and has produced no substantive evidence that the use of odd prices is superior to even prices. But that doesn't mean that marketers should change this practice.

At the same time, there are some instances in which even prices are the norm or perhaps even necessary. Theatre and concert tickets, admission to sporting events, and lottery tickets tend to be priced in even amounts, so that ticket sellers don't have to make change. Professional fees are normally expressed as even dollars. If a lawyer charged $99.99 per hour, the client might wonder why he or she has a "bargain-priced" fee and may think less of the quality of the legal advice. Many luxury items such as jewellery, golf course fees, and

**Exhibit 9.13**

Auto manufacturers know that a per-month price for a new car makes people less sensitive to the total price of the car.

**f.o.b. origin pricing** A pricing tactic in which the cost of transporting the product from the factory to the customer's location is the responsibility of the customer.

**f.o.b. delivered pricing** A pricing tactic in which the cost of loading and transporting the product to the customer is included in the selling price, paid by the manufacturer.

**zone pricing** A pricing tactic in which customers in different geographic zones pay different transportation rates.

**uniform delivered pricing** A pricing tactic in which a firm adds a standard shipping charge to the price for all customers regardless of location.

**freight absorption pricing** A pricing tactic in which the seller absorbs the total cost of transportation.

IT'S NEW. IT'S COOL.
IT'S BLUE.

Gillette·MACH3·
COOL BLUE™

Great close shave. Cool new look.

Gillette
The Best a Man Can Get™

www.MACH3.com © 2001 The Gillette Company

**Exhibit 9.14**

Gillette practises captive pricing with its razors. Once customers buy the handles, they are "captive" to the company's blade prices.

**price lining** The practice of setting a limited number of different specific prices, called price points, for items in a product line.

resort accommodations use even dollar prices to set them apart from less costly substitutes.

**PRICE LINING** Marketers often apply their understanding of the psychological aspects of pricing in a practice called **price lining**. This means that similar items in a product line sell at different prices, called price points. If you want to buy a personal computer, you will find that most manufacturers have one "stripped-down" model for about $650. Other desktop systems are offered at prices around $999, $1199, $1499, $1799, $1999, and $2500. While consumers can spend much more than $2500 on a desktop computer system, computer manufacturers have found that most consumers are prepared to pay $1500 to $2500 for a system. Rather than competing on price, these manufacturers compete on the features offered at each price point.

Why is price lining a good practice? From the marketer's standpoint, price lining is a way to maximize profits. In theory, a firm would charge each individual customer the highest price that customer was willing to pay. If the most one specific person would be willing to pay is $1499 for a personal computer, then that would be their price. If another person would be willing to pay $1999, that would be their price. But charging each consumer a different price is really not possible. Having a limited number of prices that generally fall at the top of the range customers find acceptable is a more workable alternative. Firms that use price lining assume that demand is inelastic within certain ranges, but that if prices go above that range, demand will become elastic and customers will balk. Figure 9.7 shows

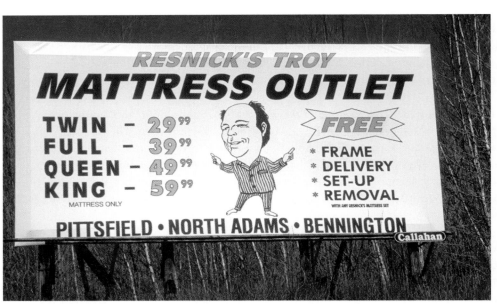

**Exhibit 9.15**

Most companies offer prices in odd dollar amounts because they think customers will be more apt to buy.

an assumed demand curve for a product for which price lining is a good strategy. This figure shows price points within price bands for different computers in a manufacturer's product line.

## Price Discounts, Terms, and Conditions

Marketers also use price discounts as a tactic in setting prices—both with customers and channel intermediaries—and for customers or distributors to get these discounts, they have to meet certain terms and conditions.

**TRADE OR FUNCTIONAL DISCOUNTS** Whether a firm sells to businesses or directly to consumers, most pricing structures are built around list prices. A **list price** is set by the manufacturer for the end customer to pay. In pricing for members of the channel, marketers recognize that pricing must ensure that retailers and wholesalers can cover their costs of doing business and make a profit (Exhibit 9.16).

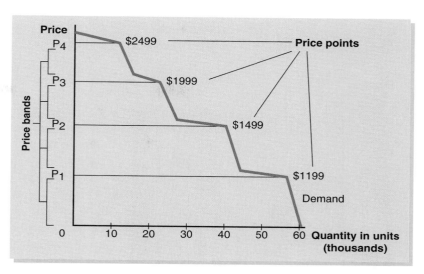

**Figure 9.7** Price Lining: Sometimes firms will offer products at standard price levels to match customer expectations.

**list price** The price the end customer is expected to pay as determined by the manufacturer.

**trade or functional discounts** Discounts off list price of products to members of the channel of distribution that perform various marketing functions.

When manufacturers develop pricing tactics for channel intermediaries, they often use **trade or functional discounts**, because the channel members perform selling, credit, storage, and transportation services that the manufacturer would otherwise have to provide. Often, setting functional discounts is simplified when a firm uses set percentage discounts off list price for each channel level.

Let's look at an example of a channel of distribution that includes a manufacturer that sells to wholesalers that in turn sell to smaller retailers. The manufacturer may state trade discounts as list price less 40/20. The first number means that 40 percent of the list price is to cover the overhead and profit requirements for the retailer—the manufacturer is suggesting that the wholesalers sell to their retail customers at list less 40 percent. If the list price of a product were $200, the price to the retailers would be:

$$\$200 - (40\% \times 200) = \$200 - \$80 = \$120$$

The second number, the 20, is the discount percentage allowed for wholesalers to cover their costs of doing business and profit. Thus, the manufacturer's selling price to the wholesaler is discounted from the retailer's price and would be:

$$\$120 - (20\% \times 120) = \$120 - \$24 = \$96$$

Note that although we talk about trade discounts being determined by manufacturers, in reality the manufacturer has little if any control over the percentage discounts. In most industries, these are standard percentages based on the margins retailers and wholesalers require to cover their overhead and profits.

**QUANTITY DISCOUNTS** Firms that sell to distribution channel members or end-user business customers often offer **quantity discounts**, or reduced prices, for purchases of larger quantities. Marketers commonly use quantity discounts as a way to encourage larger purchases from distribution channel partners.

Sometimes marketers offer buyers **cumulative quantity discounts**, which are based on a total quantity bought within a specified time period, such as a year. Cumulative quantity discounts encourage a buyer to stick with a single seller instead of moving from one supplier to another.

**quantity discounts** A pricing tactic of charging reduced prices for larger quantities of a product.

**cumulative quantity discounts** Discounts based on the total quantity bought within a specified time period.

**Exhibit 9.16**

In pricing to retailers, bicycle manufacturers have to consider the amount retailers must have to operate their business and make a profit.

**non-cumulative quantity discounts** Discounts based only on the quantity purchased in individual orders.

Cumulative quantity discounts may be rebates, in which case the firm sends the buyer a rebate cheque at the end of the discount period. In other cases, the discount is a credit against future orders. In either case, the buyer must wait until the end of the discount period to receive the discount. This delay makes cumulative quantity discounts less attractive, because the buyer must pay the non-discounted price for the goods all year long and not realize the discount until the end of the period. For businesses that operate with low gross margins, this can create some financial hardships.

**Non-cumulative quantity discounts** are based only on the quantity purchased with each individual order. Non-cumulative discounts encourage larger single orders, but do little to tie the buyer and the seller together. When a competitor makes a better discount offer, the buyer may switch.

In most cases, non-cumulative quantity discounts mean that the buyer pays a reduced price for the goods purchased—there is a simple cash discount. In other cases the discount offer is made in terms of free goods. For example, a grocer who buys 10 cases of peanut butter may get one case free.

Sometimes, offering quantity discounts can create problems for the manufacturer. For example, one Canadian publisher developed a four-volume set of encyclopedias, for which it developed a pricing structure with steep quantity discounts and a list price of $175 per set. Small, independent bookstores bought the encyclopedias priced at $125 per set, whereas large chain stores purchased in larger quantities at $75 or $80 a set. When the chain stores decided to give up some of their margin to increase sales and sold the sets at $99, below what the small independents paid the publisher, the manufacturer faced some very unhappy "former" customers.

**CASH DISCOUNTS** Using money costs money, as anyone who's ever taken out a mortgage or a college loan understands. When a firm borrows money, it must pay interest for every day it has the use of the money. Conversely, if a firm has excess cash, it is able to invest that cash and make money from its money. Thus, having cash is an advantage. For this reason many firms try to entice their customers to pay their bills quickly by offering *cash discounts*. For example, a firm selling to a retailer may state that the terms of the sale are "2 percent 10 days, net 30 days." This means that if the retailer pays the producer for the goods within 10 days, the amount due is cut by two percent. The total amount is due within 30 days, and after 30 days, the payment is late.

**SEASONAL DISCOUNTS** Seasonal discounts are price reductions offered during certain times of the year. Products such as snow blowers, lawn mowers, and water skiing equipment are priced in this way. If such products are sold only during a few months of the year, then the manufacturer must either build a large plant that has to be shut down during the off-season or build a large warehouse to store inventory until the season comes around again. Both of these options are unattractive; so to entice retailers and wholesalers to buy off-season and store the product at their locations until the right time of the year, a firm may offer seasonal discounts. Seasonal discounting is also used extensively by tourist attractions and destinations—enticing visitors in slower seasons (Exhibit 9.17).

**OTHER TERMS AND CONDITIONS** In setting prices, marketers also have to set other terms and conditions. One of these is whether they are going to accept cash only, or also accept credit card, debit card, or other forms of payment. Credit and debit card acceptance makes it more convenient for customers to pay for products but the credit card companies and banks charge the seller a commission ranging from 1 percent to 4 percent for processing the transaction and guaranteeing payment. Marketers also have to decide what currencies they are willing to accept. Canadian retailers that target tourists, for example, are often willing to accept U.S. dollars, but few are equipped or willing to provide change in U.S. dollars—because of the hassle of keeping two sets of cash registers and currencies stocked and the exchange rate risk of dealing in multiple currencies. Businesses that have a larger international trade find it advantageous make it as easy as possible for customers to buy and do business in their own currency.

## LEGAL AND ETHICAL CONSIDERATIONS IN PRICING

The free enterprise system is founded on the idea that the marketplace will regulate itself. Supplies of goods and services will be made available if there is an adequate profit incentive and prices will rise or fall according to demand. Unfortunately, some business people are greedy and/or unscrupulous. The federal and provincial governments have found it necessary to enact legislation to protect consumers and to protect businesses from predatory rivals.

The Competition Bureau, a unit of Industry Canada, is responsible for ensuring that Canadian businesses (including businesses that operate in Canada) adhere to federal laws that are designed to maintain and encourage fair competition. Most of these laws are found within statutes of the Competition Act, but others are found in the Consumer Packaging and Labelling Act, the Textile Labelling Act, and the Precious Metals Marking Act. The Competition Act was

**Exhibit 9.17**

Tourism PEI, like other destination marketing organizations, promotes seasonal discounts to attract visitors.

## SPOTLIGHT ON REAL PEOPLE  General Motors

Even before the terrorist attacks on the World Trade Center and the Pentagon, the big three North American carmakers—GM, Ford, and DaimlerChrysler—were facing large financial losses and slumping retail sales. Sales plummeted in the immediate aftermath of the September 11th attacks, and John Devine, chief financial officer of General Motors, faced the daunting prospect of low U.S. consumer confidence and a deepening recession. In response he cut prices drastically in both the United States and Canada—offering zero percent financing on both 2001 and 2002 models, effectively cutting prices by as much as $3000. Ford and Chrysler quickly matched the strategy for their 2001 models and some of the 2002s.

The incentives worked and car sales rose more than 10 percent over the previous October. GM, the first mover, was the biggest beneficiary. In Canada, GM truck sales increased 34.8 percent and total sales increased 19 percent. Ford's sales fell 10 percent and Chrysler's fell 7.5 percent. Devine was so pleased with the results that he extended the promotion through November.

Although GM's sales skyrocketed and their dealers made a lot of money, there was a price to be paid for the price cuts. GM's profit fell 58 percent in the fourth quarter to $255 million—but that was better than Ford, which lost $860 million during this period. Industry analysts suggest that the incentives didn't increase car consumption—they merely accelerated sales that would have been made in 2002 at a higher price. They also caution that those price conscious consumers are not very loyal, so the long-term benefit is dubious. Incentives can also cheapen the image of brand and erode resale values, which makes leases more expensive in the long run.

Devine acknowledges that the pricing strategy cost GM some money, but suggests that overall "it was the right thing to do." Only time will tell, but relative to the other North American auto manufacturers, he just might be right—the price cuts may have hurt the industry but at least GM got the sales.[28]

1. Given the potential problems with cutting prices, why did John Devine pursue his price cutting strategy?
2. What pricing strategy would you recommend for GM in the future?

**Competition Bureau**
http://strategis.ic.gc.ca/
epic/internet/incb-bc.nsf/
en/h_ct00000e.html

recently amended to enable civil (as well as criminal) action to more quickly and effectively stop unfair, deceptive, or otherwise anti-competitive behaviour. In this next section, we will discuss these behaviours and some of the more important regulations to combat them. A more detailed discussion is available on the Competition Bureau Web site.

## Deceptive Pricing Practices

Unscrupulous businesses may attempt to advertise or promote prices in a deceptive way. The Competition Act specifies that sellers cannot make a representation to the public that is false or misleading in a material respect. Thus, a retailer or other supplier must not claim that their prices are lower than a competitor's, unless it is true. Firms cannot promote a going-out-of-business sale, unless they are going out of business. Similarly, sellers cannot make false or misleading representation as to the ordinary selling price of a product. For example, a retailer cannot promote a 50 percent-off sale unless they have sold a substantial volume of the product at the "regular" or higher price within a reasonable period of time. An "introductory low price" cannot be promoted unless the price goes up to its "regular" level within a reasonable period of time. What is "reasonable" and "substantial" is a matter for the civil courts to decide. The Canadian Competition Bureau recently fined women's fashion retailer Suzy Shier Inc. $1 million for misleading consumers about how much they were saving on items marked "on sale" (Exhibit 9.18).[29]

**bait and switch** An illegal marketing practice in which an advertised price special is used as bait to get customers into the store with the intention of switching them to a higher-priced item.

Another deceptive pricing practice is the **bait and switch**, a tactic in which a retailer advertises an item at a very low price—the *bait*—to lure customers into the store, does not have reasonable quantities available, and then tries to get customers to buy a different, more expensive, item—the *switch*. They might tell the customer, "The advertised item is really poor quality. It doesn't have important features. There have been a lot of problems with that one. I can tell you're a really smart shopper—you know poor quality when you see it." Simply encouraging consumers to purchase a higher-priced item is an acceptable sales technique—called "trading up"—but it is a civil offence to advertise a lower-priced item when there are not reasonable quantities available. It is not considered "bait-and-switch" when a product is not available because of circumstances beyond the retailer's control or when customers are offered a "rain check," a promise to fulfill at a later date, when supplies are replenished.

**predatory pricing** The strategy of selling products at unreasonably low prices to drive competitors out of business.

Other deceptive practices are selling a product at a price above the advertised price and double ticketing, or selling a product at the higher of two prices communicated to the consumer on, accompanying, or promoting the product. Selling at a price above the advertised price is a civil court issue, while double ticketing is a criminal offence.

## Predatory Pricing

**Predatory pricing** is a strategy of selling products at unreasonably low prices to drive a rival out of the market or substantially reduce competition, then raising prices to recoup the sacrificed returns and earn higher profits. Although predatory pricing is a criminal offence under section 50(1)(c) of the Competition Act, setting prices for the purpose of taking business away from competitors is normal competition. It is very difficult to prove that low prices are "unreasonable" or that an intentional "strategy" is being followed, and few organizations have been charged under this section of the Act.

**Exhibit 9.18**
Suzy Shier Inc. was recently fined $1 million for misleading price advertising.

A low price is not necessarily a predatory price. **Loss-leader pricing**, for example, is a retailer's strategy of offering products below cost to draw consumers into their stores. Once in the store, the consumers are expected to buy other items with higher margins. The city of Vancouver, for example, has a reputation for having the lowest CD prices in the world. Stores like A&B Sound, Sam the Record Man, and Future Shop, compete aggressively with international chains like HMV and Virgin Records. A $12.79 CD brings customers into the stores, where they tend to buy $30 to $40 worth of CDs, and may buy stereo equipment or other electronic products while they are there.[30]

**loss-leader pricing** The pricing strategy of setting prices below cost to attract customers into a store.

## Price Discrimination

The Competition Act also prohibits **price discrimination**. Price discrimination is a supplier practice of granting price concessions or other advantages to one purchaser, but not making them available to competing purchasers that are buying articles of like quality and quantity.[31] It applies only to the sale of goods, not leases, licences, or the consignment of goods or the sale of services. Dry cleaners charge more to clean a woman's shirt than a man's shirt. Movie theatres charge students and seniors less than other adults. These practices are not illegal. Price discrimination only applies to competing business purchasers, not end users or consumers, and it does not apply to concessions (such as discounts, rebates, guarantees, or shipping costs) negotiated on a particular transaction. As with the predatory pricing statute, price discrimination, a criminal offence, is difficult to prove. The Consumers Group for Fair Gas Prices, for example, took the case of Porter's Automotive Parts and Service in Foxtrap, Newfoundland, to the Competition Bureau, alleging that the major Canadian gasoline suppliers were selling gas to their own corporate-owned gas stations at a lower price than to the independents. The Competition Bureau found no evidence to support the allegation that gas suppliers had charged Porter's a higher price than another dealer in the area buying a similar volume.[32]

**price discrimination** The illegal practice of offering the same product of like quality and quantity to different business customers at different prices, thus lessening competition.

## Price Maintenance

**Price maintenance**, or price fixing, occurs when two or more companies conspire to keep prices at a certain level. The Federal Court of Canada imposed a fine of $2.25 million on Chinook Group Limited of Toronto for its participation in an international conspiracy to fix prices and share markets for chlorine chloride, an important additive widely used in the animal feed industry.[33] A criminal offence under section 61 of the Competition Act, price maintenance can take two forms: horizontal and vertical.

**price maintenance** The collaboration of two or more firms in setting prices, usually to keep prices high.

HORIZONTAL PRICE FIXING *Horizontal price fixing* occurs when competitors making the same product jointly determine what price they will charge. This kind of price fixing keeps prices high by eliminating competition. Canadian courts convicted and fined the head of a Swiss vitamin and fine chemicals company, who conducted conversations with other multinational vitamin producing companies to fix prices and allocate sales volumes for numerous bulk vitamins and related products.[34] In industries, such as the Canadian gasoline industry, in which there are few sellers, there may be no specific price-fixing agreement, but sellers will still charge the same price to "meet the competition." Such parallel pricing is not of itself considered price fixing. There must be an exchange of pricing information between sellers to indicate price-fixing actions.

## Good or Bad Decision?

The Competition Act prohibits a company from predatory pricing—selling below cost to drive a competitor out of business. The Competition Bureau (**http://cb-bc.gc.ca/epic/internet/incb-bc.nsf/en/home**) expressed concerns when Air Canada purchased Canadian Airlines and ended up with an 80 percent share of the air travel market. There was concern that, as WestJet moved to introduce flights in Central and Eastern Canada, Air Canada would reduce fares to a point that would drive the competition out.[35] In general, predatory pricing charges are hard to prove because reducing prices to stimulate business is the very essence of competition. Should a company have the right to charge whatever it would like for its products—even if it loses money in the short run—if this pricing decision is part of its overall business strategy?

**VERTICAL PRICE FIXING** Sometimes manufacturers or wholesalers attempt to force retailers to charge a certain price for their product. This is called *vertical price fixing*, a criminal offence under the Competition Act. Retail stores are free to set whatever price they choose without interference or coercion by the manufacturer or wholesaler. Manufacturers and wholesalers can provide a "suggested retail price," but they cannot retaliate against retailers who chose not to follow the suggestion. Manufacturers or wholesalers are free to set prices when they own the retail outlet. The same is true for consignment selling, in which retailers do not actually ever own the product but simply agree to offer it for sale and to accept a percentage of the selling price for their efforts.

**BID RIGGING Bid rigging** is collusion between suppliers responding to a request for bids or tenders, where the suppliers reduce or eliminate competition in the bidding process and trade off opportunities to "win" the business with margins that are higher than would otherwise be attained. This might include: suppliers agreeing to submit token bids that are priced too high; suppliers abstaining from bidding or withdrawing bids; pre-selected suppliers submitting the lowest bid on a systematic or rotating basis; or suppliers not competing in designated geographic regions or for specific customers. These activities are all criminal offences.

**bid rigging** Collusion between suppliers responding to bid requests to lessen competition and secure higher margins.

## MAKING PRICING DECISIONS

Pricing decisions, like product decisions, are interrelated with all other marketing mix decisions and are made with an understanding of the internal and external decision environment. Let's take a look at these relationships.

### Marketing Mix Considerations

**Gucci**
www.gucci.com

**PRICE AND PRODUCT** The price of the product must cover the costs of doing business, but price also sends a *signal* about product quality. For example, the prices of Rolex and Gucci watches, such as the one in Exhibit 9.19, tell consumers much about the products—that they're made from durable, precision parts—and that those who can afford them are probably in an upper-income class. And although experts and the media often try to tell women that most makeup and skin care products have identical ingredients and are pretty much the same, the premium prices charged for certain brands continue to convince consumers that higher price means a better product. Sometimes it does, and sometimes it doesn't.

The stage of the product's life cycle also affects pricing. Early in the life cycle, a single firm may be the only producer of a highly desirable product. This firm is a *monopoly supplier*, so it's able to charge a premium price. Later, as competitors enter the market, prices often go down. For example, Novell Inc. sold Netware 4.0 to business customers. This product, which links up to 1000 PCs into a common network, sold for as much as $48 000 in the early growth phase, but, as the market grew, Microsoft decided to enter with a product similar to Novell's but priced at $35 000 less.[36]

**PRICE AND DISTRIBUTION** We must study pricing decisions from the viewpoint of each member of the channel of distribution—the manufacturers, wholesalers, and retailers—that help get the product to consumers. Will the pricing plan allow each channel member to be successful in reselling the

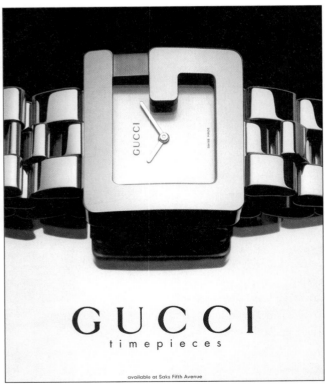

**Exhibit 9.19**
Gucci knows that its high price means a quality timepiece for many consumers.

product to end customers? Is the **margin** a wholesaler or retailer earns—the difference between their cost and their selling price—too low to cover their costs?

margin   The difference between the cost of the product and the selling price of the product.

Manufacturers usually want channel partners to perform marketing, selling, and physical distribution tasks. By taking their costs into account, channel members can figure out the margin they need to operate at a profit; a margin that covers the channel member's shipping costs, inventory costs, customer credit, overhead, and marketing and selling costs. Marketers must take these margins into consideration in deciding on a final selling price for a product. In any case, manufacturers are legally restricted from forcing channel partners to resell a product at a given price, for such control would hamper competition and hurt consumers. So, a pricing plan must appeal to channel partners on its own merits.

Consider the plight of such Canadian magazine wholesalers as Metro News or The News Group, who are intermediaries between publishers and magazine retailers. Traditionally, publishers received 50 percent of the retail price, distributors (who take the magazines from the publishers and deliver them to the wholesalers) 10 percent, and wholesalers 40 percent, which was split evenly with retailers. Retailers, in an attempt to increase their own profitability and combat price discounters, have recently sought relationships with wholesalers outside their sales region and have demanded an additional four to eight percent of the split.[37] To win contracts in this more competitive marketplace, wholesalers have increased their marketing costs, cut prices, and engaged in mergers and acquisitions. They are now seeking better terms from the publishers, who are already facing financial pressures from new media and international competitors. The publishers now need to rethink their channel and pricing strategy.

The relationship between place and price also means that marketers select retail channels that match their product's price and image. For example, a shopper would not expect to find a Rolex watch in Sears or Wal-Mart, nor expect to see Timex watches on display at Birks.

**PRICE AND COMMUNICATION** Pricing is strongly related to communication activities, if for no other reason than the firm needs to be sure it has enough revenue to pay for their advertising and promotion. It is just as important that the advertising strategies justify the cost of the product. For example, an ad for an expensive fragrance should project luxury, quality, and status imagery to convince shoppers that they are getting "quality" for their money. Even ads for high-end building materials, such as the Corian countertops in Exhibit 9.20, create a luxury appeal through advertising.

**PRICE AND RELATIONSHIP MANAGEMENT** Pricing is also strongly tied to relationship management. High-priced products often have sufficient margins to support a closer and more responsive relationship with customers. SMED, a Calgary-based builder of office interiors, for example, entertains key clients and prospective clients at a $14-million alpine retreat and takes them salmon fishing in the Queen Charlotte Islands to build relationships and gain client trust.[38] Individualized attention on such a grand scale is not possible when lower margins or purchase volumes result in less profit per customer.

**SMED**
www.smed.ca

## Environmental Considerations

**THE ECONOMY** Economic trends have an important role in directing pricing strategies. The business cycle, inflation, economic growth, and consumer confidence all help to determine whether one pricing strategy or another will succeed. But the upswings and downturns in a national economy do not affect all product categories or all regions equally. Devaluation of the Canadian dollar relative to the United States in the 1990s made American imports relatively expensive but made Canadian exports inexpensive for American consumers. Marketers need to understand how economic trends will affect their particular business.

During recessions, consumers grow more price sensitive. They switch to generic brands to get a better price and patronize discount stores and warehouse outlets. Even wealthy

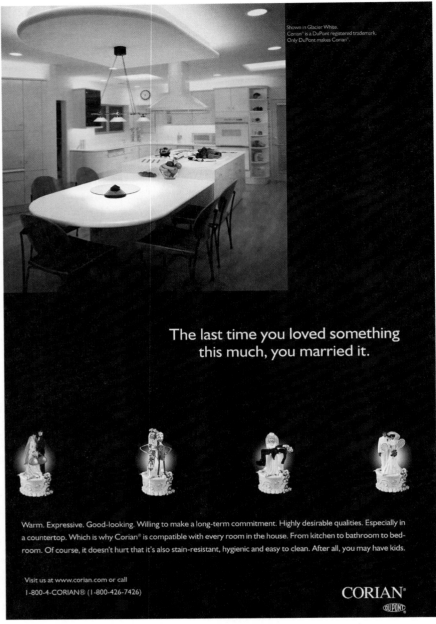

The last time you loved something
this much, you married it.

Warm. Expressive. Good-looking. Willing to make a long-term commitment. Highly desirable qualities. Especially in a countertop. Which is why Corian® is compatible with every room in the house. From kitchen to bathroom to bedroom. Of course, it doesn't hurt that it's also stain-resistant, hygienic and easy to clean. After all, you may have kids.

Visit us at www.corian.com or call
1-800-4-CORIAN® (1-800-426-7426)

Shown in Glacier White.
Corian® is a DuPont registered trademark.
Only DuPont makes Corian®.

CORIAN®

**Exhibit 9.20**

Even for building materials such as Corian countertops, advertising must justify the cost of high-end products.

households, relatively unaffected by recession, tend to cut back on conspicuous consumption, if for no other reason than to avoid attention. As a result, during periods of recession, many firms find it necessary to cut prices to levels at which costs are covered but the company doesn't make a profit to keep factories in operation. Unfortunately, price sensitivity tends to persist for a time even when a recession ends.[39] During such periods, marketers need to consider what pricing strategies will be helpful in regaining pre-recession sales and profit levels.

Recession had an even greater impact on Japanese consumers in the early 1990s. Unlike Canadian consumers, the Japanese were used to paying high prices all the time to satisfy an inefficient, multi-layered distribution system. However, this recession opened the door to discount retailing. Specialty retailers bought directly from manufacturers and were able to sell goods at least a third below department stores' prices. The trend has gained momentum, and bargain hunting is becoming a consumer sport in Japan.[40]

Economic trends also influence a firm's ability to increase prices, because they affect what consumers see as an acceptable or unacceptable price range for a product. For example, inflation accustoms consumers to price increases; but they can grow fearful for the future and whether they will have enough money to meet basic needs. In such a case, they may cut back on purchases. Then, as in periods of recession, inflation may cause marketers to lower prices and temporarily sacrifice profits to maintain sales levels. On the other hand, hyperinflation of 30 to 40 percent a month, such as Brazil experienced in the 1990s, causes consumers to spend all of their money as fast as they receive it. Pricing is particularly challenging in a hyperinflation environment.

**CONSUMERS** Another important environmental influence on price is consumer behaviour. Much of what we've said about pricing depends on economists' notions of a customer who evaluates price in a logical, rational manner. For example, the concept of demand is expressed by a smooth demand curve, which assumes that if a firm lowers a product's price from $10 to $9.50 and then from $9.50 to $9 and so on, customers will simply buy more and more. In the real world, though, it doesn't always work that way. Let's look at consumer considerations in setting prices.

**Buyers' Pricing Expectations** Often consumers base their perceptions of price on what they perceive to be the customary or fair price. For example, for many years a candy bar or a pack of gum was five cents. Consumers would have perceived any other price as too high or low. It was a nickel candy bar—period. When costs went up or inflation kicked in, the candy makers shrank the size of the bar instead of changing the price. Eventually, inflation prevailed and consumers' salaries rose, and the candy bar goes for 15 to 20 times one nickel today—a price that consumers would have found unacceptable even a decade ago.

When the price of a product is above or even sometimes when it's below what consumers expect, they are less willing to purchase the product. If the price is above their expectations, they will perceive it as a rip-off. If it is below expectations, consumers may think the product quality is unsatisfactory. By understanding the pricing expectations of their customers, marketers are better able to develop pricing strategies that meet those expectations.

Sometimes consumers' perceptions of the customary price of a product depend on their **internal reference price**—based on past experience, consumers have a set price or a price range in their mind that they refer to in evaluating a product's cost. The reference price may be the last price paid, or it may be the average of all the prices they know of similar products (Exhibit 9.21). No matter what the brand, the normal price for a standard loaf of sandwich bread is about $1.49. In some stores, it may be $1.39 and in others $1.59, but the average is $1.49. If consumers find a loaf of bread priced much higher than this—perhaps $2.99—they will feel it is overpriced and grab a competing brand. If they find bread priced significantly lower—perhaps $0.59 or $0.69—they may shy away from the purchase, wondering "what is wrong" with the bread.

Marketers may try to influence consumers' expectations of what a product should cost by using reference-pricing strategies. For example, manufacturers may show their price compared to competitors' prices in advertising. Similarly, a retailer will display a product next to a higher-priced version of the same or a different brand. The consumer must choose between the two products with different prices. Two quite different results are likely.

On the one hand, if the prices (and other characteristics) of the two products are fairly close, it is likely that the consumer will feel the product quality is similar. This is called an *assimilation effect*. The customer might think, "The price is about the same; they must be alike. I'll be a smart shopper and select the one that saves me a few dollars." And so the customer chooses the item that is priced lower, because the low price made it look attractive next to the high-priced alternative. This is why store brands of deodorant, vitamins, pain relievers, and shampoo sit beside national brands (see Exhibit 9.22), often accompanied by a shelf sign pointing out how much shoppers can save by purchasing the store brands.

On the other hand, if the prices of the two products are far apart, a *contrast effect* may result. In this case the consumer feels that the large difference in price means that there is a large difference in quality. "Gee, this lower-priced one is probably not as good as the higher-priced one. I'll splurge on the more expensive one." Using this strategy, an appliance store may place an advertised $800 refrigerator next to a $1199 model to make the customer believe the "bottom of the line" model just won't do.

**Price-Quality Inferences** Imagine that you are in a shoe store looking for a new pair of running shoes. You notice one pair priced at $89.99. On another table you see a second pair displayed. It looks almost identical to the first pair, but the price is only $24.95. Which pair do you want? Which pair do you think is the better quality? Many of us will pay the higher price, because we believe the bargain-basement shoes won't be worth the price—at any price.

> **internal reference price** A set price or a price range in consumers' minds that they refer to in evaluating a product's price.

**Exhibit 9.21**

Most consumers have an internal reference price when it comes to buying food staples like bread.

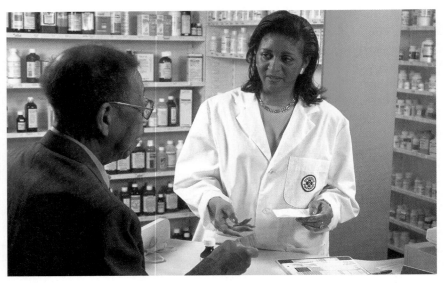

**Exhibit 9.22**

Reference pricing strategies: Pharmacists sometimes need to explain why a brand-name drug costs more than a generic drug.

Consumers make *price-quality inferences* about a product when they use price as a cue or an indicator for quality. If consumers are unable to judge the quality of a product through examination or prior experience—direct evidence—they will usually assume that the higher-priced product is the higher-quality product.

Does it make sense to believe that a product is better quality just because it has a higher price tag? The answer is: sometimes. In many cases, it is true that a higher-priced product is better. Many of us have bought a bargain-priced pair of sneakers, a private-label brand of cereal, or a less expensive brand of cellophane tape only to be disappointed. These experiences lead rational decision makers to associate price with quality, when quality cannot be otherwise perceived, especially when they have little prior experience in evaluating the item.

**THE PRICE ELASTICITY OF DEMAND** Marketers also need to know how sensitive customers are to *changes* in price. In particular, it is critical to understand whether a change in price will have a large or a small impact on demand. How much can a firm increase or decrease its price before seeing a marked change in sales? If the price of a pizza goes up $1, will people switch to subs or burgers? What would happen if the price goes up $2? $3? $5? **Price elasticity of demand** is a measure of the sensitivity of customers to changes in price: If the price changes by 10 percent, what will be the percentage change in demand for the product? The word *elasticity* reminds us that changes in price usually cause demand to stretch or retract like a rubber band.

> **price elasticity of demand** The percentage change in unit sales that results from a percentage change in price.

Price elasticity of demand is calculated as follows:

$$\text{Price elasticity of demand} = \frac{\text{percentage change in quantity demanded}}{\text{percentage change in price}} = \frac{(Q_1 - Q_2)/Q_1}{(P_1 - P_2)/P_1}$$

**Elastic and Inelastic Demand** Sometimes customers are very sensitive to changes in prices, and a change in price results in a substantial change in the quantity demanded. In such cases, demand is said to be **elastic**. In other situations, a change in price has little or no effect on the quantity that consumers are willing to buy, and demand is said to be **inelastic**.

> **price elastic** When a percentage change in price results in a larger percentage change in the quantity demanded.

> **price inelastic** When a percentage change in price results in a smaller percentage change in the quantity demanded.

For example, using the formula above, suppose the pizza maker finds (from experience or from marketing research) that lowering the price of her pizza by 10 percent (from $10 per pie to $9) will cause a 15 percent increase in demand. She would calculate the elasticity of demand as 0.15 divided by 0.10 (or 15 divided by 10). The price elasticity of demand would be 1.5. If the price elasticity of demand is greater than 1, demand is elastic; that is, consumers respond to the price decrease by demanding more. Or, if the price increases, consumers will demand less.

When demand is elastic, changes in price and in total revenues (total sales) work in opposite directions. If the price is increased, revenues decrease. If the price is decreased, there will be an increase in total revenues. With elastic demand, the demand curve shown in Figure 9.8 is more horizontal. For the pizza maker, with an elasticity of demand of 1.5, a decrease in price will increase her total sales.

**Figure 9.8** Price Elastic and Inelastic Demand Curves

In some instances, demand is inelastic so that a change in price results in little or no change in demand. For example, if the 10 percent decrease in the price of pizza resulted in only a 5 percent increase in pizza sales, then the price elasticity of demand calculated would be 5 divided by 10, which is 0.5 (less than 1), and our pizza maker faces *inelastic demand*. When demand is inelastic, price and revenue changes are in the same direction; that is, increases in price result in increases in total revenue, whereas decreases in price result in decreases in total revenue. With inelastic demand, the demand curve shown in Figure 9.8 becomes more vertical. Generally, the demand for necessities is inelastic. Even large price increases do not cause us to buy less food or to give up our telephone.

If demand is price inelastic, can marketers keep raising prices so that revenues and profits will grow larger and larger? And what if demand is elastic? Does it mean that marketers can never raise prices? The answer to these questions is "no." Elasticity of demand for a product often differs for different price levels and with different percentages of change. In the 1950s and 1960s, the price of gasoline was less than 12 cents a litre. There were the rare "gas wars" (see Exhibit 9.23), when the price of gas was less than 9 cents a litre. In those years, if the price of gasoline had increased 20 percent or more, demand would have decreased as consumers refused to pay the higher prices and simply stayed home—demand was elastic at the low price. If the price of gasoline dropped 10 cents, many consumers would decide to take more trips, drive across the country and see Victoria, PEI, or Niagara Falls. Today, gasoline prices are seldom less than 80 cents a litre, and consumers have become used to changes in gasoline prices of 5 to 10 cents a litre or more. Now a 20 percent price change is a common occurrence, making gasoline demand *price inelastic*.

**Influences on Demand Elasticity** Other factors can affect price elasticity and sales. Consider the availability of *substitute* goods or services. If a product has a close substitute, its demand will be elastic; that is, a change in price will result in a change in demand, as consumers move to buy the substitute product. For example, Coke and Pepsi may be considered close substitutes by all but the most die-hard cola fans. If the price of Pepsi goes up, many people will buy Coke instead. Marketers of products with close substitutes are less likely to compete on price, recognizing that doing so could result in less profit for everyone as consumers switch from one brand to another.

Price elasticity also depends on the time period marketers are considering. Demand that is inelastic in the short term may become elastic in the long term. In general, the longer the time period, the greater the likelihood that demand will be more elastic. Here again, the role of substitutes matters because longer time periods make it possible for substitutes to

**Exhibit 9.23**

Because demand for gasoline was price elastic, competing service stations fought for valuable customers with low, low prices in the 1960s. Now, gasoline is thought to be inelastic—at least within the range of 70 to 90 cents a litre.

enter the market. If the price of oil increases, there may not be much immediate change in the quantity demanded. However, in the long term, demand will build for alternatives for home heating, such as gas, electric, and solar power. Utilities may build more electric power plants, and auto manufacturers will develop viable electric cars and buses, and hybrid cars such as the one shown in Exhibit 9.24.

There is also an *income effect* on demand. This means changes in income affect demand for a product, even if its price remains the same. For *normal goods*, such as clothing and housing, and for luxury goods, demand is income elastic. This means that as income increases, the amount purchased increases. For necessities such as salt, toilet tissue, and toothpaste, demand is income inelastic, because changes in income do not have much impact on demand. Consumers can't do without these products. For some *inferior goods,* as income increases, demand decreases; if, in a period of economic recession, household income decreases, there is likely to be an increase in sales of dried beans, an inexpensive source of protein, whereas the number of steaks consumed goes down. But if the economy improves and incomes rise, consumers will be able to afford and demand steaks instead of beans.

Finally, the changes in prices of *other* products affect the demand for an item, a phenomenon called *cross-elasticity of demand.* When products are substitutes for each other, an increase in the price of one will increase the demand for the other. For example, if the price of bananas goes up, consumers may instead buy more strawberries, blueberries, or apples. However, when products are complements—that is, when one product is essential to the use of a second—then an increase in the price of one decreases the demand for the second. For example, if the price of gasoline goes up, consumers may drive less and, thus, demand for tires will also decrease.

**Exhibit 9.24**

The adoption of hybrid cars or electric cars is an example of how technologies and environmental change may make gasoline prices elastic again.

**CONSUMER TRENDS** Culture and demographics determine how consumers think and behave and so have a large impact on all marketing decisions. Marketers who continuously monitor the consumer environment are in a position to make better pricing decisions. These are some current trends:

- Consumers have grown disinterested in fancy stores with big markups. Grey Advertising agency calls these consumers "precision shoppers." They are more choosy, less inclined to shy away from lesser-known brands, and drawn to warehouse stores that offer inexpensive self-serve products.[41] Marketers of everything from autos to suits are scrambling to find ways to offer value and build bonds with customers who are weary of glitzy promotions and overpriced merchandise.

- Consumers want to be able to afford tokens of success. In the last decade, sales of products such as Lee Valley tools, Calvin Klein fragrances, and BMW cars soared because they offered consumers a unique prestige product image—driving a BMW tells other drivers that "you've made it." Much of the success Starbucks has enjoyed is a result of their gourmet coffee being an "affordable luxury."

- Many of the women who opted for a career in their twenties are hearing the ticking of their biological clocks as they enter their late thirties and early forties. But couples having babies later in their lives are often better off financially than younger parents, and they are far more willing to spend whatever it costs to give their babies the best. For producers of products for babies and children, this means that price resistance is rather low within the group. Such parents have no problem spending $50 or more for a Beatrix Potter musical crib mobile and don't even flinch at the $75 price tag on a Wedgwood china Peter Rabbit cereal bowl and mug.

**THE COMPETITION** Decision makers must always consider how the competition will respond to their pricing actions. They know that consumers' expectations of what constitutes a fair price depend on what the competition is charging. The Marriott hotel chain, for example, monitors the room rates of Hilton, Hyatt, and other chains.

In the cut-throat fast-food industry, when Burger King trotted out its 99-cent Whopper, McDonald's retaliated with a 55-cent Big Mac (see Exhibit 9.25), and third-place Wendy's increased promotion of its 99-cent chicken nuggets and Double-Stack cheeseburgers.[42] It's not always a good idea to fight the competition with lower and lower prices. Pricing wars, like those in the fast-food industry, can change consumers' perceptions of what is a "fair" price, leaving them unwilling to buy at previous price levels. This will be a challenge in Coke's new premium pricing strategy as years of discounting have conditioned consumers to expect to pay less than $2.99 for a two-litre bottle. In addition, when firms focus on price competition, they often ignore the need to satisfy other customer wants. For instance, many consumers have become dissatisfied with traditional burgers at any price and are looking for restaurants that offer better-tasting meals.

The type of competitive environment in which an industry operates—whether it's an oligopoly, monopolistic competition, or pure competition—also influences price decisions. Generally, firms that do business in an oligopoly, in which the market has few sellers and many buyers, are more likely to adopt *status quo* pricing objectives, in which the pricing of all competitors is similar. Such objectives are attractive to oligopolistic firms because avoiding

**Exhibit 9.25**

In a price war strategy, McDonald's reduced the Big Mac's price to 55 cents when part of a Meal Deal.

price competition allows all players in the industry to remain profitable. The Canadian gasoline industry is an oligopoly, in which a few large petroleum refiners, such as Irving Oil, Shell, and Petro-Canada, control most of the market.

In a state of monopolistic competition, in which there are many sellers each offering a slightly different product, it is possible for firms to differentiate products and to focus on non-price competition. Thrifty Foods, a Vancouver Island grocery chain, for example, faces competition from Canada Safeway, the Real Canadian Superstore (Loblaw's), Save-On-Foods, Costco, other warehouse clubs, and other independent food retailers. This level of competition makes it difficult for Thrifty Foods to compete on price. Instead they focus on being competitively priced with superior quality, choice, service, and retail innovation. To combat consumer perceptions that their prices were higher than others, the company introduced a new tag line, "We never lower our standards—just our prices," and has experienced increased market share despite increased competition from big-box discounters.

Firms in a purely competitive market have little opportunity to raise or lower prices. Rather, the price of soybeans, corn, or fresh peaches is directly influenced by supply and demand. When bad weather hurts crops, prices go up. And prices for almost any kind of fish have increased dramatically since health-conscious consumers began turning away from beef and other red meat.

**INTERNATIONAL ENVIRONMENTAL INFLUENCES** Different situations influence pricing decisions by firms conducting international trade, including the *currency exchange rate*. Japanese auto sales in Canada soared by 36 percent in 1997, and total Japanese imports doubled.[43] This increase in market share was fuelled by a lower yen and higher U.S. dollar that made North American models more expensive for Canadian consumers.

In international markets, national or local government strategies can lead to differences in the prices competitors charge for products in global markets. Government **price subsidies** to domestic industries, in the form of either an outright payment or a tax relief, allow some firms to sell their products at prices often below production costs. Prairie farmers face this situation as low grain prices and U.S. and European subsidies have combined to put Canadian farmers at a severe competitive disadvantage; they are seeking as much as one billion dollars in federal and provincial aid to make up for lost revenue.[44] American forest companies claim that Canada's software lumber is unfairly subsidized and have successfully lobbied for import restrictions.[45]

Want to take a luxury cruise? There'll be plenty of room thanks to European taxpayers. Between 1997 and 2000, European shipbuilders built over 30 new cruise ships. Cruise ship prices are low because of European Union government subsidies (up to nine percent of the price of the vessels) designed to keep ship-building labour on the job.[46]

**price subsidies** Government payments made to protect domestic businesses or to reimburse them when they must price at or below cost to make a sale. The subsidy can be a cash payment or tax relief.

# PRICING WITH ELECTRONIC COMMERCE

As we have seen, pricing for "bricks-and-mortar" firms is a complex decision process. But with the advent of the Internet, a whole new set of options appeared. Many experts suggest that technology is creating a pricing revolution that might change pricing forever—and create the most efficient market ever, some say. Because sellers are connected to buyers around the globe as never before through the Internet, corporate networks, and wireless setups, marketers can offer consumers deals tailored to a single person at a single moment.[47]

For firms that want to sell to other businesses (B2B firms), the Internet means that they can change prices rapidly to adapt to changing costs. For consumers who have lots of stuff in the attic they need to put in someone else's attic (C2C e-commerce), the Internet means an opportunity for consumers to find ready buyers. And for B2C firms, firms that sell to consumers, the Internet offers other opportunities. In this section we will discuss some of the more popular Internet pricing strategies.

# Dynamic Pricing Strategies

One of the most important opportunities offered by the Internet is **dynamic pricing**, where the price can easily be adjusted to meet changes in the marketplace (Exhibit 9.26). Posting merchandise for sale on the Web means the costs of price changes are negligible. If a retail store wants to change prices, new price tags must be placed on items, new store display signage and media advertising must be created and displayed, and new prices input into the store's computer system. For business-to-business marketers, catalogues and price lists must be printed and distributed to salespeople and to customers. These activities can be very costly to a firm, so firms simply don't change their prices very often. Because the cost of changing prices on the Internet is practically zero, firms are able to respond quickly and, if necessary, frequently, to changes in costs, changes in supply, and/or changes in demand. Tickets.com adjusts concert ticket prices based on supply and demand.

Because it's so easy to change prices on the Internet, firms can test different pricing strategies. For example, if a firm wants to see if a 5 percent increase in price will affect sales, it might try the new pricing strategy on every twentieth customer and then see if the rate of sales decreases among that group of customers. As a result, the company reports it has been able to increase revenue by as much as 45 percent.[48]

**dynamic pricing** Pricing strategy in which the price can easily be adjusted to meet changes in the marketplace.

# Auctions

Hundreds of Internet **online auctions** allow shoppers to bid on everything from Beanie Babies to health and fitness equipment to a Wayne Gretzky hockey stick. Auctions provide a second Internet pricing strategy. Perhaps the most popular auctions are the C2C auctions such as those on eBay. The eBay auction is an open auction, meaning that the buyers all know the highest price bid at any point in time. In many Internet auction sites the seller can set a reserve price, a price below which the item will not be sold.

Many B2B sites offer reverse-price auctions in which buyers ask sellers to submit quotations for a desired product. The supplier with the lowest bid wins the sales. Priceline.com offers customers goods and services in first-price, sealed-bid auctions (Exhibit 9.27). This means that potential buyers may offer a single price to a potential seller of a product (such as an airline ticket). In the case of Priceline.com, bidders guarantee their bids with a credit

**online auctions** E-commerce that allows shoppers to purchase products through online bidding.

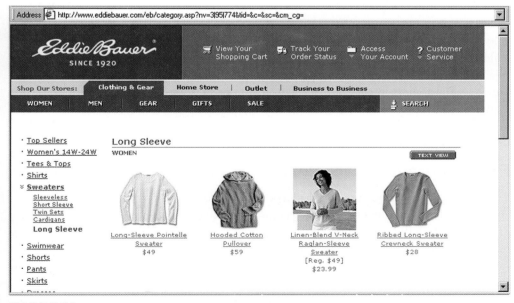

**Exhibit 9.26**

Online retailers have an advantage over bricks-and-mortar retailers in that they can use dynamic pricing. They can easily and quickly change prices to adjust to supply, demand, and costs.

**Exhibit 9.27**

Priceline.com uses a "first price" auction strategy for airline tickets, hotel rooms, even cruises. Customers make a bid and Priceline checks to see if any suppliers are willing to sell at that price.

card. Priceline then checks to see if any airline is willing to sell a ticket for or below the bid price.

## Price Discrimination

For years, some catalogue marketers have sent out more than one catalogue version with different prices based on what they know different customer segments are willing to pay. Customers in one area code may receive a catalogue with prices that are 10 or 15 percent higher on many items than customers who live in a different area code area. This practice, called price discrimination, is even more easily implemented on the Web in situations in which Internet marketers know more about customers who shop on the Web and can segment them easily and quickly.

Price discrimination means that marketers classify customers based on some characteristic that indicates what they are willing or able to pay. Movie theatres offer lower prices to children and *Maclean's* magazine offers college students lower subscription rates. The downside is that customers who pay the higher price usually aren't thrilled about this if they find out. When customers found out that Amazon.com was testing prices using a price discrimination strategy, they were outraged. The random price test charged some customers 3 to 5 percent more than other customers for DVD movies. Amazon.com refunded $3.10 each to more than 6000 customers.

## Pricing Advantages for Online Shoppers

The Internet also creates unique challenges for marketers in terms of prices. As we've already discussed, consumers or business customers are gaining more control over the buying process. With the availability of search engines and "shopbots" they are less at the mercy of firms handing out prices that they must accept. The result is that customers have become more price sensitive. For example, online drugstores have been stealing customers from traditional pharmacies by offering drastically lower prices: As one illustration, a comparison study found Rogaine priced at $53.99 at Rite Aid while at the same time the same anti-baldness product could be purchased online for $47.39 at More.com.[49] (That's a hair-raising difference!)

Detailed information about what products actually cost manufacturers, available from sites such as consumerreports.org, can give consumers more negotiating power when shopping for new cars and other big-ticket items. Finally, e-commerce potentially can lower consumers' costs due to the gasoline, time, and aggravation saved by avoiding a trip to the mall.

# Real People, Real Decisions

## How It Worked Out at the Brentwood Bay Lodge and Spa

After considering the fine art gallery's three commission options, Leanne Cadden decided to implement option 2. All artists would receive 50 percent of the art sale, The fine art gallery would receive 40 percent towards department overhead, operating, and marketing costs, and 10 percent would be donated to the charity on behalf of Brentwood Bay Lodge and Spa. Everyone would be under the same guidelines and there would be no special treatment.

As expected, some artists did not like this arrangement. Cadden lost one artist who had sold over $400 000 in art the previous year, because she would not offer 60 percent commissions. However, because this project had so much to offer in the way of high quality standards in all aspects of the resort,

including its clientele, Cadden was able to start with an elite list of 20 featured artists for the 2004 opening. Most of the artists on board were extremely well-known and had great sales histories; others were chosen for the potential that Cadden saw in their work. These artists saw the advantages of reaching BBL's clientele and valued the higher than average promotional support being offered by the fine art gallery.

Cadden sold more than $17 000 of art in the first week of business following her opening art show. She learned that she needs systems to make purchasing art easier and she needs to educate the other lodge staff on the art, where its located, and how to handle a sales transaction so art can be sold when she is not there.

# CHAPTER SUMMARY

## 1. Explain the importance of pricing and how prices can take both monetary and non-monetary forms.

Price, the amount of outlay of money, goods, services, or deeds given in exchange for a product, can be monetary or non-monetary. Bartering occurs when consumers or businesses exchange one product for another. Pricing is important to firms, because it creates profits and influences customers to purchase. Pricing decisions are tied to decisions about the rest of the marketing mix. Prices must allow channel members to cover their costs and make a profit. Prices vary during stages in the product life cycle. Prices must cover the cost of promotions, and promotions must justify the product price.

## 2. Understand the pricing objectives that marketers typically have in planning pricing strategies.

Effective pricing objectives are designed to support corporate and marketing objectives and often focus on sales (to maximize sales or to increase market share), or they may specify a desired level of profit growth or profit margin. At other times, firms may develop pricing objectives for competitive effect, to increase customer satisfaction, or to communicate a certain image to prospective customers. Pricing objectives need to be flexible to adapt to different geographic areas and time periods.

## 3. Understand the pricing strategies used to achieve different pricing objectives.

The most commonly used pricing strategies are based on cost. Though easy to calculate and "safe," cost-based strategies do not consider demand, the competition, the stage in the product life cycle, plant capacity, or product image. Cost-based strategies include cost-plus pricing—markup on cost or markup on selling price—and price-floor pricing and these help organizations achieve profit or target return objectives.

Pricing strategies based on demand require that marketers estimate demand at different prices to be certain they can sell what they produce. Such strategies include target cost pricing which starts with the desired price and the product (and its costs) is designed to meet that price. Yield management sets different prices for different market segments, based on their willingness and ability to pay. Variable (custom) pricing is when prices are negotiated on a customer-by-customer basis. Skimming strategy attempts to maximize profits by charging a high price for new products.

Strategies to achieve market share objectives include value pricing (everyday low pricing), frequent discounting, penetration pricing (for new products), and trial pricing (for new products). All of these strategies involve low prices to stimulate demand.

Firms that focus on customer needs in developing pricing strategies may consider everyday low price (EDLP) or value pricing strategies. If a new product has unique customer benefits and demand is inelastic, a firm can charge a high skimming price to recover research, development, and promotional costs. If the firm needs to encourage more customers and discourage competitors from entering the market, it may use a very low penetration price. Trial pricing means setting a low price for a limited time.

Strategies to achieve competitive objectives include a price leader strategy, often used in an oligopoly where it is best for all to avoid competition. In parity pricing, a firm sets the same price as competitors. Finally, strategies to achieve image enhancement or positioning objectives include premium pricing and prestige pricing.

## 4. Apply pricing tactics to set price points.

There are numerous tactics marketers use in setting prices. These include two-part pricing where individual products like cell phones have an initial cost and a usage cost (time). Pricing for multiple products includes price bundling (selling two or more products together for one price) and captive pricing, where there is a base price plus ongoing supply or operating costs—such as with a printer and toner or ink. Geographic pricing takes into account different tactics for charging for delivery costs. Price discounts are the trade, quantity, cash, and seasonal discounting tactics used to stimulate demand from customers and distributors.

Psychological pricing tactics include odd (even) number pricing and price lining—the tactic of having a standard range of prices for a product line, such as found for televisions and computers.

5. **Understand key implementation and legal issues with respect to pricing.**

   Most marketers seek to avoid unethical or illegal pricing practices. Deceptive pricing practices include illegal bait-and-switch pricing and superficial discounting. The federal Competition Act prohibits predatory pricing, price discrimination, horizontal or vertical price maintenance, and bid rigging.

6. **Understand some of the environmental factors that affect pricing strategies, including the Internet.**

   Like other elements of the marketing mix, pricing is influenced by a variety of internal and external environmental factors. External factors include economic trends, such as inflation and recession, and the firm's competitive environment, such as the number and size of competing firms. Pricing can also be influenced by consumer behaviour and changing consumer trends, and by differences in international market environments. Internal environment considerations include product costs and other elements of the marketing mix. The Internet provides opportunities for dynamic pricing, auctions, and price discrimination, but creates challenges for marketers in that customers have easy access to competitor prices.

# CHAPTER REVIEW

## Marketing Concepts: Testing Your Knowledge

1. Explain how pricing decisions are important to firms.
2. Explain variable costs, fixed costs, average variable costs, average fixed costs, and average total costs.
3. What is break-even analysis? How do marketers use break-even analysis?
4. What are some common pricing objectives and strategies to achieve them?
5. What are the advantages and disadvantages of pricing strategies based on demand? Explain yield management.
6. For new products, when is skimming pricing more appropriate and when is penetration pricing the best strategy? When would trial pricing be an effective pricing strategy?
7. Explain key pricing tactics used by marketers and when they would be appropriate.
8. Explain these unethical or illegal pricing practices: bait and switch; predatory pricing; price discrimination; price maintenance; bid rigging.
9. How are pricing decisions interrelated with other elements of the marketing mix?
10. What are some ways in which external environmental factors affect price planning?
11. What is price elasticity and what external influences affect demand elasticity?
12. What are the pricing implications of the Internet?

## Marketing Concepts: Discussing Choices and Issues

1. Governments sometimes provide price subsidies to specific industries; that is, they reduce a domestic firm's costs so that they can sell products on the international market at a lower price. What reasons do governments (and politicians) use for these government subsidies? What are the benefits and disadvantages to domestic industries in the long run? How about to international customers? Who would benefit or lose if all price subsidies were eliminated?

2. Critics of business often accuse marketers of taking advantage of consumers by setting prices that are far above the cost of producing the good or service—sometimes 10 or 20 or more times the cost. How do you feel about this? What reasons might a manufacturer of luxury products have for setting very high prices? Why might a pharmaceutical firm set the prices of its life-saving medicines higher than the cost of production requires?

3. With a price leadership strategy, firms can avoid price competition and yet not be guilty of illegal collusion—getting together to set prices. Although it is legal, is a price leadership strategy ethical? How does a price leadership strategy hurt and how does it help the industry? What benefits does it provide and what problems does it pose for customers?

4. Everyday low pricing strategies have met with limited success. What do you think are the advantages and disadvantages of EDLP? Are some products more suited to it than others? Why have customers not been more responsive to EDLP? What do you think its future will be?

5. Two-part pricing and payment pricing are pricing tactics that are designed to make price more palatable to customers and to better meet their needs. But do these policies always benefit consumers? What are the advantages and disadvantages of these pricing approaches for the average consumer? For business customers?

6. Technology is said to be creating a pricing revolution. How is electronic commerce changing pricing strategies? In what ways are such changes good for customers? In what ways are the changes good for sellers?

## Marketing Practice: Applying What You've Learned

1. Assume that you are the director of marketing for a large Rocky Mountain ski resort. It is essential that the resort maintain a high occupancy rate during the skiing season. Pricing is an important part of your marketing strategy, because the demand for rooms at your resort is very price elastic. For this reason, you feel that you should develop contingency pricing plans for use during changes in the economic environment (inflation and recessions, for example). List the economic conditions that might warrant changes in the pricing strategy, and give your recommendations for each possibility.

2. Assume that you are the assistant director of marketing for a firm that manufactures a line of hair-care products (e.g., shampoos, conditioners). This morning, your boss came into your office and announced that she is going to recommend a dramatic price increase. You respond by saying, "Well, I guess that means we need to totally revamp our marketing plan." To this, she replies, "No, all we're going to do is to raise the price. We're not going to mess with anything else." After she leaves you think, "I've got to convince her that we can't make pricing decisions without considering the other elements of the marketing mix. It's all interrelated."

   In a role-playing situation with one of your classmates, explain to your boss why you think the marketing department should consider the implications of the price increase on the other marketing mix elements, what you feel these implications are, and what recommendations for change might be suggested.

3. As the vice-president for marketing in a firm that markets computer software, you must regularly develop pricing strategies for new software products. Your latest product is a software package that automatically translates any foreign language e-mail messages into the user's preferred language. You are trying to decide on the pricing for this new product. Should you use a skimming price, a penetration price, or something in between? With a classmate taking the role of another marketing professional with your firm, argue in front of your class the pros and cons for each alternative.

4. Assume that you are working in the marketing department of a firm that manufactures furnaces and air conditioners. Previously, your firm has limited its operations to manufacturing units for other OEM companies. Now your firm is expanding. You will be manufacturing your product for sale with your own brand name and will be selling to heating and air-conditioning distributors across the country. What pricing objectives, strategies, and tactics will you adopt?

5. Assume that you and your friend have decided to go into business together manufacturing wrought iron birdcages. You know that your fixed costs (rent on a building, equipment, for example) will be $60 000 a year. You expect your variable costs to be $12 per birdcage.

   a. If you plan on selling the birdcages to retail stores for $18, how many must you sell to break even; that is, what is your break-even quantity?

   b. Assume that you and your partner feel that you must set a goal of achieving $10 000 profit with your business this year. How many units would you have to sell to make that amount of profit?

c. What if you feel that you will be able to sell no more than 5000 birdcages? What price will you have to charge to break even? To make $10 000 in profit?

## Marketing Mini-Project: Learning by Doing

Organizations develop pricing strategies to meet pricing objectives. These objectives may be related to sales, profit, the competition, customer satisfaction, or the image of the product. The purpose of this mini-project is to help you understand how different pricing objectives are important in marketing planning.

Many universities are having trouble filling up their existing dormitory space, as more and more students choose to live off campus in houses or in apartments. Identify your university's existing pricing objectives and develop recommendations for changes.

1. First, with two or three of your classmates, interview someone who participates in your university's pricing of dormitory space. It may be the vice-president for student affairs, the dean of students, the director of student life, or the vice-president for business and finance. Try to find out:

   a. The current prices charged for dormitory space.

   b. What the pricing objectives for dormitory space are.

   c. How the prices are calculated.

   d. The part that costs, demand, customer satisfaction, and competitive housing prices play in setting the dorm prices.

2. Next talk with students in your school to find out:

   a. Students' attitudes toward the prices charged for dormitory space.

   b. What a customer-pleasing price would be for dormitory space.

   c. The type and price of alternative housing used by students.

   d. Any other relevant student attitudes toward dormitory housing.

3. Develop a report that includes your findings and the recommendations you would make to your university. Be sure to focus on the pricing objectives currently in use and the alternative objectives that might be considered. What pricing strategies do your findings suggest? Present your results to your class.

## Real People, Real Surfers: Exploring the Web

Barter exchanges are organizations that facilitate barter transactions between buyers and sellers. Many of the Canadian exchanges are members of the International Reciprocal Trade Association (IRTA) or the American National Association of Trade Exchanges (NATE).

First, visit the IRTA (**www.irta.net**) or NATE (**www.nate.org**) Web pages. Using links from those home pages to member exchanges or using an Internet search engine, locate and explore several barter exchange Web pages. Based on your Internet experience, answer the following questions:

1. What are the benefits to a business of joining a barter exchange?

2. What types of products are bartered?

3. How does a trade actually work with a barter exchange?

4. How does the exchange make its money? Who pays the exchange, and how much is charged?

5. Assuming the goal of barter exchange Web sites is to attract new members, evaluate the different Web sites you visited. Which Web site do you think was best? What features of the site would make you want to join if you were the owner of a small business? What features of the other sites made them less appealing than this one?

## Chapter 9 **Pharmaceutical Pricing Strategy**

American citizens and seniors are literally getting sick of the soaring costs of U.S. prescription drugs, and people are looking to Canada for a solution. Unlike the United States, Canada has a prescription drug price cap that makes prescription drugs cost, on average, 67 percent less than they do south of the border.[50] This massive price gap is enticing millions of Americans to re-import drugs from Canada via the Internet and to make quick trips across the border; a trend that the U.S. government is concerned with.

The FDA and federal regulators alike stress that pharmaceutical re-importation from Canada is both illegal and unsafe.[51] However this argument holds little credibility as the drugs were produced in the same plants as those sold in the United States. In 2002 the pharmaceutical industry was the thirteenth largest contributor to political candidates injecting $21.9 million dollars into lobbying efforts, 80 percent of which went to the Republican Party.[52] There is little doubt that the FDA and federal regulators are acting in harmony with the wishes of the large pharmaceutical companies—known as Big Pharma.

In 2002 more than one million U.S. patients bought prescription drugs from Canada without a single reported case of any harm.[53] Many people, including Illinois governor Blagovevich, believe that the U.S. Federal Government's primary interest is in protecting the pharmaceutical industry.[54] The U.S. government is considering passing legislation that makes it legal to re-import drugs from Canada. This legislation would allow American pharmaceutical wholesalers, pharmacists, and individuals access to Canadian vendors selling their drugs at low, government-controlled prices. This would enable millions of Americans—not just a handful of bus-riding seniors and Web surfers—to enjoy Canadian style discounts.[55] The catch is that companies such as Pfizer, GlaxoSmithKline, AstraZeneca, and Wyeth, who have already limited shipping to Canada, would further restrict Canadian bound drug exports; essentially stripping Canadian drug cupboards. However, because pharmaceutical prices in Canada are still 30 percent to 50 percent higher than in most other parts of the world—cutting Canadian sales would impact the pharmaceutical companies' bottom line.

Another proposed solution to the issue is to impose price controls in the United States. This is unlikely to be a popular choice because it is against the interest of Big Pharma who would lose an estimated $600 billion over the next decade.[56] This loss of revenue could lead to cutting research and development work, which could reduce medical breakthroughs. "Today, 15 of the 20 top-selling pharmaceuticals world wide, a list that includes life-saving medicines such as the cholesterol-lowing Lipitor and the anti-psychotic Zyprexa, were created in the United States; none in Canada, and just 5 in the rest of the world."[57] Although controlling drug prices would be great on the wallet in the short run, it may be prevent companies from discovering and creating life-saving pharmaceuticals in the future. Critics argue that most pharmaceutical companies spend about 40 percent of their revenue on marketing—some of which could pay for the R&D.[58] U.S. consumers are paying for the research and development that benefits consumers all around the world.

The rising prices of U.S. pharmaceuticals are forcing some seniors to decide between medication and groceries. Millions of people have already chosen to get their medication from Canada but the U.S. government is not happy with this present situation. Some suggest that increasing patent protection is best, others think re-importing from Canada is better, and some believe that price controls in the United States are the answer. Each proposed solution has its downfalls. Is there a solution that would allow seniors in the United States to afford medication, allow Canadians to keep their drug cabinets stocked, and allow the Big Pharma companies to keep earning enough revenue to invest sufficient money into R&D?

## Things to Think About

1. If you were a Big Pharma executive, what pricing strategies would you adopt in the United States, in Canada, and in the rest of the world?

2. If you were head of the U.S. Federal Drug Administration, what pricing strategy, if any, would you legislate?

3. Do you think it is fair for pharmaceutical companies to restrict shipment to Canada so Americans won't be able to re-import as many pharmaceuticals?

4. Is the argument of the critics valid—is it reasonable to expect pharmaceutical companies to spend less on marketing and divert that money to R&D?

## Access Toyota

After Toyota introduced its no-hassle, no-negotiating "Access Toyota" pricing strategy, many Canadian consumers were relieved that they wouldn't have to bargain for a fair price on a new car. Toyota's idea was to present car buyers with a fixed sticker price that could not be negotiated. This pricing policy seemed like a great idea until interested Toyota car buyers went to dealerships that did not employ the "Access Toyota" policy. When car buyers shopped around, they realized that the $400 difference between the regularly advertised ticketed price and the Access program price was menial compared to the average $900 negotiated difference at non-Access dealerships. Despite this difference, Access program dealerships were not willing to budge on their prices. This fixed pricing scheme incorporated in the Access Toyota program was brought to the attention of the Competition Bureau of Canada, which investigated the fairness and competitiveness of the program. Although Toyota was found not guilty, it chose to pay for all legal and court fees; shortly after the court case ended, Toyota made a $200 000 donation to a Canadian charity. While dealers always have the discretion to sell their cars at whatever prices they choose, Toyota Access dealers have chosen to stick to the program and not budge a dollar.

## Questions

1. Do you think the Access Toyota program is an appropriate pricing strategy for a car retailer?
2. On what basis would the Competition Bureau have investigated this pricing strategy?
3. What risks does Toyota run in having some dealers adopt this program and others not?

Source: This case was prepared by Brock Smith and is based on *Disclosure*, "Access Toyota," # 20212.

To develop marketing strategies to meet the goals of an organization effectively and efficiently, it is essential that marketers understand and use a variety of financial analyses. This appendix provides some of these basic financial analyses, including a review of the income statement and balance sheet as well as some basic performance ratios. In addition, this appendix includes an explanation of some of the specific calculations that marketers use routinely in determining price.

## INCOME STATEMENT AND BALANCE SHEET

The two most important documents used to explain the financial situation of a company are the income statement and the balance sheet. The *income statement* (which is sometimes referred to as the profit and loss statement) provides a summary of the revenues and expenses of a firm—that is, the amount of income a company received from sales or other sources, the amount of money it spent, and the resulting income or loss that the company experienced.

The major elements of the income statement are

**Gross sales:** the total of all income the firm receives from the sales of goods and services.

**Net sales revenue:** the gross sales minus the amount for returns and promotional or other allowances given to customers.

**Cost of goods sold** (sometimes called the *cost of sales*): the cost of inventory or goods that the firm has sold.

**Gross margin** (also called *gross profit*): the amount of sales revenue that is in excess of the cost of goods sold.

**Operating expenses:** expenses other than the cost of goods sold that are necessary for conducting business. These may include salaries, rent, depreciation on buildings and equipment, insurance, utilities, supplies, and property taxes.

**Operating income** (sometimes called *income from operations*): the gross margin minus the operating expenses. Sometimes accountants prepare an *operating statement*, which is similar to the income statement except that the final calculation is the operating income—that is, other revenues or expenses and taxes are not included.

**Other revenue and expenses:** income and/or expenses other than those required for conducting the business. These may include such items as interest income/expenses and any gain or loss experienced on the sale of property or plant assets.

**Taxes:** the amount of income tax the firm owes calculated as a percentage of income.

**Net income** (sometimes called *net earnings* or *net profit*): the excess of total revenue over total expenses.

Table 9.A1 shows the income statement for an imaginary company, DLL Incorporated. DLL is a typical merchandising firm. Note that the income statement is for a specific year and includes income and expenses from January 1 through December 31 inclusive. The following comments explain the meaning of some of the important entries included in this statement.

- DLL Inc. has total or gross sales during the year of $253 950. This figure was adjusted, however, by deducting the $3000 worth of goods returned and special allowances given to customers and by $2100 in special discounts. Thus the actual or net sales generated by sales is $248 850.

- The cost of goods sold is calculated by adding the inventory of goods on January 1 to the amount purchased during the year and then subtracting the inventory of goods on December 31. In this case, DLL had $60 750 worth of inventory on hand on January 1. During the year the firm made purchases in the amount of $135 550. This amount, however, was reduced by purchase returns and allowances of $1500 and by purchase discounts of $750, so the net purchase is only $133 300.

There is also an amount on the statement labelled "Freight-In." This is the amount spent by the firm in shipping charges to get goods to its facility from suppliers. Any expenses for freight from DLL to its customers (Freight-Out) would be an operating expense. In this case, the Freight-In expense of $2450 is added to net purchase costs. Then these costs of current purchases are added to the beginning inventory to show that during the year the firm had a total of $196 500 in goods available for sale. Finally, the inventory of goods held on December 31 is subtracted from the goods available, for the total cost of goods sold of $136 200. For a manufacturer, calculation of the cost of goods sold would be a bit more complicated and would probably include separate figures for such items as inventory of finished goods, the "work-in-process" inventory, the raw materials inventory, and the cost of goods delivered to customers during the year.

**Table 9.A1** DLL Inc. Income Statement for the Year Ended December 31, 20XX

| | | | |
|---|---|---|---|
| Gross Sales | | | $253 950 |
| Less: Sales Returns and Allowances | | $ 3000 | |
| Sales Discounts | | 2100 | 5100 |
| Net Sales Revenue | | | $248 850 |
| **Cost of Goods Sold** | | | |
| Inventory, January 1, 20XX | | $ 60 750 | |
| Purchases | $135 550 | | |
| Less: Purchase Returns and Allowances | 1500 | | |
| Purchase Discounts | 750 | | |
| Net Purchases | $133 300 | | |
| Plus: Freight-In | 2450 | 135 750 | |
| Goods Available for Sale | | 196 500 | |
| Less: Inventory, December 31, 20XX | | 60 300 | |
| Cost of Goods Sold | | | $136 200 |
| Gross Margin | | | 112 650 |
| **Operating Expenses** | | | |
| Salaries and Commissions | | 15 300 | |
| Rent | | 12 600 | |
| Insurance | | 1 500 | |
| Depreciation | | 900 | |
| Supplies | | 825 | |
| Total Operating Expenses | | | 31 125 |
| Operating Income | | | 81 525 |
| **Other Revenue and (Expenses)** | | | |
| Interest Revenue | | 1500 | |
| Interest Expense | | (2250) | (750) |
| Income before Tax | | | 80 775 |
| Taxes (40%) | | | 32 310 |
| Net Income | | | $ 48 465 |

- The cost of goods sold is subtracted from the net sales revenue to get a gross margin of $112 650.

- Operating expenses for DLL include the salaries and commissions paid to its employees, rent on facilities and/or equipment, insurance, depreciation of capital items, and the cost of operating supplies. DLL has a total of $31 125 in operating expenses, which is deducted from the gross margin. Thus DLL has an operating income of $81 525.

- DLL had both other income and expenses in the form of interest revenues of $1500 and interest expenses of $2250, making a total other expense of $750, which was subtracted from the operating income, leaving an income before tax of $80 775.

- Finally, the income before tax is reduced by 40 percent ($32 310) for taxes, leaving a net income of $48 465. The 40 percent is an average amount for federal and provincial corporate income taxes incurred by most firms.

The *balance sheet* lists the assets, liabilities, and stockholders' equity of the firm. Whereas the income statement represents what happened during an entire year, the balance sheet is like a snapshot; it shows the firm's financial situation at one point in time. For this reason, the balance sheet is sometimes called the *statement of financial position*.

Table 9.A2 shows DLL Inc.'s balance sheet for December 31. Assets are any economic resource that is expected to benefit the firm in the short or long term. Current assets are items that are normally expected to be turned into cash or used up during the next twelve months or during the firm's normal operating cycle. Current assets for DLL include cash, securities, accounts receivable (money owed to the firm and not yet paid) inventory on hand, prepaid insurance, and supplies: a total of $84 525. *Long-term assets* include all assets that are not current assets. For DLL, these are property, plant, equipment, furniture, and fixtures less an amount for depreciation, or $45 300. The total assets for DLL are $129 825.

A firm's *liabilities* are its *economic obligations*, or debts that are payable to individuals or organizations outside the firm. *Current liabilities* are debts due in the coming

**Table 9.A2** DLL Inc. Balance Sheet: December 31, 20XX

**Assets**
*Current Assets*

| | | |
|---|---|---|
| Cash | $ 4275 | |
| Marketable Securities | 12 000 | |
| Accounts Receivable | 6900 | |
| Inventory | 60 300 | |
| Prepaid Insurance | 300 | |
| Supplies | 150 | |
| Total Current Assets | | 84 525 |

*Long-Term Assets—Property, Plant and Equipment*

| | | | |
|---|---|---|---|
| Furniture and Fixtures | $42 300 | | |
| Less: Accumulated Depreciation | 4500 | 37 800 | |
| Land | | 7500 | |
| Total Long-Term Assets | | | 45 300 |
| Total Assets | | | $129 825 |

**Liabilities**
*Current Liabilities*

| | | |
|---|---|---|
| Accounts Payable | $70 500 | |
| Unearned Sales Revenue | 1050 | |
| Wages Payable | 600 | |
| Interest Payable | 300 | |
| Total Current Liabilities | | 72 450 |

*Long-Term Liabilities*

| | | |
|---|---|---|
| Note Payable | | 18 900 |
| Total Liabilities | | 91 350 |

*Stockholders' Equity*

| | | |
|---|---|---|
| Common Stock | 15 000 | |
| Retained Earnings | 23 475 | |
| Total Stockholders' Equity | | 38 475 |
| Total Liabilities and Stockholders' Equity | | $129 825 |

year or in the firm's normal operating cycle. For DLL, the current liabilities—the accounts payable, unearned sales revenue, wages payable, and interest payable—total $72 450. *Long-term liabilities* (in the case of DLL, a note in the amount of $18 900) are all liabilities that are not due during the coming cycle. *Stockholders' equity* is the value of the stock and the corporation's capital or retained earnings. DLL has $15 000 in common stock and $23 475 in retained earnings for a total stockholders' equity of $38 475. Total liabilities always equal total assets—in this case, $129 825.

## IMPORTANT FINANCIAL PERFORMANCE RATIOS

How do managers and financial analysts compare the performance of a firm from one year to the next? How do investors compare the performance of one firm with that of another? Often, a number of different financial ratios provide important information for such comparisons. Such ratios are percentage figures comparing various

income statement items to net sales. Ratios provide a better way to compare performance than simple dollar sales or cost figures for two reasons. They enable analysts to compare the performance of large and small firms, and they provide a fair way to compare performance over time, without having to take inflation and other changes into account. In this section we will explain the basic operating ratios. Other measures of performance that marketers frequently use and that are also explained here are the inventory turnover rate and return on investment (ROI).

## Operating Ratios

Measures of performance calculated directly from the information in a firm's income statement (sometimes called an operating statement) are called the *operating ratios*. Each ratio compares some income statement item to net sales. The most useful of these are the *gross margin ratio, the net income ratio, the operating expense ratio, and the returns and allowances ratio*. These ratios vary widely by industry but tend to be important indicators of how a

**Table 9.A3** (Hypothetical) Operating Ratios for DLL Inc.

| | | | | | |
|---|---|---|---|---|---|
| Gross margin ratio | = | $\dfrac{\text{gross margin}}{\text{net sales}}$ | = | $\dfrac{\$112\ 650}{248\ 850}$ | = 45.3% |
| Net income ratio | = | $\dfrac{\text{net income}}{\text{net sales}}$ | = | $\dfrac{\$\ 48\ 465}{248\ 850}$ | = 19.5% |
| Operating expense ratio | = | $\dfrac{\text{total operating expenses}}{\text{net sales}}$ | = | $\dfrac{\$\ 31\ 125}{248\ 850}$ | = 12.5% |
| Returns and allowances ratio | = | $\dfrac{\text{returns and allowances}}{\text{net sales}}$ | = | $\dfrac{\$\ 3000}{248\ 850}$ | = 1.2% |

firm is doing within its industry. The ratios for DLL Inc. are shown in Table 9.A3.

- The *gross margin ratio* shows what percentage of sales revenues are available for operating and other expenses and for profit. With DLL, this means that 45 percent, or nearly half, of every sales dollar is available for operating costs and for profits.

- The *net income ratio* (sometimes called the *net profit ratio*) shows what percentage of sales revenues are income or profit. For DLL, the net income ratio is 19.5 percent. This means that the firm's profit before taxes is about 20 cents of every dollar.

- The *operating expense ratio* is the percentage of sales needed for operating expenses. DLL has an operating expense ratio of 12.5 percent. Tracking operating expense ratios from one year to the next or comparing them with an industry average gives a firm important information about how efficient its operations are.

- The *returns and allowances ratio* shows what percentage of all sales are being returned, probably by unhappy customers. DLL's returns and allowances ratio shows that only a little over 1 percent of sales are being returned.

## Inventory Turnover Rate

The *inventory turnover rate*, also referred to as the stock-turn rate, is the number of times inventory or stock is turned over (sold and replaced) during a specified time period, usually a year. Inventory turnover rates are usually calculated on the basis of inventory costs, sometimes on the basis of inventory selling prices, and sometimes by number of units.

For our example, DLL Inc., we know that for the year, the cost of goods sold was $136 200. Information on the balance sheet enables us to find the average inventory. By adding the value of the beginning inventory to the ending inventory and dividing by 2, we can compute an average inventory. In the case of DLL, this would be

$$\frac{\$60\ 750 + \$60\ 300}{2} = \$60\ 525$$

Thus

$$\text{Inventory turnover rate (in cost of goods sold)} = \frac{\text{costs of goods sold}}{\text{average inventory at cost}}$$

$$= \frac{\$136\ 200}{\$60\ 525} = 2.25 \text{ times}$$

## Return on Investment (ROI)

Firms often develop business objectives in terms of return on investment, and ROI is often used to determine how effective (and efficient) the firm's management has been. First, however, we need to define exactly what a firm means by investment. In most cases, firms define investment as the total assets of the firm. In order to calculate the ROI, we need the net income found in the income statement and the total assets (or investment), which is found on the firm's balance sheet.

Return on investment is calculated as follows:

$$\text{ROI} = \frac{\text{net income}}{\text{total investment}}$$

For DLL Inc., if the total assets are $129 825, then the ROI is

$$\frac{\$48\ 465}{\$129\ 825} = 37.3\%$$

Sometimes return on investment is calculated by using an expanded formula.

$$\text{ROI} = \frac{\text{net profit}}{\text{sales}} \times \frac{\text{sales}}{\text{investment}}$$

$$= \frac{\$48\ 465}{\$248\ 850} \times \frac{\$248\ 850}{\$129\ 825} = 37.3\%$$

This formula makes it easy to show how ROI can be increased and what might reduce ROI. For example, there are different ways to increase ROI. First, if the management focuses on cutting costs and increasing efficiency, profits may be increased while sales remain the same.

$$ROI = \frac{net\ profit}{sales} \times \frac{sales}{investment}$$

$$= \frac{\$53\ 277}{\$248\ 850} \times \frac{\$248\ 850}{\$129\ 825} = 41.0\%$$

But ROI can be increased just as much without improving performance simply by reducing the investment—by maintaining less inventory, for instance.

$$ROI = \frac{net\ profit}{sales} \times \frac{sales}{investment}$$

$$= \frac{\$48\ 465}{\$248\ 850} \times \frac{\$248\ 850}{\$114\ 825} = 42.2\%$$

Sometimes, however, differences among the total assets of firms may be related to the age of the firm or the type of industry, which makes ROI a poor indicator of performance. For this reason, some firms have replaced the traditional ROI measures with *return on assets managed* (ROAM), *return on net assets* (RONA), or *return on stockholders' equity* (ROE).

## PRICE ELASTICITY

Price elasticity, discussed in Chapter 9, is a measure of the sensitivity of customers to changes in price. Price elasticity is calculated by comparing the percentage change in quantity to the percentage change in price.

$$Price\ elasticity\ of\ demand = \frac{percentage\ change\ in\ quantity}{percentage\ change\ in\ price}$$

$$E = \frac{(Q_2 - Q_1)/Q_1}{(P_2 - P_1)/P_1}$$

where $Q$ = quantity and $P$ = price.

For example, suppose the manufacturer of jeans in Chapter 9 increased its price from $30 a pair to $35. But instead of 40 000 pairs being sold, sales declined to only 38 000 pairs. The price elasticity would be calculated as follows:

$$E = \frac{(38\ 000 - 40\ 000)/40\ 000}{(\$35 - 30)/\$30} = \frac{-0.05}{0.167} = 0.30$$

Note that elasticity is usually expressed as a positive number even though the calculations create a negative value.

In this case, a relative small change in demand (5 percent) resulted from a fairly large change in price (16.7 percent), indicating that demand is inelastic. At 0.30, the elasticity is less than 1.

On the other hand, what if the same change in price resulted in a reduction in demand to 30 000 pairs of jeans? Then the elasticity would be

$$E = \frac{(30\ 000 - 40\ 000)/40\ 000}{(\$35 - 30)/\$30} = \frac{-0.25}{0.167} = 1.50$$

In this case, because the 16.7 percent change in price resulted in an even larger change in demand (25 percent), demand is elastic. The elasticity of 1.50 is greater than 1. Note: Elasticity may also be calculated by dividing the change in quantity by the average of $Q_1$ and $Q_2$ and dividing the change in price by the average of the two prices. We, however, have chosen to include the formula that uses the initial quantity and price rather than the average.

## Economic Order Quantity

The amount a firm should order at one time is called the *economic order quantity* (EOQ). Every time a firm places an order, there are additional costs. By ordering larger quantities less frequently, the firm saves on these costs. But it also costs money to maintain large inventories of needed materials. The EOQ is the order volume that provides both the lowest processing costs and the lowest inventory costs. The EOQ can be calculated as follows:

1. Determine the *order processing cost*. This is the total amount it costs a firm to place an order from beginning to end. Typically, this might include the operating expenses for the purchasing department, costs for follow-up, costs of record keeping of orders (data processing), costs for the receiving department, and costs for the processing and paying of invoices from suppliers. The simplest way to calculate this is to add up all these yearly costs and then divide by the number of orders placed during the year.

2. Next, calculate the *inventory carrying cost*. This is the total of all costs involved in carrying inventory. These costs include the costs of capital tied up in inventory, the cost of waste (merchandise that becomes obsolete or unusable), depreciation costs, storage costs, insurance premiums, property taxes, and opportunity costs.

The formula for calculating EOQ is

$$EOQ = \sqrt{\frac{2 \times units\ sold\ (or\ annual\ usage) \times ordering\ cost}{unit\ cost \times inventory\ carrying\ cost\ (\%)}}$$

For example, suppose an office supply store sells 6000 cases of pens a year at a cost of $12 a case. The cost to the store for each order placed is $60. The cost of carrying the pens in the warehouse is 24 percent per year (this is a typical inventory carrying cost in many businesses.) Thus, the calculation is

$$EOQ = \sqrt{\frac{2 \times 6000 \times \$60}{\$12 \times 0.24}} = \sqrt{\frac{\$720\ 000}{\$2.88}} = 500$$

The firm should order pens about once a month (it sells 6000 cases a year or 500 cases a month).

# Weldwood
the measure of quality

# Dimension Lumber

| Species: | SPF | Spruce-Pine-Fir |
| | D.Fir | Douglas Fir |

**MC:** All lumber is kiln-dried(K.D.) to a maximum moisture content of 19%

**Grade stamp:** All lumber products graded #3 or Utility and higher have a grade stamp showing the grading agency, mill number, species, grade, and "KD – HT" (Kiln-Dried and Heat-Treated). This means lumber is dried to a maximum moisture content of 19% and achieves a minimum core temperature of 56 °C for a minimum of 30 minutes.

Economy grades are not grade stamped, but are stamped "HT" (Heat-Treated).

**Products:** KD SPF –CLS/ALS dimension lumber graded to NLGA rules or better

| NOMINAL SIZE | ACTUAL SIZE | PKG SIZE | LENGTHS | #2 & BTR | STD & BTR | #3 | UTILITY | ECONOMY |
|---|---|---|---|---|---|---|---|---|
| 2 x 3 | 1½" x 2½" | 399 | 8' to 16' | ✔ | | ✔ | | ✔ |
| 2 x 4 | 1½" x 3½" | 294 | 8' to 20' | ✔ | ✔ | ✔ | ✔ | ✔ |
| 2 x 6 | 1½" x 5½" | 189 | 8' to 20' | ✔ | | ✔ | | ✔ |
| 2 x 8 | 1½" x 7¼" | 147 | 8' to 20' | ✔ | | ✔ | | ✔ |
| 2 x 10 | 1½" x 9¼" | 105 | 8' to 20' | ✔ | | ✔ | | ✔ |
| 2 x 12 | 1½" x 11¼" | 84 | 8' to 20' | ✔ | | ✔ | | ✔ |

KD D.Fir –CLS/ALS dimension lumber graded to NLGA rules or better

| NOMINAL SIZE | ACTUAL SIZE | PKG SIZE | LENGTHS | #2 & BTR | STD & BTR | #3 | UTILITY | ECONOMY |
|---|---|---|---|---|---|---|---|---|
| 2 x 4 | 1½" x 3½" | 294 | 8' to 20' | ✔ | ✔ | ✔ | ✔ | ✔ |
| 2 x 6 | 1½" x 5½" | 189 | 8' to 20' | ✔ | | ✔ | | ✔ |
| 2 x 8 | 1½" x 7¼" | 147 | 8' to 20' | ✔ | | ✔ | | ✔ |
| 2 x 10 | 1½" x 9¼" | 105 | 8' to 20' | ✔ | | ✔ | | ✔ |

**Specialty products:** MSR (Machine Stress Rated) Lumber
D.Fir Lamstock – L3 & Btr
"Hiline" appearance grade lumber
Odd length lumber – 7' to 15'
Rough Grn SPF timber – 4 x 4 to 10 x 10 – 9' to 16'

**Packages:** Poly-wrapped packages (except economy grades)
Steel-strapped

**Grading agencies:** AFPA, CLMA, NFPA

Weldwood of Canada Limited
604 662 2790
www.weldwood.com

# CHAPTER 10
## Channels and Supply Chain Strategy

## CHAPTER OBJECTIVES

WHEN YOU HAVE COMPLETED YOUR STUDY OF THIS CHAPTER, YOU SHOULD BE ABLE TO

1. Explain what a distribution channel is and what functions distribution channels perform.

2. Describe some of the types of wholesaling intermediaries found in distribution channels.

3. Discuss the steps in planning distribution channel strategies.

4. Describe what a supply chain is, how it is related to a value chain, and how logistics is used to implement the value chain.

# Real People, Real Decisions

## Meet **Mike Nomura,** a Decision Maker at Weldwood of Canada

Mike Nomura is the Manager of Marketing & Customer Development, Offshore Export, for Weldwood of Canada, a large forest products company based in Vancouver, British Columbia. Mike went to school in both the Japanese and Canadian school systems, attended the British Columbia Institute of Technologies (Wood Science), and took postgraduate Marketing courses before getting his first job as a technician at an R&D company specializing in superconductor based medical and geological exploration machines.

Mike identified the forest industry as an industry with major earnings potential in British Columbia and he went after the export market where he could use his bicultural background. While his technical degree gave him a good foundation in the forest products industry, allowing him to get his foot in the door to his first lumber job, he feels nothing can beat on-the-job experience.

Over a five-year period beginning in 1994, he increased sales by over 250 percent. Although 1997 and 1998 saw dramatic downturns in lumber exports to Japan, Mike and his team were alone in achieving an increase in market share during this period. This can be attributed to Mike's relentless focus on the needs of the customer.

This single-minded customer focus was put to the test when one of Weldwood's key customers in Japan decided to dramatically shift their channel of distribution strategy. Weldwood of Canada's offshore department was enjoying a good, solid business relationship with one of the largest homebuilders and developers of wood frame apartments in Japan—Daito Trust Construction. Daito builds more than 10 000 units annually and the majority of building materials had been sourced and supplied by their material procurement group, Trans-Pac Housing, in Vancouver. Weldwood had worked extremely hard to capture a large portion of Trans-Pac Housing's business (and, ultimately, Daito's trust).

In 2002, Daito caught many of their suppliers off guard when it announced that it was permanently closing its Vancouver office, and that it would now be conducting all material procurement activities directly from Japan. The company created a brand new department, with all new personnel, and it seemed as though the relationships built with their Vancouver office over the years simply would evaporate.

It was indeed starting over for Weldwood—Daito chose to deal with *all* available suppliers, not only in Canada, but worldwide. Weldwood found itself in a tough situation because Daito's position was that, "whoever can provide the most attractive deals will get our business." Mike knew that if he was going to continue serving this company, he had to get creative, and fast!

After conducting a careful assessment of the customer's needs, Mike decided to present Daito four options.

**Option 1.** Weldwood would effectively replace the old Trans-Pac, and fulfill all of its functions. Weldwood would purchase on Daito's behalf, provide quality control, and take responsibility for loading and shipping to various ports in Japan. This option carried a lot of risk. Weldwood would be stepping away from its traditional role of supplying wood products to take on purchasing and warehousing, as well as quality control for other supplier's products. The advantage was that Weldwood would become the exclusive supplier and it would control 100 percent of Daito's requirements.

**Option 2.** Find ways to enjoy the same relationship with Daito that Weldwood had with Trans-Pac. Weldwood would continue to supply their portion, close to 50 percent of Daito's needs, and deal directly with Daito. The difference would be that while Trans-Pac had previously handled shipping, Weldwood would offer to manage shipping its portion to Daito directly. This option carried the least risk, but little gain. Protecting the status quo, Weldwood would continue to enjoy the relationship with Daito that it had with Trans-Pac, with the addition of shipping revenues.

**Option 3.** Do nothing, with the confidence that Weldwood would prove to be a supplier of choice once Daito reviewed the options, and the relationship would be maintained as with Trans-Pac before them. This option required the least effort, waiting for Daito to come to Weldwood. The likelihood of continuing to supply 50 percent of the customer's needs was a definite possibility, without the cost or effort of starting from scratch with a new business proposal, which may or may not be accepted. However, this option could turn into a "pricing game" with other suppliers.

**Option 4.** Partner with another supplier to cover Weldwood's inability to supply certain products that Daito required. Between the two companies, attempt to provide almost all of Daito's requirements. This option would require a high degree of coordination between two competing suppliers, and would be logistically demanding. Products from both would have to be coordinated and bundled together, and shipped on a "just-in-time" basis, to avoid costly warehousing. The advantage was that Weldwood would control a much larger portion of Daito's requirements than in the past, and would be able to charge a premium for the extra service provided. The amount of coordination and effort required to make things work could be daunting. Weldwood would be responsible for the quality of everything that was shipped to Daito, whether it produced the product or not.

Now, join Mike and his team at Weldwood. Which option would you choose, and why?

# CHANNELS OF DISTRIBUTION: THE FINAL FRONTIER

Channels of distribution may be the final "frontier" for competitive success. After years of hype, many consumers no longer believe that "new and improved" products really are new and improved. Competitors usually easily match aggressive pricing strategies. Advertising and other forms of marketing communications are so commonplace that they have lost much of their impact. Marketers know that channels of distribution may be the only one of the four Ps for which there is an opportunity for sustainable competitive advantage. That's why Weldwood of Canada puts special emphasis on their distribution strategy.

Book retailers are well aware of the major criteria people use to choose a bookstore: Selection, availability, pricing, and knowledgeable staff. Because the convenience of buying a book is important to customers, book retailers such as Chapters and Indigo try to make channels of distribution a competitive advantage. By channels, we mean making goods and services available where and when customers need and want them. Banks and trust companies, for example, make it easy for people to access their services by locating instant tellers where people are likely to need money: Malls, grocery stores, and airport lounges. Canadian Imperial Bank of Commerce, for example, teamed up with Loblaw Companies Limited to offer "President's Choice Financial," in-store no-fee banking, with low mortgage rates and no-minimum balance savings accounts paying interest above CIBC's own products.[1] The other major banks also have kiosks in supermarkets—this makes good sense since as many as 10 000 to 30 000 shoppers pass by each week.[2]

**Chapters.Indigo.ca**
www.chapters.indigo.ca

For those who don't even have time to run out to the grocery store, the Internet is fast becoming an important place for consumers to shop for everything from tulip bulbs to mortgages to exotic vacations. Chapters.indigo.ca and Amazon.com Inc., among others, make books available to consumers any time and any place. The Internet enables even small firms with limited resources to enjoy the same competitive advantages as their largest competitors in terms of making their products available to customers around the globe.

This chapter is about the science and art of distributing goods and services to customers. First, we'll discuss distribution channels and how marketers make smart decisions in developing distribution strategies. We'll also talk about supply chains and the importance of supply chain strategy for business success.

# THE IMPORTANCE OF DISTRIBUTION: YOU CAN'T SELL WHAT ISN'T THERE!

You have identified and profiled your target market(s). You have created your product and priced it. You're not done. You need to get it to your customer. In today's marketplace, marketers must work hard to get their products to consumers, who no longer have the leisure time available to "shop 'til they drop" for goods and services.

## What Is a Distribution Channel?

A **channel of distribution** is a series of firms or individuals that facilitates the movement of a product from the producer to the final customer. In many cases, channels include an organized network of manufacturers, wholesalers, and retailers that develop relationships and work together to make products conveniently available to buyers.

Distribution channels come in different shapes and sizes. The bakery around the corner where you buy your cinnamon rolls is a member of a channel, as is the baked goods section at the local supermarket, the espresso bar at the mall that sells biscotti to go with your double mocha cappuccino, and the bakery outlet store that sells day-old rolls at a discount.

A channel of distribution consists of, at a minimum, a producer—the individual or firm that manufactures or produces a good or service—and a customer. This is a *direct channel*. For example, when you buy a kilogram of strawberries at a farm where they're grown, that's a direct channel. Firms that sell their own products through catalogues, 800 numbers, the Internet, or factory outlet stores use direct channels.

**channel of distribution** The series of firms or individuals that facilitates the movement of a product from the producer to the final customer.

**channel intermediaries** Firms or individuals such as wholesalers, agents, brokers, or retailers that help move a product from the producer to the consumer or business user.

But channels often are *indirect*, because they include one or more **channel intermediaries**, firms or individuals such as wholesalers, agents, brokers, and retailers, that in some way help move the product to the consumer or business user. For example, strawberry farmers may choose to sell their berries to a produce wholesaler that, in turn, sell cases of the berries to supermarkets and restaurants that, in turn, sell to consumers.

## Functions of Distribution Channels

Distribution channels perform a number of different functions that make the flow of goods from the producer to the customer possible. These functions must be handled by someone, be it the producer, a channel intermediary, or even the customer. They can be shifted from one member of the channel to another, such as when customers pick up new chairs from the warehouse instead of having them delivered to their home, but they cannot be eliminated. Channels that include one or more intermediaries can often accomplish certain distribution functions more effectively and efficiently than can a single organization.

Channels provide time, place, and ownership utility for customers. They make desired products available when, where, and in the sizes and quantities that customers want them. Take, for example, flowers such as those shown in Exhibit 10.1. The flowers are harvested and electronically sorted by growers, auctioned to buyers in Amsterdam, shipped by air to importers in Mississauga, where they are inspected for insects and disease, transported to wholesalers around the country, and finally distributed to local florists who make them available to their customers. The channel members—the growers, the auction house, the importers, the wholesalers, and the local florists—all work together to create just the right bouquet for flower lovers.

A second function of distribution channels is increasing the efficiency of the flow of goods from producer to customer. How would we buy groceries without our modern system of supermarkets? We'd have to get our milk from a dairy, our bread from a bakery, our tomatoes and corn from a local farmer, and our flour from a flourmill. And forget about specialty items, like Twinkies or Coca-Cola. The companies that make these items would have to handle literally millions of transactions to sell to every individual who craved a junk-food fix.

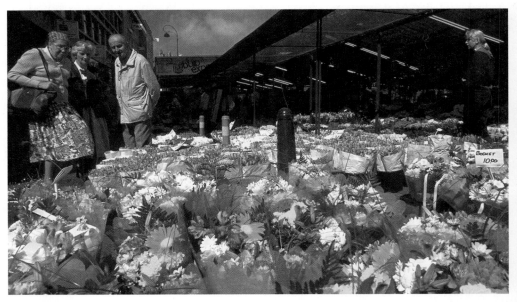

**Exhibit 10.1**

An efficient distribution system facilitates getting flowers from greenhouses to flower lovers—all in the same day.

Distribution channels create efficiencies by reducing the number of transactions necessary for goods to flow from many different manufacturers to large numbers of customers. This occurs in two ways. With **bulk breaking**, wholesalers and retailers purchase large quantities (usually cases) of goods from manufacturers but sell only one or a few at a time to many different customers. Channel intermediaries also reduce the number of transactions by **creating assortments**—providing a variety of products in one location—so that customers can conveniently buy many different items from one seller at one time.

Figure 10.1 provides a simple example of how distribution channels reduce hassles in our lives. This illustration includes five manufacturers and five customers. If each producer sold its product to each individual customer, 25 different transactions would have to occur, which is a very inefficient way to distribute products. But with a single intermediary who buys from all five manufacturers and sells to all five customers, the number of transactions is cut to 10. If there were 10 manufacturers and 10 customers, an intermediary would reduce the number of transactions from 100 to just 20. Do the math: channels are efficient.

Channel intermediaries also perform a number of **facilitating functions**, which make the purchase process easier for customers and manufacturers. For example, intermediaries often provide important customer services, such as offering credit to buyers. Most of us like to shop at department stores because, if we are not happy with the product, we can take it back to the store, where customer service personnel are happy to give us a refund (at least in theory). These same customer services are even more important in business-to-business markets in which customers purchase larger quantities of higher-priced products than in consumer markets. Some wholesalers and retailers assist the manufacturer by providing repair and maintenance service for products they handle. An appliance, television, stereo, or computer dealer may serve as an authorized repair centre, provide maintenance contracts, and sell essential supplies to customers.

Finally, international distribution channels can make global marketing easier. Even small companies can be successful in global markets by relying on distributors that know local customs and laws.

We've discussed what a distribution channel is and some of the functions it performs. What are the different types of channel intermediaries and channel structures?

**bulk breaking** Dividing larger quantities of goods into smaller lots to meet the needs of buyers.

**creating assortments** Providing a variety of products in one location to meet the needs of buyers.

**facilitating functions** Functions of channel intermediaries that make the purchase process easier for customers and manufacturers.

**Figure 10.1** Reducing Transactions via Intermediaries

**Exhibit 10.2**

Many distribution channel members provide customer services. Appliance and electronics retailers such as Future Shop provide repair and warranty services for the products they sell.

## THE COMPOSITION AND STRUCTURE OF CHANNELS

How can you get your hands on a new Phish T-shirt? There are several ways. You could pick one up at your local music store or directly over the Internet. You might buy an "official Phish concert T-shirt" from vendors during a show. Alternatively, you might get a "deal" on a bootlegged, unauthorized version of the same shirt being sold from a suitcase by a shady person standing *outside* the stadium. It might even be possible to buy it on the Home Shopping Network. Each of these distribution alternatives traces a different path from producer to consumer. Let's look at the different types of wholesaling intermediaries and at different channel structures. We'll focus on retailers, which are usually the last link in the chain, in the next chapter.

## Types of Wholesaling Intermediaries

**wholesaling intermediaries** Firms that handle the flow of products from the manufacturer to the retailer or business user.

**independent intermediaries** Channel intermediaries that are not controlled by any manufacturer but rather do business with many different manufacturers and many different customers.

**merchant wholesalers** Intermediaries that buy goods from manufacturers (take title to them) and sell to retailers and other business-to-business customers.

**take title** To accept legal ownership of a product and the accompanying rights and responsibilities of ownership.

**Wholesaling intermediaries** are firms that handle the flow of products from the manufacturer to the retailer or business user. There are many different types of consumer and business-to-business wholesaling intermediaries. Some of these are independent, but manufacturers and retailers can own them, too. Table 10.1 summarizes the important characteristics of each.

**INDEPENDENT INTERMEDIARIES** **Independent intermediaries** do business with many different manufacturers and many different customers. Because they are not owned or controlled by any manufacturer, they make it possible for many manufacturers to serve customers throughout the world while keeping prices low.

**Merchant wholesalers** are independent intermediaries that buy goods from manufacturers and sell to retailers and other business-to-business customers. Because merchant wholesalers **take title** to the goods—they actually have legal ownership of the goods—they assume certain ownership risks and can suffer losses if products get damaged, become out-of-date or obsolete, are stolen, or just don't sell. At the same time, because they own the products, they are free to develop their own marketing strategies including setting the prices they charge their customers.

*Full-service merchant wholesalers*, as the name suggests, provide a wide range of services for their customers. These services may include delivery, credit, product-use assistance, repairs, advertising and other promotion support, and market research. Full-service wholesalers often have their own sales force to call on businesses and organizational customers.

One type of full-service merchant wholesaler is a *rack jobber* (Exhibit 10.3). Rack jobbers supply retailers with such specialty items as health and beauty products, magazines, and books. Rack jobbers get their name because they own and maintain the product display racks in grocery, drug, and variety stores. These wholesalers visit their retail customers on a regular basis to maintain levels of stock and refill their racks with merchandise.

**Table 10.1** Types of Intermediaries

| Intermediary Type | Description | Advantages |
|---|---|---|
| *Independent intermediaries* | Do business with many different manufacturers and many different customers | Used by most small- to medium-sized firms |
| *Merchant wholesalers* | Buy (take title of) goods from producers and sell to organizational customers; either full or limited function | Allow small manufacturers to serve customers throughout the world while keeping costs low |
| *Rack jobbers* | Provide retailers with display units, check inventories, and replace merchandise for the retailers | Useful when retailers require merchandising services from manufacturers |
| *Cash-and-carry wholesalers* | Provide products for small business customers who purchase at wholesaler's location | To distribute low-cost merchandise for small retailers and other business customers |
| *Truck jobbers* | Deliver perishable food and tobacco items to retailers | For perishable items when delivery and some sales functions are required |
| *Drop shippers* | Take orders from and bill retailers for products drop-shipped from manufacturer | Facilitate transactions for bulky products |
| *Mail-order wholesalers* | Sell through catalogues, telephone, or mail order | For products sold to small organizational customers at a reasonable price |
| *Merchandise agents and brokers* | Provide services in exchange for commissions | Sellers do not give up legal ownership of product |
| *Manufacturers' agents* | Independent salespeople; carry several lines of noncompeting products | Supply sales function for small and new firms |
| *Selling agents Export/import agents* | Handle entire output of one or more products | Handle all marketing functions for small manufacturers |
| *Commission merchants* | Receive commission on sales price of product | Primarily in agricultural products markets |
| *Merchandise brokers Export/import brokers* | Identify likely buyers and bring buyers and sellers together | In markets where there are lots of small buyers and sellers |
| *Manufacturer owned* | Operations limited to one manufacturer | Control |
| *Sales branches* | Like wholesalers, maintain some inventory in different geographic areas | When firms must provide service to customers in different geographic areas |
| *Sales offices* | Carry no inventory; in different geographic areas | Reduce selling costs and provide better customer service |
| *Manufacturers' showrooms* | Products attractively displayed for customers to visit | When desirable for customers to examine merchandise at a central location |

Source: Adapted from J. Thomas Russell and W. Ronald Lane, *Kleppner's Advertising Procedure*, 11th ed. (Upper Saddle River, NJ: Prentice Hall, 1990); William Wells, John Burnett, and Sandra Moriarty, *Advertising: Principles and Practice*, 3d ed. (Upper Saddle River, NJ: Prentice Hall, 1995).

In contrast, *limited-service merchant wholesalers* provide fewer services for their customers. Like full-service wholesalers, they take title to merchandise, but they are less likely to provide such services as delivery, credit, or marketing assistance to retailers.

- *Cash-and-carry wholesalers* provide low-cost merchandise for retailers and industrial customers that are too small for other wholesalers' sales representatives to call on. Customers pay cash for products and provide their own delivery. Some popular cash-and-carry product categories include groceries, office supplies, building materials, and electrical supplies.

- *Truck jobbers* carry their products to small business customer locations for their inspection and selection. Truck jobbers often supply such perishable items as fruit, vegetables, and meats to small grocery stores. The bakery truck jobber shown in Exhibit 10.4 calls on supermarkets, checks the stock of bread on the shelf, removes any outdated items, and suggests how much bread the store needs to order.

- *Drop shippers* are limited-function wholesalers that take title to the merchandise but never actually take possession of it. Drop shippers take orders from and bill retailers and industrial buyers, but the merchandise is shipped directly from the manufacturer. Because they take title to the merchandise, they assume the same risks as other merchant

**Exhibit 10.3**

Rack jobbers are full-service merchant wholesalers. These intermediaries own and maintain product display racks in retail stores.

wholesalers. Drop shippers are important to both the producers and customers of bulky products such as coal, oil, or lumber.

- *Mail-order wholesalers* sell products to small retailers and other industrial customers, often located in remote areas, through catalogues rather than a sales force. They usually carry products in inventory and require payment in cash or by credit card before shipment. Mail-order wholesalers supply such products as cosmetics, hardware, sporting goods, and general merchandise.

**merchandise agents or brokers** Channel intermediaries that provide services in exchange for commissions but never take title to the product.

- **Merchandise agents or brokers** are another major type of independent intermediary. Agents and brokers provide services in exchange for commissions. They may or may not take possession of the product, but they never take title—they do not accept legal ownership of the product. Agents normally represent buyers or sellers on an ongoing basis, whereas clients employ brokers for a short period of time.

- *Manufacturers' agents*, also referred to as *manufacturers' reps*, are independent salespeople who carry several lines of non-competing products. They have contractual arrangements with manufacturers, which outline territories, selling prices, and other specific aspects of the relationship. These agents have little, if any, supervision and are compensated with commissions based on a percentage of what they sell. Manufacturers' agents often develop strong customer relationships and provide an important sales function for small and new companies.

- *Selling agents*, including export-import agents, market a whole product line or one manufacturer's total output. They are often seen as independent marketing departments because they perform the same functions as full-service wholesalers but do not take title to products. Unlike manufacturers' agents, selling agents have unlimited territories and control the pricing, promotion, and distribution of their products. Selling agents are found in the furniture, clothing, and textiles industries.

- *Commission merchants* are sales agents who receive goods, primarily agricultural products, such as grain or livestock, on consignment—they take possession of products without taking title. Although sellers may state a minimum price they are willing to take for their products, commission merchants are free to sell the product for the highest price they can get. Commission merchants receive a commission on the sales price of the product.

**Exhibit 10.4**

Bakery truck jobbers make sure supermarkets have enough bread to meet customer demands.

- *Merchandise brokers* including export-import brokers are intermediaries that facilitate transactions in markets such as real estate, food, and used equipment in which there are many small buyers and sellers. Brokers identify likely buyers and sellers and bring the two together in return for a fee received when the transaction is completed.

   **MANUFACTURER-OWNED INTERMEDIARIES** Sometimes manufacturers set up their own channel intermediaries. In this way, they can have separate business units that perform all of the functions of independent intermediaries *and* maintain complete control over the channel.

- *Sales branches* are manufacturer-owned facilities that, like independent wholesalers, carry inventory and provide sales and service to customers in a specific geographic area. Sales branches are found in such industries as petroleum products, industrial machinery and equipment, and motor vehicles.

- *Sales offices* are manufacturer-owned facilities that, like agents, do not carry inventory but provide selling functions for the manufacturer in a specific geographic area. Because they allow members of the sales force to be located close to customers, they reduce selling costs and provide better customer service.

- *Manufacturers' showrooms* are manufacturer-owned or leased facilities in which products are permanently displayed for customers to visit. Manufacturers' showrooms are often located in or near large merchandise marts, such as the furniture market in High Point, North Carolina, where Palliser Furniture goes to showcase its products.

## Types of Distribution Channels

Firms face many choices when structuring distribution channels. Should they sell directly to consumers and business users? Would they benefit by including wholesalers, retailers, or both in the channel? Would it make sense to sell directly to some customers but use retailers to sell to other customers? There is no single best channel for all products. The marketing manager must select a channel structure that creates a competitive advantage for the firm and its products based on the size and needs of the target market. Here are some factors marketers need to consider.

channel levels  The number of distinct categories of intermediaries that populate a channel of distribution.

In developing place or distribution strategies, marketers first consider different **channel levels**, or the number of distinct categories of intermediaries that make up a channel of distribution. Many different factors have an impact on this decision. What channel members are available? How large is the market, how frequently do consumers purchase the product, and what services do they require?

Figure 10.2 summarizes the different structures a distribution channel can take. The producer and the customer are always members, so the shortest channel possible has two levels. Using a retailer adds a third level; a wholesaler adds a fourth level; and so on. Different channel structures exist for both consumer and business-to-business markets.

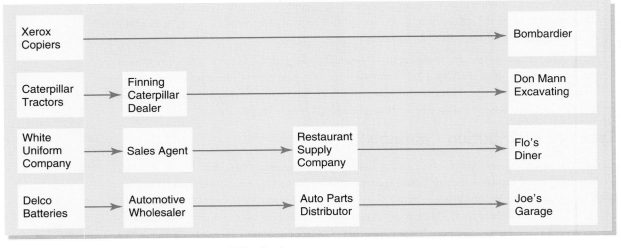

**Figure 10.2** Different Types of Channels of Distribution

**CONSUMER CHANNELS** The simplest channel is a direct channel. Why do some manufacturers sell directly to customers? One reason is that a direct channel may allow the manufacturer to serve its customers better and at a lower price than is possible using a retailer. By using direct channels, strawberry farmers make sure their customers have fresher strawberries than if they sell the berries through a local supermarket. Furthermore, if the farmers sell the berries through a supermarket, their price will be higher because of the supermarket's costs of doing business and required profit on the berries. In fact, sometimes the direct channel is the *only* way to sell the product, because using intermediaries may increase the price above what consumers are willing to pay.

One of the newest means of selling direct is through the Internet. Nick Clark and his family were trying to think of an idea for a family-owned business. The main difficulty was that the brothers, sisters, and spouses were scattered between Kelowna, Calgary, and Bowen Island, British Columbia. The Internet provided an excellent opportunity for the whole family to work together. Tina Clark, Nick's sister-in-law, suggested that they market and distribute her father's smoked salmon, and BlackBear was created (Exhibit 10.5). The Internet has enabled BlackBear to send products from Moscow to Singapore. Their line has expanded from salmon to a wide range of products, which includes clothing and jewellery. Interestingly, retail stores found out about BlackBear through the Internet and requested to carry the products through regular affiliated retail distribution channels.

**BlackBear**
www.blackbear.net

Another reason to use a direct channel is control. When the manufacturer handles distribution, it maintains control of pricing, service, and delivery—all elements of the transaction. Because distributors and dealers carry many products, it can be difficult to get their sales force to focus on selling one product. In a direct channel, a producer works directly with customers, gaining insights into trends, customer needs and complaints, and the effectiveness of its marketing strategies.

Why do manufacturers choose to use indirect channels to reach consumers? An important reason is that often customers are familiar with certain retailers or other intermediaries—it's where they always go to look for what they need. Getting customers to change their normal buying behaviour—for example, convincing consumers to buy their laundry

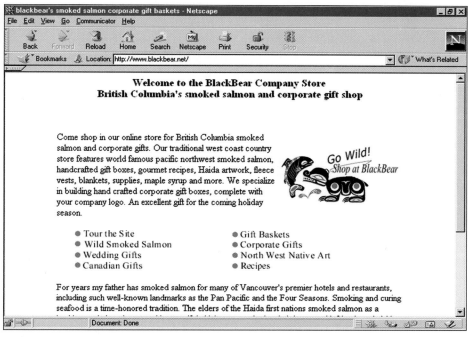

**Exhibit 10.5**

The Internet allows a small business, BlackBear, to reach customers around the globe, making it an international competitor.

detergent or frozen pizza from a catalogue or over the Internet instead of from the corner supermarket—might be difficult, although e-commerce grocery businesses such as GroceryGateway are finding that many consumers will change their behaviour if presented with the right offer.[3] In addition, intermediaries help manufacturers in all the ways described earlier. By creating utility and transaction efficiencies, channel members make manufacturers' lives easier and enhance their ability to reach customers.

The *manufacturer–retailer–consumer channel* in Figure 10.2 is the shortest indirect channel. GE uses this channel when its sells small appliances through such large retailers as Zellers or Sears. Because the retailers buy in large volume, they can buy at a low price, which they pass on to shoppers. The size of these retail giants also means that they can provide the physical distribution functions, such as transportation and storage, which wholesalers handle for smaller retail outlets.

The *manufacturer–wholesaler–retailer-consumer channel* is a common distribution channel in consumer marketing. For example, a single ice-cream factory can supply four or five regional wholesalers. These wholesalers then sell to 400 or more retailers, such as grocery stores. The retailers in turn each sell the ice cream to thousands of customers. In this channel, the regional wholesalers combine many manufacturers' products to supply to grocery stores. Because the grocery stores do business with many wholesalers, this arrangement results in a broad selection of products.

**BUSINESS-TO-BUSINESS CHANNELS** Business-to-business distribution channels, as the name suggests, facilitate the flow of goods from a producer to an organizational or business customer such as a factory or a hospital. Generally, business-to-business channels parallel consumer channels—they may be direct or indirect. The simplest indirect channel in industrial markets is the single intermediary—a merchant wholesaler referred to as an *industrial distributor* rather than a retailer—buying products from a manufacturer and selling them to business customers.

Direct channels are more common to business-to-business markets than to consumer markets, because business-to-business marketing often means selling high-dollar, high-profit items—a single piece of industrial equipment may cost hundreds of thousands of dollars—to a market made up of only a few customers. In such markets, it pays for a company to develop its own sales force and sell directly to customers at a lower cost than if it used intermediaries. The Internet is used as a direct channel in business-to-business markets as well. For example, for standardized goods such as car parts, automobile manufacturers use the Internet to ask competing suppliers to bid on a piece of business. The supplier who can meet manufacturer specifications at the lowest price wins the bid.

**DISTRIBUTION CHANNELS FOR SERVICES** Because services are intangible, there is no need to worry about storage, transportation, and the other functions of physical distribution. In most cases, the service travels directly from the producer to the customer. However, some services do need an intermediary, an *agent* who helps the parties complete the transaction. Examples include insurance agents, stockbrokers, and travel agents.

**DUAL DISTRIBUTION SYSTEMS** Figure 10.2 shows simple distribution channels; but life is rarely that simple. Manufacturers, dealers, wholesalers, retailers, and customers alike may actually interact with more than one type of channel. These are *dual* or *multiple distribution systems.*

The pharmaceutical industry provides a good example of multiple channel usage. Pharmaceutical companies distribute their products in at least three channel types. First, they sell to hospitals, clinics, and other organizational customers directly. These customers buy in quantity, purchase a wide variety of products, and, because pills are dispensed one at a time rather than in bottles of 50, require different product packaging than when the products are sold to other customers. Pharmaceuticals' second channel is an indirect consumer channel in which the manufacturer sells to large drug retailer chains that distribute the medicines to their stores across the country. Some of us would rather purchase our prescriptions in a more personal manner from a local independent drugstore. In this channel, the manufacturer sells to drug wholesalers that in turn supply these independents.

We have discussed what distribution channels and channel intermediaries are and the role of channel members in the distribution of goods and services. We know that not all channels are alike: Some are direct and simple, but indirect channels can be quite complex. The next section is about how marketers plan channel strategies to meet customer needs better than the competition—the all-important competitive advantage.

## PLANNING A CHANNEL STRATEGY

Do customers want products in large or small quantities? Do they insist on buying them locally, or will they purchase from a distant supplier? How long are they willing to wait to get the product? Intelligent marketers want to know. Distribution planning is best accomplished when marketers follow the steps in Figure 10.3. In this section, we'll look at how manufacturers decide on distribution objectives, examine what influences distribution decisions, and discuss how firms select distribution strategies and tactics.

Firms that operate within a channel of distribution—manufacturers, wholesalers, and retailers—may do some distribution planning. In this section, our perspective focuses on distribution planning of producers or manufacturers rather than intermediaries, because they, more often than intermediaries, take a leadership role in creating a successful distribution channel.

**Figure 10.3** Steps in Distribution Planning

## Channel Objectives

The first step in deciding on a distribution plan is to develop appropriate objectives that support the organization's overall marketing goals. How can distribution work with the other elements of the marketing mix to increase profits? To increase market share? To increase volume of sales?

In general, the overall objective of any distribution planning is to make a firm's product available when, where, and in the quantities customers want and need at a minimum cost. More specific distribution objectives, however, depend on characteristics of the product and the market. For example, if the product is bulky, a primary distribution objective may be to minimize shipping costs. If the product is fragile, a goal may be to develop a channel that minimizes handling. In introducing a new product to a mass market, a channel objective may be to provide maximum product exposure or to make the product available close to where customers live and work. Sometimes marketers make their product available where similar products are sold so that consumers can compare prices.

## Evaluating the Environment

After setting the distribution objectives, marketers must consider their internal and external environments. The organization must examine such issues as its own ability to create distribution channels, what channel intermediaries are available, the ability of customers to access these intermediaries, and how the competition distributes its products. Should a firm use the same retailers as its competitors? Sometimes, to ensure customers' undivided attention, a firm sells its products in outlets that don't carry the competitors' products. In other cases, a firm uses the same intermediaries as its competitors because customers expect to find the product there. Finally, by studying competitors' distribution strategies, marketers can learn from their successes and failures. For example, if the biggest complaint of competitors' customers is delivery speed, developing a system that allows same-day delivery can make the competition pale in comparison.

# Choosing a Distribution System

Planning distribution strategies means making at least three decisions. Distribution planning includes decisions about the number of levels in the distribution channel, but distribution strategies also involve decisions about channel relationships—whether a conventional system or a highly integrated system will work best. A final decision relates to the distribution intensity or the number of intermediaries at each level of the channel.

CONVENTIONAL, VERTICAL, AND HORIZONTAL MARKETING SYSTEMS Participants in any distribution channel form an interrelated system. To develop a successful distribution strategy, marketers must consider the different types of systems and select the one that best meets their needs. In general, these systems take one of three forms: conventional, vertical, and horizontal marketing systems.

A **conventional marketing system** is a multiple-level distribution channel in which members work independently of one another. Their relationships are limited to simply buying and selling from one another. Each firm seeks to benefit with little concern for other channel members. Even though channel members work independently, most conventional channels are highly successful. For one thing, all members of the channel are working for the same goals—to build demand, reduce costs, and improve customer satisfaction. And the channel members know that it's in everyone's best interest to treat other channel members fairly.

A **vertical marketing system (VMS)** is a channel in which there is cooperation among channel members at two or more levels of the channel—the manufacturing, wholesaling, and retailing levels. Firms in a VMS work together and depend on each other, like links in a chain. Members share information and provide services to other members, recognizing that such coordination makes everyone more successful in reaching a desired target market.

There are three types of vertical marketing systems: administered, corporate, and contractual. In an administered VMS, channel members remain independent but voluntarily agree to work together. In a corporate VMS, firms have ownership control of some or all of a distribution channel, such as when a manufacturer buys agent companies.

In a contractual VMS, cooperation is enforced by contracts, legal agreements that spell out each member's rights and responsibilities and how they will cooperate. In a wholesaler-sponsored VMS, wholesalers get retailers to work together under their leadership in a voluntary chain. Retail members of the chain use a common name, cooperate in advertising and other promotion, and even develop their own private-label products. Examples of wholesaler-sponsored chains are IGA (Independent Grocers' Alliance) food stores, Ace Hardware stores, and Island Farms Dairy (BC).

In other cases, retailers themselves organize a cooperative marketing channel system. A *retailer cooperative* is a group of retailers that has established a wholesaling operation to help them compete more effectively with the large chains. Each retailer owns shares in the wholesaler operation and is obligated to purchase a certain percentage of inventory from the cooperative operation. The Calgary Co-op and True Value Hardware Stores are examples of retailer cooperatives.

*Franchise organizations* are a third type of contractual VMS. In these organizations, channel cooperation is explicitly defined and strictly enforced through contractual arrangements in which a franchiser (a manufacturer or a service provider) allows an entrepreneur to use the franchise name and marketing plan for a fee. In most franchise agreements, the franchiser provides a variety of services for the franchisee, such as helping train employees, giving access to lower prices for needed materials, and helping pick a location with visibility. In return, the franchiser receives a percentage of revenue from the franchise owner. Usually the franchisees are also allowed to use the franchiser business format, but they are required to follow that format to the letter.[4] For example, a McDonald's franchisee is not allowed to change the menu or the physical decor of the restaurant. It's important that customers know

**conventional marketing system** A multiple-level distribution channel in which channel members work independently of one another.

**vertical marketing system (VMS)** A channel of distribution in which there is cooperation among members at the manufacturing, wholesaling, and retailing levels.

**True Value Hardware Stores**
www.truevalue.com

that they can get the same Big Mac in Toronto that they will find in Corner Brook, Newfoundland.

Canada is the franchise capital of the world—with more than 1300 franchise operations and 64 000 outlets generating more than a million jobs and $100 billion a year in revenues.[5] Although relatively high-cost food-service franchises ($60 000 to $1 million) represent about 40 percent of all outlets, some of Canada's hottest franchises are in consumer and business services—Web site design, window cleaning, tutoring, maid services, dog walking and house painting—with franchise fees under $30 000.

From the manufacturer's perspective, franchising a business is a way to develop widespread product distribution with minimal financial risk while, at the same time, maintaining control over product quality. From the entrepreneur's perspective, franchises, such as The Great Canadian Bagel, shown in Exhibit 10.6, are a popular way to get a start in business.

In a **horizontal marketing system**, two or more firms at the same channel level agree to work together to get their product to the customer. Air Canada and Lufthansa, for example, cooperate in providing passenger air service. To increase passenger volume for both airlines, they share a common flight code. This means that travel agents who book passengers on one of the airlines flights will be more likely to book a connecting flight on the other airline. To increase customer benefits, they also share frequent-flyer programs and airport clubs.[6]

**horizontal marketing system** An arrangement within a channel of distribution in which two or more firms at the same channel level work together for a common purpose.

**INTENSIVE, EXCLUSIVE, AND SELECTIVE DISTRIBUTION** Distribution strategy decisions also mean determining how many wholesalers and retailers will carry the product within a given market. This may seem like an easy decision: Distribute the product through as many intermediaries as possible. However, if the product goes to too many outlets, there may be inefficiency and duplication of efforts. For example, if there are too many Honda dealerships in town, there will be many unsold Hondas sitting on dealer lots, and no single dealer will be successful. But, if there are not enough wholesalers or retailers carrying a product, total sales of the manufacturer's products (and profits) will not be maximized. If customers have to drive hundreds of kilometres to find a Honda dealer, they may settle for a Ford or a Chevy. Thus, a distribution objective may be to either increase or decrease the level of market penetration.

**intensive distribution** Selling a product through all suitable wholesalers or retailers that are willing to stock and sell the product.

The three basic choices are intensive, exclusive, and selective distribution. Table 10.2 summarizes the five decision factors—company, customers, channels, constraints, and competition—and how they help marketers determine the best fit between distribution system and marketing goals.

**exclusive distribution** Selling a product only through a single outlet in a particular region.

**Intensive distribution** aims at maximizing market coverage by selling a product through all wholesalers or retailers that will stock and sell the product. Marketers use intensive distribution for such products as chewing gum, soft drinks, milk, and bread that are quickly consumed and must be frequently replaced. Intensive distribution is necessary for these products, because availability is more important than any other consideration in customers' purchase decisions.

In contrast to intensive distribution, **exclusive distribution** means limiting distribution to a single outlet in a particular region. Marketers sell pianos,

**Exhibit 10.6**

The Great Canadian Bagel is a franchise bagel shop that is a Canadian icon.

**Table 10.2** Characteristics That Favour Intensive over Exclusive Distribution

| Decision Factor | Intensive Distribution | Exclusive Distribution |
|---|---|---|
| Company | Oriented toward mass markets | Oriented toward specialized markets |
| Customers | High customer density | Low customer density |
| | Price and convenience are priorities | Service and cooperation |
| Channels | Overlapping market coverage | Non-overlapping market coverage |
| Constraints | Cost of serving individual customers is low | Cost of serving individual customers is high |
| Competition | Based on a strong market presence, often through advertising and promotion | Based on individualized attention to customers, often through relationship marketing |

cars, executive training programs, television programs, and many other products with high price tags through exclusive distribution arrangements. These strategies are typically used with products that are high priced and have considerable service requirements and when there is a limited number of buyers in any single geographic area. Exclusive distribution enables wholesalers and retailers to recoup the costs associated with long selling processes for each customer and, in some cases, extensive after-sale service.

Not every situation neatly fits a category in Table 10.2. For example, consider professional sports. Customers might not shop for games in the same way they shop for pianos. They might go to a game on impulse, and they don't require much individualized service. Nevertheless, professional sports employ exclusive distribution. The team's cost of serving customers is high, due to those million-dollar player salaries and multimillion-dollar stadiums.

The alert reader (especially one who is also a sports fan) may note that there are some exceptions to the exclusive distribution of sports teams: New York has two football teams and two baseball teams; Chicago fields two baseball teams. Market coverage that is less than intensive distribution, but more than exclusive distribution, is **selective distribution**. Selective distribution fits when demand is so large that exclusive distribution is inadequate, but selling costs, service requirements, or other factors make intensive distribution a poor fit. Although a White Sox baseball fan may not believe that the Cubs franchise is necessary (and vice versa), major league baseball and even some baseball fans think the Chicago market is large enough to support both teams (Exhibit 10.7).

Selective distribution strategies are suitable for shopping products, such as household appliances, computers, and electronic equipment, for which consumers are willing to spend time visiting different retail outlets to compare product alternatives. For producers, selective distribution means freedom to choose only those wholesalers and retailers that have a good credit rating, provide good market coverage, serve customers well, and cooperate effectively. Wholesalers and retailers like selective distribution because it results in higher sales and profits than are possible with intensive distribution in which sellers often have to compete on price.

**selective distribution**
Distribution using fewer outlets than in intensive distribution but more than in exclusive distribution.

## Developing Distribution Tactics

As with planning for the other marketing Ps, the final step in distribution planning is developing the distribution tactics necessary to implement the distribution strategy. These decisions are usually about the type of distribution system to use—a direct or indirect channel, a conventional or an integrated channel. Distribution tactics relate to the implementation of these strategies, such as selecting individual channel members and managing the channel.

**SELECTING CHANNEL PARTNERS** When firms agree to work together in a channel relationship, they become partners in what is normally a long-term commitment. Like a marriage, it is important to both manufacturers and intermediaries to select channel partners wisely or they'll regret the match later. In evaluating intermediaries, manufacturers try to answer such questions as: Will the channel member contribute substantially to our profitability? Does the channel member have the ability to provide the services customers want? What impact will a potential intermediary have on channel control? For example, what small- to mid-sized firm wouldn't jump at the chance to have its products distributed by retail giant Canadian Tire? With Canadian Tire as a channel partner, a small firm could double, triple, or quadruple its business. Actually, more than one firm, recognizing that size means power in the channel, has decided against Canadian Tire, because they are not willing to relinquish control of their marketing decision making.

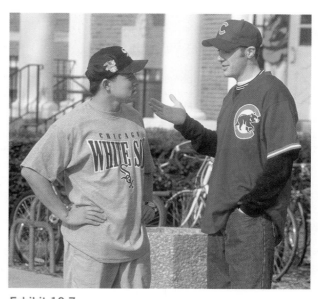

Another important consideration in selecting channel members is competitors' channel partners. For example, because people spend time comparing different brands when purchasing certain products (consumer durable goods, for example), firms need to make sure their products are displayed near similar competitors' products. If most competitors distribute their electric drills through mass merchandisers, a manufacturer has to make sure its brand is there as well.

**Exhibit 10.7**

Selective distribution: Chicago baseball fans have a choice between the White Sox and the Cubs.

A firm's dedication to social responsibility may also be an important determining factor in the selection of channel partners. Many firms have developed extensive programs to recruit minority-owned channel members.

**MANAGING THE CHANNEL OF DISTRIBUTION** Once a manufacturer develops a channel strategy and aligns channel members, the day-to-day job of managing the channel begins. The **channel leader** is the dominant firm that controls the channel. A firm becomes the channel leader because it has power relative to other channel members. This power comes from different sources:

- A firm has *economic power* when it has the ability to control resources.
- A firm such as a franchiser has *legitimate power* if it has legal authority to call the shots.
- A firm has *reward* or *coercive power* if it engages in exclusive distribution and has the ability to give profitable products and to take them away from the channel intermediaries.

Although producers have traditionally held the role of channel leader, a firm at any level of distribution can emerge as a channel leader. When retailers were much smaller than they are now, manufacturers tended to assume leadership in consumer goods markets. Procter & Gamble, for instance, developed customer-oriented marketing programs, tracked market trends, and advised retailers on the mix of products most likely to build sales. As large retail chains evolved and began harnessing customer data via technology, such giant retailers as Canadian Tire and Home Depot began to assume a leadership role.

Because manufacturers, wholesalers, and retailers depend on one another for success, channel cooperation helps everyone. High intermediary profit margins, training programs, cooperative advertising, and expert marketing advice are invisible to end customers but are important motivating factors in the eyes of wholesalers and retailers.[7] Victoria's Rogers' Chocolates, for example, has found ways to help its retail channel partners become more successful. By improving the speed and accuracy of reorders, retailers are able to maintain inventory levels necessary to satisfy customers while avoiding ordering errors.

Relations among members in a channel are not always wonderful. Because each firm has its own unique set of objectives, channel conflict may threaten a manufacturer's distribution strategy. Such conflict most often occurs between firms at different levels of the same distribution channel. Incompatible goals, poor communication, and disagreement over roles,

**Canadian Tire**
www.canadiantire.com

**channel leader** A firm at one level of distribution that takes a leadership role, establishing operating norms and processes that reduce channel conflicts, reduce costs, and enhance delivered customer value.

**Rogers' Chocolates**
www.rogerschocolates.com

## SPOTLIGHT ON REAL PEOPLE     McAfee Associates

Most software companies distribute their products in stores. William Larson, the 40-year-old CEO of McAfee Associates, does things differently. McAfee licenses its network security and management software programs that detect viruses and facilitate backup storage for two-year periods. Unlike other companies that sell major upgrades every 18 months or so, McAfee sends out mini-upgrades to licensees over the Internet—for free. Because distribution over the Internet is so inexpensive, McAfee boasts a 95 percent gross margin, the highest in the software business. This form of distribution also builds loyalty—renewal rates among licensees run at 85 percent. Now McAfee has developed other management software products that it also sells over the Internet at prices as much as 50 percent lower than competitors. This distribution strategy ensures that this maker of anti-virus programs will stay healthy for some time to come.[8]

1. What distribution channel does McAfee use?
2. What other channels are available to the firm?
3. How does McAfee's distribution strategy differ from that of other software manufacturers?

responsibilities, and functions cause conflict. For example, a manufacturer is likely to feel the firm would enjoy greater success and profitability if intermediaries carry only its brands, but the intermediaries believe they will do better if they carry a number of brands.

## Distribution Channels and the Marketing Mix

How are decisions about channel of distribution interrelated with the other three Ps? For one thing, channel decisions affect pricing. Marketers that distribute products through mass merchandisers such as Zellers and Canadian Tire will have different pricing objectives and strategies than those that sell to specialty stores.

Distribution decisions can sometimes give a product a distinct position in its market. For example, Peter van Stolk, the creator of Jones Cola, realized that he couldn't compete with the US$200 million Coke and Pepsi spent on advertising, so he chose to try to increase sales through unusual distribution channels. Rather than remain unnoticed on supermarket shelves and convenience stores, van Stolk chose to distribute his product in tattoo and body-piercing parlours, hair salons, sex shops, and fashion stores—anywhere that Coke and Pepsi won't go or won't be taken.

**logistics** The process of designing, managing, and improving the movement of products through the supply chain.

## Good or Bad Decision?

When a firm engages in illegal distribution practices, the marketer loses in a number of ways. The effort spent in building a distribution system is lost, competition gains ground, and courts may impose high fines on a guilty firm. To avoid costly setbacks, marketers must understand the basic legal constraints of channel arrangements. Here are some of the most common offenders:

- Exclusive dealing contracts: a written agreement allowing the retailer to carry a firm's products only if it does not carry other brands.

- Exclusive territories: an agreement stating that only one wholesaler or retailer will be allowed to sell the manufacturer's products in that geographic area.

- Tying contracts: an agreement in which a producer requires that a wholesaler or retailer purchase one or more of its other products along with the desired product.

Why do you think these practices spell bad business, and for whom?

## LOGISTICS: IMPLEMENTING THE VALUE CHAIN

Marketing textbooks tend to depict the practice of marketing as 90 percent planning and 10 percent implementation. In the real world, many managers would argue that this ratio should be reversed. Marketing success is very much the art of getting the timing right and delivering on promises. That's why marketers place so much emphasis on efficient **logistics**, the process of designing, managing, and improving the movement of products through the supply chain. Logistics includes purchasing, manufacturing, storage, and transport. To understand logistics, we must first examine the concept of supply chain management.

## The Supply Chain

The **supply chain** includes all the firms that engage in activities that are necessary to convert raw materials into a good or service and put it in the hands of a consumer or business customer. Thus, **supply chain management** is the management of flows among the firms in a supply chain to maximize total profitability.

The difference between a supply chain and a channel of distribution is the number of members and their function. A supply chain consists of those firms that supply the raw materials, component parts, and supplies necessary for a firm to produce a good or service *plus* the firms that facilitate the movement of that product to the ultimate users of the product, that is, the channel members. As shown in Exhibit 10.8, a supply chain can be complicated and sophisticated, and often software is needed to ensure a link in the chain does not break.

Figure 10.4 provides a simple example of a supply chain for a computer maker such as Hewlett-Packard. Of course, Hewlett-Packard uses hundreds of suppliers in manufacturing its computers and sells those items through hundreds of online and off-line retailers worldwide. And it is noteworthy that the role individual firms play within the supply chain depends on your perspective. If we are looking at Hewlett-Packard's supply chain, Intel is a supplier and Best Buy is a member of its channel of distribution. From Intel's perspective, Hewlett-Packard is a customer. From the perspective of Best Buy, Hewlett-Packard is a supplier.

Another way to look at the supply chain is as a value chain. The **value chain** concept looks at the supply chain from the perspective of adding value.[9] As a product "flows" from a producer to the consumer, other firms add value by providing supporting materials (such as packaging), financing, providing a physical space to store or display the item, and so on. So, every firm in the channel of distribution occupies a position on a value chain whether that firm is "upstream" (it is involved fairly early on in the process) or "downstream" (relatively closer to the point where the product reaches the consumer).

Let us see how a value chain works in our computer example. Intel takes raw materials such as silicon and adds value by turning them into chips. Intel ships these chips to Hewlett-Packard, which combines them with the other components of a computer, again adding value. Best Buy takes the finished product and adds value by providing display, sales support, repair service, financing, and so forth for the customer. Ideally, then, the product a consumer "catches" in the value stream has been transformed as it journeys from the source of the stream to its end (Exhibit 10.9).

## The Lowdown on Logistics

Logistics was originally a military term used to describe everything needed to deliver troops and equipment to the right place, at the right time, and in the right condition. In business, logistics is similar in that its objective is to deliver exactly what the consumer wants—at the right time, in the

**supply chain** All the firms that engage in activities necessary to turn raw materials into a good or service and put it in the hands of the consumer or business customer.

**supply chain management** The management of flows among firms in the supply chain to maximize profitability.

**value chain** The concept of a supply chain that looks at how each firm receives inputs, adds value to these inputs, and then passes them along to the next firm in the value chain.

**Exhibit 10.8**

A supply chain can be complicated and sophisticated software is often needed to be sure a link in the chain doesn't break.

| Raw Materials → | Parts Suppliers → | Manufacturer → | Resellers → | Consumers |
|---|---|---|---|---|
| Plastic | Intel Chips | | CompuSmart | Paula |
| Aluminum | Sony CD-ROM | | Best Buy | David |
| Copper | Microsoft Software | Hewlett-Packard | Microwarehouse.com | Angela |
| Silicon | Seagate Hard Drives | | Office Depot | Ann |

**Supplier Network**       **Channel of Distribution**

**The Supply Chain**

**Figure 10.4** Supply Chain

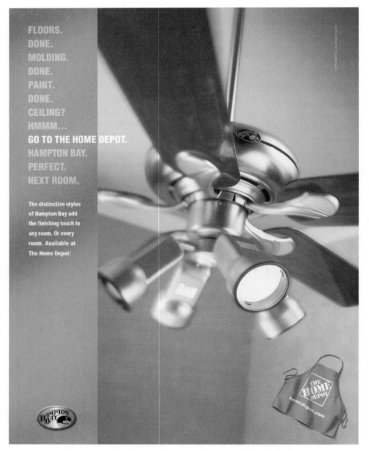

**Exhibit 10.9**

In a value chain, each member firm adds value to the product as it moves downstream. Retailers like Home Depot provide classes on how to install what customers buy there.

right place, at the right price. The application of logistics is essential to the efficient management of the supply chain. Just as it's said, "an army travels on its stomach" (meaning it cannot function without adequate supplies), so a business relies on efficient planning to be sure it has what it needs to contribute its part to the value chain.

## Logistics Functions

In developing logistics strategies, marketers must make decisions related to the five functions of logistics: order processing, warehousing, materials handling, transportation, and inventory control. For each decision, managers must consider how to minimize costs while maintaining the service customers want.

**ORDER PROCESSING** Order processing includes the series of activities that occurs between the time an order comes into the organization and the time a product goes out the door. After an order is received, it is typically sent electronically to an office for record keeping and then to the warehouse to be filled. When the order reaches the warehouse, personnel there check to see if the item is in stock. If it is not, the order is placed on back-order status. That information is sent to the office and then to the customer. If the item is available, it is located in the warehouse, packaged for shipment, and scheduled for pickup by either in-house or external shippers.

Many firms have automated this process. Once an order is in the system, all of the other steps occur automatically. Inventories are continuously updated in computer databases so that a sales representative who calls on customers or telemarketers who take orders by phone know immediately whether the product is in stock.

**WAREHOUSING** Whether we speak of fresh-cut flowers, canned goods, or computer chips, at some point goods (unlike services) must be stored. Storing goods allows marketers to match supply with demand. For example, toys and other gift items are big sellers at Christmas, but toy factories operate 12 months of the year. **Warehousing**—storing goods in anticipation of sale or transfer to another member of the channel of distribution—

**warehousing** Storing goods in anticipation of sale or transfer to another member of the channel of distribution.

**Exhibit 10.10**

By warehousing goods, marketers can match supply with demand.

enables marketers to provide time utility to consumers by holding onto products until consumers need them (Exhibit 10.10).

Part of developing effective logistics is deciding how many warehouses a firm needs, where, and what type they should be. A firm determines the location of its warehouse(s) by the location of customers and access to major highways, airports, or rail transportation. The number of warehouses often depends on the level of service customers require. If customers generally require fast delivery (today or tomorrow at the latest), then it may be necessary to store products in a number of different locations where they can be delivered to the customer within a few days.

Firms use private and public warehouses to store goods. With private warehouses, firms have a high initial investment but they also lose less inventory due to damage. Public warehouses are an alternative, allowing firms to pay for a portion of warehouse space. Most countries offer public warehouses in all large cities and many smaller cities to support domestic and international trade. A *distribution centre* is a warehouse that stores goods for short periods of time and that provides other functions, such as breaking bulk.

**MATERIALS HANDLING** **Materials handling** is the moving of products into, within, and out of warehouses. When goods come into the warehouse, they must be physically identified, checked for damage, sorted, and labelled. Next they are taken to a location for storage. Finally, they are recovered from the storage area for packaging and shipment. The goods may be handled over a dozen separate times. Procedures that limit the number of times a product must be handled decrease the likelihood of damage and reduce the cost of materials handling.

**TRANSPORTATION** Logistics decisions take into consideration the modes of transportation and the individual freight carriers a firm needs to use to move products among channel members. Making transportation decisions entails a compromise between minimizing cost and providing the service customers want. As shown in Table 10.3, modes of transportation, including railroads, pipelines, water transportation, motor carriers, and airways, differ in the following ways:

- *Dependability:* the ability of the carrier to deliver goods safely and on time.

- *Cost:* the total transportation costs for moving a product from one location to another, including any charges for loading, unloading, and in-transit storage.

- *Speed of delivery:* the total time for moving a product from one location to another, including loading and unloading.

**materials handling** The moving of products into, within, and out of warehouses.

- *Accessibility:* the number of different locations the carrier serves.
- *Capability:* the ability of the carrier to handle a variety of different products (e.g., large and small, fragile and bulky).
- *Traceability:* the ability of the carrier to locate goods in shipment.

Each mode of transportation has strengths and weaknesses that make it a good choice for different transportation needs. Table 10.3 summarizes these.

*Railroads.* Railroads are best for carrying heavy or bulky items, such as coal and other mining products, agricultural products, forest products, steel, automobiles, and large machines over long distances. Railroads are about average in their cost and provide moderate speed of delivery. Although rail transportation provides dependable, low-cost service to many locations, trains simply cannot carry goods to every community in the country, and they can't go over the oceans. These problems with rail transportation have been solved in recent years. *Piggyback services* allow low-cost rail transportation for shipping to a larger number of destinations. Truck trailers are loaded onto trains and carried as close to their destination as possible. Truck, train, and ship transportation has been similarly combined to provide *fishyback services.* Combining truck and air transportation is called *birdyback service.* Problems of excessive handling and damage have been reduced by *containerization*, in which large quantities of goods are sealed in large protective containers for transit.

*Water.* Ships and barges, like railroads, carry large, bulky, non-perishable goods and are very important in international trade. Water transportation is quite low in cost but is very slow.

*Trucking.* Arnold Bros. Transport Ltd. promises "on the road and on time!" Trucks or motor carriers, such as those operated by Arnold Bros. in Exhibit 10.11, are the most important carrier for consumer goods, especially for shorter hauls. Motor carrier transportation allows flexibility because trucks can travel to those locations missed by boats, trains, and planes. Trucks are also able to carry a wide variety of products, including perishable items.

Although costs are fairly high for longer-distance shipping, trucks are economical for shorter deliveries. Because trucks provide door-to-door service, product handling is minimal, reducing the chance of product damage.

**Table 10.3** A Comparison of Transportation Modes

| Transportation Mode | Dependability | Cost | Speed of Delivery | Accessibility | Capability | Traceability | Most Suitable Products |
|---|---|---|---|---|---|---|---|
| Railroads | average | average | moderate | high | high | low | heavy or bulky goods such as automobiles, grain, steel |
| Water | low | low | slow | low | moderate | low | bulky, nonperishable goods such as automobiles |
| Trucks | high | high for long distances; low for short distances | fast | high | high | high | a wide variety of products including those that need refrigeration |
| Air | high | high | very fast | low | moderate | high | high-value items such as electronic goods and fresh flowers |
| Pipeline | high | low | slow | low | low | moderate | petroleum products and other chemicals |
| Internet | high | low | very fast | potentially very high | low | high | services such as banking, information, and entertainment |

*Air.* Air transportation is the fastest and most expensive transportation mode. It is ideal to move high-value items, such as some mail, electronic goods, fresh-cut flowers, and live lobsters. Passenger airlines, air-freight carriers, and express delivery firms such as Federal Express and Parcel Post provide air transportation. Air transportation, especially the overnight services provided by express delivery firms, is becoming more and more important in the development of international markets—particularly for e-commerce where customers expect fast delivery. Ships, however, remain the major mover of international cargo, with Vancouver, Halifax, and Montreal being Canada's busiest ports.

*Pipeline.* Pipelines are used to carry such petroleum products as oil and natural gas and a few other chemicals. Pipelines primarily flow from oil or gas fields to refineries. They are very low in cost, require little energy, and are not subject to disruption by weather.

*The Internet.* The Internet is revolutionizing many distribution channels. Although scientists haven't yet figured out how to transport goods electronically, marketers of services such as banking, news, and entertainment are taking advantage of distribution opportunities provided by the Internet. Small entrepreneurs as well as larger firms such as Roots, Molson Canada, and the Bank of Montreal, have set up Web sites to make their products readily available to a worldwide market.

**INVENTORY CONTROL** A final activity of physical distribution is **inventory control**, developing and implementing a process to ensure that the firm always has goods available to meet customers' demands—no more and no less. Firms store goods, or create an inventory, for many reasons. For manufacturers, the pace of production may not match seasonal demand, and it may be more economical to produce snow skis year round than to produce them only during the winter season. For channel members that purchase goods from manufacturers or other channel intermediaries, it may be economical to order a product in quantities that don't exactly parallel demand. For example, delivery costs make it prohibitive for a retail gas station to place daily orders for just the amount of gas people will use that day. Instead, stations usually order truckloads of gasoline, holding their inventory in underground tanks. Finally, the consequences of stock-outs may be very negative. Hospitals must keep adequate supplies of blood, IV fluids, drugs, and other supplies on hand to meet emergencies, even if some items go to waste.

Inventory control has a major impact on the costs of physical distribution. If supplies of products are too low to meet fluctuations in customer demand, a firm may have to make expensive emergency deliveries or lose customers to competitors. If inventories are above demand, unnecessary storage expenses and the possibility of damage or deterioration occur.

Increasingly manufacturers are turning to quick-response, continuous replenishment, and just-in-time inventory management systems to ensure that their products are available for customers when and where they are needed and to improve the bottom lines of all channel partners. VF Corporation, maker of Lee and Wrangler jeans, uses a computerized market-response system that keeps records on what consumers buy each day from the register scanners of each of their key retail partners, automatically enters an order based on what items have been sold, and ships new jeans to arrive within three days.[10]

**Exhibit 10.11**

Arnold Bros. Transport Ltd. is one of Canada's largest independent transportation companies and a leading player in the North American transportation scene.

**inventory control** Activities to ensure that goods are always available to meet customers' demands.

# Real People, Real Decisions

## How It Worked Out at Weldwood of Canada

Weldwood presented all options to Daito, with emphasis on Option 4 as the favourite. Weldwood's weakness was an inability to supply sufficient "studs" (a wood product used in home construction) for Daito's needs, so it partnered with a competitor who could guarantee sufficient product supplies. The result was a new relationship where Weldwood arranged for a wide variety of building materials and products—including some the company didn't even produce—to be packaged and delivered to Daito's various job sites in Japan.

Thus, Mike was able to offer the customer a more comprehensive product mix and provide "one stop" shopping. Further, Mike promised the customer various other services such as quality control and shipping coordination at a cost. His overall strategy was to expand Weldwood's business with the customer and maximize the returns on goods and services provided.

Weldwood was able to offer Daito considerable goods and services at a profit, while Daito still realized considerable savings. The arrangement has worked out very well for Weldwood. Its sales volumes have more than doubled, with very attractive net margins.

Mike succeeded in this case because he has learned over time that assessing the customer's needs correctly can be very difficult; sometimes customers themselves do not know what their needs are or where the solutions may lie.

Mike's advice for career success is to know what gives you the most fulfillment and pursue your dreams. In his own case he derives the most satisfaction by concluding large deals and knowing that his actions have a significant impact on the growth of a certain housing segment. He loves being accountable for the entire marketing strategy—market development, pricing, channels, and marketing communications.

# CHAPTER SUMMARY

1. **Explain what a distribution channel is and what functions distribution channels perform.**

   A distribution channel is a series of firms or individuals that facilitates the movement of a product from the producer to the final customer. Channels provide time, place, and ownership utility for customers and reduce the number of transactions necessary for goods to flow from many manufacturers to large numbers of customers by breaking bulk and creating assortments. Channel members make the purchasing process easier by providing important customer services.

2. **Describe some of the types of wholesaling intermediaries found in distribution channels.**

   Wholesaling intermediaries are firms that handle the flow of products from the manufacturer to the retailer or business user. Merchant wholesalers are independent intermediaries that take title to a product and include both full-function wholesalers and limited-function wholesalers. Merchandise agents and brokers are independent intermediaries that do not take title to products. Manufacturer-owned channel members include sales branches, sales offices, and manufacturers' showrooms.

   Distribution channels vary in length from the simplest two-level channel to longer channels with three or more channel levels. Consumer distribution channels include direct distribution, in which the producer sells directly to consumers, and indirect channels, which may include a wholesaler and/or a retailer. Business-to-business channels may also be either direct or indirect and often include industrial distributors. Distribution channels for services are usually direct but may include an agent intermediary. Many firms are part of more than one type of channel, participating in dual or multiple distribution systems.

3. **Discuss the steps in planning distribution channel strategies.**

   Marketers begin channel planning by developing channel objectives and considering important environmental factors. Conventional marketing systems include multiple levels of intermediaries that work independently. Vertical marketing systems (VMS) are channels in which there is cooperation at the different levels and may be administered, corporate, or contractual. Horizontal marketing systems are composed of firms at one channel level that work together.

   Distribution planning also includes decisions about the number of channel members at each level. Intensive distribution includes all possible intermediaries, exclusive distribution has only one intermediary per region, and selective distribution includes a few but not all outlets in a region. Distribution tactics include the selection of individual channel members and management of the channel.

4. **Describe what a supply chain is, how it is related to a value chain, and how logistics is used to implement the value chain.**

   The supply chain includes all the firms that engage in activities that are necessary to turn raw materials into a good or service for a consumer or business customer including those in the marketing channel of distribution. Every firm occupies a position on a value chain. Companies add value to inputs received from firms upstream. Logistics is the process of designing, managing, and improving supply chains, including all those activities that are required to move products through the supply chain. Logistics activities include order processing, warehousing, materials handling, transportation, and inventory control.

# CHAPTER REVIEW

## Marketing Concepts: Testing Your Knowledge

1. What is a channel of distribution? What are channel intermediaries?
2. Explain the functions of distribution channels.
3. List and explain the types of independent and manufacturer-owned wholesaling intermediaries.
4. What is a direct channel? An indirect channel?
5. Explain the steps in distribution planning.
6. What are conventional, vertical, and horizontal marketing systems?
7. Explain intensive, exclusive, and selective forms of distribution.
8. What is a channel leader?
9. What is a supply chain? How is it related to a value chain?
10. What activities are involved in logistics?
11. What are the advantages and disadvantages of shipping by rail? By air? By ship? By truck?

## Marketing Concepts: Discussing Choices and Issues

1. You have probably heard someone say, "The reason products cost so much is because of all the intermediaries." Do intermediaries increase the cost of products? Would consumers be better off or worse without intermediaries?
2. Many entrepreneurs choose to start a franchise business rather than "go it alone." Do you think franchises offer the typical businessperson good opportunities? What are some positive and negative aspects of purchasing a franchise?
3. As colleges and universities are looking for better ways to satisfy their customers, an area of increasing interest is the distribution of their product—education. Describe the characteristics of your school's channel(s) of distribution. What types of innovative distribution might make sense for your school to try?

## Marketing Practice: Applying What You've Learned

1. Assume that you have recently been hired as the director of marketing for a medium-sized furniture manufacturer. Your firm specializes in producing small tables and chests, each of which is made unique with a hand-painted design. As your firm is beginning to expand into new regions of the country, you must consider whether an intensive, selective, or exclusive distribution system is best for your product.
   a. Develop an outline listing the pros and cons of each type of system for your product.
   b. Decide which you will recommend, and say why.
2. As the one-person marketing department for a candy manufacturer (your firm makes high-quality, hand-dipped chocolates of only natural ingredients), you are considering making changes in your distribution strategy. Your products have previously been sold through a network of food brokers who call on specialty food and gift stores. But you think that it would be good for your firm to develop a corporate VMS (vertical integration). In such a plan, a number of company-owned retail outlets would be opened across the country. The president of your company has asked that you present your ideas to the company executives. In a role-playing situation with one of your classmates, present your ideas to your boss, including the advantages and disadvantages of the new plan compared to the current distribution method.
3. Assume that you have recently been given a new marketing assignment by your firm. You are to head up development of a distribution plan for a new product line—a series of do-it-yourself instruction CDs for home gardeners. These CDs would show consumers how to plant trees and shrubbery and bulbs, how to care for their plants, how to prune, and so on. You know that in developing a distribution plan, it is essential that you understand and consider a number of internal and external environmental factors. Make a list of the information you will need before you can begin developing the distribution plan. How will you adapt your plan based on each of these factors?

## Marketing Mini-Project: Learning by Doing

In Canada, the distribution of most products is fairly easy. There are many independent inter-mediaries (wholesalers, dealers, distributors, and retailers) that are willing to cooperate to get the product to the final customer. Our highway system combines with rail, air, and water trans-portation to provide excellent means for moving goods from one part of the country to another. In many other countries, the means for distribution of products are far less efficient and effec-tive.

For this mini-project, you and one or more of your classmates should first select a consumer product, probably one that you normally purchase. Then use either or both library sources and other people (e.g., retailers, manufacturers, dealers, classmates) to gather information to do the following:

1. Describe the path the product takes to get from the producer to you. Draw a model to show each of the steps the product takes. Include as much as you can about transportation, ware-housing, materials handling, order processing, and inventory control.

2. Select another country in which the same or a similar product is sold. Describe the path the product takes to get from the producer to the customer in that country.

3. Determine if the differences between the two countries cause differences in price, availabil-ity, or quality of the product.

4. Make a presentation to your class on your findings.

## Real People, Real Surfers: Exploring the Web

Chapters.indigo.ca (**www.chapters.indigo.ca**) is one of many book retailers that are seeking to develop a competitive advantage through distribution, by offering customers online shopping services. Some other leaders in Internet shopping are Amazon.com (**www.amazon.com**) and Barnes & Noble (**www.bn.com**).

Explore these or other book and music selling sites. Based on your experience, answer these questions.

1. Describe the online shopping services offered by Chapters.

2. Describe the online shopping services offered by the other retailers you have researched.

3. What differences do you see in the online shopping services offered to consumers by the different booksellers?

4. Distribution planning seeks to make products available to customers when and where they want them. Do all customers want book-shopping services available on the Internet? What book-related services do you think consumers and business customers want on the Internet? What services do you think they would prefer through a different distribution channel? Which segments of customers do you think prefer online book shopping to the in-store experience?

5. Of the booksellers that you have studied, which do you think provides a competitive advan-tage for customers like yourself, and why?

6. What is your overall opinion of the bookseller Web sites you visited? What is it about the sites that makes them appealing to potential customers? Is adequate information about the service provided? Is one site easier to navigate than the other? Based on the design of the Web site, which customers do you think each bookseller is most interested in attracting?

Steven Poirier, vice-president of sales and marketing for Moosehead Brewery, considered his options for increasing sales of the popular Moosehead brands of beer. Having operated as a craft brewery for 127 years in Saint John, New Brunswick, Moosehead Brewery now distributes its beer to every province in Canada, except Saskatchewan and Quebec, and sells it internationally in over 60 countries. Although Moosehead is a profitable company, Poirier and the other executives realized that there was still unused capacity in their production facilities. To increase efficiency, Moosehead investigated the viability of additional distribution markets. Quebec seemed like the next logical step for distribution. The province is densely populated, with 7.3 million residents, and is the second largest beer consumption market in Canada, consuming 5.3 million hectolitres a year. As Quebec and New Brunswick are neighbouring provinces, distribution costs would be significantly less than shipping to other markets.

Poirier considered the company's usual marketing strategy. Moosehead's basic strategy focuses on selling their product as a premium Canadian lager. Their approach in each market differs, based on volume, market conditions, as well as distributor and government regulations. Within Canada, Moosehead starts out with a strong licensee push to generate trial and awareness, as this is the most cost-effective way to promote the product. It then begins to overlay advertising through print, radio, and billboards and signs. It could use a similar strategy in Quebec, taking into account language and cultural differences.

Poirier, very familiar with the Canadian food and beverage industry—having worked for Bacardi Rum and McCain Foods—realized that there would be challenges to distributing Moosehead products in Quebec. New Brunswick and Quebec have historically struggled with high inter-provincial trade barriers, and there were strong labour and corporate lobby groups that wanted to keep Moosehead out of the province.

The push against Moosehead was being led by a smaller Quebec brewery, whose product is not selling well in the New Brunswick market. The Quebec company believes that the New Brunswick regulations are causing the poor sales. Their product, however, is sold at a very high premium price and is a Belgian-style beer, quite different in taste from English-style ales and lagers. It is also difficult to compare the regulations of out-of-province product, as the New Brunswick and Quebec practices are structured differently.

New Brunswick marks up out-of-province beer by an additional $59 per hectolitre, but also guarantees 100 percent retail distribution. Quebec, however, is not involved in the liquor industry, so it does not offer any distribution services. Subcontracting the distribution costs a company a minimum of $48 per hectolitre, but this does not provide any guarantee of listings. To list the product, most breweries need to account for another $24 per hectolitre. Moosehead believes that these factors will contribute to higher costs when selling in Quebec. However, the provincial regulators do not recognize this.

Other challenges involve physical distribution and channel management. In British Columbia and Ontario, all alcoholic beverages are sold through government-owned liquor distribution branches (LDB). Trucks carrying Moosehead beer have relatively few stops to deliver product to the LDBs. In-store promotions are typically coordinated centrally and are similar for each of the government retail outlets, making promotion management fairly straightforward. In Alberta and Quebec, however, alcohol is sold to independent retailers or retail chains. Each retailer is responsible for negotiating contracts as well as for obtaining and promoting product. The breweries also have to assume the cost of warehousing the inventory. Selling beer in these provinces is similar to selling other retail products, such as cola or toothpaste, and requires a stronger channel management program. Moosehead would also have to ensure that the labels follow Quebec language regulations.

To balance these challenges, Moosehead already has very high brand awareness in Quebec. Their initial studies indicate that retailers are very interested in stocking Moosehead beer, and the company is confident that it will attain high-volume sales. Sales are excellent in areas surrounding Quebec. Although the two major Canadian breweries enjoy a 90 percent market share, Moosehead has the largest market share of the "smaller breweries." Poirier feels he could maintain Moosehead's premium image and pricing in the Quebec market because of this brand awareness.

After much thought and analysis, Poirier thought that entering the Quebec market made sense for Moosehead. It was not clear, however, how best to do this. Poirier knew that he needed to devise a market entry strategy for Quebec, make marketing mix decisions consistent with this strategy and the Quebec market, and focus particularly on distribution and relationship management issues. There would be implementation issues, but he didn't know if any of these would be insurmountable.

## Things to Think About

1. What marketing mix and market entry strategy would you recommend for Moosehead?

2. How would you manage Moosehead's relationships with Quebec retailers and other key stakeholders?

3. What issues, barriers, or limitations would need to be overcome to implement your strategy? Do any of these seem insurmountable?

4. What additional research or analysis would you want to conduct before implementing your launch strategy?

## Super Bacteria—Part 1

As Sam the entrepreneur says in this video, "Having a good product is just the beginning. It is all about getting it out there." Sam correctly recognizes that channels of distribution play a vital role in the success or failure of a product. His first invention, a hammock, didn't make it big in the marketplace initially (but at the end of the video we see that sales from the hammock are paying Sam's mortgage).

His new product is a disinfectant spray made entirely from plant extracts. Sam claims it is extremely effective and completely non-toxic to the consumer (the first child-safe disinfectant). He wants a piece of the $1.6 billion market for this product category. So, he formed a company along with his mother. The idea was born when Sam's wife visited a rather dirty public washroom and wished she had a disinfectant spray. Made from thyme, Sensible has been approved by Health Canada as an all-natural disinfectant. (Sam later changes its name to Benefect as Sensible sounds too "fluffy.")

However, he will be competing against big corporations who make powerful brands such as Lysol and Clorox, and who have the power to spend more per commercial than the entire sum of money Sam has ever made. How, then, can Sam succeed?

He and his investors initially consider licensing, an arrangement where they give the rights to another manufacturer who will be responsible for sales, while Sam keeps the royalties. But Sam does not like the idea because if the arrangement does not work, he will have wasted time not growing the business on his own.

Sam hires John Gibbons, a broker who matches products with retailers. Together they make a pitch to Shoppers Drug Mart. Expectations are high after the first meeting: Shoppers Drug Mart may want to carry the product in all its stores. Like any typical entrepreneur, Sam is ecstatic, but John cautions him that all he *may* be given is shelf space on the retail floor.

Now, the real work begins. Sam hires a salesperson with a proven track record, a logo consultant, and an image consultant who helps him position the brand in a competitive marketplace. The brand's message is all ready, but there is one hitch: Shoppers Drug Mart has not yet placed an order. And it never does. Why does Shoppers pull the plug on Sam's product? The answer is simple: it cannot "delist" other established brands on its shelves to make room for Benefect.

## Questions

1. Do you agree with Sam that having a good product is just the beginning; it's all about getting the product out into the marketplace? Does this mean that, among the marketing mix elements, channels of distribution (place) is the most important?

2. Given your understanding of the product and its benefits, evaluate whether Sam should have
   a. a conventional, vertical, or horizontal marketing system.
   b. intensive, exclusive, or selective distribution.

3. What other distribution channels would you recommend for Benefect?

Source: This case was prepared by Ajay Sirsi and is based on "Super Bacteria," *Venture* #885.

# CHAPTER 11
## Retailing and E-tailing

## CHAPTER OBJECTIVES

WHEN YOU HAVE COMPLETED YOUR STUDY OF THIS CHAPTER, YOU SHOULD BE ABLE TO

1. Define retailing and describe how retailers evolve over time.

2. Describe how retailers are classified.

3. Understand the importance of store image to a retail positioning strategy, and explain some of the actions a retailer can take to create a desired image in the marketplace.

4. Describe the major forms of non-store retailing.

5. Describe the opportunities and barriers to e-tailing.

# Real People, Real Decisions

## Meet **Dawn Robertson,** a Decision Maker at Federated Direct

Dawn Robertson is President and Chief Merchandising Officer at Federated Direct. After obtaining a Bachelor of Science degree in Fashion Merchandising from Auburn University in 1977, Dawn secured a job as a buyer and executive trainee with Davidson's, then a division of R.H. Macy & Co. Before joining Federated, Dawn was president and chief executive officer of McCrae's, a division of Saks, Inc.

Discount stores, catalogue companies, and online upstarts have been grabbing business right and left from department stores. Being the president and chief merchandising officer at Federated Direct, the Federated department stores' consumer catalogue and e-commerce division, Dawn Robertson looked for ways to outperform these rivals. She saw one opportunity for growth in the bridal business, especially since increasing numbers of baby boomers' kids would be at the age to get married over the next decade. Since Federated added an Internet component to its Bridal Registry operation, the total bridal business (both in-store and online) now reported to her.

Under the right conditions, Dawn was convinced Federated could acquire new customers and win the lifetime loyalty of millions of brides and grooms. In fact, her research showed that over half of women who get engaged shop at new stores as they prepare for the Big Day—and three years later 96 percent of them are still shopping at those stores. That's a relationship worth cultivating.

Even though Federated Stores, which include Macy's East and West, Bloomingdale's, Rich's, Lazarus, Goldsmiths, Burdines, and The Bon Marche, were recognized as the leaders in Bridal Registry, younger consumers in greater numbers were going to newer, cooler specialty stores. To make matters worse, Dawn knew that a poor bridal registry experience could poison the relationship brides, grooms, and their wedding guests have with a store. She also recognized that Federated was not alone in seeing the potential of this business: Competition is fierce as retailers such as Bed, Bath and Beyond; Target; and Crate and Barrel lure droves of engaged couples to their registries.

Two other trends factored into Dawn's thinking: (1) Offering engaged couples personalized bridal consulting, once the advantage of the department store, was eroding as Web-savvy women were doing research online, (2) With the exception of certain brands of china, specialty and discount stores were carrying the same merchandise as traditional department stores at cheaper prices.

So, Dawn reviewed customer feedback gathered from 15 000 customer surveys, 10 focus groups, and evaluations of competitors conducted by Federated staff. The research found that consumers liked Federated's bridal merchandise overall, but in-store service and visual displays were in need of work. And, unlike some of its competitors' private label offerings, Federated store brands did not evoke an emotional connection with its customers. Also Dawn learned that brides- (and grooms-) to-be love using the scanning gun that lets them scan in the items they want to register without the need for a salesperson. However, this cool tool was no longer novel or rare. Many stores, even discounters, offered a self-scan option.

Dawn had three options to enhance Federated's bridal services business.

**Option 1.** Offer a total bridal solution. Maintain the existing bridal registry business (the product offerings and service), but invest in buying bridal dress and tuxedo businesses, while developing alliances with a national florist and a bridal magazine to make Federated the "Total Bridal Location." This strategy would differentiate Federated from its competitors by offering a broad selection of services that the bride and groom need. But, this option would require a significant investment. And, these extra businesses would not be a core competency—it's difficult for big retailers to compete with smaller stores on customer service.

**Option 2.** Slowly enhance registry offerings. Improve Federated's bridal offerings slowly without adding significant investment. Focus on providing better in-store training to sales representatives and better merchandise selection, particularly in the china and crystal categories that make up 50 percent of bridal sales. This conservative financial strategy would slightly increase sales and bridal registrations without draining the company of time and money. However, this strategy would not deter competitors from taking away bridal registry market share, and it would not establish Federated as a leader in this category.

**Option 3.** Completely redo the bridal registry. Totally revamp Federated's core bridal business and give it a new marketing push. This strategy would require significant change in merchandise selection, pricing policies, and customer service. Such a radical move could either succeed beautifully or fail miserably. It would take management's time away from other initiatives, cost a lot of money, and be difficult to execute across both Federated's bricks-and-mortar and online operations.

Now, put yourself in Dawn Robertson's shoes: Which option would you choose, and why?

# RETAILING: SPECIAL DELIVERY

Shop 'til you drop! For many people, obtaining the product is half the fun. Others would rather walk over hot coals than spend time in a store. Marketers need to find ways to deliver products and services that please both types of consumers. **Retailing** is the final stop on the distribution path—the process by which goods and services are sold to consumers for their personal use.

A retail outlet is often more than simply a place where you buy something. The retailer adds or subtracts value from the offering with its image, inventory, service quality, location, and pricing policy. In many cases, the shopping experience is what is being bought as well as the products we take home. That's what visitors to the Discovery Channel store in Washington, DC, get when they meet up with a life-size model of a *Tyrannosaurus rex* on the main floor of the four-level store. The place feels like a museum with such attractions as a cockpit from a vintage World War II plane.[1] Similarly, part of IKEA's strategy is to make the store a shopping destination with experiences that encourage shoppers to spend more time there.

Retailers are a special breed of marketers. They assemble and present products, often from many different manufacturers, in ways that make them appealing and accessible, and often develop unique and exciting store images that are similar to the product branding strategies we've already discussed. In this chapter, we explore the different types of retailers, comparing and contrasting them along some key dimensions, keeping in mind that today's shoppers have so many retail choices—boutiques, department stores, ordering by phone, and clicking on a Web site. How does a retailer—whether a traditional one operating a store or a non-store retailer selling via television, phone, or computer—lure the consumer? These important marketing questions get more difficult to answer as the competition for customers intensifies. We start with an overview of where retailing has been and where it's going.

**retailing** The final stop in the distribution channel by which goods and services are sold to consumers for their personal use.

**IKEA**
www.ikea.com

## Retailing: A Mixed (Shopping) Bag

Retailing is big business. About one in eight Canadian workers is employed in retailing, and the sales from more than 180 000 retail stores represents about 6.2 percent of Canada's gross domestic product.[2] Although we tend to associate huge chains like IKEA, Canadian Tire, and The Bay with retailing activity, most retailers (about 75 percent) are independent small businesses.[3] Some retailers, such as Home Depot and Costco, are also wholesalers, which provide goods and services to businesses as well as end consumers. We saw how the wholesaling process works in the previous chapter. Now, we'll focus on the process that delivers goods and services to individuals for their personal use.

Retailers provide many benefits to consumers. Some save people time or money by providing an assortment of merchandise under one roof. Others search the world for the most exotic delicacies, allowing shoppers access to goods they would otherwise never see. Still others, such as Chapters and Indigo bookstores, provide us with interesting environments in which to spend our leisure time and, they hope, our money.

## The Evolution of Retailing

Retailers have taken many forms over time, including the simple peddler who hawked his wares from a horse-drawn cart, a majestic urban department store, an intimate boutique, and a huge hypermarket which sells everything from potato chips to snow tires. Old types of retailers routinely give way to new variations, as economic, social, and cultural developments change the face of society. That horse-drawn cart has been replaced by the cart that sits in the middle of your local mall, selling new-age jewellery or monogrammed golf balls to passersby en route to grab a plate of sushi in the food court or catch a movie at a state-of-the-art theatre. As times change, different types of retailers emerge, often replacing

**wheel-of-retailing hypothesis** A theory that explains how retail firms change, becoming more upscale as they go through their life cycle.

**retail life cycle** A process that focuses on the various retail life cycle stages from introduction to decline.

**Office Depot**
www.officedepot.ca

older, outmoded types. How can we understand and predict what the dominant types of retailing will be tomorrow or 10 years from now to be sure that we keep in step?

**THE WHEEL OF RETAILING** One of the oldest and simplest explanations for these changes is the **wheel-of-retailing hypothesis**. This states that new types of retailers find it easiest to enter the market by offering goods at lower prices than competitors.[4] After they gain a foothold, they gradually trade up, improving their facilities, increasing the quality of merchandise, and offering amenities like parking and gift wrapping. This upscaling results in greater investment and operating costs, so the store must raise its prices to remain profitable, which then makes it vulnerable to still newer entrants that can afford to charge lower prices. And so the wheel turns. The wheel of retailing helps to explain the development of some, but not all, forms of retailing. For example, some retailers never trade up; they simply continue to occupy a niche as discounters. Others, such as upscale specialty stores, start out at the high end. Let's take a look at a more satisfying explanation.

**THE RETAIL LIFE CYCLE** Retailers sell products; but in a way, retailers also *are* products, because they provide benefits such as convenience or status to consumers and they must offer a competitive advantage over other retailers to survive. A better way to understand how retailers evolve is the **retail life cycle**. Like the product life cycle, this perspective recognizes that retailers are born, they live, and eventually they die. The life cycle approach allows us to categorize retail stores in terms of the conditions they face at different points in the cycle.[5]

In the *introduction* stage, the new retailer is often an aggressive entrepreneur who takes a unique approach to doing business. This may mean competing on the basis of low cost, as the wheel of retailing suggests. However, the new guy on the block may enter the market by offering a distinctive assortment or a different way to distribute items, such as through the Internet. In this initial stage, profits are low due to high development costs.

As the business enters the *growth* stage, the retailer catches on with shoppers, and sales and profits rise. But a new idea doesn't stay new for long. Others start to copy it, and competition increases, so the retailer needs to expand what it offers. Often the retailer responds by opening more outlets and developing systems to distribute goods to these new stores, which may cut profits, as the firm invests in new buildings and fixtures.

In the *maturity* stage, the industry has over expanded, and intense competition makes it difficult to maintain customer loyalty. Profits decline, as retailers resort to price cutting to keep their customers. This pattern applies to department stores like The Bay and fast-food chains like McDonald's. Office supply superstores are entering the mature phase of the retail life cycle, which means they need to find ways of differentiating themselves other than price. For example, Office Depot enlisted the help of cartoon character Dilbert, the stereotypical cubicle dweller, to forge a distinctive identity claiming: "Business is crazy. Office Depot makes sense."[6]

In the *decline* stage, retail businesses, like the general store or the peddler, become obsolete, as newer ways of doing business emerge. The outmoded retailer does not have to fold its tent at this stage: Marketers that anticipate these shifts can avert decline by changing to meet the times. For example, full-service gas stations had difficulty competing with self-service discount outlets. Many responded by adding variety stores to their retail mix for drivers wanting to buy a tank of gas and groceries at the same location, as seen in Exhibit 11.1. Canada Safeway is doing the opposite—adding gasoline to their retail mix.[7]

## The Evolution Continues: What's "in Store" for the Future?

As our world continues to rapidly change, retailers are scrambling to keep up. Three important factors motivate innovative merchants to reinvent the way they do business.

**DEMOGRAPHICS** As noted in Chapter 2, keeping up with changes in population characteristics is at the heart of many marketing developments. Retailers can no longer afford to stand by and assume that their customer base is the same as it has always been. They are

**Exhibit 11.1**

Full-service gas stations fight off decline by adding products to their retail mix.

coming up with new ways to sell their products to diverse groups. Major demographic factors altering the face of retailing include:

- *Convenience for working women:* Some retailers are expanding their hours of operation, because many harried women have time to shop only at night. Others, including dry cleaners and pharmacies, are adding drive-up windows to meet demands for convenience and security. In some areas, from financial services to interior decorating and clothing, enterprising individuals have turned time shortage into a business opportunity by offering their services as shopping consultants for those unwilling or unable to shop on their own. Many major department stores also fill this need by offering the services of their own in-house consultants at no charge.

- *Catering to specific age segments:* Retailers are recognizing that there are many opportunities to specialize in providing for the needs of different age groups. For example, IKEA is responding to its me-too rivals by developing Children's IKEA, which sells furniture and related products for kids. The company recruited psychologists to assist in creating 600 new products for this market, from egg-shaped cribs to fabric dolls.[8]

- *Recognizing ethnic diversity:* Although members of every ethnic group can usually find local retailers that understand and cater to their specific needs, larger companies must tailor their strategies to the cultural makeup of specific areas. George Michel, president of the Toronto-based Burger King Restaurants of Canada, for example, recognized that catering to multiculturalism would benefit the company. With 25 percent of the Toronto population of Chinese descent, Michel began the "Now we're speaking the same language" ad campaign in Cantonese, focusing on strategic locations. Burger King also rolled out its veggie burger to ethnic markets to appeal to non-beef-eating East Indian and East Asian markets.[9] Canada's native peoples represent an under-served market niche. In the three Prairie Provinces they make up at least 10 percent of the population, half of them are under 30, their education levels are soaring, and land-claim settlements (across Canada) are forecasted to be $15 billion by 2010.[10]

**TECHNOLOGY** Technology is revolutionizing retailing. In-store video channels entertain customers by giving messages about local events or showing ads.[11] Some stores feature

**Exhibit 11.2**

Food for future thought: New database technology puts supermarkets in the high-tech fast lane.

talking posters that contain a human body sensor that speaks up when a shopper approaches.[12] Other stores (Exhibit 11.2) are experimenting with wireless networks that allow shoppers to scan in their own items as they shop, eliminating the need for checkout lines.[13] When shoppers enter a store, whatever chip-enabled device they are carrying—a cellphone, palm computer, or smart card—interacts with a store's computer system to update the shopper's buying profile and provide the shopper with individualized communications, coupons, and other incentives.[14] And widespread use of the personal computer has turned many homes into virtual malls, as consumers surf the Web from the comfort of their own chairs.

Some of the most profound changes are not even visible to shoppers, such as advanced electronic **point-of-sale (POS) systems**,

**point-of-sale (POS) systems** Retail computer systems that collect sales data and are hooked directly into the store's inventory control system.

which collect sales data, are hooked directly into the store's inventory control system, and place timely orders to ensure that the store does not stock out of an item. Birks Jewellers, for example, uses their new POS system for this purpose; but in the future, the chain expects to use it for such marketing applications as analyzing trends and planning local sales.[15]

Other technological innovations will radically change the way we shop in the future. One leading retailer predicts that in the year 2010: "Each consumer will have a personal preference card, so a store will know your tastes, clothing sizes, and even your current household decor. When shopping for furniture, a design consultant will call up a 3-D image of your living room, and show you how your new purchases will actually look in the room. Or, forget about endlessly trying on clothes—holographic imaging will let you 'see' yourself in a new suit or dress."[16] As Exhibit 11.3 shows, sophisticated body scanners already exist that can read a person's exact dimensions and send this information to machines that produce clothing precisely tailored to individual proportions.

**GLOBALIZATION** As we know, the world is becoming a smaller place. Retailers are busy expanding to other countries and bringing with them innovations and management philosophies that change the way local firms do business. Many international retailers, such as IKEA, Blockbuster Entertainment, Home Depot, and Toys 'R' Us (Exhibit 11.4), are prominent in Canadian retailing, while some Canadian retailers such as Roots, La Senza, and Mark's Work Wearhouse have made significant inroads in the United States and other parts of the world.[17] Cinnaroll Bakeries Ltd., a Western Canadian cinnamon bun retailer, has 10 Cinnzeos franchises in the Philippines and has signed an agreement for 50 more Cinnzeos throughout Southeast Asia.[18]

Of course, an understanding of global retailing means recognizing that retailing differs from country to country. In many developing countries, the retailing industry is made up of small individual retailers (Exhibit 11.5). In many parts of the develop-

**Exhibit 11.3**

Body scanners can read a person's exact dimensions and send this information to machines that produce precisely tailored clothing.

ing world, kiosks, small street corner stands, sell cigarettes, soft drinks, snacks, and batteries—the products of convenience stores.

## TYPES OF RETAILERS

We've seen that exciting things are happening in the world of retailing. But the field of retailing covers a lot of ground—from mammoth department stores to sidewalk vendors to Web sites. This section provides an overview of the different types of retailers. Retail managers need to understand the competitive environment in which they operate to make decisions about the ways to offer their merchandise to the public and to compare the productivity of their business to similar retailers.

**Exhibit 11.4**
International retailers, such as Toys 'R' Us, are prominent in Canadian retailing.

## Classifying Retailers by What They Sell

One of the most important strategic decisions a retailer makes is *what* to sell—its **merchandise mix**. This choice is similar to settling on a market segment: If a store's merchandise mix is too limited, it may not have enough potential customers; if it is too broad, the retailer runs the risk of being a "jack of all trades, master at none." A retailer's **merchandise assortment**, or merchandise mix, is the variety and selection of products it sells. It has both breadth and depth.

**merchandise mix** The total set of all products offered for sale by a firm, including all product lines sold to all consumer groups.

**merchandise assortment** The range of products sold.

**Exhibit 11.5**
In planning expansion to other countries, companies must consider the way retailing is done in each country. In China, many independent retailers take their merchandise to open markets in pedicarts.

**Merchandise breadth**, or variety, is the number of different product lines available. A *narrow assortment*, such as that found in convenience stores, means that its customers can buy only a limited selection of product lines, such as candy, cigarettes, and soft drinks. A *broad assortment*, such as that in a warehouse store, means there is a wide range of items from eyeglasses to barbecue grills.

**Merchandise depth** is the variety of choices available for each specific product. A *shallow assortment* means that the selection within a product category is limited, so a factory outlet store may sell only white and blue men's dress shirts all made by the same manufacturer and only in standard sizes. In contrast, a men's specialty store may feature a *deep assortment* of dress shirts, but not much else, in exotic shades and in hard-to-find sizes. Figure 11.1 illustrates these assortment differences for one product, science fiction books.

The strategy of carrying a mixture of merchandise items that are not directly related to each other is called **scrambled merchandising**. This strategy is exemplified by Blockbuster Entertainment Group, which defines its merchandise mix in terms of products a customer might want when spending an evening at home, including food items and other goods. In addition to stocking your favourite James Bond video, the stores sell candy, soda, and even private-label popcorn to complete the couch potato experience.

In deciding what merchandise assortment to offer, retailers need to strike a balance between the profitability of the mix and ensuring that they have the depth and breadth required to satisfy their customers. On the profitability side, they consider the markup on particular items, projected sales volume, and gross margin (revenues minus cost of goods sold, calculated as a percentage of sales). Gross margin, however, does not consider the costs of operating the store. Knowing a store's gross margin is useful, because it is a performance measure that allows the retailer to compare how it is doing relative to similar stores. The retailer also can compare how much different product lines within the store are contributing to profits. Usually, stores that mark up items substantially will have higher gross margins than those that sell products closer to what they actually cost the store to buy.

**Inventory turnover**, or *stock turn*, is the average number of times a year a retailer expects to sell its inventory. For example, a candy store owner can expect to sell the "same" pack of gum hundreds or thousands of times a year. A jewellery store owner may need to sell only one diamond ring per year to make the same profit as the gum retailer selling a thousand packs a year. So the candy store owner hopes to sell a greater volume of merchandise to compensate for razor-thin margins. All retailers, regardless of gross margin, try to encourage more rapid turnover, because this helps guarantee that their merchandise will be "fresh" and that expenses associated with storing the products will be minimized.

Overly rapid turnover, however, results in greater costs, because products must be bought in smaller quantities. The retailer, then, can't take advantage of volume discounts offered by the manufacturer or wholesaler, and delivery charges are higher for small shipments. Successful retailers try to balance gross margin and inventory turnover. The Gap, for example, started by selling items with thin profit margins, such as inexpensive jeans and T-shirts. When competitors began imitating this strategy, the company boosted profits by modifying its merchandise mix to include more higher-margin items, such as hats and handbags.[19]

**STORE TYPES** We have seen that retailers differ in the breadth and depth of their assortments. Let's review some of the major forms these retailers take.

*Convenience stores*, such as Mac's or 7-Eleven, are neighbourhood retailers that carry a limited number of frequently purchased items, including basic food

| | Breadth | |
|---|---|---|
| | Narrow | Broad |
| **Shallow** | Airport Bookstore: a few *Star Trek* books | Zellers: a few *Star Trek* books and a limited assortment of *Star Trek* T-shirts and toys |
| **Deep** | Dwarf Books: thousands of Sci-Fi titles; no other categories | Chapters: many titles, next to hundreds of romance novels |

**Figure 11.1** Merchandise Selection for Science Fiction Books

products, newspapers, and sundries (Exhibit 11.6). They cater to consumers willing to pay a premium for the ease of buying staple items close to home. In other words, they meet the needs of those who are pressed for time, who buy items in smaller quantities, or who shop at irregular hours.

*Supermarkets*, such as Loblaws or Safeway, are food stores that carry a wide selection of edible and non-edible products. Although the large supermarket is a fixture in North America, it has not caught on to the same extent in other parts of the world. Europeans, for example, are used to walking or bicycling to small stores near their homes. They tend to have smaller food orders per trip and to shop more frequently. Wide variety is less important than quality and local ambience, though those habits are changing as huge hypermarkets have grown in popularity.

*Specialty stores*, such as La Senza, Mark's Work Warehouse, and Lee Valley Tools (Exhibit 11.7), have narrow and deep inventories. They do not sell a lot of product lines, but they offer good selection of brands within the lines they do sell. Some retailers are even establishing specialty store-within-stores, such as The Bay's in-store vitamin boutique.

*General merchandise discount stores*, such as Zellers and Wal-Mart, offer a broad assortment of items at low prices and with minimal service. Some discount stores, such as Army & Navy and Toronto's Honest Ed's, are **off-price retailers**. These stores obtain surplus merchandise from manufacturers and offer these brand name, fashion-oriented goods at low prices.

**off-price retailers** Retailers that buy excess merchandise from well-known manufacturers and pass the savings on to customers.

*Warehouse clubs*, such as Costco and the Loblaws warehouse stores, are a new version of the discount store. These establishments do not even pretend to offer any of the amenities of a store; a bargain mentality is reinforced by merchandise that is displayed, often in its original box, in a cavernous, bare-bones facility. These clubs often charge a modest membership fee to consumers and small businesses, which buy a broad assortment of food and non-food items in bulk sizes. The typical warehouse shopper is likely to have a large family and a relatively high income and can afford to pay several hundred dollars to "stock up" on staples during one shopping trip.[20]

*Factory outlet stores*, such as Danier Leather Factory Outlet, are another type of discount retailer. These stores are owned by a manufacturer and sell off its defective merchandise or excess inventory.[21] Although the assortment is not wide, because a store carries only

**Exhibit 11.6**

Convenience stores such as 7-Eleven offer consumers just that, convenience, by carrying a limited number of frequently purchased items.

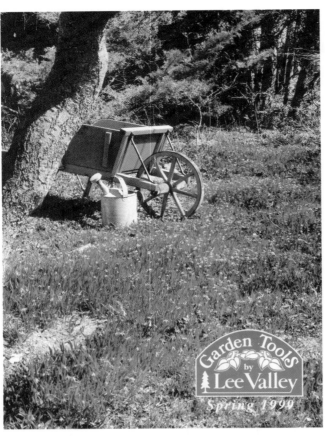

**Exhibit 11.7**

Lee Valley Tools is a specialty store targeting woodworking, gardening, and other hobby enthusiasts.

**hypermarkets** Retailers with the characteristics of both warehouse stores and supermarkets; hypermarkets are several times larger than other stores and offer virtually everything from grocery items to electronics.

**REI**

www.rei.com

products made by one manufacturer, a recent trend is for different factory outlet stores to cluster together in the same location to form an *outlet mall*.

*Department stores*, such as The Bay and Sears, sell a broad range of items and offer a deep selection organized into different sections of the store. Department stores have encountered serious problems in recent years, exemplified by the bankruptcy of Eaton's and its subsequent sale to Sears. Specialty stores have lured department store shoppers away with deeper, more cutting-edge fashion selections and better service. They have also been squeezed by mass merchandisers, catalogues, and e-commerce retailers, which can offer many of the same items at lower prices, because they don't have to shoulder expenses involved in elaborate fixtures or high salaries for knowledgeable salespeople.

**Hypermarkets** combine the characteristics of warehouse stores and supermarkets. Popular in Europe and Latin America, these huge establishments are several times larger than other stores. A supermarket might be 3700 to 4600 square metres, whereas a hypermarket takes up 18 500 to 28 000 square metres, the equivalent of four football fields. They offer one-stop shopping, often for over 50 000 items, and feature restaurants, beauty salons, and children's play areas (Exhibit 11.8). They haven't caught on as well in North America, where so many discount stores, malls, and supermarkets are available, and consumers find the hypermarkets to be so large that finding items and checking out is too time-consuming.[22]

## DEVELOPING A STORE POSITIONING STRATEGY: RETAILING AS THEATRE

Although stores can be distinguished by the breadth and depth of their assortments, we are less likely to say "I'll go to that store because their assortment is broad," and are more likely to say "That place is neat, I like going there." Stores can entertain us, they can bore us, they can make us angry or make us sad. In today's competitive marketplace, retailers have to do more than offer good inventory at reasonable prices. They need to position their stores so that they offer a competitive advantage over other stores also vying for the shopper's attention. Let's see how they do that.

Walk into REI, a Seattle-based store that sells gear for climbing, cycling, skiing, and camping. REI is more than that, though. As Exhibit 11.9 shows, the store features a 20-metre-high, artificial climbing rock, a vented area for testing camp stoves, and an outdoor trail to check out mountain bikes. Buying a water pump? Test it in an indoor river. Eyeing that new Gore-Tex jacket? See how it holds up in a simulated rainstorm.[23]

Many retailers recognize that much of what they do is really theatre. At a time when it is possible to pick up a phone or log onto a computer to buy many items, a customer must have a reason to make a trip to a store instead. True, you can probably buy that jacket over the Internet, but try getting your computer to rain on it.

Shoppers are an audience to entertain. The "play" can cleverly employ stage sets (store design) and actors (salespeople) that together create a "scene." For example, think about buying a pair of sneakers. Athletic shoe stores are a far cry from the old days, when a tired shoe salesman (much like Al Bundy in the TV show *Married with Children*) waded through box after box of shoes as kids ran amok across dingy floors. Now salespeople may be dressed in black-striped referee outfits, and stores like Foot Locker are ablaze with neon, with the shoes displayed in clear acrylic walls appearing to float.[24] All these special effects make the buying experience less about buying and more about having an experience. As one marketing strategist commented, "The line between retail and entertainment is blurring."[25]

Ontario's Liquor Control Board (LCBO) recognized the importance of entertainment to attract customers and motivate purchases. They created a 1850-square-metre mega liquor store in Toronto's Bayview Village shopping centre (Exhibit 11.10), which has 1600 different wines, 250 foreign and domestic beers, music listening stations, a gift-wrapping centre, and a demonstration kitchen for cooking presentations and wine tasting seminars—turning what was once a mundane trip to the liquor store into a great shopping experience.[26] What tools are available to the retailing playwright?

**Exhibit 11.8**

Continente, a Spanish hypermarket, offers one-stop shopping and includes a variety of smaller stores within the store.

## Store Image

When people think of a store, they often have no trouble describing it in the same terms they might a person. They use words like *exciting*, *depressed*, *old-fashioned*, *tacky*, or *elegant*. **Store image** is how the target market perceives the store—its market position relative to the competition. For example, Holt Renfrew's department store is seen by many as chic and fashionable, especially compared to a more traditional competitor such as The Bay. These

**store image** The way a retailer is perceived in the marketplace relative to the competition.

**Exhibit 11.9**

The REI store in Seattle provides a unique shopping experience.

**Exhibit 11.10**

Ontario's Liquor Control Board recognizes the importance of entertainment in retail concepts.

**atmospherics** The use of colour, lighting, scents, furnishings, and other design elements to create a desired store image.

**traffic flow** The direction in which shoppers move through the store and what areas they pass or avoid.

images don't just happen. Just as brand managers do for products, store managers work hard to create a "personality."

In developing a desirable store image, the resourceful retailer has a number of choices. Ideally, all of these elements should work together to create a clear, coherent picture that meets consumers' expectations of what that particular shopping experience should be.

**Atmospherics** is the use of colour, lighting, scents, furnishings, sounds, and other design elements to create a desired setting. Marketers manipulate these to create a certain "feeling" about the retail environment. U.S. retailer Kinney's Colorado Stores, which sell high-end outdoor clothing, has taken this to an extreme. Their stores are designed to make the shoppers feel they're out in nature: The stores pipe in new-age background music, interrupted occasionally by the sound of a thunderstorm or a babbling brook. Motion sensors in the ceiling activate displays as a shopper approaches—a person who walks near an arrangement of beach shoes, for example, may hear the sound of waves crashing.[27] The owners of these stores believe that getting people "into the mood" makes them more likely to buy what they see.

**STORE DESIGN: SETTING THE STAGE** The elements of store design should correspond to management's desired image. A bank lobby needs to convey respectability and security, because people need to be reassured about the safety of their money. In contrast, a used bookstore might create a disorderly look, so shoppers will think treasures lie buried beneath piles of tattered novels. One of the most innovative restaurant store designs in Canada is the Movenpick Marché in Toronto's BCE Place. This 400-seat restaurant has several rooms, each decorated in different styles, such as French bistro. The cafeteria-style restaurant offers stations throughout the store where customers can watch their dinner of sushi, spit-roasted Cornish hen, or fresh pasta being prepared. An in-store bakery, ice-cream parlour, and fruit and vegetable stand allow customers to complete their grocery shopping after dinner, a feature especially attractive to busy businesspeople.

Some specific design decisions management must make are:

- *Store layout.* This is the arrangement of merchandise in the store. The placement of fixtures such as shelves, racks, and cash registers is important, because store layout determines **traffic flow**—how shoppers move through the store and what areas they pass or avoid. A *grid layout*, usually found in supermarkets and discount stores, consists of rows of neatly spaced shelves that are at right angles or parallel to one another. This configuration is useful when management wants to systematically move shoppers down each aisle, ensuring that they pass through such high-margin sections as deli and meat. Figure 11.2 illustrates how a grid layout in a supermarket helps to regulate traffic flow. A typical strategy is to place staple goods in more remote areas. The designers know that traffic will move to these areas, because staples are purchased frequently. They try to place impulse goods in spots shoppers will pass on their way elsewhere; then they place eye-catching displays to catch people's attention. In contrast, a *free-flow layout* is more often used in department and specialty stores, because it is conducive to browsing. A retailer might arrange merchandise in circles or arches or perhaps in separate areas, each with its own distinct image and merchandise mix.

- *Fixture type and merchandise density.* Just as we form impressions of people from the way they decorate their homes, our feelings about stores are affected by furnishings, fixtures (shelves and racks that display merchandise), and even how much "stuff" is packed into

**Figure 11.2** A Typical Grid Layout for a Supermarket

the sales area. Generally, clutter conveys a lower-class store. Upscale stores allocate space for sitting areas, dressing rooms, and elaborate displays of merchandise. A southern California shopping centre called the Lab attracts its target audience of mall rats aged 18 to 30 by using unusual furnishings—concrete walls, a fountain made of oil drums, and an open-air living room filled with thrift-shop furniture to craft a laid-back image its patrons call "the anti-mall."

- *The sound of music.* An elegant restaurant softly playing Mozart in the background is worlds apart from a raucous place such as the Hard Rock Café, where loud rock 'n' roll is essential to the atmosphere. One owner of a 7-Eleven convenience store discovered the power of music when he figured out how to deter groups of teenagers who were loitering in his store. He piped in "classics" from the 1940s and 1950s, and soon they were gone.[28]

- *Colour and lighting.* Marketers use colour and lighting to set a mood. Red, yellow, and orange are warm colours (fast-food chains use a lot of orange to stimulate hunger), whereas blue, green, and violet signify elegance and cleanliness. Light colours make one feel more serene, whereas bright colours convey excitement. Nova Scotia's Bolands food stores, for example, moved all their fruits and vegetables onto one 3.5-metre wall of produce, painted the wall black, and highlighted the whole section with spotlights. This treatment, added to the addition of a few new and exotic varieties of produce, drew customers to the produce and increased sales.[29]

**THE ACTORS: STORE PERSONNEL** Store personnel should complement a store's image. Each employee has a part to play, complete with props and costumes. Movie theatres sometimes dress ushers in tuxedos, and many store employees are provided with scripts to use when they present products to customers. At the Loblaws store at Queen's Quay (see Exhibit 11.11), for example, counter staff help to create a fun and entertaining atmosphere

**Exhibit 11.11**

Counter staff at this Loblaws complement the store's image by helping to create an engaging atmosphere.

by engaging customers with banter and hucksterisms—the seafood counter clerk, for example, yelling "fresh fish, get your fresh fish here."[30]

Although the presence of knowledgeable sales personnel is important to shoppers, they generally rate the quality of service they receive from retail personnel as low, often because stores don't hire enough people to wait on their customers.[31] In one survey, 62 percent of shoppers said they had decided to not buy a product in a store in the past six months because sales clerks were unavailable to help them.[32] Retailers are working hard to upgrade service quality, though they often find that the rapid turnover of salespeople makes this a difficult goal to achieve. Perhaps they can learn from Japanese retailers: A visitor to a Japanese store is greeted by an enthusiastic, polite employee who bows profusely.[33]

**PRICING POLICY: HOW MUCH FOR A TICKET TO THE SHOW?** When consumers form an image of a store in their minds, the *price points*, or price ranges, of its merchandise often play a role. Ed Mirvish uses humour and poetry to communicate his concept of Honest Ed's, for example: "Honest Ed's for the birds—his prices are cheap, cheap, cheap." Similarly, Daffy's, a U.S. off-price retailer, advertises: "Friends Don't Let Friends Pay Retail." In recent years, department stores have been hurt by consumers' desires for bargains. The response of many department stores was to run frequent sales, a strategy that often backfired because many consumers would buy *only* when the store held a sale. Many stores, such as Zellers and Home Depot, have reduced the number of sales they run in favour of an everyday low-pricing (EDLP) strategy. Loblaws supports their premium shopping experience with prices that are often slightly higher than the competitors'. They have recognized, however, that premium merchandise and pricing need to be supported by premium store designs, and that the building itself contributes a lot to the customer experience.[34]

## Building the Theatre: Store Location

Realtors list the three most important factors in buying a home as "location, location, and location." The same is true in retailing. Wal-Mart's success is not due to what it is but *where* it is. Wal-Mart was the first mass merchandiser to locate in small and rural market areas. When choosing a site, its planners consider such factors as proximity to highways and major traffic routes. By carefully selecting "undiscovered" areas, the company has been able to negotiate inexpensive leases in towns with expanding populations, an important strategy for Wal-Mart because it means access to markets hungry for a store that offers such a wide assortment of household goods.[35] This section reviews some important aspects of retail locations.

**TYPES OF STORE LOCATIONS** As Figure 11.3 shows, there are four basic types of retail locations—a business district, a shopping centre, a free-standing entity, or a non-traditional location.

- *Business districts.* A *central business district (CBD)* is the traditional downtown business area in a town or city. Many people are drawn to the area to shop or work, and public transportation is usually available. CBDs have suffered in recent years due to concerns about security, lack of parking, and the lack of customer traffic on evenings and weekends. To combat these problems, many cities provide such incentives as tax breaks to encourage the opening of stores and entertainment areas like Toronto's St. Lawrence Market as shown in Figure 11.3. These vibrant developments are called *festival marketplaces*, and they have done much to reverse the fortunes of aging downtown areas.

- *Shopping centres.* A shopping centre is a group of commercial establishments owned and managed as a single property. They range in size and scope from *strip centres* to massive *super-regional centres*, such as the West Edmonton Mall, shown in Figure 11.3, the world's largest retail centre—a 492 370-square-metre complex complete with a theme-room hotel, amusement park, water park, full-sized indoor skating rink, deep sea adventure area that houses dolphins and submarines, casino, and shooting gallery.[36] Strip malls offer quick and easy access to basic conveniences such as dry cleaners and video rentals, though shoppers seeking more exotic goods need to look elsewhere. Shopping malls offer variety and the ability to combine shopping with entertainment. On the other hand, rents tend to be higher, so it's difficult for stores such as home-improvement centres to be profitable. In addition, small specialty stores may find it hard to compete with a mall's *anchor stores*, the major department stores that typically draw many shoppers.

- *Free-standing retailers.* Some stores, usually larger ones such as Kids 'R' Us (Figure 11.3), are free-standing, located by themselves in a separate building. These retailers benefit from lower rents and fewer parking problems. However, the store must be attractive enough on its own to be a destination point for shoppers, because it can't rely on spillover from consumers visiting other stores at the same place.

- *Non-traditional store locations.* Innovative retailers find new ways to reach consumers. Many entrepreneurs use *carts*, small, movable stores that can be set up in many locations including inside malls, airports, or other public facilities, or *kiosks* that are slightly larger and offer store-like facilities, including telephone hookups and electricity. As Exhibit 11.12 shows, Sunglass Hut sells nothing but sunglasses in its kiosk. Its assortment is narrow and deep. Carts and kiosks are relatively inexpensive and a good way for new businesses to get started. Mall operators need to be careful about regulating carts, because they may block a store or sell merchandise that is incompatible with a desired image.

**SITE SELECTION: CHOOSING WHERE TO BUILD** Retailers used to simply choose to build a store on a site where an adequate number of people saw it. Sam Walton, the founder of Wal-Mart, used to fly over an area in a small plane until he found a spot that appealed to him. No more. Now such factors as long-term population patterns, the location of competitors, and the demographic makeup of an area factor into retailers' decisions. The choice of where to open a new store should reflect the company's overall growth strategy. It should be consistent with long-term goals and be in a place that allows the company to best support the outlet. For example, a chain with stores and an extensive warehouse system in Ontario may not be wise to open a new store on Vancouver Island, because the store would be an "orphan" cut off from the company's supply lines.

**West Edmonton Mall**
www.westedmall.com

A central business district is often found in downtown areas. Although North American retailers have been deserting city centres for the past 20 years, these downtown areas are now staging a comeback. Such sophisticated developments as Toronto's St. Lawrence Market (shown here) and Queen's Quay, Winnipeg's The Forks, and Vancourver's Granville Market are bringing shoppers back to the city cores.

A shopping centre features one or more anchor stores, usually major department stores that initially attract shoppers, who then discover the other small, specialty stores in the centre. Shopping centres have the advantages of (1) providing heavy traffic flow (especially for small stores that would not attract so many people if they were on their own), (2) the sharing of costs (such as advertising and promotion) among tenants, and (3) a clean (and usually safe) environment. It seems likely that large malls will continue to evolve as entertainment centres and for recreational shopping, featuring a greater mix of movie theatres, restaurants, and hobby and bookstores.[a] The West Edmonton Mall is the world's largest retail centre, featuring a wide variety of shopping and entertainment experiences.

A freestanding store is not located near other stores. This locational strategy, used by some big chains like Kids 'R' Us, has the advantage of offering a lack of direct competition, lower rents, and adaptability. The store has the freedom to alter its selling space to accomodate its own needs. On the other hand, the store had better be popular because it cannot rely on the drawing power of neighbour stores to provide it with customer traffic.

A nontraditional location offers products to shoppers in convenient places. Canadian banks and financial institutions are opening branches and kiosks in large grocery stores. McDonald's has located inside Wal-Mart stores to entice customers to take a McBreak from shopping.

Source: Chip Walker "Strip Malls: Plain But Powerful," *American Demographics*, October 1991, 48(4).

**Figure 11.3** Types of Store Locations

Location planners look at many factors when selecting a site. A store's targeted consumer segment is a key determinant of where it locates. For example, a new, growing community would be appealing for hardware stores that can supply hammers and drywall to home owners, whereas upscale dress stores and travel agencies might find better locations in more established areas where people have the income to spend on fashion items and vacations. Planners also want to find a place that is convenient to customers in the store's **trade area**, the geographic zone that accounts for the majority of its sales and customers.[37] A *site evaluation* considers such specific factors as traffic flow, number of parking spaces available, ease of delivery access, visibility from the street, local zoning laws that determine the types of buildings, parking, and signage allowed, as well as such cost factors as the length of the lease and the amount of local taxes.

Planners also consider such population characteristics as age profile (Is the area witnessing an influx of new families?), community life cycle (Is the community relatively new, stable, or in decline?), and mobility (How often are people moving in and out of the area?).

**trade area** A geographic zone that accounts for the majority of a store's sales and customers.

**Exhibit 11.12**

Sunglass Hut uses kiosks to provide shades to the masses.

Planners also have to consider the degree of competition they will encounter by locating in one place rather than another.

## E-TAILING AND OTHER NON-STORE RETAILING

Many products are readily available in places other than traditional "bricks and mortar" stores. For example, the familiar Avon ladies, who sell cosmetics and other beauty products to millions of women around the world, show that a retailer need not be a store. Avon is continuing to explore new ways to give customers access to its products. Customers can place orders by phone, fax, catalogue, via the Internet, or through a sales representative. Avon has even tested a 30-minute infomercial to sell its products on television.[38]

Avon's success at giving customers alternatives to traditional store outlets illustrates the increasing importance of **non-store retailing**, which is any method a firm uses to complete an exchange that does not require a customer visit to a store. North Americans spend almost $70 billion through catalogues, TV shopping channels, the Internet, and other non-store formats.[39] Many retail stores even offer non-store alternatives to buying their merchandise, such as using catalogues and Web sites. As the founder of the Neiman-Marcus department store acknowledged: "If customers don't want to get off their butts and go to your stores, you've got to go to them."[40]

Two major types of non-store retailing are **e-tailing** and **direct marketing**. Customers are exposed to merchandise through print, broadcast, or electronic media and then purchase the products over the Internet, by phone, or by mail. In this section, we'll review the major forms of non-store retailing, starting with the newest—buying on the Internet.

## E-tailing

Throughout this book, we have talked about electronic commerce—conducting business transactions and communication over networks and through computers. In the chapter on customer (organizational) buying behaviour we discussed electronic commerce's place in business-to-business (B2B) markets. In this chapter, our focus is on e-tailing, electronic commerce in business-to-consumer (B2C) markets.

**non-store retailing** Any method used to complete an exchange with a product end user that does not require a customer visit to a store.

**e-tailing** Offering products for sale directly to consumers via the Internet.

**direct marketing** Exposing a consumer to information about a good or service through a non-personal medium and convincing the customer to respond with an order.

Industry Canada and market research firms forecast annual growth of 50 to 70 percent through 2005 and expect worldwide e-commerce sales of US$1.9 to $3 trillion.[41] So even in the aftermath of some "dot.bombs," there is a lot of excitement about e-tail opportunities.

**WHO SHOPS ONLINE?** Almost 60 percent of Canadian have tried to buy something online.[42] Traditionally (a couple of years ago), Internet shoppers tended to be better educated, younger men who were better off financially. Increased access to the Internet at work, school, libraries, and home, however, has reduced demographic differences in online shopping. The profile of online consumers now mirrors those of other shoppers: Online shoppers are now, on average, older, increasingly female, less affluent, and less highly educated than they once were.[43]

**WHY DO THEY SHOP ONLINE?** Consumers shop online to achieve a variety of benefits, known as the six Cs: cost, choice, convenience, customization, communication, and control (see Figure 11.4). Many consumers shop online to get lower prices and to reduce the psychological cost of comparison-shopping: Product information is just a click away, and there are **bots**, electronic shopping agents that help consumers find the lowest prices.

Other consumers shop online because of choice and convenience—accessibility to products from around the corner to around the world, the ability to buy them from the comfort of their home or office, and the ability to have them delivered right to their homes or, in the case of gifts, directly to others, gift wrapped with a personalized card. Lingerie sellers, like Montreal-based Linda Lingerie, La Senza (Exhibit 11.13), and La Vie en Rose, provide a convenient, more private online shopping experience that is particularly attractive to men buying lingerie for women.[44] They make it convenient by using standard sizing, offering easy-to-follow sizing charts, making product out of Lycra which accommodates different sizes and shapes, and having flexible return policies.

For others, the main motivation is customization—being able to buy something made specifically for your needs. Procter & Gamble, for example, hired Calgary-based interactive marketing agency Critical Mass to create Reflect.com, a site that allows consumers to buy cosmetic products that have been customized and packaged just for them.[45]

Still others are attracted to buying online because of their ability to have interactive communication with e-tailers. **Push technology** allows marketers to automatically send customers relevant information, specified by consumer preferences; while e-mail, chat rooms, and call centres allow consumers to talk back.

Finally, online shopping gives customers greater control over the shopping experience, and allows them to engage e-tailers on their own terms and make more informed purchase decisions. Internet **portals**, such as Canoe.ca and Sympatico.ca assist consumers to navigate the Internet, find products, and make informed choices.

**WHAT DO THEY BUY?** Although still in its infancy, electronic commerce is transforming the way we shop. Buyers now have access to millions of stores around the world without leaving their computers, and often they can easily get crucial information before making a purchase. For example, Intel is working on a site for Ticketmaster that allows the customer to move around a virtual replica of a concert hall or a sports arena to test the view from different seats before buying tickets: Try doing that over the phone.[46] Clearwater Fine Foods of Nova Scotia sells fresh lobster, shipped to your door anywhere in North America within 24 hours. Ordering might be done by fax, but it's easier to track your dinner over the Internet using software supplied by courier companies like UPS and Federal Express.

Travel services, computer hardware and software, financial services, collectibles, autos, health and beauty

---

**bots** Electronic robots or shopping agents that help consumers find products and prices on the Internet.

**Linda Lingerie**
www.lindalingerie.com

**La Senza**
www.lasenza.com

**La Vie en Rose**
www.lavieenrose.com

**Reflect.com**
www.reflect.com

**Clearwater Fine Foods of Nova Scotia**
www.cffi.com

**push technology** Internet tools that allow marketers to send information they think is relevant to consumers directly to their computers.

**portals** Gateways to the Internet that assist consumers to navigate the Internet and customize their experience.

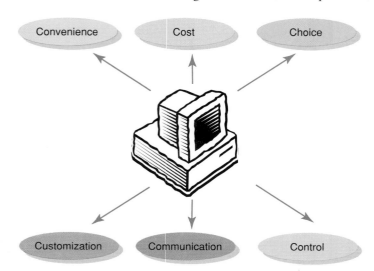

**Figure 11.4** The Six Cs of E-tailing

products, toys, books, and videos are fast-moving online items. Products that can actually be delivered electronically over the Internet, such as computer software, news, music, videos, electronic games, financial services, airline and other tickets, and maybe even books are naturals for e-tailing—the convenience of buying these products online may soon make other forms of distribution obsolete.

Table 11.1 illustrates other consumer products that have the potential to do well online. This is not an exhaustive list: Every day innovative entrepreneurs are demonstrating business models for selling new product categories online.

## Critical Success Factors

We are just beginning to see the enormous potential of electronic commerce in retailing. The success of this non-store format will depend on the ability of retailers to offer sites that are entertaining and informative, and that are worth revisiting again and again even after the novelty wears off. Gap, for example, offers a Web site with a page (shown in Exhibit 11.14) that allows the shopper to mix and match colours and styles on the computer, a service that can't be matched by a conventional catalogue. Blast Radius, a three-year-old Vancouver-based Web design company with production offices in Toronto, New York, and Los Angles, won gold and silver Clio awards for the interactive sites they designed for Casio and Lego, respectively.[47] These sites keep consumers involved, bring them back, and help build brand loyalty.

**Exhibit 11.13**

Lingerie retailer La Senza stresses convenience as a main benefit to shopping online.

**Gap**
www.gap.com
**Casio**
www.gshock.com
**Lego**
www.lego-media.com

**Table 11.1** Consumer Products That Have the Potential to Do Well Online

| Characteristic | Description | Example |
|---|---|---|
| Straight rebuys | Consumers have product and brand experience and just want another one as conveniently and cost effectively as possible | packaged goods, household items, health, flowers, personal care products |
| Commodities | No or few perceived differences between brands and price is a key buying criteria | produce, electricity, recycling services, telephone services |
| "Low-touch" items | Items that don't need to be tried on or fitted, felt, or smelled (Although once body shapes and sizes are determined even custom clothes can be bought online.) | |
| Have high retail margins | Direct to consumer distribution may provide significant cost savings | toys, cosmetics, clothes |
| Can be customized | Can be targeted to very narrow audiences around the world | computers, cars, clothing, music |
| Expensive to inventory | Difficult and expensive to offer wide selections in traditional retail settings | cars, computers, household appliances |
| Invite comparison shopping | Products that are highly differentiated or where they are many options and where consumers can save time and effort by comparing product features and prices | consumer electronics, household furniture and fixtures |
| Difficult to find | Where supply is limited or geographically inaccessible | collectibles, specialty goods, antiques, art |

**Exhibit 11.14**

Advanced technology allows the Gap to let surfers mix and match its apparel items on the company's Web site.

**scalability** The ability of organizations to get bigger without a big rise in expenses.

Branding (discussed in Chapter 8) is particularly important in e-tailing, as customers need to know what to look for online and need some way to assess the trustworthiness of online suppliers. That's why many e-tailers are spending, on average, 32 percent of revenues on marketing communications, where traditional retailers typically spend about five percent.[48]

A second critical success factor is building loyalty. This is where Canadian e-tailers excel, with 47 percent of their revenues coming from repeat customers compared to 31 percent for U.S. e-tailers.[49] As Figure 11.5 shows, speed of delivery, cost of delivery, responsiveness of customer service, and return policy are key factors in driving customer satisfaction, a key determinant of customer loyalty. We will have more to say about the relationship between customer satisfaction and customer loyalty in Chapter 15.

Branding and customer loyalty are also key issues for traditional retailers. Where e-tail organizations really stand out is in their **scalability**, their ability to get bigger without a big rise in expenses. Once a Web site is set up, it is accessible anywhere in the world. It also allows marketers such as Bluenile.com to almost infinitely expand the depth and breadth of their product assortment, as long as they can deliver the product to the customer (see the Spotlight on Real People, below).

Another problem is that people need "touch-and-feel" information before buying many products. For this reason, companies such as Tupperware, Amway, and Mary Kay discourage Internet sales. Executives at Tupperware want shoppers to be able to "burp" their plastic containers to appreciate their airtight qualities.[50] This is one reason that Just White Shirts

## SPOTLIGHT ON REAL PEOPLE  Bluenile.com

Amy Smith is what happens when true love meets the Internet. The 31-year-old fell in love with an engagement ring she saw at Tiffany & Co., the high-end jewellery store. When she got home she went to Bluenile.com, a jewellery e-tailer, and after using the site's guides to master the Four Cs of diamonds (colour, cut, clarity, and carats), she picked one costing US$10 000. But, what surprised this consumer was that Bluenile.com beat Tiffany & Co.'s price by almost $6000. Amy thought to herself, "Why are the offline retailers so expensive?"

Welcome to the Web's second act, being led by jewellery e-tailers such as Bluenile.com, founded by Mark Vadon, a discouraged engagement ring shopper, and Ben Elowitz.

Bluenile.com went public in May 2004. Selling diamonds, double-strand pearl necklaces, sterling silver bangle bracelets, and more, online jewellers made up about US$2 billion of the industry's US$45 billion in revenues in 2003. These e-tailers are textbook examples of how the Web fundamentally undercuts traditional ways of doing business.

They run their business by knocking out the intermediaries and expensive stores to lower costs, then offer the consumer lower prices. Amazon.com, for example, is betting it can make money on 15 percent markups instead of the industry's usual 60 percent to 100 percent. "We believe over time customers figure these things out," says Thomas J. Szkutak, Amazon's Chief Financial Officer.[51]

1. Do you think upscale retailers such as Tiffany & Co. face troubles from online retailers, or do you think their image and cachet afford them protection?
2. Some authors argue that neighbourhood jewellery stores face the biggest threat from jewellery e-tailers. Do you agree? What can neighbourhood stores do to insulate themselves from the online attack?
3. What other goods and services do you think are prime candidates for following Blue Nile's business model? Provide a rationale for your choice.

and Black Socks of Mississauga decided to open a bricks-and-mortar warehouse outlet in Toronto to support their Internet and mail-order sales (Exhibit 11.15)—some buyers just have to touch the fabric and feel the weight of the cotton.[52]

Many consumers are still reluctant to buy over the Internet due to their concerns about security. They are understandably reluctant to provide such sensitive information as credit card numbers. Technological advances, such as digital signatures, may help to ensure that valuable personal information is secure, and pre-paid e-cards may reduce the risk of others using your credit card number.[53] The governments of Ontario and Saskatchewan have passed e-commerce bills to ensure that electronic contracts, documents, and signatures have the same legal effect as non-electronic versions to protect both consumers and businesses.[54]

As major marketers beef up their presence on the Web, some are concerned that inventory sold online will cannibalize store sales. That is not a concern of Future Shop: This electronics retailer has one of Canada's busiest Web sites, with over 100 000 visits each month.

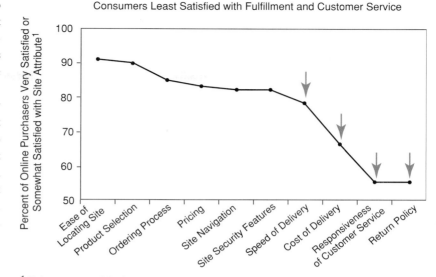

**Consumers Least Satisfied with Fulfillment and Customer Service**

[1] Relates to use of the Internet for personal (as opposed to business) reasons

**Figure 11.5** Determinants of E-customer Satisfaction

**Just White Shirts and Black Socks**
www.executive-lifestyle.com

**Exhibit 11.15**

Some non-store retailers are opening traditional storefronts to support their brands.

The site is fully integrated with their stores in a "clicks and mortar" concept, so that consumers can decide to buy online or just browse online and go to a traditional Future Shop store to purchase. The retail stores provide their customers with a tangible point of reference, places where they can go and see the products.[55]

Manufacturers also face a problem. If they sell their products directly on the Web, they will anger stores that carry their merchandise. Companies such as Mattel are experimenting with online marketing and are finding that consumers appreciate access to hard-to-find items, such as Share a Smile Becky, a wheelchair-bound friend of Barbie that many small toy stores don't stock. Still, these companies must be sure they don't antagonize the many stores on which they still rely to sell their products.[56]

In addition, electronic retailing has the potential to increase price competition, because the Web surfer can look for the same branded item offered on numerous Web sites and just buy it wherever it's cheapest, regardless of whether the business is located next door or in another continent. Indeed, shopping bots already scan cyberspace for bargains; these electronic agents (such as the ones found at www.compare.net and www.webmarket.com) automatically access many sites and compare prices.

**Mattel's Barbie**
www.barbie.com

## Direct Marketing

Although e-tailing has gained significant attention in the marketplace, there are more established forms of non-store retailing, by which customers are exposed to merchandise through print or electronic media and then purchase the products by phone or mail. Let's look at the most popular types of direct marketing, starting with the oldest—buying through the mail. The communications functions of direct marketing will be discussed in Chapter 13.

MAIL ORDER In 1872, Aaron Montgomery Ward and two partners put up $1600 to mail a one-page flyer that listed their merchandise with prices, hoping to spur a few more sales for their retail store.[57] The mail-order industry was born. Today, consumers can buy just about anything through the mail. Mail order comes in two forms: catalogues and direct mail.

catalogue   A collection of products offered for sale in book form, usually consisting of product descriptions accompanied by photos or illustrations of the items.

CATALOGUES A **catalogue** is a collection of products offered for sale in book form, usually consisting of product descriptions accompanied by photos or illustrations of the items. Catalogues came on the scene within a few decades of the invention of moveable type in the fifteenth century, but they've come a long way since then.[58] The early Canadian catalogues pioneered by innovators such as Sears and Eaton's were designed for people in remote areas who lacked access to stores.

Today, the catalogue customer is likely to be an affluent career woman with access to more than enough stores but who does not have the time or desire to go to them. Canadians spend about $2 billion through domestic and foreign catalogues.[59] Catalogue mania extends well beyond clothing and cosmetics purchases. Dell and Gateway, direct-selling computer companies, each have annual sales of over $1 billion. Bridgehead, an Ottawa-based Oxfam affiliate, has a catalogue that features housewares, gifts, foods, and other items imported through "fair trade" deals with the Third World. Although the Internet is starting to replace the function of catalogues, large retailers such as Canadian Tire and IKEA continue to make extensive use of catalogues to make shopping more convenient for consumers. The trend, however, is to replace much of the catalogues with Internet sales.[60] Zellers, however, uses catalogues and the Internet to reach key target audiences. They created a new Zellers Special Delivery Baby Catalogue and online baby-gift registry. Baby-related tips are offered throughout the catalogue courtesy of *Today's Parent* magazine, and there is as an integrated loyalty program for Club Z members and their babies.[61]

direct mail   A brochure or pamphlet offering a specific product or service at one point in time.

DIRECT MAIL Unlike a catalogue retailer that offers a variety of merchandise through the mail, **direct mail** is a brochure or pamphlet offering a specific product or service at one point in time. Although e-mail is increasingly used for the same purpose, Canada Post expects to continue to deliver about 4.7 billion pieces of direct mail each year.[62] A direct mail offer has an advantage over a catalogue because it can be personalized. Direct mail also is widely used by charities, political groups, and other not-for-profit organizations.

## Direct Selling

**Direct selling** occurs when a salesperson presents a product to one individual or a small group, takes orders, and delivers the merchandise. This form of non-store retailing works well for such products as vacuum cleaners, nutritional products, and educational materials—products that require a great deal of information to sell. Most people involved in direct selling are independent agents who buy the merchandise from the company and then resell it to consumers.

**DOOR-TO-DOOR SALES** Although door-to-door selling is popular in some countries such as China, it is declining in North America, because few women are home during the day and those who are home are reluctant to open their doors to strangers. Companies that used to rely on door-to-door sales have had to adapt their retailing strategies. Finding that many of its female customers work during the day, Avon now sells to them at the office during lunch and coffee breaks. Similarly, Tupperware features rush-hour parties at the end of the work-day and finds that about 20 percent of its sales come from outside the home. An employee of Mary Kay cosmetics, which has also adopted this strategy, offered another explanation for its success: "Working women buy more in the office because they are not looking at the wallpaper that needs replacing. They feel richer away from home."[63]

**PARTIES AND NETWORKS** About three-quarters of direct sales are made in the consumer's home, sometimes at a home shopping party, at which a company representative makes a sales presentation to a group of people who have gathered at a friend's.[64] People who attend may get caught up in the "group spirit," buying things they would not normally buy if alone.[65] This technique is called a **party plan system**.

Another form of non-store retailing, epitomized by the Amway Company, is **multilevel marketing**, or network marketing (Exhibit 11.16). In this system, a master distributor recruits other people to become distributors as well. Master distributors sell the company's products to the people they entice to join and receive commissions on all the merchandise sold by the people they recruit. Despite the growing popularity of this technique, some network systems are illegal. They are really **pyramid schemes** in which the initial distributors profit by selling merchandise to other distributors, and very little product ever gets bought by consumers.[66]

**TELEMARKETING** **Telemarketing** is direct selling conducted over the telephone. It is definitely easier and less expensive than door-to-door selling. Recent surveys indicate that one out of six North Americans felt it difficult to resist a telemarketing pitch; on the other hand, about one in three complained of feeling cheated at one time by a telemarketer.[67]

## Automatic Vending

Coin-operated vending machines are a tried-and-true way to sell convenience goods, especially cigarettes and drinks. These machines are appealing because they require minimal space and personnel to maintain and operate.

Some of the most interesting innovations are state-of-the-art vending machines, which dispense everything from Ore-Ida french fries to software. French consumers can even purchase Levi's jeans from a machine called Libre Service, which offers the pants in 10 different sizes. Due to their frenetic lifestyles, the Japanese are avid users of vending machines. These machines, a cluster of which can be found on many street corners, dispense virtually all of life's necessities, plus many luxuries people in other countries would not consider obtaining from a machine. The list includes jewellery, fresh flowers, frozen beef, pornography, business cards, underwear, and even the names of possible dates.[68]

**direct selling** An interactive sales process, in which a salesperson presents a product to one individual or a small group, takes orders, and delivers the merchandise.

**party plan system** A sales technique that relies heavily on people getting caught up in the "group spirit," buying things they would not normally buy if alone.

**multilevel marketing** A system in which a master distributor recruits other people to become distributors, sells the company's product to the recruits, and receives a commission on all the merchandise they sell.

**pyramid schemes** An illegal sales technique, in which the initial distributors profit by selling merchandise to other distributors, with the result that consumers buy very little product.

**telemarketing** A sales technique in which direct selling is conducted over the telephone.

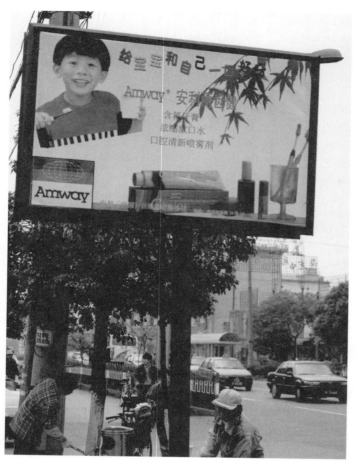

**Exhibit 11.16**

Amway uses a multilevel network, one type of direct selling, to sell its many products. Amway's global expansion includes China, where Amway products have gained popularity.

**direct-response TV** Television programming, such as infomercials or shopping channels, which elicits direct orders for products from the viewing public.

In general, vending machines are best suited to the sales of inexpensive merchandise and food and beverages. Most consumers are reluctant to buy pricey items from a machine. New vending machines may spur more interest, however, as technological developments such as video kiosk machines that let people see the product in use, the ability to accept credit cards as payment, and inventory systems that signal the operator when malfunctions or stock-outs occur loom on the horizon.

## Direct-Response Television

Almost as long as there has been television there has been **direct-response TV** (DRTV)—television programming that is intended to elicit direct orders, typically by phone, from viewers. Where the original DRTV pioneers were entrepreneurs who couldn't get their products into traditional channels, their approach of selling products on TV was so successful that it soon became mainstream for more established companies and brands.[69] DRTV is still an important marketing tool for two reasons: It works and it is measurable, so you can tell how well it is working.

**HOME SHOPPING NETWORKS** Television channels that exist solely to sell products let shopping junkies indulge themselves without leaving their living rooms.[70] In Canada, shoppers can frequent the Home Shopping Channel; the U.S. equivalent is QVC, which sells products at the rate of $39 per second around the clock. To date, the typical North American home shopping customer is in a low-income bracket, and the most frequently purchased product is inexpensive jewellery.

## Good or Bad Decision?

When it is abused, telemarketing embodies the most negative aspects of marketing. Even though some consumers are open to telephone sales pitches, many resent being interrupted at home. Sometimes, it's hard to tell the difference between a legitimate sales call and a scam. Many telemarketing scams hawk fishy credit card deals, scholarships, and vacation packages. Many governments have enacted tougher regulations on the telemarketing industry. Should marketers be allowed to "break and enter" into consumers' homes via the telephone to push their products, even if what they are selling is legitimate? What rules would you impose on telemarketing?

# Real People, Real Decisions

## How It Worked Out at Federated Direct

Dawn chose option 3. Federated developed a strategy to revamp its bridal registry business. To attract younger couples and change shoppers' perceptions of its bridal registry, the retailer developed a list of the "Top 10 Reasons to Register with Federated." These reasons were the core of the marketing strategy:

1. Creating your registry is FUN, FAST, and EASY—With the latest technology, including touch-screen kiosks, in-store scanner guns, and online registrations.
2. Personalized service—Meet with professional bridal consultants at our Premier Stores to customize a registry that fits your lifestyle.
3. Best selection—Of china, crystal, flatware, housewares, and home textiles under one roof!
4. Locking in Low Registry Prices Is a Piece of Cake!—On the day that you register, you will lock in the lowest price of the last 60 days for the next year to be used by you and your guests.
5. Guests Buy Gifts With Ease . . . And Confidence—By visiting 400 stores of the most highly recognized nameplates across the USA, shopping online, or by calling our toll-free number.

6. Great Brands You Know . . . And Trust—Choose from the most respected national brand names plus our own exclusive brands that you won't find anywhere else.
7. New, Exciting Shower Gifts—A selection of great gift ideas is available through our special shower gift in-store displays.
8. Reliable Delivery—The most popular items are always in stock and shipped to you within 5 days.
9. Special Savings—With our additional 10% off completion program for brides in all Home areas.
10. Hassle-Free Returns—With our one-stop return desk.

Early returns showed a dramatic increase in the number of bridal registrations across the stores. Dawn is hopeful that Federated's revamped courtship of brides and grooms will be a match made in heaven!

The gutsy move made by Dawn is no surprise given her motto in life: "Dream big and dare to fail," a quote from the explorer Norman Vaughan. Dawn's advice is to make a commitment to a course of action, regardless of what you do in life, and give it your best.

**Exhibit 11.17**

Macy's revamped bridal registry offers younger couples what they want.

# CHAPTER SUMMARY

### 1. Define retailing and describe how retailers evolve over time.

Retailing is the process by which goods and services are sold to consumers for their personal use. The wheel-of-retailing hypothesis suggests that new retailers compete on price and, over time, become more upscale, leaving room for other new, low-price entrants. The retail life cycle theory suggests retailing institutions are introduced, grow, reach maturity, and then decline. Three factors that motivate retailers to change are changing demographics, technology, and globalization.

### 2. Describe how retailers are classified.

Retailers can be classified according to the type of products sold, whether they carry items having high or low gross margins and high or low turnover rates. Merchandise assortment is described in terms of breadth and depth, which refer to the number of product lines sold and the amount of variety available for each.

### 3. Understand the importance of store image to a retail positioning strategy, and explain some of the actions a retailer can take to create a desired image in the marketplace.

Store image is the result of many elements working together to create a desirable shopping experience and to ensure that shoppers view a store favourably compared to the competition. Colour, lighting, scents, furnishings, and other design elements, or atmospherics, are used to create a "feel" for a store environment. Atmospheric decisions include: store layout, which determines traffic flow and influences the desired customer behaviour in the store; the use of store fixtures and open space; the use of sound to attract (or repel) certain types of customers; and the use of colour and lighting that can influence customers' moods. The number and type of store personnel are selected to complement the store image. Pricing of products sold in the store contributes to shoppers' perceptions. A store's location also contributes to its image: Major types of retail locations include central business districts, shopping centres, free-standing retailers, and non-traditional locations such as kiosks.

### 4. Describe the major forms of non-store retailing.

Non-store retailing includes e-tailing and direct marketing, such as traditional mail-order shopping, direct-selling, vending machines, direct-response television shopping, and online shopping. Mail-order retailing includes catalogues and direct-mail advertisements sent to consumers. Popular direct selling techniques include the home shopping party, door-to-door sales, and telemarketing. The growing electronic marketplace uses both the power of more traditional television infomercials and home shopping networks and the growing popularity of computer online services and the World Wide Web.

### 5. Describe the opportunities and barriers to e-tailing.

E-tailing, online exchanges between companies and consumers, is growing rapidly. E-tailing benefits include greater convenience and greater product variety for consumers and opportunities for specialized businesses, lower business costs, and instantaneous delivery of some products for marketers. For consumers, the downside of e-tailing is that they have to wait to receive products, security issues, and the inability to touch and feel products. For Internet-only marketers, success on the Internet may be difficult to achieve, whereas cannibalization may be a problem with traditional retailers' online operations.

# CHAPTER REVIEW

## Marketing Concepts: Testing Your Knowledge

1. How does the wheel-of-retailing hypothesis explain changes in retail outlets? How does the retail life cycle concept explain these changes?

2. What are some environmental trends that will have a major impact on the future of retailing?

3. How are gross margins and turnover rates used to classify retailers? Describe the differences in merchandise assortments for convenience stores, supermarkets, specialty stores, discount stores, department stores, and hypermarkets.

4. What is meant by store atmospherics? How can the elements of atmospherics be used to increase the store's success? How are store personnel a part of store image?

5. What are the different types of store locations? What are the advantages and disadvantages of each?

6. How do retail store location planners evaluate potential store sites?

7. Describe the major types of non-store retailing.

8. Describe some of the changes that are expected in the growing electronic marketplace.

9. Explain the different types of direct marketing.

## Marketing Concepts: Discussing Choices and Issues

1. The wheel-of-retailing theory suggests that the normal path for a retailer is to enter the marketplace with lower-priced goods and then to increase quality, services, and prices. Why do you think this happens? Is it the right path for all retailers? Why or why not?

2. Discount retail stores such as Wal-Mart seem to be getting larger and larger. Is there an optimal size for retailers? Can retail stores get too big? Why or why not?

3. Owners of stores that make effective use of atmospherics believe that getting people "in the mood" makes them more likely to buy. Do you feel that store atmospherics influence your purchase behaviour? Is this sort of planned store setting ethical?

## Marketing Practice: Applying What You've Learned

1. All your life you've wanted to be an entrepreneur and own your own business. Now you're ready to graduate and you've decided to open a combination coffee shop and bookstore in a location near your college or university. You know that to attract both the student market and other customers from the local community, you will have to carefully design the store image. Develop a detailed plan that specifies how you will use atmospherics to create the image you desire.

2. In your job with a marketing consulting firm, you are often asked to make recommendations for store location. Your current client is a local caterer that is planning to open a new retail outlet for selling take-out gourmet dinners. You are examining the possible types of locations: the central business district, a shopping centre, free-standing entity, or some non-traditional location. Outline the advantages and disadvantages of each type of location. Present your recommendations to your client.

3. Assume you are the vice-president of marketing for Elegant Evenings, a chain of women's lingerie stores. Your firm sells exclusive designer lingerie in boutiques located in shopping malls across the country. With a changing marketplace, your firm is considering whether there is a need to develop some type of non-store retailing operation. You consider the opportunities for marketing your products via

   a. catalogues

   b. direct mail

   c. television infomercials

   d. television home shopping network

   e. World Wide Web

   Outline the pros and cons of each for your firm.

4. Assume you are the director of marketing for a national chain of convenience stores. Your firm has about 80 stores located in central and eastern Canada. The stores are fairly traditional both in design and in the merchandise they carry. Because you want to be proactive in your marketing planning, you are concerned that your firm may need to consider significant changes due to the current demographic, technological, and global changes in the market-place. You think it is important to discuss these things with the other executives at your firm. Develop a presentation that includes:

    a. a discussion of the demographic changes that will affect your stores.

    b. a discussion of the technological changes that will affect your stores.

    c. a discussion of how global changes may pose problems and opportunities for your organization.

    d. your recommendations for how your firm might meet the challenges faced in each of these areas.

## Marketing Mini-Project: Learning by Doing

This project is designed to help you understand how store atmospherics play an important role in consumers' perceptions of a retail store.

1. Select two retail outlets where students in your college or university are likely to shop. Try to select two stores that have different images but that sell the same types of products.

2. Visit each store and write down a detailed description of its atmosphere—colours, materials used, types of displays, lighting fixtures, product displays, store personnel, and so on.

3. Survey some of the students in your college or university. Develop a brief questionnaire asking about the perceptions of the two stores you are studying. Include questions about the quality of merchandise, prices, competence and friendliness of the store personnel, the attitude of management toward customer service, and so on. What is the "personality" of each store?

4. Develop a report of your findings. Compare the description of the stores with the results of the survey. Explain how the different elements of the store atmosphere create each store's image.

## Real People, Real Surfers: Exploring the Web

Many retailers have Internet sites. The Hudson's Bay Company (**www.hbc.com/bay**), Sears (**www.sears.ca**), and Future Shop (**www.futureshop.com**) are three examples. Explore these or other retailer sites and answer the following questions.

1. Describe each retailer's Web site. What information is available on each site? How easy was each to navigate? What information did you find interesting and useful on each site? What did you find that you didn't expect to find at a retailer site? What was lacking at each site?

2. How do the retailers' Web sites communicate the image or personality of their stores? How are they alike? How are they different? If you had no information except that available on the Web, would you know what types of products are sold, whether the products sold are expensive, prestige products or low-priced products, and what types of consumers each retailer is attempting to attract to their stores? How does each site use graphics or other design elements to represent the "setting" as retailers do in their stores? How do they communicate the type of consumer they consider to be their primary market?

3. Why do you think customers visit a retailer's Web site? To find a local store? To learn about career opportunities? To find out whether a certain product is available in the store? To shop online? Or for some other reason? How well does each site you explored satisfy these customer needs?

4. What recommendations would you make to each retailer to improve its Web site?

While online retailing is growing, so far it has not been associated with luxury brands. While the range of luxury brands offered over the Internet is widening, the dollar sales value remains small compared with sales through traditional bricks-and-mortar channels. Tiffany was the first luxury brand to go online in 1999 in the United States, followed by the United Kingdom in December 2001. Gucci sells handbags, shoes, and other leather goods through its Web site. Other famous luxury brand names such as Louis Vuitton and Hermes sell online in the United States.

Why this caution in embracing online retailing? One answer may lie in preserving the mystique associated with the high-end brand. David Cutler, manager of communications for Rolex in the United Kingdom says, "There is nothing to beat being served by a well-qualified adviser, feeling the weight of a watch and having it sized to your wrist." Such argument for personalized service has been made before, perhaps with some merit. According to a report published in May 2004 by Ledbury Research, which specializes in the luxury market, just over one in three affluent consumers in the United Kingdom would be prepared to buy a watch online, while fewer than one in four would consider buying jewellery over the Internet.

However, it appears that consumer attitudes can change. Tiffany has reported strong growth online since 2001. Also, affluent consumers have shown strong appetite for the European online retailer, Net-a-Porter, which sells ready-to-wear women's fashion from such designers as Chloe and Missoni to a global market.

Another reason for the luxury brands' hesitancy to jump on the online bandwagon may be the association of e-commerce with price discounting. To avoid this (and preserve their cachet and markups) online retailers offer a very high level of service. Net-a-Porter, for example, adheres to designers' recommended retail prices, and focuses on being "high-frills." "If a customer asks us to delay delivery until after her holiday, we offer to deliver to her resort," says Natalie Massenet, managing director of Net-a-Porter. When the purchase arrives, she adds, it comes beautifully wrapped "like a hat box carried by a hotel porter in a 1950s film-set."

There are several reasons why a luxury brand may consider going online:

- Being online enables the brand to acquire an instant presence in global markets. Niche brands benefit the most from this technological tool. "The Internet has allowed us to develop secondary markets in Scandinavia and Eastern Europe that we would otherwise have struggled to serve," says Brian Tickle, director of e-commerce at Orient-Express, the travel group and train operator that owns or part-owns a string of exclusive hotels.

- An online presence enables the brand to serve affluent consumers who may not live in traditional capitals of style, where luxury brands have historically had their outlets. A recent survey by the *Financial Times* of London shows that there are more billionaires in Moscow than in New York.

- There is an increasing willingness by affluent consumers to bypass traditional channels and shop online.

- Customers of the future—today's teenagers—may have different buying motivations than their parents. These young consumers, well versed in the art of shopping online without the need for touch or personalized service, could revolutionize the way luxury brands are sold.

Source: Based on Alicia Clegg, "Profits in the laptop of luxury," *Financial Times*, 13 May 2004: 11.

## Things to Think About

1. Go to your local library and compare the consumer research done in the United Kingdom with consumer attitudes in Canada. Are Canadian consumers more venturesome when it comes to buying high-end luxury items over the Internet?

2. What factors do you think account for changing consumer attitudes toward buying luxury brands online?

3. Do you think it is a good idea for a luxury brand to have an online presence? Why or why not?

4. Visit the Web sites of Tiffany, Gucci, Hermes, Louis Vuitton, and Net-a-Porter. Next, visit the Web sites of non-luxury brands such as Amazon.com and Tesco (the British supermarket chain). Compare the two sets of Web sites. What recommendations do you have for luxury brands to compete online?

## Montreal Sandwich—Part 2

Lina's Sandwiches is a franchise operation from Paris, where there are 29 locations. The concept is simple: luxury sandwiches sold in an appealing ambience. The Lina's Sandwiches franchise "book" is complete, with details on how to set up the store, cook sandwiches, and serve the customer. However, the book is silent on the subject of how to actually raise the cash to start up the business. Frederick, the entrepreneur, has borrowed from his mother, a friend, and a local bank. Frederick is thinking big, with plans to expand across Canada.

But starting a retail store is no easy task, as Frederick soon finds out. First, you have to get the required licenses from the government. Then, you have to line up contractors to do the actual construction of the retail establishment. Frederick does his own research, visiting other restaurants to see how they create a certain atmosphere, and what is on their menus. Finally, reliable suppliers have to be lined up.

Frederick goes shopping for restaurant equipment and realizes, with shock, just how expensive things are. He quickly goes $80 000 over budget, so he has to make adjustments to his dream store: the washroom is chopped, and he has to settle for less expensive heating and air conditioning systems and less expensive furniture. But this is not enough. He still has to finance another $40 000 to $50 000. Fortunately, his friend steps in to make up the difference.

The opening of the store is constantly delayed. Frederick does not open in the fall, as originally anticipated, but in early January.

## Questions

1. Do you think Frederick made the right choice of retail location for his store (Place Ville Marie in Montreal)? Why or why not?
2. What problems does Frederick run into before he even opens his retail store? What do you think he could have done to minimize some of his problems?
3. If you were a banker lending money to Frederick, what would you expect to see in his retail "business plan"?
4. Your best friend wants to start a retail store. Make a list of critical success factors necessary for a retail operation to succeed.

Source: This case was prepared by Ajay Sirsi and is based on "Montreal Sandwich," *Venture* #893.

# CHAPTER 12
## Integrated Marketing Communications

## CHAPTER OBJECTIVES

WHEN YOU HAVE COMPLETED YOUR STUDY OF THIS CHAPTER, YOU SHOULD BE ABLE TO

1. Explain the concept of integrated marketing communications and its implementation, and why some marketers resist it.

2. Explain the steps involved in developing a communications plan.

3. List, describe, and contrast the elements of the communications mix.

4. Explain how marketing communication strategies can be evaluated.

5. Explain the content and purpose of a communications brief.

# Real People, Real Decisions

## Meet **David Edward,** a Decision Maker at Cormark Communications

David Edward is president of Cormark Communications, a full-service agency that practises integrated marketing communications, with offices in London, Toronto, and Calgary. It is a member of Maxxcom, a communications holding company, which has created the fourth largest advertising network in Canada. Cormark provides communications counsel, strategic planning, advertising, promotion, and direct marketing to a diverse client base in the financial services, life sciences, agriculture, business-to-business, packaged goods, and retail sectors.

After earning a BBA from Wilfrid Laurier University, Edward gained 16 years of agency management experience with Ogilvy & Mather, Saatchi & Saatchi, and Grey Canada, managing such clients as Toyota, British Airways, SmithKline Beecham, American Express, and Effem Foods. In addition to his presidential duties, Edward takes an active role in the strategic management of key accounts like Pfizer Animal Health.

The Cormark Pfizer Animal Health Team was given the task of launching a new pharmaceutical product for the treatment of arthritis in dogs. Rimadyl had been successfully launched in the U.S. market the previous year, and Pfizer was looking for similar success in Canada.

The U.S. campaign was a high-budget, multilayered communication campaign that targeted both consumers and veterinarians. Media included television, magazines, direct mail, video production, in-clinic collateral, and veterinary detail pieces. The benchmark had been established, and a successful strategy and campaign had been developed. Cormark's task was to ensure similar success for Pfizer's first major direct-to-consumer launch of a product in Canada. A typical new product launch could take six months to plan and execute—Cormark and Pfizer Canada had 90 days. The agency had three options.

**Option 1.** Cormark could use existing U.S. materials. The U.S. agency responsible for the launch of Rimadyl was also a member of the Maxxcom network. Cormark had access to all materials, the strategy, and the teams responsible for the U.S. launch. There were no issues in sourcing material. In fact, Cormark's professional relationship with the U.S. agency meant materials could be sourced and used at a savings for the Pfizer Canada client. Cormark used this relationship to understand the strategy and how the materials were used in the marketplace. Given the success in the United States and the market similarities, using the U.S. materials would offer several benefits. It would be cost efficient—costs sunk into production of material could be allocated to media spending or other marketing activities to promote the launch—and time efficient—time otherwise spent on the production of communications materials could be spent on other marketing activities, particularly impor-

tant given the launch timetable. In addition, using the materials would seem to provide some guarantee of success in the Canadian market.

**Option 2.** Cormark could build on a good thing by taking the best of the available U.S. launch materials and adapting them for use in Canada. Given the variety of materials and the multitude of messages, they could tailor a campaign for Canada that would be based on the "best of the best." This option would ensure a role for the agency in the launch. Materials could be adapted to address perceived market differences or any differences in consumer behaviour that might exist between Canadians and Americans. Costs would be minimized, as adaptation would be limited to copy platforms and claims. Strategic direction and major sunk production costs would be preserved. In the interests of synergy, North–South relationships, and cost, this option would be a pragmatic way to preserve Canadian identity in the communications.

**Option 3.** Cormark could create new communications materials for the Canadian launch, thus taking advantage of the learning in the United States and building on its success. With the U.S. results in hand and access to the strategy, Cormark could create materials designed to beat the U.S. benchmark and provide Pfizer Canada the opportunity to better the U.S. results with a Canadian success story. A case could be made that market conditions and consumer behaviour were not identical to those in the U.S. launch. In the United States, Rimadyl was a first in class product belonging to a new generation of non-steroid anti-inflammatory drugs (NSAIDs) while in Canada Rimadyl was second to market. In addition, there was the important French market to consider in Canada, which often requires separate strategy and communications materials. A "made in Canada" solution would ensure that Cormark and Pfizer Canada controlled the launch and managed the launch process to Canadian standards and Canadian expectations. An investment in new Canadian materials takes a longer-term view of the market in terms of payback and assumes that original work meets the financial hurdles and budget requirements for the launch.

Cormark and Pfizer Canada concluded that all of the options could be achieved in the 90-day launch timetable. They conducted qualitative research with consumers and veterinarians to probe usage and attitudes: The Cormark team concluded that the U.S. strategy and its key messages were effective with Canadian consumers, who were generally similar to their U.S. counterparts; but Canadian veterinarians held different perspectives.

Now, join David Edward and the Cormark–Pfizer decision team. Which option would you choose, and why?

# TAILORING MARKETING COMMUNICATIONS TO CUSTOMERS

To reach customers, it is essential to get to know them and to talk their language—to communicate well. Sometimes, it's as simple as creating an image for your product or company that matches customer preferences. For example, when research showed that the image of courier service UPS Canada was that of a boring, traditional, and old-fashioned company, they knew that change was needed. A new communications campaign was developed to liven up UPS's image. It focused on their trusted and approachable drivers overcoming all obstacles to deliver their packages, with a tagline of "Moving at the speed of your business." It worked. Customers now use words like "dynamic" and "contemporary" to describe the company.[1]

**UPS Canada**
www.ups.com/canada

The coordination of a marketer's efforts to influence attitudes or behaviour used to be commonly called **promotion**. While this term fit well as one of the four Ps of the marketing mix, it implies a one-way (asymmetrical) conversation from marketer to customer. Promotion-oriented companies focus on disseminating favourable information about products and services to mass audiences, or on using research to develop messages to persuade specific, targeted audiences to engage in desired behaviour.[2] Today, technologies ranging from the Internet to digital wireless communication to "smart" products allow marketers to become much more interactive with customers. Many consumers expect to enter into a dialogue with an organization—to be informed, not manipulated, and to be assisted in making decisions, not sold.

**promotion** The coordination of a marketer's communications efforts to influence attitudes or behaviour toward a product or service.

**Marketing communications** is the term now used most frequently to describe the vital roles of informing consumers and customers about the relative value of products, and developing trust and other relational bonds that facilitate ongoing exchange relationships. Marketing communications plays these roles for every type of business, whether its goal is to sell suits to executives or to encourage government to decrease taxes on gasoline. New two-way (symmetrical) approaches to communications strategies help build better relationships—there is greater mutual understanding with two-way ongoing dialogue, more balance in relationships, and consequently greater commitment to brands and companies on the part of consumers and customers that usually results in greater long-term profitability.[3]

**marketing communications** Informing consumers and customers about the relative value of products, and developing trust and other relational bonds that facilitate ongoing exchange relationships.

Marketing communications can take many forms—quirky television commercials, sophisticated magazine ads, Internet banner ads using the latest interactive technology, glaring billboards, funky T-shirts, or blimps drifting lazily over football stadiums. Some of these communications activities are intended to communicate key messages to target audience. Others provide incentives to buy specific products. In each case, the communication is intended to accomplish specific goals:

- Communications *inform* consumers about new goods and services, and where they can be obtained.[4]
- Communications *remind* consumers to continue using products.
- Communications *persuade* consumers to choose one product over others.
- Communications *create* complex brand images and identities in the minds of consumers.
- Communications *build* relationships with customers.

## COMMUNICATIONS STRATEGY

Virtually everything an organization says and does is a form of communication. The ads it creates, the packages it designs, even the uniforms its employees wear contribute to the picture people have of the company and its products. In a broad sense, every element of the marketing mix is actually a form of communication. After all, the price of a product, where it is sold, and even the nature of the product itself contribute to the impression of the item in people's minds.

# Integrated Communications Strategy

In the past, companies made little effort to coordinate the messages consumers received. An advertising campaign would run independently of a sweepstakes, which in turn had no relation to a series of company-sponsored community events. The consumer, however, does not see these items in isolation but instead as one stream of communication. It was often confusing and ineffective. But let's see how the rules are changing in the marketing communication business.

**COORDINATING COMMUNICATIONS MESSAGES** A broader view of the communications process, as shown in Figure 12.1, has spurred the development of an exciting new perspective on communication strategy. **Integrated marketing communications (IMC)** is the practice of unifying all marketing communication tools and corporate and brand messages to communicate in a consistent way to and with stakeholder audiences[5] In a survey of marketing executives, IMC was rated the most important factor in marketing strategy—more important than consumer lifestyle changes, economic trends, new retail formats, or globalization.[6]

The IMC philosophy recognizes that customers absorb information about a product or an organization from many sources, not all of which are formal communication messages or even under the marketer's control. It takes the recipients' perspective—anticipating every opportunity in which they see information about the good, service, or organization—and then ensures that each of these exposures communicates the desired message and elicits the intended response.[7] As Figure 12.1 illustrates, this approach still relies on a variety of communication tools and approaches, but it emphasizes that some are planned, some are unplanned, that all marketing mix decisions and contact points (such as the cleanliness of bathrooms, convenience of parking, or even employee appearances) send messages to consumers or business customers, and they must all be used in harmony to reach targeted consumers. Figure 12.1 also suggests that different elements in an IMC strategy may have greater or lesser relevance to consumers or customers during different stages of their decision process from pre-purchase, to purchase, to post-purchase evaluation.

Tourism British Columbia follows an IMC strategy of a low-cost integrated system aimed at impacting consumer buying decisions.[8] It starts with identifying consumer needs

> **integrated marketing communications (IMC)** IMC is the practice of unifying all marketing communication tools and corporate and brand messages to communicate in a consistent way to and with stakeholder audiences.

**Figure 12.1** The Integrated Marketing Communications Perspective

Adapted from Figure 1.2, *Introduction to Marketing Communications*, First Canadian Edition, John Burnett, Sandra Moriarty, and E. Stephen Grant, Prentice Hall, 2001.

and interests, then develop programs to motivate consumers involving distribution outlets (including sales offices), a Web site, a call centre, print ads, direct television (DRTV), direct mail, and a guide distributed as a 28-page newspaper free-standing insert. The ***BC Escapes®**** campaign (Exhibit 12.1) was launched in 1998 using this IMC strategy, targeting high-income, time-compressed consumers in San Francisco, Los Angeles, and Chicago with either airfair only or airfare plus accommodation four- or five-day spring getaway offers. In 2000, the ***BC Escapes®*** campaign was expanded to target other U.S. and Canadian cities and attracted nearly 60 000 visitors, generating $43 million in revenue from a $5 million campaign investment. Tourism British Columbia attributes its success to the IMC strategy with a direct call to action and a 100 percent accountable, measurable tracking system.

**THE EMERGING IMC PERSPECTIVE** The IMC perspective is still new and evolving. At many companies, it is more of an idea than a reality. However, many advertising agencies, communication companies, and marketing organizations are beginning to develop their own ideas of what an IMC strategy should look like. These approaches tend to share a number of characteristics:

- They focus on customers' need for communications rather than on the message.

- They rely on the use of a customer database or detailed primary research to precisely focus their audiences and messages.

- They strive to send consistent messages using diverse communications vehicles.

- They plan for carefully timed message deliveries to provide a continuous stream of consistent information to recipients.

- They use several communication tools plus product design and packaging to communicate.

## Roadblocks to IMC

The idea of coordinating all elements of communication seems so sensible that you may wonder why all communications strategies are not done this way. Unfortunately, many marketers resist the IMC approach or have trouble implementing it.[9] Following are some of the barriers to acceptance.

The approach requires changes in the way marketers plan and implement communication strategies. Many companies are financially driven rather than customer driven, and there is a general resistance to change in organizations. Finally, many executives specialize in one aspect of communication, such as advertising or sales promotion, and are reluctant to branch out into other areas.

*page 15*

*page 22*

### Get away from it all. Or to it all.

Send for your free BC Escapes® guides filled with over 100 pages of remarkable experiences and special accommodation offers. One night's stay starts at just $59, but only for a limited time.

Call 1-800 HELLO BC®
or visit HelloBC.com/calgary

SUPER, NATURAL
BRITISH
COLUMBIA
CANADA

Price quoted is per room based on double occupancy, excluding taxes, and is subject to change. Some restrictions may apply. Subject to availability. See guides for details.

**Exhibit 12.1**

Tourism British Columbia used an IMC approach in developing their series of ***BC Escapes®*** campaigns.

*® Registered trade-mark of Tourism British Columbia. Used under license.

The IMC approach can assign relatively more importance to aspects of communication other than advertising. Some executives are reluctant to divert part of their communications budget from glamorous ads to coupons or contests, and some advertising agencies don't want to relinquish this piece of their business to other companies specializing in running sweepstakes or hosting town hall meetings.

Brand managers and associate brand managers develop communication strategies at lower levels after senior planners have already developed the larger marketing strategy. But the IMC approach requires upper-level management to view other aspects of the marketing mix, such as packaging or pricing decisions, as part of the communication strategy. A successful IMC approach requires a company-wide commitment, from the CEO down, to putting the customer first and communicating interactively with customers in many different channels. Some firms find it hard to change their habits.

Some advertising agencies have not bought into the concept of IMC. Since they often do not have the full services required to deliver comprehensive programs, the solutions they offer their clients focus on their area of specialization, such as advertising or public relations.

## COMMUNICATIONS THEORY

Like other marketing mix decisions, marketing communication strategy is based on a solid understanding of the target market, the decision environment, and marketing concepts, principles, and theory. In this next section we will explore the central communication theory and models on which communication decisions are based

### The Communications Model

With either one-way or two-way communications, the consumer is the focal point: A message is transmitted on some medium from a sender to a receiver who (it is hoped) is paying attention and understands the sender. Regardless of how messages are sent, whether as a hat with a Roots logo on it or a sales pitch from an Aveda representative, messages are designed to capture receivers' attention and relate to their needs. With two-way communications, the receiver sends a message back to the original sender, opening a dialogue between the parties.

Any ways that marketers reach out to consumers, from simple highway billboards to customized messages sent via e-mail to busy executives, are part of the basic communications process. The **communications model** specifies that a number of elements are necessary for communication to occur—a source, a message, a medium, and a receiver. Figure 12.2 shows the communications model.

**ENCODING BY THE MARKETER** It is one thing for marketers to create an idea about a product in their minds and quite another to express that idea so that other people get the same picture. **Encoding** is the process of translating an idea into a form of communication that will convey the desired meaning. Consider how different companies have used a dog to symbolize their brands. Microcell's Fido, a personal communication (PCS) product, has successfully used dogs in its communications to help us draw linkages to their services being as faithful and companionable as "man's best friend." RCA has introduced a second dog (a puppy) into its logo to communicate that they are always innovating—the best of old and new. And Greyhound Bus Lines has successfully used a greyhound dog to convey fast and sleek service. Many other animals have been used by many other companies to convey brand meaning: Can you think of some?

**THE SOURCE** The **source** is the organization or individual sending the message. Marketers must choose a real person (e.g., company president Dave Thomas for Wendy's fast-food restaurants), hire an actor or model (e.g., Canadian country singer Shania Twain for Revlon), or create a character (e.g., Mr. Peanut for Planters Peanuts) who will represent the source.

**communications model** The elements necessary for meaning to be transferred from a sender to a receiver.

**encoding** The process of translating an idea into a form of communication that will convey meaning.

**source** An organization or individual that sends a message.

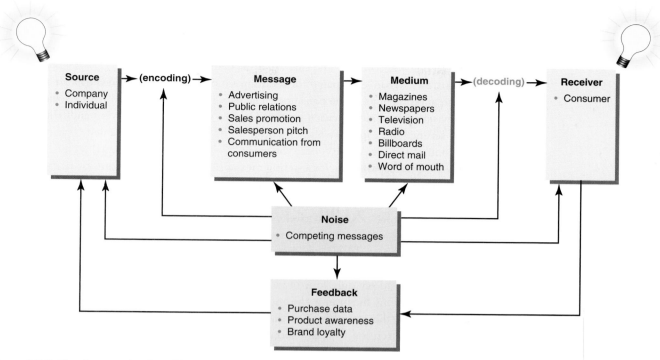

**Figure 12.2** The Communications Model

**THE MESSAGE** The **message** is the actual communication sent from a sender to a receiver. The message should ideally accomplish four objectives (though a single message can rarely do all of these): It should get *attention*, hold *interest*, create *desire*, and produce *action*. These communications goals are known as the **AIDA model** (Figure 12.3). Here we'll review some different forms the message can take, as well as how the information in the message can best be structured.

*Type of appeal:* Because there are many ways to say the same thing, marketers must choose what type of appeal, or message strategy, they will use when encoding the message. To illustrate how the choice of an appeal can result in a different communication, compare two

**message** The communication in physical form that goes from a sender to a receiver.

**AIDA model** The communication goals of attention, interest, desire, and action.

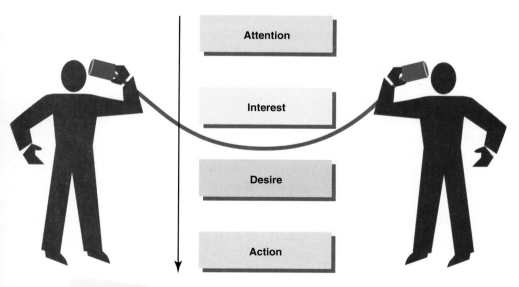

**Figure 12.3** AIDA Model

strategies selected by rival car companies to promote similar automobiles. A few years ago, Toyota and Nissan both introduced a large luxury car that sold for over $50 000. Toyota's advertising for its Lexus model used a *rational appeal*, which focused on the technical advancements in the car's design. This approach is often effective for promoting products that are technically complex and that are a substantial investment.

In contrast, Nissan's campaign for its Infiniti model used an *emotional appeal*, an attempt to arouse good feelings in the consumer. The new car was introduced with a series of print and television ads, which focused on the Zen-like experience of driving and featured long shots of serene landscapes. As one executive with the campaign explained, "We're not selling the skin of the car; we're selling the spirit."[10]

*Structure of the appeal:* Many marketing messages are similar to debates or trials, in which someone presents arguments and tries to convince the receivers to shift their opinions accordingly. The way the argument is presented can be important. Most messages merely present one or more positive attributes about the product or reasons to buy it: These are *supportive arguments* or *one-sided messages*. An alternative is to use a *two-sided message*, with both positive and negative information. Two-sided ads can be quite effective, but marketers do not use them very often.[11] A related issue is whether the argument should draw conclusions: Should the ad say only "our brand is superior," or should it add the message that the consumer should buy the brand? The answer depends on the consumer's motivation to think about the ad and the complexity of the arguments. If the message is personally relevant, people will pay attention to it and spontaneously draw their own conclusions. However, if the arguments are hard to follow or the person's motivation to follow them is lacking, it is safer for the ad to make these conclusions explicit.[12]

**THE MEDIUM** No matter how the message is encoded, it must then be transmitted via a **medium**, a communications vehicle used to reach members of a target audience. This vehicle can be television, radio, a magazine, personal contact, a billboard, or even a product logo printed on a coffee mug (Exhibit 12.2). Ideally the attributes of the product should match those of the medium. For example, magazines with high prestige are more effective at communicating messages about overall product image and quality, whereas specialized magazines do a better job of conveying factual information.[13]

**DECODING BY THE RECEIVER** Communication cannot occur unless there is a **receiver** to intercept the message. Assuming that the customer is even paying attention—a big assumption in our overloaded, media-saturated society—the meaning of the message is interpreted in light of that individual's unique experiences. **Decoding** is the process whereby a receiver assigns meaning to a message. We hope that the target consumer will decode the message the way we had intended. Effective communication occurs only when the source and the receiver have a mutual *frame of reference*. They must share the same understanding about the world. Grabbing the receiver's attention is more likely if the message source is someone the receiver likes, the message is creatively executed, and the medium is one the receiver typically notices. Furthermore, it helps if the subject of the message is something that is personally relevant. The most enticing shampoo ad in the world probably won't be noticed by a bald man.

To improve the abilities of organizations to focus their communications efforts on receptive receivers, companies are slicing the mass market into smaller and smaller target audiences. In a truly interactive environment, communications efforts will look more like door-to-door selling than like television advertising. Even the Coca-Cola Company, which has long been known for extravagant network productions, is looking for alternatives to big-budget, mass-market commercials. One recent campaign, produced by Creative Artists Agency, has 24 ads in many moods and styles developed for 20 different television networks. These range from one done in a "quick-cut" style for MTV to a *Star Trek*-style spot called "Spaceship," intended to appeal to teenage boys.[14] These changes make sense, because the more recipients can identify with the message, the greater the probability they will reach for a Coke.

**medium** A communications vehicle through which a message is transmitted to a target audience.

**receiver** The organization or individual that intercepts and interprets the message.

**decoding** The process by which a receiver assigns meaning to the message.

**NOISE** The communications model also acknowledges that messages often are blocked by **noise**, which is anything that interferes with effective communication. Competing marketing communications cause noise, as do other things happening in the environment that divert the receiver's attention. Marketers try to minimize noise by placing their messages where there is less likely to be distractions or competition for consumers' attention. For example, companies such as Calvin Klein often buy a block of advertising pages in a magazine to be sure the reader sees only pictures of their clothing. Some advertisers such are now using black and white ads in colour magazines or on television to break through the noise. Corporate Communications Limited, Aliant Telecom, and Halifax Regional Police, for example, teamed up to create an anti-bullying public service announcement (Exhibit 12.3). The television spot shows white words on a plain black background with voiceovers of bullying taunts from both boys and girls and the tag line: "Just because you don't see it, doesn't mean it's not going on."

**FEEDBACK** To complete the communications loop, the source receives **feedback**, or reactions, from receivers. These reactions to the message help the marketer gauge the appeal's effectiveness and fine-tune it. Obtaining feedback reminds us of the importance of conducting marketing research to verify that a firm's strategies are working. The area of feedback is where newer symmetrical communications techniques based on IMC outperform the traditional asymmetrical approaches. By listening to the feedback provided by consumers and customers, organizations can be more responsive to the information needs of consumers and develop closer and stronger relationships with them. Developing these relationships, seen as increasingly important, will be discussed further in Chapter 15.

## The FCB Grid

There are many other communication frameworks and models. In Chapter 5 we introduced the FCB grid that categorized consumer decisions as being primarily thinking (cognitive) or feeling (affective) and high involvement or low involvement. This model has useful communication implications as different communication strategies and tactics are appropriate in each of the four quadrants (Figure 12.4).

High involvement–thinking decisions, for example, call for informative communication strategies and tactics such as comparative advertising or demonstrations and detail accommodating media such as print, infomercials, and the Internet. Low involvement–feeling decisions, on the other hand, call for image-oriented strategies and tactics such as life-style advertising or sex appeals and immediate response media such as point of purchase displays. We will further discuss communication strategies and tactics later in this chapter.

There are a number of limitations associated with the FCB grid, including its simplicity, its inability to differentiate product attitudes and motivations from brand attitudes and motivations, and its lack of recognition of the need to create brand awareness before brand attitudes.[15] There are more sophisticated models such as the Rossiter and Percy RPG grid[16] but these models are best left to advanced marketing communication classes. Because of its simplicity, the FCB Grid is widely used and it provides a useful way to think about marketing communication strategy. It also relates nicely to value creation strategies. "Thinking"

**Exhibit 12.2**

Electronic devices like PDAs and cell phones are now being used as communication medium by marketers. Bell Mobility recently partnered with the World Wrestling Entertainment Canada to offer a phone for WWE fans, enabling the WWE to target electronic communication.

**noise** Anything that interferes with effective communication.

**feedback** Receivers' reactions to the message.

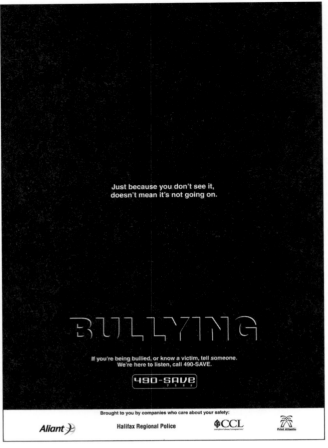

Just because you don't see it,
doesn't mean it's not going on.

BULLYING

If you're being bullied, or know a victim, tell someone.
We're here to listen, call 490-SAVE.

490-SAVE

Brought to you by companies who care about your safety:

Aliant          Halifax Regional Police          CCL          Print Atlantic

**Exhibit 12.3**

Distinctive black and white ads can help break through the noise of colour images.

decisions are concerned with functional value and cost-sacrifice value while "feeling" decisions are concerned with experiential and symbolic value.

## DEVELOPING COMMUNICATION PLANS AND BRIEFS

A marketing manager has to identify the specific combination of communication tools that will meet the company's objectives in the most effective and cost-efficient way. To ensure that companies develop an IMC strategy, the smart manager first develops a **communications plan**, a framework for developing, implementing, and controlling the firm's communication activities.[17]

Advertising (communication) agencies typically have three main functional areas: communication strategy, creative, and media placement. Large agencies may also have in-house market research and Internet/mobile communication capability. Communication planning and strategy is the domain of the "suits"—the account management people with business diplomas and degrees who understand target audiences, marketing strategy, communication theory, and how to develop the strategic elements of a communication plan. An effective communication plan addresses the elements illustrated in Figure 12.5. A communications brief is a summary (typically three or four pages) of the elements in Figure 12.5 that is used by the creative team to ensure that the creative execution is on-strategy.

**communications plan** A framework that outlines the strategies for developing, implementing, and controlling the firm's communication activities.

| | | Thinking (Rational / Cognitive) | Feeling (Emotional / Affective) |
|---|---|---|---|
| **High Involvement** | **Creative Strategy** | **Informative Communication**<br><br>Specific information<br>Demonstrations<br>Comparitive advertising | **Affective Communication**<br><br>Strong creative execution<br>Visual appeals<br>Impactful communication |
| | **Media Strategy** | Long Copy Formats<br>Magazine & Newspaper<br>Infomercials<br>Internet | Large Spreads (Space)<br>Inserts & Other Special Images<br>Television & Other Rich Media<br>Interactive Media |
| **Low Involvement** | **Creative Strategy** | **Habitual Communication**<br><br>Reminder communication<br>Repetition<br>Memorable music and slogans | **Reactive Communication**<br><br>Attention-getting<br>Impulse-trigger<br>Image-oriented |
| | **Media Strategy** | Small-space ads<br>TV shorts or radio<br>Point of sale | Billboards / outdoor<br>Point of sale<br>Newspaper |

**Figure 12.4** FCB Grid Communication Implications

# Marketing Objectives, Situation, Target Markets, and Target Audiences

Marketing communication strategy is designed to achieve marketing objectives such as those discussed in Chapter 2 and, as previously discussed, is based on an understanding of the decision environment and specific target markets. We will discuss the influences of the decision environment after reviewing communications mix alternatives. The target market is identified from research and segmentation decisions, which we discussed in Chapter 4. A **target audience** is the group or set of individuals or organizations with whom you want to communicate. This may be the same as the target market but often target audiences are more specific. For example, the target market for Burton Snowboards may be status-conscious boarders, 15- to 25-years-old, but the target audience for a specific communication campaign may be female status-conscious boarders, 15- to 25-years-old, living in greater Vancouver.

There may be more than one target audience within a target market. For example, if the audiences have different media watching and reading habits, live in different geographic areas reached by different TV or radio stations, or are persuaded by different types of information or appeals. Target audience profiles are also typically more detailed than target market profiles—particularly in the areas of media use and communication strategy and tactic preferences or responsiveness. For example, an account executive working on a campaign for Pioneer Stereo was assigned to hang out with guys who were likely prospects to buy car stereos. His observations resulted in an advertising campaign that incorporated the phrases they used to describe their cars: "My car is my holy temple, my love shack, my drag racer of doom…."[18] To make our communications more effective we need to know their values, attitudes, interests, opinions, and anything else that might affect how they receive, process, store, and use information. This additional information helps marketers to hone their integrated communications strategies to successfully reach consumers with the right message, in the right place, at the right time, and with the right offer.

- Marketing Objectives
- Situation (marketing mix, SWOT, and other analyses) & Assumptions
- Target Markets
- Target Audiences & Profiles
- Communication Objectives
- Communication Strategy
- Positioning Statement and Key Messages
- Communication Tactics (themes, approaches)
- Budget Reality Check
- Communications Mix
- Creative Execution
- Media Scheduling and Placement
- Budget Allocation
- Evaluation

**Figure 12.5** Stages in Developing the Communications Plan

**target audience** A highly segmented group of people who receive and respond similarly to marketing messages.

# Establish Communications Objectives

The point of developing a communications strategy is to connect the marketing plan to consumers, to let them know that the organization has a product to meet their needs in a timely and affordable way. It's bad enough when a product comes along that people don't want or need; perhaps a bigger marketing sin is to have a product that they do want, but fail to let them know about it. As creative as some advertisers or salespeople are, it is rare that any one communication element could cause a consumer who has never heard of a product to become aware of it, prefer it over competing products, and buy it on the spot. An exception is novelty or impulse items, which are bought on a whim. Think of this communications road as an uphill climb (see Figure 12.6)—as the hill gets steeper, the later steps, which are forming a preference for the product and actually buying it, get tougher. During this climb, many people drop out, so only a small proportion of the target market actually reaches the top of the hill to become loyal customers. Each part of this path can entail different communications objectives to "push" people to the next level in their decision processes (see Chapters 6 and 7 for a review of decision models).

To understand how this process works, consider how a company would have to adjust its communications objectives as it tries to establish a presence in the market for a new men's cologne called Hunk. Let's say that the primary target market for the cologne is single men, aged 18 to 24, who care about their appearance and who are into health, fitness, and working out. The company would want to focus on some communications methods (such as advertising) and less on others (such as personal selling). These are some steps the company might take to promote Hunk:

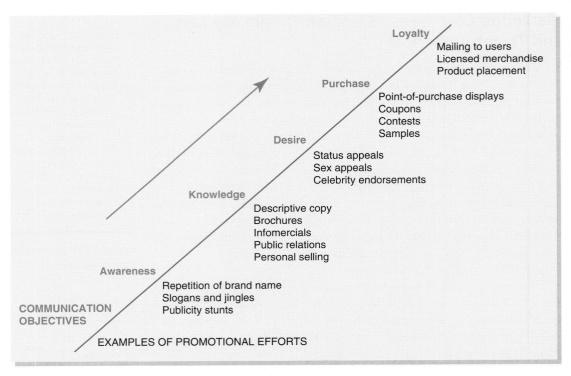

**Figure 12.6** Up the Communications Road

- *Create awareness.* The first step is to make members of the target market aware that there's a new brand of cologne on the market. This would be accomplished by simple, repetitive advertising in magazines, on television, and on the radio that feature the brand name (Exhibit 12.4). The selection of the specific magazines, television shows, and radio stations would be based on knowing what men 18 to 24 years old are reading, watching, and listening to. The company might even undertake a *teaser campaign*, in which interest is heightened by not revealing the exact nature of the product (e.g., newspaper ads that simply proclaim, "Hunk is coming!"). The communication objective might be to create an 80 percent awareness of Hunk cologne among 18- to 24-year-old men in the first two months in the three Prairie Provinces.

- *Inform the market.* The next step would be to provide prospective users with knowledge about the benefits the new product has to offer, that is, how it is positioned relative to other fragrances (see Chapter 8). Perhaps the cologne has a light, slightly mentholated scent that smells vaguely like liniments men use after a workout. Communication efforts would focus on messages and images that emphasize this position. The objective at this point might be to communicate the connection between Hunk and muscle building, so that 75 percent of the target market becomes interested in the product.

- *Create desire.* The next task is to create favourable feelings toward the product and to convince at least some portion of this group that it is preferable to other colognes they now wear. Communications at this stage might emphasize splashy advertising spreads in magazines, perhaps including an endorsement by a well-known celebrity "hunk," such as Arnold Schwarzenegger. The specific objective might be to create positive attitudes toward Hunk cologne among

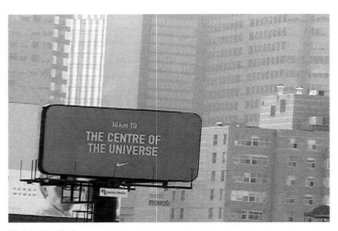

**Exhibit 12.4**

This Nike billboard was part of a campaign designed to create awareness and interest for the inaugural Nike RunTO 10K event in Toronto.

50 percent of the target market and brand preference among 30 percent of the target market.

- *Encourage trial.* The company now needs to get some of the men who have formed a preference for the product to splash it on. A communications plan might encourage trial by mailing samples of Hunk to members of the target market, inserting scratch-and-sniff samples in bodybuilding magazines, placing elaborate displays in stores that dispense money-saving coupons, or even sponsoring a contest in which the winner gets to have Arnold Schwarzenegger as his personal trainer for a day. The specific objective now might be to encourage trial of Hunk among 25 percent of 18- to 24-year-old men in the first two months in the three Prairie Provinces.

- *Build loyalty.* Now, the company must focus on building loyalty: convincing customers to keep buying the cologne after they've gone through the first bottle. Communications efforts must maintain ongoing communications with current users to reinforce the bond they feel with the product. This will be accomplished with some mix of strategies, including periodic advertising, special events for users, and maybe even the development of a workout clothing line bearing the fragrance's logo. The objective might be to develop and maintain regular usage of Hunk cologne over 18 months among 10 percent of men from 18- to 24-years-old in the three Prairie Provinces.

In Chapter 8 we discussed the concept of the product life cycle. Marketers recognize that different communication objectives are particularly relevant in each life cycle stage. In the introduction stage, marketers need to make consumers or customers aware of their offering and help them become knowledgeable about it. In the growth stage, when competition increases, marketers pay most attention to creating desire and differentiating their brands. In the maturity stage, the focus is mostly on increasing market share, encouraging trial from new users, or encouraging users to switch brands, and building loyalty. In the decline stage the focus is predominately encouraging loyal customers to repeat their purchases and increase consumption. It should be noted, however, that all communication objectives are evident in marketing campaigns at each stage of the product life cycle as marketers need to help consumers complete their decision process at each stage.

## Communication Strategy

The communication strategy describes the overall approach to the communication. Toyota, for example, recently combined its advertising and public relations departments into one integrated team to create an IMC strategy for the launch of the Echo Hatchback, integrating public relations, cinema advertising, direct marketing, Internet marketing, and traditional advertising.[19] You will learn more about these communication mix elements shortly.

IMC is one way to describe an overall strategy. Another is whether the strategy is a **push strategy** or a **pull strategy**. A push strategy means that the company is seeking to move its products through the channel by convincing channel members to offer them and entice their customers to select these items. In this case, communication efforts will focus on personal selling and sales promotions, such as exhibits at trade shows. The company relying on a pull strategy is counting on consumers to learn about and express desire for its products, thus convincing retailers to respond to this demand by stocking these items. In this case, efforts will focus on media advertising to stimulate interest among end consumers.

**push strategy** Moving products through the channel by convincing channel members to offer them.

**pull strategy** Moving products through the channel by building desire for the products among consumers, who convince retailers to stock the items.

In describing the overall communication strategy, marketers also need to specify what kind of communication they are developing. Communication specialist James Grunig[20] identifies two fundamental dimensions governing communication strategy: the direction of the communication (one-way vs. two-way) and the purpose behind the communication (asymmetrical vs. symmetrical). One-way communication is where the marketing organization sends messages to audiences without expecting or desiring feedback. With two-way communication, the objective is to develop a relationship with customers (or other stakeholders), solicit feedback from them, and as the marketing organization, be willing to change your own behaviour. In asymmetrical communication the intent is to persuade customers (or other stakeholders) to engage in behaviour beneficial to the marketing organization by only communicating selective positive benefits or one side of the story. Thus one-way asymmetrical communications is the "hit and run" approach taken by some marketing organizations like some used car salesmen, or insurance salesmen, that use "hard sell" tactics to convince people to buy their products—not caring particularly if customers will be satisfied with their purchase decision, as there are lots of other customers. Two-way asymmetrical communication is where organizations and customers (through advocacy organizations) try to persuade each other, without really engaging in a give-and-take dialogue. This approach can be seen in the marketing of controversial social issues like the building of casinos where both advocates and proponents try to persuade elected officials to support or reject casino development applications. Symmetrical communication is a balanced approach where a marketing organization communicates both the positive and negative information about their products to help consumers make an informed choice of which products best suit their needs. While this model, like any other simplification has its limitations, the four approaches suggested by this $2 \times 2$ matrix are evident in practice. Grunig advocates the practice of the two-way symmetrical model of communications and this is the approach most consistent with the marketing concept (Chapter 1).

## Positioning Statement and Key Messages

Once the overall approach to the communication strategy is established, marketers need to decide what they want to communicate to their audience(s). In Chapter 3 we discussed the concept of positioning. A positioning statement is a one- to three-sentence summary of the product positioning—how you want a product to be known in the minds of customers as being different from, and better than, competitive offers.

Benjamin Moore, for example, recently changed their corporate positioning statement to be "Benjamin Moore is in the business of helping discerning customers create an atmosphere, express their style and personality, and add value to their homes, through the use of colour."[21]

**Benjamin Moore**
www.benjaminmoore.ca

They then conducted extensive research to understand their target audience of home decorators and learned that home decorators constantly scour magazines, rip out pages, and put them into a file for later use, seeking inspirational decorating ideas for their home. They captured their positioning for this audience in the expression "Colour as Inspiration," and developed a personalized "My Scrapbook," feature in the Benjamin Moore Web site.

Communication purists would suggest that the positioning statement should focus on the one, maybe two, ways in which a marketing organization wants their product to be differentiated for a particular audience. Under this perspective, the positioning statement is similar to the concept of a unique selling proposition (USP)—the number one message a marketer wants to convey to an audience. A good example of a USP is "M&M's melt in your mouth, not in your hands." Other USP examples were described in Chapter 3 in the positioning discussion.

Other key messages are what you want to communicate to your target market, and these are typically listed in a communication plan in order of priority. That way, the marketer can evaluate the communication media and assess how many messages can be reasonably communicated by that media. Billboards, for example, can only typically accommodate one message. A 30-second radio spot might accommodate three or four messages. Magazine and newspaper ads can accommodate more messages.

## Communication Tactics

The communications tactics section discusses the themes and approach(es) that will break through the perceptual screens, get the attention of the target audience, and be consistent with the overall strategy and positioning. An **advertising appeal** is the central idea of the ad and a **creative concept** is how that idea will be expressed through visuals, text, music, and other design elements. While advertising appeals and creative concepts are typically the domain of the creative department within an agency (see below), a communications plan needs to set some boundaries on the creative process to ensure the creative is on strategy and is consistent with the communication objectives, target audience, and positioning.

Communication experts come up with many ingenious ways to express a concept (Exhibit 12.5). Consistent with the FCB grid, some marketers use an emotional appeal complete with dramatic colour or powerful images, whereas others bombard the audience with facts. Some feature sexy people or stern-looking experts (even professors from time to time). Different appeals can work for the same product, from a bland "talking head" to a montage of animated special effects. An attention-getting way to say something profound about cat food or laundry detergent is more art than science, but we can describe some common appeals.

- *Informative Appeals:* Gives consumers one or more clear reasons why one product is a good choice for solving a problem. The format focuses on a need and points out how the product can satisfy it.

- *Comparative Advertising.* A *comparative advertisement* explicitly names two or more competitors. The Pepsi challenge is an example of a comparative advertising campaign that has been used successfully over a long period of time. Comparative ads like the Pepsi challenge can be very effective, but there is a risk of turning off consumers who don't like the negative tone. This is especially a problem in cultures that don't take kindly to impolite messages. For instance, Tokyo's five major television networks pulled a Pepsi comparative ad, because Japanese viewers found it offensive to be too blunt.[22]

- *Demonstration:* The ad shows a product "in action" to prove that it performs as claimed. "It slices, it dices!" This appeal helps sell products that people "use." The ad in Exhibit 12.6 demonstrates the poor performance of unnamed Goodyear tire competitors in a very creative and attention-getting way.

- *Testimonial:* A celebrity, an expert, or a "typical person" states the product's effectiveness. The use of *celebrity endorsers* is a common but expensive strategy. It is particularly effective for mature products, which need to differentiate themselves from competitors. 3M Canada, for example, used comedian Steve Smith (otherwise known as Red Green) as the spokesperson for one of its mature products—the Scotch brand duct tape.[23] Chrysler dropped Celine Dion (and walked away from a US$14 million contract!) as a celebrity endorser of their Pacifica crossover car (part SUV, station wagon, and minivan) after finding she was too young to appeal to the Pacifica's target market.[24]

- *Slice-of-Life:* A slice-of-life format presents a (dramatized) scene from everyday life. Today, advertisers are trying to expand their definition of "everyday life." An ad for Spray 'n' Wash Stain Stick from Dow Chemical, for example, shows a mother and her Down syndrome child. The mother comments, "The last place we need another challenge is the laundry room." One advertising critic described the spot as "the most crassly contrived slice-of-life in advertising history." But the American National Down Syndrome Congress applauded the ad and awarded Dow its annual media award.[25]

**advertising appeal**   The central idea or theme of a communication message.

**creative concept**   How the advertising appeal will be expressed through visuals, text, music, and other design elements.

**3M Canada**
http://cms.3m.com/cms/CA
/en/1-30/cuRucFQ/view
.jhtml

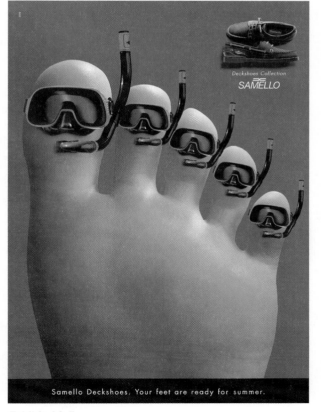

**Exhibit 12.5**

Advertising creatives find unique ways to express a concept.

**Exhibit 12.6**

This Goodyear tire ad demonstrates the benefit of having Goodyear tires.

- *Lifestyle:* A lifestyle format shows a person or persons attractive to the target market in an appealing setting (Exhibit 12.7). The advertised product is "part of the scene," implying that the person who buys it will attain the lifestyle. For example, a commercial shown on MuchMusic might depict a group of snowboarders having fun and then taking time to drink a McCain fruit drink. A fantasy format is a variation of the lifestyle approach in which the viewer is encouraged to imagine being transported to a novel or exotic situation. Ads for some Canadian lotteries show fantasy lifestyles that ticket purchasers can achieve if they win the lottery. R K Swamy/BBDO used a lifestyle appeal to sell the Performa by focusing on how the machine empowers children to pursue their potential. They created print ads and television commercials that plugged the Performa by showing parents and children using it to expand their horizons. The goal was to create ad messages that are warm and friendly, "feel-good" ads that would humanize the technology behind Apple's products and show potential buyers how the home computer could improve their lives.

- *Fear Appeals:* This format highlights the negative consequences of using or not using a product. Fear appeals are often used to get the attention of audiences of social messages like not drinking and driving, not smoking, and safe sex. The Quebec government and their agency Marketel, for example, recently developed a campaign to help increase awareness of AIDS and expose the source of the danger. While the images are provocative and disturbing, the intent was to get their audience's attention. Fear appeals are also used by private sector marketers, but typically with less disturbing images aimed at illustrating the problem of not buying a particular good or service. The British Columbia Automobile Association, for example, developed a campaign that humorously showed the problems of not having a BCAA membership, and being stranded in potentially scary situations.

- *Sex Appeals:* Some ads appear to be selling sex rather than products. This was the case in a recent ad for Carlsberg beer, run by Labatt Breweries of Canada, in which three women are shown discussing a boyfriend's willingness to perform a particular sexual act. These ads and many others rely on sexuality to get consumers' attention.

- *Humorous Appeals:* Humorous ads can be an effective way to break through advertising clutter. But humour can be tricky: What is funny to one person may be offensive to another. Different cultures also have different senses of humour.

## Budget Reality Check

Communication budgets do not determine communication strategy but communication budgets do inform strategy—in that marketers need to be aware of what can be achieved with a particular budget. The strategies and tactics used to communicate with a $50 000 budget may be the same as the strategies and tactics used to communicate with a $500 000 budget, but the impact will be different as the $500 000 can buy more, and perhaps different, exposure to an audience. Table 12.1 shows examples of what different media cost for single placement (one ad, one time). Costs fall significantly when multiple placements are booked and most media sell packages of space, bundling attractive time slots with less attractive time slots at a discounted rate. However, as you can see from the "list" prices, communication is not inexpensive. Knowing the approximate budget for a communication campaign helps marketers decide what communication mix elements can realistically be used.

## Communications Mix

We've discussed integration as key to effective communication strategy. Now let's look at the elements that marketers must coordinate in their IMC efforts. Within the marketing mix, the communication elements that the marketer controls or influences are the **communications mix**. These include advertising, sales promotions, public relations, direct marketing, personal selling, and word-of-mouth. The term *mix* implies that a company's communication strategy is focused on more than one element, so part of the challenge is to combine these different communications tools effectively. Another challenge is to ensure that the communications mix works in harmony with the overall marketing mix, which combines elements of communication with distribution, price, and product decisions to position the firm's offering in people's minds. These other marketing mix elements, after all, also communicate. A product design, for example, can send a powerful message: Honda Motor Company introduced to the Japanese market a model called the City, which it deliberately designed to attract young drivers. The car featured a very high roof that made the City look like a toy. This playful quality appealed to Japan's young consumers, and the design theme was reinforced by fun and carefree communication messages.[26]

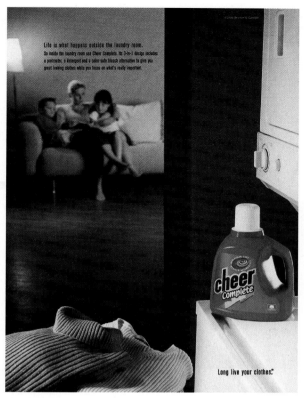

**Exhibit 12.7**

Lifestyle advertising shows consumers who are attractive to the target market in an appealing setting. Here, Cheer focuses on family living in an appeal for clean laundry.

## SPOTLIGHT ON REAL PEOPLE     Rethink on Target

Not many people would choose to leave a secure, high-income job with a successful multinational advertising agency to launch an uncertain and risky entrepreneurial start-up. But that is exactly what Ian Grais, Chris Staples, and Tom Shepansky did when they left Jarvis DDB in Vancouver in 1999 to launch the small ad agency Rethink. Rethink started with three partners working out of a condemned building in Coal Harbour, and four years later it has earned an impressive reputation, numerous powerhouse clients and staff, and was the recipient of the prestigious award of Marketing's Top Agency of the Year in 2003.[27]

Rethink prides itself on its no frills, complete creativity vision, and this is making them more effective than ever. Rethink has scored clients all over North America, and is developing creative, smart, popular, and effective advertisement campaigns. When Rethink developed advertisements for Clover Leaf Tuna, sales went up 35 percent; similarly Rethink's "fresh obsessed" slogan for Michigan's

largest grocery chain has brand recognition up nearly 20 percent.

One key to their success is they really understand target audiences (Exhibit 12.8). For example, Ian Grais recently completed his tenth campaign for Vancouver's Playland, which focuses on the lingering effects of the rides. In a radio ad (which offended four of seven Vancouver radio stations), listeners hear a man talking about having taken his kids to Playland the previous weekend to colleagues in an elevator. The man starts vomiting causing his colleagues to also vomit. Print ads showed how the Playland feeling lasts by depicting older adults with their hair on end in dishevelled clothes with their wrinkles falling upside down (they hung actors upside down in gravity booths). The intent was to offend and gross-out anyone over the age of 18—which they did![28] Grais understood that tweens and young teens would think it humorous and memorable and that was the intended audience.

1. What allows a small advertising agency to compete with large national or international agencies?
2. What type of tactic was used in the Playland campaign to get the attention of the target audience?
3. What research could Rethink do to even better understand the tween and young teen Playland customer?

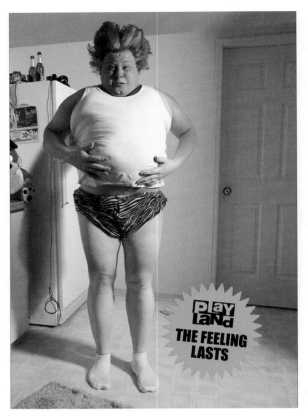

**Exhibit 12.8**

Rethink understood its target audience in creating a campaign for Playland that focused on the lasting effects of the rides.

**COMMUNICATIONS MIX ELEMENTS** Marketing communications can be categorized along two basic dimensions: the type of communication and the source (see Table 12.2). From the customer's perspective, there are two types of communication: marketers are trying to deliver a message about their product or organization or they are providing an incentive to purchase or otherwise change consumer behaviour.[29] The customer identifies the source of these messages or incentives as either the organization or a presumed independent source, such as friends, magazine editorials, or expert opinion. There are also two main methods of transmitting messages and incentives—those that communicate to a mass audience and those that communicate person to person. This latter distinction is becoming blurred, however, as technological advances such as the Internet, smart checkout scanners, and interactive television enable what has traditionally been considered tools of mass media—advertising, sales promotion, and public relations—to be used to reach individual consumers with personal appeals. In this section, we'll briefly describe the elements of the communications mix, which are covered in more detail in Chapter 13. Some of the pros and cons of each element are also presented in Table 12.3.

**ADVERTISING** For many, **advertising** is the most familiar and visible element of the communications mix. Advertising is non-personal communication from an identified sponsor using paid space, primarily in mass media. Because it can convey rich and dynamic images, such as the ones in the Dunlop Tire ad in Exhibit 12.9, advertising creates and reinforces a distinctive brand identity. This helps marketers both persuade customers to select their product and build bonds with buyers by presenting them with familiar brand images and logos time after time. Advertising is also useful in communicating factual information about the product or reminding consumers to buy their favourite brand. However, advertising sometimes suffers from a credibility problem, because cynical consumers tune out messages they think are biased or are intended to sell them something they don't need. It can also be very expensive for firms, so they must take great care to ensure their messages are effective.

**communications mix** The major elements of marketer-controlled communications, including advertising, sales promotions, marketing public relations, direct marketing, and personal selling.

**Honda Motor Company**
www.honda.com

**advertising** Non-personal, paid communication from an identified sponsor, primarily using mass media.

**Table 12.1 Media Cost Examples**

| 30-Second Television: National Exposure | | Magazine Full-Page, 4-Colour | |
|---|---|---|---|
| CTV – Survivor | $209 000 | MacLean's | $32 600 |
| CBC – The National | $8000 | BC Business | $4630 |
| TSN – PGA Golf | $1200 | EnRoute | $7500 |
| Teletoon (National) | $500–$3000 | Chatelaine | $43 840 |
| MuchMusic (12pm–6 pm) | $525 | Toronto Life | $12 960 |
| | | Famous Magazine | $25 000 |
| **Newspaper ?-Page, Black + 1-Colour** | | | |
| The Globe & Mail (National) | $8204 | **30-Second Radio** | |
| The Gazette (Montreal) | $2446 | Montreal CINW - AM | $75–$105 |
| Times Columnist (Victoria) | $929 | Vancouver CKNW (afternoon) | $135 |
| | | Edmonton CFCW- AM | $117–$147 |
| | | Toronto CJCL - AM | $130–$235 |
| | | Fredericton CFXY - FM | $56–$62 |

Note: Rates are approximate and change frequently. Significant volume- and package-based discounts are available.

**Table 12.2** Types of Marketing Communications

| | | Identified as Marketer | Not Identified as Marketer |
|---|---|---|---|
| METHOD OF TRANSMISSION | **Mass Media** | Advertising, Sales promotion | Public relations |
| | **Personal** | Personal selling | Word of mouth |

**PERSONAL SELLING** The most personal way to communicate with consumers is by direct interaction, which can occur in person, by phone, or even over an interactive computer link. Personal selling occurs when a company representative comes in direct contact with a customer or group of customers to inform them about a product or service and to encourage them to make a purchase. This type of communication activity is most often seen in the business-to-business market, but everyone has experienced a door-to-door representative selling Girl Guide cookies or sales clerks in clothing stores asking if they can be of assistance. Salespeople are a valuable communications medium, because customers can ask questions and the salesperson can immediately address objections and relay product benefits.

Personal selling can be tremendously effective, especially for big-ticket consumer items and for industrial products for which the "human touch" and developing tailored solutions is essential. It can be so effective that some marketers, if given a choice, might well abandon other forms of communication and simply dispatch a salesperson to every customer's house or office. Unfortunately, this form of communication is also the most expensive, and it can be difficult to ensure that all salespeople are delivering the same message with the same impact.

**Table 12.3** A Comparison of Elements of the Communications Mix

| Communications Element | Pros | Cons |
|---|---|---|
| Advertising | The marketer has control over what the message will say, when it will appear, and who is likely to see it. | Often expensive to produce and distribute. May have low credibility and/or be ignored by audience. |
| Sales promotion | Provides incentives to retailers to support one's products. Builds excitement for retailers and consumers. Encourages immediate purchase and trial of new products. Price-oriented promotions cater to price-sensitive consumers. | Short-term emphasis on immediate sales rather than a focus on building brand loyalty. The number of competing promotions may make it hard to break through the promotional clutter. |
| Public relations | Relatively low cost. High credibility. | Lack of control over the message that is eventually transmitted, and no gurarantee that the message will ever reach the target. Hard to track the results of publicity efforts. |
| Personal selling | Direct contact with the customer gives the salesperson the opportunity to be flexible and modify the sales message to coincide with the customer's needs. The salesperson can get immediate feedback from the customer. | High cost per contact with customer. Difficult to ensure consistency of message when it is delivered by many different company representatives. The credibility of salespeople often depends on the quality of their company's image, which has been created by other promotion strategies. |

TESTED FOR THE UNEXPECTED. ⊳DUNLOP

**Exhibit 12.9**

This German ad uses bizarre imagery to attract customers to its advertising.

interactive marketing Two-way communications, in which customized marketing communications elicit a measurable response from individual customers.

**DIRECT MARKETING** Direct marketing was introduced in Chapter 11 as a form of non-store retailing. The tools of direct marketing—catalogues, direct mail, the Internet, and direct response television—also play a significant communications role and are part of the communications mix. Some of these tools, such as the Internet and direct mail, are interactive: They can be customized to elicit measurable direct responses from individual customers and allow marketers to provide further customized information based on that response. Use of these interactive tools is called **interactive marketing**. The desired response is typically an order—a first-order response. But other intermediate responses might be desired, such as a request for more information, agreeing to a sales demonstration, or providing feedback on a provided sample—second-order responses. Coupon Radio, a car radio system that is now being tested, lets drivers request more information (e.g., about a band they hear on the radio, or to get names and addresses of retailers that sell an advertised product), all while cruising along in their cars.[30] It may sound strange, but another kind of second-order response is a request to *not* receive any more information from the company. We assume that a priority of any communication campaign is to get more customers. Interactive marketers sometimes operate with the opposite goal in mind: to *reduce* their customer base. They know that their efforts will be most effective when they are communicating only with customers who are interested in what they have to offer.

Direct marketing typically focuses on short-term, single transaction responses or a set of responses leading to a purchase decision. Database marketing, a related concept that will be discussed later in the chapter, focuses on building ongoing relationships and brand loyalty over time. The secret to effective direct marketing is developing an effective customer database, which contains enough detail in its target market profiles about customer needs, wants, interests, preferences, purchase behaviour, consumption behaviour, and media habits to enable the marketer to tailor messages to very specific categories of consumers. In the case of direct mail, messages are often personalized, not only by using the consumers' name and address, but also by using personal information from the database in the content of the message.

public relations Communications strategies to build good relationships with an organization's publics.

**PUBLIC RELATIONS** **Public relations** is a set of communication tools that organizations use to establish and maintain contact with the various publics (stakeholders) on whom their success depends. Public relations components of the communications mix seek to nurture a long-term positive relationship between the organization and its customers, suppliers, distributors, employees, shareholders, legislators, and other parties who affect or are affected by the achievement of the organization's objectives, and a positive image for the organization and its products in the long term. Public relations efforts are often associated with **publicity**—writing press releases and developing relationships with journalists who write stories or articles about an organization and its products. The communication results of publicity efforts are typically identified by consumers as being from an independent source.

Public relations activities also include staging events, commissioning surveys of people's feelings about issues related to a product, signing and working with a celebrity spokesperson, and responding to product recalls or other crises. These are all activities that consumers identify with the organization. Tourism PEI, for example, recently used roving PEI ambassadors to tour New Brunswick tourist attractions in specially detailed cars like the one in Exhibit 12.10 (suggesting fun adventure), to entice Quebecers visiting New Brunswick to come over to PEI during their holiday. This PR campaign was highly successful, but drew the wrath of New Brunswick tourism officials and government ministers.

**SALES PROMOTION** Sales promotions are programs, such as contests or store demonstrations, that marketers design to build interest in or encourage purchase of a product or service during a specified time period. Unlike other forms of communication that are message oriented, sales promotions are incentives, which are primarily intended to stimulate immediate action, such as coupons, rebates, or bonuses that might stimulate a purchase. Increasingly, however, organizations such as airlines (e.g., Air Canada), grocery stores (e.g., Canada Safeway), and gas stations (e.g., Petro-Canada) are using continuity or loyalty programs, which give discounts, bonuses, or redeemable "points" to members or frequent customers with the intention of building long-term loyalty to the organization. Sales promotions are a form of mass appeal, because they target groups of consumers or retailers to receive special offers or merchandise, invite these people to participate in some activity, or call attention to some event or product feature.

**THE INTERNET AND OTHER ELEMENTS** The IMC concept, illustrated in Figure 12.1 on page 386, suggests that marketers can use many other communications elements to communicate messages and incentives to customers—word-of-mouth communication, brand placement (such as in movies or on TV shows), third-party endorsements (such as Greenpeace recommending an environmentally friendly product), and third-party incentives (such as government subsidies for buying emergency preparedness kits). Marketers don't control third-party endorsements or incentives, but they can influence the third parties through public relations and political lobbying.

Word-of-mouth communication occurs when consumers tell their friends, relatives, or other people about their product experiences. A recommendation from a friend or relative can be a powerful influence on the buying behaviour of others. Marketers try to influence positive word-of-mouth by creating positive product experiences for customers, but also through communications. L'Oréal, for example, recently launched a new brand called "Open, Vibrantly Natural Colour Gel" aimed at a new target market for L'Oréal, young women 16 to 25. Using a mix of traditional, non-traditional, and electronic media L'Oréal implemented a strategy to encourage young women to tell their friends about the product. Over 50 percent of visitors to their Web site sent Open e-cards to their network of friends.[31]

**publicity** Unpaid communication about an organization appearing in the mass media.

**Exhibit 12.10**

Tourism PEI used vehicles like this one to attract Quebec tourists in New Brunswick to PEI.

The Internet and electronic devices such as personal digital assistants and cell phones provide a unique environment for messages that include text, audio, video, hyperlinking, and personalization, not to mention opportunities for interaction with customers and other stakeholders. Web sites can come alive with the right mix of technical wizardry and good design. One advantage of the Web is that companies can give customers a "feel" for their products or services before they buy. Even nightclubs are going to the Web to draw virtual crowds.[32] Sites such as groovetech.com, thewomb.com, raveworld.net, and digitalclubnetwork.com feature real-time footage of what's happening in the clubs. No more big, beefy bouncers to worry about!

The Internet is also increasingly being used by companies to encourage word-of-mouth communications. This approach, called **viral marketing**, was used by Virgin Music Canada when promoting a new alternative band A Perfect Circle. The company wanted to target fans of the rock band Tool (one of the members of A Perfect Circle is also the lead singer for Tool), who tend to be Internet-savvy 15- to 25-year-old males. Virgin Music Canada obtained the names of fans of Tool from *Watch* magazine, a Canadian publication that targets teens. Virgin Canada then selected five fans from Toronto and provided them with downloadable song samples from A Perfect Circle and information about the band. Virgin was hoping that these fans would then discuss the new band in online chat rooms and on other Web sites; this did happen. The five chosen teens were pleased that they were the first five kids to find out about the band and were happy to share their "find" with others online.[33]

Although the original users of viral marketing received the word-of-mouth pitches from customers for free, many companies have upped the ante by offering premiums and free products if customers tell friends who become customers. Procter & Gamble generated 2 million referrals when it offered consumers a free styling hair spray and entry into a sweepstakes for every 10 friends who visited the Web site for P&G's new Physique shampoo.[34]

**viral marketing** Marketing activity in which a company recruits customers to be sales agents and spread the word about the product.

## Influences on the Communication Strategy, Tactics, and Mix

Some products need personal selling, whereas others are best sold in other ways. Industrial goods and services, as well as big-ticket consumer items, are more likely to have a greater emphasis on personal selling in their communication mix; whereas it would be too costly for Colgate to hire door-to-door salespeople to promote its toothpaste. Many consumer products, such as cologne, tend to rely more on advertising, especially when the buyer selects the brand because of an image the manufacturer has carefully created for it. Using consumer sales promotion techniques such as coupons and premiums is very important to Procter & Gamble's sales of Tide detergent, but those same tactics would cheapen the image of Rolex or Mercedes. To compete for shoppers' attention, many companies allocate part of their communication efforts to in-store displays and even live product demonstrations to add the personal touch.

The communications mix must vary over time, because some elements are better for accomplishing the marketer's objectives at different points in time than are others. As we saw in the Hunk cologne example, the stage of the product life cycle (see Chapter 7) influences the communications mix.

# Good or Bad Decision?

Consumers are spending increasingly more time in front of the TV and computer screen gaming, and marketers who don't want to be shut out are pushing their way right into the media. "The gaming industry's financial influence is irrefutable. Larger than the motion picture box office in terms of revenue, and growing at three times the pace, gaming is a path to more than 145 million customers of all ages," states Jack Clues CEO of ad agency SMG.[35] The allure of video games for marketers is twofold as they provide an interactive avenue to target a coveted demographic, in an immersive content that keeps consumers engaged. Dole bananas has had huge success and recognition for stamping their logo on all the hundreds of bananas collected in the popular kids Nintendo game *Super Monkey Ball*. Both Burton and McDonalds are a few of the advertisements scattered on the sidelines of the most popular game in the world, FIFA soccer series. The gaming industry is booming with computer games and interactive entertainment estimated to grow to $41.3 billion in 2007.[36] What do you think—is this is a communication vehicle marketers should not ignore or should games be ad free?

In the introduction phase, the objective is to build awareness of the product among consumers and to rely on a push strategy. Advertising is the primary communication tool for creating awareness, and a publicity campaign to generate news reports about the new product may help. At this stage, sales promotion can be used to encourage consumers to try a new product or service. Distributors are also often given incentives to stock the new item.

In the growth phase, communication efforts must start to focus on communicating specific product benefits. Advertising increases, whereas sales promotions that encourage trial often decline, because people are more willing to try the product without being offered an incentive.

The opposite pattern often occurs during the maturity phase in which many people have tried or used the product. As sales stabilize, the goal is to persuade people to switch from a competitor's product, often when they see few important differences between competitors in a category. Sales promotions, particularly coupons and special price deals, increase—but sales promotion is not the only way to gain market share in a mature market. Familiprix, a Quebec pharmacy chain, managed to increase sales by 23 percent and awareness from 19 percent to 52 percent in a mature market through a series of 15-second ads demonstrating, with humour, the positioning that Familiprix pharmacies are close by and understand health issues. The ads depicted common family health issues and a Familiprix pharmacist jumping to the rescue exclaiming "Ah! Ha! Familiprix!" The campaign became such a pop-culture sensation that consumers, school children, and media personalities began adopting the tag line in their conversations.[37]

All bets are off during the decline phase. As sales plummet, the company dramatically reduces spending on all elements of the communications mix. Sales will be driven by the continued loyalty of a small group of users who keep the brand alive until it is sold to another company or discontinued as part of a harvesting strategy (see Chapter 2). The decline in sales further discourages the company from investing any more money in promoting the product, which may be left to wither on the vine. Alternatively, the company may decide to try to revive the brand and dedicate a modest budget to restoring sales.

This was the case with Clorox Canada. Market research found that by the late 1990s, the Glad garbage bags brand was timeworn. Clorox needed to revive its whole line of garbage bags and food protection products: They decided to go "retro" and revived a famous Canadian ad icon, the Man from Glad (Exhibit 12.11). They took him out of the old suburban setting and placed him in the technical surroundings of a high-performance testing lab, where he watched technicians demonstrate the strength and dependability of Glad products to the slogan "Glad. Depend on it." Canadians watched new Man from Glad television ads, read magazine ads, saw promotions in their local grocery store, and responded very positively. The re-emphasis on the Man from Glad has put Glad close to surpassing its main competitor to take over the top position in the disposable container category.[38]

## Creative Execution

**Creative strategy** is the process that turns a concept into a communications piece or element. It's one thing to know what a company wants to say about itself and its product, and quite another to figure out exactly how to say it. The creative process has been described as the "spark between objective and execution." The Novell ad in Exhibit 12.12 demonstrates how even business-to-business products, such as computer software and services, can come to life with the right creative strategy.

creative strategy   The process that turns a concept into an advertisement.

It is unlikely that one communication element can achieve all of the communications objectives discussed previously, so marketers work in campaigns—a set of related elements that collectively deliver the objectives desired. Each element in a campaign (a television ad, a newspaper ad, a brochure, etc.) typically has a different objective. The goal of a campaign is to present a series of messages and repeat it to a sufficient degree that the audience will progress through the AIDA stages described earlier in this chapter. To do this, the creative

**Exhibit 12.11**

Clorox Canada restored sales of Glad garbage bags by reviving the "Man from Glad" icon.

**media planning** The process of developing media objectives, strategies, and tactics for use in an advertising campaign.

**eProvisioning solutions:**
the way to get everyone in your company
**working in uNison.**

As part of the Novell® one Net vision, the employee eProvisioning Solution Framework gives you a simple way to provide, change or update the information, communication resources and applications employees need to be 100 percent productive on their first day and every day thereafter. (Plus, you'll have the security to revoke that access just as simply if an employee's status changes.) This increased productivity optimizes revenue and accelerates profit growth, going straight to your company's bottom line. That's the power of the Novell eProvisioning Solution Framework. **To find out how Novell and its partners can make eProvisioning solutions work for you, visit** www.novell.com/eprovisioning

**Novell.**
the power to chaNge

© Copyright 2001 Novell, Inc. All rights reserved. Novell is a registered trademark and the power to change is a trademark of Novell, Inc., in the United States and other countries.

**Exhibit 12.12**

Business products like software can be given a distinctive identity through advertising.

team (art directors, mechanical artists, copywriters, photographers, and others) must develop a "big idea," a concept that expresses aspects of the product, service, or organization in a tangible, attention-getting, memorable manner. Then the concept must be executed in different media—such as print advertising, point-of-purchase materials, packaging, etc. Recognizing the concept of diffusion of innovation (Chapter 7) campaign elements need to be repeated—where the innovators may have acted already and tried a product, there will be many in the early and late majority who are not yet aware of a product.

## Media Scheduling and Placement

**Media planning** is a problem-solving process for getting a message to a target audience in the most effective fashion. The decisions include audience selection and where, when, and how frequent the exposure should be. There is no such thing as one perfect medium for marketing communications. The choice depends on the specific target audience, the objective of the message, and the budget. For the communication to be effective, the media planner must match up the profile of the target market with that of specific media vehicles. For example, 80 percent of Chinese Canadian consumers in Vancouver read Chinese Canadian newspapers.[39] Thus, a marketer trying to reach this segment might allocate a significant share of the communication budget to buying space in these newspapers.

The media planner's first task in deciding where to place the communication is to find out when and where people in the target market are most likely to be exposed to the communication. This is the **aperture**, the best "window" to reach that type of person. For example, many people who drive to work in the morning listen to the radio, so their aperture would include this medium at this time. Sun-Rype, for example, wanted to reach moms with a message that its product "Fruit to Go" was nutritious (100 percent fruit) and reach kids with a message that these snacks were cool and tasty. Magazine ads, such as the one in Exhibit 12.13, were chosen as the way to reach both audiences, separately, with specific messages. Mom-targeted media included lifestyle and parenting magazines, while magazines distributed through schools, movie theatres, and direct to home were used to reach kids.[40]

**MEDIA CHOICES** There are numerous paid and unpaid media outlets for communicating to audiences. Paid for media such as television, radio, print, and outdoor media will be discussed in Chapter 13—when we further discuss communication tactics.

A company's Web site is becoming an increasingly important way to communicate interactively with consumers and support other forms of advertising. Kellogg Canada has set up several Web sites to support its advertising and communication goals for individual products. For example the site for Kellogg's Special K cereal uses the slogan from its television and magazine ads, "Look good on your own terms," and is designed for women, the cereal's primary target market. As users enter the site, they are shown an ad for Special K before the Web page loads. Once on the site, visitors can see recipes using the product, participate in chat rooms, or ask questions of fitness and nutrition experts. Through its Web site, Kellogg Canada is able to reinforce advertising activities in more traditional media and potentially reach new consumers with their ads and other promotional messages.

**MEDIA SCHEDULING: WHEN TO SAY IT** After choosing the advertising media, the planner then creates a **media schedule** that specifies the exact media to use, when, and how often the message should appear. Figure 12.7 shows a hypothetical media schedule for the communication of a new video game. Note that much of the advertising reaches its target audience in the months just before Christmas, and that much of the expensive television budget is focused on advertising during specials just before the holiday season. The company's Web site is used in the media schedule as a constant reinforcement of the paid advertising placed in other media.

The media schedule outlines the planner's best estimate of which media will be most effective in attaining the advertising objective(s), and which specific media vehicles will do the most effective job. The media planner considers such factors as the match between the demographic and psychographic profile of a target audience and the people reached by a media vehicle, the communication activities of competitors, and the capability of a medium to convey the desired information adequately. The planner must also consider the compatibility of the product with editorial content: After all, viewers might not respond well to a lighthearted ad for a new snack food during a sombre documentary on world hunger.

When analyzing media, the planner is interested in assessing **advertising exposure**, the degree to which the target market will see an advertising message in a specific medium. Media planners talk in terms of **impressions**, which measure the number of people who will be exposed to a message placed in one or more media vehicles. For example, if one million people watch a miniseries on CTV,

**aperture** The best place and time to reach a person in the target market group.

**Kellogg Canada**
www.kelloggs.ca

**media schedule** The plan that specifies the exact media to use and when.

**advertising exposure** The degree to which the target market will see an advertising message placed in a specific vehicle.

**impressions** The number of people who will be exposed to a message placed in one or more media vehicles.

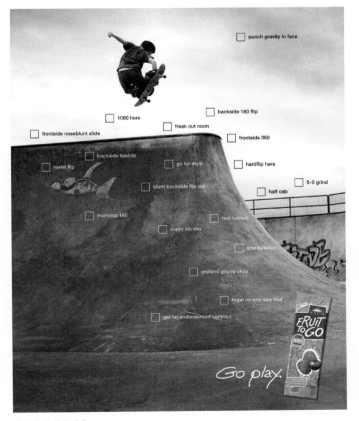

**Exhibit 12.13**

Sun-Rype used targeted magazines to reach moms and kids with different messages.

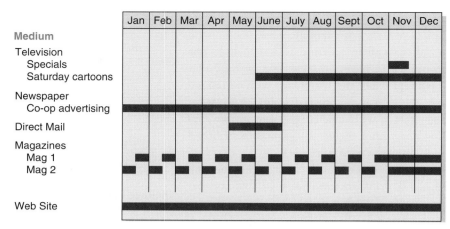

**Figure 12.7** A Media Schedule for a Video Game

each time an advertiser runs an ad during that program, it receives one million impressions. If the advertiser's spot runs four times during the program, the impression count would be four million, even though some of these impressions would represent repeated exposure to the same viewers.

To calculate the exposure a message will have if placed in a certain medium, planners consider two factors: reach and frequency. **Reach** is the percentage of the target market that will be exposed to the media vehicle. This measure is particularly important for widely used products when it's important to get the message to as many consumers as possible. **Frequency** is the number of times a person in the target group would be exposed to the message. This is important with products that are complex or are targeted to relatively small markets for which multiple exposures to the message are necessary to make an impact.

For example, say a media planner wants to get Club Med advertising to university and college students. The advertiser learns that 25 percent of that target market reads at least a few issues of *Rolling Stone* each year (reach). The advertiser may also determine that these students are likely to see three of the twelve monthly ads that Club Med will run in *Rolling Stone* during the year (frequency). Now, the planner calculates the magazine's **gross rating points (GRPs)** by multiplying reach times frequency, which in this case compares the effectiveness of *Rolling Stone* to alternative media. By using this same formula, the planner can then compare the GRP number of another magazine or the GRP of placing an ad on television or on a bus or any other advertising medium.

Although some media vehicles deliver superior exposure, they may not be cost efficient. More people will see a commercial aired during the Stanley Cup playoffs than during a 3:00 a.m. rerun of a horror movie. But the advertiser could run late-night commercials every night for a year for the cost of one 30-second Stanley Cup spot. For example, a 30-second ad on CBC that would be shown across the country could cost as little as $100 or as much as $46 000, depending on when it was run. Similarly, a 30-second ad on TSN could be as little as $100 or as much as $20 000.[41]

To compare the relative cost-effectiveness of different media and of spots run on different vehicles in the same medium, media planners use a measure called **cost per thousand (CPM)**. This figure compares the relative cost effectiveness of different media vehicles that have different exposure rates and reflects the cost to deliver a message to 1000 people. For example, the cost for a Canadian company to do banner advertising on DoubleClick averages $30 to $40 CPM.[42] A medium's popularity with consumers determines how much advertisers must pay to put their message on it. Television networks are concerned with getting good ratings, because their advertising rates are determined by how many viewers their programming attracts. Similarly, magazines and newspapers try to boost circulation and Web sites to justify raising ad rates.

**MEDIA SCHEDULING: HOW OFTEN TO SAY IT** After deciding where to advertise, the planner must decide when and how often. What time of day? Frequently for a few weeks, or occasionally for a long time? After selecting the media schedule, the planner turns to the overall pattern the advertising will follow.

A *continuous schedule* maintains a steady stream of advertising throughout the year. This is most appropriate for products that sell on a regular basis, such as shampoo or bread. Some advertising professionals maintain that continuous advertising sustains market leadership even if total industry sales fall.[43] On the downside, some messages can suffer from *advertising wearout*, because people tune out the same old ad messages.

A *pulsing schedule* varies the amount of advertising throughout the year, based on when the product is likely to be in demand. S.C. Johnson & Son, for example uses a pulsing schedule to communicate its Off! brands of bug repellents more heavily in the summer months. *Flighting* is an extreme form of pulsing in which advertising appears in short, intense bursts alternating with periods of little to no activity. It can produce as much brand awareness as a steady dose of advertising at a much lower cost, if the messages from the previous flight were noticed and made an impact.

## Budget and Allocation

In an ideal world, setting the budget for communications would be simple: Spend whatever it takes to accomplish the stated objectives. In reality, firms often view communications costs as an expense rather than as an investment that will lead to greater profits. When sales are declining or the company is operating in a difficult economic environment, it is often tempting to cut costs by reducing spending on advertising, sales promotions, and other "soft" activities whose contributions to the bottom line are hard to quantify. When this is the case, marketers must try to justify these expenses to others in the firm.

Economic approaches to budgeting rely on marginal analysis (discussed in Chapter 9), in which the organization spends money on communications as long as the revenues realized by these efforts continue to exceed the costs of the communications themselves. This perspective assumes that promotions are always intended solely to increase sales when, in fact, these activities may have other objectives, such as enhancing a firm's image. Also, the effects of communications often lag. For example, a firm may have to spend a lot on communications when it first launches a product without seeing any return on this investment for quite awhile. Because of these limitations, most firms rely on two budgeting techniques: top down and bottom up.

**Top-down budgeting techniques** require top management to establish the overall amount that the organization wishes to devote to communication activities, and this amount is then divided among advertising, public relations, and other communication departments.

The most common top-down technique is the **percentage-of-sales method**, in which the communication budget is based on last year's sales or on estimates for this year's sales. The percentage is an industry average provided by trade associations that collect objective information on behalf of member companies. The advantage of this method is that it reminds the organization that spending on communication does result in profits.

Unfortunately, this method implies that sales cause communication outlays, rather than viewing sales as the outcome of communication efforts. As sales drop, firms might be reluctant to spend more on communication, when the drop might be due to environmental changes, such as a change in economic conditions or a rival's recent introduction of a new product. If so, cutting communication spending might not help the firm in the long run.

The *competitive-parity method* is simply matching whatever competitors are spending. Some marketers think this approach is justified, saying the decision simply mirrors the best thinking of others in the business. However, this method often results in each player maintaining the same market share year after year. This method also assumes that the same dollars spent on communication by two different firms will yield the same results, but spending a lot of money doesn't guarantee a successful communication. Firms certainly need to monitor their competitors' communication activities, but they must combine this information with their own objectives and abilities.

The problem with top-down techniques is that budget decisions are based more on established practices than on communication objectives. Another approach is to begin at the beginning: Identify communication goals and allocate enough money to accomplish them. That is what **bottom-up budgeting techniques** attempt. For example, some marketers

**top-down budgeting techniques** Allocation of the promotion budget that is based on the total amount to be devoted to marketing communications.

**percentage-of-sales method** A method for promotion budgeting, in which the promotion budget is based on a percentage of either last year's sales or on estimates for this year's sales.

**bottom-up budgeting techniques** Allocation of the promotion budget that is based on identifying promotional goals and allocating enough money to accomplish them.

construct a *payout plan* that attempts to predict the revenues and costs associated with a product over several years and matches communication expenditures to this pattern—spending more on communication in the first year to build market share, for example, and then less after the product catches on.

This bottom-up logic is at the heart of the **objective-task method**, which is gaining in popularity. Using this approach, the firm first defines the specific communication goals it hopes to achieve, such as increasing by 20 percent the number of consumers who are aware of the brand. It then tries to determine what kind of communication efforts it will take to meet that goal. Although this is the most rational approach, it is hard to implement, because it obliges managers to specify their objectives and attach dollar amounts to them. This method requires careful analysis and a bit of "guesstimating."

**ALLOCATE THE BUDGET TO A SPECIFIC COMMUNICATIONS MIX** Once the organization has decided how much to spend on communications, it must divide its budget among the elements in the communications mix. Although advertising used to get the lion's share of the communications budget, sales promotions are now playing a bigger role in marketing strategies. As MasterCard's vice-president of promotions observed, marketers who once relied on sales promotions solely to create a short-term response now see them as "a permanent, integral part of the brand."[44] For example, although the typical NASCAR racing car, such as the one in Exhibit 12.14, is covered with the logos of tobacco and motor oil companies, other marketers such as Hewlett-Packard, Universal Studios, and even banking giant HSBC (Hong Kong and Shanghai Banking Corp.) are changing their communications mix by sponsoring racing teams. They are joining the race to capture the attention of the 460 million people who watch these events as they are broadcast to 201 countries.[45] Several factors influence how companies divide up the communications pie:

- *Organizational factors:* Characteristics of the specific firm influence how it allocates its money. These characteristics are the complexity and formality of the company's decision-making process, preferences within the company for advertising versus sales promotions or other elements in the communications mix, past experiences with specific communications vehicles, as well as the "comfort level" of the firm's advertising and communications agencies with developing different kinds of marketing communications. Nestlé, the

**objective-task method** A promotion budgeting method in which an organization first defines the specific communications goals it hopes to achieve and then tries to calculate what kind of promotional efforts it must take to meet these goals.

**Nestlé**
www.nestle.com

**Exhibit 12.14**

Many companies have shifted their promotional dollars to sponsor sporting events, such as NASCAR racing.

giant Swiss company, for example, shifted about 20 percent of its advertising budget into sales promotion and direct-response efforts over a two-year period after the company determined that its communications dollars would be more effective there.[46]

- *Market potential:* Consumers in some markets will be more likely to buy the product. For example, the marketers of Hunk might find that men in blue-collar occupations would be more interested in the product than men in professional occupations. It makes sense for marketers to allocate more resources to television shows, radio stations, magazines, and other media or communication vehicles that also target people in blue-collar occupations.

- *Market size:* As a rule, larger markets are more expensive places in which to communicate. The costs of buying media (such as spots on local television) are higher in major metropolitan areas. But the sheer density of highly populated areas makes it easier to reach large numbers of consumers at the same time. Advertising is good for mass-market products, whereas personal selling is good for specialized or highly technical products.

## Evaluation

The final stage in developing a communications plan is to set criteria and methods to determine whether the plan is working. The marketer needs to determine whether the communications objectives are adequately translated into marketing communications that are reaching the right target market.

It would be nice if a marketing manager could simply report, "Our new $3 million communications campaign for our revolutionary glow-in-the-dark surfboards resulted in $15 million in new sales!" Unfortunately, it is not so easy. Because there are many factors at work in the marketing environment, other events such as a manufacturing problem encountered by a rival board manufacturer, a coincidental photograph of a movie star riding one of the boards, or even renewed interest in surfing may have caused those new sales instead.

A retail advertiser once complained: "I am certain that half the money I spend on advertising is completely wasted. The trouble is, I don't know which half."[47] Despite this admonition, there are ways to monitor and evaluate the company's communications efforts. The catch is that the effectiveness of some forms of communication is easier to determine than others. As a rule, sales promotions are the easiest to evaluate because they occur during a fixed period of time and can be directly tied to sales.

Direct measures of advertising effectiveness are difficult to design. It is hard to determine just how many sales were the result of a specific ad campaign. Advertising researchers measure brand awareness, recall of product benefits communicated through advertising, and even the image of the brand before and after an advertising campaign. **Posttesting** is conducting research on consumers' responses to advertising messages they have seen or heard (as opposed to pretesting, which collects reactions to messages before they're actually placed in "the real world"). Ironically, many creative ads that are quirky or even bizarre make an advertising agency look good within the industry but are ultimately unsuccessful, because they don't communicate what needs to be said about the product itself. As one consultant observed, "There is so much emphasis on the creative aspect of the ads, sort of 'Aren't we clever?' that the message is lost."[48]

In some cases, the ads are popular but they send the wrong message to consumers. For example, a lot of people remember Joe Isuzu, the lying car salesman whose television commercials were popular for two years but were no help to Isuzu's car sales during that time.[49] As one advertising executive explained, "The humor got in the way. All you remembered was that car salesmen are dishonest, and the car salesman you remembered most was from Isuzu."[50] Three measures of the impact of an advertisement are *unaided recall*, *aided recall*, and *attitudinal measures*. **Unaided recall** tests, by telephone survey or personal interview, how much of an ad a person remembers during a specified period of time, sometimes by

**posttesting** Research conducted on consumers' responses to actual advertising messages they have seen or heard.

**unaided recall** A research technique conducted by telephone survey or personal interview that asks how much of an ad a person remembers during a specified period of time.

**aided recall** A research technique that uses clues to prompt answers from people about advertisements they might have seen.

**attitudinal measures** A research technique that probes a consumer's beliefs or feelings about a product before and after being exposed to messages about it.

**Adobe Defy the Rules site**
www.defytherules.com

asking the person to write down what the ad said. An **aided recall** test uses clues to prompt answers. For example, a researcher might show a group of consumers a list of brands and ask them to choose which items they have seen advertised within the past week. **Attitudinal measures** probe a bit more deeply by testing consumer beliefs or feelings about a product before and after being exposed to messages about it. If, for example, Dove antiperspirant's ads about the product being good for the skin make enough consumers believe that this is an important attribute for antiperspirants, marketers can consider the advertising campaign successful.

Measuring the effectiveness of marketing communications is easier if the audience is requested to respond in some way—such as calling a 1-800 number or going to a Web site. For example, in the Adobe ad in Exhibit 12.15, the company wants people to visit the "defytherules" site; if Adobe wanted to measure the effectiveness of the ad, it might use number of visits to the Web site advertised as one measure of this. Most often, however, advertisers research consumer response to advertising through posttesting. The effectiveness of banner advertising is even easier to measure, since the number of visitors coming to a Web site through a banner ad is directly measurable.

A firm can analyze and compare the performance of salespeople in different territories, though again it is often difficult to rule out other factors that make some sales forces more effective than others. Public relations activities are perhaps the hardest to assess, because they often are intended to result in building favourable relationships over a longer period of time.

**EVALUATING INTEGRATED MARKETING COMMUNICATIONS** The IMC perspective takes a broad view of the world: Learning about a good or service comes from many sources, and beliefs develop over time. For these reasons, traditional measurement techniques that focus on the impact of one message at one point in time are not adequate to assess the impact of an entire communications program. Instead, marketers track consumer responses to communications efforts and interactions with the brand and/or company over time.[51] They also conduct research to assess consumer attitudes toward the brand and/or organization. Although they don't always accurately predict purchases, customers' attitudes toward an item still are important pieces of information, especially when changes in attitudes are tracked over time. Ideally these pieces of information are collected on an ongoing basis and fed back into a database, where they will be used to update and refine the integrated strategy.[52]

# COMMUNICATION BRIEFS

Communication plans are internal documents created by organizations that provide rationale for, and guide, their communication strategy for a specified period of time. People in an in-house creative department or communication/advertising agency do not have time to read a lengthy communication plan. They rely on a communications brief, which is typically a one- to three-page summary of the elements of a communications plan that precedes creative execution (see Figure 12.5 on page 393)—and for small projects it may replace the communications plan if the other elements of a communication plan are considered in the brief. The advantage of writing a formal communication brief, rather than just explaining the strategy for a campaign to the creative team is that verbal explanations can be misinterpreted or modified in sequential telling within the creative team. If a lot of time is wasted in wrestling projects back on track (and at rates of $100 to $150 dollars an hour

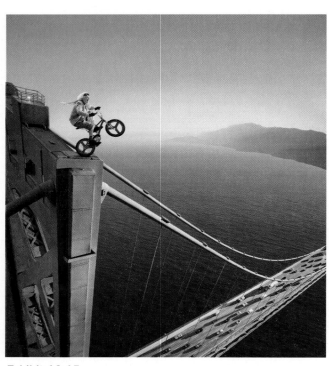

**Exhibit 12.15**

The number of people visiting the "defytherules" Web site would be one way of measuring the effectiveness of this ad.

for each person in the room), it can be very expensive not having a clear understanding of the creative task. It is not easy capturing the essence of a 15- to 25-page communications plan into a 1- to 3-page brief, but as one marketing executive suggested "the creative has to be brief so the brief has to be creative."[53] The idea is to set the strategic parameters in which the creative team operates and to gain agreement from the client that the brief represents the intended strategy. One retired president of a large New York agency described this as the brief needing to be "as hard and brilliant as a diamond, and as tight and confining as a pair of handcuffs."[54] For example, the heart of the creative brief for the now acclaimed Absolut Vodka campaign (Exhibit 12.16) was "You can do anything you want creatively, but you must always show the product and no headline can be longer than two words and one of those words must be Absolut."[55]

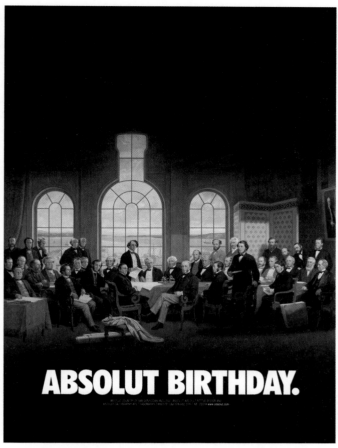

**Exhibit 12.16**

A very tight creative brief helped focus the creative team to create the famous Absolut Vodka campaign.

# Real People, Real Decisions

## How It Worked Out at Cormark Communications

The Cormark team chose Option 2, maintaining the U.S. strategic platform but rebuilding key sections of the strategy to meet the needs of the Canadian marketplace. They concluded that the communications materials were directionally right but needed some modification to fit the Canadian marketplace and regulatory context, particularly for the veterinary market. They based this decision primarily on their market research. The hybrid option of customizing the U.S. strategy allowed Cormark and Pfizer Canada to control the Canadian product launch and move directionally correct and successful U.S. material to strategically accurate and insightful material that was right for the Canadian market.

There were two significant differences in the Canadian launch program. One was the significantly smaller budget requiring tighter targeting of messaging for efficiency. The sec-

ond was a higher degree of emotion in the message. Cormark learned through research that consumers were moved by the restoration of the dog-owner relationship that could be achieved by the use of the product.

In implementing the strategy, Cormark developed a launch blueprint for Canada. The agency determined the key audiences within the broader consumer and veterinarian target markets and determined how best to reach them. Within three months of launch, Rimadyl exceeded the annual volume objective. Post-campaign research indicated that awareness by the target markets was higher than expected. Rimadyl is well on its way to becoming a major product in the category. Since the launch, other international markets have requested the Canadian launch materials for their own local use.

# CHAPTER SUMMARY

**1. Explain the concept of integrated marketing communications and its implementation, and why some marketers resist it.**

Integrated marketing communications (IMC) programs allow marketers to communicate with consumers on a continual basis by coordinating the communications messages and media. IMC often uses customer databases to stay in touch with the market. In an IMC strategy, contact management means that communications occur when customers will be receptive to them. The type of message is influenced by the communications objectives, the characteristics of the customer group, and the exposure situation. The effectiveness of the IMC strategy may be assessed through transactional data, by customers' second-order responses, or by customer attitudes. Some marketers resist IMC, because it requires changing accepted ways of doing things, decreases emphasis on advertising, puts an increased focus on communications, and requires major changes in advertising agencies.

**2. Explain the steps involved in developing a communications plan.**

A communications plan is an internal document that develops the communication strategy for an organization, product line, or brand. It starts with a summary of the marketing objectives and situational context, then specifies the target markets and profiles the target audiences. Communication objectives are then identified followed by a description of communication strategy, positioning and key messages, and tactics (themes or approaches) that will be used to break through perceptual screens of receivers. A communications mix is then chosen, informed by a budget reality check. This part of the plan is often summarized in a communications brief for the creative team in order to keep the creative on strategy. The plan concludes with specification of the creative execution, media scheduling and placement, budget allocation, and evaluation criteria and methods.

**3. List, describe, and contrast the elements of the communications mix.**

The five major elements of marketing communications are known as the communications mix. Personal selling provides direct contact between a company representative and a customer. Direct marketing is direct impersonal communication focused on short-term, single transaction responses or a set of responses leading to a purchase decision. Advertising is nonpersonal, paid-for communication from an identified sponsor using mass media. Sales promotions stimulate immediate sales by providing incentives to the trade or to consumers. Publicity and public relations activities seek to influence the attitudes of various publics.

**4. Explain how marketing communication strategies can be evaluated.**

Marketers need to conduct research to determine if specific advertisements are effective. Posttesting research may include recall tests or attitudinal measures, which examine whether the message had an influence on the target market. If the communication has a direct response element to it (1-800 number, Web site sign in, etc.) it is easier to measure its effectiveness.

**5. Explain the content and purpose of a communications brief.**

A communications brief is a summary of a communications plan that is used by the creative team to develop the creative concept and execution for a campaign. The brief typically summarizes the elements of the communications plan up to creative execution, but might also include summaries of the other elements if the brief is used instead of a formal communications plan.

# CHAPTER REVIEW

## Marketing Concepts: Testing Your Knowledge

1. What is integrated marketing communications (IMC)?

2. What is marketing communication? What are the goals of communication?

3. How does communication theory help marketers develop more effective communication strategies?

4. List and describe the elements of the communications mix.

5. List and explain the steps in the development of a communications plan.

6. Why should communication objectives be phrased in terms of communications tasks? What are some examples of communications task objectives?

7. How does the communications mix vary with push versus pull strategies? How does it vary in different stages of the product life cycle (PLC)?

8. Explain each of the following budgeting methods:

   a. percentage-of-sales method

   b. competitive-parity method

   c. objective-task method.

9. What are some methods for evaluating the effectiveness of marketing communication?

## Marketing Concepts: Discussing Choices and Issues

1. Increasingly, marketers are seeking new ways to communicate with consumers. Advertising is being placed on washroom walls, in high-school cafeterias, and even in the halls of university and college classroom buildings. Develop debate arguments for and against this proliferation of commercial messages.

2. One reason to build a database is to advance a political or social agenda by identifying and mobilizing a core of supporters. For example, Philip Morris has built a database with 26 million names, which the tobacco company uses to rally customers to the cause of smokers' rights. What are the ethical issues related to this usage of databases?

3. Advertisers who spend millions of dollars for ads during special events such as the Olympics may be more interested in achieving aesthetic goals—having the most highly rated ad—than in selling products. Does it make sense for advertisers to focus on aesthetic goals rather than on marketing goals? Explain.

4. Some argue that IMC is just a passing fad in marketing communications. What do you think?

## Marketing Practice: Applying What You've Learned

1. As a marketing consultant, you are frequently asked by clients to develop recommendations for communications strategies. Outline your recommendations for the use of different communications mix elements for one of the following products:

   a. a new brand of laundry detergent

   b. a familiar brand of cereal

   c. a political candidate

   d. equipment for a new manufacturing facility.

2. As the director of marketing for a small firm that markets specialty salad dressings, you are in the process of developing a communications plan. With one or more of your classmates, develop suggestions for each of the following. Then, in a role-playing situation, present your recommendations to the client.

   a. communications objectives

   b. a method for determining the communications budget

   c. the use of a push strategy or a pull strategy.

3. As an account executive for a communications services firm, you have been assigned to a new client, a manufacturer of a popular brand of toothpaste. As you begin development of the creative strategy, you are considering different types of appeals:

   a. informative appeal

   b. comparative advertising

   c. a fear appeal

   d. a celebrity endorsement

   e. a slice-of-life ad

   f. sex appeal

   g. humour

   Outline the strengths and weaknesses of using each of these appeals for advertising the toothpaste.

4. As a member of the marketing department for a manufacturer of sports equipment, you have been directed to select a new agency to do the communications for your firm. You have asked two agencies to submit proposals. One agency recommends an integrated marketing communications plan, and the second agency has developed recommendations for a traditional advertising plan. Write a memo to explain each of the following to your boss.

   a. What is different about an integrated marketing communications plan?

   b. Why is the IMC plan superior to merely advertising?

   c. Why do some agencies resist changing from traditional communications planning?

## Marketing Mini-Project: Learning by Doing

The purpose of this mini-project is to give you an opportunity to experience the advertising creative process.

1. With one or more classmates, create (imagine) a new brand of an existing product, such as a laundry detergent, toothpaste, perfume, or soft drink.

2. Develop a communications brief for this new product.

3. Develop at least three creative concepts for implementing the strategy summarized in your brief and mock-up magazines ads as one element of a campaign. Your magazine ads should have a headline, a visual, and copy to explain your product and to persuade customers to purchase your brand.

4. Present your brief and ads to your class. Discuss the advertising appeal you selected, and explain your ad executions.

## Real People, Real Surfers: Exploring the Web

Much of the advertising you see every day on television and in magazines is created by communications services companies and advertising agencies. Some of these companies are large, some very small. Some offer clients specialized services, such as "new media" advertising, while others offer a wide variety of services. To make their company stand out from the others, the different agencies develop unique personalities or corporate philosophies. Visit the Web sites of several large and small Canadian communications companies.

**Cossette Communications Group (www.cossette.com)**
**BBDO Canada (www.bbdo.ca)**
**Amoeba Corporation (www.amoebacorp.com)**
**Palmer Jarvis DDB (www.palmerjarvisddb.com)**
**Sonic Boom (www.sonicboom.com)**
**Critical Mass (www.criticalmass.ca)**

Explore the Web sites to see how they differ. Then answer these questions.

1. What is the mission of each company? How does each company attempt to position itself?

2. Who are some of the major clients of the firm?

3. How does the site demonstrate the creative ability of the company? Does the site do a good job of communicating the mission of the company? Explain.

4. If it is available, tell a little about the history of the company.

5. Of the companies you visited, which would you most like to work for and why?

6. As a client, based on your exploration of the Web sites, which company would you choose for your business and why?

Innovative sponsorship embedded into Canada's hottest Reality TV shows and one of the country's most fully integrated marketing communications strategies earned L'Oréal Canada (**www.en.loreal.ca/**) a big boost in sales, increased brand recognition, and even the 2003 marketer of the year award.[56]

Jochen Zaumseil, the CEO and President of L'Oréal Canada, is beaming about the success the Canadian Subsidiary of L'Oréal de Paris has had in 2003. Zaumseil admits that although key decisions about the company are made at the brand headquarters in Paris, Tokyo, and New York, the Canadian subsidiary has autonomy to work with the brands and to develop campaigns tailored to the Canadian culture, and for a good reason. Zaumseil says "to bring excitement to the mass market is not something that can be done in Paris. You have to go it alone by your own culture, by your own approach, and with the type of retailers in your own country." With sales up 7.8 percent, Zaumseil knows what he's talking about.[57]

Zaumseil saw how Reality TV was taking off in the United Staes, and knowing that this trend would soon show up in Canada, Zaumseil endorsed a sponsorship with the incredibly popular television shows Canadian Idol- and Quebec-based Star Academie. Star Acadamie was a huge success and after 3 million Quebec viewers were exposed to L'Oréal's Maybelline campaign, Quebec's business magazine *Commerce* estimated that the economic return was three times L'Oréal's Star Academie ad expense. L'Oréal's involvement with Canadian Idol was even more successful. "Canadian Idol was nothing less than the most significant mass-media effort major sponsor L'Oréal Canada's Division had ever done," says Sunni Boot, CEO of the media agency for L'Oréal Canada.

In addition to traditional 30-second television spots, L'Oréal had opening and closing billboards, a major presence on the Canadian Idol Web page, product placement in the show, and Idol-related sales promotions at Shoppers Drug Mart stores. Ron Szekely, Marketing Director for L'Oréal, was very pleased to be able to reach the younger demographic through the Idol sponsorship, and to see sales of L'Oréal products go up 30 percent during the Idol Promotions.[58]

Although L'Oréal had huge success with its Reality TV campaigns, its integrated marketing communication efforts did not stop there. L'Oréal's involvement with Toronto's Fashion Week, International Woman's Day, and Cirque Du Soliel enhanced L'Oréal's product concept, brand recognition, and sales even more. L'Oréal has developed an engaging interactive Web site that allows visitors to upload pictures of themselves and create new looks with L'Oréal hairstyle, colouring, and make-up products.

L'Oréal understands the concept of thinking outside the box. In 2003 its integrated marketing communications strategy was diverse, responsive, creative, and most of all, effective.

## Things to Think About

1. What makes the L'Oréal strategy an IMC strategy?

2. What are the challenges and benefits of an IMC strategy?

3. What else could L'Oréal do to effectively communicate to 18- to 34-year-old women?

4. Is IMC something that only large organizations like L'Oréal can do, or can it be done by smaller organizations?

# The Brand Man

Bernard Hadley-Beauregard, or Bernie for short, knows that for most products, branding is critical for sales success. Bernie recently quit his job with a popular Vancouver marketing company to launch his own image and branding consulting venture. He is a branding expert and has just taken on the most challenging project of his career—turning the badly named "A Very Fine Winery" of Abbotsford into a hip, new brand.

But Bernie has his work cut out for him with this struggling and broke winery, and his own brand reputation is on the line. David and Liz Avery, the owners of the eight-acre winery (and hence the name "*A Very* Fine Winery") are over $1 million in debt and will face bankruptcy in months if sales don't take a turn for the better. The Averys have been scraping by for the past few years selling their wine through buffet restaurants and independent beer and wine stores. Lately, sales have been very disappointing, and bottles of wine have started to pile up on the Averys' property (this is *not* planned "aging"). The Averys know that they need a fast and effective change if they want their dream business and life investment to survive. So they have hired "Brand-Man" Bernie to revitalize their brand and get sales rolling again.

Bernie needs his newly launched company to start off on the right foot and has his sights set on selling the Averys' wine to some of Vancouver's finest restaurants and wine stores. Bernie's challenge is to turn Avery wine into a stylish, appealing, and profitable brand before the Christmas season. A successful and complete re-branding is in the wings for the Averys, and this 180-degree change will determine whether the winery makes it through the new year, and whether Bernie will see a paycheque and a profitable company. A few obstacles, however, stand in the way, such as obtaining more financing and making the wine while the grapes are at their peak.

But most important to Bernie are his reputation and that of his recently launched branding company, which are riding on the success of the Averys' newly coined "Lotusland" wine, supported by images of Vancouver celebrities on the label. Will Bernie work his magic and make Lotusland a hit? Or will the Averys face bankruptcy and have to look for a new career?

## Questions

1. Although there can be many benefits to re-branding, what are some potential dangers associated with a complete brand transformation?
2. Why do you think this winery was struggling in the first place? Do you think that the Averys could have turned their business around themselves? Why or why not?
3. What considerations should go into choosing a brand name? Is "Lotusland" a good brand name for a wine?

Source: This case was prepared by Brock Smith and is base on *Venture*, "The Brand Man," # 913.

CUCINAetc.

CUCINARIO
E LIBRO

RISTORANTE
E TRATTORIA

TUTTI IN CUCINA   SEGRETTI DELLA
PRONTO PASTA          CUCINA

# CUCINA*etc.*™

ENGLISH EDITION

COOKING THE ITALIAN WAY

## ALLA GRIGLIA
Grill to Perfection

## TOSCANA
A Culinary Tour

## MENU CLASSICO
From *Campania* to You

www.cucinaetc.com

5,95 $ - No 5

0   55113 57038   4

01

# CHAPTER 13
## Communications Mix and Tactics

## CHAPTER OBJECTIVES

WHEN YOU HAVE COMPLETED YOUR STUDY OF THIS CHAPTER, YOU SHOULD BE ABLE TO

1. Explain the advantages and disadvantages of alternative advertising media.

2. Critique advertising.

3. Explain the role of public relations and describe the steps in developing a public relations campaign.

4. Explain what sales promotion is and describe some of the different types of trade and consumer sales promotion activities.

5. Explain the important role of personal selling in the marketing effort and list the steps in the personal selling process.

6. Explain the job of the sales manager.

# Real People, Real Decisions

## Meet **Mario Demers,** a Decision Maker at Saputo Dairy Products Canada

Mario Demers is the National Marketing Director of Saputo Dairy Products Division (Canada). Founded in 1954, Saputo is a Montreal-based cheese and food products company that has rapidly grown through acquisition since going public in 1997. After acquiring Dairy World (the B.C.-based company that owned Dairy Land and Armstrong Cheese), Saputo is now the leading dairy processor in Canada and one of the most important cheese producers in North America and Argentina. Demers graduated in 1985 with a BBA in Marketing from the Université du Québec à Montréal. Prior to joining Saputo in 2001, he spent 11 years at Quebecor Inc. as a Marketing and Sales Director, and one year as Marketing Director at the TVA Network.

The challenge Demers faced was that Saputo had developed or acquired a number of regional cheese brands, but none had national recognition, and there was no marketing vision or synergy. Saputo was well known in Quebec and some parts of Ontario for its Italian cheeses such as Mozzarella, Parmesan, and Ricotta. Armstrong was well known for its cheddar in Western Canada. Bari is a fighter brand known in Western Canada, primarily in British Columbia.

Demers recognized that maintaining a large portfolio of small cheese brands was an expensive proposition from a marketing communications point of view, as each brand had its own positioning and would need to be supported with a separate communication strategy. He thought it would make more strategic and financial sense to rationalize the brands into 3 groups: the Italian cheeses under the Saputo brand name, Canadian and English cheeses (e.g., Cheddar, Colby, Monterey Jack) under the Armstrong brand, and French and other European cheeses (e.g., Brie, Camembert, Swiss) under the Cayer brand. This brand rationalization would require some time, however, as the other brand names were liked and sought by both regional customers and regional distributors as a "local" alternative to large international brands like Kraft and Black Diamond. Demers, however, recognized the advantages of having three family brands: the ability to position each family differently, being able to leverage the current strong reputations of individual cheeses to build brand equity for a family of related cheeses, and being able to share brand reputation with any new products added to the three lines. The question became how to manage the transition. Demers considered two options.

**Option 1.** A series of national mass media advertising campaigns. Demers thought that the rationalization of the brands could be achieved through a series of large-scale television, print, and radio campaigns introducing consumers to the Saputo Corporation and the three brand families. The main advantage of a mass media approach was the relative speed at which the branding strategy could be introduced to consumers. Most consumers across Canada were already

familiar with one of the three family brands and positive associations with that brand would likely be transferred to the unfamiliar brands. This approach, however, would be very expensive—in the range of $500 000 for each 6-week campaign, and $4 million to $5 million in total to get sufficient reach and frequency. This is Kraft's approach and it can be quite effective in generating brand recognition so that when consumers see the brand in the store, they have a positive predisposition to purchase it. However, frequent campaigns are necessary to keep a brand in consumers' minds. Also, large-scale television, print, and radio campaigns do not guarantee that the product will be listed by grocery chains and independent retail stores. Consequently, this alternative might need to be implemented on a region-by-region basis where the Saputo sales force was successful in getting listings for all three of the product lines. This might prove difficult as some retailers had established relationships with other regional or specialty brands and might be unwilling or unable to break contracts to free up shelf space for Saputo products they had not previously carried.

**Option 2.** A product-placement IMC approach. Demers thought that another effective approach would be to promote the three families of Saputo cheeses more slowly by reaching current and new users through product placement in a cooking show. There has been a significant increase in interest in cooking as the baby boomer generation reaches the prime ages for home entertaining and people of the echo-boom generation are setting up apartments and learning to cook for themselves. Rather than compete with other cheese brands for product placement opportunities on established cooking shows, Demers thought that Saputo could create its own cooking show to increase general cheese consumption, and specifically to increase Saputo cheese consumption. This would be done first in Italian on a specialty channel (TLN—Tele Latino) to reach the large Italian communities in Quebec and Ontario (almost 1 million people) who were the main customers of Saputo's Italian cheeses. Then, after listing agreements could be developed for the three cheese families, the show would be produced in English on TLN and other base cable carriers to reach both the bilingual Italian communities and other English-speaking consumers in the rest of Canada.

While Demers estimated it would cost $16 000 to $20 000 to produce each 30-minute cooking show segment, he would have control over the product placement and there would be opportunities for sponsorship and advertising revenue from complementary manufacturers such as cooking appliance companies, kitchen supply stores, and producers of food complements like pasta or wine. Demers' concept was to feature one cheese and one recipe in each 30-minute show, and allocate six minutes to advertising

Saputo brands and directing consumers to Saputo retailers. The retailer featured each week would feature the Saputo cheese in their store flyer and consumers would be reminded of the cheese and recipe with in-store signage and demonstrations. This alternative had the advantages of being scaleable (starting small and then expanding the number of shows produced and where they were shown), being memorable to consumers (tied to valued content), and hav-ing a direct benefit to the grocery retailers (which would aid in securing listing agreements). The question in Demers mind was whether they could generate sufficient viewership to warrant the production costs and get the attention of the retailers and sponsors.

Now join the Saputo team, which option would you choose and why?

## COMMUNICATIONS MIX REVISITED

In the previous chapter we discussed the range of decisions involved in developing a marketing communication strategy. In this chapter we revisit the communications mix to get a deeper understanding of the tactical tools available to marketers to get their messages in front of audiences. While advertising is often the most visible of communication mix elements, organizations that follow an IMC strategy recognize that other elements can be highly effective—and that is the choice facing Mario Demers at Saputo Dairy Products Canada. Microcell Solutions, for example, supports their Fido (cellular phone system) brand's communications strategy with a strong public relations program, sales promotion, and personal selling (Exhibit 13.1). In the greater Toronto area, Microcell's objective was to increase awareness and trial of Fido and leverage the emotional relevancy of the brand to reach customers one-to-one.[1] The company linked a variety of experiences—key messages, images, sounds, and activities to the brand under the theme "Fun & Freedom." It launched the campaign with a "Fido mobile," a vintage 1942 bus pulled by a dozen dogs, which attracted significant media attention. Fun & Freedom events were held throughout greater Toronto—augmented by free photography of prospective customers and their pets, having dogs perform tricks to demonstrate Fido's feature and benefits, and allowing prospective customers to make free calls anywhere in Fido's coverage area. Fido also chose to involve Canine Vision Canada in the campaign, because both Fido and guide dogs represent freedom to their masters. Advertising supported the public relations efforts by visually linking Fido to fun and freedom imagery, such as sunglasses, beach balls, and fireworks. Sales promotions, including a grand prize sweepstakes and at-event contests for T-shirts, baseball caps, Fido phones, and airtime packages, further enhanced the overall strategy. The campaign was successful in making the Fido brand personally relevant to thousands of pet owners. Having a better understanding of these communication mix elements will allow you to make more informed communication mix decisions.

**Saputo**
www.Saputo.com

**Fido**
www.fido.ca

## ADVERTISING

Wherever we turn, we are bombarded by ads in the form of television commercials, radio spots, banner ads on the Internet urging us to "click here," or huge billboards screaming "Buy Me!" As indicated in the previous chapter, advertising is

**Exhibit 13.1**

Microcell Solutions uses public relations to support its integrated marketing communications strategy.

non-personal communication paid for by an identified sponsor using mass media to persuade or inform an audience.[2] Advertising is the most common element of a communication mix because it can be fun to create, glamorous to be involved with, and it often involves large budgets, travel, and celebrities. It gives a marketing manager or executive something tangible that says "I helped create that" inspiring, magical, humorous, provocative, or otherwise creative piece of art. Be honest, wouldn't you rather spend $200 000 of someone else's money creating a television ad with Shania Twain or Justin Timberlake than developing a coupon or hiring another sales rep? Of course, actually creating the television ad can be time consuming, heavily detail-oriented, and boring (such as waiting for the paint on the set to dry or taking five or six hours of retakes to shoot a three-second scene), but overall, advertising attracts a lot of a communication budget because it is fun to do.

Of course, advertising is also very effective. Advertising is often unparalleled in its ability to demonstrate products (particularly services), use sights and sounds to create desire, and repeat the message as often as it deems necessary for it to have an impact on receivers. Advertising is such a big part of our culture that it both reflects and shapes our culture, and it is so effective that there are laws limiting its use for vulnerable audiences like children and the promotion of socially undesirable products like cigarettes. And that's also why Canadian businesses spend close to $6 billion a year on advertising.[3]

We talked about the planning that goes behind the creation of advertising in Chapter 12. Here we will discuss how to create effective advertising and how to evaluate or critique the effectiveness of advertising.

## Creating Advertising

A poor strategy or poor execution can result in annoying, boring, or otherwise ineffective advertising. You know, the ones you flip the TV channel to avoid watching or the ones you don't even look at when reading your favourite magazine.

When people give examples of effective advertising, they are likely to recall the provocative poses in Calvin Klein ads, a ranting Molson Joe, or vomiting Playland customers—advertising that was memorable because it stood out and uniquely appealed to its intended audience. These are all examples of **product advertising**, in which the message focuses on a specific good or service. Product advertising usually has one of three purposes: educate people about the new product and what it does; convince the target audience to try it or choose it over other options; or ensure that people won't forget about the product and the things they already know about it. **Institutional advertising** promotes the activities, personality, or point of view of an organization or company, as in the ad for Pfizer shown in Exhibit 13.2. Another use of institutional advertising is to build demand for a product category, such as the Canadian egg producers' ads that encourage consumers to "Get Cracking."

Some institutional messages state a firm's position on an issue to sway public opinion, a strategy called **advocacy advertising**.[4] For example, the R.J. Reynolds company ran an ad titled "Of Cigarettes and Science," which attempted to refute arguments about the relationship between smoking and health. **Public service advertisements** (PSAs) are advertisements the media runs free of charge for not-for-profit organizations that serve society in some way, or to champion an issue such as increasing literacy or discouraging drunk driving. The ad in Exhibit 13.3 produced by Taxi advertising of Toronto for Covenant House won a Canadian Marketing Award in 2003 in the Public Service Campaign category. Often advertising agencies will take on one or more public service campaigns on a pro bono basis (for free).

**WHO CREATES ADVERTISING?** An **advertising campaign** is a coordinated, comprehensive plan that carries out promotion objectives and results in a series of advertisements placed in media over a period of time. For example, the long-running advertising campaign for Buckley's Mixture—"It tastes awful. And it works."—has included both print advertis-

**product advertising** An advertising message that focuses on a specific good or service.

**institutional advertising** An advertising message that promotes the activities, personality, or point of view of an organization or company.

**advocacy advertising** A type of public service advertising provided by an organization that is seeking to influence public opinion on an issue because it has some stake in the outcome.

**public service advertisements** Advertising run by the media without charge for not-for-profit organizations or to champion a particular cause.

**advertising campaign** A coordinated, comprehensive plan that carries out promotion objectives and results in a series of advertisements placed in media over a period of time.

ing and a series of humorous television commercials that all work together to build brand loyalty for the cough medicine. In fact, the Buckley's campaign is considered one of the most effective in Canadian advertising history. The brand is the number-one selling cough syrup in Canada, even though it spends far less on advertising every year ($458 600) than its closest competitor, Robitussin Dm ($1.7 million).[5]

Creating and executing an advertising campaign often requires many companies working together and a broad range of skilled people to do the job right. Some firms may do their own advertising by creating an *in-house agency*. In many cases, though, the firm retains one or more outside advertising agencies to develop advertising messages on its behalf. A *limited-service agency* provides one or more specialized services, such as media buying or creative development (we'll see what these tasks are later). A *full-service agency* provides most or all of the services needed to mount a campaign, including research, creation of ad copy and art, media selection, and production of the final messages. In keeping with the move to integrated communications strategies discussed in Chapter 12, most Canadian advertising agencies have transformed themselves into full-service *communications services companies*, which provide clients with advice and service in all areas of communications decision making, including advertising. Many different tasks are required to produce an advertising campaign. The ad in Exhibit 13.4 humorously illustrates the "birth" of an advertising concept, highlighting some of the major players who participate in the delivery. Big or small, an advertising agency or communications services company joins the talents of specialists who together craft a message and make the communications concept a reality.

- *Account Management:* The *account executive*, or *account manager* or *suit*, is the "soul" of the operation. This person develops the campaign's strategy for the client. The account executive supervises the day-to-day activities on the account, and is the primary liaison between the agency and the client. The account executive has to ensure that the client is happy while verifying that people within the agency are executing the desired strategy.

- *Creative Services:* *Creatives* are the "heart" of the communications effort. These are the people who actually dream up and produce the ads. They include the agency's creative director, copywriter, and art director. Creatives are the artists who breathe life into marketing objectives and craft messages that (hopefully) will excite, arouse, or interest consumers.

- *Research and Marketing Services:* Researchers are the "brains" of the campaign. They collect and analyze information that will help account executives develop a sensible strategy. They assist creatives in getting consumer reactions to different versions of ads, or by providing copywriters with details on the target group.

- *Media Planning:* The media planner is the "legs" of the campaign. The media planner helps to determine which communications vehicles are the most effective and recommends the most efficient means for delivering the ad by deciding where, when, and how often it will appear.

**Exhibit 13.2**

Institutional advertising can be used to build a corporate reputation.

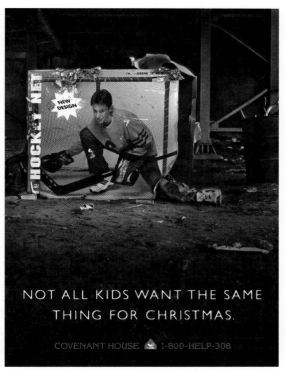

**Exhibit 13.3**

This Covenant House ad with the caption "Not All Kids Want the Same Thing for Christmas" is a public service announcement promoting donations to help get children off the streets in Canada.

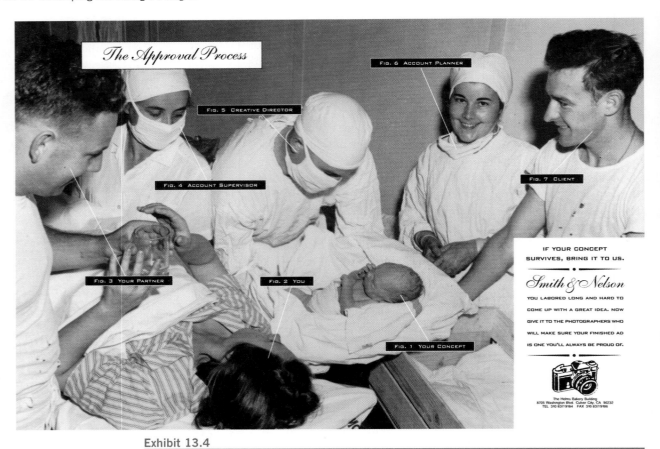

**Exhibit 13.4**

This trade ad illustrates the "birth" of an advertising concept.

## Media Choices

What does a 130-centimetre television with Dolby Surround-Sound have in common with a matchbook? Each is a media vehicle that permits an advertiser to communicate with a potential customer. Depending on the intended message, each medium has its advantages and disadvantages. Let's look at the major categories of media. The pros and cons of each type are summarized in Table 13.1.

**TRADITIONAL MEDIA** *Television.* Because of television's ability to reach so many people at once, this medium is a favourite choice for regional or national companies. Ninety-nine percent of Canadians live in households that have a TV and, on an average day, 77 percent of Canadians watch TV at least once.[6] There are two English (CBC and CTV) and two French (Radio-Canada and TVA) national television networks in Canada, which can offer both regional and national advertising exposure. There are 18 regional networks, three of which are in French. Yet another option for TV advertising is specialty channels, which provide a specific programming format (The Comedy Network) or audience (Women's Television Network) and can, therefore, provide easy access to a particular market segment.

One disadvantage of advertising on television is cost. In addition to the cost of placing ads in media, production costs range from $80 000 to $250 000 for a 30-second television ad.[7] This high cost of production has led some companies to consider advertising on TV without using commercials. *Product placement* is a method of advertising on television (and in movies), where the product is seen as part of the TV show (or movie) rather than in a separate ad. Recent product placements in Canadian TV shows include Nortel phones used on *The Newsroom*, Polaroid cameras used on *PSI Factor*, Rona building products used in the Quebec home renovation show *Ma Maison Rona,* and Sony Ericsson phones being used on *Train 48.* MMI Product Placement, the largest product placement company in Canada,

**Table 13.1** Pros and Cons of Selected Media Vehicles

| Vehicle | Pros | Cons |
|---|---|---|
| Television | Extremely creative and flexible.<br>Network TV is a cost-effective way to reach a mass audience.<br>Specialty TV allows the advertiser to reach a selected group at relatively low cost.<br>Messages have high impact because of the use of sight and sound. | The message is quickly forgotten unless it is repeated often.<br>The audience is increasingly fragmented.<br>Although the relative cost of reaching the audience is low, prices are still high on an absolute basis—often too high for smaller companies. A 30-second spot on a primetime TV sitcom costs well over $40 000.<br>Rising costs have led to more and shorter ads, which cause greater clutter. |
| Radio | Good for selectively targeting an audience.<br>Relatively low cost, both for producing a spot and for running it repeatedly.<br>Radio ads can be modified quickly to reflect changes in the marketplace.<br>Use of sound effects and music allows listeners to use their imagination to create a vivid scene. | Listeners often don't pay full attention to what they hear.<br>The small audience of most stations means ads must be repeated frequently.<br>Not appropriate for products that must be seen or demonstrated to be appreciated. |
| Newspapers | Wide exposure provides extensive market coverage.<br>Flexible format permits the use of colour, different sizes, and targeted editions.<br>Useful for comparison shopping.<br>Allows local retailers to tie in with national advertisers. | Most people don't spend much time reading the newspaper.<br>Readership is especially low among teens and young adults.<br>Short life span—people rarely look at a newspaper more than once.<br>Very cluttered ad environment.<br>The reproduction quality of images can be poor. |
| Magazines | Audiences can be narrowly targeted by specialized magazines.<br>High credibility and interest level provide a good environment for ads.<br>Advertising has a long life and is often passed along to other readers.<br>Visual quality is excellent. | Can be expensive.<br>The cost of a full-page, four-colour ad in a general-audience magazine typically exceeds $30 000.<br>Long deadlines can reduce flexibility.<br>The advertiser must generally use several magazines to reach the majority of a target market. |
| Internet Banner Advertising | Narrow targeting possible.<br>Can be cost effective.<br>Measurable. | Easily ignored.<br>Very cluttered environment.<br>Security/privacy issues may prevent consumers from clicking on banner ads. |
| Outdoor | Most of the population can be reached at low cost.<br>Good for supplementing other media. | Hard to communicate complex messages.<br>Hard to demonstrate a product's effectiveness.<br>Controversial and disliked in many communities. |

Source: Adapted from J. Thomas Russell and W. Ronald Lane, *Kleppner's Advertising Procedure*, 11th ed. (Upper Saddle River, NJ: Prentice Hall, 1990); William Wells, John Burnett, and Sandra Moriarty, *Advertising: Principles and Practice*, 3d ed. (Upper Saddle River, NJ: Prentice Hall, 1995).

claims that the advantages of product placement include image reinforcement when a "star" uses the product, brand awareness, extensive reach (during reruns as well as during first runs), and the protection of the product from zapping (since consumers often use zapping to avoid ads, not TV shows).[8]

*Radio.* One advantage of radio advertising is flexibility. Marketers can change commercials quickly, often on the spot by an announcer and a recording engineer.[9] Radio is attractive to advertisers seeking low cost and the ability to reach specific consumer segments. There are hundreds of radio stations in Canada, with formats ranging from contemporary hits to classical.[10] The growth of on-line radio also presents future opportunities for reaching large numbers of consumers in a cost-effective manner. Vancouver's Raincoast Books used radio spots about out-of-work mythical characters (Merlin, a witch, and a

**Exhibit 13.5**

Radio was a cost-effective way to reach broad audiences during the release of this Harry Potter book.

**The Globe and Mail**
www.globeandmail.ca

**computer media**
Communications media that transmit information through the Internet or via e-mail messages.

**banners** Internet advertising in the form of rectangular graphics at the top or bottom of Web pages.

**buttons** Small banner-type advertisements that can be placed anywhere on a Web page.

**permission-based marketing** E-mail advertising where online consumers have the opportunity to accept or refuse the unsolicited e-mail.

**m-commerce** Promotional and other e-commerce activities transmitted over mobile phones and other mobile devices such as personal digital assistants (PDAs).

leprechaun) as the primary medium for launch of the J. K. Rowling book *Harry Potter and the Order of the Phoenix* (Exhibit 13.5). Aired across Canada, the radio spots enabled the Canadian publisher to cost effectively reach new audiences for the book.[11]

*Newspapers.* The newspaper is one of the oldest media vehicles. Retailers in particular have relied on newspaper ads since before the turn of the century to inform readers about sales and deliveries of new merchandise. Newspapers are an excellent medium for local advertising and for events (such as sales) that require a quick response. Many newspapers, such as *The Globe and Mail* and the *National Post*, offer online versions of their papers to expand their exposure.

*Magazines.* Magazine ads provide high-quality images and can reach specific segments of consumers. New technologies such as *selective binding* allow publishers to personalize their editions so that advertisements for local businesses can be included in issues mailed to specific locations. *Desktop publishing* software allows magazines to close their pages just before going to press—no more long lead times that used to plague advertisers that wanted to hit their market with timely information.

*Directories.* Directory advertising is the most "down-to-earth," information-focused advertising medium. Today, the *Yellow Pages* has revenues of over $9.5 billion, and more than 6000 directories are published in North America alone. These listings are usually references used just before the consumer makes the decision to buy, so the advertiser has the opportunity to influence the buyer immediately before the decision.

COMPUTER MEDIA  The use of e-mail and the Internet (**computer media**) are growing in popularity as advertising media, as increasing numbers of consumers get online. Worldwide Internet advertising revenues are projected to reach $16.5 billion by the year 2005.[12] As indicated by the ad for DoubleClick in Exhibit 13.6, one potential advantage of **banner** advertising online is that advertisers can reach a large and diverse number of consumers. However, some critics believe that most banner advertising goes unnoticed by Internet users, making it an ineffective advertising strategy. Mark Pavan, CEO of the new online dating service Lemontonic doesn't think so—he is spending $4 million of his $5 million marketing budget with undisclosed online partners—the rest in print, out of home media, and product placement with the reality TV show *Hooked Up*.[13] Banner advertising isn't the only form of Internet advertising. Other forms include: **buttons**, pop-up ads, search engines and directories, sponsorships, and e-mail. These are described in Table 13.2. Of these, e-mail is particularly interesting as it allows marketers to send video (and still) images to targeted consumers—providing television-like impact at a fraction of the cost. Many marketers have found **permission-based marketing**, where the receiver either opts-in or opts-out of receiving e-mail, to be highly effective.

MOBILE MEDIA In this age of the Internet, it seems like we just get used to a dozen or so new terms when they are replaced by an equal number of new ones. M-commerce is a new buzzword that many marketers are talking about. The "m" stands for mobile. **M-commerce** is the promotional and other e-commerce activities transmitted over mobile phones and other mobile devices such as personal digital assistants (PDAs).[14]

M-commerce is prevalent in Europe and Asia. Text messaging in the Philippines is replacing traditional phone calls because of convenience and cost savings. According to the Philippine Long Distance Telephone Co., an estimated 1 million text messages are sent every day.[15]

M-commerce is now making its way to Canada and the United States. Even the MTV Music Video Awards now include a wireless advertising campaign to promote the event. Millions of consumers who use such networks as Telus, Bell Mobility, Palm, and OmniSky will get messages urging them to tune in.[16]

What's the big attraction? Although only a small proportion of the millions of users of mobile phones worldwide use their phones to check e-mail, stock quotes, and so on, that number is expected to grow dramatically in the next few years. Young people in particular are big users of cell phones. At this point about 28 percent of young people own or use a cell phone, which explains why cell phone companies such as Nokia are aggressively advertising on high school campuses.[17]

This high usage will open the door for m-commerce advertising campaigns like those now being conducted in other countries. Consider a campaign for the Kit Kat candy bar that was conducted by Nestlé in the United Kingdom. The firm's ad agency sent text messages to the cell phones of 6000 consumers ages 18 to 25 that alerted them when ads for the candy would air and invited them to take a quiz about the ad that would in turn enter them into a drawing to win a month's supply of Kit Kats (about 94 percent of British youth have cell phones with wireless messaging capability). This technique, known as *short-messaging system marketing (SMS)*, is becoming a popular way to reach customers in the United Kingdom and throughout Europe.

M-commerce messages can reach specific types of consumers. A campaign for readers of *Men's Health* magazine sent a customized daily menu via cell phone to help interested readers curb calories (doubtful those Kit Kats were on the list).[18] So what are the advantages of m-commerce to consumers? First, m-commerce provides incredible consumer convenience. You can use your mobile phone to buy tickets for a concert without standing in line. You can even buy soft drinks from a vending machine through the phone—a service already available in Europe.[19]

But the potential for m-commerce is even greater. Perhaps you're in the market for a new computer. You visit a local retailer and decide what you want. While you're there, you use your mobile phone or PDA to check prices of the same computer on the Internet. If you decide you have the best price, you'll be able to handle the transaction on your phone as well, paying for the computer through a secure Internet connection.

For marketers the opportunities for m-commerce are even more exciting. Using sophisticated *location-based technologies* including satellites, a retailer will be able to know when you are only a few blocks away from her store and she can send you messages about a special sale.[20] And as you pass McDonald's, your phone will beep to remind you how great a Big Mac combo would taste right about now. Of course, such opportunities bring a whole host of privacy issues that must be settled before these scenarios can become a reality.

For the time being there are some technological barriers that must be overcome for m-commerce to take off. At present North American consumers are put off by the reliability of these services, the difficulty of typing messages on a tiny keypad, and concerns about security and privacy since it's possible for some services to pinpoint the user's location. For these reasons about one in four people who try m-commerce stop after the first few attempts.[21] In addition, Canadian and U.S. mobile phone standards differ from those in Europe and Asia, which prevents worldwide access.

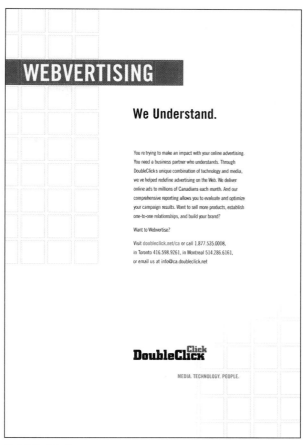

**Exhibit 13.6**

Reaching their target market with advertising is important to media planners.

### Table 13.2 Internet Advertising

| | |
|---|---|
| Banners | *Banners,* those rectangular graphics at the top or bottom of Web pages, were the first form of Web advertising. Although the effectiveness of banners remains in question (banners now receive less than a 1 percent click-through rate), they still remain the most popular form of Web advertising. One study that tested the impact of banner ads at top Web sites reported a dramatic increase in brand awareness after just one exposure and significant positive impact on intent to purchase.[22] Experts suggest banners that contain animation, effectively use colour, call for action (e.g., "click here"), and create a sense of urgency are more effective. |
| Buttons | *Buttons* are small banner-type advertisements that can be placed anywhere on a page. Early in the life of the Internet, buttons encouraging surfers to "Download Netscape Now" became a standard on many Web sites and were responsible for much of Netscape's early success. |
| Sponsorships | *Sponsorships,* much like the sponsorships of traditional radio and television programming, provide visibility for the company but, unlike banners and buttons, are not aimed at getting Web users to visit their sites. Ford sponsors a site that provides answers to women's major concerns about buying cars, safety, maintenance, and leasing rather than buying. Johnson & Johnson and its Huggies brand sponsor a parenting area on iVillage. |
| Search Engine and Directory Listings | Just as the Yellow Pages and other directories are advertising media, so too are search engines and online directory listings. Increasingly firms are paying search engines for more visible or higher placement on results lists. |
| Pop-up Ads | A *pop-up ad* is an advertisement that pops up on the screen while a Web page is being loaded or after it is loaded. Because pop-up ads take the centre of the screen while surfers are waiting for the desired page to load, they are difficult to ignore. A pop-up ad opens a separate Internet window. Web advertisers are typically charged only if people click through the windows. |
| E-mail | For advertising, *e-mail* is becoming as pervasive as radio and television. It is one of the easiest ways of communicating with consumers. |

Still, the future is bright for m-commerce: One study predicts that despite the slow start, about 90 million North Americans will be participating in m-commerce by 2007, generating more than $50 billion in revenues.[23] That's opportunity calling!

**out-of-home media**
Communications media that reach people in public places.

**OUT-OF-HOME MEDIA Out-of-home media** such as blimps, transit ads, and billboards, reach people in public places. This medium works best when it tells a simple, straightforward story.[24]

Marketers are constantly searching for new ways to get their messages out to busy people. Ads in movie theatres are popular with certain advertisers. For example, since TV viewers are also frequent movie goers, several TV networks, such as Global and the Discovery Channel (Canada), use ads in movie theatres to promote new shows.[25]

In addition, *place-based media*, which transmits messages in public places, can be an effective way to reach a captive audience. Exhibit 13.7 shows part of an ad for the Bank of Montreal Financial Group. Kitchener, Ontario-based Timeline Technologies operates video screens that transmit ads while consumers are pumping gas at gas stations. IGRABBER is a Canadian company that sells ad space on more than 1000 mini-billboards in laundromats across the country.[26]

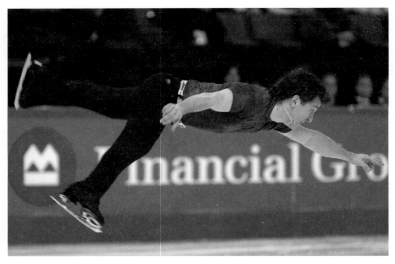

**Exhibit 13.7**

Place-based media such as rink-boards can be an effective way to communicate to a captive audience.

# Developing Effective Advertising

Once the creative team has developed a campaign concept, how does the agency know if the ideas will work? Advertisers try to minimize mistakes by getting reactions to ad messages before they are actually placed. Much of this **pretesting**, the research that goes on in the early stages of a campaign, centres on gathering basic information that will help planners make sure they've accurately defined the product's market, consumers, and competitors. This information comes from quantitative sources, such as syndicated surveys, and qualitative sources, such as focus groups, which we discussed in Chapter 4.

As the campaign takes shape, the players need to determine how well the specific advertising concepts under development will perform. **Copy testing** measures the effectiveness of ads. It seeks to determine whether consumers are receiving, comprehending, and responding to the ad according to plan. There are several copy-testing techniques.

- *Concept testing* helps determine if initial ideas will work. Respondents, who are often drawn from the target market for which the ad is intended, evaluate different creative ideas or rough copies of ad layouts.

- *Test commercials* let consumers respond to a rough version of what a television message will look like. This preliminary treatment may take the form of an *animatic* or *storyboard*, such as the one shown in Exhibit 13.8, which is a series of sketches showing frame by frame what will happen in the finished commercial.

- *Finished testing* is testing audience reactions to a fully produced commercial to see if it has motivated them to buy the product. This occurs before the commercial actually airs on television. Because production of a "real" commercial is expensive, most testing is conducted before this point.

**CRITIQUES OF ADVERTISING** You might like advertising that your friends do not and one of your friends might like an ad that you do not. Liking or disliking an ad does not determine its effectiveness. While formal measures of communication and advertising effectiveness involves an assessment of the outputs and outcomes of the communication effort (Chapter 12), advertising critique involves an assessment of the quality of the communication strategy and its execution, to the extent that these are reflected by the ad. Following

> **pretesting** A research method that seeks to minimize mistakes by getting consumer reactions to ad messages before they appear in the media.

> **copy testing** A marketing research method that seeks to measure the effectiveness of ads by determining whether consumers are receiving, comprehending, and responding to the ad according to plan.

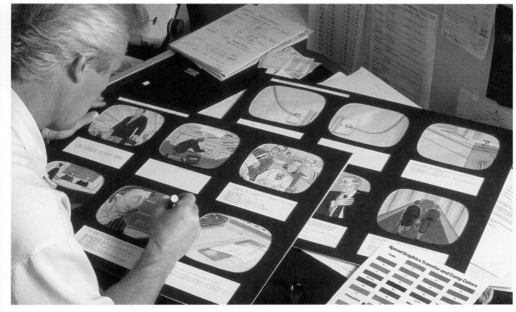

**Exhibit 13.8**

A storyboard presents preliminary ideas for an advertisement.

**Exhibit 13.9**

This German ad for a movie theatre reminds us that "Not everywhere that's dark shows great movies." As some readers might be turned-off by the imagery, a concept like this one would need to be pre-tested.

**public relations (PR)**
Communications strategies to build good relationships and corporate image with an organization's stakeholders, including consumers, stockholders, and legislators.

the communication plan outline (see Figure 12.5, page 393), an advertising critique has eight main elements (Table 13.3).

Advertising is highly effective when all of the elements in Table 13.3 are done well, are coordinated and consistent with each other, and come together with impact and creativity that supports the intended strategy. When one or more elements are not done well, the results can be a disaster. Next time you are reading a newspaper or magazine look for ads that you think are not effective—what didn't the creator(s) do well?

## PUBLIC RELATIONS

Chapter 12 noted that **public relations (PR)** helps build mutually beneficial long-term relationships and improve the image of an organization with key stakeholders—consumers, the media, shareholders, legislators, and interest groups. Public relations is crucial to an organization's ability to create and sustain a favourable relationships, corporate goodwill, and overall image. There are many types of public relations that focus on different activities and stakeholders:

- *Publicity and media relations:* unpaid communications about an organization and/or its products appearing in the mass media.

**Table 13.3 Elements of an Advertising Critique**

1. **Target Audience.** Is the target audience clear? When we dislike an ad it is often because we are not in the target audience—the ad was not meant for us, it does not strike a cord, and we just don't "get it."

2. **Communication Objectives.** Are the objectives clear? Advertising needs to be assessed against its objectives. Does the ad do what is intended for its audience? If the objectives of an ad are not clear, it is unlikely to be very effective.

3. **Overall Communications Strategy.** How appropriate is the overall communications strategy given the intended audience and objectives? Is an IMC, push or pull, or one-way or two-way symmetrical or asymmetrical strategy appropriate?

4. **Positioning Statement and Key Messages.** Does the ad clearly position the product and are the key messages clear and appropriate for the desired positioning of the brand, media used, and creative concept? If not, then the ad is not very effective. Every element in a communications strategy should reinforce the overall brand positioning.

5. **Communication Tactics.** Is the theme, approach, or tactics used to break through perceptual screens and get the attention of the audience appropriate given the audience, communication objectives, brand positioning, messages, and media? Ineffective ads do not break through the noise or do so in a way that is annoying or otherwise creates negative attitudes towards the brand. The German ad in Exhibit 13.9, for example, gets the reader's attention but could result in negative attitudes towards Cinemax.

6. **Communications Mix / Media.** Is advertising the most effective way to achieve the communication objectives with the intended audience and is the media selected, the ad placement, and scheduling appropriate given the other strategic elements?

7. **Creative Execution.** Is the creative concept appropriate for the audience, communication objectives, positioning, media, and messages? Cost effective communication also has lasting power—it doesn't get old or stale too quickly. Humour, for example, wears out quickly.

8. **Evaluation.** Does the ad include a call to action that would help the marketing organization track responses to the ad (e.g., a 1-800 number or Web address)? An ad is more effective if its creators can demonstrate its impact.

- *Corporate public relations:* managing the overall reputation and image of the organization.
- *Crisis management:* plans for the management of corporate crises, including boycotts, recalls, natural disasters, strikes.
- *Employee relations:* internal programs designed to foster positive relationships among and between organization employees.
- *Financial relations:* effective communications directed toward investors, regulators, and other financial stakeholders.
- *Public affairs:* lobbying efforts aimed at influencing policy decisions at the federal, provincial, and municipal levels of government.
- *Community relations:* grassroots management of relationships with local community stakeholders, including business owners, major employers, schools, kids' groups, and community organizations.

Although public relations is a powerful element of the communications mix, marketers often overlook it, primarily because it doesn't have the creative and visual appeal of creating an "ad." Public relations is powerful because it is interactive, helping to foster relationships. It allows corporations to build social goodwill, which can often protect them against future public issues and concerns. It also provides a higher level of credibility and believability when the communication is presented through third parties like reporters, experts, celebrities, or independent organizations such as the Consumers' Association of Canada. Finally, public relations provides an inexpensive way to reach not only consumers but also other stakeholders important to the interests of an organization.

## Objectives of Public Relations

Public relations specialists need to operate at many levels to ensure that various stakeholders receive coordinated and accurate messages about the firm. As we saw with the Fido example, public relations strategies are often used in concert with advertising, sales promotions, and personal selling to accomplish communication objectives related to:

- *Introducing new products:* When Al Galbraith earned the chance to sell 246 homes in the village at Cornwallis Park, a former military base in Nova Scotia, he enlisted a PR agency to help him develop an innovative public relations and advertising campaign. It was expected to take two years to sell the well-maintained, three- and four-bedroom homes, some of which had ocean views; Galbraith sold them all in seven weeks. One key was price—the homes were $29 900 to $49 900. A second key was getting media attention. Galbraith and his PR agency created news releases to catch the public interest angles— the developer was targeting former service men and other retirees who didn't have a lot of money, and was revitalizing a down-trodden region of Nova Scotia; these were picked up across the country.[27]
- *Supporting current products:* Ocean Spray Cranberries Ltd. sponsored research at Harvard Medical School that confirmed the "folk wisdom" that cranberry juice is an effective way to treat urinary tract infections. With the help of PR agency Cohn & Wolfe in Toronto, Ocean Spray sent press kits to food editors and other writers with a focus on health and seniors' lifestyles to promote the study published in the *New England Journal of Medicine* and to offer interviews with the leader of the research team, Dr. Jerry Avorn.[28] The strategy was to promote the product category, not the brand, but sales of Ocean Spray Cranberry juice increased significantly after the PR program.
- *Influencing government legislation:* Concerned about public outcry over the price of gasoline, Petro-Canada and other distributors developed a PR campaign to explain that more than half the price consumers pay for gasoline is tax.[29] This was intended, in part, to deflect public influence onto the federal and provincial governments.

**Ocean Spray Cranberries Ltd.**
www.oceanspray.com

- *Enhancing the image of an organization or entity:* Faced with international criticism about possible human rights abuses and restriction of trade, the Chinese government established an office in charge of "overseas propaganda" to present a more favourable image of China to the rest of the world.[30]

- *Calling attention to a firm's involvement with the community:* To help improve their corporate images, Canadian insurance companies, such as Royal Insurance, are providing financial aid and employees' time to support community initiatives, such as injury awareness campaigns, sailing regattas, block parent associations, and neighbourhood watches. These companies have realized what other organizations that support little league teams, youth associations, and community events have known all along—being involved in community interests helps win friends and influence people.[31] Many companies find value in sponsorship of large-scale events, such as the Olympic Games, the HSBC Celebration of Light (formerly the Benson & Hedges Symphony of Fire), the Montreal International Jazz Festival (Exhibit 13.10), or the Molson Indy. Public relations specialists work behind the scenes to ensure that a sponsored event receives ample press coverage and exposure for the organization. Canadian sponsorship law recently changed to ban the tobacco company sponsorship of cultural or sporting events and this has left many events searching for new sponsors. Attracting new sponsors has proven difficult for some events as sponsor organizations are increasingly questioning the value of such sponsorship, setting specific measurable communication objectives for their sponsorship, and basing sponsorship decisions on return on investment.

- *Demonstrating social responsibility:* With help from Toronto-based social marketing firm Manifest Communications, Swedish telecom giant Ericsson launched a program called Ericsson Response, a worldwide initiative to aid the cause of disaster relief by providing mobile and satellite telephones systems to humanitarian relief workers.[32] Crabtree & Evelyn of London, Ontario, donates $2 for every bath gel sold in the month of October to the Canadian Breast Cancer Foundation, which helps raise the company's visibility.[33]

- *Developing positive employee or investor relations:* Petro-Canada uses PR to influence, albeit indirectly, government legislation. It has also undertaken an internal communications program in an effort to enlist its 4500 employees in the cause to redirect public concern about gas prices—recognizing that its employees are the best ambassadors.[34] Husky Injection Moulding Systems introduced a program that allows its 3000 workers to earn company shares for acting green and helping others. While this has social responsibility and community involvement messages, it also makes employees more committed to the organization and helps shape organization culture.[35] Electronic bulletin boards, newsletters, golf tournaments, and staff picnics are among many vehicles used to develop positive employee relations. Company tours, open houses, annual reports, quarterly reports, annual general meetings, technical briefings, and one-on-one interviews are some of the methods used to develop relationships with investors and potential investors.

- *Handling communication issues and crises:* A few years ago, PepsiCo was rocked by claims that hypodermic needles had been found in Diet Pepsi cans. The company assembled a crisis team to map out a response and supplied video footage of its bottling process to reassure people that foreign objects could not be inserted at the factory. The claims turned out to be false, and PepsiCo ran ads designed to let people know there was nothing to worry about. Pepsi's calm, coordinated response averted a public relations disaster. Similarly, Bridgestone/Firestone Canada Inc. decided to act proactively and voluntarily recalled a million sport utility vehicle (SUV) tires when it was learned that some Firestone tires had failed in the United States under the conditions of high temperatures, high speed, and low tire pressure. This PR initiative will cost Bridgestone/Firestone over $212 million in Canada but is expected to foster stronger long-term relationships with SUV owners.[36] McDonald's, on the other hand, decided to sue a London, England-based environmental group in the 1980s to prevent it from publishing a pam-

**McSpotlight**
www.mcspotlight.org

phlet that accused McDonald's of numerous wrongdoings. McDonald's won the suit, but it took ten years and cost $23 million in legal fees, and the proceedings were covered by the global media for a decade. Supporters of the defendants established a Web site that is still frequently updated to bring public scrutiny to McDonald's business practices.[37]

## Planning a Public Relations Campaign

A public relations campaign is a coordinated effort to communicate with one or more of the firm's stakeholders. It requires a three-step process of developing objectives, executing, and evaluating.

The organization must first develop clear objectives for the PR program that define the message it wants people to hear. Raincoast Books, for example, wanted to ensure that it got the "most bang for the time" in terms of favourable publicity surrounding J.K. Rowling's visit to Canada. After determining the objective, the PR specialists create a campaign strategy, which includes these elements:

**Exhibit 13.10**

A sponsored event is a form of public relations. Changes in the Canadian law now ban tobacco companies like DuMaurier from sponsoring cultural or sporting events.

- A statement of the problem
- A situation analysis
- Specification of target audiences (publics)
- Messages to be communicated
- Specific program elements to be used
- A timetable and budget
- Discussion of how the program will be evaluated

The International Apple Institute, a trade group devoted to increasing the consumption of apples, had to decide if a campaign should get consumers to cook more with apples, drink more apple juice, or buy more fresh fruit. Because fresh apples brought a substantially higher price per kilogram to growers than apples used for applesauce or apple juice, the group decided to push the fresh fruit angle. It used the familiar theme "An apple a day..." and mounted a focused campaign to encourage people to eat more apples by placing articles extolling the fruit's health benefits in consumer media.

Execution of the campaign means deciding precisely how the message should be communicated to the stakeholder(s) of interest. An organization can get out its positive messages in many ways (Table 13.4), ranging from news conferences and sponsorship of charity or sporting events to creating attention-getting promotional events. Palmer Jarvis DDB Toronto created the public service announcement in Exhibit 13.11 for the Canadian Foundation for Physically Disabled Persons. It uses a strong visual to communicate the social issue of whelchair access.

## Public Relations Program Elements

Sometimes, these efforts involve lobbying government officials to persuade them to vote a certain way on pending legislation, or writing speeches for company executives to deliver.

**Table 13.4 Tools of Public Relations**

| Interactive | Proactive | Responsive | Indirect & Associative |
| --- | --- | --- | --- |
| E-mail | Newsletters | Letters to Customers | Social/Cause Advertising |
| Web Sites | News Releases | Annual Reports | Public Service Announcements |
| Open Houses | Video News Releases | Bulletin Boards | Celebrity Endorsement |
| Ceremonies | Disaster Planning | Suggestion Boxes | Product Placement |
| Meetings | Issues Management | Surveys | Fundraising |
| Events | Lobbying | Environmental Scanning | Sponsorship |
| Speeches/Addresses | Brochures | | Advertorials |
| Trade Shows & Exhibits | Pamphlets | | |
| News Conference | | | |
| Annual General Meeting | | | |
| Corporate Social Events | | | |
| Employee Volunteering | | | |

Note: Categories are illustrative; public relations tools can be used in different ways to reach different objectives.

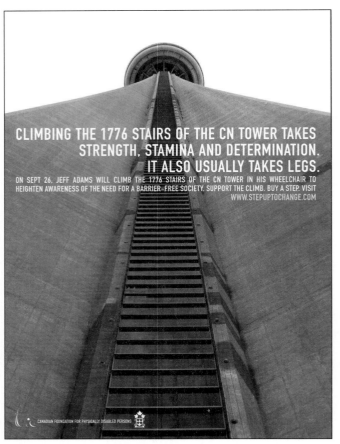

**Exhibit 13.11**

PR messages can be communicated in many ways, such as using strong visuals like the CN Tower by this ad by the Canadian Foundation for Physically Disabled Persons.

PR specialists may provide input on corporate identity materials, such as logos, brochures, building design, and even stationery, which communicate a positive image for the firm. Or the organization can simply try to get media exposure for the achievements of an employee who has done some notable charity work or for a product it developed that saved someone's life. For example, the Canadian pharmaceutical firm Boehringer Ingelheim (Canada) Ltd. sent large My Buddy dolls wearing respirator masks to Canadian pediatricians. The dolls helped doctors ease their young patients' fears about putting a mask over their mouths and noses. In return, Boehringer Ingelheim received a lot of favourable publicity when newspapers across the country featured the campaign.

As the My Buddy doll example illustrates, **publicity** is a powerful PR tool. The most common way for public relations specialists to communicate to the media is through a **press release**, a description of some event that an organization produces itself and sends to the media in the hope that a reporter will write an article about it. A newer version of this idea is a video news release (VNR), aimed at the broadcast media, that tells the story in a film format. Some of the most common types of press releases are:

- *Timely topics* deal with hot topics in the news. Levi Strauss promoted casual Fridays (and presumably sales of its casual dress pants such as Dockers and Slates) by highlighting how different corporations around the country are adopting a relaxed dress code.

- *Research stories* summarize research projects, such as articles that universities send out that highlight recent breakthroughs from faculty members or public opinion polls that are released by political parties. Ralston Purina released the results of a survey that asked people how they show love to their pets: It was picked up by media across the country, earning 22 million impressions based on readership, viewership, and circulation of the media.[38]

**publicity** Unpaid communication about an organization appearing in the mass media.

**press release** Information that an organization distributes to the media about its activities, intended to appear as publicity.

- *Consumer information releases* provide information to help consumers make better product decisions. The British Columbia Ministry of Health's Food Safe Program distributes helpful tips about properly preparing foods for Thanksgiving, barbecuing, and other seasonal activities.

Internal public relations activities aimed at employees often include company newsletters and closed-circuit television. These sources of information help keep employees informed about company plans, successes, changes, and so on. Often company newsletters are distributed outside the firm to suppliers or others outside the company.

**Sponsorships** are PR activities through which companies provide financial support to help fund an event in return for publicized recognition of the company's contribution (Exhibit 13.12). Many companies today find that their promotion dollars are far better spent on sponsoring a golf tournament, a building, an athlete or team, a symphony concert, or global events such as the Olympics or World Cup soccer competition. These sponsorships are particularly effective because consumers often connect their enjoyment of the event with the sponsor, thus creating brand loyalty.

Because different events cater to different consumers, sponsorships are a good way to target specific market segments. Philishave, for example, is the official electric shaver of the Toronto Maple Leafs and Raptors—using the team Web sites and events to promote their association with the teams and endear themselves with Toronto sports fans.

The Olympic Games offer interesting sponsorship opportunities as every two years there is worldwide media coverage of a summer or winter Olympic Games. The upcoming Vancouver–Whistler 2010 Winter Games, for example, provides British Columbian and other Canadian businesses an opportunity to launch global brands. The Kootenay Knitting Company of Cranbrook, BC, for example, supplied CBC television sports with sweaters for the 2002 Winter Games in Salt Lake City. The national and international exposure to their products allowed them to double in size. Banner Images of Milton, Ontario supplied venue banners to the 1988 Calgary Olympics and subsequent games and credits this exposure to their landing a large contract with BMW.[39]

A few years back, some companies with smaller advertising budgets developed innovative ways of getting consumers' attention—from putting stickers on apples and heads of lettuce, to placing product-related messages on the backs of theatre tickets, and flags on a golf course—became known as **guerrilla marketing**. This strategy involves "ambushing" consumers with promotional content in places they are not expecting to encounter this kind of activity.[40] Raincoast Books hired young actors dressed as Harry Potter characters, in Gryffindor scarves, to hand out train tickets at Toronto and Vancouver train stations (Exhibit 13.13). The train tickets were stamped with platform 9 ¾, in reference to the Hogwarts Express, to support the *Harry Potter and the Order of the Phoenix* book.

Today, big companies are buying into guerrilla marketing strategies big time. When RCA records wanted to create a buzz around teen pop singer Christina Aguilera, the label hired a team of young people to swarm the Web and chat about her on popular teen sites like alloy.com, bolt.com, and gurl.com. They posted information casually, sometimes sounding like fans. Just before one of her albums debuted, RCA also hired a direct marketing company to e-mail electronic postcards filled with song snippets and biographical information to 50 000 Web addresses. The album quickly went to number 1 on the charts.

**Ralston Purina Canada Inc.**
www.purina.ca

**sponsorship** A PR activity through which companies provide financial support to help fund an event in return for publicized recognition of the company's contribution.

**Olympic Business Success Stories**
www.smallbusinessbc.ca/2010/business/business_success.pdf

**guerrilla marketing** Promotional strategies that "ambush" consumers with promotional content in places they are not expecting it.

**Exhibit 13.12**

Corporate sponsorships of events or facilities, like Air Canada's sponsoring of the Air Canada Centre in Toronto, can help marketing organizations build brand loyalty.

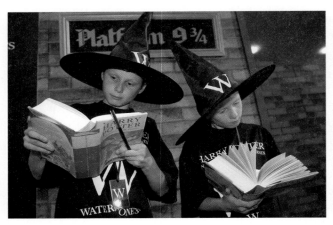

**Exhibit 13.13**

Raincoast Books used a promotional event to get people talking about the newest Harry Potter book.

One barrier to greater reliance on public relations campaigns by many organizations is the PR focus on long-term relationships across a wide variety of stakeholders, making it difficult to assess the effectiveness of specific program elements. For example, no one knows precisely what impact a series of appearances by company executives on talk shows or sponsorship of a charity event has on sales: any one effect cannot be isolated. Marketers do, however, use such research tools as focus groups, interviews, and quantitative surveys (described in Chapter 4) to measure PR effectiveness by tracking changes in attitudes, opinions, and behaviours over time. Measuring media exposure from publicity efforts is relatively more straightforward, although it is more difficult to gauge what impact that coverage has had. Table 13.5 describes some of the most common publicity measurement techniques.

## SALES PROMOTION

**sales promotion** A program designed to build interest in or encourage purchase of a product during a specified time period.

Walking into your student union, you have to be prepared to be ambushed by people eager for you to enter a contest, taste a new candy bar, or take home a free T-shirt with a local bank's name on it. These are examples of **sales promotions**, programs marketers design to build interest in or encourage you to purchase a product or service during a specified time period.[41] Sales promotions can sometimes be elaborate and far-reaching. For example, a successful promotional effort by Diet Coke capitalized on the enormous popularity of the television sitcom *Friends* when the company distributed bottle caps with the names of the show's main characters on them. Each week, a different character was shown drinking a bottle of Diet Coke in a commercial immediately after the show, and holders of caps with that person's name won a prize.

How does a sales promotion differ from advertising? They are similar in that they are both paid messages from identifiable sponsors intended to bring about a change in behaviour or attitudes. In some cases, the sales promotion itself is publicized using a traditional advertising medium, such as the Diet Coke commercials that ran after *Friends*. But although many advertising campaigns are carefully crafted to create long-term positive feelings about a brand, company, or store, sales promotions tend to focus on more short-term objectives, such as an immediate boost in sales of Diet Coke. There are exceptions, however. Perpetual promotions like McDonald's Monopoly game, Canadian Tire's "Canadian Tire money," and Tim Hortons' "Roll-up-the-rim-to-win" contest are all examples of sales promotions targeted to support or reward an existing customer base, rather than boost short-term sales.[42] Marketers also recognize that a series of short-term sales promotions can help to create long-term brand associations, image, and equity.

**Tim Hortons**
www.timhortons.com

Sales promotions are very useful if the firm has an immediate objective, such as quickly bolstering sales for a brand or encouraging consumers to try a new product. The objective may be to create enthusiasm among dealers who carry the product by convincing them to take a chance on a new product or provide more shelf space for an item they already carry. Thus, like advertising, sales promotions can be targeted to channel partners and to the firm's own employees in the form of trade promotions as well as to end consumers.

## Trade Promotions

Trade promotions take one of two forms. Some sales promotions give the retailer a discount on the product's cost or on the expense of advertising it to encourage the store to stock the item and be sure it's given a lot of attention. Other sales promotions generate awareness and increase sales by creating enthusiasm among salespeople.

**Table 13.5** Measuring Effectiveness of Publicity Efforts

| Method | Description | Pros | Cons |
|---|---|---|---|
| In-house assessment conducted by a public relations manager | Analyze media coverage in publications, looking for number of mentions and prominence of mentions. | Relatively inexpensive because the major cost is the manager's time. | Cannot guarantee objectivity in the analysis; crucial to specify up front what the relevant indicators are. |
| Awareness and preference studies | Assess company's standing in the minds of customers relative to competition. | Good for broad-based strategy setting or to demonstrate the progress of a large program. | Difficult to connect results to specific PR events and to identify which actions had what level of impact on awareness; very expensive. |
| Counting of press clippings | The basic measurement tool in PR. | Provides a quantifiable measure of press coverage; relatively inexpensive. | Quantitative only; does not consider the *content* of the press coverage. |
| Impression counts | Measure the size of the potential audience for a given article. | Because a similar measure is used to assess advertising effectiveness, provides a common measure for comparison. | Usually limited to the circulation of selected publications, so this method does not include pass-along readership; can be expensive. |

Source: Adapted from Deborah Holloway, "How to Select a Measurement System That's Right for You," *Public Relations Quarterly*, Fall 1992, 15–17.

**DISCOUNTS AND DEALS** One form of trade promotion is a price break. A manufacturer can reduce a channel partner's costs through sales promotions that give a discount on its own products. For example, a manufacturer can offer a **merchandise allowance**, which reimburses the retailer for in-store support such as shelving. A **case allowance** provides a discount to the retailer or wholesaler based on the volume of product ordered.

**INDUSTRY BOOSTING AND BOASTING** Other types of trade sales promotions increase the visibility of a manufacturer's products to channel partners (Table 13.6). Whether an elaborate exhibit at a convention or a coffee mug with the firm's logo mailed to clients, these efforts seek to keep the company's name topmost when distributors and retailers make decisions about which products to stock and push. These forms of sales promotions include:

- *Trade shows.* Hundreds of industry **trade shows** are held in Canada each year, and over 9000 shows are held in the United States. These are major vehicles for manufacturers to show off their product lines to wholesalers and retailers.[43] Large trade shows are often held in big hotels or convention centres where many companies set up elaborate exhibits to show their products, give away samples, distribute product literature, and troll for new business contacts. Some large Canadian companies, such as Home Hardware Stores Ltd. and Shoppers Drug Mart, focus their marketing strategies on private trade shows where key suppliers can interact more closely with buyers and store managers and do more deal making than is possible in a standard show where suppliers interact with many competing customers.[44]

  **Good or Bad Decision?**

In early 2003 SARS affected millions of people around the world. China was hit hard with the fatal virus and Toronto was second only to Asia in the severity of the outbreak. In response to the highly contagious virus, the World Health Organization (WHO) announced a travel advisory against the city of Toronto. In this time of crisis Toronto officials chose not to work with the WHO to try to help solve the problem. Instead officials denied the allegations and warnings, claiming that everything was under control and that the WHO was blowing the situation out of proportion.[45] The Toronto Mayor, Mel Lastman, even went in front of the world press to say that he had no idea why a travel advisory had been posted against his city. Toronto's defensive statements forced the WHO to further reinforce its warnings, and claims of city officials were further discredited by news stories covering the many SARS-related deaths in Toronto. After Toronto officials realized that their city's reputation was quickly tarnishing, they launched a $10 million dollar marketing campaign to attract visitors, including a nationally televised rock concert with the Rolling Stones. How could the public relations initiative by the city of Toronto been handled better? Was the advertising campaign a good decision?

**merchandise allowance** A promotion that reimburses the retailer for in-store support of the product.

**case allowance** A discount to the retailer or wholesaler based on the volume of product ordered.

**trade shows** Events at which many companies set up exhibits to show their products, give away samples, distribute product literature, and troll for new business contacts.

- *Promotional products.* We have all seen them—coffee mugs, visors, T-shirts, key chains, and countless other doodads emblazoned with a company logo. These are *promotional products.* Unlike licensed merchandise sold in stores, these goodies are given away free to build awareness of the sponsor. Although some of these freebies are distributed directly to consumers, many, like the 3M Post-It notes in Exhibit 13.14, are intended for channel partners, such as retailers and vendors, to build name recognition and loyalty.

- *Incentive programs.* In addition to motivating distributors and customers, some promotions are designed to light a fire under the firm's own sales force. These incentives, known as **push money**, may come in the form of cash bonuses, trips, or prizes. Mary Kay cosmetics is famous for giving its more productive distributors pink cars as a reward for their efforts. Involving employees in a promotion is a great way to get them excited about what they sell. When Frito-Lay sponsored a promotion giving away six million bags of their new Nacho Cheese Doritos around the United States in one day, one objective was to psych up its own employees. Frito-Lay had its salespeople distribute the free goodies to people on the street, and a full-page ad in *USA Today* featured employees who worked on the brand.[46]

**push money** A bonus paid by a manufacturer to a salesperson for selling its product.

**Frito-Lay**
www.fritolay.com

**rebates** Sales promotions that allow the customer to recover part of the product's cost from the manufacturer.

## Consumer Promotions

Since 1970, Gillette has run the Gillette Cavalcade of Sports promotion, using large prizes, huge display, and major sports stars to draws consumers across Canada into retail outlets to buy popular and less well-known Gillette products. Each year, it fine tunes the $2 million promotion to keep it fresh, but the basic strategy is impact—go big or go home. Year after year, it works, and the company experiences a 30 percent dollar sales increase during the event.[47]

Gillette's efforts and the Fido example, discussed earlier in the chapter, illustrate how major companies are creating unusual and attention-getting forms of promotion. As with trade promotions, sales-boosting efforts try to stimulate purchases by attracting consumers with price breaks or attracting their attention with novel incentive.

**PRICE-BASED CONSUMER PROMOTIONS** Many sales promotions aim for consumers' wallets. They emphasize short-term price reductions or refunds, thus encouraging people to choose a brand—at least while the deal is on.

- *Coupons.* Try to pick up any Wednesday newspaper without spilling a pile of coupons. Coupons are certificates redeemable for money off a purchase and are the most common price promotion. Indeed, they are the most popular form of sales promotion overall. Over 3.1 billion coupons are distributed annually in Canada, with redemptions valued at $100 million.[48] Consumers can also now find coupons online at sites like www.savingyoumoney.com.

- *Price deals, refunds, and rebates.* Manufacturers often offer temporary price reductions to stimulate sales. This price deal may be printed on the package itself, or it may be a price-off flag or banner on the store shelf. Sometimes companies offer **rebates**, which allow the customer to recover part of the product's cost directly from the manufacturer. Chapters Inc. offered a new twist on the common "scratch & save" promotion by offering Web surfers a chance to scratch a real-sounding card on their Web site.

- *Special packs.* Another form of price promotion is giving the shopper more of the product instead of lowering its price or

**Exhibit 13.14**

Many businesses put their logos on Post-It notes, used as a promotional item to keep their name in front of customers.

**Table 13.6** Sales Promotion Techniques: A Sampler

| Primary Technique | Target | Description | Example |
|---|---|---|---|
| Trade show | Industry | Many manufacturers showcase their products to convention attendees. | The National Kitchen and Bath Association organizes several shows a year. Manufacturers display their latest wares to owners of kitchen and bath remodelling stores. |
| Incentive program | Sales force | A prize is offered to employees who meet a pre-specified sales goal or who are top performers in a given time period. | Mary Kay cosmetics awards distinctive pink cars to its top-selling representatives. |
| Point-of-purchase displays | Trade and consumers | In-store exhibits make retail environment more interesting and attract consumers' attention. | The Farnam Company: As somber music plays in the background, a huge plastic rat draped in a black shroud lies next to a tombstone to promote the company's Just One Bite rat poison. |
| Push money | Trade | Salespeople are given a bonus for selling a specific manufacturer's product. | A retail salesperson at a formal wear store gets $1 every time he or she rents a particular tuxedo for a prom or wedding. |
| Promotional products | Trade | A company builds awareness and reinforces its image by giving out items with its name on them. | Beer companies send liquor store owners posters of attractive women wearing company T-shirts. |
| Cooperative promotions | Trade | Companies team up to promote their products jointly. | CompuServe and Universal Pictures ran a promotion for the mystery/thriller film *Sneakers*. CompuServe users were invited to break a series of codes contained in a special "Sneakers" file and win a trip to Hollywood. |
| Coupons | Consumers | Certificates for money off on selected products, often with an expiration date, used to encourage product trial. | Colgate-Palmolive offers 79 cents off a bottle of Teen Spirit deodorant. |
| Samples | Trade and consumers | Retailers might get a demonstration product to help in sales presentations; consumers get a free trial size of the product. | A small bottle of Pert shampoo arrives in the mail. |
| Contests/sweepstakes | Trade and consumers | A sales contest rewards wholesalers or retailers for performance; consumers participate in games or drawings to win prizes; builds awareness and reinforces image. | The Publishers' Clearing House announces its zillionth sweepstakes. |
| Bonus packs | Consumers | Additional product is given away with purchase; rewards users. | Maxell provides two extra cassettes with purchase of a pack of ten. |
| Gifts with purchase | Consumers | A consumer gets a free gift when a product is bought; reinforces product image and rewards users. | A free umbrella comes with the purchase of Lagerfeld's Photo cologne. |

Source: Some material adapted from Ajay Bhasin, Roger Dickinson, William A. Robinson, and Christine G. Hauri, "Promotion investments that keep paying off," *Journal of Consumer Marketing*, Winter 1989, 31–36; "One sneaky campaign," *Incentive*, November 1992, 93.

bundling another product for the same price.[49] Kraft Canada, for example, recently included Famous Player's movie coupons in a Post cereal promotion.

**ATTENTION-GETTING CONSUMER PROMOTIONS** Attention-getting consumer promotions stimulate interest in and publicity for a company's products. Labatt Breweries, for example, recently made a 14-stop tour of Ontario parks and beaches to promote its Kokanee brand of beer. The tour included a 7.5-metre-high inflatable glacier, bikini and muscleman contests, ultimate Frisbee games, and kayak races.[50] Some typical types of attention-getting promotions are:

- *Contests and sweepstakes.* A contest is a test of skill, while a sweepstakes is based on chance. Guinness Import Company's "Win Your Own Pub in Ireland" contest gave away an actual pub to winners of an essay contest "Why Guinness Is My Perfect Pint."[51] Tim Hortons' "Roll-up-the-rim-to-win" contest has become so ingrained in Canadian culture that Tim Hortons ran an advertising campaign in which a traveller "proved" Canadian citizenship by spouting the "Roll-up-the-rim-to-win" slogan.[52] A Kool-Aid promotion helped launch Kool-Aid Magic, a Kool-Aid product aimed at 6- to 12-year-olds that changes colour when water is added.

**premium** An item included without charge with a purchased product.

- *Premiums.* **Premiums** are items offered for free to people who have bought a product. A premium is often a novelty item, such as the free, removable tattoos called Barqtoos that Barq's root beer gives away to its customers. A Pokemon card in a box of cereal, a replica Stanley Cup in cases of Labatt's Blue, or a movie pass in Humpty-Dumpty potato chips are all examples of premiums. The latest craze in premiums is prepaid phone cards that enhance brand identification. Phone cards make ideal premiums, because they are compact in size, brand logos or graphics provide opportunities for repeat exposure, and the issuer can track card usage and build databases by determining where calls originate.[53] Labatt struck retail (and promotion award) gold for their Coldies—bottles of Labatt Blue dressed in a sleeve designed like one of 30 NHL teams (Exhibit 13.15).

**sampling** Distributing trial-size versions of a product for free to encourage people to try it.

- *Sampling.* How many people at one time or another have managed to scrape together an entire meal by scooping up free food samples at their local grocery store? **Sampling** gets people to try a product by distributing trial-size versions in stores, on street corners, or through the mail. Effem, the Canadian subsidiary of Mars Corp that owns the Whiskas brand of cat food used sampling, for example, to encourage cat owners to try Whiskas' wet pack product. It sent 250 000 samples to cat owners and increased sales by 20 percent.[54]

**point-of-purchase (POP) promotion** The use of signs or displays to influence purchases at the store.

- *Point-of-purchase promotion.* A **point-of-purchase (POP) promotion** attempts to influence consumers in the store by catching their attention with displays or signs.[55] Marketers are challenged to come up with new and innovative POP displays that will grab people's attention. For example, Bausch & Lomb conducted a promotion in Spain to encourage consumers with good vision to buy contact lenses to change their eye colour. The in-store display allowed shoppers to see what they would look like with five different colours of eyes before they actually inserted the contacts.[56] POP activities also include the use of *in-store media*, including placards on shopping carts or even closed-circuit television, which promote specific products. As the CEO of one company that produces these in-store messages put it, "Does it make any sense to spend millions of dollars talking to people in their living rooms and cars and then let them wander around a supermarket with 30 000 product choices without something to remind them to buy your product?[57]

**LOYALTY GENERATING PROMOTIONS** *Continuity programs*, *membership programs*, and *loyalty programs* are all terms used to describe the practice of awarding discounts, bonuses, or such other incentives as redeemable "points" to frequent and other high-value customers. These programs are increasingly recognized as the best retention-marketing tactic. They are used to recognize the importance of the customer, reward their ongoing patronage, establish long-term ties or bonds to the organization, and encourage loyalty. An added benefit is enabling the organization to observe and track their purchase behaviour. More than 71 percent of Canadian consumers participate in at least one loyalty program, and over 67 percent take part in four or five different programs.[58] While some companies such as Air Canada (Aeroplan) and Petro-Canada

**Exhibit 13.15**

Labatt "Coldies" are an example of a premium promotion.

(Petro-Points) have independent loyalty programs, smaller companies are able to participate in joint programs such as Air Miles, where points earned from purchases from a variety of participating organizations can be redeemed for travel on a number of sponsor airlines or for merchandise (such as theatre tickets) from member organizations.

## Promotion Strategy

Ideally, the objective of every sales promotion should be to cement the product's position in the marketplace. This may mean building awareness for a new product, enticing retailers to stock it, or kick-starting sales for an item during Christmas season. Once marketers have determined the objectives of a sales promotion, they must decide what the program will look like. If the objective is to encourage users of a competing product to try the item, a sampling program might work best. If the objective is to encourage loyal users to increase their interest in the brand, the firm might sponsor a contest or sweepstakes. If the company wants to increase its shelf space allocation, it might try a price break to retailers. Many marketers also are discovering the virtues of **cross-promotion**, in which two or more companies combine forces to create interest in their different products or services using a single promotional tool. Duracell, for example, recently teamed up with the Canadian Association of Fire Chiefs (Exhibit 13.16) to promote fire safety and support Duracell's Trusted Everywhere positioning.

A key issue for marketers is over-redemption: having too many customers redeem coupons, satisfy contest requirements, or buy cross-promoted product.[59] The classic example of this was Maytag Corporation's 1993 offer of free round-trip airline tickets to British customers who bought Hoover-brand appliances. The company placed severe restrictions on the dates of travel to limit redemption but hadn't counted on unemployed people buying the appliances just to go on the trip. It cost Maytag US$36 million to honour the promotion, and it then faced a flood of "nearly new" second-hand Hoover appliances being sold by customers who never really wanted the appliance. Marketers can now buy over-redemption insurance.

**cross-promotion**   Two or more companies combining forces and using a single promotional tool to create interest in their products or services.

## DIRECT MARKETING

We discussed direct marketing in Chapter 11 as a non-store form of retailing. Direct marketing also serves a communications function as direct mail and catalogues are print-based media that can be specifically targeted to customers and consumers. The Whiskas sampling program, previously described, was successful because the company was able to mail

**Exhibit 13.16**

A cross-promotion lets companies join forces to communicate about their products.

## SPOTLIGHT ON REAL PEOPLE     Cara's Winning Combo

Gabriel Tsampalieros CEO of Cara Operations, the parent company of some of the best-known Canadian restaurant chains, uses extensive consumer research and targeted marketing techniques to ensure the company meets and understands customer demands. Cara Operations has evolved from a Railway News Company in 1883 into a successful restaurant company that now boasts an impressive list of chains including Swiss Chalet, Harvey's, Second Cup, Kelsey's, Montana's, Outback Steakhouse, and Milestone's. Tsampalieros says Cara has its bases covered. "When you play in a geography like Canada with its limited population, you recognize that to grow a certain size, you have to have flexibility to play in different price points." Cara Operations envisions itself being the leading restaurant company in Canada; with this in mind, Cara created a central branding and research team in 1999. This team fully evaluated each brand, researched consumer's needs, and developed marketing campaigns and tactics to support their findings. This included a "brand intelligence gathering capability" that

cost $3 million dollars annually and meant developing a back-of-house support system to support the front-line brands. They gather information from 21 different sources, including focus groups, individual surveys, 7000 consumer interviews per year, and syndicated sources. The results of this branding initiative are becoming apparent today, and Cara's leading brand, Swiss Chalet, is spearheading the restaurant pack. Through restaurant upgrades, new menu offerings, takeout and delivery channels, increased advertising, special offers, such as Haagen-Dazs Ice Cream, and enhanced Web site interactivity, Cara hopes to attract younger customers, revitalize their image, and boost sales. Tsampalieros explains that each individual chain is going through some major marketing efforts each with tailor-made campaigns and initiatives, aimed at restaurant specific goals. Through marketing efforts, re-branding, and brand clarification strategies Cara hopes to attain its vision of becoming the leading restaurant company in Canada.[60]

1. How does Cara's market information support their marketing and communication decisions?
2. How else might Cara incorporate communications mix activities to enhance brand positioning?

## Valpak's Blue Envelope

• **Early Promotions**

1986 - 2001 Design Version

Initial promotions were instant win cash giveaways. Tailored specially for the Valpak envelope promotions were proprietary and did not co-brand with other products or companies.

Side 2 – Holiday Hundreds Promotion

A $100 Check May Be Inside!

$100 checks were seeded randomly into envelopes.

COX TARGET MEDIA, INC.

**Exhibit 13.17**

Cox Target Media is a firm that specializes in direct mail coupon promotions under the ValPak brand.

samples to 250 000 cat owners by buying access to a database of potential customers, having their own database from previous promotions, and by soliciting sample requests on their Web site. The key to successful direct marketing is having a solid database that allows organizations to select potential recipients that match the desired target profile. In Chapter 14 we will further discuss direct marketing and the use of databases as central tools in relationship marketing efforts.

Direct mail is becoming increasingly popular as a communications vehicle that supports other elements in a campaign. Rocky Mountaineer Railtours, for example, sent a direct mail piece to 20 000 empty nest couples who had previously requested a brochure. It drew a conversion of 3 percent (203 bookings and 511 guests) and incremental revenue of $1 million—a 25:1 return on investment.[61]

Direct mail is also used extensively in business-to-business contexts. Hewlett-Packard, for example, used direct mail to both channel partners and end-users as part of an integrated campaign to promote their SureStore AutoBackup Storage System for computer networks. For channel partners, it sent a box with the copy on the front that said, "Opening this Box is Guaranteed to Make You Richer." Inside the box were a $5 bill, product feature brochures, and a demo CD. Business executives and IT managers were also sent personalized direct mail pieces that directed them to a promotional Web site for the product. The campaign achieved a 6 percent response rate (1 percent to 3 percent is typical) from the business executives and resulted in a 32 percent increase in sales.[62]

A key benefit of direct marketing initiatives is the opportunity to elicit a measurable response from prospects or customers by directing them to a 1-800 number, or a Web site, or providing another way for customers or consumers to respond such as by mail or by fax. When a specific call to action is included in direct mail it becomes **direct response marketing**—marketing activity aimed at generating a measurable response via marketing communications.

direct-response marketing Marketing activity aimed at generating a measurable response via marketing communications.

## PERSONAL SELLING

The final piece of the promotion pie is personal selling, which is a far more intimate way to talk to the market. **Personal selling** is a company representative coming in direct contact with customers to inform them about a good or service to get a sale. Many organizations rely heavily on this immediate form of communication. The "personal touch" can be a lot more influential than information we get from mass media. And, for business-to-business marketers such as Xerox, personal selling accounts for a big chunk of sales. Many industrial products and services are too complex or expensive to be adequately explained or demonstrated in an impersonal trade advertisement.

personal selling   The part of the promotion mix that involves direct contact between a company representative and a customer.

Another advantage of relying on a good sales force is that salespeople are the firm's eyes and ears in the field. They pay attention to which competitors' salespeople are calling on customers, what new competing products have been delivered to their customers, and what new literature is on the customers' desks. Personal selling has special importance for students, because many graduates with a marketing background will enter sales jobs. Let's take a close look at how personal selling works and how sophisticated salespeople work hard to develop long-term relationships with customers.

### The Role of Personal Selling

When a man calls a 1-800 number to order a new desktop PC configured with a snappy DVD drive so his kids can play the latest Hollywood blockbuster, he is dealing with a company salesperson. When he sits in on a presentation at work by a computer technician who demonstrates a new spreadsheet software package, he is dealing with a company salesperson. And when that same man agrees over dinner at a swanky restaurant to buy a new computer network for his company, he also is dealing with a company salesperson.

For many firms, some form of personal selling is essential for a transaction (the sale) to occur, so this type of communication is an important part of an organization's overall marketing plan. Generally, a personal sales effort is more important when a firm engages in a *push strategy*, in which the goal is to push the product through the channel of distribution. As a vice-president at Hallmark Cards observed, "We're not selling *to* the retailer, we're selling through the retailer. We look at the retailer as a pipeline to the hands of consumers."[63] Personal selling also is likely to be crucial in business-to-business contexts when direct interaction with upper-level management is required to clinch a big deal—and often when intense price negotiations will occur before the deal is signed. In addition, inexperienced buyers may need the hands-on assistance that a salesperson can provide. Organizations selling products that consumers buy infrequently, such as computers, lawn mowers, and college educations, often place greater emphasis on personal selling, as do firms selling complex or very expensive products that need a salesperson to explain, justify, and sell them.

**Hallmark**
www.hallmark.com

If personal selling is so effective, why don't firms just scrap their advertising and sales promotion budgets and hire more salespeople? There are some drawbacks that limit the role played by personal selling in the communications mix.

First, when the dollar amount of individual purchases is low, it doesn't make sense to use personal selling. The cost per contact with a customer is much higher than with other forms of communication. After all, the median cost for a typical sales call is over $3200, due to salary, travel, a company car, and other expenses.[64] In comparison, the cost per contact of a national television commercial is low, even though the total cost to run the ad is high. A

30-second, prime-time commercial may be $30 000 to $40 000 (plus production costs) but with millions of viewers, the cost may be only $10 or $15 per 1000 viewers—little more than a penny per viewer.

Because salespeople—even if they are *really* energetic—can call on only a limited number of customers in a day, reliance on personal selling is effective only when a reasonable number of the customers the salespeople do see make a purchase. Because the cost of field salespeople is so great, **telemarketing**, in which person-to-person communication takes place via the telephone, fax machine, or e-mail is growing in popularity. Pharmaceutical companies Novartis, Janssen-Ortho, and Becton Dickinson, for example, make extensive use of telemarketing to launch new products. Armed with a good database and software that can handle 8000 to 10 000 outbound faxes per hour, they can communicate product information to all the 6500 pharmacies and dispensaries in Canada within one hour. They then follow up the same or next day with phone calls from a team of professional, knowledgeable telemarketers who can each place about 80 calls per day. This enables the pharmaceutical companies to effectively reach their target audience with timely information far more quickly than a regiment of in-store reps.[65]

The type of salespeople and the roles they perform vary in different firms. The person who processes a computer purchase over the phone is an **order taker**, a salesperson whose primary function is to facilitate transactions that the customer initiates. Most retail salespeople are order takers; but often wholesalers, dealers, and distributors also employ salespeople to wait on customers. The computer technician is a **technical specialist**, who contributes expertise in the form of product demonstrations, recommendations for complex equipment, and set-up of machinery. The technical specialist's job is to provide *sales support* rather than actually closing the sale, meaning that the technical specialist promotes the firm and tries to stimulate demand for a product to make it easier for others to actually make the deal.

Sometimes a person whose job is to lay this groundwork is known as a **missionary salesperson**.[66] Missionary salespeople promote the firm and try to stimulate demand for a product but don't actually complete a sale. And this support person may even be part of a sales team. Xerox, for example, competes for big accounts by sending out teams of specialists: Each Team Xerox includes customer service personnel, financial experts, and even top management in the case of important customers.[67] Finally, the person who actually convinces the customer to shell out for the computer network, probably after several weeks or months of discussions, is an **order getter**. Order getters work creatively to develop relationships with customers or to generate new sales. These salespeople find new customers, persuade customers to buy, and close the sale. Some marketers, such as Tupperware and Mary-Kay Cosmetics, recruit people to become order getters within their personal network of friends, family, and acquaintances (Exhibit 13.18). This network or multi-level marketing approach can be highly effective since the "sale rep" is someone who customers in the network know and trust.

## Approaches to Personal Selling

Personal selling is one of the oldest forms of communication, but the image of this profession has been tarnished by smooth-talking hucksters who would say anything to make a sale. In the latter part of the twentieth century, personal selling has largely redeemed itself as a profession. In most industries, it has moved from a transactional, hard-sell marketing approach to a relationship marketing approach.

**TRANSACTIONAL MARKETING: PUTTING ON THE HARD SELL** The *hard sell* is a high-pressure process. We've all been exposed to the pushy electronics salesperson who puts down the competition by telling shoppers that if they buy elsewhere they will be stuck with an inferior sound system that will fall apart in six months. These hard-sell tactics are a form of **transactional selling**, a sales technique that focuses on making an immediate sale with little or no attempt to develop a relationship with the customer. As customers, we feel

**telemarketing** The use of the telephone or fax to sell directly to consumers and business customers.

**order taker** A salesperson whose primary function is to facilitate transactions that the customer initiates.

**technical specialist** Sales support personnel with a high level of technical expertise who assist in product demonstrations.

**missionary salesperson** A salesperson who promotes the firm and tries to stimulate demand for a product but does not actually complete a sale.

**order getter** A salesperson who works creatively to develop relationships with customers or to generate new sales.

**transactional selling** A form of personal selling that focuses on making an immediate sale with little or no attempt to develop a relationship with the customer.

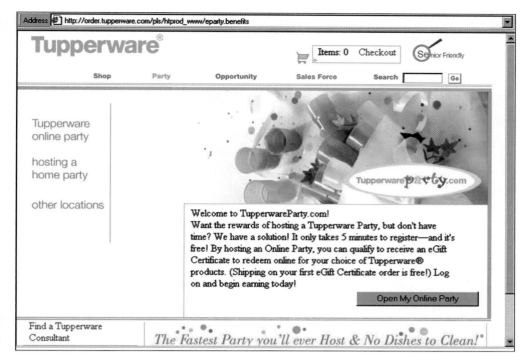

**Exhibit 13.18**

Tupperware parties used to be housebound. Now they can be held online!

manipulated by the hard sell and resent it. This technique and its depiction in movies like *GlenGarry GlenRoss* and plays like *Death of a Salesman* also contribute to the negative image many of us have of obnoxious salespeople. But not all transactional marketers are obnoxious. Jacques Gatien, president of Atlantic Promotions of Longueuil, Quebec (see Exhibit 13.19) has earned a reputation as the "jovial huckster." He is the brains behind a $115 million company that sells products like the Oskar snowbrush, Pant Saver car mat, Starfrit Rotato, T-Rex rake, and other useful products, using a combination of advertising and in-store demonstrations. His motto is: "The more you can use a demonstration to sell a product, the easier it is to sell."[68]

**RELATIONSHIP SELLING: COUNTERING THE TARNISHED IMAGE** Rather than transactional selling, today's professional salesperson is more likely to practise **relationship selling**—seeking to develop a mutually satisfying relationship with the customer.[69] Relationship selling involves winning, keeping, and developing customers. *Winning* customers means converting interested prospects into people who are convinced that the product or service holds value for them. *Keeping* customers means ensuring that the product or service delivers what was promised. *Developing* customers means satisfying them so that they can be counted on to provide future business.[70]

> **relationship selling** A form of personal selling in which the salesperson seeks to develop a mutually satisfying relationship with the consumer so they can work together to satisfy each other's needs.

## The Role of Personal Selling in the Communications Mix

The salesperson's job can be made easier with support from public relations and advertising. The business customer, having already seen the supplier's advertisements or product releases, is likely to welcome that vendor's representative. Responses to toll-free numbers included in advertising and sales promotions can provide hot sales leads to follow up with prospective customers who have already expressed interest in learning more about the product. And many salespeople obtain valuable leads at industry trade shows attended by thousands of prospective customers.

**THE SELLING PROCESS** Selling is seldom boring. Every customer, every sales call, and every salesperson are unique. Some salespeople are successful primarily because they know so much about what they sell. Others are successful because they've built strong

**Exhibit 13.19**

Jacques Gatien uses in-store product demonstrations to show customers how useful his products are.

creative selling process   The process of seeking out customers, analyzing their needs, determining how product attributes might provide benefits for them, and then communicating that information.

prospecting   A part of the selling process that includes identifying and developing a list of potential or prospective customers.

qualify prospects   A part of the selling process that determines how likely prospects are to become customers.

preapproach   A part of the selling process that includes developing information about prospective customers and planning the sales interview.

approach   The first step of the actual sales presentation in which the salesperson tries to learn more about the customer's needs, create a good impression, and build rapport.

relationships with their customers over time, and these people look forward to their visits to "chew the fat." And most salespersons understand and engage in a series of activities necessary to bring about a transaction.

Sales of complex or expensive products require careful planning. To be successful in these, the salesperson must follow the **creative selling process**—seeking out customers, analyzing their needs, determining how product attributes provide benefits, and then deciding how best to communicate that information to the targeted customers. As Figure 13.1 shows, there are seven steps in the process.

**PROSPECT CUSTOMERS Prospecting** is the process of identifying and developing a list of potential customers, called *prospects* or *sales leads*. Leads can come from existing customer lists, telephone directories, and commercially available databases. The local library usually contains directories of businesses (including those published by provincial and federal agencies) and directories of association memberships. Some companies generate sales leads through their advertising or sales promotions by letting customers request more information. One way to generate leads is through *cold calling*, when the salesperson contacts prospects "cold," without prior introduction or permission. Because it always helps to know someone rather than starting off cold, salespeople might instead seek *referrals* from other customers. Current clients who are satisfied with their purchase often give referrals, which is yet another reason to maintain good customer relationships.

**QUALIFY PROSPECTS** Just because people are willing to talk to a salesperson doesn't mean they will turn out to be good sales leads. Along with identifying potential customers, salespersons need to **qualify prospects** to determine how likely they are to become customers. Salespeople qualify prospects by asking themselves such questions as: Are the prospects likely to be interested in what I'm selling? Are they likely to switch their allegiance from what they are currently using? Is the potential sales volume large enough to make a relationship with them profitable? Can they afford the purchase? If they must borrow money to buy my product, is their credit history acceptable?

**DO A PREAPPROACH** The **preapproach** consists of compiling background information about prospective customers and planning the sales interview. Important purchases are not made lightly, so it is foolish for a salesperson to blindly call on a qualified prospect and risk losing the sale due to a lack of preparation. Salespeople try to learn as much as possible about qualified prospects before initiating a sale, such as their past history of purchases, their current needs, and, in some cases, personal information about their likes and dislikes.

Salespeople can find information about a prospect from a variety of sources. In the case of larger companies, financial data, names of top executives, and other information about business can be found in such publications as *Standard & Poor's 500 Directory* or the *Million Dollar Directory*. The inside scoop on a prospect, however, frequently comes from informal sources, such as noncompeting salespeople who have dealt with the person before. This background information helps salespeople to plan their strategy and the goals they will try to achieve when the prospect is contacted.

**MAKE THE APPROACH** After the groundwork has been laid with the preapproach, it is time to **approach**, or contact, the prospect. During the important first minutes when the salesperson initiates contact with the prospective customer, several key events occur. The salesperson tries to learn even more about the prospect's needs, create a good impression, and build rapport. If the salesperson made contact with the prospect through a referral, the salesperson will probably acknowledge this connection: "Barbara Price with Amida Industries suggested I call on you."

During the approach, the customer is deciding whether the salesperson has something beneficial to offer. The old saying, "You never get a second chance to make a good first impression," certainly rings true in this situation. A professional appearance is a signal to the prospect that the salesperson means business and is competent to handle the sale. Successful salespeople are always well groomed and wear appropriate business dress; they don't chew gum, use poor grammar or inappropriate language, mispronounce the customer's name, or seem uninterested in the job.

**MAKE THE SALES PRESENTATION** Many sales calls involve a formal **sales presentation**, in which the salesperson lays out the benefits of the product and why it is better than what competitors are offering. *Proof statements*, such as data on past sales, testimonials, guarantees, or research results, help to make the salesperson's pitch credible. And in the most effective sales presentations, the salesperson gets the would-be customer to participate by asking questions or, as we saw with Jacques Gatien, allowing the customer to try the product.

Some sales presentations are canned, which means a script has been written in advance and the same message is delivered to every prospect. This technique often provides a series of verbal prompts to which the customer is expected to respond in the desired manner. For example, office supplies salespeople might start all of their pitches with, "Would you like to see a new line of products that will revolutionize the way you run your office?" That standardized approach works fine in some cases, but the most effective sales presentations are those that are tailored to the specific needs of the customer. For example, a salesperson instead might say, "Would you be interested in getting better-quality report binders at a lower price?" after discovering during the preapproach that the office manager was under pressure from the boss to cut costs on office supplies.

Such technologies as laptop and palm computers, presentation software, digital projectors, and the Internet are enhancing the ability of sales people to make effective presentations. "Web-push" technology, for example, transmits information via any combination of telephone and Internet-enabled communication formats to a desktop computer, allowing presenters to simultaneously talk to, visually interact with, and otherwise communicate with remote audiences using in-sync multiple media formats.[71] Many marketing organizations, such as Fujitsu Siemens Computers and Tourism Queensland are putting multimedia product presentations demonstrations on the Internet, allowing customers and consumers to view them with more convenience (Exhibit 13.20).

**OVERCOME CUSTOMER OBJECTIONS** It is rare that a prospect accepts whatever the salesperson has to say and immediately makes an order. The effective salesperson anticipates *objections*, or reasons why the prospect is unwilling to commit to a purchase, and is prepared to overcome them by providing additional information or persuasive arguments. In fact, the salesperson should *welcome* objections, because they show that the prospect is at least interested enough to have considered the offer and seriously weigh its pros and cons. Handling the objection successfully may move a prospect to the decision stage. For example, the salesperson might say, "Ms. Robbins, you've said before that you don't have room to carry our new line of sleeping bags, although you admit that you may be losing some sales by carrying only one brand with very few different models. If we could determine how much business you're losing, I'd be willing to bet you'd make room for our line, wouldn't you?"

**CLOSE THE SALE** A common mistake made by salespeople is that they work very hard to open the door for the prospect but don't get the prospect to walk through that door. **Sales closing** occurs when the salesperson asks the customer straight out to buy the product and complete the transaction.

There are a variety of techniques good salespeople use to close the sale. A *last objection close* asks customers if they are ready to purchase, providing any concerns they have about the

Prospecting and Qualifying

↓

Preapproach

↓

Approach

↓

Sales Presentation

↓

Handling Objections

↓

Close

↓

Follow-Up

**Figure 13.1** Steps in the Creative Selling Process

**sales presentation** The part of the selling process in which the salesperson seeks to persuasively communicate the product's features and the benefits it will provide after the sale.

**Fujitsu Siemens Computers**
www.hpcline.com

**Tourism Queensland**
www.destinationqueensland.com/tq.cfm?pageID=167

**sales closing** The stage of the selling process in which the salesperson asks the customer to buy the product.

**Exhibit 13.20**

Tourism Queensland offers canned sales presentations to travel agents and consumers wanting more information on Queensland tourism products.

product can be addressed: "Are you ready to order if we can show you a 20 percent cost savings associated with using this software?" In a *trial close*, on the other hand, the salesperson acts as if the purchase is inevitable; all that's left is to wrap up the details: "What quantity would you like to order?" In some cases, the salesperson applies a bit more pressure by using a *standing-room-only close*, in which the salesperson indicates that if the customer does not buy now, there may not be the opportunity in the future. No matter what technique is used, it's important to close the sale rather than just assuming the transaction will happen "magically" on its own.

**FOLLOW-UP AFTER THE SALE Sales follow-up** includes arranging for delivery, payment, and purchase terms. It also means the salesperson is making sure the customer received the order and is satisfied. Follow-up also allows the salesperson to *bridge* to the next purchase. Once a relationship develops with a customer, the selling process is only beginning. Even as one cycle of purchasing draws to a close, a good salesperson is already laying the foundation for the next one.

## Sales Management

**sales follow-up** After-sales activities that provide important services to customers.

**sales management** The process of planning, implementing, and controlling the personal selling function of an organization.

No firm can succeed with just one star salesperson. Personal selling is a team effort, and this form of communication usually requires careful planning to ensure that a firm's salespeople are in the field when and where customers need them. **Sales management** is the process of planning, implementing, and controlling the personal selling function of an organization. These are some major decisions sales professionals who oversee this function must make.

**SETTING SALES FORCE OBJECTIVES** Sales force objectives state what the sales force is expected to accomplish and when. Sales managers develop specific sales force performance objectives, such as "acquire 100 new customers," "generate $100 million in sales," or even "reduce travel expenses by 2 percent." Some firms also state goals for customer satisfaction, new customer development, new product suggestions, training, or community involvement.

Sales managers also work with their salespeople to develop individual goals. *Performance goals* are measurable outcomes, such as total sales and total profits per salesperson. *Behavioural goals* specify the actions salespeople must accomplish, such as the number of prospects to identify, the number of sales calls they need to make, and the number of sales presentations they must deliver.

**sales territory** A set of customers often defined by geographic boundaries, for whom a particular salesperson is responsible.

**CREATING A SALES FORCE STRATEGY** A sales force strategy specifies how the firm will structure, size, and compensate its sales force. Each salesperson has the responsibility for a **sales territory**, a set group of customers. The territory structure allows salespeople to have an in-depth understanding of customers and their needs because they call on the same people repeatedly and get to know them on a personal level. The most common way to structure territories is by geographic boundaries to minimize travel and other field expenses. Thus, a sales territory might be Regina, Saskatchewan, the Prairie Provinces,

Western Canada, or even all of Canada, depending on the size of the sales force and how many customers are found in an area.

If the product line is technically complex or quite diverse, however, it may be better to structure sales territories based on different classes of products rather than location. This enables the salesperson to provide greater expertise to a set of customers with similar needs. Still another structure is industry specialization in which salespeople focus on a single industry or a small number of industries. For example, IBM went from a geographic sales force structure to one in which its salespeople were assigned to one of 14 different industries. In making the change, IBM executives cited a need to have salespeople who "speak the language of its customers and understand their industries."[72]

**IBM**
www.ibm.com

Putting a salesperson out into the field is an expensive proposition; so the number of people pounding the pavement for the company affects its profitability. For this reason, determining the optimal number of salespeople is an important decision. A larger sales force may increase sales, but it will also increase costs. A smaller sales force will keep costs down, but this strategy can backfire—competitors with larger sales forces may be able to develop strong customer relationships, because each of their salespeople doesn't have to call on as many customers.

**RECRUITING, TRAINING, AND REWARDING SALESPEOPLE** Because the quality of a sales force can make or break a firm, recruiting and hiring the right set of people to do the job is a top priority for sales managers. Many firms recruit people who are strategic thinkers, who have technical knowledge pertaining to the industry, and who have excellent interpersonal skills.[73] Companies use various methods to screen potential salespeople. Interviews reveal communication skills, interpersonal skills, and information about interests and capabilities. Paper-and-pencil tests can determine quantitative skills and competence in areas not easily assessed through interviews.

Although some people feel that a successful salesperson is born, not made, even the most skilled communicator has much to learn. *Sales training* allows salespeople to learn about the organization and its products and to develop the skills, knowledge, and attitudes necessary for high levels of performance. For example, training programs at Xerox focus on ways to identify customer problems. The Xerox Document University, a training facility with 250 classrooms and a curriculum of 180 courses, provides an 11-week training program for new salespeople and continuing training throughout the salesperson's career.[74] The publisher Southwestern Company runs a different sort of sales training program: Every summer, almost 4000 college students attend the company's sales school where they attend pep rallies (Exhibit 13.21), meet with sales managers, and learn how to sell books door-to-door.

An important way to motivate salespeople is by paying them well, and often this means tying compensation to performance. There are several payment systems commonly used to motivate salespeople. A *straight commission plan* is payment based solely on a percentage of sales the person

**Exhibit 13.21**
Sales schools train college students to sell by finding novel ways to motivate them.

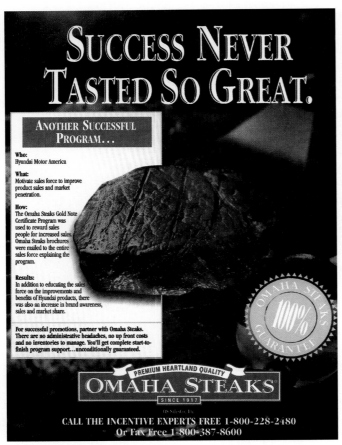

**SUCCESS NEVER TASTED SO GREAT.**

**ANOTHER SUCCESSFUL PROGRAM...**

**Who:**
Hyundai Motor America

**What:**
Motivate sales force to improve product sales and market penetration.

**How:**
The Omaha Steaks Gold Note Certificate Program was used to reward sales people for increased sales. Omaha Steaks brochures were mailed to the entire sales force explaining the program.

**Results:**
In addition to educating the sales force on the improvements and benefits of Hyundai products, there was also an increase in brand awareness, sales and market share.

For successful promotions, partner with Omaha Steaks. There are no administrative headaches, no up front costs and no inventories to manage. You'll get complete start-to-finish program support...unconditionally guaranteed.

**PREMIUM HEARTLAND QUALITY**

**OMAHA STEAKS**
SINCE 1917

**CALL THE INCENTIVE EXPERTS FREE 1-800-228-2480**
**Or Fax Free 1-800-387-8600**

**Exhibit 13.22**

Omaha Steaks markets to organizations looking for innovative incentive items.

closes. Under a *commission-with-draw plan*, earnings still are based on commission but the salesperson also receives a regular payment, or "draw," which may be charged against future commissions if current sales are inadequate to cover the draw. With a *straight salary compensation plan*, the salesperson is paid a set amount regardless of sales performance. Sometimes straight salary plans are augmented by use of a *quota-bonus plan*, in which salespeople are paid a salary plus a bonus for sales they make above their assigned quota.

In addition to basic compensation, many managers find that a variety of other incentives can also enhance the sales force effort tremendously. Such incentives can range from a free trip to the Caribbean for the top salesperson and his or her family to products like barbecues or steaks (Exhibit 13.22), or the always-appreciated extra cash. IBM invites all of their sales representatives who achieve their sales quotas and their spouses, or significant other, to "Club"—a three-day vacation / sales meeting at an expensive resort.

Although most salespeople like to work independently, supervision is essential for an effective sales force. Sales managers often require salespeople to develop monthly, weekly, and daily *call reports*, plans of action detailing which customers were called upon and what happened during the call. These reports allow the sales manager to track what the salespeople are doing in the field, and they provide marketing managers with timely information about customers' responses, competitive activity, and changes in the firm's customer base.

# Real People, Real Decisions

## How It Worked Out at Saputo Dairy Products Division

Demers and the Saputo executives chose option 2—to develop their own weekly cooking show, called *Cucina,* focused on Italian cuisine and how consumers could use Saputo cheeses to make fabulous dishes. They hired a well known food personality in the greater Toronto area named Rita DeMontis, who has been Food Editor at the *Toronto Sun* for over 25 years, guest chef personalities from famous restaurants, and a producer who was a food lover to help select recipes and ensure Saputo products were showcased in the best possible way.

This approach required less of an investment, could be tried for limited commitment and then reassessed, was focused on building demand through increased product use, and helped support the sales force in getting listings for the Saputo brand of Italian cheeses across the country. A similar strategy could then be used to develop demand for the Armstrong and Cayer family brands across the country—either by changing the theme of the show to more general cuisine, or developing a second show featuring Canadian cuisine with Armstrong products or multicultural cuisine with Armstrong and Cayer products.

Demers started with a series of 6 minute cooking spots, in Italian, in a one-hour news/sports show on TLN (part of basic cable in Toronto). Research of viewer attitudes demonstrated sufficient demand to produce thirteen 30-minute shows, in English, also on TLN. These shows in turn had sufficient following to justify the production of 39 episodes the next year, which attracted more than 100 000 viewers per show, key sponsors, and new distributors. With the ability to measure week-to-week changes in sales compared to the previous year using AC Nielsen data, Demers was able to demonstrate the financial impact of the strategy—sales at least tripled and sometimes increased ten fold.

Interest in the show was so high that Saputo began producing and selling a cooking magazine (now with distribution of 50 000 copies) and is selling DVD copies of its shows through major book retailers like Chapters. Demers recently negotiated to bring the *Cucina* show to Global, providing national exposure to his brands, an expected 400 000 viewers, and the ability to customize the Saputo advertising by region—which was not possible previously.

Implementation of the strategy was not without its challenges. What proved most difficult was coordinating a schedule that aligned featured stores and cheeses, and then creating or finding appropriate recipes.

# CHAPTER SUMMARY

## 1. Explain the advantages and disadvantages of alternative advertising media.

Television is an excellent medium for demonstrating goods, and particularly services for mass audiences. It is highly flexible from a creative concept perspective but very expensive. Radio is a cost effective way to reach selective audiences and spots can be created and changed quickly but products cannot be demonstrated and listeners do not often pay full attention to radio ads. Newspapers provide extensive market coverage and allow for informative appeals. People do not spend much time reading newspapers and they are typically thrown away once read. Magazines have a longer shelf life than newspapers, may be passed to other readers, and may be more targeted, but magazine ads can be expensive. Internet banner advertising, buttons, and pop-ups can be cost effective with measured results but they are easily ignored. Outdoor advertising (primarily billboards) can be effective in reaching broad audiences with simple messages but are not effective for complex messages.

## 2. Critique advertising.

The elements that go into a communication plan can be used as criteria to critique advertising. These include an evaluation of: the target audience, communication objectives, overall communications strategy, positioning and key messages, communication tactics, choice of communications mix / media, creative execution and ease of evaluation.

## 3. Explain the role of public relations and describe the steps in developing a public relations campaign.

The purpose of public relations is to build mutually beneficial long-term relationships and improve the image of an organization with key stakeholders, including consumers, the media, shareholders, legislators, and interest groups. An important part of this is managing publicity. Public relations is important in introducing new products; influencing legislation; enhancing the image of a city, region, or country; and calling attention to a firm's community involvement.

A public relations campaign begins with setting objectives, creating and executing a campaign strategy, and planning how the PR program will be evaluated. PR specialists often use print or video news releases to communicate timely topics, research stories, and consumer information.

## 4. Explain what sales promotion is and describe some of the different types of trade and consumer sales promotion activities.

Sales promotions are short-term programs designed to build interest in or encourage purchase of a product. Trade promotions include merchandise allowances, trade shows, promotional products, and incentive programs including push money. Consumer sales promotions include coupons, price deals, rebates, special packs, contests and sweepstakes, premiums, sampling programs, point-of-purchase promotions, and continuity (loyalty) programs.

## 5. Explain the important role of personal selling in the marketing effort and list the steps in the personal selling process.

Personal selling occurs when a company representative directly informs a client about a good or service to get a sale. Personal selling is more important for push strategies. Because of the high cost per customer contact for field sales, telemarketing is growing in popularity. Different types of salespeople include order takers, technical specialists, missionary salespeople, and order getters. Today's salesperson is less likely to practise transactional selling, that is, hard-sell tactics. Instead, salespeople today often engage in relationship selling, seeking to develop mutually satisfying relationships with customers.

The steps in the personal selling process include prospecting, qualifying the prospects, the preapproach, the approach, making the sales presentation, overcoming customer objections, closing the sale, and follow-up after the sale.

6. Explain the job of the sales manager.

Sales management means planning, implementing, and controlling the selling function. The responsibilities of a sales manager are setting sales force objectives and creating a sales force strategy, including specifying sales territories, recruiting, training, and rewarding salespeople.

# CHAPTER REVIEW

## Marketing Concepts: Testing Your Knowledge

1. What is advertising and what is its role in marketing?
2. What are the strengths and weaknesses of television, radio, newspapers, magazines, out-of-home media, and the Internet for advertising?
3. How can advertisers make sure their advertising is effective before it is placed in the media, and what criteria can be used to critique advertising?
4. What is public relations, what is publicity, and when are they likely to be an important part of the communication mix?
5. What is sales promotion? When is sales promotion more likely to be an important part of the communication mix?
6. Explain some of the different types of trade sales and consumer promotions marketers frequently use.
7. What is the role played by personal selling within the total marketing function?
8. What is the difference between transactional selling and relationship selling?
9. List the steps in the creative selling process.
10. Describe the major decisions made by sales managers.

## Marketing Concepts: Discussing Choices and Issues

1. Some people are turned off by advertising because they say it is obnoxious, that it insults their intelligence, and that advertising claims are untrue. Others argue that advertising is beneficial and actually provides value for consumers. What are some arguments on each side? How do you feel?
2. Technology through the Internet, television remotes, VCRs, and digital television is giving today's consumers more and more control over the advertising images they see. What are the implications of this for advertising as an industry?
3. Some critics denounce public relations specialists, calling them "flacks" or "spin doctors," whose job is to cover up the truth about a company's problems. What is the proper role of public relations within an organization? Should PR specialists try to put a good face on bad news?
4. Companies sometimes teach consumers a "bad lesson" with the overuse of sales promotion. As a result, consumers expect the product always to be "on deal." What are some examples of products for which this has occurred? How do you think companies can prevent this?
5. In general, professional selling has evolved from hard sell to transactional selling. Does the hard-sell style of selling still exist? If so, in what types of organizations? What do you think the future holds for these organizations? Will the hard sell continue to succeed?

## Marketing Practice: Applying What You've Learned

1. Assume that you are working in the media department of an advertising agency. You have been asked your opinion on which media to use for advertising for a local retail-clothing store.
   a. Write a memo that compares newspapers, magazines, television, radio, and outdoor advertising as vehicles for this media plan.
   b. Write a memo assessing the appropriateness of each of these media for advertising a national brand of dog food.

2. As a public relations professional employed by your college or university, you have been asked to develop recommendations for improving your school's public relations program. Write a memo to your college or university president with your recommendations.

3. Assume that you are a member of the marketing department for a firm that produces several brands of household cleaning products. Your assignment is to develop recommendations for trade and consumer sales promotion activities for a new brand of laundry detergent. Develop an outline of your recommendations for sales promotions for the new detergent.

4. Timing is an important part of a sales promotion plan. When is the best time to mail out samples, to offer trade discounts, to sponsor a sweepstakes? Assume the introduction of the new laundry detergent in question 3 is planned for April 1. Place the activities you recommended in question 3 on a 12-month calendar. In a role-playing situation, present your plan to your supervisor. Be sure to explain why you have included certain types of promotions and the reasons for your timing of each promotion activity.

5. You have been newly hired as a field salesperson by a firm that markets college and university textbooks. As part of your training, your sales manager has asked that you develop an outline of what you will say in a typical sales presentation. Write that outline.

6. As a sales manager for a firm that sells heavy construction equipment, you are evaluating the current sales force compensation plan. Currently, salespeople are paid straight commission, but you are thinking that moving to straight salary or a combination salary and commission plan might be better.

   a. With one of your classmates taking the other side, present your arguments for each option in a role-playing situation.

   b. In a similar role-playing situation, present arguments for different compensation plans that might be used in a retail-clothing store.

   c. In a similar role-playing situation, present arguments for different compensation plans that might be used by a new car sales force.

## Marketing Mini-Project: Learning by Doing

Many college and university students say that they are "absolutely, completely lost" when it comes to knowing what type of job they want, much less how to look for the ideal job. This project gives you experience in the beginning steps in the creative selling process; but in this case, your potential customers are potential employers and the "product" you will be selling is yourself. You might find the information included on the Pearson Education Canada Companion Web Site (**www.pearsoned.ca/solomon**) helpful for this project.

1. Your first task is to identify a list of characteristics of jobs you might find attractive—your target market. You may consider such characteristics as:

   a. Geographic location
   b. Size of company (local, regional, national, international)
   c. Type of business
   d. Job responsibilities
   e. Skills required

2. One method used by salespeople for identifying potential job prospects is through networking. Therefore, with one or more members of your class, seek to talk with other people for their suggestions and to find out if they know of any jobs that have the characteristics you have outlined for your target market.

3. Using the resources of your school or your college or university library, generate a list of potential employers that seem to match your target market.

4. Using library resources or personal contacts if available, find out as much as you can about each potential employer.

5. Based on the information you have gathered, classify these employers as A, B, or C leads. "A" leads warrant more of your time and effort. "C" leads warrant the least level of time and effort, because you have determined that their fit with your target market is not very good.

6. With your group, present your findings to your class.

## Real People, Real Surfers: Exploring the Web

A problem that has confronted marketers for several years is how to efficiently distribute coupons. Some companies find the Internet to be a useful medium for this. In fact, a number of Web sites have been developed solely for the purpose of distributing coupons, including:

**www.valpak.com**
**www.couponscanada.com**
**www2.hotcoupons.com/coupon/canada/**
**www.valupage.com**
**www.suzicoupon.com**

Visit several of these Web sites, or use an Internet search engine to identify other coupon sites. Then evaluate the different sites you've visited by answering the following questions.

1. Generally describe each coupon Web site you visited. What kinds of coupons were there? How do consumers take advantage of the offers?

2. What about the design of each Web site is most useful to you as a consumer?

3. Do you think the coupons offered by the Web sites are useful to many consumers? Do you think consumers visit the Web site on a regular basis? What do you think would be some of the characteristics of the type of consumer most likely to be a regular visitor to these sites?

4. As a marketer, would you be likely to try to distribute coupons for your products over the Web sites? Why or why not?

5. How would you improve each of the Web sites you visited?

## Chapter 13 Dairy Farmers of Ontario and the BC Dairy Foundation

Got Milk? This has been the mantra of milk marketers for years—and it is getting a little stale. Milk consumption levels have dropped dramatically for young adults between the ages of 16 and 23[75] and milk use in cooking has declined steadily among women 45 to 65.[76] Milk has a trial rate of 100 percent and is used in over 99 percent of homes, yet consumption is declining. Consumers know that "Milk Does A Body Good" and, according to Canada's Food Guide, they should consumer 2 to 4 servings of dairy products per day, but young people in particular have been leaving milk for other "pastures." The Dairy Farmers of Ontario and the BC Dairy Foundation have responded differently to this challenge.

The Dairy Farmers of Ontario (DFO) have retuned their highly successful Milk Calendar, a calendar/recipe book that is distributed to 2.3 million people in Ontario through newspaper

**Exhibit 13.23**

The Dairy Farmers of Ontario used celebrity endorsement and a milk calendar to appeal to young adult users.

inserts the third week of February. It is also distributed to a total of 500 000 people in Alberta, British Columbia, Saskatchewan, and the Maritimes (see Exhibit 13.23). The calendar is aimed at three audiences: core users, women 45 to 65 who are loyal, committed users who have used the calendar for over 10 years and will go out of their way to get one; infrequent users who tend to be 35 to 44 year olds who have used a Milk Calendar in the past but not every year and do not know how to get one; and low or non-users in their 20s and 30s who have not yet developed cooking and meal preparation routines.[77]

Focus group research in 1999 revealed that while consumers loved the calendar, they thought it was "tired," too conservative, and not moving quickly enough into easier, lighter recipes. In response, the DFO signed on Anne Lindsay, the "Light Hearted Cookbook" author as a celebrity endorser and her signature graced the Milk Calendar cover in 2000, 2001, and 2002. Milk sales driven by the calendar (measured by a detailed annual usage study) increased from 3.8 million litres in 1999 to 6.6 million litres in 2001 but began decreasing again in 2002.[78] Because milk sales generated by the calendar represent 12 to 15 percent of annual consumption in the province of Ontario, Joanne Morrison, program manager at the DFO, wanted to revamp the calendar to appeal to younger users and non-users.

To achieve this, the DFO switched celebrity endorsers in 2003 by signing on Christine Cushing, a young, trendy, celebrity chef and featured her and, for the first time in 27 years, a cow on the cover of the calendar. The recipes, tested for appeal, ease of preparation in Ontario malls with 200 women, and, later, taste with professionals and users, were also selected to have greater appeal to a younger audience. The DFO is also considering new distribution channels, such as in-store, to broaden its reach into the younger market.

The BC Dairy Foundation also wants to attract a similar younger user group, young adults 16 to 23, living at home. Through a series of focus groups the BC Dairy Foundation learned that these consumers were not overly negative about milk but used words like "boring," "old-fashioned," and "fattening" to describe the beverage—a brand image that the BC Dairy Foundation wanted to change. The focus group participants said they would like to be surprised by milk, and that they would like to see it behave in a non-traditional way.[79]

The BC Dairy Foundation teamed up with Palmer Jarvis DDB to organize a new and innovative milk marketing initiative, a campaign that would surprise both the primary target market and the industry itself. The "Don't take your body for granted" television and print ads asked teens: "What would life be like without your body?" The irreverent, memorable, humorous, and award-winning ads showed people with no bodies being dragged around by dogs and being thrown around a public transit bus. The ads generated significant talk about milk and changed its "boring" image among teen viewers.[80]

In addition to the amusing print and television ads, BC Dairy and Palmer Jarvis DDB came up with an advertising initiative that was totally different than anything done before; the Cold Crew street team. The Cold Crew consisted of three girls in white "Fembot" (Austin Powers) or Barbarella-style type dresses armed with misting water guns (that sprayed up to 24 metres) and three hip guys decked out in white tank tops and tear away pants. This crew toured around British Columbia promoting milk in a funky new way at both indoor and outdoor teen and young adult centred events. The crew was also equipped with "branding irons" that stamped crowds with cold crew logos, and while young adults were being branded or misted the Cold Crew guys would further entertain by breakdancing. The Cold Crew wrapped up their Milk Centred summer with the successful and original Cold Crew White Out Party in September.[81]

The Cold Crew paired with BC Dairy's humorous television and print ads helped the foundation achieve the seemingly impossible task of making a safe and un-cool beverage hip and sexy with teens.

## Things to Think About

1. Critique the strategies adopted by the DFO and BC Dairy Foundation. Do you think they will have a significant impact on milk sales?

2. What are the challenges in trying to position a brand differently for different audiences?

3. What other elements could have been incorporated in an Integrated Marketing Communications campaign?

4. As a brand or project manager responsible for milk, design a communications campaign aimed at increasing milk sales among people under 30.

## Trade Show

Trade shows and other public or private showcases of products provide an opportunity for entrepreneurs to talk with and show their products to key stakeholders, such as customers, distributors, and franchisees. To make effective use of the time and money involved in participating in a trade show, these entrepreneurs require a good strategy and an understanding of trade-show tactics.

There are more than 10 000 large trade shows and countless small ones in North America every year (some of the large shows can draw more than 18 000 attendees). Entrepreneurs need to pick the right shows with the right audiences to make the greatest use of their resources. Barry Siskind is a trade-show consultant with 13 years of experience in helping others make the best use of their trade-show dollars. Of the 100 or so objectives he has identified for a trade show, he encourages entrepreneurs to focus on two or three and implement a plan to achieve them. Segmentation is also key—he suggests that, of the possible 18 000 attendees, booth operators pursue the segment they would like to reach. With a good understanding of the target market profile and some thought given to qualifying questions, operators can identify the serious customers and spend more time developing those relationships. Siskind argues that the main job of operators at a trade show is to get people—not just anybody, but the real prospects—to like them.

He also has insights into trade-show tactics. Most people enter a trade show and immediately turn to the right. This has implications for the best booth locations and signage within a booth. U-shaped booths can be a problem because customers don't want to get stuck at the back. Siskind suggests putting a table in front of the u-shape so customers can get the key messages without coming all the way in. Corner booths draw more traffic, but the tradeoff is that they're more expensive. Although there are trade-show booth suppliers that have fancy $25 000 setups, you don't need to spend a lot of money on a trade-show booth. It's more important to be creative and build a booth with an appealing look or draw, like a retirement-planning company that used the back end of a Corvette with a surf board sticking out of it as its booth. Siskind also says that good product demonstrations are memorable; the challenge is to make them good through sound planning and practice. His parting advice? Avoid trade-show food.

## Questions

1. In what situations would trade-show participation be an important element of a communications mix?
2. How might trade shows be integrated into a broader Integration Marketing Communication Strategy?

Source: This case was prepared by Brock Smith and is based on *Venture*, "Trade Secrets," # 774.

# PART IV

Part IV

Part III

Part I

Part II

Societal Success • Business Success • Customer Success • Customer Success •

# Managing the Marketing Effort

**In Part III you learned about developing superior marketing strategies.** In this part you will learn how business organizations put these strategies down on paper (called developing a marketing plan) and how marketing strategies are actually implemented. You may be tempted to think that once a business develops and implements marketing strategy, its job is done. Think again. Smart businesses know that they cannot rest on past successes: if businesses neglect customers, customers will be lost to the competition. This part, therefore, also examines how businesses satisfy and retain customers for the long run.

# CHAPTER 14
## Developing and Implementing a Marketing Plan

### CHAPTER OBJECTIVES

WHEN YOU HAVE COMPLETED YOUR STUDY OF THIS CHAPTER, YOU SHOULD BE ABLE TO

1. Explain why firms develop and implement marketing plans.

2. Describe the steps involved in developing and implementing a marketing plan.

3. Highlight dos and don'ts in developing a strong marketing plan.

466 | Part IV: Managing the Marketing Effort

# Real People, Real Decisions

## Meet **Leonard Hendricks,** a Decision Maker at TELUS Communications

Leonard Hendricks is the Director of Product and Customer Marketing at TELUS Communications, a large Canadian telecommunications corporation. After a joint B.Sc. degree between the faculty of Business and the faculty of Agricultural Economics at the University of Alberta, Leonard joined the Agriculture division of Dow Chemicals doing inbound call answer for farmers and channel of distribution dealers.

From Dow, he moved to Andersen Consulting (now Accenture), where he worked on a consulting project for TELUS. He learned that TELUS was starting a data and IP company in Calgary. Excited by this opportunity, he joined other Andersen colleagues who had already left to work for the new TELUS company.

Leonard was motivated to choose this career path because he enjoyed business decisions and wanted to see the long-term impact of his work. While he felt consulting was a great way to learn, he did not experience the impact of his work as he moved from client to client. He says, "To me, the marketing department makes the main business decisions. Marketing generally decides where to invest scarce resources and priorities for a company to maximize benefits."

The achievement of which Leonard is most proud is when he was a core team member that performed the analysis for TELUS to expand nationally. "There was a lot of work on the new market opportunities, best approaches, etc. that enabled TELUS to invest substantial sums in this initiative," says Leonard. "Today, this non-traditional business generates over $800M per year in revenue for TELUS, which is about 18 percent of the total TELUS Communications revenue."

The non-traditional markets to which Leonard is referring are the geographic markets of Ontario and Quebec. Traditionally, TELUS had only operated in the British Columbia and Alberta marketplace. TELUS decided to expand operations in the East by initially offering Dial VPOP©. Dial VPOP are centrally managed dial-up Internet modems that are sold to Internet Service Providers (ISPs). The ISPs use the service to provide dial-up Internet service to end customers. While TELUS was a large provider of this service in the B.C. and Alberta marketplace, with the largest market share in that territory, the company was virtually unheard of in the Ontario and Quebec markets.

Leonard was faced with a classic pricing problem from a product management point of view. TELUS did not have a track record in the new markets of Ontario and Quebec but was known to most ISPs because it is the second largest telecommunications carrier in Canada. Most ISPs have either dealt with or have heard about the company. The new markets provided a challenge because TELUS would have to deal with a new set of competitors, different pricing structures, different discount plans, and different geographic needs.

Leonard considered three pricing alternatives in the new markets.

**Option 1.** Cost plus margin pricing. TELUS would calculate costs based on the investment required to provide a managed modem to an ISP. Costs would include all incremental costs to provide the service and a portion of the costs (sunk) spent to get the network in place. The advantage of this option is that TELUS would certainly cover the cost of providing the service to ISPs. It would have a predictable margin in line with company expectations. The main disadvantage of using a cost-plus-pricing model is that TELUS could charge less than the going market price and, therefore, leave money on the table. Alternatively, the cost-plus-pricing could be higher than the market price and TELUS would not sell enough.

**Option 2.** Market pricing. Other companies, including Bell Canada, the incumbent in the market, provided a very similar service. Pricing would be based on selling at the same rate as competitors. So, depending upon the price it charged, TELUS' margin would change. The advantage with market pricing is that you are aware of your competitors' pricing and can set your price accordingly. In this market, TELUS would have to decide where its pricing should be in order to attract business from competitors. "Market pricing is a great strategy to consider if gaining market share is a priority," says Leonard. The disadvantage of the market pricing approach is that market pricing is not always easy to determine. If the prices are not readily available, or the product is new and there are no major competitors, price benchmarks are difficult to attain. Another disadvantage of this option is that, if the market price were lower than your costs, you would have to sell the product at a loss. Finally, the market price could be greater than the price for substitute products and you may be missing a large portion of the market for the product.

**Option 3.** Substitute based pricing. The alternative for the ISPs was to build the service themselves, rather than buying a centrally managed service. This would entail having the right technical staff to install and manage the service and buying the piece components from the suppliers. By determining what the costs of the customers' alternatives were, TELUS would be able to justify their price based on substitute pricing. The advantage of a substitution model is that you understand the costs to your target customers and can talk to them about the savings they could expect from buying from you, rather than building it themselves. The disadvantage is you may price the service either too high relative to your competitors (and thus impact sales) or too low, below your costs. It may also be a meaningless measure against those that currently purchase the service from a competitor.

Now join Leonard's team at TELUS. Which option would you recommend in expanding to the new markets, and why?

## "IF YOU FAIL TO PLAN, YOU PLAN TO FAIL"

Whether a firm is a not-for-profit organization like the United Way, a family-based retailer like Army & Navy, or a major manufacturer like Bombardier, planning for the future is the key to prosperity. Success in the competitive world of business is not accidental; businesses that succeed do so because they are capable of developing and implementing *superior* strategies in the marketplace. A recent study tracking the fate of 160 businesses over a 10-year time period found exactly that—organizations that outperformed their industry peers did so because they developed superior strategies and they executed those strategies flawlessly.[1]

As we saw in Chapter 2, business organizations develop plans at three levels: strategic, marketing, and functional. We also saw that the marketing plan is a crucial document that links the high-level strategic plan with the functional (or operational) plans developed by various functions such as sales, HR, production, and finance.

This chapter is devoted entirely to the topic of developing and implementing marketing plans. Read this chapter carefully and practise the exercises at the end of the chapter and you will be in a position to develop winning marketing plans on your own!

## WHY DEVELOP A MARKETING PLAN?

The development of a marketing plan enables a business to set priorities regarding markets it wants to compete in (**market segments**), customers it wants to serve (**target customers**), and how it plans to serve those customers (**marketing mix strategy**).

Without such priorities, the firm will not have a viable product at a price customers are willing to pay, the means to get that product to the place customers want it, and a way to promote the product to the right customers. In other words, without the development of a sound **marketing plan**, the business tends to drift.

## WHAT HAPPENS WHEN A BUSINESS DOES NOT DEVELOP A MARKETING PLAN?

The underlying goal of all marketing strategies and plans is to create a **competitive advantage** for the business—to take what the company does really well and outperform the competition, thus providing customers with a benefit the competition cannot. A competitive advantage gives customers a reason to choose one product over another again and again.

Without a formal marketing plan outlining superior marketing strategies, most businesses underperform for years. Eventually, many of these firms go out of business. As we have repeated before, success in the competitive world of business is *earned*; it is not a right. When a business organization conducts itself without developing formal marketing plans, it faces many negative consequences as outlined in Table 14.1.[2] Without a formal marketing plan, businesses tend to engage in a lot of "pie-in-the-sky" thinking: "The market is worth $1 billion. All we have to do is capture 1 percent of it." This may be true, but without a formal strategy, how is the business going to capture 1 percent of the market?

**market segment** A marketplace opportunity or industry that a firm wants to serve (e.g., the pharmaceutical market segment, the retailing market segment).

**target customer** Customers that represent the best opportunity for a business (e.g., high-income consumers, large manufacturing organizations).

**marketing mix strategy** A combination of product strategy, pricing strategy, channel of distribution (place) strategy, and marketing communications (promotion) strategy that a business uses to satisfy the needs of the target customer.

**marketing plan** A document that describes the marketing environment, outlines the marketing objectives and strategy, identifies who will be responsible for carrying out each part of the marketing strategy, and describes how the strategy will be adjusted to respond to a changing marketplace.

**competitive advantage** The ability of a firm to outperform the competition, providing customers with a benefit the competition cannot.

### Table 14.1 Negative Consequences of Not Developing Marketing Plans

1. **The business tends to drift.**
   Lacking superior strategies, the business continually underperforms.

2. **There is a lot of "pie-in-the-sky" thinking, but no formal strategy.**
   Without formal strategies to compete in a tough marketplace, the business thinks about success, but it never comes to fruition.

3. **The business tends to waste resources trying one tactic after another.**
   Without a plan of action, the business attempts many things without knowing in advance the likehood of their success.

4. **The business lacks a "playbook."**
   A marketing plan is like a playbook for a sports team. Without a playbook, there is no accountability within different functions.

5. **There is no unity within the organization.**
   Lacking a "glue" that binds the business together, different functions work to optimize specific interests instead of focusing on the customer.

As a result, businesses without formal marketing plans tend to try one tactic, and if that does not work, they try another. They end up wasting resources. A sound marketing plan enables a business to utilize its limited resources in an optimum fashion.

As also shown in Table 14.1, a marketing plan is like a "playbook" for a sports team. Imagine the fate of a football team without a playbook! There would be complete chaos on the field. Similarly, as you will see when we turn to the topic of actually developing a marketing plan, a marketing plan clearly outlines a detailed set of tactics to implement each marketing strategy. So, everyone within the business knows exactly what they have to do and how long they have to do it.

Finally, as we saw in Chapter 2, the marketing plan provides a common foundation for the development of other functional plans (e.g., sales, HR, production, finance). Therefore, without a formal marketing plan there is no unity among the different functions in a business. Each function is motivated to act in its best interests, and not in the collective interests of the customer.

Table 14.1 explored the negative consequences of not developing superior marketing strategies encoded in the form of marketing plans. On the other hand, as shown in Exhibit 14.1, successful firms such as Sony succeed by understanding customer needs and developing superior offerings to satisfy those needs.

When Sony initially came out with a digital camera, it quickly captured over a 40 percent share of the market, even though its camera's picture quality was inferior to the competitions'. This is because Sony developed a superior marketing plan based on its understanding of customer needs. It correctly recognized that customers would be willing to sacrifice picture quality for ease of use. So, it developed a camera that would enable users to insert floppy disks into the cam-

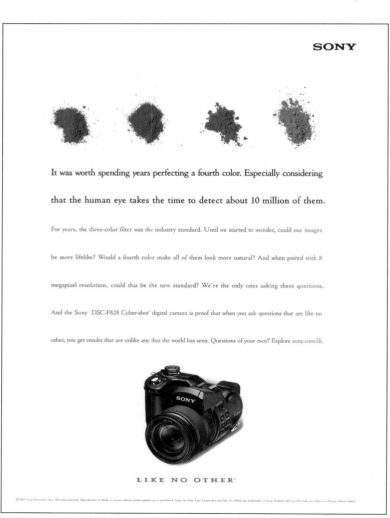

**Exhibit 14.1**

Sony succeeds by understanding customer needs and developing superior offerings to satisfy those needs.

era, take pictures, and instantly upload the pictures on their computers without the fuss of memory cards or cables.

## HOW TO DEVELOP STRONG MARKETING PLANS: THE MARKETING PLAN TEMPLATE

Table 14.2 outlines a practical template you can use to develop sound marketing plans. As can be seen from the marketing plan template, a typical marketing plan has 11 different sections. It is important to familiarize yourself with the general layout of the marketing plan. Although it may look complicated, the marketing plan actually is a very simple document that has *four* major sections as outlined in Figure 14.1.

The four sections are:

1. Understanding the marketplace in terms of customers, competitors, and other factors.
2. Designing marketing mix strategies to take advantage of marketplace opportunities.
3. Delivering the marketing plan strategies via tactical plans.
4. Managing the marketing plan efforts to ensure the plan is going according to schedule and making any necessary changes along the way.

The four major sections of the marketing plan play an important role in that the output from one section forms the input for the next section. Let us turn to this topic next.

## Using the Marketing Plan Template

Now that we have examined the marketing plan's overall structure, let us examine each of the 11 sections to see why they are there and what role they play in the overall marketing plan development.

**SECTION I. EXECUTIVE SUMMARY** The Executive Summary section is a one-page summary of the marketing plan. It shows the reader, at a glance:

Key challenges facing the business
Key strategies in place to achieve objectives
Key expected outcomes (financial and non-financial)

Therefore, reading the Executive Summary tells us what objectives will be pursued and how, and what rewards await us at the end of the plan period if we implement our strategies well.

**SECTION II. TABLE OF CONTENTS** After the Executive Summary section, a Table of Contents section appears so one can see what areas the plan covers. This helps the reader navigate more easily through the marketing plan.

## Good or Bad Decision?

It is not surprising that pharmaceutical companies' marketing plans call for heavy emphasis on new product development. These companies rely on a stream of new products to stay ahead of competitors. However, developing a new blockbuster drug is expensive, often costing in the hundreds of millions of dollars in R&D. To recoup the high cost of new product development these companies often charge high prices for their drugs. They do not lower the price even in countries where consumers cannot afford to pay high prices. Critics charge that pharmaceutical companies have a moral obligation to subsidize drug prices in poor countries. The pharmaceutical companies, on the other hand, counter that they would have no incentive to develop life-saving drugs if they subsidized prices. What do you think? Should pharmaceutical companies be mandated by law to sell their products at lower prices in poor countries?

**Figure 14.1** Major Sections of a Marketing Plan

**Table 14.2** Marketing Plan Template (see Appendix for sample marketing plan)

I.  *Executive Summary*

II. *Table of Contents*

III. *Current Market Situation. Format: 1 page text*
- What is the size of the market for the product (good, service, program, etc.)?
- Why is the market attractive?
- Sales potential (what percentage of this market can we expect to attain)?

IV. *Environmental Analysis. Format: 1 page summary text; 1 page competition matrix: ½ – 1 page trend data*
- Competitor analysis
  - Size
  - Goals
  - Market share
  - Products currently offered
  - Product quality/capability
  - Strengths
  - Weaknesses
  - How they currently serve *our* customer segments
  - Likely future moves
  - Other pertinent information that highlights their intentions in this market
  - Other competitors planning entry into this market
- Analysis of the Macro Environment
  - Demographic factors
  - Socio/cultural factors
  - Economic factors
  - Technological factors
  - Political/regulatory factors

V.  *Customer Analysis. Format: 1 – 3 pages text*
- General Statement (customers served in their needs)
- Customer trends likely to affect what (and how) customers buy and implications for our business
- Segmentation Analysis
- Customer Profile
  - Customer needs
  - Key decision-making criteria used by customers
  - Key personnel involved with decision to buy/not buy product

VI. *SWOT Analysis. Format: 2 – 3 pages of bullets*
- This is the most important section in the marketing plan. Spend a lot of time on it. The integrity of the plan depends on how you address this section.
- Opportunities/Threats Analysis
- Strengths/Weakness of Organization (to respond to opportunities and threats) Analysis
- Issues Analysis
  - What do data in sections III to V mean for us in terms of how we should be competing in the marketplace?
  - Main issues to be addressed by marketing plan based on above analyses

VII. *Objectives to Be Achieved by Marketing Plan. Format: 1 – 1½ pages*
- Financial Objectives
- Marketing Objectives (convert financial objectives into marketing objectives)
  - Size
  - Market share
  - New product objectives
  - Product modification objectives
  - Customer service objectives
  - Development of new markets

*(continued)*

**Table 14.2** *(continued)*

- Sales training objectives
- Other channel objectives
- Marketing communications objectives
- Pricing objectives
- Marketing research objectives
- Other Objectives

VIII. *Marketing Strategies. Format: 2 – 3 pages of text; 1 paragraph for each item*
- Product Strategy
  - Market segments selected and targeted
  - Product benefits
  - Positioning relative to competition (how different from competition)
  - Service strategy
  - Expected product life cycle
  - Expected product modifications/improvements; implications for new product development.
  - Development of new markets
- Channel of Distribution Strategy
- Marketing Communications Strategy
- Pricing Strategy
- Marketing Research Strategy
- Other Strategy (e.g., operations, human resources)

IX. *Tactical Plans. Format: 3 – 4 pages of text; 1 paragraph for each item; chart showing timelines and responsibilities very useful*
In this section provide details of the implementation plan. Specifically, for *each* item identified in the previous section delineate:
- What will be done?
- When will it be done?
- Who will do it (e.g., functional department or interaction between departments)?
- What help will be needed (resources)?
- Contingency plans in event of blockage of marketing plan?

X. *Budgets and Projected Profit/Loss Statement. Format: 1 page table*
May be included at start of marketing plan.
- Forecasted sales volumes, average realized price
- Cost of marketing plan elements
- Profit

XI. *Marketing Plan Control. Format: 1 – 1½ pages text; table for goals*
In this section delineate how the execution of the marketing plan will be monitored.
- Adjustment to be made to marketing plan
- Goals to be achieved by period
- Tracking of actual progress toward goals by period
- Corrective actions to be taken
- Information needed to track above; who will get the information; who will track progress; what mechanisms will be in place for corrective actions, etc.

SECTION III. CURRENT MARKET SITUATION In this section, we research the market in general to assess how attractive it is, what piece of the market we can expect to attain, what slice of the market our competitors already have, and other factors that may impact our ability to create value for customers.

SECTION IV. ENVIRONMENTAL ANALYSIS We do not operate in a vacuum within our markets. Our competitors are also trying to serve the needs of our customers through their *own* value-creation efforts. Therefore, in this section we first examine the competitive landscape to assess the strengths, weaknesses, opportunities, and threats facing our current and potential competitors.

Most importantly, we keep an eye on how they serve the needs of market segments in which we operate. Therefore, one goal of this section is to provide us with an indication of how well our competitors are doing and an early warning of actions we might need to take in our unceasing efforts to satisfy the needs of our customers. Also, in this section we examine some macro-environmental factors such as demographics, culture, and politics to assess any impact on our business. For example, we would need to know if the population is aging and how this factor would affect our business.

**SECTION V. CUSTOMER ANALYSIS** The ultimate focus of our value creation efforts is the customer. The only competitive advantage an organization has is its ability to understand and satisfy the needs of its customers. Therefore, in this section we examine customer needs and how these may be changing over time. At the end of Section V, we have completed a scan of the major forces in the marketplace. We are now ready to synthesize this information to see what it means to us (in our capabilities to serve our customers).

**SECTION VI. SWOT ANALYSIS** Collecting information about the marketplace in Sections III to V will not help us very much unless we reduce this information so we can answer one basic question: What does this all mean for us? In other words, we are asking: What are the business implications of the information we have collected about the marketplace?

Therefore, in this section we first examine the major opportunities and threats facing us in the marketplace based on our assessment in the previous sections. Then, we analyze our ability to respond to these opportunities and threats. We do this by examining our strengths and weaknesses. What we have just conducted is a SWOT analysis (strengths, weaknesses, opportunities, and threats analysis). Finally, we reduce this information by writing down the main issues our marketing plan will address based on the above analysis.

For example, our SWOT analysis may reveal that mid-size customers are an attractive opportunity, but we do not have any experience serving this market. Therefore, one key issue to be addressed by the marketing plan next year is developing capabilities (e.g., goods and services) to serve the needs of this market segment.

As you can see, up to this point, we have assessed the marketplace and we have come to certain conclusions about what major issues we will have to address during the next year. At this point it should be fairly clear what actions we will need to take to serve the market well and be an effective competitor. In other words, the marketing plan should *almost* write itself (with your help!).

**SECTION VII. OBJECTIVES TO BE ACHIEVED BY MARKETING PLAN** In the previous section we identified the major issues to be addressed by the marketing plan. However, if we left it at that, we would not have any way of monitoring the success or failure of the marketing plan. Therefore, we need to establish certain objectives to be achieved by the plan.

In this section we begin by establishing financial objectives to be achieved by the marketing plan. These objectives are stated in the form of revenues and profits. Next, we convert these financial objectives into actionable marketing objectives and highlight other functional objectives, if appropriate (e.g., sales, HR). Writing down financial objectives by themselves will not ensure that we actually achieve them. We have to perform some marketing actions to make an impact in the marketplace and thereby achieve our financial objectives. These marketing objectives enable us to develop specific marketing actions. We turn to this in the next section.

**SECTION VIII. MARKETING STRATEGIES** This section is the engine that drives the marketing plan. It outlines our efforts to create value for customers using marketing mix elements and to garner a competitive advantage for ourselves in the marketplace. We also outline any other strategies we may have to implement in our efforts to satisfy customers. Strategies by themselves will not enable us to create value for our customers unless we implement them successfully. In the next section we outline implementation (tactical) plans.

**SECTION IX. TACTICAL PLANS** In this section we examine our strategies in the previous section and, for *each* strategy, we delineate our tactical plans. We have to be very specific about what needs to be done (action steps), when it will be done, who will do it, what resources will be needed, and what we will do in case of "roadblocks" to our plan. Many marketing plans go astray because they lack this section. This is the way we assign responsibility for implementing the plan and ensuring that the plan does not get placed on a shelf somewhere to be forgotten.

**SECTION X. BUDGETS AND PROJECTED PROFIT/LOSS STATEMENT** In this section we examine what rewards we hope to attain if we design and implement our strategies correctly. We examine what revenues our marketing plan efforts will generate and what it will cost us to do business (budgets). A comparison of the two items shows a profit or loss.

**SECTION XI. MARKETING PLAN CONTROL** A marketing plan is a living, breathing document. As such, it needs to be monitored constantly to ensure goals are being met and progress is being made. If not, corrective actions should be taken to bring the plan back on track. Notice that in this section we assign responsibility for collecting information to assess whether the plan is on track or not. Without this crucial section a marketing plan is just another document that gets written but is not acted upon.

## DOS AND DON'TS IN DEVELOPING A STRONG MARKETING PLAN

Table 14.3 lists dos and don'ts that need to be followed to develop strong marketing plans.

As we discussed in Chapter 2, the marketing plan is the foundation upon which all other plans are built. Therefore, keep the focus of the marketing plan on *major* strategies and tactics to be implemented during the time period (i.e., one year) to create value for your customers. *Do not try to do it all next year.* As has been wisely suggested, you are better off being short on strategy and long on implementation, rather than the other way around.[3]

A good marketing plan should be a highly *actionable* document. So, keep the plan short (approximately 25–30 pages) and simple. As necessary, individual "brand" plans may be developed for each product (e.g., goods, services offered, programs). Do not provide information (especially in sections III to V) that is interesting but does not directly impact your strategies to serve customers. Put all supporting material in an appendix and be sure to reference appendix material in the main body of the plan.

## SPOTLIGHT ON REAL PEOPLE    Sangam Dairy

Anil Rao, the managing director of a small dairy in India, has to develop a marketing plan. His dairy buys milk directly from farmers, packages the milk in plastic pouches, and sells the product through India's weak channels of distribution. The problem with plastic pouches is that because the "cold chain" (refrigeration in the channel of distribution) is not well developed in India, milk has a tendency to spoil, and therefore, homemakers boil (and often re-boil) the milk before using it.

Mr. Rao is thinking of introducing milk in an innovative packaging format from Europe. Although still needing refrigeration, the new packaging can stand non-refrigerated formats better than the plastic pouch. Mr. Rao's biggest challenge is how to communicate the superior benefits of his package (i.e., no need to boil milk before use), change entrenched household behaviour, and charge a price premium for his product.

1. What recommendations do you have for Mr. Rao in terms of marketing plan development?
2. What factors should Mr. Rao keep in mind as he develops his marketing strategy?
3. Which elements of the marketing mix do you think should be emphasized in this problem? Are all elements equally important? In either case, provide a rationale for your answer.

**Table 14.3 Dos and Don'ts in Developing Strong Marketing Plans**

**Do:**
- Focus on key strategies and tactics
- Keep the marketing plan short and actionable
- Focus on the "so what" of data, and not on the data itself
- Develop marketing plan for a period of one year, but meet periodically to assess progress and examine marketing plan assumptions.

**Do not:**
- Forget that the marketing plan template is directional
- Forget that marketing is everyone's job

To ensure you have a short and actionable plan, focus on the "so what" of data and not on the data itself. Spend time gathering relevant information (sections III to V) and then spend a *lot* of time thinking about what the information means (section VI). This time, invested up-front, is well spent and will enable you to develop meaningful strategies and tactics as you write the plan.

Unfortunately, many marketing plans end up being very voluminous and not actionable because the marketing strategist did not follow the advice of focusing on data implications and not on the data themselves. Do not fall into this trap.

The marketing plan should be developed for a period of one year. However, it is necessary to meet periodically (e.g., every quarter) to assess progress and make any corrections to the plan.

Do not forget that the marketing plan template in this chapter is *directional*. This means that you should not view the template as a checklist. Examine each section carefully and assess what it is asking of you. For example, in the section on competitor analysis, only one thing is paramount: What are your competitors doing to take business away from you? The

# Real People, Real Decisions

## How It Worked Out at TELUS Communications

Leonard Hendricks and his team chose option 2, the market-based pricing model. TELUS wanted to enter the market with pricing in line with its competitors. This pricing model was chosen to ensure that TELUS would not be seen as too "cheap" (which would compromise the TELUS brand if the product was priced too low) or alternatively that the product would not be priced too high (and customers would not take TELUS' desire to enter this market seriously).

The end result? TELUS ended up winning several large contracts to provide service to ISPs. These contracts provide millions of dollars of profitable revenue a year to TELUS' new non-traditional operating area. Customers experienced few problems because of TELUS' experience. The Dial VPOP product enabled the company to sell additional services to the target market of ISPs.

What lessons has Leonard learned the most in his career? "Underestimating the critical need to communicate your strat-

egy, ideas, plans, and decision rationale. It sounds trite, but you can't over-communicate. In any organization, it is the people that enable your best ideas or plans to succeed. And, it is people that generally cause them to fail," says Leonard.

What advice does he have for students in preparing for a productive career? Leonard says, "Find things that interest you and pursue them. They may not be directly related to what you are studying, but don't let that stop you. If you are bored or aren't challenged you won't be successful. The thing I enjoy most about the telecommunications industry is the constant change and learning opportunities. Continual learning keeps me challenged, which is the key to enjoying your job." He also says, "Make the time before/during/after school to go to another country and travel (and work). The life experience will help tremendously and once you start working it is very difficult to get a long period of time to do it."

rest (e.g., competitor size, strengths, weaknesses) is merely background material to help you in your analysis.

Finally, do not forget that marketing is everyone's job. It is not the sole domain of the marketing department. A good marketing plan unites the entire business organization. As a marketing strategist, it is your job to champion the customer within your organization and educate others on the salient points contained within the marketing plan.

# CHAPTER SUMMARY

### 1. Explain why firms develop and implement marketing plans.

Smart businesses know that "If you fail to plan, you plan to fail." Firms, both in the for-profit and not-for-profit sector, develop and implement marketing plans because it is through sound marketing planning that they are able to utilize their resources most effectively and achieve their marketing objectives. Organizations that do not develop and implement marketing plans tend to drift because they lack superior strategies and, therefore, the business continually underperforms. A sound marketing plan is like a "playbook" for a sports team. It provides a common direction for all functions and, in this way, unites the entire organization.

### 2. Describe the steps involved in developing and implementing a marketing plan.

The marketing planning process, as demonstrated by the marketing plan template, begins with a thorough analysis of the external environment facing the firm. This includes the current market situation to ascertain marketplace attractiveness, competitor analysis, analysis of the macro environment (such as cultural or technological trends), and analysis of customer needs and trends. Taken together, the external analysis provides the firm with a set of opportunities and threats.

Next, the business evaluates the external opportunities and threats by completing a SWOT analysis. Based on the SWOT analysis, the business organization highlights key issues it must address the following year and develops some key financial and non-financial objectives it wants to achieve. The next steps in the development and implementation of a marketing plan are to formulate marketing strategies using the marketing mix elements, outline detailed tactical plans, provide budgets and profit/loss statements, and put in place mechanisms to control the implementation of the plan.

### 3. Highlight dos and don'ts in developing a strong marketing plan.

A strong marketing plan is an actionable marketing plan. To achieve this, the marketer should focus on the key strategies and tactics, keep the plan short and simple, focus on data analysis (and not the data themselves), understand that the marketing plan template is *not* a checklist, and educate the rest of the organization on the needs of the customer and major sections of the marketing plan.

Key Terms

competitive advantage, p. 467

market segment, p. 467

marketing mix strategy, p. 467

marketing plan, p. 467

target customer, p. 467

# CHAPTER REVIEW

## Marketing Concepts: Testing Your Knowledge

1. Draw a figure explaining the relationship between a strategic plan, marketing plan, and functional plan.

2. What are the key differences between a strategic plan and a marketing plan?

3. List five reasons why firms should develop marketing plans.

4. List the steps needed to develop and implement a sound marketing plan.

5. What is SWOT analysis? Why should you examine opportunities and threats *before* you examine organization strengths and weaknesses?

6. Why is it important to have a control section in a marketing plan?

7. List five dos and don'ts when developing strong marketing plans.

## Marketing Concepts: Discussing Choices and Issues

1. In this chapter, we asserted that the marketing plan provides a common foundation for the development of other functional plans. Do you see any problems with this approach?

2. Can you think of any situations where a business may not want to develop a marketing plan?

3. Critique the marketing plan template provided in this chapter. Are there any sections missing? If so, what are they? If not, provide a rationale for your answer.

## Marketing Practice: Applying What You've Learned

1. Conduct a SWOT analysis for each of the products below and outline three key issues facing these products in the next three to five years:

   a. Harley Davidson motorcycles

   b. Levi's jeans

   c. Boeing aircraft

   d. McDonald's

## Marketing Mini-Project: Learning by Doing

The purpose of this project is to gain an understanding of developing marketing plans through actual experience.

1. Select one of the following:

   a. An existing product (e.g., Crest toothpaste, John Deere tractors)

   b. An existing business (e.g., Apple Computers, your local dry cleaning establishment)

   c. A product or business you want to launch

2. Next, develop a marketing plan for your product or business. For an existing product you may have to draw certain conclusions based on your research. For example, comparing toothpaste brands in a supermarket will enable you to understanding pricing, packaging, and positioning. Depending on your product or business choice, you may not have the capability to develop detailed tactical plans (e.g., for Crest toothpaste, it will be hard to develop tactical plans; for your local dry cleaning establishment this should present no problem).

3. Present your results as a set of recommendations the product or business should follow to be a better competitor.

## Real People, Real Surfers: Exploring the Web

For the four products in the Applying What You've Learned Section, visit the company's Web site and answer these questions.

1. What objectives does the organization hope to achieve in the next five years?

2. What customers does the organization want to serve?

3. What is the external environment facing the firm (e.g., competitors, macro environmental factors)?

4. Do you think the organization's strategies are in line with the SWOT analysis you have done?

5. Develop a report based on your findings and present your recommendations to the class.

For the first time since the collapse of the Nasdaq stock market in 2000, investors are clamouring to give billions of dollars to a company that is only a few years old and whose stock may not perform well even if its business booms.[4] The company's potential is enormous, but so are its risks.

Sergey Brin and Larry Page founded Google, the dominant Web search engine, which is already profitable and appears to have strong competitive advantages. But, the company also has several question marks. For one thing, its management, for the most part, is young and inexperienced. Also, its marketing strategy is long on rhetoric, but short on specifics. To justify the high price investors are willing to pay for its stock, analysts say Google has to continue growing for many years.

That growth is far from certain. While such companies as McDonald's and Starbucks grew into the multiples of profit that investors paid for their stock price, most companies never do. McDonald's and Starbucks have very well-defined marketing strategies in place, but the same cannot be said for Google.

Although in 2003, Google had $962 million in sales and $106 million in profits, these figures are overstated because Google had unusually high tax and option expenses. What worries analysts, in the end, is Google's lack of a clear marketing strategy on how it plans to compete with its nearest rivals, Yahoo and Microsoft.

Documents filed with the Securities and Exchange Commission contain repeated pronouncements about the evils of Wall Street and its focus on short-term profits. But, the SEC filing is short on specifics about Google's business. It lacks details on important contracts between Google and its partners like America Online. Nor does it include any metrics used to measure corporate health such as number of new customers (advertisers) signed, the size of its audience, or the average price Google charges advertisers.

Scott Black, president of Delphi Management, an institutional investment firm, agrees with the accusation against Wall Street (short-term focus), but has this to say: "You've got to take people through the building blocks of business production, finance, marketing, and people. You have to give them at least some idea of what your strategic plan is." Continues Mr. Black, "Can they articulate where they're strong and where they're weak? Just to say we know more than you, that smacks of arrogance."

Source: Adapted from Alex Berenson, "Yesterday's Back! At Last, an I.P.O. to Drool Over," *The New York Times*, 2 May 2004, section 3, page 5.

## Things to Think About

1. What are some key marketing strategy issues facing companies in this industry?

2. Can you develop a SWOT analysis for Google based on your knowledge of developing marketing plans?

3. Would you invest in Google based on your knowledge of the importance of developing a superior marketing strategy? Why or why not?

## Caribbean Beer—Part 2

Although Chapter 14 reminds us that "if you fail to plan, you plan to fail," we see in the video on Banks beer that Alysha and Paula do not appear to be running their business by developing marketing plans. Rather, their approach is very typical of young entrepreneurial companies—operating by the seat of their pants, doing whatever it takes to keep the beer bottled and customers satisfied.

This is a tough business to be successful in—the major breweries control over 90 percent of the market, and over half of all new microbreweries fail.

Throughout the winter months, the brewery is plagued by machinery problems. In March, production stops for three weeks while parts are ordered from Germany. In desperation, Alysha hires a priest to bless the machinery, in the hopes that this will solve their mechanical problems. To complicate matters, the two sisters have to deal with family politics, employee turnover, missing labels, off-tasting products, rising production costs, and hard-bargaining customers.

As we see towards the end of the video, the business appears to be successful (it is at least breaking even) and things appear to have settled down. Alysha has cut costs by ten percent by going with a cheaper bottler, Banks beer is distributed in 350 stores across Ontario, the brewery is still supplying Grace (the Caribbean food distributor), and hopefully the machinery bugaboos will disappear with the blessing of the priest!

## Questions

1. Evaluate Alysha and Paula's approach to business, which appears to be one of doing whatever it takes to keep the operation moving forward. Do you think their lack of a formal marketing plan will hurt them? Why or why not?
2. Conduct a SWOT analysis for Alysha and Paula's business.
3. If you were hired by their company to develop a marketing plan, what top three to five issues do you think would be key to its success?

Source: This case was prepared by Ajay Sirsi and is based on "Caribbean Beer," *Venture* #889.

# CHAPTER 15
## Customer Satisfaction and Retention

### CHAPTER OBJECTIVES

WHEN YOU HAVE COMPLETED YOUR STUDY OF THIS CHAPTER, YOU SHOULD BE ABLE TO

1. Understand the importance of monitoring customer satisfaction and customer retention.

2. Describe what causes customer satisfaction and dissatisfaction.

3. Describe methods to measure customer satisfaction.

4. Explain why business organizations go beyond measuring customer satisfaction to monitoring customer retention.

5. Explain the importance of Customer Relationship Management (CRM) and describe how it works.

# Real People, Real Decisions

## Meet **Jamie Chiarotto,** a Decision Maker at TD Canada Trust

Jamie Chiarotto recently completed a Bachelor's in Business Administration degree at the Schulich School of Business at York University, specializing in both Marketing and Finance. Throughout his business school studies, Jamie worked part-time at TD Canada Trust, starting as a Customer Service Representative in 1999, and working his way to his present position as a Financial Services Representative. His tasks at TD Canada Trust include offering investment recommendations based on current market conditions and client needs and providing advice on, and issuing, loans, lines of credit, and mortgages.

Jamie says that the moment he began his business studies he knew that marketing and finance would be his two passions. In his studies Jamie learned that building a brand is a bottom-up phenomenon. Businesses have to ensure that every contact their customers have with their brands is a positive experience. So, at TD Canada Trust, he ensures that whenever he meets with a client he adapts to their particular needs. He wants to make them feel comfortable in their dealings with the financial institution.

Two gentlemen who had recently partnered up in a private business venture together had decided to come to TD Canada Trust to inquire about the services the bank could potentially provide them as they started their business endeavours. They each operated one of two retail businesses in the Greater Toronto Area and were looking at the different financial institutions to see which one would best suit their needs. When Jamie met with them about their small business banking services they told him the following:

- They needed comprehensive chequing account services for each of the two locations.
- They needed some sort of operating line of credit facility for each of the two locations. They suggested that they would like to each have their own line of credit for the location that they ran.
- They were extremely busy and were operating on a very strict time deadline.

The partners left Jamie the appropriate documentation and told him to be in touch within 24 hours. He had to act quickly and put together a package for the business partners. The decision involved a number of products and he had to decide the best design for a small-business-banking bundle that would meet all of their immediate and long-term needs. The problem arose when he discovered that one of the two business partners would have difficulty obtaining an operating line of credit due to a poor credit history.

Jamie's decision involved how best to proceed with the situation and he did not have a lot of time. He did not want to lose the customers to his competition because they offered a great deal of potential for business, both now and in the future. Yet, he did not want to act hastily and make a costly mistake in the process.

Jamie considered three options.

**Option 1.** Suggest to the clients that they each co-sign the other's line of credit. The advantage of this option was that both operating lines of credit were much more likely to be approved. As long as both partners were comfortable being held liable for both lines of credit, this would be ideal. However, the disadvantage was that if one of the two partners defaulted on either line of credit, both clients would be held liable.

**Option 2.** Have the partner with the poor credit bring in a third party as a co-signor. The main advantage of this option was that it avoided making both partners liable for both lines of credit. Bringing in a third party as a co-signor can sometimes be complicated though, especially in a business situation in which the co-signor would essentially become a silent partner of the business. This would probably not be convenient for either of the clients.

**Option 3.** Probe the situation further to see the reason for the bad credit. The advantage of this situation was that it was possible that the poor credit was an "explainable" situation. (An explainable situation is a justifiable and isolated incident that adversely affects a person's credit. Some clients are not even aware of such tarnishes on their credit history.) The disadvantage with this option was that it could take a little longer than Jamie had hoped to put his package together. Furthermore, if he learned that the reason for the poor credit history was not explainable, he would have lost time and would still be left with only the first two options.

Now, join Jamie and his team at TD Canada Trust. Which option would you choose, and why?

# "BUSINESS SUCCESS IS NOT DETERMINED BY THE PRODUCER BUT BY THE CUSTOMER"

Years ago, Thomas Bonoma, a Harvard professor, coined the term "marketing inertia" to describe a business organization's inability to adapt to market changes.[1] He argued that a firm's success makes it complacent; managers are reluctant to tamper with marketing strategies that have been successful in the past. The thinking is, "If it ain't broke, why fix it?"

In this book we have provided you with frameworks, concepts, and marketing tools to be successful. So, it is only fitting that in this last chapter, we show you how to avoid getting trapped by your own success.

The words echoed by the legendary Peter Drucker at the beginning of this chapter must never be forgotten.[2] Ultimately, it is the customer who determines whether a business succeeds or not. It is for this reason that business organizations pay so much attention the topic of this chapter—customer satisfaction and customer retention.

## IMPORTANCE OF MONITORING CUSTOMER SATISFACTION AND CUSTOMER RETENTION

Research has shown that customer retention (customer loyalty) is the single most important driver of long-term financial performance.[3] But, what is the key to customer retention? As shown in Figure 15.1, it is customer satisfaction, which explains why business organizations are so concerned about monitoring customer satisfaction and customer retention. To be successful, a business needs loyal (retained) customers. This is because retained customers are less costly to serve and they tend to be more price insensitive.

Think about your own behaviour for a minute. Do you have favourite brands? The firms that supply those brands do not need to spend precious marketing communication dollars to attract you because you are already familiar with the brands. Further, it is possible that, in spite of a price increase, you will continue to be loyal to this brand.

As demonstrated in Figure 15.1, customer satisfaction is the key to customer retention. According to Philip Kotler,[4] a highly satisfied customer:

**Figure 15.1** Importance of Monitoring Customer Satisfaction and Customer Retention

- Stays loyal longer
- Buys more as the company introduces new products and upgrades existing products
- Talks favourably about the company and its products
- Pays less attention to competing brands and advertising, and is less sensitive to price
- Offers product/service ideas to the company
- Costs less to serve than new customers because transactions are routinized

Given the crucial role played by customer satisfaction and customer retention, it is no wonder companies take these topics seriously, as demonstrated by the Lexus ad in Exhibit 15.1.

Lexus is well known in the industry for its high standards of customer care. When the brand was initially introduced in the mid 1980s it took on luxury car brands from Germany by going above and beyond to satisfy the customer. For example, shortly after launch, a minor defect was discovered in the car. Lexus immediately issued a recall notice, went to each Lexus owner's home, picked up the car, performed the minor repair, and delivered the car (after a thorough wash) back to its home. Such customer service has helped propel Lexus into the ranks of established luxury automobiles.

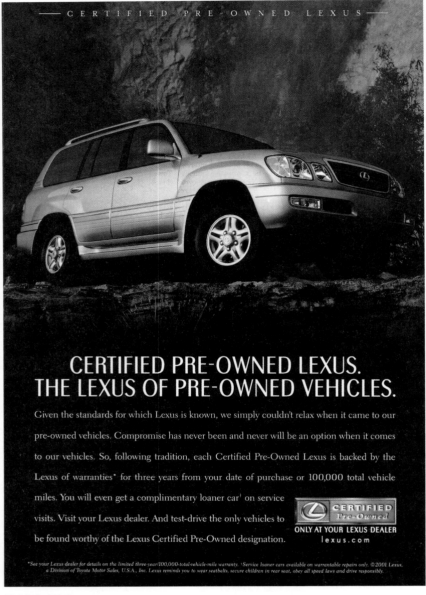

## CAUSES OF CUSTOMER SATISFACTION AND DISSATISFACTION

**Customer satisfaction** can be defined as:

Satisfaction is the consumer's fulfillment response. It is a judgment that a product or service feature, or the product or service itself, provides a pleasurable level of consumption-related fulfillment.[5]

Satisfaction is the difference between a customer's needs and expectations and the customer's perception that the good or service has met those needs and expectations. Figure 15.2, adapted from a well-known concept in services marketing called service quality, shows this.[6]

Failure to meet the customer's needs and expectations results in dissatisfaction. According to Figure 15.2, a customer can be dissatisfied because the good or service does not meet expectations. But, the customer can also be dissatisfied *even though* the good or service performs as it should if the customer's *perception* is that it does not perform as it should. For this reason, we show, in Figure 15.2, that communicating with the customer is key. *Customer communications can influence both customer expectations and customer perceptions.* HSBC knows this very well. As can be seen from Exhibit 15.2, their advertising is clearly aimed at shaping customer expectations about what they can expect from the bank: local expertise.

Let us examine Figure 15.2 in more detail to see how a business can shape customer satisfaction and dissatisfaction.

**Exhibit 15.1**

Lexus cares about its customers.

**customer satisfaction** The difference between a customer's needs and expectations and the customer's perception that the good or service has met those needs and expectations.

## Understanding Customer Needs

At the heart of any successful strategy to monitor customer satisfaction is the firm's ability to understand the needs and expectations of its customers. Most successful business organizations use a combination of the methods listed in Table 15.1. Many average or underperforming firms either do a poor job of understanding customer needs, or do a poor job of incorporating customer needs into their strategies.[7]

## Designing Goods and Services to Satisfy Customer Needs

Unless a business organization has done a first rate job of understanding customer needs, it cannot develop goods and services to satisfy its customers. Clorox, for example, uses its understanding of customer needs to make life a little easier for its customers (Exhibit 15.3).

**Figure 15.2** Customer Satisfaction and Dissatisfaction

Source: Adapted from Service Quality Model proposed by Parasuraman, Zeithaml, and Berry (1985).

# Delivering Goods and Services

The way in which a good or service is delivered affects customer perceptions and, in this way, impacts satisfaction. Business organizations go to great lengths to ensure that the delivery of goods and services to customers is seamless. Harry Rosen, a high-end clothier across Canada, demonstrates this point in its ad seen in Exhibit 15.4 on page 488. Harry Rosen not only makes it easy to find the perfect gift through its stores or online, but reassures customers through its no-hassle return policy that shopping at its stores is a breeze.

# TOOLS TO MEASURE CUSTOMER SATISFACTION

As outlined in Table 15.2 on page 489, there are different ways to measure customer satisfaction. Most customer-oriented businesses use at least one of the methods outlined in the table.

However, there are certain cautions to heed in measuring customer satisfaction.[8] When customers rate their satisfaction with an element of the company's performance (e.g.,

**Table 15.1** Tools to Understand Customer Needs

**Marketing Research**
As discussed in Chapter 4, many qualitative as well as quantitative marketing research tools are available at a firm's disposal. Common methods to understand customer needs are focus groups and surveys.

**Frontline Personnel**
Employees who come in direct contact with the customer (e.g., salesforce, customer service, technical service) are excellent sources of customer information. Unfortunately, these sources are not very well utilized in many organizations. To fully utilize these sources, it is important to develop formal mechanisms to capture, store, and disseminate frontline personnel information.

**Customer Complaints**
Strong marketing organizations make it easy for their customers to complain or offer suggestions. Procter & Gamble, for example, provides toll-free phone numbers and Web sites so customers can register a complaint or a suggestion. Such corporations correctly recognize that a customer complaint is actually a form of free marketing research.

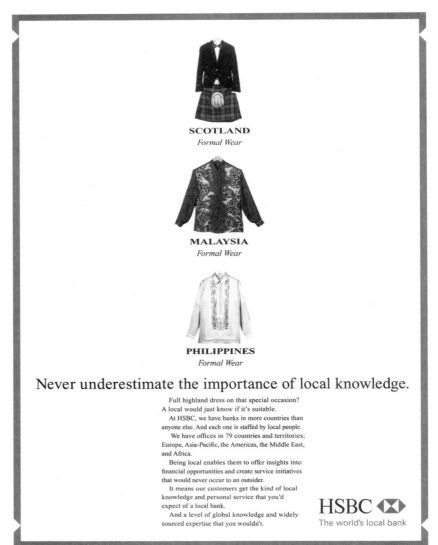

**SCOTLAND**
*Formal Wear*

**MALAYSIA**
*Formal Wear*

**PHILIPPINES**
*Formal Wear*

Never underestimate the importance of local knowledge.

Full highland dress on that special occasion?
A local would just know if it's suitable.

At HSBC, we have banks in more countries than
anyone else. And each one is staffed by local people.

We have offices in 79 countries and territories;
Europe, Asia-Pacific, the Americas, the Middle East,
and Africa.

Being local enables them to offer insights into
financial opportunities and create service initiatives
that would never occur to an outsider.

It means our customers get the kind of local
knowledge and personal service that you'd
expect of a local bank.

And a level of global knowledge and widely
sourced expertise that you wouldn't.

**HSBC**
The world's local bank

*Issued by HSBC Holdings plc.*

**Exhibit 15.2**

HSBC is shaping customer expectations.

delivery) the company needs to recognize that customers vary in their definition of this factor. To some customers, delivery may mean on-time delivery, while to others it may mean delivery accuracy. Yet, if the company detailed these terms, the customer satisfaction questionnaire would get very lengthy.

## Good or Bad Decision?

To secure customer loyalty, many firms offer loyalty programs. These programs award customers points for purchases, which can then be redeemed for goods or services. The problem is that loyalty programs have become very commonplace. It appears as if all firms are offering them. If this is the case, do you think a loyalty program is enough to buy a customer's long-term loyalty? Do you think customers can be "bought" in the first place? Why or why not?

The company should also recognize that two customers could report being "very satisfied" with the product for different reasons. Customer A could have had a very satisfactory experience with the product (e.g., a hotel stay) on this occasion, while Customer B could be basing her answer on a totality of past experiences, both good and not so good.

The timing of customer satisfaction surveys is key. Surveys should not be sent to customers immediately after the company has done something nice for them. Customers should not be

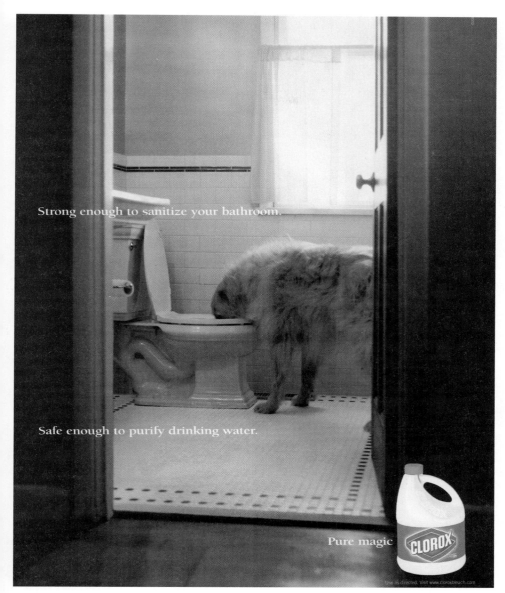

Strong enough to sanitize your bathroom.

Safe enough to purify drinking water.

Pure magic

Use as directed. Visit www.cloroxbleach.com

**Exhibit 15.3**

Clorox creates value for its customers.

bothered with questionnaires during busy time periods, for example beginning-of-year planning periods. Finally, customer satisfaction measurement should be consistent from one period to the next so meaningful comparisons can be made.

## MOVING FROM CUSTOMER SATISFACTION TO CUSTOMER RETENTION

### Why Is Monitoring Customer Satisfaction Not Enough?

The widely held belief that it is sufficient to merely satisfy a customer has shown to be false.[9] In Table 15.3 on page 490, and in many customer satisfaction surveys, a five-point scale is used to measure satisfaction, with "Very Dissatisfied" and "Very Satisfied" being the two end points. On this scale a score of 4 would mean the customer is "Satisfied." Many business organizations falsely believe that it is enough to obtain a score of 4 from a majority of customers. After all, they argue, how many customers actually give a score of 5?

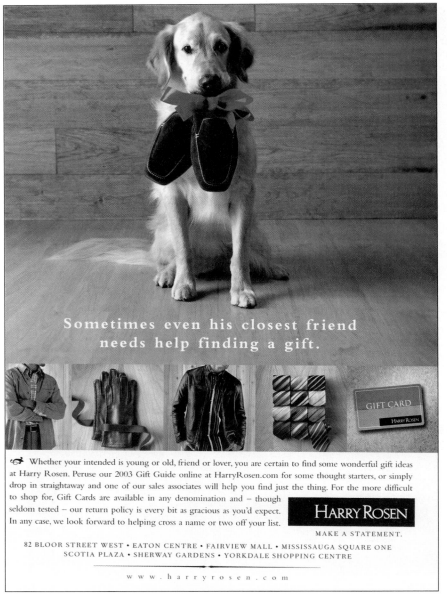

**Exhibit 15.4**

Harry Rosen: Excellence in delivering goods and services.

This belief is false because *complete* customer satisfaction is the key to customer retention. Research conducted by Xerox found that a customer who gives a score of 5 is six times more likely to be a repeat buyer than one who gives a score of 4. This is the reason why firms strive to *totally* satisfy their customers and why there is so much emphasis on customer retention as the end goal, with customer satisfaction as an antecedent variable.

Figure 15.3 demonstrates how the competitive environment affects the satisfaction-loyalty relationship. As can be seen from the figure, any drop from total satisfaction (e.g., in the automotive industry) results in a precipitous drop in customer loyalty.

## How Should You Use Customer Satisfaction Research?

The ultimate goal of customer satisfaction monitoring is to improve customer loyalty. This means achieving total customer satisfaction. Table 15.4 on page 491 outlines three stages of actions a firm can take, depending on the bulk of responses to a customer satisfaction survey.

**Table 15.2** Tools to Measure Customer Satisfaction

**Customer Satisfaction Surveys**
Most customer satisfaction surveys have three sections
(1) a global satisfaction index with the good, service, or firm (typically measured on a 5-point scale, with "Very Dissatisfied" and "Very Satisfied" being the two end points),
(2) a detailed evaluation of the goods and services offered by the firm,
(3) intentions to repurchase the firm's offerings.
A customer satisfaction survey for a fictitious business, Widget Co., is shown in Table 15.3.

**Mystery Shopping**
A form of marketing research, mystery shopping involves a researcher buying the firm's goods and services and assessing the purchase experience vis-à-vis the firm's competitors.

**Customer Complaint Analysis**
Analyzing customer complaints is another way to understand customer satisfaction.

**Lost Customer Analysis**
Some business organizations contact customers who have stopped being repeat purchasers to assess what went wrong. This provides a good assessment of customer satisfaction levels and what needs to be done to retain customers.

According to Table 15.4, a dissatisfied customer (scores of 2 or 3) is not even receiving the basic good or service expected by customers in the industry. This is the equivalent of ordering a meal in a restaurant and not receiving one. Such customers are best served by reviewing the delivery of basic goods and services and making changes to keep pace with industry and technological trends.

A score of 3 or 4 indicates a neutral customer, one who is satisfied with the basic good or service, but desires a set of supporting services (e.g., procedures in place when service delivery fails). This is similar to going to a restaurant where you are happy with the food and service, except that when the restaurant gets busy, the level of service tends to fall short. A neutral customer is best served by putting in place proactive service standards to handle situations when service delivery fails.

Finally, a score of 4 or 5 indicates a completely satisfied customer. Companies that excel at this define the good or service experience from the customer's perspective.

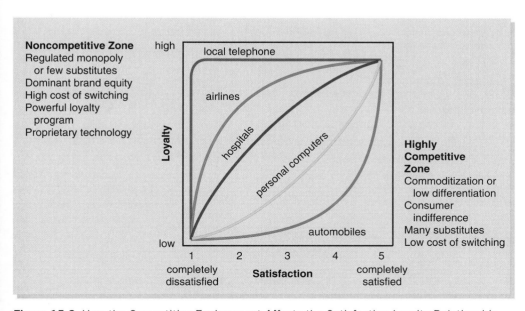

**Figure 15.3** How the Competitive Environment Affects the Satisfaction-Loyalty Relationship

### Table 15.3 Customer Satisfaction Survey, Widget Co.

Dear Customer:
We want your satisfaction level with the Widget Co. to be the highest at all times. Our goal is to ensure your complete satisfaction and earn your loyalty. Only YOU can tell us if we have met your expectations. Your candid comments will help us constantly improve our services.

Please take a few minutes and fill out this satisfaction questionnaire. You may mail it or, if you prefer, you can e-mail your comments to us.

Thank you for your business. We look forward to hearing from you and having the opportunity to serve your needs.

Sincerely,

Bella Adams, General Manager
Widget Co.


**Your Overall Widget Co. Experience**
Please rate your overall satisfaction with Widget Co.:

| Very Satisfied | Satisfied | Neutral | Dissatisfied | Very Dissatisfied |
|---|---|---|---|---|
| 5 | 4 | 3 | 2 | 1 |

Please indicate the overall reason(s) for your score above:

_____

_____

_____


**Performance Ratings**
Please rate your level of satisfaction with the following services using the 5-point scale below:

| | Very Satisfied | Satisfied | Neutral | Dissatisfied | Very Dissatisfied |
|---|---|---|---|---|---|
| | 5 | 4 | 3 | 2 | 1 |
| Widget Co. employees (overall) | 5 | 4 | 3 | 2 | 1 |
| Availability | 5 | 4 | 3 | 2 | 1 |
| Competence | 5 | 4 | 3 | 2 | 1 |
| Responsiveness | 5 | 4 | 3 | 2 | 1 |
| Professionalism | 5 | 4 | 3 | 2 | 1 |
| Product performance | 5 | 4 | 3 | 2 | 1 |
| Price-value ratio | 5 | 4 | 3 | 2 | 1 |
| Delivery | 5 | 4 | 3 | 2 | 1 |
| Technical assistance | 5 | 4 | 3 | 2 | 1 |
| Web site | 5 | 4 | 3 | 2 | 1 |
| Other _____ _____ | 5 | 4 | 3 | 2 | 1 |

**Table 15.3** *(Continued)*

Please indicate your level of agreement or disagreement with the following statements using the 5-point scale below:

| Strongly Agree | Agree | Neither Agree Nor Disagree | Disagree | Strongly Disagree |
|:---:|:---:|:---:|:---:|:---:|
| 5 | 4 | 3 | 2 | 1 |

| | | | | | |
|---|:---:|:---:|:---:|:---:|:---:|
| I plan to repurchase from Widget Co. | 5 | 4 | 3 | 2 | 1 |
| I would recommend Widget Co. to another person looking for a similar product | 5 | 4 | 3 | 2 | 1 |

Please indicate any additional comments you may have that will help us meet your needs better:

_____

_____

_____

Lexus is a good example. It recognized that most dealerships define the experience of getting a car fixed from their (i.e., internal) perspective. But, customers define the experience as the hassle of going to the dealership, dropping off the car, the inconvenience of going without a car, and the hassle involved in picking the car up. So, Lexus, in their quest to completely satisfy the customer, picks up the car at the customer's home or office, repairs and cleans the car, and drops it back at the customer's location.

## CUSTOMER RELATIONSHIP MANAGEMENT: A TOOL TO RETAIN CUSTOMERS

In the last section we discussed that monitoring customer satisfaction is not enough, the ultimate goal should be to retain customers. Experts advocate that, in order to retain customers, we should build a learning relationship with each of them.[10] In other words, technology enables us to build meaningful relationships with our customers by understanding their needs accurately, satisfying those needs in a superior fashion to our competitors, and adjusting our offerings as customer needs change. **Customer Relationship Management (CRM)** is a tool that enables a firm to do just that.

The CRM trend has been referred to as one-to-one (1:1) marketing, relationship marketing, and customer-relationship management.[11] Don Peppers, a leading writer and consultant in this area, defines CRM as " . . . managing customer relationships. If I'm managing customer relationships, it means I'm treating different customers differently, across all

> **Customer Relationship Management (CRM)** A strategy and process used by companies to identify their best customers, stay on top of their needs, and increase their satisfaction.

**Table 15.4** How to Use Customer Satisfaction Information

| | Bulk of Responses | Strategic Response |
|---|---|---|
| Stage 1 | 2 – 3 (dissatisfied) | Deliver the basic product or service elements as expected of anyone in the industry. |
| Stage 2 | 3 – 4 (neutral) | Provide an appropriate range of supporting services. Develop proactive service recovery to make amends when something goes wrong. |
| Stage 3 | 4 – 5 (satisfied) | Understand and achieve results in customers' terms. |

Source: Based on Thomas O. Jones and W. Earl Sasser, Jr., "Why satisfied customers defect," *Harvard Business Review,* November–December 1995: 88.

## SPOTLIGHT ON REAL PEOPLE    Subaru

The "Holy Grail" for a marketer is to create satisfied customers. No one believes this more than Joe Barstys. As Manager of Customer Relationships for the carmaker Subaru, Joe's job is to ensure that Subaru's customers are happy. He manages all aspects of relationship building for the company, including an after-sale survey program and an owner magazine sent to 650 000 Subaru owners quarterly. When Subaru drivers are satisfied, Joe is satisfied.

But, in today's competitive business environment, is it enough just to be satisfied? Is there a difference between being *satisfied* with something and being *loyal* to something? Joe had to find out what makes consumers loyal to a brand of car. Since 1985, his company has been conducting a survey on the purchase and service experiences of Subaru owners as part of its Subaru Owner Loyalty Program. Forms sent after purchase and during the warranty period ask Subaru buyers to rate their contentment with their car and the service they got from local dealers.

Joe realized that despite its name, the survey wasn't measuring loyalty, just *satisfaction*. In fact, virtually *all* of the industry's attempts to track customer's reactions

focused on satisfaction, including the influential J.D. Power Customer Satisfaction Index (CSI) that published consumer's evaluations of many different car models. Subaru, along with most of its competitors, had assumed that there is only a short leap from satisfaction to loyalty. If consumers were satisfied with Subaru's goods and services, they would continue to buy a Subaru in the future. But, the facts are different. Loyalty towards a car manufacturer averages around 40 percent.

Joe reworked the customer survey to ask three questions, all related to key loyalty indicators: the degree of overall owner satisfaction, how the experience at the dealership compared to past car-buying and service experiences, and the degree to which the owner would repeat the experience at that dealership. Reports sent to dealers categorized their customers by loyalty types (i.e., loyal, vulnerable, and possibly lost) based on how they responded to the three questions, allowing the dealers to review the feedback and then prioritize their actions with an eye to retaining customers rather than just fixing "things gone wrong."

1. Do you think the three reworked questions relate to key customer loyalty indicators? Why or why not?
2. Visit personal Web sites linked to sites such as geocities.com where devoted car owners have created "shrines" to certain kinds of cars. Now, formulate a list of key loyalty indicators that Subaru may want to use in consumer surveys.
3. Do you think this loyalty focus will increase repeat business for Subaru?

enterprises . . . The relationship develops a context over time, it drives a change in behaviour . . . [this] means that I have to change my behaviour as an enterprise based on a customer."[12] A CRM strategy allows a company to identify its best customers, stay on top of their needs, and increase their satisfaction.

Is CRM for all companies? Of course, CRM seems to make more sense for business-to-business companies and consumer products companies that have a limited number of customers. But, as we'll see in the next section, even soft drink and auto companies have used CRM to build customer relationships and brand loyalty.

## CRM: A New Perspective on an Old Problem

CRM is about communicating with customers and customers being able to communicate with a company one-to-one. CRM systems are applications that, through computers, CRM computer software, databases, and often the Internet, automate interactions between customers and companies. They include everything from Web sites that let you check on the status of a bill or package to *call centres* that solicit your business. The Federal Express Web site uses a CRM system to let customers track lost packages (Exhibit 15.5). When you get a phone message from the dentist reminding you about that filling appointment tomorrow, that's a CRM system. Car dealers use CRM when they call to ask how you like your new vehicle.

To appreciate the value of a CRM strategy, consider the experience of financial services firms such as Salomon Smith Barney and Fidelity Investments, both of which have adopted this new perspective. In general, an investment banker needs to manage accounts as well as open new ones—often 30 to 50 per month. The process of opening the account can take

45 minutes, not a satisfying process for the banker or for the customer. But with an automated CRM system the banker can open an account, issue a welcome letter, and produce an arbitration agreement in 10 minutes.

She can create a unique marketing communications campaign for each client based on that person's life cycle—including such variables as when a person opened an account, annual income, family situation, and desired retirement age. The marketer can generate a happy anniversary letter to clients (to commemorate when they joined the firm, not when they got married) and include an invitation to update their investment objectives.

These firms have found that this level of individualized attention results in a much higher rate of customer satisfaction and retention, so CRM creates a win-win situation.[13] This success helps to explain why CRM is hot: Industry sources estimate that, by 2005, companies will be spending US$14 billion to purchase sophisticated software that will let them build these electronic bridges.[14]

In addition to mollifying angry customers, marketers can also use CRM systems to keep better track of enthusiastic ones. For example, marketers of youth products are integrating CRM technology into their efforts in the following ways.[15]

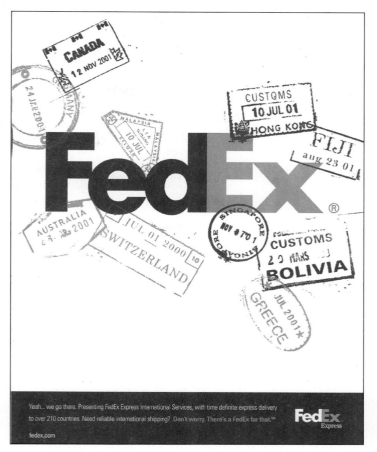

**Exhibit 15.5**

FedEx uses Internet technology to communicate with customers worldwide. From Chile to China, customers can track their packages and know where they are and when they will arrive.

- Sprite staged a "Rocket Cash" sweepstakes promotion by sending out legions of marketing representatives with handheld touch-screen devices. They hung out at concerts and on street corners and enticed young people to enter the sweepstakes by tapping their names, e-mail addresses, and birthdays into the devices on the spot. Every evening, data were uploaded to Sprite's Web site and entrants were kept informed by e-mail of their status in the sweepstakes. Needless to say, in return Sprite wound up with a great list of consumers with whom it could continue to communicate in the future.

- Bacardi held a similar sweepstakes, but in this case the rum marketer also took digital photos of drivers' licenses to verify consumers' ages.

- Ford sponsored a concert tour called Area One on behalf of its youth-oriented Focus model. At each of the tour's 17 stops, attendees could have their pictures taken next to a souped-up version of the Focus. If you wanted to see your photo, you registered your e-mail address with Ford and went to a special Web site where you could download your picture in a special frame (branded with Focus information) and e-mail the picture to your friends. Successful? Ford reported that 87 percent of the people who had their picture taken went to the Web site to retrieve them. And Ford was able to use the e-mail addresses to build relationships with these prospective customers.

Perhaps the most important aspect of CRM is that it presents a new way of looking at how to compete effectively in the marketplace. This begins with looking at customers as partners. CRM proponents suggest that the traditional relationship between customers and marketers is an adversarial one, where marketers try to sell their products and customers seek ways to avoid buying.[16] The customer relationship perspective sees customers as partners, with each partner learning from the other every time they interact. Successful firms compete by establishing relationships with individual customers on a one-to-one basis through dialogue and feedback. What does *this* customer really want?

And, of course, when we say customers we don't just mean end consumers—CRM is widely used to strengthen business-to-business relationships as well. To understand the importance of this kind of thinking, consider the experience of Dow, a giant corporation that sells US$30 billion worth of chemicals, plastics, and agricultural products each year in more than 170 countries. Although Dow uses cutting-edge manufacturing technology every day, until recently, it had literally no centralized mechanism to keep track of its many customers.

Eventually, Dow launched a major effort to install a company-wide CRM system that would be a central repository for customer information and would allow its customers to interact with Dow more efficiently—letting them access information automatically without having to deal with a large corporate bureaucracy. The result? A Web-based interface called MyAccount@Dow that lets customers log on (with a secure password, of course), enter new orders, check on the status of old orders, pay invoices electronically, and collaborate with others throughout the system. As a result, Dow lowered its customer support costs by US$15 million and is taking electronic orders of US$100 million per month.[17]

## Characteristics of CRM

In addition to having a different mind-set, companies that successfully practise CRM have different goals, use different measures of success, and look at customers in some different ways. So, CRM marketers look at their share of the customer, at the lifetime value of a customer, at customer equity, and at focusing on high-value customers.

**share of customer** The percentage of an individual customer's purchase of a product that is a single brand.

**SHARE OF CUSTOMER** Historically, marketers have measured success in a product category by their share of market. For example, if there are 100 million pairs of athletic shoes sold each year, a firm that sells 10 million of them has a 10 percent market share. If the shoemaker's marketing objective is to increase market share, it may lower the price of its shoes, increase its advertising, or offer customers a free basketball with every pair of shoes purchased. Such tactics may increase sales in the short run but, unfortunately, they may not do much for the long-term success of the shoemaker. In fact, such tactics may actually *decrease* the value of the brand by cheapening its image with giveaways.

Because it is always easier and less expensive to keep an existing customer than to get a new customer, CRM firms focus on increasing their **share of customer**, not share of market. Let's say that a consumer buys six pairs of shoes a year—two pairs from each of three different manufacturers. Let's assume one shoemaker has a CRM system that allows it to send letters to its current customers inviting them to receive a special price discount or gift if they buy more of the firm's shoes during the year. Or, the CRM system could alert the consumer when the firm received the consumer's favourite styles in stock. If the firm can get the consumer to buy three or four or perhaps all six pairs from it, it has increased its share of customer. And that may not be too difficult because the customer already buys and supposedly likes the firm's shoes.

Without the CRM system, the shoe company would probably use traditional advertising to increase sales, which would be far more costly than the customer-only direct-mail campaign. So, the company can increase sales and profits at a much lower cost than it would spend to get one, two, or three new customers.

**customer's lifetime value** The potential profit generated by a single customer's purchase of a firm's products over the customer's lifetime.

**LIFETIME VALUE OF THE CUSTOMER** With CRM, a **customer's lifetime value** is identified and is the true goal, not an individual transaction. It just makes sense that a firm's profitability and long-term success are going to be far greater if it develops long-term relationships with its customers so those customers buy from it again and again. Costs will be far higher and profits lower if each customer purchase is a first-time sale.

How do marketers calculate the lifetime value of customer? They first estimate a customer's future purchases across all products from the firm over the next 20 or 30 years. The goal is to try to figure out what profit the company could make from the customer in the future. For example, an auto dealer might calculate the lifetime value of a single customer by first calculating the total revenue that could be generated by the customer over his lifetime: the number of automobiles he would buy times the average price, plus the service the dealership would provide over the years, and even possibly the income from auto loan financing. The lifetime value of the customer would be the total profit generated from the revenue stream.

CUSTOMER EQUITY Today, an increasing number of companies are considering their relationships with customers as financial assets. Such firms measure their success by calculating the value of their **customer equity**—the financial value of customer relationships throughout the lifetime of the relationships.[18] To do this, firms compare the investments they make in acquiring customers, retaining customers, and relationship enhancement with the financial return on those investments. The goal is to reap a high return on the investments made in customer relationships and maximize the value of a firm's customer equity.

A GREATER FOCUS ON HIGH-VALUE CUSTOMERS Using a CRM approach, customers must be prioritized and communication customized accordingly. For example, any banker will tell you that not all customers are equal when it comes to profitability. Some banks now use CRM systems to generate a profile of each customer based on factors such as value, risk, attrition, and interest in buying new financial products. This automated system helps the bank decide which current or potential customers it will target with certain communications or how much effort to expend on retaining a person's account—all while cutting its costs by as much as a third.[19]

It just makes sense to use different types of communication contacts based on the value of each individual customer. For example, personal selling may constitute 75 percent of all contacts with high-volume customers, while direct mail or telemarketing is more often the best way to contact low-volume customers.

**customer equity** The financial value of a customer relationship throughout the lifetime of the relationship.

## Steps in CRM Marketing

There are four steps in CRM marketing.[20] The first step is to identify customers and get to know them in as much detail as possible. In step two, marketers need to differentiate these customers in terms of both their needs and value to the company. For step three, CRM marketers must interact with customers and find ways to improve cost efficiency and the effectiveness of the interaction. In step four, marketers need to customize some aspect of the goods or services they offer to each customer. This means treating each customer differently based on what has been learned through customer interactions. Table 15.5 suggests some activities for implementing these four steps.

**Table 15.5** Four Steps in CRM Marketing

| Step | Suggested Activities |
|---|---|
| **Identify** | Collect and enter names and additional information about your customers. |
| | Verify and update, deleting outdated information. |
| **Differentiate** | Identify top customers. |
| | Determine which customers cost the company money. |
| | Find higher-value customers who have complained about your product or service more than once. |
| | Find customers who buy only one or two products from your company but a lot from other companies. |
| | Rank customers into A, B, and C categories based on their value to your company. |
| **Interact** | Call the top three people in the top five percent of dealers, distributors, and retailers that carry your product and make sure they're happy. |
| | Call your own company and ask questions; see how hard it is to get through and get answers. |
| | Call your competitors and compare their customer service with yours. |
| | Use incoming calls as selling opportunities. |
| | Initiate more dialogue with valuable customers. |
| | Improve complaint handling. |
| **Customize** | Find out what your customers want. |
| | Personalize your direct mail. |
| | Ask customers how and how often they want to hear from you. |
| | Ask your top 10 customers what you can do differently to improve your product or service. |
| | Involve top management in customer relations. |

Source: Adapted from Don Peppers, Martha Rogers, and Bob Dorf, "Is Your Company Ready for One-to-One Marketing?" *Harvard Business Review,* January–February 1999, reprint # 99107.

# Real People, Real Decisions

## How It Worked Out at TD Canada Trust

Despite the fact that time was tight, Jamie decided to choose option 3 and probe the situation further. He worked in conjunction with the credit administrative services department to find out why the client had poor credit. He figured that the worst that could happen would be that he would be left with the original alternatives, option 3 was the best way to move forward. If he was going to win the business of the clients, he had to give them exactly what they wanted, and this was the best chance he had to do so.

Jamie dealt with TD Canada Trust's Credit Centre and learned that the reason for poor credit was an "explainable" situation. While this makes it difficult to get a client approved, it certainly makes it easier than if the poor credit was not explainable.

Jamie continued to work with the credit department and his management team and asked them to look at the bigger picture. "These business partners had a solid foundation and excellent potential. Essentially, we ended up working out a compromise with the credit centre in which the clients would both receive exactly what they wanted," says Jamie.

How did it work out? The next day Jamie met with the clients and finalized the paperwork for two accounts and two operating lines of credit. He also began discussing other products that would heighten their entire banking experience, such as payroll services, merchant services, and online banking.

Since that decision, the clients have added two new partners and two new locations. Each location does more than $250 000 in business per year and the company's business with TD Canada Trust continues to grow. All of the partners have been thrilled with their overall experience at TD Canada Trust.

Taking the extra step fits with Jamie's favourite motto: "Measure Twice . . . Cut Once." He believes in looking at the entire situation before making a final decision. In this case, it was important for him to know that he did everything within his power to gain the clients' business.

The achievement of which Jamie is most proud is the completion of a year-long study on customer loyalty strategies, which resulted in the development of a model that can be used by any business.

Jamie has some words of advice for students as they prepare for a productive career. Firstly, he says, "I have learned that it is important to spot and solve any problems within a group setting immediately. Whether the problems arise in a group at school or a group at work, problems must be addressed face first. That is, if there is a problem within a group it should be addressed and solved, rather than avoided."

Jamie learned this lesson through an experience in university in which two group members were having difficulty working together. Rather than deal with the problem, Jamie's group avoided the situation. This later blew up in their faces when the two group members had a major blowout, making it very difficult to achieve a favourable result during their future group sessions.

Jamie's second piece of advice is this: university or college is not about achieving a perfect grade point average (GPA). It is about learning and gaining experience. He believes it is more important to graduate as a well-rounded individual than to graduate with a high GPA. "Companies that are hiring newly graduated students today are not only interested in your marks," he says.

"They want to hire someone who has some sort of real life experience. If you do not have a job, then my advice is to get one. If getting a job is not possible for you, then join a club or get involved with your student government. Utilize your entrepreneurial skills and do something new and unique. Take chances, and most of all, have fun."

Recently, Jamie was recruited by Kraft Foods Canada. While leaving TD Canada Trust was not an easy decision, he is looking forward to an exciting career with Kraft Foods. "I will forever be grateful to TD Canada Trust for instilling in me the values and work ethic," says Jamie.

# CHAPTER SUMMARY

### 1. Understand the importance of monitoring customer satisfaction and customer retention.

Research has shown that customer retention (customer loyalty) is the single most important driver of long-term financial performance. Loyal customers tend to be less price sensitive and firms do not have to spend marketing communication dollars in attracting these customers. Customer satisfaction is the single most important factor that impacts customer retention. It is for this reason that firms spend time monitoring customer satisfaction and customer retention.

### 2. Describe what causes customer satisfaction and dissatisfaction.

Customer satisfaction may be defined as the difference between what a customer expects from a good or service and the customer's perception that the good or service met prior expectations. So, when perceptions equal expectations, we say the customer is satisfied. When there is a mismatch between customer perceptions and expectations, the customer is dissatisfied.

To satisfy a customer, a business organization needs to do four things well. They are:

1. Understand customer needs and expectations in an accurate fashion.
2. Develop goods and services to match customer needs.
3. Deliver goods and services in a manner that the customer expects.
4. Influence customer needs (and expectations) and customer perceptions via marketing communications.

### 3. Describe methods to measure customer satisfaction.

There are four main methods used to measure customer satisfaction.

1. Customer Satisfaction Surveys. Most customer satisfaction surveys have three sections: A global satisfaction index with the good, service, or firm (typically measured on a five-point scale—"Very Dissatisfied" and "Very Satisfied" being the two end points); A detailed evaluation of the goods and services offered by the firm; Intentions to repurchase the firm's offerings.
2. Mystery Shopping. A form of marketing research, mystery shopping involves a researcher buying the firm's goods or services and assessing the purchase experience against the firm's competitors.
3. Customer Complaint Analysis. Analyzing customer complaints is another way to understand customer satisfaction.
4. Lost Customer Analysis. Some business organizations contact customers who have stopped being repeat purchasers to assess what went wrong. This provides a good assessment of customer satisfaction levels and what needs to be done to retain customers.

### 4. Explain why business organizations go beyond measuring customer satisfaction to monitoring customer retention.

Research has shown the merely satisfying customers is not enough; the ultimate goal should be customer retention. This is because even satisfied customers can migrate to the competition. Only totally satisfied customers become repeat purchasers.

### 5. Explain the importance of Customer Relationship Management (CRM) and describe how it works.

CRM is important because it presents organizations a new way of looking at how to compete effectively in the marketplace. This begins with looking at customers as partners. CRM proponents suggest that the traditional relationship between customers and marketers is an adversarial one, where marketers try to sell their products, and customers seek ways to avoid buying. Instead, CRM's goal is to establish a learning relationship with each customer, with the business organization changing its offering of goods and services in response to (or even ahead of) changing customer needs.

A four-step process is involved in implementing CRM:

1. Identify. This step involves collecting and storing information about customers such as their buying patterns and needs.

2. Differentiate. This step involves differentiating among customers to identify the most attractive customers we should be serving.

3. Interact. This step involves initiating more dialogue with our best customers. For example, in this step we may develop a better way to handle customer complaints.

4. Customize. This step involves personalizing the elements of the marketing mix (product, price, channel of distribution, and marketing communications) to develop a one-to-one relationship with customers.

# CHAPTER REVIEW

## Marketing Concepts: Testing Your Knowledge

1. Provide a definition of customer satisfaction in your own words.

2. What is the difference between customer satisfaction and customer retention? Why are these terms so important to a business organization?

3. What are some ways in which we can measure customer satisfaction? Describe the pros and cons of each.

4. What cautions should we heed in customer satisfaction measurement?

5. Why do we focus on customer retention? What are some factors that affect customer retention?

6. What is CRM and why is it important?

7. Describe steps in implementing a CRM system.

## Marketing Concepts: Discussing Choices and Issues

1. In this chapter we argue that customer satisfaction and retention are key to business success. Do you agree? Describe situations where these variables may not be the best options for a firm.

2. Can you design a method to measure customer satisfaction that we have not discussed in this chapter?

3. Do you think CRM is the best way to retain customers? Can you think of other ways business organizations have used to retain customers?

## Marketing Practice: Applying What You've Learned

1. Working with four to six classmates, select a product that you all use. Identify the different brands used by each person in the group and find out what product attributes contribute to satisfaction or dissatisfaction. Summarize your findings.

2. You have been asked by your college or university's admission director for help in conducting a student satisfaction study. Advise her on the main study methods you can use in this situation.

3. Go to your library and search for business organizations that have installed a CRM system. Provide a report on their experiences, both good and bad. What recommendations do you have in successfully implementing a CRM strategy?

## Marketing Mini-Project: Learning by Doing

The purpose of this mini-project is to apply your learning of customer satisfaction and customer retention.

1. Select any good, service, or company—preferably one that is well-known.
2. Develop a customer satisfaction survey for the good, service, or company.
3. Administer the survey with a small sample (~20) of consumers.
4. Diagnose the customer satisfaction findings and provide recommendations.
5. Report your findings to the class.

## Real People, Real Surfers: Exploring the Web

Visit the Web site of the American Customer Satisfaction Index (ACSI) at **www.theacsi.com/**. The ACSI is a measure of quality of goods and services as experienced by consumers.

Write a report on the ACSI based on these questions.

1. Why was the ACSI developed?
2. How does it work? How are data collected?
3. What are the main findings from last year? What industries scored high and what industries scored low?
4. What are some reasons for high or low customer satisfaction scores?

As far back as 1965, Ray A. Kroc, the founder of McDonald's Corp., declared, "I don't know what we'll be serving in the year 2000, but we'll be serving more of it than anybody." In the year 2000, true enough, McDonald's was the number one fast-food chain in the world with 41 000 restaurants in 121 countries.

Kroc's prediction was on the money, and McDonald's has dominated the fast-food business for more than 30 years. But, as the new century is unfolding, cracks are beginning to appear in the golden arches.

The first McDonald's restaurant opened in 1937 in a parking lot east of Pasadena, California, where happy customers ate hot dogs (the most popular item on the menu) served by teenage carhops. When consumer tastes changed, the golden arches changed, too. Indoor restaurants replaced carhops. And in the 1960s, the Big Mac made McDonald's stand out from other burger joints.

When consumers became tired of beef in the early 1980s, McDonald's introduced bite-size chunks of fried chicken. McDonald's gave consumers what they wanted—seemingly before they knew what they wanted. And in the process, McDonald's became a global icon, even succeeding in countries like France where a one- (or two-) hour break for lunch is still sacrosanct.

But, it is not easy to remain top dog. By the late 1990s Burger King and Wendy's were closing in. McDonald's seemed to lose its competitive edge. McDonald's last successful new product had been the Chicken McNugget, introduced in 1983. In the 1990s McDonald's had experimented with pizza and veggie burgers and had unsuccessfully tried to enter the adult fast-food market with the ill-fated Arch Deluxe, an adult burger with Dijon mustard sauce.

Then, to make matters worse, McDonald's had confused customers with a series of discounting strategies. Even though McDonald's still had a large percentage of the fast-food burger market, the data verified that McDonald's faced serious problems. In 2003, McDonald's faced its first quarterly loss since going public in 1965. This could be attributed to a weak global economy and lingering fears about mad-cow disease, but there were other problems as well. Research done at the University of Michigan suggested that consumers rated McDonald's lowest of all U.S. fast-food chains in terms of satisfaction—for the eighth consecutive time.

In the recent past, McDonald's had tried a number of strategies to improve its status. In 1998, it had required all restaurants (in the United States) to install a made-to-order cooking system designed to improve the taste of burgers and compete with rivals, but many franchises complained that the system slowed down delivery of food to customers—an important component of customer satisfaction.

Some members of the McDonald's marketing team suggested that the company needed a product development strategy—that there ought to be ways to squeeze new profits by adding items to the current menu. Another idea that had been thrown around was to build on McDonald's brand value to sell totally different products—for example, take advantage of McDonald's popularity with kids to sell a line of toys. Some thought that McDonald's could continue expansion into international markets. McDonald's earns over half of its profits from its international division. But new international expansion meant going past the "easy" markets such as Paris and Moscow into more challenging markets such as Germany and Japan. And, there was substantial anti-American feeling in some countries.

Of course, none of these strategies would solve the problem many felt to be the primary reason for McDonald's low growth—customer satisfaction. While McDonald's had focused on building more stores, what consumers really wanted was better food and more variety. Many consumers who eat fast food at least once a month said that Wendy's and Burger King offered better-tasting food. In a *Business Week*/Harris poll, McDonald's ranked 87th out of 91 in the taste of their food—just behind Hooters. These same consumers ranked taste and quality as very important factors in restaurant choice, whereas they rated convenience and speed as much less important. As the new millennium unfolds, McDonald's has to figure out its recipe for continued McProfits.

Sources: "Burger and fries a la francaise," *The Economist*, 17–23 April 2004: 60; Mack Ballon, "McDonald's looking for a break," *Los Angeles Times*, December 15, 2001, Part 3, Page 1.

## Things to Think About

1. What is the strategic decision facing McDonald's?

2. What factors are important in understanding the decision situation?

3. What has McDonald's done recently to enhance customer satisfaction?

4. What recommendations do you have to improve customer satisfaction at McDonald's?

5. How would you solve the problems facing McDonald's? Make a list of its problems and suggest possible solutions.

After Shoppers Drug Mart pulls the plug on the tentative deal to place Benefect on its shelves, Sam has to find other opportunities for his product. Soon, another opportunity presents itself in the form of Purity Life Products, Canada's biggest seller of all things natural. But Purity wants an exclusive licensing deal; it does not want other customers selling Benefect. It wants the brand all to itself, and it wants to build a store brand.

Sam has a new problem to contend with now—should he simply hand over his "goldmine" to Purity? Should he satisfy the needs of Purity and build a relationship with one customer exclusively, or should he maintain control over his brand? This time, Sam pulls the plug on the deal. He does not want to retain just one customer, because he feels this would limit his opportunities.

As you can see, Sam makes a very bold decision because, in the meantime, the bills are piling up; the business needs to have some cash inflow. Mark, the salesperson, is out drumming up sales with retailers, but the tight budget is cramping his style. However, he remains optimistic. Over a few months, Mark picks up 100 new retail accounts. The word of mouth on the product is generating attention in the marketplace.

Towards the end of the video, we see that Sam has a new investor on board, so he can explore other opportunities. Benefect gains U.S. government approval, so Sam can distribute his product south of the border. He also inks a distribution deal with Purity under the Benefect name, and his product now retails in health food stores. Also, Sears uses Benefect to clean air ducts in customers' homes.

Ultimately, it appears as if Sam's gutsy decision to not keep just one customer happy has paid off.

## Questions

1. In spite of how Sam's story ends in the video, do you think he makes the right decision not to do an exclusive licensing deal with Purity? Why or why not?
2. In this chapter, we discuss the concepts of customer satisfaction and customer retention. Who, in your opinion, is the customer for Benefect? Is it the retailer or the end consumer? Provide a rationale for your answer.
3. Based on your answer above, design a short customer satisfaction survey Sam can use to learn about his customers.

Source: This case was prepared by Ajay Sirsi and is based on "Super Bacteria," *Venture* #885.

## COMPANY OVERVIEW

Green Nature Landscaping Inc. (GNL) is a sole proprietorship owned by John Jones. It provides landscape maintenance and design services to homes, apartment buildings, and condominiums in the metro area. The company employs three full-time employees and 15 part-time employees on an as-needed basis. John has a profit-sharing plan for all his employees. John and the three full-time employees make all the strategic decisions for the company, with John acting as the company's CEO.

GNL is a five-year-old company. John has spent his entire career in the garden and landscaping business. He started when he was in high school, working for the local nursery. For a while, he worked for a large landscaping firm in its operations department. John loves the industry and knows the market quite intimately. GNL currently has 150 maintenance contracts in place, and John is working on 20 design projects for homeowners.

## EXECUTIVE SUMMARY

There are three key issues GNL must address next year:

- Attracting and keeping service-oriented, price insensitive customers who want to invest in landscaping services to enhance the value of their properties.

- Differentiating landscaping services from the competition. Given the relatively low entry barriers in this industry, new entrants tend to undercut existing players. This makes customers very price sensitive.

- Tackling the issue of seasonality. Currently, once the summer season is over, GNL's business dries up until spring. The length of the winter months affects GNL's revenue-generating season.

To address these three issues, GNL will implement some key strategies, which are outlined below.

### Market Segmentation and Product Strategy

GNL will reexamine its current segmentation scheme to focus on customers who appreciate quality service and who are willing to pay a higher price for the service. It

---

[1] This sample marketing plan is provided for illustration purposes only, and depicts a fictitious business organization. Sections of the marketing plan have been abbreviated.

will refocus product efforts on providing excellent customer service and new product innovation. GNL will exit the residential and condo markets and will focus solely on (and build expertise in) the homeowner market segment.

### Pricing Strategy

GNL will focus on a premium pricing strategy. In general, prices will be 10 to 50 percent higher than the competition, depending on the type of service.

### Channel of Distribution (Place) Strategy

GNL will emphasize staff training to provide excellent customer service. New products will be distributed through relationships developed with Shorewood nurseries in the metro area.

### Marketing Communications (Promotion) Strategy

GNL recognizes that building a premium brand is key in the marketplace. To achieve this, GNL will focus on aspects of landscaping that have previously been ignored by competitors: garden nutrition innovation, personalized advice, and turnkey garden solutions for homeowners.

If the above strategies are implemented correctly, GNL anticipates these outcomes next year:

- A greater brand recognition in the metro area and an increase of brand awareness from 25 percent to 45 percent

- A market share increase of 15 percent to a total of 3.5 percent of the market

- Sales revenues of $250 000

- A return on investment of 15 percent

## CURRENT MARKET SITUATION

In 2003, gross revenues for the landscaping industry were estimated at approximately $5 billion by the horticulture industry association. The industry is very fragmented, with approximately 5000 firms of all sizes competing for market share.

The market is very attractive because of these factors:

- Market size: annual revenues of approximately $5 billion

- Market growth rate: the horticulture industry association estimates that this industry will grow by approximately 10 percent annually for the next 10 years
- Ease of entry: low overhead costs and easy availability of industry and technical information
- Opportunity to earn profit margins of up to 20 percent
- Ready availability of part-time labour

GNL's current market share is estimated at 2.5 percent. Each percentage point of market share is approximately worth $75 000 in revenue. GNL estimates that, over time, the industry will consolidate as weak players either exit the marketplace or are bought out by stronger competitors. In five years, GNL expects its market share to double to approximately 5 percent.

# ENVIRONMENTAL ANALYSIS
## Competitor Analysis

The market for landscaping services is very fragmented, with approximately 5000 players competing in a very intense fashion. These firms vary widely in terms of their size, product lines, quality of service, brand positioning, and price. Firms range from small one-man companies (often operating from the owner's basement) to large operations with hundreds of employees.

Most landscaping companies operate within one of two market segments: residential and commercial, although many companies serve both market segments. Landscaping companies can be grouped into the following categories:

- Maintenance: includes tree maintenance, grass cutting, and lawn care (seeding, fertilizing, weed control)
- Design and construction: includes the design of a landscape and its implementation (planting trees, bushes, and flowerbeds; using stone; etc.)
- Full-service landscaping: includes design, construction, and maintenance

GNL's main competitors in this industry are outlined below.

**GREEN DESIGN** Green Design is focused on the design and construction of landscapes. It blends Japanese and western landscaping techniques. Green Design's strategy is to position itself as the specialist who designs landscapes that need minimal maintenance.

GNL's marketing research reveals that Green Design could face problems in the future as its melding of eastern and western landscaping design tends to confuse customers.

**ACME LANDSCAPE INC.** Acme is a full-service company that positions itself as a specialist in new home landscaping, as well as renovation of existing properties. It currently serves the needs of both residential and commercial customers. This approach is problematic in that the needs of these customers vary greatly and it is difficult to serve distinct needs successfully at the same time.

**DONE RIGHT INC.** Done Right's main focus is on garden maintenance. It offers its customers a choice of three different packages, with three different prices. This menu-based approach seems to be working well for Done Right. However, this limits the kinds of services it can offer the customer.

Although Done Right has seen steady growth for the past five years, its growth appears to be slowing. This is probably due to the consumer trend of viewing a landscape as more than just a garden.

**GARDEN ARTISTS INC.** Garden Artists is a small company that positions itself as the "un-corporation." Because it is small, it claims it can provide the customer with specialized and custom services that the big players just can't offer. Garden Artists charges a price premium for its service, and has a loyal client base. However, it is not a very innovative company—it prefers to stick with traditional landscaping methods.

Garden Artists is one of the oldest players in the market. Currently, it is run with an iron fist by Mr. Greenhaven, the company's founder. Rumour has it that Mr. Greenhaven is due to retire in the next three years. His son, Ron, is expected to take over at that time. Ron is a risk taker who will most certainly introduce innovative management techniques to the company.

**SAVE-THE-PLANET GARDENS** Save-the-Planet Gardens has found a niche in the marketplace. It focuses on consumers who want organic, chemical-free products for their gardens. Its customers tend to be very environmentally conscious, and are willing to pay a higher price for pesticide-free products. Since the size of this segment is small, the ability for Save-the-Planet Gardens to grow and capture market share is restricted.

**GREAT GARDEN CARE** A large corporation, Great Garden Care has the advantage of purchasing power due to its size. It uses this advantage to pass cost savings on to its customers by pricing its services lower than its competitors. But its size also has certain disadvantages, including customer complaints that the staff does not provide excellent customer service. Although part-time labour is readily available in the industry, labour turnover tends to be high. High labour turnover is the prime cause of poor customer service, as new employees have to be trained constantly to offer the level of service Great Garden Care wants to provide to its customers.

## Business Implications of Competitor Analysis

In order to be a more effective competitor, GNL needs to refocus its efforts. Right now, it's striving to be "all things to all people" by competing in multiple market segments. Successful competitors in this industry (like Save-the-Planet Gardens) tend to offer only a few services, but do an excellent job of implementation. This enhances customer satisfaction, resulting in customer retention.

## Analysis of the Macro Environment

**DEMOGRAPHIC AND SOCIO-CULTURAL FACTORS** The population of the metro area is booming: one million more people are expected to move into the metro area within the next 10 years. This creates a need for more housing and, naturally, the need for garden and landscaping services. Furthermore, there is a trend toward an aging population that has more discretionary income to spend on landscaping services.

**TECHNOLOGICAL FACTORS** There have been many innovations in the lawn-care service sector. Pesticide manufacturers are focusing on developing more powerful—yet environmentally gentle—ingredients. Also, products have been developed that can perform multiple lawn-care tasks simultaneously. For example, only a few years ago a lawn-care business would have to buy many different chemicals to impart nutrition to grow a healthy lawn. Today, that job can be done with elements that combine different chemicals into one molecule.

**ECONOMIC FACTORS** The economic malaise plaguing the nation for the last few years is behind us. Economic forecasts show a robust economy with plenty of jobs and rising incomes for the next five years. This trend bodes well for the landscaping industry as people tend to spend more on their gardens during economic boom times.

## CUSTOMER ANALYSIS

## Customer Segments

There are two main customer segments in this market: residential and commercial. Residential customers tend to be more price insensitive, but require more hand-holding in terms of services. Commercial customers like high-rise apartment-building owners and condominium corporations tend to be more price sensitive, but less demanding in terms of services required.

## Customer Needs and Trends

There is a trend among consumers to have a garden, and not just a lawn. In the past, consumers were satisfied with having a manicured lawn in their yards. Today, the trend is to "bring the inside outside"—consumers want their outside environment to be just as comfortable as their inside environment.

Consumers have a need for a "one-stop" supplier who can provide them with every service from garden design to maintenance at a reasonable cost. This segment of the market is currently underserved because most landscaping businesses do not know how to combine different aspects of landscaping (design and maintenance) to offer one-stop shopping.

Because of the population influx into the metro area, housing prices have gone up. A survey by the real estate board shows that houses with well-landscaped exteriors sell for 10 to 25 percent more than houses with ordinary gardens. This statistic has not gone unnoticed by homeowners.

Consumers are becoming more environmentally conscious, but the segment of consumers willing to pay a price premium for environmentally friendly products and organic materials remains small. Although consumers want to treat the environment gently, they don't want to pay more for eco-friendly goods and services.

There is a small, but growing, customer segment called the do-it-yourself (DIY) segment. While DIY consumers like to receive professional advice, they prefer to do their own gardening. This segment mainly consists of older consumers with a high percentage of disposable income.

## SWOT ANALYSIS

### Opportunities

- Growth of the residential market. Housing starts in the metro area in 2003 totalled more than 75 000 units.
- Metro population growth is fuelled by immigrants who have little or no landscaping knowledge.
- Increasing discretionary income to spend on landscaping services.
- Opportunity to serve neglected customer needs such as one-stop shopping.
- Opportunities to leverage advances in technology.
- Opportunities to partner with software makers to provide drawing services to the DIY market.
- New product innovation opportunities such as partnering with real estate agencies to offer property appreciation services.
- Expansion opportunities in related businesses such as garden centres, nurseries, and composting facilities.

- Fragmented industry creates opportunities for service-oriented supplier.

**Threats**

- Fragmented industry means a much more intense level of competition, making it hard for players to differentiate themselves.

- Low entry barriers in industry results in the rapid formation of new businesses.

- New entrants tend to undercut existing players. This makes customers price sensitive.

- Environmentalists are lobbying to halt the use of certain types of pesticides. If approved, this will certainly raise the cost of doing business. Higher costs cannot be passed on to the consumer in all cases.

- Seasonal nature of the business. Length of the winter months affects ability to earn revenue.

**Strengths**

- Expertise in the industry. John's educational background in the sciences and industry experience combine to provide customers with broad, but accurate, information.

- Ability to provide customers with personalized service. Customer satisfaction is a key success factor in this industry.

- Low overhead costs.

- Good labour relations. GNL's profit sharing program attracts and keeps employees. Lower employee turnover means better customer service, which leads to higher customer satisfaction and customer retention.

**Weaknesses**

- Size of the firm is a weakness as larger players can negotiate purchasing agreements with suppliers of chemicals, equipment, etc. These larger firms can pass on these savings to customers.

- Lack of access to capital. Cash flow is a perennial problem for GNL.

## KEY ISSUES TO BE ADDRESSED BY THE MARKETING PLAN NEXT YEAR

There are three key issues GNL must address next year:

1. *Attracting and keeping service-oriented customers who want to invest in landscaping services to enhance the value of their properties.* This issue is important because there is a need for one-stop-shop suppliers—landscape firms that can provide the customer a full roster of services from landscape design to maintenance. This is one way to make customers price insensitive.

2. *Differentiating landscaping services from the competition.* Given the relatively low entry barriers in this industry, new entrants tend to undercut existing players. This makes customers very price sensitive.

3. *Tackling the issue of seasonality.* Currently, once the summer season is over, GNL's business dries up until spring.

## OBJECTIVES TO BE ACHIEVED BY THE MARKETING PLAN

### Financial Objectives

- Acquire sales revenues of $250 000.

- Get a return on investment (ROI) of 15 percent.

### Marketing and Sales Objectives

- Create greater brand recognition in the metro area. Increase of brand awareness from current 25 percent to 45 percent.

- Increase the market share by 15 percent to a total of 3.5 percent of the market.

- Develop new market opportunities by creating a "garden visualizer" software program that will enable property owners to see what their gardens will actually look like on a computer screen.

- Expand into real estate appreciation services by partnering with real estate agencies.

- Obtain 25 new service contracts and three new design projects next year.

## MARKETING STRATEGIES

### Market Segmentation Strategy

GNL will exit the commercial (high-rise apartment buildings and condominiums) market segment, as these customers tend to be very price sensitive and very demanding. GNL will focus exclusively on the residential market segment, enabling the company to specialize in one segment. Segment specialization has advantages, particularly in that the knowledge gained in one segment can be passed on to customers via enhanced customer service.

GNL will pursue customers selectively. Some customers tend to be very price sensitive and not interested in investing in their gardens. GNL will not compete for their business. The focus will be on attracting and retaining the price insensitive segment of the market that demands a higher level of service with a one-stop-shop approach.

## Product Strategy

GNL will provide a higher quality of service to the service-conscious customer. Services will include:

- Providing personal, site-specific, and customized service to suit each client's needs. GNL staff will consult with a client to determine client objectives before recommending a course of action.

- Partnering with Retail Technologies Inc. to develop a software program that is easy to use for home consumer use. This software program will allow the DIY consumer to design a garden on screen and look at the final product before buying plants at the local nursery. Retail Technologies has a product that is currently used to design retail-store environments. John has a good relationship with Retail Technologies and is certain that its product can be modified for use in the landscaping business.

- Partnering with selected real-estate agencies to offer homeowners "property appreciation" services. Given the real estate boom in the metro area, homeowners wanting to sell their properties are looking for ways to enhance their property values. An appealing landscape is one way to enhance the value of a property.

- Expanding into the leaf-raking and snow-removal business to combat the seasonal nature of the landscaping business. John sees this as an opportunity to keep his part-time staff employed year round. Employee turnover is a big problem in this industry; when there is turnover, customer service tends to be low. Keeping employees throughout the year is one way to keep motivation levels high.

## Pricing Strategy

GNL will pursue a premium pricing strategy. It will price goods and services between 10 to 50 percent higher than the competition.

## Channel of Distribution Strategy

- GNL will train its staff to provide excellent customer service, focusing on diagnosing a customer's landscape needs and providing custom services.

- It will partner with Shorewood Nurseries to sell software products throughout the metro area.

- It will offer software products for sale at local book stores.

- GNL will partner with selected real-estate agencies to offer property appreciation services to homeowners.

## Marketing Communications Strategy

- GNL will build a premium landscape firm brand.

- GNL will increase its brand awareness.

## TACTICAL PLANS

| Item | Person Responsible | Timeline | Resources Required |
|---|---|---|---|
| Market segmentation strategy | John Jones | Q1 | Memo to employees on GNL strategy. |
| Customer-service quality | John Jones | Q1 | Half-day workshop with full- and part-time staff to discuss customer-service quality needs. |
| Software product | John Jones<br>Terry Adams | Q2 | Initial contact with Retail Technologies has been made.<br>Terry Adams to work with software technician to modify retail software.<br>$5000 |
| Property appreciation service | John Jones | Q2 | Contact select real-estate agencies.<br>Develop partnership with agencies. |
| Leaf-raking and snow-removal services | John Jones | Q3 | $5000 for purchase of equipment.<br>$2000 for advertising. |
| Shorewood Nurseries contract | Sarah Parker | Q2 | Meet with Shorewood operations manager to discuss product placement and pricing. |
| Bookstores product placement | Sarah Parker | Q2 | Negotiate fees. |
| Web site development | John Jones<br>Jamie Kennedy | Q1 | $10 000 |
| Loyalty program | Jamie Kennedy | Q1 | $2000 |

# BUDGETS AND PROJECTED PROFIT AND LOSS STATEMENT

|  | This Year | Next Year |
|---|---|---|
| Marketing-plan budget | $15 000 | $24 000 |
| Sales | $175 000 | $250 000 |
| Profit | $70 000 | $120 000 |
| Market share | 2.5% | 3.5% |
| ROI | 9% | 15% |

# MARKETING-PLAN CONTROL

GNL will use several tools to evaluate and control the marketing plan. First, GNL will use monthly trend analysis to examine sales by market segment. This analysis will enable GNL to take corrective action as necessary. Second, GNL will monitor customer and employee feedback weekly to quickly identify problems (such as problems in customer service) to keep customers satisfied.

Finally, GNL will conduct a marketing audit in mid-year and again at year-end to evaluate the effectiveness and efficiency of its marketing programs. In this way, GNL can pinpoint areas for improvement and prepare contingency plans for emerging problems.

# ENDNOTES

## Chapter 1

1. Ani Hadjian, "Communicate, innovate," *Fortune*, Autumn/Winter 1993: 25.
2. "AMA board approves new definition," *Marketing News*, 1 March 1985: 1.
3. Michael R. Solomon, "Deep-seated materialism: The case of Levi's 501 jeans," in Richard Lutz (ed.) *Advances in Consumer Research* 13, Las Vegas: Association for Consumer Research, 1986: 619–22.
4. Peter F. Drucker, *Management: Tasks, Responsibilities, Practices*, New York: Harper & Row, 1972: 64–5.
5. "McCain drops genetically altered spuds," *Calgary Herald*, 29 November 1999: D5.
6. Peter F. Drucker, *Management*, New York: Harper & Row, 1973.
7. Randall Lane, "Prepackaged celebrity," *Forbes*, 20 December 1993: 86.
8. Bill Saporito, "Behind the tumult at P&G," *Fortune*, 7 March 1994: 74(6).
9. Linda Grant, "Mattel gets all dolled up," *U.S. News & World Report*, 13 December 1993: 72(4).
10. Adapted from Carly Fiorina's talk given at the Schulich School of Business, York University, October 28, 2003.
11. Theodore Levitt, "Marketing myopia," *Harvard Business Review*, July–August 1960: 45–56.
12. *Canadian Business*, 26 December 1997: 66–7.
13. "IKEA insists suppliers protect environment," *The Globe and Mail*, 25 November 1999.
14. "Dear Chrysler: Outsiders' advice on handling the odometer charge," *The Wall Street Journal*, 26 June 1987: 19.
15. Larry Edwards, "The decision was easy," *Advertising Age* 2, 26 August 1987: 106. For research and discussion related to public policy issues, see Paul N. Bloom and Stephen A. Greyser, "The maturing of consumerism," *Harvard Business Review*, November/December 1981: 130–9; George S. Day, "Assessing the effect of information disclosure requirements," *Journal of Marketing*, April 1976: 42–52; Dennis E. Garrett, "The effectiveness of marketing policy boycotts: Environmental opposition to marketing," *Journal of Marketing* 51, January 1987: 44–53; Michael Houston and Michael Rothschild, "Policy-related experiments on information provision: A normative model and explication," *Journal of Marketing Research* 17, November 1980: 432–49; Jacob Jacoby, Wayne D. Hoyer, and David A. Sheluga, *Misperception of Televised Communications*, New York: American Association of Advertising Agencies, 1980; Gene R. Laczniak and Patrick E. Murphy, *Marketing Ethics: Guidelines for Managers*, Lexington, MA: Lexington Books, 1985: 117–23; Lynn Phillips and Bobby Calder, "Evaluating consumer protection laws: Promising methods," *Journal of Consumer Affairs* 14, Summer 1980: 9–36; Donald P. Robin and Eric Reidenbach, "Social responsibility, ethics, and marketing strategy: Closing the gap between concept and application," *Journal of Marketing* 51, January 1987: 44–58; Howard Schutz and Marianne Casey, "Consumer perceptions of advertising as misleading," *Journal of Consumer Affairs* 15, Winter 1981: 340–57; Darlene Brannigan Smith and Paul N. Bloom, "Is consumerism dead or alive? Some new evidence," in Thomas C. Kinnear (ed.) *Advances in Consumer Research* 11, Provo, UT: Association for Consumer Research, 1984: 569–73.
16. Quoted in Alice Z. Cuneo, "SegaSoft Online games tap into cultlike mind-set," *Advertising Age*, 7 April 1997: 3.
17. William Leiss, Stephen Kline, and Sut Jhally, *Social Communication in Advertising: Persons, Products, and Images of Well-Being*, Toronto: Methuen, 1986; Jerry Mander, *Four Arguments for the Elimination of Television*, New York: Morrow, 1977.
18. George Stigler, "The economics of information," *Journal of Political Economy*, 1961: 69.
19. William Leiss, Stephen Kline, and Sut Jhally, *Social Communication in Advertising: Persons, Products, and Images of Well-Being*, Toronto: Methuen, 1986.
20. Andrew Wahl, "Tickets to rise," *Canadian Business*, 30 April 1999: 26–32.

## Chapter 2

1. David Greising, "I'd like the world to buy a Coke," *BusinessWeek*, 13 April 1998: 70–6.
2. Theodore Levitt, "Marketing myopia," *Harvard Business Review*, September–October 1975: 1ff.
3. Seth Lubove, "Aim, focus and shoot," *Forbes*, 26 November 1990: 67, 68, 70.
4. Joshua Levine, "Badass sells," *Forbes*, 21 April 1997: 142–8.
5. Tom Seery, "RV makers targeting new niche, " *Post and Courier (Charleston, SC)*, 25 May 1997: 1–2D.
6. Jeffrey Zygmont, "In command at Campbell," *Sky*, March 1993: 52–62.

7. Thomas Petzinger Jr., "The front lines: Aly Abulleil finds facts by tracking feelings," *The Wall Street Journal Interactive Edition*, 4 September 1998.

8. An influential argument for this perspective can be found in Theodore Levitt, "The globalization of markets," *Harvard Business Review*, May–June 1983: 92–102.

9. Juliana Koranteng, "Reebok finds its second wind as it pursues global presence," *Advertising Age International*, January 1998: 18.

10. Terry Clark, "International marketing and national character: A review and proposal for an integrative theory," *Journal of Marketing*, 54, October 1990: 66–79.

11. Norihiko Shirouzu, "Snapple in Japan: How a splash dried up," *Wall Street Journal*, 15 April 1996: B1 (2).

12. Sara Hope Franks, "Overseas, it's what inside that sells," *Washington Post National Weekly Edition*, 5–11 December 1994: 21.

13. William Echikson, "The trick to selling in Europe," *Fortune*, 20 September 1993: 82.

14. Nikhil Deogun and Jonathan Karp, "For Coke in India, Thumbs Up is the real thing," *Wall Street Journal*, 29 April 1998: B1 (2).

15. Bradley Johnson, "Unisys touts service in global ads," *Advertising Age*, 3(2), 15 February 1993: 59.

16. Sinclair Stewart, "Tim Hortons brews new U.S. campaign," *Strategy Magazine*, 27 September 1999: 3.

17. Sak Onkvisit and John J. Shaw, *International Marketing: Analysis and Strategy*, 2nd ed., New York: Macmillan, 1993.

18. "Kodak alleges Fuji photo is dumping color photographic paper in the U.S.," *Wall Street Journal*, 22 February 1993: B6.

19. Andrea Mandel-Campbell, "McCain tries to thaw South American biz," *Marketing Magazine*, 7 October 1996: 5.

20. www.thebodyshop.ca

21. Quote by John Shad, former chairman of the U.S. Securities and Exchange Commission, in N. Craig Smith and John A. Quelch, *Ethics in Marketing*, Homewood, IL: Richard D. Irwin, 1993.

22. "Shareholders and General Public Say Corporations Should Balance Profits with Social Responsibilities, Poll Reveals," press release, Canadian Democracy and Corporate Accountability Commission, http://www.corporate-accountability.ca, 9 January 2002.

23. www.mbnet.mb.ca/crm/law/cac01.html

24. www.geocites.com/WallStreet/Floor/3105/RIGHTS.html

25. Joan C. Szabo, "Business pitches in after Andrew," *Nation's Business*, October 1992:37–9.

26. Mark Abley, *The Ice Storm: January, 1998*, Montreal: McClelland and Stewart.

27. Advertising Standards Canada, "1998 Ad Complaints Report," www.canad.com.

28. www.environmentalchoice.com

29. Catherine Arnst, Stanley Reed, Gay McWilliams, and De'Ann Weimer, "When green begets green," *Business Week* 10 November 1997: 98–106.

30. Catherine Arnst, Stanley Reed, Gay McWilliams, and De'Ann Weimer, "When green begets green," *Business Week* 10 November 1997: 98–106.

31. Nancy Arnott "Marketing with a passion," *Sales & Marketing Management,* January 1994: 64–71.

32. www.avon.com/about/women/global/current_programs.html.

33. www.equalopportunity.on.ca/enggraf/business/labert.html.

34. Patricia Digh, "America's largest untapped market: Who they are, the potential they represent," *Fortune*, 2 March 1998: S1–S12.

## Chapter 3

1. Industry Canada, *Small Business Quarterly*, Spring 2000, www.strategis.ic.gc.ca.

2. Eve Lazarus, "Sizing up the sizzle," *Marketing Magazine*, 5 June 2000: 17.

3. "Seizing the occasion," *Marketing Magazine Online*, August 13, 2001.

4. Craig Saunders, "Peachtree invests in brand-building," *Strategy Magazine*, 27 March 2000: 1.

5. Judann Pollack, "Kraft's Miracle Whip targets core consumers with '97 ads," *Advertising Age*, 3 February 1997: 12.

6. Robert L. Burr, "Market segments and other revelations," *Journal of Services Marketing* 1, Fall 1987: 59–67.

7. "Vital signs," *Financial Post*, 1 April 1999: C8.

8. "How Ocean Spray gave cranberries some sparkle," *The New York Times*, 26 November 1992: D1.

9. Bill Guns, president, SRI Consulting, personal communication, 1998.

10. Environics Research Group Web site, www.erg.environics.net/tribe/default.asp.

11. Caitlin Kelly, "A Jones for a Soda: Peter van Stolk is bottling success in Fufu Berry and Vanilla Coke flavours," *The Ottawa Citizen*. Jan 15, 2000, pg. B2.

12. Jennifer Lawrence, "Gender-specific works for diapers—almost too well," *Advertising Age*, 8 February 1993: S-10.

13. Keith Morgan, "Designed by women, Volvo concept car will please both sexes," *The Gazette*. Montreal, Que.: Mar 30, 2004. pg. E.1.

14. Astrid Van Den Broek, "Not so tough a sell," *Marketing Magazine*, 19/26 July 1999.

15. Kathleen Martin, "Boys Read." *Marketing Magazine,* January 20, 2003.]

16. David K. Foot and Daniel Stoffman, *Boom, bust and echo 2000: Profiting from the demographic shift in the new millennium*, Macfarlane Walter & Ross, Toronto, 1998.

17. David K. Foot and Daniel Stoffman, *Boom, bust and echo 2000: Profiting from the demographic shift in the new millennium*, Macfarlane Walter & Ross, Toronto, 1998.

18. David K. Foot and Daniel Stoffman, *Boom, bust and echo 2000: Profiting from the demographic shift in the new millennium*, Macfarlane Walter & Ross, Toronto, 1998: 124.

19. "Kids with cash," *Marketing Magazine*, 29 November 1999: 76.

20. Liza Finlay, "A lot more than just a piggy bank," *Marketing Magazine*, 4/11 January 1999: 14.

21. Statistics Canada, Cansim Matrix #6367, www.statcan.ca/ english/pgdb/people/populat/demo10a.htm.

22. Charles M. Schaninger and William D. Danko, "A conceptual and empirical comparison of alternate household life cycle markets," *Journal of Consumer Research* 19, March 1993: 580–94.

23. James Careless, "Condos find their niche," *Marketing Magazine*, 25 January 1999: 12.

24. www.statcan.ca; Statistics Canada, *The Population Census of Canada, 2000.*

25. Bill Keenan, "Snob appeal," *Marketing Magazine*, 8 May 2000: 15.

26. Michael R. Solomon, Judith L. Zaichkowsky, and Rosemary Polegato, *Consumer Behaviour: Buying, Having and Being*, Canadian Edition, Toronto: Prentice Hall Canada Inc., 1999: 476.

27. Danny Kucharsky, "Quebec's distinct specialty TV," *Marketing Magazine*, 20 March 2000: 22.

28. "1996 Census: Ethnic origin, visible minorities," *Statistics Canada Daily*, 17 February 1998.

29. Deanie Kolybabi, "Time for a closer look at the Aboriginal market," *Marketing Magazine*. September 22, 2003.

30. Julie McCann, "Native niches," *Marketing Magazine*, 14 September 1998: 15–7.

31. Ken Waldie, "Out of the gate, financing aboriginal enterprises," *Summit*, November 1998: 56.

32. "1996 Census: Ethnic origin, visible minorities", *Statistics Canada Daily*, 17 February 1998.

33. Eun-Mi (Liz) Adams, "The big piece of the mosaic," *Marketing Magazine*, 21 June 1999: 16–7.

34. "2001 Census: Household Income Groups (24) in Constant 2000 dollars," Statistics Canada.

35. Eun-Mi (Liz) Adams, "The big piece of the mosaic," *Marketing Magazine*, 21 June 19/99: 16–7.

36. Astrid Van Den Broek, "Cozying up to kosher," *Marketing Magazine*, 5 June 2000:18–9.

37. Carey Toane, "Veering off from the mainstream," *Marketing Magazine*, 5 June 2000: 24.

38. Eun-Mi (Liz) Adams, "The big piece of the mosaic," *Marketing Magazine*, 21 June 1999: 16–7.

39. Terra Boots to Take Down Billboards. CBC News Online. October 8, 2003. www.cbc.ca/stories/2003/10/08.

40. David Menzies, "It's Only Advertising," *Marketing Magazine,* January 12, 2004.

41. "The rich list: How the rich spend their money," *The National Post*, 22 April 2000, www.nationalpost.com/content/features/rich-list/spend.html.

42. Jo Marney, "When the urge hits," *Marketing Magazine*, 29 March 1999.

43. Canada Post Web site, www.canadapost.ca/cpc2/dirmlfiles/geopost.pdf.

44. Thomas V. Bonoma and Benson P. Shapiro, *Segmenting the Organizational Market*, Lexington, MA: Lexington Books, 1983.

45. Sinclair Stewart, "Grand & Toy launches The Stockroom," *Strategy Magazine*, 7 June 1999: D10.

46. Bruce Gillespie, "Get Ready For the New Wave," *National Post*, Nov. 24, 2003 pg FE.01.F.

47. Debbie Shork, "A matter of taste," *Marketing Magazine*, 22 May 2000: 14.

48. Heather Paris and Henry Wong, "Toyota sells functional fun," *Marketing Magazine*, 20 March 2000: 27.

49. Jeannette Hanna, "How to expand your brand," *Marketing Magazine*. April 1, 2002.

50. William Echikson, "Aiming at high and low markets," *Fortune*, 22 March 1993: 89.

51. William Echikson, "Aiming at high and low markets," *Fortune*, 22 March 1993: 89.

52. Becky Ebenkamp, "No Dollars for Bowling," *Brandweek*, 27 March 2000: 56–8.

53. Kathleen Martin-James, "Peak pita performance," *Marketing Magazine*, 10 April 2000: 18.

54. Michael Treacy and Fred Wiersama. "Customer Intimacy and Other Value Disciplines". *Harvard Business Review*. Jan-Feb 1993: 84–93.

55. Ian P. Murphy, "Beverages don't mean a thing if they ain't got that zing," *Marketing News*, 14 April 1997: 1.

56. Shawna Cohen, "Energizing elixirs," *Marketing Magazine*, 3 April 2000: 12–3.

57. Chris Daniels, "Little porn shop going mainstream," *Marketing Magazine*, 29 May 2000.

58. Eve Lazarus, "Lemon-aid," *Marketing Magazine*, 11 October 1999: 15.

59. Cassies Awards: Listerine Mouthwash and PocketPaks, *Marketing Magazine Online*, November 18, 2002.

60. Martin R. Lautman, "End-benefit segmentation and prototypical bonding," *Journal of Advertising Research*, June/July 1991: 9–18.

61. "The University Crunch," *Maclean's Magazine*, November 18, 2002, 21–62.

62. Industry Canada, *Small Business Quarterly*, Spring 2000, www.strategis.ic.gc.ca.

## Chapter 4

1. Ken Deal, "The eyes and ears of business," *Marketing Magazine*, 17 May 1999: 1.

2. Chris Flanagan, "Proof positive," *Marketing Magazine*, 17 May 1999: 15.

3. Daniel Erasmus, "A common language for strategy series: Mastering information management," *National Post (National Edition)*. Don Mills, Ont.: Sep 18, 2001. pg. M.10.

4. Daniel Erasmus, "A common language for strategy series: Mastering information management," *National Post (National Edition)*. Don Mills, Ont.: Sep 18, 2001. pg. M.10.

5. S.J. Diamond, "Trend tracking," *Los Angeles Times*, 29 March 1993: E1.

6. www.speakers.com/popcorn.htm, accessed 2 August 1998.

7. Statistics Canada Web site, www.statcan.ca/english/IPS/Data/63–224-XPB.html.

8. SurveySite Web site, www.surveysite.com.

9. Michael R. Solomon and Elnora W. Stuart, *Marketing: Real People, Real Choices*, Upper Saddle River, NJ: Prentice Hall, 1997.

10. Yumiko One, "An ad for smudge-proof makeup rubs a big marketer the wrong way," *Wall Street Journal*, 12 April 1996: B1.

11. Peter R. Peacock, "Data mining in marketing: Part I," *Marketing Management*, Winter 1998: 9–18.

12. Peter R. Peacock, "Data mining in marketing: Part I," *Marketing Management*, Winter 1998: 9–18.

13. Paul C. Judge, "Do you know who your most profitable customers are?" *Business Week Online*, September 14, 1998, Accessed at www.Businessweek.com/1998/37/B3595144.html.

14. Paul Ferriss, "'Ice cream' powers Mercedes-Benz," *Marketing Magazine*, June 9, 2003: 2.

15. Cyndee Miller, "Sometimes a researcher has no choice but to hang out in a bar," *Marketing News*, 3 January 1994: 16(2).

16. Lauren Sherman, "Dancing into the hearts of teens," *Marketing Magazine*. January 20, 2003: 10.

17. Annetta Miller, "You are what you buy," *Newsweek*, 4 June 1990: 59(2).

18. "Special report: Research: What role should research play?" *Strategy Magazine*, 1 September 1997: 23.

19. Terry Taciuk, "Guiding consumer apathy," *Marketing Magazine Online*. May 5, 2003.

20. David Kiley, "At long last, Detroit gives consumers the right of way," *Adweek*, 6 June 1988: 25–7.

21. Jack Weber, "Absorbing some changes," *Quirk's Article # 101*, November 1994, accessed via www.quirks.com, 26 January 1998.

22. "Special report: Research: What role should research play?" *Strategy Magazine*, 1 September 1997: 23.

23. "Special report: Research: What role should research play?" *Strategy Magazine*, 1 September 1997: 23.

24. Nancy Vonk, "Fun with dull numbers," *Marketing Magazine*, 10 April 2000: 26.

25. Mark MacDonald, "Workshops improving service," *Nanaimo Daily News*. Nanaimo, B.C.: Apr 29, 2003. pg. A.4.

26. Kelly Shermach, "Art of communication," *Marketing News*, 8 May 1995: 2.

27. Srikumar Rao, "Diaper-Beer Syndrome," *Forbes* (6 April 1998): 128(3).

28. Erica Zlomislic, "Special report: Legitimate researchers combat 'sugging'," *Strategy Magazine*, 14 April 1997: 40.

29. David Bosworth, "Bayer posts DM survey to health care professionals," *Strategy Magazine*, 16 August 1999: D5.

30. Fawzia Sheikh, "Kiosks ASK shoppers for their views," *Marketing Magazine*, 15 February 1999: 3.

31. Rebecca Piirto Heath, "The digital interviewer," *Marketing Tools*, August 1997: 28(3).

32. Peter Krasilovsky, "Surveys in cyberspace," *Marketing Tools*, November/December 1996: 18(4).

33. Michael J. McCarthy, "James Bond hits the supermarket: Stores snoop on shoppers' habits to boost sales," *Wall Street Journal*, 25 August 1993: B1(2).

34. Chris Daniels, "Real life research," *Marketing Magazine*, 17 May 1999: 15–6.

35. Chris Daniels, "Real life research," *Marketing Magazine*, 17 May 1999: 15–6.

36. Bait Car: Media Innovation Awards. *Marketing Magazine*. November 5, 2003.

37. Mike Galetto, "Turning trash to research treasure," *Advertising Age*, 17 April 1995: I-16.

38. Michael J. McCarthy, "James Bond hits the supermarket: Stores snoop on shoppers' habits to boost sales," *Wall Street Journal*, 25 August 1993: B1(2).

39. Bruce L. Stern and Ray Ashmun, "Methodological disclosure: The foundation for effective use of survey research," *Journal of Applied Business Research* 7, 1991: 77–82.

40. Alan E. Wolf, "Most colas branded alike by testy magazine," *Beverage World*, 31 August 1991: 8.

41. Janet Simons, "Youth marketing: Children's clothes follow the latest fashion," *Advertising Age*, 14 February 1985: 16.

42. Gary Levin, "New adventures in children's research," *Advertising Age*, 9 August 1993: 17.

43. Alan Radding, "Consumer worry halts data-bases," *Advertising Age*, 11 February 1991: 28.

44. Alan Radding, "Consumer worry halts data-bases," *Advertising Age*, 11 February 1991: 28.

45. Amanda Maltby, "Adapting to Canada's new privacy rules," *Marketing Magazine*. November 3, 2003: 16–8.

46. Jan Larson, "It's a small world, after all," *Marketing Tools*, September 1997: 47–51.

47. Tara Parker-Pope, "Nonalcoholic beer hits the spot in Mideast," *Wall Street Journal*, 6 December 1995: B1(2).

48. SurveySite Web site, www.surveysite.com.

49. Jean Halliday, "Automakers involve consumers," *Advertising Age*, 31 January 2000: 82.

50. Jack Neff, "Safe at any speed," *Advertising Age*, 24 January 2000: 1, 12.

51. Sue Cummings, "Online music surveys look for future hits," *New York Times On Line*, 2 February 2001.

52. Jack Neff, "P&G weds data, sales," *Advertising Age*, 23 October 2000: 76.

53. James Heckman, "Turning the focus online," *Marketing News*, 28 February 2000: 15; Judith Langer, "'On' and 'offline' focus groups: Claims, questions," *Marketing News*, 5 June 2000: H38.

54. Dana James, "Precision decision," *Marketing News*, 27 September 1999: 24–25.

55. Erik Bruenwedel, "Poll position," *Brandweek*, 20 March 2000: 82.

56. Thomas L. Greenbaum, "Focus groups vs. online," *Advertising Age*, 14 February 2000: 34.

## Chapter 5

1. James R. Bettman, "The decision maker who came in from the cold," in Leigh McAllister and Michael Rothschild (eds.) *Advances in Consumer Research* 20, Provo, UT: Association for Consumer Research, 1990; John W. Payne, James R. Bettman, and Eric J. Johnson, "Behavioral decision research: A constructive processing perspective," *Annual Review of Psychology* 4, 1992: 87–131; Robert J. Meyer and Barbara E. Kahn, "Probabilistic models of consumer choice behavior," in Thomas S. Robertson and Harold H. Kassarjian (eds.) *Handbook of Consumer Behavior*, Englewood Cliffs, NJ: Prentice Hall, 1991: 85–123.

2. "Condoms cause concern among student consumers," *Chronicle, The University of B.C. Alumni Magazine* 53 (2), Summer 1999.

3. Vaughn, Richard, "How advertising works: A planning model revisited." *Journal of Advertising Research*, 26 (1), 57–66.

4. "Touch looms large as a sense that drives sales," *BrandPackaging* (May/June 1999): 39–40.

5. Abraham H. Maslow, *Motivation and personality*, 2nd ed., New York: Harper & Row, 1970.

6. Clayton Alderfer. *Existence, relatedness, & growth*, New York: Free Press, 1972.

7. Robert A. Baron and Donn Byrne, *Social psychology: Understanding human interaction*, 5th ed., Boston: Allyn & Bacon, 1987.

8. Rebecca Piirto Heath, "You can buy a thrill: Chasing the ultimate rush," *American Demographics I*, June 1997: 47–51.

9. Linda L. Price and Nancy Ridgway, "Development of a scale to measure innovativeness," in Richard P. Bagozzi and Alice M. Tybout (eds.) *Advances in Consumer Research* 10, Ann Arbor, MI: Association for Consumer Research, 1983: 679–84; Russell W. Belk, "Three scales to measure constructs related to materialism: Reliability, validity, and relationships to measures of happiness," in Thomas C. Kinnear (ed.) *Advances in Consumer Research* 11, Ann Arbor, MI: Association for Consumer Research, 1984: 291; Gordon R. Foxall and Ronald E. Goldsmith, "Personality and consumer research: Another look," *Journal of the Market Research Society* 30(2) 1988: 111–25; Ronald E. Goldsmith and Charles F. Hofacker, "Measuring consumer innovativeness," *Journal of the Academy of Marketing Science* 19(3) 1991: 209–21; Terence A. Shimp and Subhash Sharma, "Consumer ethnocentrism: Construction and validation of the CETSCALE," *Journal of Marketing Research* 24, August 1987: 282.

10. Emily Yoffe, "You are what you buy," *Newsweek*, 4 June 1990: 59.

11. Jeffrey F. Durgee, "Self-esteem advertising," *Journal of Advertising*, 14(4) 1986: 21.

12. Mark Etting, "How to make perfect patties," *Marketing Magazine*, 26 October 1998: 47.

13. Jennifer Gilbert, "New teen obsession," *Advertising Age*, 14 February 2000: 38.

14. Benjamin D. Zablocki and Rosabeth Moss Kanter, "The differentiation of life-styles," *Annual Review of Sociology I,* 1976: 269–97.

15. Alan R. Hirsch, "Effects of ambient odors on slot-machine usage in a Las Vegas casino," *Psychology & Marketing* 12(7), October 1995: 585–94.

16. Marianne Meyer, "Attention shoppers!" *Marketing and Media Decisions* 23, May 1988: 67.

17. Eben Shapiro, "Need a little fantasy? A bevy of new companies can help," *The New York Times,* 10 March 1991: F4.

18. Brad Edmondson, "Pass the meat loaf," *American Demographics,* January 1989: 19.

19. Robert La Franco, "Wallpaper sonatas," *Forbes,* 25 March 1996: 114; Louise Lee, "Background music becomes hoity-toity," *The Wall Street Journal,* 22 December 1995: B1(2).

20. Bernice Kanner, "Trolling in the aisles," *New York,* 16 January 1989: 12; Michael Janofsky, "Using crowing roosters and ringing business cards to tap a boom in point-of-purchase displays," *The New York Times,* 21 March 1994: D9.

21. Stephanie Whittaker, "Stopping them cold," *Marketing Magazine,* 5 April 1999.

22. Wendy Cuthbert, "Gadgets and gizmos," *Strategy Magazine,* 27 September 1999: 21.

23. John P. Robinson, "Time squeeze," *Advertising Age,* February 1990: 30–3.

24. Leonard L. Berry, "Market to the perception," *American Demographics,* February 1990: 32.

25. Richard W. Pollay, "Measuring the cultural values manifest in advertising," *Current Issues and Research in Advertising,* 1983: 71–92.

26. Michael Adams, "Clouds over Canada: The new social climate," www.erg.enviornics.net/news/default.asp?aID=400.

27. "Cashing in on the new nationalism," *Marketing Magazine,* 22 May 2000: 26.

28. Shawna Steinberg, "Oh, Canada in the spotlight," *Marketing Magazine,* 2 November 1998: 10–1.

29. Chris Daniels, "Canucks vs. Yanks," *Marketing Magazine,* 22 May 2000: 26–7.

30. Elliot Ettenberg, "Red, White, and Red, eh." *Marketing Magazine, 10* November, 2003: 8.

31. Tony Spencer, "Going Canadian," *Marketing Magazine,* 7 September 1998: 23.

32. Helena Katz, "Distinctly Quebecois," *Marketing Magazine,* 26 April 1999: 13.

33. Jack Kohane, "Wampole Canada taps into sappy idea," *Marketing Magazine,* 5 October 1998: 2.

34. Danny Kucharsky, "Migrating to Montreal," *Marketing Magazine,* July 14/21, 2003: 8.

35. October 25, 2003, "What's In a Name? GM Embarrassed over LaCrosse," by Trevor Hofmann, Canadian Auto Press, www.auto123.com/en/info/news/news,view.spy?artid=18027.

36. Brandon Watson, "The new frontiers," *Marketing Magazine,* 21 June 1999: 14.

37. Astrid Van Den Broek, "Speaking the same language," *Marketing Magazine,* 21 June 1999: 13.

38. Michelle Warren, "Telus, Fat Free tailor Indian ad effort," *Marketing Magazine,* 17 November, 2003: 3.

39. Joanne Thomas Yaccato, "Through the gender lens," *Marketing Magazine,* 30 June/7 July, 2003: 14.

40. Robert Beaudoin and Daniel Charron, "Answering the needs of female drivers," *Marketing Magazine,* 30 June /7 July, 2003: 16.

41. Chris Daniels, "The rize of men's mags," *Marketing Magazine,* 22 September, 2003: 18.

42. "Canada's hole-y grail," *Marketing Magazine,* 6 September 1999: 30.

43. www.rcpsych.ac.uk/press/preleases/pr/pr_308.htm.

44. Richard P. Coleman, "The continuing significance of social class to marketing," *Journal of Consumer Research* 10, December 1983: 265–80.

45. J. Michael Munson and W. Austin Spivey, "Product and brand-user stereotypes among social classes: Implications for advertising strategy," *Journal of Advertising Research* 21, August 1981: 37–45.

46. Stuart U. Rich and Subhash C. Jain, "Social class and life cycle as predictors of shopping behavior," *Journal of Marketing Research* 5, February 1968: 41–9.

47. Michael Shnayerson, "The champagne city," *Vanity Fair,* December 1997: 182–202.

48. Nathan Kogan and Michael A. Wallach, "Risky shift phenomenon in small decision-making groups: A test of the information exchange hypothesis," *Journal of Experimental Social Psychology* 3, January 1967: 75–84; Nathan Kogan and Michael A. Wallach, *Risk Taking,* New York: Holt, Rinehart and Winston, 1964; Arch G. Woodside and M. Wayne DeLozier, "Effects of word-of-mouth advertising on consumer risk taking," *Journal of Advertising,* Fall 1976: 12–9.

49. Donald H. Granbois, "Improving the study of customer in-store behavior," *Journal of Marketing* 32, October 1968: 28–32.

50. Robert D. Hof, "Special report: Internet communities," *Business Week,* 5 May 1997: 63(8).

51. Len Strazewski, "Tupperware locks in new strategy," *Advertising Age,* 8 February 1988: 30.

52. Kathleen Debevec and Easwar Iyer, "Sex roles and consumer perceptions of promotions, products, and self: What do we know and where should we be headed," in Richard J. Lutz (ed.) *Advances in Consumer Research* 13, Provo,

UT: Association for Consumer Research, 1986: 210–4; Lynn J. Jaffe and Paul D. Berger, "Impact on purchase intent of sex-role identity and product positioning," *Psychology & Marketing*, Fall 1988: 259–71.

53. Kathleen Debevec and Easwar Iyer, "Sex roles and consumer perceptions of promotions, products and self"; Deborah E. S. Frable, "Sex typing and gender ideology: Two facets of the individual's gender psychology that go together," *Journal of Personality and Social Psychology* 56(1), 1989: 95–108; Lynn J. Jaffe and Paul D. Berger, "Impact on purchase intent of sex-role identity and product positioning," Keren A. Johnson, Mary R. Zimmer, and Linda L. Golden, "Object relations theory: Male and female differences in visual information processing," in Melanie Wallendorf and Paul Anderson (eds.) *Advances in Consumer Research* 14, Provo, UT: Association for Consumer Research, 1986: 83–7; Leila T. Worth, Jeanne Smith, and Diane M. Mackie, "Gender schematicity and preference for gender-typed products," *Psychology & Marketing* 9, January 1992: 17–30.

54. James Pollock, "Home Hardware drops handyman slogan," *Marketing Magazine*, 24 February 1997: 2.

55. Everett M. Rogers, *Diffusion of Innovations*, 3rd ed., New York: Free Press, 1983.

56. Steven A. Baumgarten, "The innovative communicator in the diffusion process," *Journal of Marketing Research* 12, February 1975: 12–8.

57. Robert V. Kozinets, "E-tribalized marketing?: The strategic implications of virtual communities of consumption," *European Management Journal* 17, 3 (June 1999): 252–64.

58. Tom Weber, "Net's hottest game brings people closer," *The Wall Street Journal Interactive Edition*, 20 March 2000.

59. Quoted in Marc Gunther, "The newest addiction," *Fortune*, 2 August 1999: 123.

60. Greg Jaffe, "No MTV for Widespread Panic just loads of worshipful fans," *The Wall Street Journal Interactive Edition*, 17 February 1999.

61. Amy Harmon, "Illegal kidney action pops up on eBay's site," *The New York Times on the Web*, 3 September 1999.

62. Ravi S. Achrol and Philip Kotler, "Marketing in the network economy," *Journal of Marketing* 63 (Special Issue 1999): 146–63.

63. Bob Tedeschi, "Product reviews from anyone with an opinion," *The New York Times on the Web*, 25 October 1999.

64. "Dunkin' Donuts buys out critical Website," *The New York Times on the Web*, 27 August 1999.

65. Bradley Johnson, "febrezekilldogs.com (and birds too)," *Advertising Age*, 10 May 1999: 8.

66. Nicholas Kulish, "Still bedeviled by satan rumors, P&G battles back on the Web," *The Wall Street Journal Interactive Edition*, 21 September 1999.

## Chapter 6

1. *US Statistical Abstract*, 1997: 330.

2. B. Charles Ames and James D. Hlaracek, *Managerial Marketing for Industrial Firms*, New York: Random House Business Division, 1984; Edward F. Fern and James R. Brown, "The industrial/consumer marketing dichotomy: A case of insufficient justification," *Journal of Marketing*, Spring 1984: 68–77.

3. www.census.gov/pub/epcd/www/naics/html.

4. Terry Lefton, "Sprint positions as biz solution," *Brandweek*, 11 July 1994: 6.

5. Statistics Canada, Consolidated federal, provincial, territorial, and local government revenue and expenditures, www.statcan.ca/english/pgdb/State/Government.

6. Government of Canada Web site, www.canada.gc.ca/depts.

7. MERX home page, www.merx.ca/english2/about.html.

8. Daniel H. McQuiston, "Novelty, complexity, and importance as causal determinants of industrial buyer behavior," *Journal of Marketing*, April 1989: 66–79.

9. J. Joseph Cronin Jr. and Michael H. Morris, "Satisfying customer expectations: The effect on conflict and repurchase intentions in industrial marketing channels," *Journal of the Academy of Marketing Science*, Winter 1989: 41–9; Thomas W. Leigh and Patrick F. McGraw, "Mapping the procedural knowledge of industrial sales personnel: A script-theoretic investigation," *Journal of Marketing*, January 1989: 16–34; William J. Qualls and Christopher P. Puto, "Organizational climate and decision framing: An integrated approach to analyzing industrial buying," *Journal of Marketing Research*, May 1989: 179–92.

10. Ruby Roy Dholakia, "Decision-making time in organizational buying behavior: An investigation of its antecedents," *Journal of the Academy of Marketing Science*, Fall 1993: 281–92.

11. Neville Nankivell, "Total change: Canadian companies reach out online," *Financial Post*, 26 April 2000: E3.

12. Eve Lazarus, "Cafeteria Blues," *Marketing Magazine Online*, 19 January, 2004.

13. Ruby Roy Dholakia, "Decision-making time in organizational buying behavior: An investigation of its antecedents," *Journal of the Academy of Marketing Science*, Fall 1993: 281–92.

14. Tom Venetis, "Extranets take over for EDI," *Computer Dealer News*, 15(39), 15 October 1999: 15.

15. Simon Tuck "Point2.com mines success in heavy equipment," *The Globe and Mail*, 22 June 2000: T1.

16. Lori Enos, "Canada poised for B2B boom," *E-Commerce Times*, 11 January, 2001.

17. Neville Nankivell, "Total change: Canadian companies reach out online," *Financial Post*, 26 April 2000: E3.

18. www.worldbid.com.

19. Debbie Barrett, "Taking a page from efficiency's book: Tiny technology tools save city workers lots of frustration and create new ways to bond," *Technology in Government* 6(9), Spring 1999: 29.

20. Tom Venetis, "Extranets take over for EDI," *Computer Dealer News*, 15(39), 15 October 1999: 15.

21. Kimberly Chapman, "A matter of life and death," *Network World Canada* 9(15), 13 August 1999: 20.

22. Erik Heinrich, "What can work: one buyer, many sellers," *Toronto Star*, 23 October 2003: K.02.

23. Kevin Ferguson, "Purchasing in packs," *Business Week*, 1 November 1999.

24. Marie Clarke, "Strategies: Pulling together," *Canadian Business*, November 1988.

25. Wendy Stueck, "Onvia lets small firms buy like big business," *The Globe and Mail*, 22 June 2000: T9.

## Chapter 7

1. Information obtained from the Woodstream Corporation.

2. Lee D. Dahringer, "Marketing services internationally: Barriers and management strategies," *Journal of Services Marketing* 5, Summer 1991: 5–17, Table 2.

3. Jim Carlton, "Support lines' busy signals hurt PC makers," *Wall Street Journal*, 6 July 1995: B1 (2).

4. Lou W. Turkey and Douglas L. Fugate, "The multidimensional nature of service facilities: Viewpoints and recommendations," *Journal of Services Marketing* 6, Summer 1992: 37–45.

5. David H. Maister, "The psychology of waiting lines," in J. A. Czepiel, M. R. Solomon, and C. F. Surprenant, eds., *The Service Encounter: Managing Employee/Customer Interaction in Service Businesses*, Lexington, MA: Lexington Books, 1985: 113–24.

6. Richard Gibson, *Wall Street Journal Interactive Edition*, 3 September 1998.

7. Norma Ramage, "Flames score with marketing plan," *Marketing Magazine*, 6 December 1999: 4.

8. Astrid Van Den Broek, "ING expansion includes cafés and Web," *Marketing Magazine*, 5 April 1999: 4.

9. Michael T. Kaufman, "About New York: The nail salon of the 90s: Massages for the clothed," *The New York Times*, 1 December 1993: B3.

10. Rachel Lipton, "You don't have to be a celebrity . . . to live like one," *National Post*, 24 April 1999: 25.

11. "Employment by industry, population 15 years of age and over," Statistics Canada, CANSIM, Matrix 3472, www.statcan.ca/english/pgdb/Economy/Economic/econ40.htm.

12. John A. Czepiel, Michael R. Solomon, and Carol F. Surprenant, eds., *The Service Encounter: Managing Employee/Customer Interaction in Service Businesses*, Lexington, MA: D.C. Heath and Company, 1985.

13. *The Economist*, December 13–19, 2003: 79.

14. Caryne Brown, "Making money making toys," *Black Enterprise*, November 1993: 68–77.

15. Roman G. Hiebing and Scott W. Copper, *Instructor's Manual: The Successful Marketing Plan*, Lincolnwood, IL: NTC Business Books, 1992.

16. Lindsay Elliott, "What were they thinking?" *Realm*, Winter 1998: 29.

17. James Dao, "From a collector of turkeys, a tour of a supermarket zoo," *The New York Times*, 24 September 1995: F12.

18. IRAP Web site. http://irap-pari.nrc-cnrc.gc.ca

19. John Gray, "U.S. optical company eyes Vancouver market," *Strategy Magazine*, 15 February 1999: 7.

20. Craig Saunders, "Canada test ground for Korean appliance manufacturer," *Strategy Magazine*, 5 June 2000: 5.

21. "Test marketing a new product: When it's a good idea and how to do it," *Profit Building Strategies for Business Owners*, March 1993: 14.

22. George Anders, "Vital statistic: Disputed cost of creating a drug," *The Wall Street Journal*, 9 November 1993: B1.

23. Edmund L. Andrews, "When imitation isn't the sincerest form of flattery," *The New York Times*, 9 August 1990: 20.

24. William M. Bulkeley, "PictureTel to introduce $6,000 system to make PCs work as video telephones," *The Wall Street Journal*, 16 July 1993: B8.

25. Mark De Wolf, "Barq's bites into Canadian root beer market," *Strategy Magazine*, 7 July 1997: 8.

26. Everett Rogers, *Diffusion of Innovations*, New York: Free Press, 1983: 247–51.

27. Beth Hitchcock, "Pore wars," *Marketing Magazine*, 12 April 1999: 16–7.

28. Christopher Power, Kathleen Kerwin, Ronald Grover, Keith Alexander, and Robert D. Hof, "Flops," *Business Week* 3332, 16 August 1993: 77.

29. Everett Rogers, *Diffusion of Innovations*, New York: Free Press, 1983: Chapter 6.

30. Statistics Canada, *Market Research Handbook*, www.statcan.ca; and Statistics Canada, "Selected dwelling characteristics and household equipment," 1995, 1993, 1991, 1990, 1987, 1984, 1981, www.statcan.ca.

31. Thomas S. Robertson and Yoram Wind, "Organizational psychographics and innovativeness," *Journal of Consumer Research* 7, June 1980: 24–31.

**Chapter 8**

1. David Todd, "Dentyne Ice locks lips with youth target," *Strategy Magazine*, 8 May 2000: B14.

2. Wendy Cuthbert, "Big Rock brews up marketing push: Alberta brewer wants stronger foothold in Ontario and B.C.," *Marketing Magazine,* 20 July 1998: 1.

3. Ian P. Murphy, "All-American icon gets a new look," *Marketing News,* 18 August 1997: 6.

4. Brian Dunn, "Taking on Tropicana," *Marketing Magazine*, 2 November 1998: 16.

5. Astrid Van Den Broek, "Germ warfare," *Marketing Magazine*, 29 November 1999: 15.

6. Jo Marney, "Too much of a good thing," *Marketing Magazine*, 24 January 2000: 21.

7. www.ford.com/archive/edselhistory.html; www.lvrj.com/lvrj home/1998/Mar-29-Sun=1998/news/; www.theautochannel.

8. "Warner-Lambert strips Listerine," *Marketing Magazine*, 3 July 2000: 2.

9. Ed Brown, "Thwacking away for 66 years," *Fortune*, 4 August 1997: 40.

10. Gail Tom, Teresa Barnett, William Lew, and Jodean Selmonts, "Cueing the consumer: The role of salient cues in consumer perception," *Journal of Consumer Marketing*, 1987: 23–27.

11. Suzanne Steel, "Hudson's Bay Company set to join KFC, CIBC, IBM, O&Y and TD," *Financial Post*, 11 February 1999.

12. Andrea Coutu, "Covering their assets," *Realm*, Spring 1999: 33; Body Blockers Web site at www.bodyblocker.com.

13. Hugh Graham, "Launch annals of marketing," *Report on Business Magazine*, October 1998: 16–7.

14. David Aaker and Erich Joachimsthaler, "Brand leadership," *Brandweek*, 21 February 2000.

15. Kevin Lane Keller, "The brand report card," *Harvard Business Review*, January–February 2000.

16. Lesley Daw, "Pillsbury turnover," *Marketing Magazine*, 14 July 1997: 11–2.

17. Susan Caminiti, "How to win back customers," *Fortune*, 14 June 1993: 118; Craig Saunders, "Holt's launches private label promo blitz," *Strategy Magazine*, 31 July 2000: 3.

18. Betsy Spethmann and Karen Benezra, "Co-Branding or be damned," *Brandweek*, 21 November 1994: 21–4.

19. Keith McArthur, "Co-branding roulette," *The Globe and Mail*, 14 June 2000: www.theglobeandmail.com.

20. Stan Sutter, "Lessons in ingenuity," *Marketing Magazine*, 15 May 2000: 30; and Shawna Cohen, "The Pill is controversial once again," *Marketing Magazine*, 15 May 2000: 3.

21. Jack Neff, "P&G redefines the brand manager," *Advertising Age*, 13 October 1997: 1,18,20.

22. Pam Weisz, "Lever plans P&G-like moves," *Brandweek*, 10 January 1994: 1,6.

23. Gary Hoover, Alta Campbell, and Patrick J. Spain, *Hoover's Handbook of American Business 1994*, Austin: The Reference Press, 1994.

24. James B. Treece, "The great refrigerator race," *Business Week*, 15 July 1993: 78–81; "Whirlpool wins prize of $30 million to build efficient refrigerator," *The Wall Street Journal*, 30 June 1993: B8.

25. Zachary Schiller, "Frigidaire's run for the cold cash," *Business Week*, 15 July 1993: 81.

**Chapter 9**

1. Laura Pratt, "Trading places," *Financial Post Magazine*, March 1998: 97–100.

2. Michael L. Rothschild, "Marketing communications in nonbusiness situations or why it's so hard to sell brotherhood like soap," *Journal of Marketing*, Spring 1979: 11–20.

3. Kenneth Labich, "What will save the U.S. airlines," *Fortune*, 14 June 1993: 98–101.

4. Leslie Vreeland, "How to be a smart shopper," *Black Enterprise*, August 1993: 88.

5. Melissa Campanelli, "The price to pay," *Sales and Marketing Management*, September 1994: 96.

6. Andrew E. Serwer, "What price brand loyalty?" *Fortune*, 10 January 1994: 103–4; Richard Gibson, "General Mills to cut prices of 3 cereals and curb discounts," *The Wall Street Journal* 222(116), 14 December 1993: A10; Richard Gibson, "Kellogg boosts prices on many cereals; average 2.6% rise may meet resistance," *The Wall Street Journal*, 8 February 1994: A3, A8.

7. Judann Pollack, "Post's price play rocked category, but did it work," *Advertising Age*, 1 December 1997: 24.

8. Betsy McKay, "Coca-Cola sets prices at premium," *The Globe and Mail*, 16 November 1999: B18.

9. Joseph Pereira, "Early coupon campaign by Toys "R" Us may spark price war among discounters," *The Wall Street Journal*, 29 October 1993: B1.

10. Norma Ramage, "Nevada Bob's tries new brand stance," *Marketing Magazine*, 13 September 1999.

11. Steward Washburn, "Pricing basics: Establishing strategy and determining costs in the pricing decision," *Business Marketing*, July 1985, reprinted in Valerie Kijewski, Bob Donath, and David T. Wilson, eds., *The Best Readings from Business Marketing Magazine*, Boston: PWS-Kent Publishing Co., 1993: 257–69.

12. Steven Theobald, "Bay boss reverses upmarket tide," *The Telegram (St. John's)*, 3 July 1999: 26.

13. Greg Winter, "What keeps a bottom line healthy? Weight loss," *The New York Times*, 2 January 2001, accessed at www.nytimes.com/2001/01/02/business/02WEIG.html, 3 January 2001.

14. Ken Popovich and Mary Jo Foley, "Dell remains committed to pricing strategy," *eWeek*, 9 April 2001, accessed at www.eweek.com/articles/0,3658,s=701&a=9334,00.asp, 22 February 2002.

15. Tony Wong, "Some like it hot at Coca-Cola: Soft-drink maker exploring vending machines that raise the price of a can of pop when the weather warms up," *The Toronto Star*, 29 October 1999: Section Head, NEWS.

16. Jennifer Merritt, "The belle of the golf balls," *Business Week*, 29 July 1996: 6.

17. Zachary Schiller, "'Value pricing' pays off," *Business Week*, 1 November 1993: 32–3.

18. Jack Neff, "Diaper battle puts EDLP on injured list," *Advertising Age*, 14 August 1995: 3, 33.

19. Sebastian Rupley, "The PowerPC revolution," *PC/ Computing*, February 1994: 129–31; Marc Dodge, "New power chips," *PC/Computing*, February 1994: 116–7.

20. Jim Carlton, "Apple to launch Macintosh PowerPCs priced at level to gain market share," *Wall Street Journal*, 14 March 1994: B4.

21. Michael D. Mondello, "Naming your price," *Inc.*, July 1992: 159.

22. Paul Marck, "Telus pilot program serves up everything but the popcorn," *Edmonton Journal*, 22 February 2000: A-1.

23. Susanne Craig, "Wal-Mart has radically changed the retail scene," *The Financial Post*, 21 December 1996: 41.

24. "Challenging the high price at the pumps: Consumers force an inquiry on the gas industry," *Maclean's* 109(23), 3 June 1996: 17,19.

25. Michael MacDonald, "Charge against Irving Oil just a distraction: Liberal MP," *Canadian Press Newswire*, 1 October 1999.

26. Betsy McKay, "Coca-Cola sets prices at premium," *The Globe and Mail*, 16 November 1999: B18.

27. Douglas Lavin, "Goodbye to haggling: Savvy consumers are buying their cars like refrigerators," *Wall Street Journal*, 20 August 1993: B1, B3.

28. Alex Taylor III, "Soaring sales—but at a price," *Fortune*, 12 November 2001; Steve Erwin, "GM truck sales jump; Ford, Chrysler sales sink," *Ottawa Citizen*, 2 November 2001, p. E3.

29. "Bogus bargains cost Suzy Shier $1 million." *The Times Colonist*, 14 June 2003: E2.

30. Mike Roberts, "World beats a path to Vancouver's cheap CDs," *The Province (Vancouver)*, 1 August 1999: B1.

31. "Price discrimination enforcement guidelines," news release, Competition Bureau, Industry Canada, 1992-08-17.

32. Chris Flanagan, "Gas price group takes on the giants," *The Telegram (St. John's)*, 20 May 1999: 1.

33. Ryan Cleary, "Price-fixing charge dismissed," *The Telegram (St. John's)*, 21 March 2000: 1.

34. "Canadian participant in an international price-fixing conspiracy for a feed additive fined $2.25 million," news release, Competition Bureau, Industry Canada, 1999-09-24; "Former Roche executive convicted and fined for international conspiracies under the *Competition Act*," news release, Competition Bureau, Industry Canada, 1999-09-27.

35. "Federal watchdog has concerns over airline merger, says Globe," *Canadian Press Newswire*, 7 October 1999.

36. Jim Carlton, "Microsoft takes aim at Novell by cutting software price $35,000," *The Wall Street Journal* 222, 22 September 1993: B6.

37. Anita Lahey, "Wholesale war," *Marketing Magazine*, 27 April 1998.

38. Peter Verburg, "His party, your hangover," *Canadian Business*, 27 August 1999: 36–9.

39. Rahul Jacob, "The economy: Girding for worse," *Fortune*, 18 October 1993: 10.

40. Yumiki Ono, "As discounting rises in Japan, people learn to hunt for bargains," *The Wall Street Journal*, 31 December 1993: 1, 8.

41. Jacob Rahul, "Beyond quality and value," *Fortune*, Autumn/Winter 1993: 8(3).

42. George Burns, "McDonald's: Now it's just another burger joint," *Business Week*, 17 March 1997: 38; Bill McDowell and Laura Petrecca, "Burger King ads take slap at McD's," *Advertising Age*, 10 February 1997: 12.

43. Alisa Priddle, "Japanese car makers gaining ground," *The Edmonton Journal*, 8 December 1998: 18.

44. Lloyd Robertson, "Prairie farmers say the need as much as one billion dollars in aid to deal with a looming crisis in farm income," broadcast transcript, CTV National News, 4 November 1998.

45. Steve Mertl, "Forest industry battles switch to boardroom," *Times Colonist (Victoria)*, 12 October 1999: E1.

46. William G. Flanagan, "Thanks for the subsidies," *Forbes*, 7 July 1997: 120–7.

47. Amy E. Cortese and Marcia Stpeanek, "Goodbye to fixed pricing?" *Business Week,* 4 May 1998: 71–84.

48. Walter Baker, Mike Marn and Craig Zawada, "Price smarter on the Net," *Harvard Business Review,* February 2001, accessed at www.hbsp.harvard.edu/rcpt/filestream .asp?otype=s&ey=69541836& prodno=R0102J&order_id=1136431& type.pdf, 22 February 2002.

49. Jennifer Gilbert, "Drugstores wage a pricey online battle," *Advertising Age* (30 August 1999): 26.

50. "Bitter pill for the drug industry", *The Montreal Gazette*, 10 August 2003:A12., Business editorial.

51. Theresa Agovino, "US battle over Canadian drugs intensifies", *The Ottawa Citizen*, Business Article, 14 October 2003:C.2.

52. Theresa Agovino, "US battle over Canadian drugs intensifies," *The Ottawa Citizen*, Business Article, 14 October 2003:C.2.

53. David Gratzer, "American drugs, Canadian problems", Business Opinion, Editorials, *National Post*, 12 August 2003:A15.

54. Theresa Agovino, "US battle over Canadian drugs intensifies," *The Ottawa Citizen*, Business Article, 14 October 2003:C.2.

55. David Gratzer, "American drugs, Canadian problems", Business Opinion, Editorials, *National Post*, 12 August 2003:A15.

56. "Bitter pill for the drug industry", *The Montreal Gazette*, 10 August 2003:A12., Business editorial.

57. David Gratzer, "American drugs, Canadian problems", Business Opinion, Editorials, *National Post*, 12 August 2003:A15.

58. "Bitter pill for the drug industry", *The Montreal Gazette*, 10 August 2003:A12., Business editorial.

## Chapter 10

1. Thu Hien Dao, "Banks jump on kiosk bandwagon," *Financial Post* 2(58), 1 January 2000: C6.

2. G. Bruce Knecht, "Banks bag profits with supermarket branches," *The Wall Street Journal*, 20 May 1994: B1, B8.

3. Zena Olijnyk, "GroceryGateway struggles to meet heavy demand: phenomenal growth. Hoping for help from warehouse and new software," *Financial Post*, 18 May 2000: C9.

4. Jeffrey A. Tannenbaum, "Chain reactions," *Wall Street Journal*, 15 October 1993: R6.

5. Charise Clark, "The new face of franchising: From cool concepts to creative financing methods, franchising offers hot new growth opportunities," *Profit: The Magazine for Canadian Entrepreneurs* 18 (8), December 1999/January 2000: 36–40.

6. Robert L. Rose and Bridget O'Brian, "United, Lufthansa form marketing tie, dealing a setback to American Airlines," *The Wall Street Journal*, 4 October 1993: A4.

7. Allan J. Magrath, "The gatekeepers," *Across the Board*, April 1992: 43–6.

8. Scott Woolley, "The new distribution," *Forbes*, 4 November 1996: 164–5.

9. Richard Norman and Rafael Ramirez, "From value chain to value constellation: Designing interactive strategy," *Harvard Business Review*, July-August, 1993.

10. Scott Woolley, "Replacing inventory with information," *Forbes*, 24 March 1997: 54–8.

## Chapter 11

1. Jennifer Steinhauer, "Interactive stores make shopping an experience," *New York Times News Service* online, 28 February 1998.

2. Jacobson Consulting Inc., *The Retail Sector in Canada*, report prepared for the Retail Council of Canada, www.retailcouncil.org.

3. Michael Levy and Barton A. Weitz, *Retailing Management*, 3rd ed., Boston: Irwin/McGraw-Hill, 1998.

4. Stanley C. Hollander, "The wheel of retailing," *Journal of Retailing*, July 1960: 41.

5. William R. Davidson, Albert D. Bates, and Stephen J. Bass, "The retail life cycle," *Harvard Business Review*, November–December 1976: 89.

6. Gail DeGeorge, "Dilbert to the rescue," *Business Week*, 4 May 1998: 166.

7. "Safeway gas stations pose challenge to big oil," *The Globe and Mail*, 15 August 2000: B10.

8. Julia Flynn, "IKEA's new game plan," *Business Week*, 6 October 1997: 99 (2).

9. Astrid van den Broek, "Speaking the same language: Burger King cooks up a multicultural marketing menu," *Marketing Magazine*, 21 June 1999.

10. Judy Waytiuk, "The new native niche," *Marketing Magazine*, 22 May 2000: 13.

11. Robert E. Calem, "Coming to a cash register near you: Multimedia," *New York Times*, 31 July 1994: F7.

12. Marianne Meyer, "Attention shoppers!" *Marketing and Media Decisions*, May 1988: 67–70.

13. Gary Robins, "Wireless POS systems," *STORES*, February 1994: 47 (2).

14. Raju Mudhar, "Food for future thought: New database technology puts supermarkets in the high-tech fast lane," *Marketing Magazine*, 18 October 1999.

15. Diane Forget, chief systems, POS, Henry Birks & Sons, personal communication.

16. Alfred F. Lynch, "Training for a new ball game: Retailing in the 21st century," *The Futurist*, July/August 1992: 36–40.

17. Arthur Good and Stephen Granovsky, "Retail goes global," *Canadian Business Review* 22(2), Summer 1995: 31–3.

18. Norma Ramage, "Canadian cinnamon buns savoured in Asia," *Marketing Magazine*, 19 June 2000: 6.

19. Mitchell Russell, "The Gap dolls itself up," *Business Week*, 21 March 1994: 46.

20. Julie Liesse, "Welcome to the club," *Advertising Age* 2, 1 February 1993: 3 (2).

21. Debra Hazel, "The factory outlets' best of times: Belz's and other centers beat the recession," *Chain Store Age Executive*, November 1992: 39–42.

22. Michael Levy and Barton A. Weitz, *Retailing Management*, 3rd ed., Boston: Irwin/McGraw-Hill, 1998.

23. Jennifer Steinhauer, "Interactive stores make shopping an experience," *New York Times News Service* online, 28 February 1998.

24. "A wide world of sports shoes: Fixtures enhance appeal of world foot locker," *Chain Store Age Executive*, January 1993: 176–81.

25. Wendy Marx, "Shopping 2000," *Brandweek* 20 (2), 9 January 1995: 20.

26. Chris Eby, "A toast to opening of booze behemoth," *National Post*, 24 February 1999: B1.

27. "The sound of retail," *Chain Store Age*, January 1996: 3C–6C.

28. "Lobbyists against noise pollution pick up some unexpected allies," *Wall Street Journal*, 1 June 1990: B1.

29. "Design therapy: New trends in supermarket design can create moods that can enhance sales," *Canadian Grocer* 107(2), February 1993: 102–10.

30. George Condon, "Retailing as entertainment!: Is it fun to shop in your store?" *Canadian Grocer* 112(6), July/August 1998: 14–9.

31. "Service: Retail's no. 1 problem," *Chain Store Age*, 19 January 1987.

32. Elaine Underwood, "Mall busters, like crime, a boon for home shopping," *Brandweek*, 17 January 1994: 18 (2).

33. Stephanie Strom, "Bold stroke in Japan's art of retailing," *New York Times*, 23 April 1993: D1 (2).

34. Zena Olijnyk, "Supermarket chic. He's been raising food retailing to new heights: Architect Leslie Rebanks has transformed what used to be big boxes that sold groceries into cultural phenomena," *Financial Post*, 24 April 2000: C1,C4.

35. Kate Fitzgerald, "All roads lead to...," *Advertising Age*, 1 February 1993: S-1.

36. "Service memorial for Jacob Ghermazian," *Canadian Press Newswire*, 4 January 2000.

37. Michael Levy and Barton A. Weitz, *Retailing Management*, 3rd ed., Boston: Irwin/McGraw-Hill, 1998.

38. Pat Sloan, "Avon looks beyond direct sales," *Advertising Age*, 22 February 1993: 32; Seema Nayyar, "Avon calling, by fax, phone, and infomercial," *Brandweek*, 22 February 1993: 22–3.

39. John Browning and Spencer Reiss, "Encyclopedia of the new economy, Part I," *Wired*, March 1998: 105 (8).

40. Stratford Sherman, "Will the information superhighway be the death of retailing?" *Fortune*, 18 April 1994: 99(5), 110.

41. Boston Consulting Group and Retail Council of Canada, *The Canadian Online Retailing Report*, joint research project, June 19, 2000, www.bcg.com/media_center; "E-commerce: Shopping around the Web," *The Economist*, 26 February 2000: 65–93; A.C. Neilsen, *The Canadian Internet Survey*, Industry Canada, 12 April 2000.

42. Boston Consulting Group and Retail Council of Canada, *The Canadian Online Retailing Report*, joint research project, June 19, 2000, www.bcg.com/media_center.

43. http://www.shop.org/research/summary.htm.

44. Danny Kucharsky, "Log-ons & lace," *Marketing Magazine*, 24 January 2000.

45. John Grey, "Internet rewriting marketing rules: P&G," *Strategy: The Canadian Marketing Report*, 13 March 2000: 5.

46. Richard Covington, "Companies find the net helps trap surprising source of revenue,"

*International Herald Tribune*, accessed via ssnewslink, 23 February 1998.

47. Timothy J. Mullaney, "Jewellery Heist," *Business Week*, May 10, 2004, P. 82.

48. Patricia Sellers, "Inside the first e-Christmas," *Fortune*, 1 February 1999: 71; Boston Consulting Group and Retail Council of Canada, *The Canadian Online Retailing Report*, joint research project, June 19, 2000, www.bcg.com/media_center.

49. Boston Consulting Group and Retail Council of Canada, *The Canadian Online Retailing Report*, joint research project, June 19, 2000, www.bcg.com/media_center.

50. Lisa Napoli, *New York Times News Service Online*, 26 February 1998, accessed via ssnewslink.

51. Eve Lazarus, "Blast off," *Marketing Magazine*, July 2000: 12.

52. Andrew Tausz, "The Internet rewards Dell's directness," *Financial Post*, 17 April 2000: E1.

53. John Browning and Spencer Reiss, "Encyclopedia of the new economy, Part I," *Wired*, March 1998: 105 (8).

54. Richard Mackie, "Ontario unveils e-biz act," *The Globe and Mail*, 14 June 2000: B5.

55. "Future Shop is a veteran of the e-commerce world," *The Globe and Mail*, 30 November 1999: E21.

56. Dana Canedy, "Buying Barbie, Legos and Beanie Babies online," *New York Times News Service*, 27 July 1998.

57. Frances Huffman, "Special delivery," *Entrepreneur*, February 1993: 81 (3).

58. Paul Hughes, "Profits due," *Entrepreneur*, February 1994: 74 (4).

59. Margaret Nearing, "A comfy place to shop: Canadians' increasing fondness for catalogue ordering is spurring red-hot sales growth," *Marketing Magazine*, 7 December 1998.

60. Zena Olinjnyk, "Sears shuts call centre: Internet more profitable," *Financial Post*, 12 May 2000: C6.

61. "Zellers delivers baby catalogue," *Marketing Magazine*, 21 June 1999: 3.

62. David Carr, "The limits of e-mail," *Marketing Magazine*, 24 April 2000.

63. Kate Ballen, "Get ready for shopping at work," *Fortune*, 15 February 1988: 95.

64. Michael Levy and Barton A. Weitz, *Retailing Management*, 3rd ed., Boston: Irwin/McGraw-Hill, 1998; Len Strazewski, "Tupperware locks in new strategy," *Advertising Age*, 8 February 1988: 30.

65. Peter Wilkinson, "For your eyes only," *Savvy Woman*, January 1989: 68.

66. Mario Brossi and Joseph Marino, *Multilevel Marketing: A Legal Primer*, Washington, DC: Direct Selling Association, 1990.

67. Linda Lipp, "Telephones ringing off the hook," *Journal and Courier*, 19 May 1994.

68. James Sterngold, "Why Japanese adore vending machines," *New York Times*, 5 January 1992: A1 (2).

69. Ian French, "Brand-based DRTV that sells: Rules to live by in the brave new world of direct response," *Marketing Magazine*, 24 April 2000.

70. "How Videotex offers special potential in France," *Business Marketing Digest* 17, 1992: 81–4.

## Chapter 12

1. Rob Pashko, "No more yawns," *Marketing Magazine*, 31 January 2000.

2. J. Grunig, *Excellence in Public Relations and Communications Management*, New Jersey: Lawrence Erlbaum Associates, Inc., 1992.

3. J. Grunig, *Excellence in Public Relations and Communications Management*, New Jersey: Lawrence Erlbaum Associates, Inc., 1992.

4. Leiss et al., *Social Communication*; George Stigler, "The economics of information," *Journal of Political Economy*, 1961: 69.

5. William D. Wells, John Burnett, and Sandra Moriarty, *Advertising: Principles and Practice*, Prentice Hall. London: 2002.

6. Scott Hume, "Integrated marketing: Who's in charge here?" *Advertising Age*, 22 March 1993: 3(2).

7. Don E. Schultz, Stanley I. Tannenbaum, and Robert F. Lauterborn, *Integrated Marketing Communications: Pulling It Together and Making It Work*, Chicago: NTCBusiness Books, 1993; Melanie Wells, "Purposeful grazing in ad land," *Advertising Age*, 11 April 1994: S-12.

8. Lesley Young, "Great escapes," *Marketing Magazine Online*, 20 August 2001.

9. Don E. Schultz, Stanley I. Tannenbaum, and Robert F. Lauterborn, *Integrated Marketing Communications: Pulling It Together and Making It Work*, Chicago: NTC Business Books, 1993.

10. Michael Lev, "For car buyers, technology or Zen," *New York Times*, 22 May 1989: D1.

11. Linda L. Golden and Mark I. Alpert, "Comparative analysis of the relative effectiveness of one- and two-sided communication for contrasting products," *Journal of Advertising* 16, 1987: 18–25; Kamins, "Celebrity and non-celebrity advertising in a two-sided context,"; Robert B. Settle and Linda L. Golden, "Attribution theory and advertiser credibility,"

*Journal of Marketing Research* 11, May 1974: 181–5.

12. Frank R. Kardes, "Spontaneous inference processes in advertising: The effects of conclusion omission and involvement on persuasion," *Journal of Consumer Research* 15, September 1988: 225–33.

13. Gert Assmus, "An empirical investigation into the perception of vehicle source effects," *Journal of Advertising* 7, Winter 1978: 4–10; Stephen Baker, *Systematic Approach to Advertising Creativity*, New York: McGraw-Hill, 1979.

14. Patricia Sellers, "The best way to reach your buyers," *Fortune*, Autumn/Winter 1993: 15 (4).

15. John R. Rossiter, Larry Percy, Robert J. Donovan, "A better advertising planning grid," *Journal of Advertising Research*, New York: Oct/Nov 1991, 31(5): 11.

16. John R. Rossiter, Larry Percy, Robert J. Donovan, "A better advertising planning grid," *Journal of Advertising Research*, New York: Oct/Nov 1991, 31(5): 11.

17. George E. Belch and Michael A. Belch, *Introduction to Advertising & Promotion: An Integrated Marketing Communications Perspective* 2nd ed., Homewood, IL: Irwin, 1993.

18. Scott Hume, "Integrated marketing: Who's in charge here?" *Advertising Age*, 22 March 1993: 3(2).

19. Richard Rotman, "When worlds combine," Marketing Commentary, *Marketing Magazine*, 29 September 2003: 8.

20. James Grunig, *Excellence in Public Relations and Communication Management*, New Jersey: Lawrence Erlbaum Associates, Publishers, 1992.

21. Emily Rayson, "Capturing the joy of online experiences", *Marketing Magazine Online*, 1 March 2004.

22. Juliette Walker, "Pepsi-Coke spat raises questions about ad policies," *Japan Times Weekly International Edition,* 24–30 June 1991:7.

23. "Green promotes 'handyman's helper'," *Marketing Magazine*, 3 July 2000: 3.

24. Joanne Laucius, "Celine Dion and Chrysler make for a bad mix, ad experts say," *The Times Colonist*, 27 November 2003: A3.

25. Kevin Goldman, "Ad with disabled children stirs controversy," *Wall Street Journal,* 3 September 1993: B8.

26. Katsumi Hoshino, "Semiotic marketing and product conceptualization," in Jean Umiker-Sebeok (ed.), *Marketing and Semiotics: New Directions in the Study of Signs for Sale*, Berlin: Mouton de Bruyter, 1987: 41–56.

27. Eve Lazarus, "Rethink's fresh obsession," *Marketing Magazine*, 24 Nov 2003: 11–14.

28. Eve Lazarus, "Rethink tunes in playland," *Marketing Magazine*, 2 June 2003: 4.

29. D. Schultz and B. Barnes, *Strategic Brand Communication Campaigns*, 5th ed., Lincolnwood IL: NTC Publishing, 1999.

30. Michael Wilke, "A radio entrepreneur reaches for the interactive age," *New York Times*, 4 September 1994: F7.

31. Ron Szekely, "L'Oréal generates buzz," *Marketing Magazine*, 7 January 2002.

32. Khanh T.L. Tran, "Lifting the velvet rope: Night clubs draw virtual throngs with webcasts," *The Wall Street Journal Interactive Edition,* 30 August, 1999.

33. Don E. Schultz, Stanley I. Tannenbaum, and Robert F. Lauterborn, *Integrated Marketing Communications: Pulling It Together and Making It Work*, Chicago: NTC Business Books, 1993.

34. Ibid.

35. Chris Powell, "Get in the game," *Marketing Magazine*, 28 July/3 August 2003: 11.

36. Chris Powell, "Get in the game," *Marketing Magazine*, 28 July/3 August 2003: 11.

37. Danny Kucharsky, "Ah! Ha!: How a brilliant ad concept sparked a pop culture sensation and pumped up the profile of Quebec's Familiprix," *Marketing Magazine*, 9 June 2003: 8–10.

38. "The man from Glad—He's back," *Marketing Magazine*, 20 March 2000.

39. "P&G stages live advertising," *Marketing Magazine*, 1 May 2000.

40. Barb Grant, "Getting the right balance," *Marketing Magazine*, 22 September 2003.

41. Gert Assmus, "An empirical investigation into the perception of vehicle source effects," *Journal of Advertising* 7, Winter 1978: 4–10; Stephen Baker, *Systematic Approach to Advertising Creativity*, New York: McGraw-Hill, 1979.

42. Patricia Sellers, "The best way to reach your buyers," *Fortune*, Autumn/Winter 1993: 15 (4).

43. James P Masciarelli, "Are you managing your relationships?" *Management Review New York* 87(4): 41–5.

44. Jonathan Berry, "Wilma! What happened to the plain old ad?" *Business Week*, 6 June 1994: 54–5.

45. Tom Buerkle, "Advertisers find a formula they like in auto racing," *International Herald Tribune* [on-line] 10 March 1998, accessed via ssnewslink.

46. Patricia Sellers, "Winning over the new consumer," *Fortune*, 27 July 1991: 113.

47. Charles Goodrum and Helen Dalrymple, *Advertising in America: The First 200 Years,* New York: Harry N. Abrams, 1990.

48. Kevin Goldman. "The message, clever as it may be, is lost in a number of high profile campaigns," *Wall Street Journal,* 27 July 1993: B1 (2).

49. Charles Goodrum and Helen Dalrymple, *Advertising in America: The First 200 Years,* New York: Harry N. Abrams, 1990.

50. Kevin Goldman "Knock, Knock. Who's there." The same old funny ad again," *Wall Street Journal,* 2 November 1993: B10.

51. Curt Barry, "Building a database," *Catalog Age,* August 1992: 65–8.

52. John F. Yarbrough, "Putting the pieces together," *Sales and Marketing Management,* September 1996: 70.

53. Bruce MacDonald, "The Art of the Brief," *Marketing Magazine,* 27 October 2003: 36–38.

54. Bruce MacDonald, "The Art of the Brief," *Marketing Magazine,* 27 October 2003: 36–38.

55. Bruce MacDonald, "The Art of the Brief," *Marketing Magazine,* 27 October 2003: 36–38.

56. Danny Kucharsky, "Highlighting the Canadian approach: L'Oreal Canada," *Marketing Magazine,* 8/15 December 2003: 25.

57. Danny Kucharsky, "Marketer of the Year: L'Oréal," *Marketing Magazine,* 9 Feb 2004: 9–14.

58. Danny Kucharsky, "Highlighting the Canadian approach: L'Oréal Canada," *Marketing Magazine,* 8/15 December 2003: 25.

## Chapter 13

1. Danielle D'Agostino, "Teaching brands new tricks: Fido's PR campaign worked by leveraging off the visual icon of the dog," *Marketing Magazine,* 28 February 1999: 28.

2. William Wells, John Burnett, and Sandra Moriarty, *Advertising Principles and Practice,* 2nd ed., Engelwood Cliffs, NJ: Prentice Hall, 1992.

3. A.C. Nielsen Canada, "1999 advertising trends in Canada," www.acnielsen.ca/sect_adtrends/adtrends-en.htm.

4. Bob D. Cutler and Darrel D. Muehling "Another look at Advocacy advertising and the boundaries of commercial speech," *Journal of Advertising* 20, December 1991: 49–52.

5. Lara Mills, "Campaigns with legs," *Marketing Magazine,* 15 May 2000: 12–4.

6. Canadian Media Directors' Council, *1999/2000 Canadian Media Directors' Council Media Digest:* 16.

7. James Careless, "Where's the price tag?" *Marketing Magazine,* 31 January 2000.

8. Philip Hart, "Product placement comes of age in Canada," *Marketing Magazine,* 18 November 1996: 20.

9. Phil Hall, "Make listeners your customers," *Nation's Business,* June 1994: 53R.

10. Canadian Media Directors' Council, *1999/2000 Canadian Media Directors' Council Media Digest:* 27.

11. Paul-Mark Rendon, "Radio works magic for Potter tome," *Marketing Magazine,* 30 June/7 July 2003.

12. www.cyberatlas.internet.com/markets/advertising/article/0,,5941_440981,,00.html.

13. Chris Powell, "Lemontonic connects to Hooked Up," *Marketing Magazine,* 16 February 2004: 4.

14. William Safire, "M-Commerce," *The New York Times Magazine,"* accessed at www.nytimes.com/library/magazine/home/20000319mag-onlanguage.html on 27 February 2002.

15. Michael Bociurkiw, "Text messaging thrives in the Phillippines," *Forbes,* (10 September 2001): 28.

16. "MTV adds wireless ads to mix," 23 August 2001, CNN.com, http://cnn.career.printthis.clickability.com/pt/printThis?clickMap=p.

17. Sheree R. Curry, "Wireless trend taking hold," *Advertising Age,* 25 June 2001: 2.

18. Dana James, "RU PYNG ATTN?: Europeans find text messaging the right marketing call," *Marketing News,* 7 January 2000: 4.

19. Olga Karif, "Online extra: Mobile commerce is coming—modestly, eventually," *Business Week Online,* E-Biz, 14 May 2001, accessed 26 February 2002.

20. Ibid.

21. "M-commerce report," *New Media Age,* 30 November 2000: 56.

22. Lisa Marie Petersen, "Outside chance," *MediaWeek,* 15 June 1992: 20–3.

23. Mike Dano, "M-commerce will outperform e-commerce," RCR Wireless News, 20, 2 April 2001: 4.

24. Gene Koprowsky, "Eyeball to eyeball," *Critical Mass* (Fall 1999): 32 (5).

25. Astrid Van De Broek, "TV Network's ads go to the movies," *Marketing Magazine,* 3 April 2000: 3.

26. Altaf M. Khan, "New ways to get in faces," *Marketing Magazine,* 10 April 2000: 33.

27. Michael Bernard, "The great house sale," *Marketing Magazine,* 23 February 1998.

28. Anita Lahey, Michael McCullough, and Gail Chiasson, "Placing products," *Marketing Magazine,* 12 August 1996.

29. Patrick Allossery, "Petro-Canada to list its costs per litre in public relation bid: Posted on the pumps," *Financial Post,* 14 March 2000: C6.

30. Ni Chen and Hugh M. Culbertson, "Two contrasting approaches of government public relations in mainland China," *Public Relations Quarterly,* Fall 1992: 36–41.

31. John Swinimer, "Untarnished: Rolling up their sleeves to polish up what is widely seen as a mudied image, insurance companies and

industry associations are cleaning it off by getting involved in worthy causes and community projects," *Canadian Underwriter*, February 1993: 12–3.

32. "Ericsson, Manifest team on aid," *Marketing Magazine*, 8 May 2000.

33. Anita Lahey, Michael McCullough, and Gail Chiasson, "Placing products," *Marketing Magazine*, 12 August 1996.

34. Patrick Allossery, "Petro-Canada to list its costs per litre in public relation bid: Posted on the pumps," *Financial Post*, 14 March 2000: C6.

35. Tony Van Alphen, "Husky Injection Molding adds altruism to the mix," *Canadian Press Newswire*, 21 January 2000.

36. Roma Luciw, "Bridgestone recalls Canadian tires: About a million of affected brands are on selected SUVs and trucks," *The Globe and Mail*, 11 August 2000: A1.

37. Rick Hall, "Lessons of the McLibel case," *Marketing Magazine*, 25 January 1999.

38. Anita Lahey, Michael McCullough, and Gail Chiasson, "Placing products," *Marketing Magazine*, 12 August 1996.

39. www.smallbusinessbc.ca/2010/business/ business_success.pdf.

40. Kerry J. Smith, "It's for you," *PROMO: The International Magazine for Promotional Marketing,* 41(4), August 1994.; Sharon Moshavi, "Please deposit more cents," *Forbes*, 16 August 1993: 102.

41. Howard Stumpf and John M. Kawula, "Point of purchase advertising," in S. Ulanoff (ed.), *Handbook of Sales Promotion*, New York: McGraw Hill, 1985; Karen A. Berger, *The Rising Importance of Point-of-Purchase Advertising in the Marketing Mix*, Englewood, NJ: Point-of-Purchase Advertising Institute.

42. Liza Finlay, "Perpetual promotions," *Marketing Magazine*, 31 May 1999: 11–2.

43. Melinda Grenier Guiles, "Wooing press and public at auto shows," *Wall Street Journal,* 8 January 1990: B1.

44. Fawzia Sheikh, "Do your own thing," *Marketing Magazine*, 14 July 1997: 14.

45. Ron Piovesan, "Toronto's PR bungle on SARS," *Marketing Magazine*, 12 May 2003: 7.

46. Jennifer Lawrence, "Tracy-Locke Division works for the big event," *Advertising Age*, 17 May 1993: S-2, S-7.

47. Louise Gagnon, "The big one," *Marketing Magazine*, 14 April 1997: 12.

48. Dagmara Lewkowicz, "Couponing shifts away from food: The real growth is in categories like hair care," *Marketing Magazine*, 13 April 1998.

49. Don E. Schultz, William A. Robinson, and Lisa A. Petrison, *Sales Promotion Essentials,* 2nd ed., Lincolnwood, IL: NTC Business Books, 1993.

50. "Sampling debuts PowerBar in East," *Marketing Magazine: Newsline*, 7 June 1999.

51. Kate Fitzgerald, "Guinness looks to its past to fresh 5th pub giveaway," *Advertising Age*, 30 March 1998: 46.

52. Liza Finlay, "Perpetual promotions," *Marketing Magazine*, 31 May 1999: 11–2.

53. Kerry J. Smith, "It's for you," *PROMO: The International Magazine for Promotion Marketing*, August 1994: 41(4); Sharon Moshavi, "Please deposit no cents," *Forbes*, 16 August 1993: 102; *The Point-of-Purchase Advertising Industry Fact Book*, Englewood, NJ: The Point-of-Purchase Advertising Institute, 1992.

54. Lesley Young, "Smart sampling wins award and new cat owners," *Marketing Magazine*, 3 Nov 2003: 14.

55. Kerry J. Smith, "It's for you," *PROMO: The International Magazine for Promotion Marketing*, August 1994: 41(4); Sharon Moshavi, "Please deposit no cents," *Forbes*, 16 August 1993: 102; *The Point-of-Purchase Advertising Industry Fact Book*, Englewood, NJ: The Point-of-Purchase Advertising Institute, 1992.

56. "Bausch & Lomb makes eyes with consumers in Spain," *PROMO: The International Magazine for Promotion Marketing*, October 1994: 93.

57. Patricia Sellers, "Winning over the new consumer," *Fortune*, 29 July 1991: 113.

58. Lara Mills, "Marketers face up to new challenges," *Marketing Magazine*, 24 May 1999: 4.

59. Lara Mills, "Too much of a good thing," *Marketing Magazine*, 19/26 August 1996.

60. "Rocky Mountaineer's direct mail response goes off the rails," *Marketing Direct*, 16 April 2001.

61. "Hewlett-Packard's S.A.S. reseller and end user promotion," Promo Report, *Marketing Magazine*, 29 October 2001.

62. Sarah Dobson, "Cara's winning combo," *Marketing Magazine,* 28 October 2002: 10–12.

63. Jaclyn Fierman, "The death and rebirth of the salesman," *Fortune*, 25 July 1994: 38(7), 88.

64. "A user's guide to the sales manager's budget planner," *Sales and Marketing Management*, 28 June 1993: 6–10.

65. Greg Weatherdon, "The telemarketing edge: Combining it with broadcast faxing creates a powerful tool for drug companies," *Marketing Magazine*, 19 October 1998: 25.

66. Dan C. Weilbaker, "The identification of selling abilities needed for missionary type sales," *Journal of Personal Selling & Sales Management* 10, Summer 1990: 45–58.

67. W. David Gibson, "Fielding a force of experts," *Sales and Marketing Management*, April 1993: 88–92; Henry Canaday, "Team selling works!" *Personal Selling Power*, September 1994: 53–8.

68. Jack Branswell, "The gadget king," *Marketing Magazine*, 12 June 2000.

69. Martin Everett, "This is the ultimate in selling," *Sales and Marketing Management*, August 1989: 28.

70. Maurice G. Clabaugh Jr. and Jessie L. Forbes, *Professional Selling: A Relationship Approach*, New York: West, 1992.

71. André Mazerolle and Eva A. Lau, "A teleconference on steroids: Web-push technology offers the next best thing to being there at a press conference," *Marketing Magazine*, 15 March 1999.

72. Melissa Campanelli, "Reshuffling the deck," *Sales and Marketing Management*, June 1994: 83–90.

73. W. David Gibson, "Fielding a force of experts," *Sales and Marketing Management*, April 1993: 88–92.

74. W. David Gibson, "Fielding a force of experts," *Sales and Marketing Management*, April 1993: 88–92.

75. Sarah Dobson, "Moo juice marketers," *Marketing Magazine*, 26 May 2003: 9–16.

76. Angela Scardillo, "Making milk cool," *Marketing Magazine*, 11 August 2003: 26.

77. Angela Scardillo, "Making milk cool," *Marketing Magazine*, 11 August 2003: 26.

78. Angela Scardillo, "Making milk cool," *Marketing Magazine*, 11 August 2003: 26.

79. Sarah Dobson, "Moo juice marketers," *Marketing Magazine*, 26 May 2003: 9–16.

80. Sarah Dobson, "Moo juice marketers," *Marketing Magazine*, 26 May 2003: 9–16.

81. Sarah Dobson, "Moo juice marketers," *Marketing Magazine*, 26 May 2003: 9–16.

## Chapter 14

1. Nitin Nohria, William Joyce, and Bruce Roberson, "What really works," *Harvard Business Review*, July 2003: 42.

2. Ajay Sirsi, *Marketing Led—Sales Driven: How Successful Businesses Use the Power of Marketing Plans and Sales Execution to Win in the Marketplace*, Trafford Publishing, 2004.

3. Jim Collins, *Good To Great*, Harper Business, 2001.

4. Alex Berenson, "Yesterday's Back! At Last, an I.P.O. to Drool Over," *The New York Times*, 2 May 2004, section 3, page 5.

## Chapter 15

1. Thomas Bonoma, "Market success can breed 'marketing inertia'," *Harvard Business Review*, September–October 1981: 115.

2. Peter Drucker, *Management: Tasks, Responsibilities, Practices*, New York: Harper & Row, 1973.

3. Frederick F. Reichheld and W. Earl Sasser, Jr., "Zero defections: Quality comes to services," *Harvard Business Review*, September–October 1990.

4. Philip Kotler and Ronald E. Turner, *Marketing Management: Analysis, Planning, Implementation and Control*, Canadian Ninth Edition, Toronto: Prentice-Hall Canada.

5. Richard L. Oliver, *Satisfaction, a Behavioral Perspective on the Consumer*, New York: McGraw-Hill, 1997.

6. A. Parasuraman, Valerie A. Zeithaml, and Len L. Berry, "A conceptual model of service quality and its implications for future research," *Journal of Marketing*, 49 (Fall 1985), 41–50.

7. Thomas O. Jones and W. Earl Sasser, Jr., "Why satisfied customers defect," *Harvard Business Review*, November–December 1995: 88.

8. Philip Kotler and Ronald E. Turner, *Marketing Management: Analysis, Planning, Implementation and Control*, Canadian Ninth Edition, Toronto: Prentice-Hall Canada.

9. Thomas O. Jones and W. Earl Sasser, Jr., "Why satisfied customers defect," *Harvard Business Review*, November–December 1995: 88.

10. B. Joseph Pine II, Don Peppers, and Martha Rogers, "Do you want to keep your customers forever?" *Harvard Business Review*, March–April 1995: 103.

11. "A crash course in customer relationship management," *Harvard Management Update* (March 2000): HBS reprint #U003B.

12. Quoted in Cara B. DiPasquale, "Navigate the maze," Special Report on 1:1 Marketing, *Advertising Age*, 29 October 2001: S1 (2).

13. Jim Middlemiss, "Users say CRM is worth the effort," www.wallstreetandtech.com (Third Quarter 2001): 17–8.

14. Mel Duvall, "Charting customers: Why CRM spending remains strong even in tight times," *Interactive Week* 8, 20 August 2001: 23.

15. Kate Fitzgerald, "Events a big 1st step," *Advertising Age*, 29 October 2001: S4.

16. Susan Fournier, Susan Dobscha, and David Glen Mick, "Preventing the premature death of relationship marketing," *Harvard Business Review*, January–February 1998.

17. Mel Duvall, "Charting customers: Why CRM spending remains strong even in tight times," *Interactive Week* 8, 20 August 2001: 23.

18. Robert C. Blattberg, Gary Getz, and Mark Pelofsky, "Want to build your business? Grow your customer equity," *Harvard Management Update,* August 2001: HBS reprint #U0108B, 3.

19. Tonia Bruyns, "Banking on targeted marketing," *Business 2.0,* 7 November 2001.

20. Don Peppers, Martha Rogers, and Bob Dorf, "Is your company ready for one-to-one marketing," *Harvard Business Review,* January–February 1999.

# GLOSSARY

**80/20 rule** A marketing rule of thumb that 20% of purchasers account for 80% of a product's sales.

**acceleration principle (multiplier effect)** A marketing phenomenon in which a small percentage change in consumer demand can create a large percentage change in business-to-business demand.

**advertising** Non-personal, paid communication from an identified sponsor, primarily using mass media.

**advertising appeal** The central idea or theme of a communication message.

**advertising campaign** A coordinated, comprehensive plan that carries out promotion objectives and results in a series of advertisements placed in media over a period of time.

**advertising exposure** The degree to which the target market will see an advertising message placed in a specific vehicle.

**advocacy advertising** A type of public service advertising provided by an organization that is seeking to influence public opinion on an issue because it has some stake in the outcome.

**AIDA model** The communication goals of attention, interest, desire, and action.

**aided recall** A research technique that uses clues to prompt answers from people about advertisements they might have seen.

**aperture** The best place and time to reach a person in the target market group.

**approach** The first step of the actual sales presentation in which the salesperson tries to learn more about the customer's needs, create a good impression, and build rapport.

**atmospherics** The use of colour, lighting, scents, furnishings, and other design elements to create a desired store image.

**attitude** A learned predisposition to respond favourably or unfavourably to stimuli based on relatively enduring evaluations of people, objects, and issues.

**attitudinal measures** A research technique that probes a consumer's beliefs or feelings about a product before and after being exposed to messages about it.

**baby boomers** The largest age segment in Canada, it includes people who were born between 1947 and 1966.

**bait and switch** An illegal marketing practice in which an advertised price special is used as bait to get customers into the store with the intention of switching them to a higher-priced item.

**banners** Internet advertising in the form of rectangular graphics at the top or bottom of Web pages.

**bartering** The practice of exchanging a good or service for another good or service of like value.

**behavioural learning theories** Theories of learning that focus on how consumer behaviour is changed by external events or stimuli.

**behavioural segmentation** Technique that divides consumers into segments on the basis of how they act toward, feel about, or use a product or service.

**benefit** The outcome sought by a customer that motivates buying behaviour.

**benefit segmentation** A segmentation approach that groups consumers or customers based on the benefits or value they seek in buying and using products.

**bid rigging** Collusion between suppliers responding to bid requests to lessen competition and secure higher margins.

**bots** Electronic robots or shopping agents that help consumers find products and prices on the Internet.

**bottom-up budgeting techniques** Allocation of the promotion budget that is based on identifying promotional goals and allocating enough money to accomplish them.

**brand** A name, term, symbol, or any other unique element of a product, which identifies one firm's product(s) and sets them apart from the competition.

**brand concept** How the marketer wants the brand to be positioned.

**brand equity** The value of a brand to an organization.

**brand extension** A new product sold with the same brand name as a strong existing brand.

**brand image** How consumers perceive the positioning of the brand.

**brand loyalty** A pattern of repeat product purchases, accompanied by an underlying positive attitude toward the brand, which is based on the belief that the brand makes products superior to its competition.

**brand manager** A manager who is responsible for developing and implementing the marketing plan for a single brand.

**brand personality** A distinctive image that captures a product or service's character and benefits.

**break-even analysis** A method for determining the number of units that a firm must produce and sell at a given price to cover all its costs.

**bulk breaking** Dividing larger quantities of goods into smaller lots to meet the needs of buyers.

**business-to-business (B2B) e-commerce** Internet exchanges between two or more businesses or organizations.

**business-to-business marketing** The marketing of goods and services that business and organizational customers need to produce other goods and services for resale or to support their operations.

**business ethics** Rules of conduct for an organization.

**business portfolio** The group of different products or brands owned by an organization and characterized by different income-generating and growth capabilities.

**buttons** Small banner-type advertisements that can be placed anywhere on a Web page.

**buy class** One of three classifications of business buying situations that characterize the degree of time and effort required to make a decision in a buying situation.

**buying centre** The group of people in an organization who influence and participate in purchasing decisions.

**buying group** The coordination of purchasing among member organizations to realize economies of scale and other efficiencies.

**cannibalization** The loss of sales of an existing product when a new item in a product line or product family is introduced.

**capacity management** The process by which organizations adjust their offerings in an attempt to match demand.

**captive pricing** A pricing tactic for two items that must be used together; one item is priced very low and the firm makes its profit on another, high-margin item essential to the operation of the first item.

**case allowance** A discount to the retailer or wholesaler based on the volume of product ordered.

**case study** A comprehensive examination of a particular firm or organization.

**catalogue** A collection of products offered for sale in book form, usually consisting of product descriptions accompanied by photos or illustrations of the items.

**causal research** Techniques that attempt to understand cause-and-effect relationships.

**cause marketing** A marketing strategy in which an organization serves its community by promoting and supporting a worthy cause or by allying itself with a not-for-profit organization to tackle a social problem.

**centralized purchasing** A business buying practice in which an organization's purchasing department does the buying for all of the company.

**channel intermediaries** Firms or individuals such as wholesalers, agents, brokers, or retailers that help move a product from the producer to the consumer or business user.

**channel leader** A firm at one level of distribution that takes a leadership role, establishing operating norms and processes that reduce channel conflicts, reduce costs, and enhance delivered customer value.

**channel levels** The number of distinct categories of intermediaries that populate a channel of distribution.

**channel of distribution** The series of firms or individuals that facilitates the movement of a product from the producer to the final customer.

**classical conditioning** Learning that occurs when a stimulus eliciting a response is paired with another stimulus that initially does not elicit a response on its own but will cause a similar response over time because of its association with the first stimulus.

**co-branding** An agreement between two brands to work together in marketing new or existing products.

**code of ethics** Written standards of behaviour to which everyone in the organization must subscribe.

**cognitive dissonance** The regret or remorse buyers may feel after making a purchase.

**cognitive learning theory** A theory of learning that stresses the importance of internal mental processes and that views people as problem solvers, who actively use information from the world around them to master their environment.

**communications mix** The major elements of marketer-controlled communications, including advertising, sales promotions, marketing public relations, direct marketing, and personal selling.

**communications model** The elements necessary for meaning to be transferred from a sender to a receiver.

**communications plan** A framework that outlines the strategies for developing, implementing, and controlling the firm's communication activities.

**competitive advantage** The ability of a firm to outperform the competition, providing customers with a benefit the competition cannot.

**competitive bids** A business buying process in which two or more suppliers submit proposals (including price and associated data) for a proposed purchase and the firm providing the better offer gets the bid.

**competitive effect objective** Pricing that is intended to have an effect on the marketing efforts of the competition.

**computer media** Communications media that transmit information through the Internet or via e-mail messages.

**concentrated targeting strategy** Focusing a firm's efforts on offering one or more products to a single segment.

**conformity** A change in beliefs or actions as a reaction to real or imagined group pressure.

**consideration set** The set of alternative brands the consumer is considering for the decision process.

**consumer** The ultimate user of a good or service. Can be an individual or an organization.

**consumer-to-consumer (C2C) e-commerce** Communications and purchases that occur among individuals without directly involving the manufacturer or retailer.

**consumer behaviour** The process individuals or groups go through to select, purchase, and use goods, services, ideas, or experiences to satisfy their needs and desires.

**consumer interviews** One-on-one discussions between a consumer and a researcher.

**consumer orientation** A management philosophy that focuses on being proactive and responsive in identifying and satisfying consumer needs and wants.

**consumer satisfaction/dissatisfaction** The overall feelings or attitude a person has about a product after purchasing it.

**consumerism** A social movement that attempts to protect consumers from harmful business practices.

**continuous innovation** A modification of an existing product that sets one brand apart from its competitors.

**contribution margin** The price an organization receives less its variable costs.

**conventional marketing system** A multiple-level distribution channel in which channel members work independently of one another.

**cookies** Text files inserted by a Web site sponsor into a Web surfer's hard drive that allow the site to track the surfer's moves.

**copy testing** A marketing research method that seeks to measure the effectiveness of ads by determining whether consumers are receiving, comprehending, and responding to the ad according to plan.

**cost-plus pricing** A method of setting prices in which the seller totals all the unit costs for the product and then adds the desired profit per unit.

**cost of ownership** A pricing strategy that considers the lifetime cost of using the product.

**cost per thousand (CPM)** A measure used to compare the relative cost effectiveness of different media vehicles that have different exposure rates: the cost to deliver a message to 1000 people or homes.

**creating assortments** Providing a variety of products in one location to meet the needs of buyers.

**creative concept** How the advertising appeal will be expressed through visuals, text, music, and other design elements.

**creative selling process** The process of seeking out customers, analyzing their needs, determining how product attributes might provide benefits for them, and then communicating that information.

**creative strategy** The process that turns a concept into an advertisement.

**cross-promotion** Two or more companies combining forces and using a single promotional tool to create interest in their products or services.

**cross-sectional design** Type of descriptive technique that involves the systematic collection of quantitative information at one point in time.

**cultural diversity** A management practice that actively seeks to include people of different sexes, races, ethnic groups, religions, and sexual preferences in an organization's employees, customers, suppliers, and distribution channel partners.

**culture** The values, beliefs, customs, and tastes that a group of people value.

**cumulative quantity discounts** Discounts based on the total quantity bought within a specified time period.

**custom marketing strategy** Approach that tailors specific products and the messages about them to individual customers.

**customer equity** The financial value of a customer relationship throughout the lifetime of the relationship.

**Customer Relationship Management (CRM)** A strategy and process used by companies to identify its best customers, stay on top of their needs, and increase their satisfaction.

**customer satisfaction** The difference between a customer's needs and expectations and the customer's perception that the good or service has met those needs and expectations.

**customer satisfaction objective** Pricing that is intended to maximize customer satisfaction and retention.

**customer value** What the customer gets in the purchase, use, and ownership of a product relative to the costs and sacrifices incurred.

**customer's lifetime value** The potential profit generated by a single customer's purchase of a firm's products over the customer's lifetime.

**data mining** Sophisticated analysis techniques to take advantage of the massive amount of transaction information now available.

**decline stage** The final stage in the product life cycle, in which sales decrease as customer needs change.

**decoding** The process by which a receiver assigns meaning to the message.

**demand** Customers' desire for products coupled with the resources to obtain them.

**demand-based pricing** A price-setting method based on estimates of demand at different prices.

**demand curve** A plot of the quantity of a product that customers will buy in a market during a period of time at various prices if all other factors remain the same.

**demographics** Variables that describe objective characteristics of a population or group.

**derived demand** The demand for business or organizational products that is derived from demand for consumer goods or services.

**descriptive research** Tool that probes more systematically into the problem and bases its conclusions on large numbers of observations.

**differentiated targeting strategy** Developing one or more products for each of several distinct customer groups and making sure these offerings are kept separate in the marketplace.

**diffusion** The process by which the use of a product spreads throughout a population.

**direct-response marketing** Marketing activity aimed at generating a measurable response via marketing communications.

**direct-response TV** Television programming, such as infomercials or shopping channels, which elicits direct orders for products from the viewing public.

**direct mail** A brochure or pamphlet offering a specific product or service at one point in time.

**direct marketing** Exposing a consumer to information about a good or service through a non-personal medium and convincing the customer to respond with an order.

**direct selling** An interactive sales process, in which a salesperson presents a product to one individual or a small group, takes orders, and delivers the merchandise.

**discontinuous innovation** A totally new product that creates major changes in the way we live.

**disintermediation** The process of eliminating interaction between customers and service providers.

**dumping** Pricing products lower in a foreign market than they are offered in the home market.

**dynamic pricing** Pricing strategy in which the price can easily be adjusted to meet changes in the marketplace.

**dynamically continuous innovation** A change in an existing product that requires a moderate amount of learning or behaviour change.

**e-tailing** Offering products for sale directly to consumers via the Internet.

**early adopters** Those who adopt an innovation early in the diffusion process but later than the innovators.

**early majority** Those whose adoption of a new product signals a general acceptance of the innovation.

**embodying** The inclusion of a service with a purchase of a physical good.

**encoding** The process of translating an idea into a form of communication that will convey meaning.

**environmental stewardship** A position taken by an organization to protect or enhance the natural environment as it conducts its business activities.

**ethnography** A detailed report on observations of people in their own homes or communities.

**evaluative criteria** The dimensions that consumers use to compare competing product alternatives.

**exchange** The process by which some transfer of value occurs between a buyer and a seller.

**exclusive distribution** Selling a product only through a single outlet in a particular region.

**experimental pricing** A strategy of experimenting with prices until the price that generates the highest profitability is found.

**experiments** Techniques that test prespecified relationships among variables in a controlled environment.

**exploratory research** Technique that marketers use to generate insights for future, more rigorous studies.

**external environment** The uncontrollable elements outside of an organization that may affect its performance either positively or negatively. These include demographic/social/cultural factors, economic factors, competitive factors, regulatory factors, and technological factors.

**f.o.b. delivered pricing** A pricing tactic in which the cost of loading and transporting the product to the customer is included in the selling price, paid by the manufacturer.

**f.o.b. origin pricing** A pricing tactic in which the cost of transporting the product from the factory to the customer's location is the responsibility of the customer.

**facilitating functions** Functions of channel intermediaries that make the purchase process easier for customers and manufacturers.

**family brand** A brand that a group of individual products or individual brands share.

**family life cycle** A means of characterizing consumers based on the different family stages they pass through as they grow older.

**feedback** Receivers' reactions to the message.

**fixed costs** Costs of production that do not change with the number of units produced.

**focus group** A product-oriented discussion among a small group of consumers led by a trained moderator.

**freight absorption pricing** A pricing tactic in which the seller absorbs the total cost of transportation.

**frequency** The number of times a person in the target group will be exposed to the message.

**frequent discounting** A strategy of frequently using sale prices to increase sales volume.

**geodemography** Segmentation technique that combines geography with demographics.

**goods** Tangible products we can see, touch, smell, hear, or taste.

**government markets** Federal, provincial, and local governments that buy goods and services to carry out public objectives and to support their operations.

**green marketing** A marketing strategy that supports environmental stewardship by creating an environmentally founded differential benefit in the minds of consumers.

**grey market** The importing of products by an unauthorized party, who then sells them for a fraction of the price.

**gross rating points (GRPs)** A measure used for comparing the effectiveness of different media vehicles: average reach times frequency.

**growth stage** The second stage in the product life cycle, during which the product is accepted and sales rapidly increase.

**guerrilla marketing** Promotional strategies that "ambush" consumers with promotional content in places they are not expecting it.

**heuristics** A mental rule of thumb that leads to a speedy decision by simplifying the process.

**hierarchy of needs** An approach that categorizes motives according to five levels of importance, the more basic needs being on the bottom of the hierarchy and the higher needs at the top.

**horizontal marketing system** An arrangement within a channel of distribution in which two or more firms at the same channel level work together for a common purpose.

**hypermarkets** Retailers with the characteristics of both warehouse stores and supermarkets; hypermarkets are several times larger than other stores and offer virtually everything from grocery items to electronics.

**image enhancement objective** Pricing intended to establish a desired image or positioning to prospective customers.

**impressions** The number of people who will be exposed to a message placed in one or more media vehicles.

**independent intermediaries** Channel intermediaries that are not controlled by any manufacturer but rather do business with many different manufacturers and many different customers.

**industrial psychographics** The application of psychographics to the business-to-business context.

**inelastic demand** The demand for products does not change because of increases or decreases in price.

**information search** The process whereby a consumer searches for appropriate information needed to make a reasonable decision.

**innovation** A product that consumers perceive to be new and different from existing products.

**innovators** The first segment (roughly 2.5 percent) of a population to adopt a new product.

**institutional advertising** An advertising message that promotes the activities, personality, or point of view of an organization or company.

**integrated marketing communications (IMC)** IMC is the practice of unifying all marketing communication tools and corporate and brand messages to communicate in a consistent way to and with stakeholder audiences.

**intensive distribution** Selling a product through all suitable wholesalers or retailers that are willing to stock and sell the product.

**interactive marketing** Two-way communications, in which customized marketing communications elicit a measurable response from individual customers.

**internal environment** The controllable elements inside an organization, including its people, its facilities, and how it does things that influence the operations of the organization.

**internal reference price** A set price or a price range in consumers' minds that they refer to in evaluating a product's price.

**intranet** An internal corporate communication network that uses Internet technology to link company departments, employees, and databases.

**introduction** The first stage of the product life cycle, in which slow growth follows the introduction of a new product in the marketplace.

**inventory control** Activities to ensure that goods are always available to meet customers' demands.

**inventory turnover** The average number of times a year a retailer expects to sell its inventory.

**involvement** The relative importance of perceived consequences of the purchase to a consumer.

**joint demand** The demand for two or more goods that are used together to create a product.

**judgment** A pricing strategy that draws on past experience of the marketer in setting appropriate prices.

**just in time (JIT)** Inventory management and purchasing processes that manufacturers and resellers use to reduce inventory to very low levels and ensure that deliveries from suppliers arrive only when needed.

**knock-off** A new product that copies with slight modification the design of an original product.

**laggards** The last consumers to adopt an innovation.

**late majority** The adopters who are willing to try new products when there is little or no risk associated with the purchase, when the purchase becomes an economic necessity, or when there is social pressure to purchase.

**learning** A relatively permanent change in behaviour caused by acquired information or experience.

**licensing** An agreement in which one firm sells another firm the right to use a brand name for a specific purpose and for a specific period of time.

**lifestyle** The pattern of living that determines how people choose to spend their time, money, and energy and that reflects their values, tastes, and preferences.

**list price** The price the end customer is expected to pay as determined by the manufacturer.

**logistics** The process of designing, managing, and improving the movement of products through the supply chain.

**longitudinal design** Technique that tracks the responses of the same sample of respondents over time.

**loss-leader pricing** The pricing strategy of setting prices below cost to attract customers into a store.

**m-commerce** Promotional and other e-commerce activities transmitted over mobile phones and other mobile devices such as personal digital assistants (PDAs).

**margin** The difference between the cost of the product and the selling price of the product.

**marginal analysis** A method that uses costs and demand to identify the price that will maximize profits.

**market** All of the customers and potential customers who share a common need that can be satisfied by a specific product, who have the resources to exchange for it, who are willing to make the exchange, and who have the authority to make the exchange.

**market fragmentation** Creation of many consumer groups due to a diversity of distinct needs and wants in modern society.

**market manager** A manager who is responsible for developing and implementing the marketing plans for products sold to a specific customer group.

**market position** The way in which the target market perceives the offering in comparison to competitors' brands.

**market potential** The maximum demand expected among consumers in a segment for a product or service.

**market segment** A distinct group of customers within a larger market, who are similar to one another in some way and whose needs differ from other customers in the larger market; a marketplace opportunity or industry that a firm wants to serve (e.g., the pharmaceutical market segment, the retailing market segment).

**marketing** The process of planning and executing the conception, pricing, promotion, and distribution of ideas, goods, and services to create exchanges that satisfy individual and organizational objectives.

**marketing communications** Informing consumers and customers about the relative value of products, and developing trust and other relational bonds that facilitate ongoing exchange relationships.

**marketing concept** A business orientation that focuses on achieving organizational objectives by understanding customer needs, the associated costs of satisfying them, and thinking about the best way to satisfy those needs.

**marketing decision support system (MDSS)** The data, analysis software, and interactive software that allow managers to conduct analyses and find the information they need.

**marketing information system (MIS)** Procedure developed by a firm to continuously gather, sort, analyze, store, and distribute relevant and timely marketing information to its managers.

**marketing intelligence** A method by which marketers get information about everyday happenings in the marketing environment.

**marketing mix** A combination of the product itself, the price of the product, the place where it is made available, and the activities that introduce it to consumers, which creates a desired response among a set of predefined consumers.

**marketing mix strategy** A combination of product strategy, pricing strategy, channel of distribution (place) strategy, and marketing communications (promotion) strategy that a business uses to satisfy the needs of the target customer.

**marketing plan** A document that describes the marketing environment, outlines the marketing objectives and strategy, identifies who will be responsible for carrying out each part of the marketing strategy, and

describes how the strategy will be adjusted to respond to a changing marketplace.

**marketing research** The process of collecting, analyzing, and interpreting data about customers, competitors, and the business environment in order to make a specific marketing decision.

**marketplace** Any location or medium used to conduct an exchange.

**mass customization** Approach that modifies a basic product or service to meet the needs of an individual.

**mass market** All possible customers in a market, regardless of the differences in their specific needs and wants.

**materials handling** The moving of products into, within, and out of warehouses.

**maturity stage** The third and longest stage in the product life cycle, in which sales peak and profit margins narrow.

**media planning** The process of developing media objectives, strategies, and tactics for use in an advertising campaign.

**media schedule** The plan that specifies the exact media to use and when.

**medium** A communications vehicle through which a message is transmitted to a target audience.

**merchandise agents or brokers** Channel intermediaries that provide services in exchange for commissions but never take title to the product.

**merchandise allowance** A promotion that reimburses the retailer for in-store support of the product.

**merchandise assortment** The range of products sold.

**merchandise breadth** The number of different product lines available.

**merchandise depth** The variety of choices available for each specific product.

**merchandise mix** The total set of all products offered for sale by a firm, including all product lines sold to all consumer groups.

**merchant wholesalers** Intermediaries that buy goods from manufacturers (take title to them) and sell to retailers and other business-to-business customers.

**message** The communication in physical form that goes from a sender to a receiver.

**mission statement** A formal statement in an organization's strategic plan that describes the overall purpose of the organization and what it intends to achieve in terms of its customers, products, and resources.

**missionary salesperson** A salesperson who promotes the firm and tries to stimulate demand for a product but does not actually complete a sale.

**modified rebuy** A buying situation classification that business buyers use to categorize a previously made purchase that involves some change and that requires limited decision making.

**motivation** An internal state that drives us to satisfy needs by activating goal-oriented behaviour.

**multicultural marketing** The practice of recognizing and targeting the distinctive needs and wants of one or more ethnic subcultures.

**multilevel marketing** A system in which a master distributor recruits other people to become distributors, sells the company's product to the recruits, and receives a commission on all the merchandise they sell.

**multiple sourcing** The business practice of buying a particular product from many suppliers.

**national or manufacturer brands** Brands that the manufacturer of the product owns.

**need** Recognition of any difference between a consumer's actual state and some ideal or desired state.

**new-task buy** A new business-to-business purchase that is complex or risky and that requires extensive decision making.

**New Era orientation** A management philosophy in which marketing decision making means a devotion to excellence in designing and producing products that benefit the customer plus the firm's employees, shareholders, and fellow citizens.

**niche marketing** A type of concentrated targeting strategy where the market segment chosen is relatively small

**noise** Anything that interferes with effective communication.

**non-cumulative quantity discounts** Discounts based only on the quantity purchased in individual orders.

**non-store retailing** Any method used to complete an exchange with a product end user that does not require a customer visit to a store.

**nonprobability sample** A sample in which personal judgment is used in selecting respondents.

**North American Industry Classification System (NAICS)** The numerical coding system that the United States, Canada, and Mexico use to classify firms into detailed categories according to their business activities and shared characteristics.

**not-for-profit institutions** Organizations with charitable, educational, community, and other public service goals that buy goods and services to support their functions and to attract and serve their members.

**objective-task method** A promotion budgeting method in which an organization first defines the specific communications goals it hopes to achieve and then tries to calculate what kind of promotional efforts it must take to meet these goals.

**off-price retailers** Retailers that buy excess merchandise from well-known manufacturers and pass the savings on to customers.

**online auctions** E-commerce that allows shoppers to purchase products through online bidding.

**operant conditioning** Learning that occurs as the result of rewards or punishments.

**operating costs** Costs involved in using a product.

**operating variables** The production technology used, the business customer's degree of technical, financial, or operations expertise, and whether the prospect is a current user or non-user of the product.

**opinion leader** A person who is frequently able to influence others' attitudes or behaviours by virtue of his or her active interest and expertise in one or more product categories.

**opportunity cost** The value of something that is given up to obtain something else.

**order getter** A salesperson who works creatively to develop relationships with customers or to generate new sales.

**order taker** A salesperson whose primary function is to facilitate transactions that the customer initiates.

**out-of-home media** Communications media that reach people in public places.

**outsourcing** The business buying process of obtaining outside vendors to provide goods or services that otherwise might be supplied in-house.

**party plan system** A sales technique that relies heavily on people getting caught up in the "group spirit," buying things they would not normally buy if alone.

**penetration pricing** A pricing strategy in which a firm introduces a new product at a very low price to encourage more customers to purchase it.

**perceived risk** The belief that use of a product has potentially negative consequences, either financial, physical, or social.

**percentage-of-sales method** A method for promotion budgeting, in which the promotion budget is based on a percentage of either last year's sales or on estimates for this year's sales.

**perception** The process by which people select, organize, and interpret information from the outside world.

**perceptual map** A picture of where products or brands are located in consumers' minds.

**permission-based marketing** E-mail advertising where online consumers have the opportunity to accept or refuse the unsolicited e-mail.

**personal selling** The part of the promotion mix that involves direct contact between a company representative and a customer.

**personality** The psychological characteristics that consistently influence the way a person responds to situations in the environment.

**place** The availability of the product to the customer at the desired time and location. Also known as channels of distribution.

**point-of-purchase (POP) promotion** The use of signs or displays to influence purchases at the store.

**point-of-sale (POS) systems** Retail computer systems that collect sales data and are hooked directly into the store's inventory control system.

**portals** Gateways to the Internet that assist consumers to navigate the Internet and customize their experience.

**positioning** Developing a marketing strategy aimed at influencing how a particular market segment perceives a product or service as being differentiated in comparison to the competition.

**posttesting** Research conducted on consumers' responses to actual advertising messages they have seen or heard.

**preapproach** A part of the selling process that includes developing information about prospective customers and planning the sales interview.

**predatory pricing** The strategy of selling products at unreasonably low prices to drive competitors out of business.

**premium** An item included without charge with a purchased product.

**press release** Information that an organization distributes to the media about its activities, intended to appear as publicity.

**prestige pricing** A strategy where prices are set significantly higher than competing brands.

**pretesting** A research method that seeks to minimize mistakes by getting consumer reactions to ad messages before they appear in the media.

**price** The value that customers give up, or exchange, to obtain a desired product; the seller's assignment of value to a product.

**price-floor pricing** A method for calculating price in which, to maintain full plant operating capacity, a portion of a firm's output may be sold at a price that covers only marginal costs of production.

**price bundling** Selling two or more goods or services as a single package for one price.

**price discrimination** The illegal practice of offering the same product of like quality and quantity to different business customers at different prices, thus lessening competition.

**price elastic** When a percentage change in price results in a larger percentage change in the quantity demanded.

**price elasticity of demand** The percentage change in unit sales that results from a percentage change in price.

**price fixing** An illegal business practice in which firms decide in advance on a common price for their product.

**price inelastic** When a percentage change in price results in a smaller percentage change in the quantity demanded.

**price leadership (follower)** The firm that sets price first in an industry; other major firms in the industry follow the leader by staying in line.

**price lining** The practice of setting a limited number of different specific prices, called price points, for items in a product line.

**price maintenance** The collaboration of two or more firms in setting prices, usually to keep prices high.

**price subsidies** Government payments made to protect domestic businesses or to reimburse them when they must price at or below cost to make a sale. The subsidy can be a cash payment or tax relief.

**primary research** Research conducted by or for a single firm to provide information for a specific marketing decision.

**private exchanges** Systems that link an invited group of suppliers and partners over the Web.

**probability sample** A sample in which each member of the population has some known chance of being included in the sample.

**problem recognition** The process that occurs whenever the consumer sees a significant difference between his or her current state of affairs and some desired or ideal state. This recognition initiates the decision-making process.

**producers** The individuals or organizations that purchase products for use in the production of other goods and services.

**product** A tangible good, a service, an idea, or some combination of these that, through the exchange process, satisfies consumer or business customer needs; a bundle of attributes including features, functions, benefits, and uses.

**product adoption** The process by which a consumer or business customer begins to buy and use a new good, service, or an idea.

**product advertising** An advertising message that focuses on a specific good or service.

**product category manager** A manager who is responsible for developing and implementing the marketing plan for all of the brands and products within a product category.

**product life cycle** Concept that explains how products go through four distinct stages from birth to death: introduction, growth, maturity, and decline.

**product line** A firm's total product offering designed to satisfy a single need or desire of target customers.

**product mix** The total set of all products a firm offers for sale.

**product orientation** Management philosophy that emphasizes the most efficient ways to produce and distribute products.

**product usage segmentation** A segmentation approach that groups consumers or business customers based on the amount of a product purchased or consumed or how the product is used.

**profit objective** Pricing products with a focus on a target level of profit growth or a desired net profit margin.

**projective techniques** Tests that marketers use to explore people's underlying feelings about a product, especially appropriate when consumers are unable or unwilling to express their true reactions.

**promotion** The coordination of a marketer's communications efforts to influence attitudes or behaviour toward a product or service.

**prospecting** A part of the selling process that includes identifying and developing a list of potential or prospective customers.

**psychographic segmentation** A segmentation approach that groups people based on their attitudes, beliefs, values, lifestyles, or other psychological orientations.

**public relations (PR)** Communications strategies to build good relationships and corporate image with an organization's stakeholders, including consumers, stockholders, and legislators.

**public service advertisements** Advertising run by the media without charge for not-for-profit organizations or to champion a particular cause.

**publicity** Unpaid communication about an organization appearing in the mass media.

**pull strategy** Moving products through the channel by building desire for the products among consumers, who convince retailers to stock the items.

**push money** A bonus paid by a manufacturer to a salesperson for selling its product.

**push strategy** Moving products through the channel by convincing channel members to offer them.

**push technology** Internet tools that allow marketers to send information they think is relevant to consumers directly to their computers.

**pyramid schemes** An illegal sales technique, in which the initial distributors profit by selling merchandise to other distributors, with the result that consumers buy very little product.

**qualify prospects** A part of the selling process that determines how likely prospects are to become customers.

**quantity discounts** A pricing tactic of charging reduced prices for larger quantities of a product.

**reach** The percentage of the target market that will be exposed to the media vehicle.

**rebates** Sales promotions that allow the customer to recover part of the product's cost from the manufacturer.

**receiver** The organization or individual that intercepts and interprets the message.

**reciprocity** A trading partnership in which two firms agree to buy from one another.

**reference group** An actual or imaginary individual or group that has a significant effect on an individual's evaluations, aspirations, or behaviour.

**relationship marketing** A marketing philosophy that focuses on building long-term relationships with customers, suppliers, distributors, and other key stakeholders to satisfy mutual needs.

**relationship selling** A form of personal selling in which the salesperson seeks to develop a mutually sat-

isfying relationship with the consumer so they can work together to satisfy each other's needs.

**reliability** The extent to which research measurement techniques are free of errors.

**repositioning** Redoing a product's position to respond to marketplace changes.

**representativeness** The extent to which consumers in a study are similar to a larger group in which the organization has an interest.

**research design** A plan that specifies what information marketers will collect and what type of study they will do.

**resellers** The individuals or organizations that buy finished goods for the purpose of reselling, renting, or leasing to others to make a profit and to maintain their business operations.

**retail life cycle** A process that focuses on the various retail life cycle stages from introduction to decline.

**retailing** The final stop in the distribution channel by which goods and services are sold to consumers for their personal use.

**reverse marketing** A business practice in which a buyer firm shapes a supplier's products and operations to satisfy its needs.

**sales closing** The stage of the selling process in which the salesperson asks the customer to buy the product.

**sales follow-up** After-sales activities that provide important services to customers.

**sales management** The process of planning, implementing, and controlling the personal selling function of an organization.

**sales or market share objective** Pricing products to maximize sales or to attain a desired level of sales or market share.

**sales presentation** The part of the selling process in which the salesperson seeks to persuasively communicate the product's features and the benefits it will provide after the sale.

**sales promotion** A program designed to build interest in or encourage purchase of a product during a specified time period.

**sales territory** A set of customers often defined by geographic boundaries, for whom a particular salesperson is responsible.

**sampling** Distributing trial-size versions of a product for free to encourage people to try it; the process of selecting respondents who statistically represent a larger population of interest.

**scalability** The ability of organizations to get bigger without a big rise in expenses.

**scenarios** Possible future situations that futurists use to assess the likely impact of alternative marketing strategies.

**scrambled merchandising** A merchandising strategy that offers consumers a mixture of merchandise items that are not directly related to each other.

**secondary research** Research collected for a purpose other than the decision at hand.

**segment profile** A description of the typical customer in a segment.

**segmentation** The process of dividing a larger market into smaller pieces, based on one or more meaningful, shared characteristics.

**segmentation variables** Bases for dividing the total market into fairly homogenous groups, each with different needs and preferences.

**selective distribution** Distribution using fewer outlets than in intensive distribution but more than in exclusive distribution.

**self-concept** An individual's self-image that is composed of a mixture of beliefs, observations, and feelings about personal attributes.

**selling orientation** A managerial view of marketing as a selling function, or a way to move products out of warehouses to reduce inventory.

**service encounter** The actual interaction between the customer and the service provider.

**services** Intangible products that are exchanged directly from the producer to the customer.

**sex roles** Society's expectations about the appropriate attitudes, behaviours, and appearance for men and women.

**share of customer** The percentage of an individual customer's purchase of a product that is a single brand.

**single-source data** Information that is integrated from multiple sources, to monitor the impact of marketing communications on a particular customer group over time.

**single sourcing** The business practice of buying a particular product from only one supplier.

**skimming price** Charging a very high, premium price for a new product.

**slotting allowance** A fee paid by a manufacturer to a retailer in exchange for agreeing to place products on the retailer's shelves.

**social class** The overall rank or social standing of groups of people within a society according to the value assigned to such factors as family background, education, occupation, and income.

**social marketing concept** An orientation that focuses on satisfying consumer needs while also addressing the needs of the larger society.

**social profit** The benefit an organization and society receive from the organization's ethical practices, community service, efforts to promote cultural diversity, and concern for the natural environment.

**social responsibility** A management practice in which organizations seek to engage in activities that have a positive effect on society and promote the public good.

**source** An organization or individual that sends a message.

**sponsorship** A PR activity through which companies provide financial support to help fund an event in return for publicized recognition of the company's contribution.

**stakeholders** Individuals or organizations who affect, or are affected by, the activities of a firm.

**status symbols** Products that consumers purchase to signal membership in a desirable social class.

**stimulus generalization** Behaviour caused by a reaction to one stimulus that occurs in the presence of other similar stimuli.

**store image** The way a retailer is perceived in the marketplace relative to the competition.

**store or private-label brands** Brands that are owned and sold by a specific retailer or distributor.

**straight rebuy** A buying situation in which business buyers make routine purchases that require minimal decision making.

**strategic business units (SBUs)** Individual units within the firm that operate like separate businesses, with each having its own mission, business objectives, resources, managers, and competitors.

**strategic planning** A managerial decision process that matches an organization's resources and capabilities to its market opportunities for long-term growth and survival.

**subculture** A group within a society whose members share a distinctive set of beliefs, characteristics, or common experiences.

**supply chain** All the firms that engage in activities necessary to turn raw materials into a good or service and put it in the hands of the consumer or business customer.

**supply chain management** The management of flows among firms in the supply chain to maximize profitability.

**survey** A questionnaire that asks participants about their beliefs or behaviours.

**switching costs** Costs involved in moving from one brand to another.

**SWOT analysis** An analysis of an organization's strengths and weaknesses and the opportunities and threats in its external environment.

**syndicated research** Research by firms that collect data on a regular basis and sell the reports to multiple firms.

**take title** To accept legal ownership of a product and the accompanying rights and responsibilities of ownership.

**target audience** A highly segmented group of people who receive and respond similarly to marketing messages.

**target costing** A process in which firms identify the quality and functionality needed to satisfy customers and what price they are willing to pay before the product is designed; the product is manufactured only if the firm can control costs to meet the required price.

**target customer** Customers that represent the best opportunity for a business (e.g., high-income consumers, large manufacturing organizations).

**target marketing strategy** Dividing the total market into different segments based on customer characteristics, selecting one or more segments, and developing products to meet the needs of those specific segments.

**target markets** The market segment(s) on which an organization focuses its marketing plan and toward which it directs its marketing efforts.

**technical specialist** Sales support personnel with a high level of technical expertise who assist in product demonstrations.

**telemarketing** The use of the telephone or fax to sell directly to consumers and business customers.

**test marketing** Testing the complete marketing plan in a small geographic area that is similar to the larger market the firm hopes to enter.

**top-down budgeting techniques** Allocation of the promotion budget that is based on the total amount to be devoted to marketing communications.

**total contribution** Contribution margin multiplied by the number of units sold.

**total unit cost** Variables costs plus average fixed costs per unit.

**trade area** A geographic zone that accounts for the majority of a store's sales and customers.

**trade or functional discounts** Discounts off list price of products to members of the channel of distribution that perform various marketing functions.

**trade shows** Events at which many companies set up exhibits to show their products, give away samples, distribute product literature, and troll for new business contacts.

**trademark** The legal term for a brand name, brand mark, or trade character; a trademark legally registered by a government obtains protection for exclusive use in that country.

**traffic flow** The direction in which shoppers move through the store and what areas they pass or avoid.

**transactional selling** A form of personal selling that focuses on making an immediate sale with little or no attempt to develop a relationship with the customer.

**trial pricing** Pricing a new product low for a limited period of time to lower the risk for a customer.

**umbrella pricing** A strategy of ducking under a competitor's price by a fixed percentage.

**unaided recall** A research technique conducted by telephone survey or personal interview that asks how much of an ad a person remembers during a specified period of time.

**undifferentiated (mass) targeting strategy** Appealing to a broad spectrum of people.

**uniform delivered pricing** A pricing tactic in which a firm adds a standard shipping charge to the price for all customers regardless of location.

**usage occasions** Indicator used in one type of market segmentation based on when consumers use a product most.

**validity** The extent to which research actually measures what it was intended to measure.

**VALS™ (Values and Lifestyles)** Psychographic system that divides people into eight segments.

**value chain** The concept of a supply chain that looks at how each firm receives inputs, adds value to these inputs, and then passes them along to the next firm in the value chain.

**value pricing or every day low pricing (EDLP)** A pricing strategy in which a firm sets prices that provide ultimate value to customers.

**variable costs** The costs of production (raw and processed materials, parts, and labour) that are tied to, and vary depending on, the number of units produced.

**variable pricing** A flexible pricing strategy that reflects what individual customers are willing to pay.

**venture teams** Groups of people within an organization who work together focusing exclusively on the development of a new product.

**vertical marketing system (VMS)** A channel of distribution in which there is cooperation among members at the manufacturing, wholesaling, and retailing levels.

**viral marketing** Marketing activity in which a company recruits customers to be sales agents and spread the word about the product.

**want** The desire to satisfy needs in specific ways that are culturally and socially influenced.

**warehousing** Storing goods in anticipation of sale or transfer to another member of the channel of distribution.

**wheel-of-retailing hypothesis** A theory that explains how retail firms change, becoming more upscale as they go through their life cycle.

**wholesaling intermediaries** Firms that handle the flow of products from the manufacturer to the retailer or business user.

**yield management pricing** A practice of charging different prices to different customers in order to manage capacity while maximizing revenues.

**zone pricing** A pricing tactic in which customers in different geographic zones pay different transportation rates.

# CREDITS

## Chapter 1

**4** Lanyon Phillips Communications Inc., Bill Downie, Art Director and Peter Lanyon, Chairman/Chief Creative Officer; **6, 21** Vancouver Sun photo/Dick Didlick; **9** Durex Canada, a division of SSL Canada Inc.; **10** The Fund for Animals; **11** Reebok; **15** Copyright 2003 Hewitt Associates LLC. Used with permission; **16** Churchill & Klehr Photography; **17** Ford Motor Company, Detroit; **19** Courtesy of the American Association of Advertising Agencies; **21** Lanyon Phillips Communications Inc., Bill Downie, Art Director and Peter Lanyon, Chairman/Chief Creative Officer.

## Chapter 2

**28** Used with permission of Sony Nordic A/S; **30, 52** Henrik Kaas; **35** Philip Morris Co., Inc.; **38** Dave G. Houser/Corbis; **41** Courtesy of Xerox; **42 (top)** AP Photo/Chiaki Tsukumo; **42 (bottom)** Paridiset DDB; **44** Ben & Jerry's Homemade Holdings, Inc.; **49** Toyota Motor North America; **50** © 2000 Avon Canada Inc.; **51** Shell Canada Limited.

## Chapter 3

**60** Ford Motor Company of Canada, Ltd.; **62, 94** Roman Pylypczak Photography; **63** Joe McBride/Tony Stone Images; **64** "Coca-Cola," "Coke" and "Vanilla Coke" appear courtesy of Coca-Cola Ltd. www.vanillacoke.com appears courtesy of The Coca-Cola Company; **65** Courtesy of Thermohair; **66** Beef Information Centre; **67** Courtesy of Club Med Canada; **69** Reprinted by permission of Covenant House. Created by Taxi Advertising; **70** Used with permission of Ducane Gas Grills Co.; **73 (top)** Elaine Thompson/CP Photo Archive; **73 (bottom)** Courtesy of *Fuel* Magazine; **74 (top)** Courtesy of Terra Canada; **74 (bottom)** Dick Hemingway; **76** Dick Hemingway; **77 (top)** Courtesy of Royal Bank/Aboriginal Banking, artwork by Linda Rostad; **77 (bottom)** Courtesy of CFMT-TV; **78 (top)** Courtesy of Grand & Toy; **78 (bottom)** © 2004 Dell Inc. All Rights Reserved; **80** Soya World Inc.; **83** Hard Candy, Inc.; **85 (left)** Courtesy of WestJet; **85 (right)** Used with permission of BC Ethic USA; **86 (top)** The Buckley's Company; **86 (bottom)** Dick Hemingway; **89** Corbis/S.I.N; **90** Courtesy of Pfizer Canada.

## Chapter 4

**102, 104, 131, 133** Courtesy of SurveySite; **106** Photo by Paul Shambroom/Photo Researchers, Inc.; **107** Reproduced with the permission of the Minister of Public Works and Government Services 2004; **109** Released with permission by Dun and Bradstreet Canada; **110** Courtesy of *Marketing Magazine*; **111** Ad courtesy of Ford Motor Company; **114** Courtesy of Lowe Roche Advertising; **116** Courtesy of Sights and Sounds; **117 (top)** Courtesy of Centrica; **117 (bottom)** Dick Hemingway; **118** Georgia-Pacific Corp.; **120** Decision Insight, Inc.; **122** Photo by Jeff Greenberg/PhotoEdit; **123** photoresearchers/firstlight.ca; **124 (top)** Courtesy of ICBC; **124 (bottom)** Louie Psihoyos/Matrix International, Inc.; **126** Dick Hemingway; **129** Courtesy of Shoppers Drug Mart; **132 (top)** Used with permission of Amazon.com; **132 (bottom)** Courtesy of Mind/Share Inc.

## Chapter 5

**146** Courtesy of MegaBloks; **148, 173** Michel Benayan; **151** "Coca-Cola," "Coke" and "Vanilla Coke" appear courtesy of Coca-Cola Ltd.; **152** Photo: Pfizer Canada Inc.; **153** Courtesy of Google, Inc.; **154** Apple Canada; **158 (top)** Pepsi-Cola Company; **158 (bottom)** Courtesy of Benetton; **160** © 2002 Time Inc. Reprinted with permission; **161 (top)** Courtesy of National Fluid Milk Processor Promotion Board and Lowe Worldwide Inc.; **161 (bottom)** Benjamin Moore Co., Limited; **162** Richard Sheinwald/Bloomberg News/Landov; **163** Courtesy of David K. Foot, Professor of Economics, University of Toronto; **164** Courtesy of Rainforest Cafe; **165** Courtesy of Molson Canada; **166** Courtesy of www.canoe.ca; **167** Courtesy of TELUS Mobility; **169** Henry Diltz/CORBIS/MAGMA; **170** CP Photo.

## Chapter 6

**180** David W. Cerny/Reuters/Landov; **182, 201** Marion Lay; **183** Courtesy of Bombardier Inc.; **185 (top)** Keith Dannemiller/CORBIS/MAGMA; **185 (bottom)** Photograph reprinted Courtesy of Caterpillar Inc.; **186** Neil Rabinowitz/Corbis; **187** BMW of North America, Inc.; **190** Courtesy of Gowlings; **191** Greater Vancouver Transportation Authority; **192** Federal Express; **193 (top)** Courtesy of Canon Canada; **193 (bottom)** Ralf-Finn Hestoft/SABA Press Photos, Inc.; **197** CP Photo; **199** Courtesy of Future Shop;

**200** Used with permission of Excelon;
**201** eSecurityOnline.com.

## Chapter 7

**212** Churchill & Klehr Photography;
**214, 233** Much and House; **215** Churchill & Klehr Photography; **220** Courtesy of Air Canada; **221** Ann States/SABA Press Photos, Inc.; **222** Procter & Gamble, Inc.; **224** UPI/Corbis; **226** Courtesy of Mastercard International; **228** Warner-Lambert Canada Inc.; **229** "Barq's" trademarks are used with permission; **231** Jergens Canada Inc.;
**232 (top)** Denis Cahill/CP Photo Archive;
**232 (bottom)** Courtesy of SAIC; **233** Renaissance Cosmetics, Inc.

## Chapter 8

**240** Dick Hemingway; **242, 256** Julie Desrosier;
**244 (top)** Volkswagen of America, Inc.;
**244 (bottom)** Volkswagen of America/FPG International LLC; **246** Photo used with permission of Bombardier Inc. Traxter™ XT are trademarks of Bombardier Inc. and/or its subsidiaries;
**247** Courtesy of Procter & Gamble Inc.;
**248** Victorinox® and Swiss Army™ are registered trademarks; **249** Ad courtesy of Hitachi, Ltd.;
**250 (top)** Warner-Lambert Canada Inc.;
**250 (bottom)** Jessica Wecker Photography;
**251** Kraft Canada Inc.; **252** © 2000 Clarica Life Insurance Company. All rights reserved; **253** The A&W Rootbeer Company; **255** AP/Wide World Photos.

## Chapter 9

**264** Courtesy of Brentwood Bay Lodge;
**266, 305** Leanne Cadden; **268** Jim Young/Reuters/Landov; **270** Courtesy of Palliser;
**273** Saturn; **274** Courtesy of Burton Snowboards;
**278** Michael Newman/PhotoEdit; **279** Used with permission of Dell Computer Corporation;
**280** Tibor Bognar/CORBIS/MAGMA;
**281** Kyodo/Landov; **282** "Trade-mark reproduced with the permission of Zellers Inc."; **284** Malaysia Airlines/Albert Pointdexter; **285** Courtesy of Sanyo; **286** Lee Valley Tools Ltd.; **287** Suzuki;
**288 (top)** Used with permission of Gillette Inc.;
**288 (bottom)** Majorie Farrell/The Image Works;
**290** Mongoose; **291** Tourism P.E.I.; **292** Dick Hemingway; **294** Gucci America Inc.; **296** Tursack Incorporated; **297** Dick Hemingway; **298** Blair Seitz/Photo Researchers, Inc.; **300 (top)** Cliff Otto/Los Angeles Times; **300 (bottom)** Issei Kato/Landov; **301** Teri Stratford; **303** Used with permission of Eddie Bauer Inc.; **304** Courtesy of Priceline.com.

## Chapter 10

**318** Weldwood of Canada Limited; **320, 342** Mike Nomura; **322** John Elk III; **324** Boris Spremo/CP Photo Archives; **326** AP/Wide World Photos;
**327** L. Migdale/Stock Boston; **329** BlackBear Company Store; **333** Alene M. McNeill; **335** Jim Whitmer; **337** Used with permission of Business Objects; **338** Used with permission of Home Depot; **339** SuperStock, Inc.; **341** Arnold Bros. Transport Ltd.

## Chapter 11

**350, 375** Used with permission of Macy's Corporation; **352, 375** Dawn Robertson;
**355** Courtesy of Petro-Canada;
**356 (top)** Dominion Stores/Alene M. McNeill;
**356 (bottom)** R.A. Flynn, Inc./TC2;
**357 (bottom)** Elnora Stuart; **359** Photo by David Young-Wolff/PhotoEdit; **360** Lee Valley Tools Ltd.;
**361 (top)** Elnora Stuart; **361 (bottom)** Courtesy REI; **362** Alene M. McNeill; **364** Dick Hemingway;
**366 (top left)** Toronto Corporate Services;
**366 (top right)** Canapress/Dave Buston;
**366 (bottom left)** AP/Wide World Photos;
**366 (bottom right)** PhotoEdit, Jim Mone;
**367** Samcor Communications Company;
**369** Courtesy of La Senza; **370** The Gap;
**371** Just White Shirts & Black Socks;
**374** M. Antman/The Image Works.

## Chapter 12

**382** Henry Ausloos/AGE/firstlight.ca;
**384, 413** Dave Chidley; **387** © 2004 - Copyright of Tourism British Columbia. Used under license. All rights reserved; **391** Courtesy of Bell Canada, the WWE, and Rethink Communications; **392** Halifax Regional Police; **394** Courtesy of Nike Canada;
**397** DM9 Advertising; **398** Courtesy of Goodyear;
**399** © The Procter & Gamble Company. Used by permission; **400** Courtesy of RETHINK; 402 BBDO Duesseldorf; **403** Tourism P.E.I;
**406 (top)** GLAD is a registered trademark of the GLAD Products Company and is used with permission. Copyright 1999, The GLAD Products Company. Reprinted with permission;
**406 (bottom)** Courtesy of Novell; **407** Sun-Rype Products Ltd.; **410** Canapress/David Duprey;
**412** Adobe and the Adobe logo are trademarks of Adobe Systems Incorporated; **413** Under permission by V&S Vin & Sprit AB (publ). "ABSOLUT COUNTRY OF SWEDEN VODKA & LOGO, ABSOLUT, ABSOLUT BOTTLE DESIGN AND ABSOLUT CALLIGRAPHY ARE TRADEMARKS OWNED BY V&S VIN & SPRIT AB (publ). © 2004 V&S VIN & SPRIT AB (publ)."

## Chapter 13

**420** Courtesy of Saputo; **422, 453** Mario Demers; **423** Microcell Solutions Inc.; **425 (top)** Pfizer Canada Inc.; **425 (bottom)** Reprinted by permission of Covenant House. Created by Taxi Advertising; **426** Courtesy of Smith & Nelson; **428 (left and right)** CP Photo; **429** Digital Pulp, 2000; **430** Frank Gunn/CP Photo; **431** Tom Lyle/Medichrome/The Stock Shop, Inc.; **432** Cinemaxx; **435** Canapress/Paul Chaisson; **436** Boivin Consulting Group; **437** © Ron Stroud/Masterfile; **438** Adam Butler/CP Photo Archive; **440** Used with permission of 3M; **442** Labatt Breweries of Canada; **443** Courtesy of Gillette Canada Company and CAFC; **444** Val-Pak DMS, Inc.; **447** Used with permission of Tupperware; **448** Phil Norton/Gazette Photos Montreal; **450** Tourism Queensland (Australia); **451** The Southwestern Company; **452** Used with permission of Omaha Steaks; **458** Courtesy of Dairy Farmers of Canada. Photography: Philip Rostron-Instil Productions Inc.

## Chapter 14

**464** Courtesy of TELUS Mobility. Creative developed by TAXI advertising and design; **466, 474** Leonard Hendricks; **468** Courtesy of Sony Canada.

## Chapter 15

**480** Reprinted by permission of Eden Robbins Photography Inc., Getty Images, and TD Canada Trust; **482, 497** Jamie Chiarotto; **484** Courtesy of TeamOne Advertising. Photograph by Rick Rusing; **486** Creative Agency: Low & Partners. Photographer: Richard Pullar; **487** CLOROX® and the CLOROX logo are registered trademarks of The Clorox Company. Used with permission; **488** Reprinted courtesy of Paul Alexander www.paul-alexander.com; **493** FedEx.

# COMPANY/NAME INDEX

# SUBJECT INDEX